D0651511

3000 800063 419.

St. Louis Community College

Florissant Valley Library
St. Louis Community College
3400 Pershall Road
Ferguson, MO 63135-1499
314-513-4514

· HISTORICAL DICTIONARIES
OF WAR, REVOLUTION, AND CIVIL UNREST
Jon Woronoff, Series Editor

1. *Afghan Wars, Revolutions, and Insurgencies*, by Ludwig W. Adamec. 1996. *Out of print. See No. 30.*
2. *The United States–Mexican War*, by Edward H. Moseley and Paul C. Clark Jr. 1997.
3. *World War I*, by Ian V. Hogg. 1998.
4. *The United States Navy*, by James M. Morris and Patricia M. Kearns. 1998.
5. *The United States Marine Corps*, by Harry A. Gailey. 1998.
6. *The Wars of the French Revolution*, by Steven T. Ross. 1998.
7. *The American Revolution*, by Terry M. Mays. 1999.
8. *The Spanish–American War*, by Brad K. Berner. 1998.
9. *The Persian Gulf War*, by Clayton R. Newell. 1998.
10. *The Holocaust*, by Jack R. Fischel. 1999.
11. *The United States Air Force and Its Antecedents*, by Michael Robert Terry. 1999.
12. *Civil Wars in Africa*, by Guy Arnold. 1999. *Out of Print. See No. 34.*
13. *World War II: The War Against Japan*, by Anne Sharp Wells. 1999.
14. *British and Irish Civil Wars*, by Martyn Bennett. 2000.
15. *The Cold War*, by Joseph Smith and Simon Davis. 2000.
16. *Ancient Greek Warfare*, by Iain Spence. 2002.
17. *The Vietnam War*, by Edwin E. Moïse. 2001.
18. *The Civil War*, by Terry L. Jones. 2002.
19. *The Crimean War*, by Guy Arnold. 2002.
20. *The United States Army, a Historical Dictionary*, by Clayton R. Newell. 2002.
21. *Terrorism, Second Edition*, by Sean K. Anderson and Stephen Sloan. 2002.
22. *Chinese Civil War*, by Edwin Pak-wah Leung. 2002.
23. *The Korean War: A Historical Dictionary*, by Paul M. Edwards. 2002.
24. *The "Dirty Wars,"* by David Kohut, Olga Vilella, and Beatrice Julian. 2003.

25. *The Crusades*, by Corliss K. Slack. 2003.
26. *Ancient Egyptian Warfare*, by Robert G. Morkot. 2003.
27. *The French Revolution*, by Paul R. Hanson. 2004.
28. *Arms Control and Disarmament*, by Jeffrey A. Larsen and James M. Smith. 2005.
29. *The Russo–Japanese War*, by Rotem Kowner. 2005.
30. *Afghan Wars, Revolutions, and Insurgencies, Second Edition*, by Ludwig W. Adamec. 2005.
31. *War of 1812*, by Robert Malcomson. 2006.
32. *Arab–Israeli Conflict*, by P. R. Kumaraswamy. 2006.
33. *Nuclear, Biological, and Chemical Warfare*, by Benjamin C. Garrett and John Hart. 2007.
34. *Civil Wars in Africa, Second Edition*, by Guy Arnold. 2008.
35. *Northern Ireland Conflict*, by Gordon Gillespie. 2008.

Historical Dictionary of Civil Wars in Africa

Second Edition

Guy Arnold

*Historical Dictionaries of War,
Revolution, and Civil Unrest, No. 34*

The Scarecrow Press, Inc.
Lanham, Maryland • Toronto • Plymouth, UK
2008

SCARECROW PRESS, INC.

Published in the United States of America
by Scarecrow Press, Inc.
A wholly owned subsidiary of
The Rowman & Littlefield Publishing Group, Inc.
4501 Forbes Boulevard, Suite 200, Lanham, Maryland 20706
www.scarecrowpress.com

Estover Road
Plymouth PL6 7PY
United Kingdom

Copyright © 2008 by Guy Arnold

All rights reserved. No part of this publication may be reproduced,
stored in a retrieval system, or transmitted in any form or by any
means, electronic, mechanical, photocopying, recording, or otherwise,
without the prior permission of the publisher.

British Library Cataloguing in Publication Information Available

Library of Congress Cataloging-in-Publication Data

Arnold, Guy.
  Historical dictionary of civil wars in Africa / Guy Arnold. — 2nd ed.
    p. cm. — (Historical dictionaries of war, revolution, and civil unrest ; 34)
  Includes bibliographical references.
  ISBN-13: 978-0-8108-5766-7 (hardcover : alk. paper)
  ISBN-10: 0-8108-5766-9 (hardcover : alk. paper)
    1. Revolutions—Africa—Encyclopedias. 2. Civil war—Encyclopedias.
  3. Africa—History, Military—Encyclopedias. I. Title.
  DT21.5.A76 2007
  960—dc22 2007024894

∞The paper used in this publication meets the minimum requirements of
American National Standard for Information Sciences—Permanence of
Paper for Printed Library Materials, ANSI/NISO Z39.48-1992.
Manufactured in the United States of America.

Contents

Editor's Foreword (*Jon Woronoff*)   vii

Preface   ix

Acronyms and Abbreviations   xi

Map   xxi

Chronology   xxiii

Introduction   xxix

THE DICTIONARY   1

Bibliography   433

About the Author   491

Editor's Foreword

For over a century, Africa has experienced a violent cycle of warfare. First came the wars of colonial conquest, then the armed struggles for independence, and finally a series of civil wars. These civil wars have many causes, including the struggle over artificial frontiers inherited from colonialism, friction and rivalry among different ethnic and religious groups, and the crude desire for power of some African leaders. During the Cold War, the situation was further exacerbated by intervention or "aid" from the former colonial powers and new superpowers. Although it has not been easy to prevent or contain these wars, increasingly efforts are being made by the United Nations, other international organizations, and African organizations such as the African Union to provide peacekeeping and provide care for refugees.

For a continent that is poorly known and badly misunderstood to begin with, it is often hard to find useful information about underlying situations, groups and people involved, and even the course of wars—which is why this *Historical Dictionary of Civil Wars in Africa* is such an important book. The chronology tracks when civil wars erupted or were resolved, and which ones still continue; the introduction puts the warfare into historical, political, and geographical context; the dictionary provides a wealth of information on each of the wars, the more prominent leaders involved (both those who make war and those who try to bring peace), liberation movements, and political parties and organizations; and the substantial bibliography presents indispensable information for those who want to know more.

Guy Arnold, who wrote the first and now the second edition of this volume, is a freelance writer and has become an acknowledged authority on Africa and the third world. He has been writing about Africa for four decades and his books have covered events in many African countries, including Kenya, Nigeria, and South Africa. He has also written *Wars in the Third World since 1945, Historical Dictionary of Aid and Development Organizations,* and *Historical Dictionary of the Non-Aligned Movement and the Third World.* The second edition of this *Historical Dictionary of Civil Wars in Africa* is not only updated, but it is also considerably expanded, since there are sadly now 30 civil wars instead of the 20 in the first edition. It is an important resource for anyone concerned with current events in Africa.

Jon Woronoff
Series Editor

Preface

In the eight years since the first edition of the *Historical Dictionary of Civil Wars in Africa* appeared, much has changed, yet the level of violence on the continent remains high. Thirty civil wars are now recorded as opposed to 20 in the first edition. In Sudan, the 20-year-old war between north and south has finally come to an end, but another civil war has replaced it in the huge Darfur province. In the Congo (former Zaire), following the civil war that ended Mobutu's long tyranny, another war followed. This was known as Africa's Great War and involved a number of Congo's neighbors. In West Africa, Côte d'Ivoire, long seen as one of the region's most stable countries, descended into a civil war that split the country between north and south.

Dictionary entries cover a number of categories: civil wars, of which there are now 30; liberation or other movements, such as the African National Congress (ANC) or Popular Movement for the Liberation of Angola (MPLA), which are involved in such wars; leading political or military figures, such as Idi Amin of Uganda or Laurent Kabila of the Democratic Republic of Congo; external countries or organizations that have attempted peacekeeping or mediation roles—the Commonwealth, France, the United Nations, the United States—or have intervened in other ways; and specific events connected with the wars, such as the Setif uprising of 1945 in Algeria (which was a defining moment in the deteriorating relationship between France and its north African colony) or the Nkomati Accord of 1984 between Mozambique and South Africa. In addition, there are a number of entries covering topics such as aid, the churches, or mercenaries that have obvious relevance. The principal entries cover the civil wars, which are Algeria (2), Angola, Burundi, Central African Republic, Chad, Comoros, Congo (Africa's Great War), Congo (Zaire) (2), Congo (Brazzaville), Côte d'Ivoire, Darfur, Eritrea/ Ethiopia, Ethiopia, Liberia, Mozambique, Nigeria (2), Ogaden War,

Rwanda, Sierra Leone, Somalia, South Africa, Sudan (2), Uganda (2), Zanzibar, and Zimbabwe.

The introduction attempts to disentangle the civil and other wars, such as the liberation struggles (which often overlap), and to relate the endless cycle of African violence that has been a feature of the continent in the period since 1945 (and especially since 1960) to other crucial factors, including the after-effects of recent colonialism, the impact of the Cold War on the continent, the general weakness of state systems in Africa, and the extent to which external powers have been drawn into Africa's conflicts. Finally, questions are addressed that have been raised in acute form during the 1990s, such as when (if ever) it is right to intervene in the internal affairs of another state; whether all states should be regarded as permanently inviolable; and whether the separation of fundamentally antagonistic ethnic groups, such as the Hutus and Tutsis of Burundi and Rwanda, would not be better than attempting to keep intact states in which genocidal massacres appear to have become the periodic norm. Although this is a historical dictionary, wars in Africa, sadly, are an ongoing phenomenon and in a number of cases the civil wars dealt with in the first edition were still in progress eight years later. Three entries concern wars in what is now named the Democratic Republic of Congo (DRC). They could have been brought together in a single narrative, but it would have been too long and indigestible. Instead, they appear in alphabetical rather than chronological sequence under the appropriate name of the country at the time: Congo, Democratic Republic of: Africa's Great War (1998–2003); Congo, Republic of the (later Zaire) (1960–65); and Zaire (DRC) (1997–98).

In this dictionary, only civil wars have been dealt with in depth, though others may be mentioned when it is relevant to the overall picture. Items in boldface indicate separate dictionary entries.

ACKNOWLEDGMENTS

I would like to express my particular thanks to Tom Ofcansky and Toungara and Aimable Twagilamana for their assistance with the bibliography and to the series editor, Jon Woronoff.

Acronyms and Abbreviations

ACDL	Association for Constitutional Democracy in Liberia
ADF	Allied Democratic Forces
AEC	African Economic Community
AENF	Alliance of Eritrean National Forces
AFDL	Alliance des Forces Démocratiques pour la Libération du Congo/Zaire/Alliance of Democratic Forces for the Liberation of the Congo/Zaire
AFL	Armed Forces of Liberia
AFRC	Armed Forces Revolutionary Council
AFU	All African Union
AIAI	Al-Itihaad al-Islamia/Union of Islam
AIS	Armée Islamique du Salut/Islamic Army of Salvation
ALN	Armée de Libération Nationale/National Liberation Army
AMIS	African Union Mission in Sudan
AML	Les Amis du Manifeste et de la Liberté/Friends of the Manifesto and of Liberty
ANAF	Anya-Nya Armed Forces
ANC	African National Congress
ARPCT	Alliance for the Restoration of Peace and Counter-Terrorism
CAF	Central African Federation
CDR	Coalition pour la Défense de la République/Coalition for the Defense of the Republic
CEMAC	Communauté Economique et Monétaire de l'Afrique Centrale/Economic and Monetary Community of Central Africa
CHOGM	Commonwealth Heads of Government Meeting

CIA	Central Intelligence Agency
CIO	Central Intelligence Organization
CMSN	Comité Militaire du Salut National/Military Committee of National Salvation
CNAG	Commission Nationale pour l'Amnestie Générale/National Commission for General Amnesty
CNDD	Conseil National pour la Défense de la Démocratie/National Council for the Defense of Democracy
CNRA	Conseil National de la Révolution Algérienne/National Council of the Algerian Revolution
CNSP	Comité National de Salut Publique/National Committee of Public Salvation
CONACO	Conféderation Nationale des Associations Congolaises/National Confederation of Congolese Associations
CONAKAT	Conféderation des Associations Katangaises/Confederation of Katangese Associations
COPWE	Commission for the Organization of a Party of the Workers of Ethiopia
COSATU	Confederation of South African Trade Unions
CRUA	Comité Révolutionnaire pour l'Unité et l'Action/Revolutionary Committee for Unity and Action
DFSS	Democratic Front for the Salvation of Somalia
DLF	Darfur Liberation Front
DPKO	Department of Peacekeeping Operations
DUP	Democratic Unionist Party
EC	European Community
ECOMOG	Economic Community Monitoring Group
ECOWAS	Economic Community of West African States
EDU	Ethiopian Democratic Union
ELF	Eritrean Liberation Front
ELF-PLF	Eritrean Liberation Front-Popular Liberation Forces
EPDM	Ethiopian People's Democratic Movement
EPG	Eminent Persons Group
EPLF	Eritrean People's Liberation Front
EPRDF	Ethiopian People's Revolutionary Democratic Front
EPRP	Ethiopian People's Revolutionary Party
EU	European Union

FAC	Forces Armées Congolaises/Congolese Armed Forces
FAC	Front d'Action Commune/Front for Common Action
FAFN	Forces Armées des Forces Nouvelles/Armed Forces of the New Forces
FAN	Forces Armées du Nord/Armed Forces of the North
FANCI	Forces Armées Nationales de Côte d'Ivoire/Armed Forces of Côte d'Ivoire
FANT	Forces Armées Nationales Tchadiennes/National Armed Forces of Chad
FAP	Forces Armées Populaires/Popular Armed Forces
FAPLA	Forcas Armadas Populares de Libertação de Angola/ Popular Armed Forces for the Liberation of Angola
FARDC	Forces Armées de la République Démocratique du Congo/Armed Forces of the Democratic Republic of Congo
FAT	Forces Armées du Tchad/Armed Forces of Chad
FAZ	Forces Armées du Zaire/Armed Forces of Zaire
FDC	Forum for Democratic Change
FDD	Forces pour la Défense de la Démocratie/Forces for the Defense of Democracy
FDLR	Forces Démocratiques pour la Libération de Rwanda/ Democratic Forces for the Liberation of Rwanda
FDP	Front Démocratique et Patriotique/Democratic and Patriotic Front
FDU	Forces Démocratiques Unies/United Democratic Forces
FIS	Front Islamique du Salut/Islamic Salvation Front
FLEC	Frente da Libertação do Enclave de Cabinda (also Front pour la Libération de l'Enclave de Cabinda)/ Liberation Front for the Cabinda Enclave
FLN	Front de Libération Nationale/National Liberation Front
FMG	Federal Military Government
FNLA	Frente Nacional da Libertação de Angola/National Front for the Liberation of Angola
FPI	Front Populaire Ivorien/Ivorian Popular Front
FRELIMO	Frente da Libertação de Moçambique/Mozambique Liberation Front

FRODEBU	Front Burundien pour la Démocratie/Burundian Democratic Front
FROLINAT	Front de Libération Nationale du Tchad/Chad National Liberation Front
FRONSA	Front for the National Salvation of Uganda
FRPI	Front Patriotique de la Résistance d'Ituri/Patriotic Resistance Front of Ituri
FRUD	Front for the Restoration of Unity and Democracy
FUC	Front Uni pour le Changement/United Front for Change
GDP	Gross Domestic Product
GIA	Groupe Islamique Armée/Armed Islamic Group
GNP	Gross National Product
GPRA	Gouvernement Provisoire de la République Algérienne/Provisional Government of the Algerian Republic
GRAE	Governo Revoluçionario de Angola no Exilo/Revolutionary Government of Angola in Exile
GSU	General Service Unit
GUNT	Gouvernement d'Union Nationale de Transition/National Union Transitional Government
ICC	International Criminal Court
ICRC	International Committee of the Red Cross
ICTR	International Criminal Tribunal for Rwanda
IFP	Inkatha Freedom Party
IGAD	Intergovernmental Authority on Development
IMF	International Monetary Fund
INPFL	Independent National Patriotic Front of Liberia
IRC	International Red Cross
IWG	International Working Group
JEM	Justice and Equity Movement
JMC	Joint Military Commission
JTF	Joint Task Force
KPCS	Kimberley Process Certification Scheme
LRA	Lord's Resistance Army
LURD	Liberians United for Reconciliation and Democracy
MDC	Movement for Democratic Change

MDDI	Mouvement pour la Démocratie et le Développement Intégrale/Movement for Democracy and Integral Development
MEND	Movement for the Emancipation of the Niger Delta
MFA	Movimento das Forças Armadas/Movement of the Armed Forces
MIA	Mouvement Islamiste Armée/Armed Islamic Movement
MINURCA	United Nations Mission to the Central African Republic
MISAB	Inter-African Mission to Monitor the Bangui Accords
MJP	Mouvement pour la Justice et la Paix/Movement for Justice and Peace
MLC	Mouvement pour la Libération du Congo/Movement for the Liberation of the Congo
MNC	Mouvement National Congolais/National Congolese Movement
MOG	Military Observer Group
MOJA	Movement for Justice in Africa
MONUC	United Nations Mission in the Democratic Republic of Congo
MPA	Mouvement du Peuple Anjouaniste/Anjouan People's Movement
MPCI	Mouvement Patriotique de la Côte d'Ivoire/Patriotic Movement of Côte d'Ivoire
MPIGO	Mouvement Populaire Ivoirien du Grand Ouest/ Popular Ivorian Movement of the Great West
MPLA	Movimento Popular para a Libertação de Angola/ Popular Movement for the Liberation of Angola
MPLT	Mouvement pour la Libération du Tchad/Movement for the Liberation of Chad
MPR	Mouvement Populaire de la Révolution/Popular Movement of the Revolution
MPS	Mouvement Patriotique du Salut/Patriotic Salvation Movement
MRC	Mouvement Révolutionnaire du Congo/Revolutionary Movement of the Congo

MRND	Mouvement Révolutionnaire National pour le Développement/National Revolutionary Movement for Development
MRNDD	Mouvement Républicain National pour la Démocratie et le Développement/National Republican Movement for Democracy and Development
MTLD	Mouvement pour le Triomphe des Libertés Démocratiques/ Movement for the Triumph of Democratic Liberties
NATO	North Atlantic Treaty Organization
NCP	National Congress Party
NDA	Northern Democratic Alliance
NDP	National Democratic Party
NDPVF	Niger Delta People's Volunteer Force
NECC	National Education Crisis Committee
NEPAD	New Partnership for Africa's Development
NGO	non-governmental organization
NIF	National Islamic Front
NMG	National Military Government
NP	National Party
NPFL	National Patriotic Front of Liberia
NPP	National Patriotic Party
NPRC	National Provisional Ruling Council
NRA	National Resistance Army
NRM	National Resistance Movement
OAS	Organisation de l'Armée Secrète/Secret Army Organization
OAU	Organization of African Unity
OIOS	(UN) Office of Internal Oversight Services
OLF	Oromo Liberation Front
ONLF	Oromo National Liberation Front
OPDO	Oromo People's Democratic Organization
OPEC	Organization of Petroleum Exporting Countries
OS	Organisation Secrète/Secret Organization
PAC	Pan-Africanist Congress
PAIGC	Partido Africano da Independência da Guine e Cabo Verde/African Party for the Independence of Guine and Cape Verde

PARMEHUTU	Parti du Mouvement de l'Émancipation du Peuple Hutu/Party of the Movement for the Emancipation of the Hutu People
PDA	Partido Democratico Angolana/Angolan Democratic Party
PDP	People's Democratic Party
PLAN	People's Liberation Army of Namibia
PLF	Popular Liberation Front
PMAC	Provisional Military Administrative Council
PPA	Parti Populaire Algérien/Algerian Popular Party
PRP	Parti de la Révolution Populaire/Popular Revolution Party
PUSIC	Party for Unity and Safeguarding the Integrity of Congo
RCC	Revolutionary Command Council
RCD	Rassemblement Congolais pour la Démocratie/Rally for Congolese Democracy
RENAMO	Resistência Nacional Moçambicana/Mozambican National Resistance
RND	Rallé National Démocratique/National Democratic Rally
RPF	Rwanda Patriotic Front
RRA	Rahanwayu Resistance Army
RUF	Revolutionary United Front
SACP	South African Communist Party
SADF	South African Defence Force
SALF	Somali Abo Liberation Front
SCS	Supreme Council of State
SLA	Somali Liberation Army
SNA	Somali National Alliance
SNM	Somali National Movement
SPLA	Sudan People's Liberation Army
SPLM	Sudan People's Liberation Movement
SRC	Supreme Revolutionary Council
SRRC	Somali Reconciliation and Restoration Council
SSA	Somali Salvation Alliance
SSDF	Somali Salvation Democratic Front
SSIM	South Sudan Independence Movement

SSU	Sudan Socialist Union
SWAPO	South West Africa People's Organization
TANKS	Tanganyika Concessions
TNG	Transitional National Government
TPLF	Tigre People's Liberation Front
UDF	United Democratic Front
UDI	Unilateral Declaration of Independence
UDMA	Union Démocratique du Manifeste Algérien/ Democratic Union of the Algerian Manifesto
UDPS	Union pour la Démocratie et le Progrès Social/Union for Democracy and Social Progress
UGEMA	Union Générale des Étudiants Mohametains Algériens/General Union of Algerian Muslim Students
ULIMO	United Liberation Movement of Liberia
UN	United Nations
UNAMIR	UN Assistance Mission in Rwanda
UNAMSIL	UN Mission to Sierra Leone
UNAVEM	(I, II, III) UN Angola Verification Mission
UNHCR	United Nations High Commissioner for Refugees
UNICEF	UN Children's Fund
UNIR	Union Nationale pour l'Indépendence et la Révolution/National Union for Independence and Revolution
UNITA	União Nacional para a Independência Total de Angola/National Union for the Total Independence of Angola
UNLF	Uganda National Liberation Front
UNMEE	UN Mission to Ethiopia and Eritrea
UNOCI	UN Operation in Côte d'Ivoire
UNOMIL	UN Observer Mission in Liberia
UNOMOZ	UN Operation in Mozambique
UNOMSA	UN Observer Mission in South Africa
UNOMUR	UN Observer Mission Uganda-Rwanda
UNOSOM	(I, II, III) UN Operation in Somalia
UNTAF	UN Task Force
UPA	União das Populaçoes de Angola/Union of the Angolan People

UPA	Union Populaire Algérienne/Popular Algerian Union
UPC	Uganda People's Congress
UPC	Union of Congolese Patriots
UPRONA	Union pour le Progrès National/Union for National Progress
USC	United Somali Congress
WFP	World Food Programme
WNBF	West Nile Bank Front
WSLF	Western Somali Liberation Front
ZANLA	Zimbabwe African National Liberation Army
ZANU	Zimbabwe African National Union
ZAPU	Zimbabwe African People's Union
ZIPRA	Zimbabwe People's Revolutionary Army

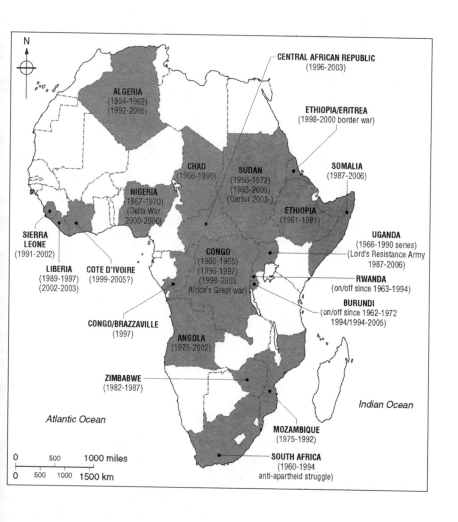

N

CENTRAL AFRICAN REPUBLIC
(1996-2003)

ALGERIA
(1954-1962)
(1992-2005)

ETHIOPIA/ERITREA
(1998-2000 border war)

CHAD
(1966-1990)

SUDAN
(1956-1972)
(1983-2005)
(Darfur 2003-)

SOMALIA
(1987-2006)

NIGERIA
1967-1970)
(Delta War
2000-2006)

ETHIOPIA
(1961-1991)

SIERRA
LEONE
(1991-2002)

UGANDA
(1966-1990 series)
(Lord's Resistance Army
1987-2006)

CONGO
(1960-1965)
(1996-1997)
(1998-2003)
Africa's Great war)

LIBERIA
(1989-1997)
(2002-2003)

COTE D'IVOIRE
(1999-2005?)

RWANDA
(on/off since 1963-1994)

BURUNDI
(on/off since 1962-1972
1994/1994-2005)

CONGO/BRAZZAVILLE
(1997)

ANGOLA
(1975-2002)

ZIMBABWE
(1982-1987)

Indian Ocean

Atlantic Ocean

MOZAMBIQUE
(1975-1992)

0   500   1000 miles

0   500   1000   1500 km

SOUTH AFRICA
(1960-1994
anti-apartheid struggle)

Chronology

1945 End of World War II; United Nations is established; Nationalist uprising at Setif in Algeria.

1947 Uprising against French in Madagascar.

1948 The National Party wins election in South Africa, heralding the beginning of the apartheid era.

1952 Outbreak of Mau Mau rebellion in Kenya; King Farouk overthrown in Egypt.

1954–62 War of independence (civil war) in Algeria.

1956 The Suez Crisis leads to first Soviet involvement in Africa; Sudan independence sparks growing rift between North and South that will soon develop into civil war.

1959 Hutu uprising against dominant Tutsi in Rwanda, which is not yet independent.

1960 Seventeen African colonies become independent; Sharpeville massacre in South Africa (21 March); Belgian Congo independent (30 June); Katanga secedes and disturbances develop into civil war—to 1965.

1961 Liberation struggle against the Portuguese launched in Angola.

1962–91 Eritrea launches war of secession against Ethiopia; the war becomes part of a wider civil war involving the Tigrayans and the Oromo.

1963 Formation of the Organization of African Unity (OAU); Liberation struggle launched against the Portuguese in Guinea Bissau.

1963 Hutus massacre Tutsis in Rwanda.

1964 Revolution in Zanzibar ends Arab domination; Liberation struggle against the Portuguese launched in Mozambique.

1965 Unilateral Declaration of Independence (UDI) by the white minority government in Rhodesia.

1966–90 Civil wars between North and South in Chad, involving French and Libyan interventions.

1967–70 Civil war in Nigeria.

1971 Idi Amin comes to power in Uganda.

1972 Hutu uprising against Tutsi domination in Burundi; End of first civil war in Sudan.

1974 Beginning of "creeping" revolution in Ethiopia; downfall of Haile Selassie; Overthrow of the Caetano government in Portugal signals end of Portugal's African empire.

1975 Angola becomes independent and civil war follows—to 1994; Mozambique becomes independent; the Rhodesian (white) government helps create opposition (RENAMO), leading to civil war—to 1992.

1976 Soweto uprising in South Africa.

1977–78 Ogaden War between Ethiopia and Somalia.

1979 Fall of Idi Amin after pro-Obote forces invade Uganda from Tanzania; a period of instability follows.

1980–86 Civil wars in Uganda; Yoweri Museveni emerges as victor.

1980–90 South Africa employs "destabilization" tactics against its neighbors, the Frontline States.

1982–87 "Dissidents" War in Zimbabwe.

1984– Renewal of North-South civil war in Sudan.

1987–88 Battle of Cuito Cuanavale in Angola, a defining point in the civil war.

1988 A year of negotiations according to the Crocker Plan, leads to a settlement between Angola, Namibia and South Africa; the Cubans leave Angola and Namibia becomes independent (March 1990); Massacres in Burundi.

1988–96 Civil war in Somalia and the fall of Siad Barre (1991).

1990–94 Violence in South Africa until the all-race elections of April 1994 bring an African National Congress victory and Nelson Mandela becomes the country's first black president.

1990–96 Civil war in Liberia; end of the Samuel Doe government (1990); Charles Taylor emerges as victor and wins presidential elections of July 1997.

1991–98 Civil war in Sierra Leone; deposed President Ahmad Tejan Kabbah is restored to power in 1998 with help from the Economic Community of West African States (ECOWAS) and Great Britain.

1992– Outbreak of civil war in Algeria between government and Islamic extremists.

1994 Genocidal massacres against Tutsi set off by extremist Hutus in Rwanda (possibly one million killed); Tutsi Rwanda Patriotic Front takes control of Rwanda.

1996–97 Civil war in Zaire: opponents of Mobutu Sese Seko are led by Laurent Kabila (with assistance from Rwanda and Uganda); Mobutu is overthrown (May 1997) and Kabila renames Zaire the Democratic Republic of Congo (DRC).

1998 Border confrontation between Eritrea and Ethiopia; Civil war erupts in Democratic Republic of Congo as former allies fall out with Kabila; the region becomes extremely unstable; Rwanda and Uganda support the rebels; Angola, Namibia, and Zimbabwe send troops to support Kabila.

1999 Heavy involvement of ECOMOG forces in Sierra Leone; Massacre of civilians in Eastern Congo; President Henri Konan Bedie of Côte d'Ivoire overthrown in coup; prelude to civil war.

2000 Mandela becomes peace facilitator for Burundi; Renewed fighting between Eritrea and Ethiopia; A new ceasefire agreed in Democratic Republic of Congo, which does not hold; Paul Kagame, a Tutsi, elected president of Rwanda; Britain sends 700 troops to bolster UN forces in Sierra Leone; Laurent Gbagbo inaugurated as president of Côte d'Ivoire; A comprehensive peace agreement ends 19-month war between Eritrea and Ethiopia.

2001 Kabila assassinated in DRC; his son Joseph becomes president; Hutu rebels attack Bujumbura, capital of Burundi, displacing 200,000; Rebel Revolutionary United Front (RUF) and pro-government Kamajor militia agree to end hostilities in Sierra Leone; Final OAU summit is held in Lusaka before it is replaced by the African Union (AU); President Pierre Buyoya of Burundi signs a power-sharing agreement to end eight years of civil war.

2002 Death of Jonas Savimbi effectively brings war in Angola to an end; President Ahmed Tejan Kabbah lifts state of emergency in Sierra Leone; Uganda and Rwanda agree to withdraw their troops from Democratic Republic of Congo; Fighting between factions in Abidjan, Côte d'Ivoire, and death of Robert Guei; Agreement upon a transitional government in DRC to last 30 months to elections.

2003 Upsurge of Islamist related violence in Algeria; Meeting in Marcoussis in France to resolve north-south confrontation in Côte d'Ivoire leads to massive anti-French riots in Abidjan; DRC government and main rebel groups agree to draft constitution in Pretoria; Joseph Kabila sworn in as head of transitional DRC government; Charles Taylor resigns as president of Liberia and flees to Nigeria.

2004 Lord's Resistance Army massacres 200 in refugee camp in northern Uganda; Pan-African Parliament inaugurated in Addis Ababa; Repeated claims made that ethnic cleansing was being carried out in Darfur by government-supported Janjawid militias; Sudan government and Sudan People's Liberation Army (SPLA) sign peace agreement.

2005 President Yoweri Museveni of Uganda orders new military offensive against Lord's Resistance Army (LRA); Report discloses UN peacekeepers involved in sexual abuse scandals in DRC; A comprehensive peace agreement signed by Sudan government and SPLA to end 20 years of civil war; UN peacekeepers launch offensive against rebels on Ituri Province of DRC; President Gbagbo of Côte d'Ivoire and rebels agree to end hostilities and disarm; African Union peacekeeping force in Darfur seeks logistical support from the European Union (EU) and the North Atlantic Treaty Organization (NATO); First African woman president, Ellen Johnson-Sirleaf, elected in Liberia.

2006 Death of John Garang in helicopter crash threatens to disrupt Sudan peace; Elections in DRC give Joseph Kabila a clear lead but not 50 percent of vote, and a run-off in October gives Kabila a clear majority; Uganda government and the LRA agree to end war; Ethiopian troops invade Somalia to suppress a government of the Union of Islamic Courts.

Introduction

Ever since 1945, and still more since 1960, the "annus mirabilis" of independence, the African continent has suffered from a series of wars. These have ranged from the liberation struggles against former colonial powers Great Britain, France, and Portugal to power struggles between factions in the aftermath of independence, border or adjustment wars between newly independent states, civil wars between ethnic or ideological groups or both, and wars which, whatever their origins, became intertwined with the Cold War, attracting interventions by major powers from outside the continent. Such wars, moreover, with their often multiple causes, have varied enormously in scope and duration.

There are problems in defining a civil war: at what point, for example, do domestic unrest and demonstrations or riots against a particular regime qualify to be described as a civil war rather than merely civil disturbances? And when does a civil war become an international war? To take one example, between 1966 and 1990 Chad was in a more or less permanent state of civil war; yet this was greatly complicated by Libyan ambitions in the north for, although Libya intervened on one side in Chad's civil war, its real objective was to gain control of the uranium-rich Aozou Strip.

At least two of the liberation struggles against the colonial powers, that in Algeria against the French and the Mau Mau rebellion against the white settlers in Kenya, also displayed many characteristics of civil wars. The Algerian independence struggle, which lasted from 1954 to 1962, saw one million *colons* (the name given to the French settlers) assisted at the struggle's height by 500,000 French troops pitted against nine million indigenous Algerians. Although this was primarily a nationalist struggle for independence, the fact that many of the *colons* were second- or third- or even fourth-generation settlers who regarded Algeria as their home provided this most brutal of wars with all the hallmarks of a civil war. In contrast, the Mau Mau struggle in Kenya was on a much smaller scale and, though at one level comparable to the war in Algeria, was more a colonial than a civil war.

The long-drawn-out anti-colonial wars against the Portuguese in Angola and Mozambique were nationalist liberation struggles, yet, in each case, these wars formed the prelude to subsequent power struggles to obtain political mastery in the newly independent countries which emerged. And here too the power struggles were to be complicated by ethnic alignments, interventions by interested neighbors, and Cold War considerations.

Like civil wars everywhere, those in Africa, with hardly an exception, drew in outside powers. The United States and the Soviet Union became involved in Angola, Ethiopia, and Mozambique for Cold War reasons. Neighbors became involved in Burundi, Rwanda, Uganda, or Zaire, either in order to limit the spread of violence across borders into their own countries, or in support of the faction which most favored their interests. Britain and France became involved (in Nigeria or Congo Brazzaville, for example) in order to maintain or extend their influence from the colonial past, which was then on the wane. The United Nations (UN) and the Organization of African Unity (OAU) mounted, or attempted to mount, peacekeeping operations, though rarely with much success. The Economic Community of West African States (ECOWAS) mounted interventions in the civil wars in both Liberia and Sierra Leone during the 1990s, and these can be seen as the first real attempts at regional peacekeeping in Africa. Mercenaries have appeared all over the continent in pursuit of their dubious trade; and few combatants in any of these civil wars had much difficulty in obtaining the means to continue their struggles, either from international arms traders or from outside powers with a vested interest in the war in question.

BURUNDI AND RWANDA

The terrible genocidal massacres that occurred in Rwanda in 1994 and continued to affect both that country and Burundi thereafter have raised a question that would have been regarded as unthinkable a few years earlier: should the world community, through the instrument of the United Nations, consider controlled ethnic cleansing—the reorganization of the

Tutsi and Hutu peoples in those two countries by resettlement and partition into separate entities—as the only viable solution that might prevent further genocide in the future? The forced movement of peoples, ethnic cleansing, is not new and can be traced back historically at least as far as the Assyrian Empire. The term came into modern usage during the civil wars in disintegrating Yugoslavia during the first half of the 1990s. As a result, the forced separation of peoples, if all else fails, may come to be seen as the least unacceptable solution in a situation where suspicions and hatreds between two ethnic groups have become so deeply ingrained that persuading them to continue living together, mixed as one people, is patently unworkable.

The Hutu-Tutsi confrontations in Burundi and Rwanda, which have steadily escalated ever since independence, also pose fundamentally awkward questions about the workings of democracy. In both countries, the Hutus represent a majority of approximately 85 percent, while the Tutsis are in the position of being permanent minorities of approximately 15 percent. In these circumstances, and given the deep fears to be found on both sides, democracy in the form of one-person one-vote will result in the permanent rule of the majority ethnic group over the minority group. Should some alternative form of government be considered? It is easy for outsiders, in the guise of the United Nations or the big powers, to insist upon the superiority of democracy over other forms of government, but if that democracy works to the permanent disadvantage of one group, with no prospect of change, then an alternative form of government needs to be considered.

THE TRIBAL BASIS OF WARS

Wars in Africa have often been tribal-based in ways that have not been so evident elsewhere in the world, although the 1991–1995 disintegration of Yugoslavia was totally tribal in its nature. Ethnic or tribal suspicions exacerbate existing ideological or political divisions so that, for example, a post-independence power struggle may also become an ethnic war. The long-drawn-out civil war between North and South in Sudan embraces a number of strands that reinforce each other: the majority in the North are both Muslim and Arab, or Arabicized peoples, while the minority in the South are largely black Nilotic groups (with their own tribal antagonisms) who are either Christian or follow various traditional African religions, but are not Muslim. In addition, there exists a historical racial divide between North and South, with the Northerners seeing the South as a source of slaves. Furthermore, the concentration of political power and the control of the country's wealth have lain overwhelmingly with the North ever since independence. In these circumstances, the civil war which began shortly after independence, and then enjoyed a truce under Gaafar Mohammed Nimeiri from 1972 to 1984 before breaking out again, was predictable. The peace, so laboriously worked out over the last years of the 20th and first of the 21st centuries, envisages the possibility that after six years, should it so wish, the South may secede from Sudan and go its own way.

Until the late 1990s, such a suggestion would have been treated as anathema by the OAU, whose charter made the borders of its newly independent member states inviolable. Yet more than 40 years after the formation of the OAU, Africa was coming to accept that another inviolable principle, that there must never be interference in the internal affairs of another state, should no longer automatically apply. In Burundi, Liberia, and Sierra Leone—to mention but three troubled states—the OAU (now the African Union), ECOWAS, and the neighboring states have each argued that there is a higher principle mandating intervention when genocide or a civil war threatens people's lives, liberties, and human rights.

THE EFFECTS OF THE END OF COLONIALISM

In Asia civil wars have been ideological (Vietnam) and religious (Afghanistan), as well as being about wealth and poverty. In Latin America they have been about the political Left versus the Right, the "haves" versus the "have-nots." In Africa these same factors have operated with the addition of all of the strains and complications arising out of the most recent period of the "end of empires," with all its ensuing succession problems. Many of the civil wars in Africa have broken out, more or less directly, as a result of the end of colonialism. The centralizing tendencies of the European colonizers created artificial states whose principal unifying factor was the presence of the colonial power, such as the British in Nigeria, the French in Chad, and the Portuguese in Angola.

The Nigerian civil war illustrates a number of these post-colonial problems. As the British expanded into what became Nigeria during the second half of the 19th century, they created not one, but several colonial structures, which they only brought together into a single large colony on the eve of World War I in 1914. Subsequently, until independence in 1960, the British colonial administrators became fierce rivals as they safeguarded the interests of their different regions in Nigeria—the North, the West, and the East. These colonial rivalries were carried over into the post-independence era since, in any case, they already represented ethnic or tribal divisions, as between the Hausa-Fulani of the North, the Yoruba of the West, and the Ibos of the East. As long as the British, as the colonial power, held the center, Nigeria was ruled as a single entity, although there were many centrifugal forces at work. But once the British departed, a power struggle developed as to who, or which region, should also control the central government. Eventually the regional pulls became too great to control effectively from the center, resulting in the attempted breakaway of the eastern region as Biafra in 1966–1967, which led to the civil war of 1967–1970.

The results of colonialism go deep and not least in the ways in which western sources have explained subsequent wars in Africa. Too frequently, western explanations for developments in Africa are racist in tone and assume a degree of tribalism which, it is suggested, is unique to the African continent. At least, after the Yugoslav debacle of 1991–1995, such attitudes will be less easy to sustain. Nonetheless, European and American observers tend to see Africa from their own perspectives and are likely to explain what happens on the continent in terms of their own perceptions of democracy and human rights. When an empire comes to an end, it invariably leaves a series of vacuums behind it. In the Africa of the 1960s and 1970s, not one but four European empires—those of Belgium, Britain, France, and Portugal came to an end, and so it is hardly surprising that the continent has suffered from a series of political and power implosions. It is the need to fill these vacuums that lies at the center of much of the violence that has troubled Africa over the 50 years since 1960.

In its dealings with Africa during the 1990s, the West has overemphasized the value of democracy, as though that political system alone can solve the continent's problems. Yet, as attractive as democracy may be (as the least oppressive of political systems), it does not always answer the immediate needs of a country just emerging from a civil war. As with so many other of Africa's problems, alternative approaches must be examined. On the one hand, it is insulting to suggest that because African states are new or young they are incapable of handling democracy; on the other hand, it is naive to imagine that only a democratic approach will solve their problems. Democracy, for example, was manifestly not the answer in Rwanda during the 1990s.

THE AFRICAN ATTITUDE TOWARD ETHNIC PROBLEMS

In the heady 1960s of newly found independence, African leaders refused to talk in ethnic terms—tribalism was a taboo subject—and instead insisted upon the united nationalist nature of their new countries: their people were Nigerians, Kenyans, Zambians, and so on. Yet tribalism kept rearing its head and in almost every case where democracy was established, it was largely tribally based. In Tanzania, President Julius Nyerere could justify the one-party state on the grounds of preventing separate political parties identifying themselves with separate tribal groups.

But Tanzania was almost unique in having a variety of small tribes, none of which was in a position to dominate the others. The more usual pattern would involve three or four major tribes, which either had long histories of antagonism, or at least suspicion toward one another, or else had gone their separate ways until the exigencies of European colonialism had brought them into closer contact. In the deeply troubled states of Burundi and Rwanda, moreover, there were for all practical purposes two tribes, one with a permanent and massive majority, the other destined always to be a minority. As a result, the minority Tutsis tried various non-democratic means of seizing and then holding on to power for themselves. The Hutus, frustrated by such tactics, turned to violence, although both sides in this long-lasting confrontation have employed equally atrocious acts of violence toward each other. In their particular case, to insist upon a democratic system dependent upon one-person one-vote is simply to ensure that permanent control would lie with the Hutus at the expense of the Tutsis. It is this type of situation, in these two tiny landlocked countries, that raises two critical yet explosive questions: First, does such a situation justify outside intervention? And second, can a clear case be made in this instance for a UN-enforced policy of ethnic cleansing, whose end result would be to create two separate states, one each for these two tribal groups?

THE UNITED NATIONS IN AFRICA

The end of the Cold War raised the hope that at last the United Nations would be able to play a more active role worldwide in keeping the peace. During the 1990s Africa certainly provided many opportunities for United Nations action—in Somalia, Burundi, Rwanda, Zaire (now the Democratic Republic of Congo), Congo (Brazzaville), Angola, Mozambique, Liberia, Sierra Leone—yet its record has, on the whole, been dismal. This is only in part the fault of the United Nations, which is bedeviled by power politics at the top among the members of the Security Council or, when it does intervene, finds itself starved of the funds and sufficient personnel or backup to do an effective job. Nonetheless, the United Nations provided some important leads during the 1990s that will bear fruit in the new century. In 1991 the secretary-general, Javier Perez de Cuellar, said: "It is now increasingly felt that the principle of non-interference within the essential domestic jurisdiction of states cannot be regarded as a protective barrier behind which human rights could be massively or systematically violated with impunity. . . . The case for not impinging on sovereignty, territorial integrity and political independence of states is by itself indubitably strong. It would only weaken if it were to carry the implication that sovereignty . . . includes the right to mask slaughter or the launching of systematic campaigns of decimation or forced exodus, civil strife or insurrection."

His successor as secretary-general, Boutros Boutros-Ghali, believed that the United Nations had the right to intervene in any conflict to enforce the peace regardless of sovereignty. Boutros-Ghali also believed that problems arising from "poverty, social unrest and humanitarian tragedies in just one state, if left unchecked, might reach a magnitude that is capable of disrupting the stability of the entire region." And it was Boutros-Ghali who revived the earlier UN idea of devolving peacekeeping responsibilities to regional authorities. He, in turn, was succeeded by Kofi Annan, the first black African to hold the post of UN secretary-general, at a time of unprecedented change and harsh problems in his own continent.

REGIONAL PEACEKEEPING

The regional intervention in the Liberian civil war by the Economic Community of West African States (ECOWAS) during the 1990s, marked an important advance in African efforts at peacekeeping. Earlier interventions, such as those by Morocco to support Zaire's Mobutu Sesi Seko during the Shaba wars at the end of the 1970s or Tanzania's intervention in Uganda in 1979, had taken place, but these were designed to support a particular side in a national quarrel and did not qualify as peacekeeping operations. The ECOWAS interventions by means of ECOMOG (the ECOWAS Monitoring Group) were an attempt by West African countries, led by Nigeria, to end the civil wars first in Liberia and then in Sierra Leone and were undertaken with the blessings of both the UN and the Organization of African Unity. As operations, these ECOMOG interventions were far from perfect (though certainly no less successful than other exercises by the UN) and they had the merit of being all-African efforts and, as such, they fitted in with the newly emerging UN orthodoxy of regional peacekeeping. Nigeria is the only West African power with the capacity to intervene effectively in neighboring states and, therefore, was the natural leader of the ECOMOG operation, although this was assisted by forces from Côte d'Ivoire, The Gambia, Ghana, Guinea, and Senegal. Between 1990 and 1994 ECOMOG brokered numerous peace accords or truces in Liberia and though these were constantly broken (as were similar accords in Yugoslavia), the process could still be seen as a breakthrough for Africa which, for the first time, assumed direct and primary responsibility for peacekeeping operations on the continent.

Africa not only suffers from the after-effects of recent colonialism; it is also especially subject to projections of its image by outsiders rather than by Africans. In part, this is a consequence of the general weakness of the African media; in part, it results from a deeply one-sided and often racist western media, led by the former European colonial powers, which projects Africa as the former colonial powers wish to see it, in the light of their own recent withdrawal from control. In consequence, most outsiders see Africa as a backward, deeply troubled continent, unable to cope with its own problems. This image, which often suits a western world that is loathe to see newly independent countries set out on paths of their own, has been enhanced by the residues of colonialism and interference by aid donors, the World Bank, or the International Monetary Fund (IMF), in countries that are simply too weak economically to resist such external pressures. When seeking reasons to explain African civil wars or the breakdown of law and order, the western (ex-colonial) explanation, too often, is that independence came too soon; this explanation implies that a continuing colonial presence would have prevented such breakdowns. At one level this is true, but it ignores the fact that colonialism did not solve problems of ethnic rivalry or other divisive elements in the colonial states that had been created, but either sat on them so that the territory would operate as the metropolitan power wished or sometimes exacerbated them by pursuing policies of "divide and rule." Thus, however long the colonial powers might have remained, the problems would still have surfaced when they left.

TYPES OF CIVIL WAR

African civil wars, broadly, have been of three kinds: racial, ideological, or for political power, though in most cases these motivations have overlapped. Divided as many African countries are between a number of equally balanced ethnic groups with distinct and often antagonistic traditions, it is hardly surprising that the ethnic factor has played a significant part in many of the continent's conflicts. When ideological factors are added to the ethnic mix—some form of Marxism versus western-oriented free enterprise during the Cold War, for example—or when divisions of rival groups seek control of the political system in the immediate aftermath of independence, the violent results should hardly come as a surprise. Since, moreover, the great majority of African countries achieved their independence within a decade or so of one another, comparable arguments for division and conflict had a contagious effect upon the continent as a whole.

Many African leaders and intellectuals have blamed colonialism for their troubles and a good deal of blame is deserved; yet with regard to particular problems where colonialism might justly have been blamed for subsequent civil wars, African leaders have kept conspicuously quiet. Combinations of diverse peoples under single European colonial umbrellas resulted in complex political legacies once the colonial powers withdrew, as in the case of Nigeria. Yet African nationalisms have ensured that no post-independence government will consider whether a country might be better off if two divisive elements were in fact separated. Ethiopia fought a 30-year war, first under Emperor Haile Selassie and then under the Marxist Dergue of Mariam Mengistu, before ceding Eritrea's right to become a separate state.

The map of the world is changing all the time and rigid insistence that boundaries are forever inviolate runs contrary to political pragmatism and existing realities. In the Africa of the 1990s, at least two countries or regions ought to have been examined in terms of asking whether some form of partition would not be more realistic and humane than the existing and apparently open-ended conflicts: the first was Sudan and the second, Burundi and Rwanda. In the case of Sudan, a partition between North and South (now on the agenda) would coincide with religious, ethnic, and historical divisions and the two resultant countries might then both be able to prosper. In the case of Burundi and Rwanda (given their turbulent history of mass slaughters since independence), partition and reorganization into separate entities consisting of Hutus and Tutsis, at least presents an alternative that might bring to an end the years of brutal conflict that have bedeviled these two countries since independence.

EXTERNAL INTERVENTIONS

Given the general weakness of the African continent with its tiny proportion of world trade, dependence upon aid, and overall vulnerability to external pressures, it is unrealistic to suppose that it can escape interference from outside. That being the case, it is important, insofar as it is possible to do so, to channel and control such interventions. What then should be the role of the United Nations? It has tried peacekeeping valiantly enough, despite its many handicaps, and during the 1990s was involved in Angola, Burundi, Namibia, Mozambique, Rwanda, Somalia, and South Africa. Angola, Burundi, Rwanda, and Somalia may be seen as failures, the others as moderate success stories. The move toward regional peacekeeping as in Liberia makes sense for the future, and if regional powers—the obvious ones being Nigeria and South Africa—have the formal backing of the African Union (AU) and the United Nations, they are likely to become the core countries in any future peacekeeping operations.

The role of the major powers is more problematic: they demonstrated quite clearly in the case of Rwanda (in 1994), for example, that they did not wish to become involved in any major peacekeeping role (and this despite the limited "in-out" exercise carried out by France). At the same time they are prone to intervene when they believe their interests to be involved, as with France in the 1997 civil war in Congo (Brazzaville). What appears to be the most likely development in the future—there were indications of this during the ECOWAS intervention in Liberia—would be for external powers to provide financial and logistical support for a regional peacekeeping operation led by a country such as Nigeria.

Almost without exception, civil wars in Africa have drawn in supporters from outside: either self-interested African neighbors or greater powers bent upon safeguarding their interests in the region. Throughout the years from 1960 onward, whenever civil strife became a factor in an African country, there existed the background fear that external intervention would follow, and over these years there have been British, Belgian, French, Soviet, and American interventions. Sometimes interventions have been carried out under the umbrella of the United Nations, while in other cases they have been covert, with aid from a source such as the Central Intelligence Agency (CIA) being channeled indirectly into the area of conflict. At any rate, the success of liberation struggles signaled an immediate switch to power struggles for ultimate political mastery, as for example in Angola and Mozambique. Meanwhile, the creation of the one-party state, which has been a particularly African phenomenon over this period, has invited violent opposition inasmuch as the physical overthrow of a one-party regime is often seen as the only way of changing governments. Centralized state power under charismatic and often corrupt leaders cannot easily be dislodged but when, finally, the opposition is no longer prepared to accept such dictatorships (as happened in Zaire during 1997) the result is a civil war.

Wars of all kinds attract intervention and this may come in many guises. Apart from military assistance to one or the other side, or efforts at peacekeeping, a war situation attracts offers of aid—for humanitarian purposes, to enable an interested outside power to maintain a footing in the country, or to assist in the subsequent rebuilding and rehabilitation of a war-ravaged territory. Similarly, wars attract non-governmental organizations (NGOs), which become involved for humanitarian purposes, although their presence sometimes does more harm than good.

CONCLUSION

The period since the end of the Cold War in 1990 has seen a number of civil wars worldwide, and at least some lessons may perhaps be learned from them. A good many efforts at conflict mediation have been attempted in Africa, though few have had much success. The first lesson to be learned is that peace agreements too often reflect the "reasoning" of the mediators as opposed to the "aspirations" of the combatants. As long as this is the case, such agreements are liable to be broken almost as soon as they are made, and certainly as soon as one or the other side sees an advantage in breaking such an agreement. Furthermore, a mediator is unlikely to have any success if one side in a conflict believes it is on the verge of winning outright. This was the situation in 1997 when President Nelson Mandela of South Africa attempted to mediate in the Zaire conflict: there was no reason why Laurent Kabila should stop an advance, which by that time, showed every sign of succeeding absolutely. Mediation, as a general rule, is only likely to succeed when both sides are either evenly balanced and have reached a particular level of exhaustion or war weariness, or have reluctantly embarked upon hostilities that they both wish to terminate (a condition that is somewhat rare). Further, the mediator or peacekeeper must be seen to be impartial. In Somalia during 1993, for example, once the Americans were seen to be demonizing General Mohammed Farah Aideed, their presence in the country became counterproductive. Mediation that attempts to return a country to the status quo before the outbreak of hostilities will not succeed, since it is equivalent to taking the side of the government or regime that is under attack.

Perhaps the most important lesson for Africa to emerge from the conflicts of the 1990s is that, increasingly, the continent is on its own. The compulsions of the Cold War have passed and with them have also passed the "aid age" and the need for the two sides in the Cold War to seek allies. As the world enters the era of economic globalization, Africa is beginning to realize how little it matters on a global economic scale, and though this may seem a harsh judgment, facing up to it could also herald a new African realism. While they may have had only limited success, both the countries which intervened in Liberia and Sierra Leone under the umbrella of ECOWAS, and the neighbors of Burundi and Rwanda which tried to limit the awful slaughter, had largely assumed—and rightly—that they could expect little assistance from outside the continent. In the future, increasingly, peacekeeping in Africa must come from its regional powers led by the AU and backed by the United Nations.

The Dictionary

– A –

ABBAS, FERHAT (1899–1985). One of the older generation of nationalists, pharmacist Ferhat Abbas, formed the Union Populaire Algérienne (UPA) in 1938. The UPA advocated the assimilation of Algerians into French culture through increased education and the extension of the franchise. Before this time, in 1936, Ferhat Abbas had written: "Algeria is French soil, and we are Frenchmen with the personal status of Muslims." He also claimed that he was unable to discover any trace of an Algerian nation. By 1940, Ferhat Abbas had changed his stand and had come to oppose total assimilation, calling instead for an autonomous Algerian state federated with France. On 10 February 1943, he submitted a manifesto to the French and Allied authorities in Algiers in which he demanded self-determination for Algerians, complete liberty and equality of Algeria's inhabitants without distinction of race or religion, and the recognition of the Arab language as official and equal in status with French. On 14 March 1944, with the support of Messali Hadj and his Parti Populaire Algérien (PPA)/Algerian Popular Party, which had also started in the 1930s, Ferhat Abbas launched Les Amis du Manifeste et de la Liberté (AML)/Friends of the Manifesto and of Liberty. The AML pursued the nationalist objectives laid down by Ferhat Abbas in his 1943 Manifesto to the Allies. Following the **Setif** uprising of May 1945, the AML was proscribed and Ferhat Abbas was arrested by the French authorities; he was released under the terms of an amnesty in March 1946.

He then formed the Union Démocratique du Manifeste Algérien (UDMA)/Democratic Union of the Algerian Manifesto, which polled 71 percent of the Algerian votes and captured 11 of the 18 seats allotted Algeria in the 2 June 1946 elections to the French Constituent

Assembly. On 9 August 1946 when the Assembly met, Ferhat Abbas advanced proposals for the creation of an autonomous Algerian state to be federated with France. The Assembly refused to discuss it. In an address to the Assembly of 23 August 1946 Ferhat Abbas said: "The Algerian personality, the Algerian fatherland, which I did not find in 1936 amongst the Muslim masses, I find here today. The change that has taken place in Algeria is visible to the naked eye, and neither you nor I can have the right to ignore it." However, the Assembly passed the Statute of Algeria (on which 15 Algerian deputies abstained), turning Algeria into a group of departments. The UDMA then withdrew from the Assembly and refused to take part in the forthcoming elections. Between 1947 and 1951, increased rigging of votes and discrimination against nationalists in Algeria formed the prelude to the coming struggle. However, the nationalists began to split between the more old-fashioned who wished to pursue only peaceful means and those who advocated violence. On 1 November 1954, the **Front de Libération Nationale** (FLN)/National Liberation Front was founded and launched the revolution. Ferhat Abbas was still a moderate and opposed the use of violence and in *La République Algérienne* on 12 November 1954, he wrote: "We continue to be persuaded that violence will settle nothing."

As the war escalated, the Algerian leaders began to flee the country; at a news conference in Cairo on 26 April 1956, Ferhat Abbas pledged his allegiance to the FLN. On 18 September 1958, the FLN established a government in exile in Tunis: **Gouvernement Provisoire de la République Algérienne** (GPRA)/Provisional Government of the Algerian Republic with Ferhat Abbas as its leader. This represented the height of his career, but also the end of his real political influence. In 1961 the GPRA split over the question of whether it should concentrate on exercising diplomatic pressures or intensify the armed struggle. At Tripoli in August 1961 Ferhat Abbas was removed from his position as head of the GPRA and replaced by the more radical Ben Khedda.

AFEWERKE, ISSAYAS (1946–). Issayas Afewerke spent the quarter century of his adult life from 1966, when he reached the age of 20, first as a guerrilla fighter in **Eritrea** until he became the leader of the **Eritrean People's Liberation Front** (EPLF) and then, after 1993, as head of state of the newly independent Eritrea. In 1991, he entered Asmara at the head of a victorious guerrilla army to form an Eritrean government. Afewerke, whose father was a clerk in the civil service, was born in Asmara in 1946; after attending high school he went to University College at Addis Ababa, though he only completed a year of studies before he left the university to join the **Eritrean Liberation Front** (ELF).

He was sent to the People's Republic of China for a year's training and on his return was made commissioner (in charge) of an ELF territorial command. In 1970, however, the ELF was split by factional arguments with part breaking away to form the EPLF; Afewerke joined the latter group in which he was given the command of a fighting unit. In 1977, Afewerke was promoted to the position of deputy secretary-general of the EPLF and 10 years later, in 1987, he rose to the position of secretary-general, the effective leader of the EPLF. Although he began his political career as a Marxist, Afewerke became increasingly pragmatic as he came closer to wielding real power and eventually was ready to adopt parliamentary democracy. In 1991, following the occupation of Asmara, he became the chairman of the provisional government of Eritrea; its principal task was to prepare the people for a referendum which would decide the future of the country—whether it should remain linked to **Ethiopia** or become totally independent. The referendum was held during April 1993 and the people voted by an overwhelming 99.8 percent for independence. Afewerke was then elected president of the new state by the National Assembly.

Subsequently, Eritrea under Afewerke proved an uneasy neighbor to the three countries with which it had borders. In 1995, he took the lead in coordinating opposition to the Islamist military regime in **Sudan** when he announced publicly his readiness to provide arms to Sudanese groups seeking to overthrow their government. Afewerke then predicted that the government of Sudan was on the verge of collapse and later accused Sudan of providing logistical support to Ethiopia in the war that had erupted between Eritrea and Ethiopia in 1998. In 1999, Sudan supported opposition groups aiming to overthrow Afewerke. However, Qatar hosted a reconciliation meeting between the leaders of Sudan and Eritrea. After five years of "confrontation" by Afewerke, diplomatic relations between Eritrea and

Sudan were restored in January 2000. President **Omar Ahmed al-Bashir** of Sudan visited Eritrea in February and Afewerke returned the visit in October. Subsequent relations between the two countries remained uneasy.

Meanwhile, a border dispute with **Ethiopia** in May 1998 led to a full-scale war between the two countries. In February 1999, after eight months of truce, the war with Ethiopia broke out again and only in December 2000 did President Afewerke and Prime Minister **Meles Zenawi** of Ethiopia sign a peace agreement to mark the formal end of the 19-month border war between the two countries. This agreement did not end the dispute and, in 2004, Afewerke complained to the United Nations that Ethiopia should be compelled to implement the 2002 border ruling. In April 2005, Afewerke said that the inevitability of war with Ethiopia was "a firm conclusion that we have reached." This conclusion, he said, was based on "our assessment that Ethiopia harbors expansionist ambitions and will act on them." *See also* ERITREA–ETHIOPIA BORDER WAR.

AFRICAN NATIONAL CONGRESS (ANC). The African National Congress, which was founded in 1912, is Africa's oldest political party and was originally created to oppose white and especially Afrikaner domination after **South Africa** became a self-governing Dominion of the British **Commonwealth** in 1910. The National Party under Dr. D. F. Malan won the elections of 1948 with a platform based upon the separation of the races and the dominance of the white minority (apartheid). In 1950, when the government introduced its Population Registration Bill for classification into racial groups, the ANC council of action decided to cease all cooperation with the government.

Throughout the 1950s, using a variety of tactics though condemning violence, the ANC opposed apartheid as it was systematically introduced to cover all aspects of South African life. In a conference at Kliptown in 1955, the ANC adopted its "Freedom Charter" in which appeared the statement: "South Africa belongs to all who live in it, black and white, and that no government can justly claim authority unless it is based on the will of the people."

In 1961, following the Sharpeville massacre of 21 March 1960, the ANC abandoned its non-violent policy. Already on 5 April 1960, in the immediate aftermath of Sharpeville, both the ANC and the Pan-Africanist Congress (PAC) had been declared illegal organizations. Following the ban, the ANC went underground in South Africa while establishing offices in various key capitals in Africa, Europe, and North America. On 16 December 1961, the ANC published the manifesto of Umkhonto we Sizwe (Spear of the Nation), its newly formed armed wing. Umkhonto we Sizwe began its campaigns by blowing up buildings and power pylons. It was the nucleus of a later army, although initially it conducted its actions without violence to life. It sent members abroad for guerrilla training and on 10 May 1963 was banned by the government. By 1976, the leadership of Umkhonto we Sizwe consisted of Joe Modise (leader), **Chris Hani** (political commissioner), and **Joe Slovo** (chief of staff in **Mozambique**). In 1977, it claimed that 55,000 persons had undergone training in the "army of the ANC." Its attacks upon targets in South Africa were stepped up at the end of the 1970s and included the SASOL I and SASOL II fuel plants.

On 30 January 1981, the chief of the South African Defence Force (SADF) announced that the planning and control headquarters of the ANC at Matola (Maputo) in Mozambique had been destroyed. The incidence of attacks mounted was increased sharply in 1982. During the 1980s South African hit squads targeted ANC activists in countries outside the Republic, killing Ruth First (the wife of Joe Slovo) by letter parcel bomb in Maputo in 1982 and Dulcie September, who was shot in Paris in 1988. Although the South African government always claimed that it was able to cope with ANC threats, this was often denied by the efforts it made to "take out" ANC headquarters or other targets inside Mozambique, Lesotho, Swaziland, or Botswana under its policy of destabilization.

The 1984 **Nkomati Accord** between South Africa and Mozambique was a blow to the ANC, which was now denied transit facilities through Mozambique. **Nelson Mandela** who, with his close friend **Oliver Tambo**, had become the most prominent ANC leader at the beginning of the 1960s, and had been sentenced to life imprisonment in 1964 on charges of treason, was offered release from prison on 31 January 1985 by President P. W. Botha if he would renounce violence. But Mandela replied from prison that the ANC had turned to violence "only when other forms of resistance were no longer open to us." An ANC meeting at Kabwe in Zambia during June 1985 decided to adopt a policy of assassination of police councillors and other collaborators, thus abandoning its previous policy of not attacking persons and only destroying inanimate objects. At the same meeting, the ANC elected non-blacks to its national executive committee, including Joe Slovo.

The ANC's president was Oliver Tambo, who had arranged to flee South Africa at the beginning of the 1960s to organize international support for the ANC while Mandela remained to organize internal resistance. At a press conference in Lusaka, Zambia, in January 1986, Tambo announced an escalation of ANC political and military action and said that the ANC would organize "mass units" among the local population in South Africa. On 19 May 1986, units of the SADF raided ANC targets in Botswana, Zambia, and **Zimbabwe** in a deliberate exercise to undermine the work of the Commonwealth Eminent Persons Group (EPG), whose members were then in South Africa to negotiate a dialogue between the government and the black majority. Zimbabwe's President **Robert Mugabe** said such raids would not prevent his country from supporting the ANC.

On 15 January 1987, in a broadcast from Addis Ababa, Tambo stated that the ANC had created "mass democratic organizations" inside South Africa including street committees, the Confederation of South African Trade Unions (COSATU), the United Democratic Front (UDF), the National Education Crisis Committee (NECC), and various affiliates. Tambo called upon "the young lions of our revolutionary struggle"—the comrades—to act as a "disciplined revolutionary force." As the ferment grew in South Africa during the later 1980s, the ANC published (9 August 1988) its Constitutional Guidelines for a democratic South Africa. The document was the result of two years' discussion and revision of the 1955 Freedom Charter. The occasion of Mandela's 70th birthday in June 1988 sparked off worldwide celebrations and calls for his release.

In 1989, President P. W. Botha resigned and was succeeded by **F. W. de Klerk** as president. De Klerk quickly saw that the only way forward for South Africa was for the government to come to terms with the ANC and other African parties and organizations. On 2 February 1990, he lifted the ban on the ANC and 32 other radical opposition groups, and on 11 February released Mandela unconditionally.

On 13 December 1990, Oliver Tambo returned to South Africa after 30 years in exile.

Between February 1990 and April 1994, the ANC consolidated its position in South Africa as the leading African political party and became the principal negotiator with the government. In the elections of April 1994, the ANC polled 62.7 percent of the votes, the National Party 20.4 percent, the Inkatha Freedom Party 10.5 percent, the Freedom Front 2.2 percent, the Democratic Party 1.7 percent, the PAC 1.2 percent, and the African Christian Democratic Party 0.5 percent. Nelson Mandela was sworn in as president of South Africa on 10 May 1994, and the ANC subsequently dominated the government of national unity until the National Party withdrew from it in 1996.

AFRICAN UNION (AU). At the beginning of the 21st century, the African Union replaced the **Organization of African Unity** (OAU). Somewhat reluctantly, at its annual summit of 2000 in Lome, Togo, the OAU had adopted a Libyan-sponsored resolution to turn the OAU into the African Union. A new African Union Charter was to replace the 1963 OAU Charter as well as the 1991 Abuja Treaty that had established the African Economic Community. A number of countries, led by **South Africa** and **Nigeria**, were reluctant to move too fast because they felt that Africa, with its many problems, was not yet ready to embark upon continental unity. However, the move to transform the OAU into the AU took on a momentum of its own. In July 2001, the OAU held its final annual summit in Lusaka, Zambia, before transforming itself into the African Union, which was loosely modeled upon the European Union (EU). The Constitutive Act, establishing the AU, had been adopted at the OAU summit in Lome the previous year and by May 2001, two-thirds of the OAU's 53 members had ratified it. Amaru Essy, the former foreign minister of **Côte d'Ivoire**, succeeded the OAU's long-lasting secretary-general Salim Ahmed Salim as secretary-general, for a year in which he was to create the framework of the AU. Unlike the OAU, the AU was to be based upon principles of good governance and was to work for the economic development of the continent as a whole. Funds for the new organization were urgently required, for it was to be more elaborate than the OAU. AU institutions, apart from a Pan-African Parliament, were to be a council of heads of state, a central bank, a court of justice, and (a long term aim) a single Afro-currency. The first AU summit was scheduled to meet in Durban, South Africa, in 2002.

Libya's leader, **Muammar al-Gaddafi**, saw the AU as his brainchild, but South Africa's President, Thabo Mbeki, was determined to preserve the organization's credibility for western **aid** donors and feared that an AU dominated by Gaddafi would derail the New Partnership for African Development (NEPAD), which had obtained the backing of **Great Britain**'s prime minister Tony Blair and the other Group of Eight (G8) leaders. Despite much lobbying by Gaddafi to have the first AU summit in Sirte, Libya, Thabo Mbeki got his way and in July 2002 African leaders arrived in Durban to mark the end of the OAU and the launch of the AU. However, there were deep divisions between the "repressive" old leaders and the new "democrats" determined to reform the continent's leadership. Thabo Mbeki, who became the first chair of the AU, said that the much-criticized OAU, now at the end of its life, had effectively pursued its twin goals of promoting African unity and eradicating colonialism.

The principal aims of the AU were as follows: to promote the unity, solidarity and cooperation of African states; to defend their sovereignty; to promote democratic principles, human rights, and sustainable development; and to accelerate the political and socioeconomic integration of the continent. All 53 members of the OAU joined the new organization and only Morocco, which had quit the OAU in the 1980s over the issue of Western Sahara, remained outside. The Durban summit adopted NEPAD as its socio-economic development program and established a "peer review" system whose object was to judge whether an AU member was behaving improperly, for example, in terms of good governance. However, no pressures were exerted upon **Zimbabwe** over the political harassment of opponents of President **Robert Mugabe**'s ruling party. In one crucial respect, the AU laid down a clear principle of intervention in member states as follows: Article Four of the Constitution, paragraph (h), states: "The right of the union to intervene in a Member State pursuant to a decision of the Assembly in respect of grave circumstances, namely war crimes, genocide and crimes against humanity."

The first annual summit of the AU, after its launch in Durban, was held in Maputo, **Mozambique**, in July 2003. The summit elected Alpha Oumar Konare of Mali as its first president for a term of four years. **Kofi Annan**, the **United Nations** secretary-general, called for "African responsibility" and said "democracy means more than holding elections." It was up to Africa, he said, to create a healthy climate for "intra regional trade."

AID. Aid has always been used as an instrument of politics. In a civil war situation, apart from aid as **military assistance**, it is provided to bolster one or the other side in the struggle. Its provision can be especially important when a civil war is coming to an end and the donors wish to ensure that the winning side is helped to overcome the problems of rehabilitation, which it faces, so that it may rejoin the ranks of acceptable economic powers. The denial of aid may be as effective as its supply: the psychological and international impact of a refusal by aid donors to provide assistance to a government, which is at war with part of its people, may be profound, indicating international disapproval and, conversely, encouraging the other side in the struggle to hope that its cause is approved and, therefore, has a greater chance of triumphing. In the long series of wars in **Chad**, for example, **France** provided aid to the various governments which emerged in N'Djamena, less perhaps as a sign of approval than in order to ensure that it continued to maintain a foothold and influence in the country. In 1997, following the coup in **Sierra Leone**, **Great Britain** and other donors reduced the level of their aid to purely humanitarian assistance as a sign of their disapproval, while at the same time, exerting diplomatic and other pressures upon the new, illegitimate regime to reverse its coup and return the country to its elected government.

During the second half of the 1980s, the European Community (EC) provided approximately $600 million of aid to the government of **Mozambique** for the rehabilitation of the port of Beira. In this particular case, the provision of aid illustrated a number of donor motivations. First, it was signaling a clear choice by supporting the government of the ruling **Frente da Libertação de Moçambique** (FRELIMO)/Mozambique Liberation Front, even though this was a proclaimed Marxist party, as opposed to the opposition **Resistência Nacional Moçambicana** (RENAMO)/Mozambican National Resistance; by so doing the Community was making a moral as well as political judgment upon RENAMO. Second, although Mozambique under FRELIMO (1975–90) was a proclaimed Marxist state, clear signals were emerging that its preference was for a western rather than a communist link, and aid from the EC was designed to reinforce this preference. Third, since Mozambique controls the vital series of rail and road links to the Indian Ocean ports that serve the landlocked countries and regions of the interior—Malawi, Swaziland, Zambia, and **Zimbabwe** (as well as the Transvaal in **South Africa**)—it was in both western and the interior countries' interests to support the FRELIMO government in Maputo.

Fourth, Mozambique was entirely surrounded by **Commonwealth** countries (and South Africa, which would rejoin the Commonwealth in 1994) and these were then members of the Frontline States and exerted strong pressures upon Britain to assist Mozambique. Finally, at that time, Britain was resisting all pressures to apply sanctions against South Africa, and by providing substantial aid to Mozambique instead, hoped to persuade African and Commonwealth countries that, despite its stand on South Africa, it was nonetheless committed to opposing apartheid.

In a quite different case, United States aid over many years to **Joseph-Désiré Mobutu**'s **Zaire**, despite his appalling record, was in part designed to secure channels from his country into **Angola** to support the anti-Marxist forces of **Jonas Savimbi** and his **União Nacional para a Independência Total de Angola** (UNITA)/National Union for the Total Independence of Angola, which were waging a civil war against the government of the Marxist **Movimento Popular para a Libertação de Angola** (MPLA)/Popular Movement for the Liberation of Angola.

Aid provided to one side in a civil war, which is designated for peaceful purposes only—for example, for medical supplies or food for displaced populations—serves a double purpose, since by relieving the recipients of the necessity to meet these obligations themselves, it releases scarce resources for the purchase of arms. Aid, then, may play a crucial role assisting one or the other side in a civil war, even if the donor refuses to become involved in the supply of arms. *See also* MILITARY ASSISTANCE.

AIDEED, GENERAL MUHAMMAD FARAH (AYDID) (1930–96).

Muhammad Farah Aideed was born in Beletweyne, Italian Somaliland,

and died of battle wounds in Mogadishu in August 1996. He received military training in Italy and was promoted to captain in the Somali army immediately following independence in 1960. After **Siad Barre** had made himself head of state following a successful coup in 1969, he appointed Aideed his military chief of staff. Aideed's promotion was short lived, however, since Barre did not trust him and had him imprisoned for six years from 1969 to 1975.

After his release, his military capabilities ensured that he was used at a high level during the **Ogaden War** of 1977–1978 when he was promoted to brigadier general and was placed in an advisory role directing the war. Barre continued to view Aideed with suspicion, seeing him as a threat to his own position, and in 1984 he sent him as **Somalia**'s ambassador to India where he remained until 1989. Aideed then went to Italy where he became the leader of a dissident faction which sought to overthrow Barre.

He returned to Somalia in 1991 after Barre had been forced to leave Mogadishu, but discovered that his rival, **Ali Mahdi Mohammed,** had stolen a march on him and been proclaimed interim president. Once Barre had left the country, factional fighting divided Somalia; Aideed emerged as leader of one faction and his followers came to control the greater part of Mogadishu. He was to achieve a high international profile following the arrival of some 28,000 **United States** marines at the end of 1992; their stated purpose was to ensure that humanitarian supplies reached the large numbers of Somalis who had become refugees and were close to starvation as a result of the civil war. Aideed's troops repeatedly prevented the U.S. marines from gaining control in Mogadishu, with the result that violence between his faction and the U.S. forces constantly escalated during 1993.

The U.S. forces, technically working under the authority of the **United Nations,** made the mistake of demonizing Aideed. A UN resolution ordered his arrest, but he was never captured, despite strenuous U.S. efforts. In the end he was seen to triumph when the United Nations aborted its resolution. However, Aideed's success in defying both the Americans and the United Nations did not continue after the withdrawal of UNOSOM-II, and he himself was mortally wounded in the ongoing factional fighting in August 1996. Aideed was a classic warlord figure rather than a statesman, which was what post-Barre Somalia required.

ALGERIA (1954–62). The bitter war waged between the French settlers (*colons*), with the backing of the French army, and the indigenous people of Algeria over the years 1954 to 1962 was in part a straightforward nationalist war of liberation to gain independence from **France** and partly a civil war, since a large proportion of the *colons* had been born in Algeria and some were second- or third-generation Algerians who regarded the country as their home and had come to see themselves as the ruling elite.

Background and Beginnings

By 1945, after 115 years of French colonization (the French had spent much of the first 50 years fighting to gain control of the territory), there were more than one million European settlers (not all French) in the country. Between them they controlled most of the wealth. On the other hand, the majority of the nine million indigenous Muslim people were poor. Algeria was to be affected by the general Africa-wide demands for independence that soon became apparent after the end of World War II, as well as by the rising nationalism in its neighbors, Morocco and Tunisia. In 1945, at **Setif**, nationalists flew their flags, and in the course of a popular uprising, about 80 French settlers were killed. There followed indiscriminate French reprisals in which an estimated 1,500 Algerians were killed as well a further 90 French, although nationalist estimates suggested that 45,000 Algerians were killed while independent observers placed the death toll at between 10,000 and 15,000. The longstanding nationalist leader, **Ferhat Abbas**, who had created the nationalist movement Les Amis du Manifeste et de la Liberté in 1944, was arrested and the AML was proscribed by the French authorities. Further disturbances were to follow in October 1945 and May 1946. Even so, the nationalists at this time tended to be moderate. In 1946, the Parti du peuple Algérien (Algerian People's Party), which had been operating underground, emerged as the Mouvement pour le Triomphe des Libertés Démocratiques (MTLD)/Movement for the Triumph of Democratic Liberties and the AML joined it. A militant group led by **Ahmed ben Bella,** who had fought for the Free French in Italy, broke away in 1947 to form the **Organisation Secrète** (OS)/Secret Organization, which advocated an armed struggle. Agitation for reform now steadily increased. In 1950, ben Bella and other members of the OS, in an early resort to violence, robbed the Oran Post Office. In 1952, Ferhat Abbas was tried for a minor offense, yet three lawyers—a Muslim, a Christian, and a Jew—defended him in a gesture of solidarity that ought to have been noted by the administration. Also in 1952, the acting head of the MTLD, Ahmed Mezerna, sought support from Egypt while the head of the Association of Algerian Ulama toured Arab countries in a search for scholarships for Algerians wishing to study further Arabic.

In March 1954, nine members of the OS, led by ben Bella and Belkacem Krim, formed the **Comité Révolutionnaire pour l'Unité et l'Action** (CRUA)/Revolutionary Council for Unity and Action to prepare for an armed struggle. These young radicals rejected the leadership of men such as Messali Hadj, who had formed the MTLD at the end of World War II, as too moderate; they issued a leaflet claiming their aim to be the restoration of a sovereign Algerian state. CRUA now became the **Front de Libération Nationale** (FLN)/National Liberation Front, which argued that Algeria had fallen behind other Arab states and that this could only be changed by an armed struggle. The FLN advocated democracy within an Islamic framework and said that any resident of Algeria would qualify for citizenship in the new state. On 1 November 1954, the FLN and its armed wing, the Armée de Libération Nationale (ALN)/National Liberation Army, launched the revolution in the city of Algiers with attacks on police stations, garages, gas works, and post offices. There were 15 deaths.

The Civil War

National Liberation Front strategy consisted of widespread guerrilla action with raids, ambushes, and sabotage that would make the administration unworkable at home. Abroad, it would carry on a diplomatic offensive directed both at the **United Nations** and at securing Arab support. Early FLN actions included raids on French army installations and European farms, plantations, and vineyards. In the aftermath of the first violence about 2,000 members of the MTLD were arrested in the Batna and Aures region, although the MTLD had not been in favor of such an uprising and nationalist journals still advocated peaceful negotiations rather than violence. But as the violence escalated, some prominent nationalists fled Algeria while pledging their assistance to the FLN cause from abroad. Before long the authorities were resorting to torture to obtain information, and the nationalists were regularly using terrorist tactics.

In February 1955, **Jaques Soustelle** came to Algeria as governor-general and attempted some reforms, but these proved too few and too late. On 20 August 1955, uprisings at Ain Abid, 44 kilometers from Constantine, and at the mine of al-Alia near Skikda, led to massacres of Europeans that were followed by summary executions of Muslims. There was a change of government in Paris at the beginning of 1956 and Guy Mollet came to power as prime minister. He appointed the moderate General Georges Catroux as governor-general, but when Mollet himself visited Algiers, he was bombarded with tomatoes by angry Europeans. Mollet gave way to European demands for tough action; Catroux was withdrawn as governor-general and replaced by the pugnacious Socialist Robert Lacoste who initiated a policy of pacification or forcible repression. During 1956, the war took on a more international aspect as the FLN obtained growing support from the Arab world, and especially Nasser's Egypt; following the independence of its neighbors, Morocco and Tunisia, the FLN was able to seek sanctuary across the borders in those two countries. France had hoped to gain friends in the Arab world by giving independence to these two Maghreb countries, allowing it to concentrate upon holding Algeria (which by then was known to have oil and natural gas resources), but the strategy did not work.

The actual numbers of the active, militant FLN were probably no more than 9,000 at this time, but they received support from a large part of the total Algerian population. France, meanwhile, had built up its armed forces in Algeria to about 500,000 troops. The rebels exercised substantial control in the remoter regions where they collected money and took reprisals against Muslims who did not support them. By May 1956, the majority of the formerly non-committed nationalist leaders had swung round to support the FLN and Ferhat Abbas; Tawfiq al-Madani of the Association of Algerian Ulama joined the FLN leaders, who had their headquarters in Cairo. In 1957, the French government refused to contemplate independence for Algeria, instead sending large numbers of additional troops to crush the rebellion. During this year about 1,200 FLN members mounted an extensive urban terrorist war in Algiers; this was countered by the French "paras" who were only able to defeat the campaign after the widespread use of torture to obtain information. The result was to win the battle but to lose the "hearts and minds" of the people. At the same time France erected barbed wire barriers along the borders with Morocco and Tunisia, in which countries, by then, an estimated 25,000 to 30,000 FLN troops were based.

At the end of 1961, there were an estimated 5,000 Algerian guerrillas in the field. The insurgents employed machine guns, mortars, recoilless rifles, bangalore torpedoes, and captured French equipment. The French deployed a large part of their army against the insurgents but were unable to bring the revolt under control. The war was responsible for great brutalities: whole populations were moved so as to cut them off from the FLN guerrillas, and by 1959 an estimated two million Arabs (25 percent of the population) had been forced to leave their villages. The French carried out "killer" raids on villages suspected of harboring guerrillas. Many of the whites in their territorial units became brutal in their tactics and indiscriminate in their targets, while in certain police stations and military detention centers a new breed of torturer appeared. The Arabs were the main victims but so too were Europeans if they were seen to collaborate with the Arabs. French doctors were known to take part in the torture sessions although later they denied all knowledge of such activities.

The members of the FLN could be equally brutal toward the *colons*, carrying out indiscriminate killings in bars or at other social gatherings in Algiers and other cities; the French on isolated farms were also targets. In addition, outrages were carried out against targets in France by both Algerians and members of the **Organisation de l'Armée Secrète** (OAS)/Secret Army Organization.

The FLN built up military and civilian committees that carried on the war nationwide. These committees raised taxes, recruited new FLN members, and acted as an alternative government to the French. Egypt and Syria provided the FLN with arms, other Arab countries supplied money. Meanwhile, in April 1956, the colons had formed the OAS, which drew support from sections of the French army. The OAS refused to negotiate with the FLN. In February 1958, provoked by Tunisian support for the FLN, the French air force bombed the Tunisian border village of Saqiyat Sidi Yusuf, where the casualties included women and children. An Anglo-American mediating mission then negotiated the French withdrawal from Tunisian ports, including the naval base at Bizerta. During the last days of April 1958, the Maghreb Unity Congress, consisting of representatives from Morocco, Tunisia, and the FLN, met in Tangier, Morocco. The Congress recommended the creation of an Algerian government in exile as well as a secretariat to promote Maghreb unity. On 18 September 1958 the **Gouvernement Provisoire de la République Algérienne** (GPRA)/Provisional Government of the Algerian Republic was established in Tunis with Ferhat Abbas as its leader. Back in Paris the Algerian war had provoked a full-scale political crisis, which brought **Charles de Gaulle** to power on 1 June 1958. Though at first, de Gaulle gave the impression that he was the strong man who would secure the future of the *colons* in Algeria, in fact, he was to recognize the inevitable and bring about a French withdrawal and the independence of Algeria in 1962.

After holding a referendum in France that approved his new constitution, de Gaulle offered to negotiate a ceasefire with the FLN and on 16 September 1959, he promised self-determination for Algeria within four years. A series of secret meetings between the FLN and the French government were held in June 1960 (Paris), 1961 (Geneva), and January 1962 (Rome), leading to the signing of a ceasefire on 18 March 1962, at Evian-les-Bains. The *colons*, who felt they had been betrayed by de Gaulle, turned to extreme methods in April 1961 when they backed an unsuccessful army insurrection led by General **Raoul Salan** and three other generals, Maurice Challe, Edmond Jouhaud, and Andre Zeller. De Gaulle assumed emergency powers and the revolt was crushed within four days. After the arrest of General Salan by French forces, the OAS continued its resistance against the French army.

The negotiations with the French had produced disagreements in the GPRA, and Ferhat Abbas was removed from the leadership and replaced by ben Khedda, while Belkacem Krim became minister of the interior and Saad Dahlad foreign minister. On 28 March 1962, a provisional government was formed in Algiers with Abderrahman Fares as president. In a referendum of 1 July 1962, 91 percent of the Algerian electorate (six million) voted for independence and only 16,000 against. Independence was proclaimed by de Gaulle on 3 July, the GPRA came to Algiers in triumph and there were three days of rejoicing by the nationalists.

The Aftermath

The European population of Algeria now departed on a massive, very nearly total, scale and the majority, nearly one million, returned to France. These included most of the country's senior administrators, although about 10,000 teachers courageously decided to remain, often finding themselves in exposed positions. In addition, there were the Algerians (harkis) who had remained loyal to the French and had often fought for them as well; many of these quit independent Algeria and settled in France. The casualties of this war have been variously estimated: one estimate suggests that 10,000 French officers and men and 250,000 nationalists were killed, while many villages were destroyed and up to two million peasants were relocated. On the other hand, official French estimates put the overall figures considerably higher for French casualties and lower for nationalists: 17,250 French officers and men killed and a further 51,800 wounded between 1954 and the end of 1961, with an additional 1,000 French civilian casualties. This same estimate suggests that 141,000 nationalists were killed, although the FLN was to claim that Muslim casualties were four times that number. Other FLN claims suggested a high of one million killed altogether—fighting, in concentration camps, under torture, or during the removal of populations. The war also witnessed massive destruction of property—schools, bridges, government buildings, medical centers, railway depots, social centers, and post offices, as well as farms and great damage to crops.

At independence, the GPRA found itself divided between Colonel **Houari Boumedienne**, who commanded the FLN army in Tunisia (he was supported by ben Bella who had been released from prison by the French) and the more moderate members of the GPRA. The secretary-general of the FLN, Muhammad Khidr, also supported the ben Bella/Boumedienne axis. There was a brief period of skirmishing, which might have developed into a post-independence civil war when Boumedienne was dismissed by the government for plotting a coup. He advanced with his troops on Algiers, but the new head of government, ben Khedda, fled. The conflict ended when ben Bella was recognized as prime minister, Boumedienne as chief of staff, and Khidr as head of party organization. Elections, which were held on 20 September 1962, were won by the ben Bella/Boumedienne faction of the

FLN. However, ben Bella and Boumedienne differed sharply in their approach to government, with the former being the more radical of the two, the latter a greater pragmatist. Although ben Bella was popular, he became increasingly dictatorial; at the same time, he promised Algerian support to other revolutionary movements. In April 1963, Muhammad Khidr resigned and then fled Algeria with FLN funds; he was later assassinated in Madrid. Ben Bella, meanwhile, became more dictatorial and began to eliminate actual or potential political rivals.

On 19 June 1965, to forestall the increasingly dictatorial tendencies of ben Bella, who would probably have established a Marxist state, Boumedienne and the army mounted a coup and deposed him. At first, Boumedienne had little popular support, yet he was to rule Algeria as an austere socialist until his death in 1978. On coming to power, Boumedienne set up a military Council of the Revolution and tried to create a "true socialist society." While the FLN accepted Boumedienne, the hard Left went into exile.

In the post-independence period, a love-hate relationship developed between Algeria and France. Oil and gas allowed Algeria to develop a modern economic sector and provide much-needed fuels for Europe; it became a "hawk" in the councils of OPEC during the 1970s and was generally seen to belong to the radical wing of African countries in the **Organization of African Unity** (OAU).

The war had a traumatic impact upon France and, for example, was the reason why France collaborated with Britain in the abortive invasion of Egypt (Suez) in 1956 (because of Nasser's support for the FLN). The war also led to the downfall of the Fourth Republic in France and the rise to power of de Gaulle in 1958. The wholesale flight of the *colons* to France in 1962 was a contributory cause of the rise of the National Front, while in Algeria the OAS carried out acts of revenge. The war also contributed to the growth of radical French literature, its most notable writers being **Albert Camus** and **Frantz Fanon**.

ALGERIA, THE ISLAMIST WAR (1992–2006). During the 1990s Algeria was subjected to one of the most brutal civil wars in recent history, with torture by the authorities, massacres of whole villages by Islamists, apparently indiscriminate killings, and hard line attitudes on both sides that eschew any compromise.

Background and Beginnings

Two factors, working in parallel, were the principal causes of the growing rift that led to civil war in Algeria during the 1990s. The first was the growth of fundamentalist Islamic forces, which were seen as an alternative to secular government. The second was the failure of the one party state of the **Front de Libération Nationale (FLN)**/National Liberation Front to satisfy the economic and political needs of the people. During 1988, the country witnessed the worst rioting and social unrest since 1962. In October, rioting occurred in Algiers, Annaba, Oran, and elsewhere and went on for several days with government buildings and state-owned shops as the main targets. Eventually the riots and demonstrations were suppressed by the army, with 159 deaths (the official figure) or 500 deaths, according to other estimates. Despite government claims that the riots had been incited by Islamic fundamentalists, the more likely reason was simply popular dissatisfaction with harsh economic conditions. The economic hardships resulted from the 1986 fall in oil prices and consequent government austerity measures, which had led to a 30 percent devaluation. Within the ranks of the ruling FLN, factions opposed to the austerity measures had further inflamed the general discontent. In response to the riots, the government quickly increased consumer supplies while also promising constitutional reforms, which would make government directly responsible to the Popular Assembly rather than the FLN, although critics suggested the reforms seemed more designed to strengthen the hand of the president. In fact, the reforms that followed allowed President Chadli Benjedid to dominate the FLN Congress of November after a referendum of 3 November, which secured a 92 percent vote for the reforms. On 22 December, Benjedid was re-elected for a third five-year term as president.

Political and economic reforms followed in 1989, and the new constitution of February dropped the word socialism and permitted multi-partyism as well as granting the right to strike. A new law of July 1989 forbade political parties to base their programs upon either language or religion, while a second law required a party to obtain 10 percent of the vote in a constituency in order to qualify for representation. Further, in a multi-party constituency, any party obtaining above 50 percent of the vote would take all the seats. These new laws were thought to favor the incumbent ruling party, the FLN. The government also took control of the media, and the FLN took over leading newspapers. Algerian journalists were to become targets for assassination in this war (69 had been killed by December 1996) and, according to a communique later issued by the Groupe Islamique Armée (GIA)/Armed Islamic Group: "If a journalist can't tell the truth he must stop work—and that if he doesn't stop, he must die."

By September 1989, five political parties (apart from the FLN) had registered while within the FLN a struggle had developed for ultimate control between President Benjedid and the old hierarchy of the party. The Gulf Crisis of 1990 (following the Iraqi invasion of Kuwait) produced massive pro-Iraqi demonstrations in Algiers, with the Front Islamique du Salut (FIS)/Islamic Salvation Front as well as secular nationalists opposing any U.S. presence in the Gulf. Political reforms continued through 1990 and all political exiles, including former President **Ahmed ben Bella**, were allowed to return to Algeria. By mid-year, some 25 political parties had been recognized by the government. On 12 June 1990, the first elections were held under the new laws for town councils and provincial assemblies. The parties complained that the government was rushing them, that they had not had time to prepare, and that the FLN had denied a request for a postponement. In the event, the elections proved a huge setback for the government and FLN: 65 percent of the electorate voted, with the FIS obtaining 54 percent of the vote against the FLN's 28 percent. The FIS took control of 32 out of 48 wilayats, mainly in the densely populated coastal regions. The FLN was split by recriminations and the premier, Mouloud Hamrouche, and four other senior ministers resigned from the FLN politburo. After stalling for a while, President Benjedid promised that elections to the National Assembly would be held early in 1991.

The turning point was to come in 1991. Following its victories in the municipal elections the previous June, the FIS insisted upon general and presidential elections in 1991; the government promised legislative but not presidential elections for June. The FLN now appeared to be in national decline although its members dominated the old Assembly. Meanwhile, the government carried out a number of economic reforms designed to move Algeria toward a full market economy. It also doubled the number of parliamentary constituencies and removed electoral abuses, but the FIS objected to these reforms on the grounds that the new seats represented gerrymandering in favor of the FLN. The government mounted various hostile pressures against the FIS whose members were accused of growing violence. At the same time, FIS administrative capacity was shown to be seriously lacking in those municipal centers which it had captured in the previous year's elections. By mid-1991, the FIS was facing internal troubles of its own, which resulted in a split between the moderates under Abassi Madani and the radicals under Ali Belhadj. FIS objections to the electoral reforms led to a general strike and demonstrations, giving the army an excuse to proclaim a state of siege on 5 June, which it maintained to 29 September. By that time most of the FIS leadership had been arrested and the party—apparently—disbanded.

The postponed legislative elections were held on 27 December 1991 and, to the dismay of the government and the FLN, the FIS made huge gains, winning 188 of 430 National Assembly seats outright while also leading in 150 of the remaining seats, where a second round of voting would be held. The FLN, on the other hand, only won 16 seats (as opposed to 295 in the 1987 elections) while the Socialists took 20. The second round of voting was scheduled for 15 January 1992, when the FIS would only need to win 30 more seats to obtain an absolute majority. Fearing these results, the armed forces took control of the country: first they forced President Benjedid to resign and then, on 11 January, cancelled the elections and declared a state of emergency. The army then created a High State Council (HSC) and invited the long-exiled Muhammad Boudiaf (who had spent 28 years in Morocco) to return home and head the HSC. Meanwhile, the security services proceeded to dismantle the party structures of the FIS; they arrested 9,000 of its members who were interned in camps in the Saharan desert. On 4 March, the FIS was formally banned.

The stage was now set for escalating violence by the "dispossessed" FIS. The FIS soon turned to urban terrorist tactics, which it aimed at the new military regime, targeting security services personnel. By October, 150 had been killed. Boudiaf did not prove to be as pliant as the HSC, who had recalled him, no doubt expected; he tried to move Algeria back to its experiment in democracy and attempted to create a new mass movement, the Assemblée Patriotique, while also launching an anti-corruption campaign. However, on 29 June, Boudiaf was assassinated by a member of his personal bodyguard, and though Islamic extremists were blamed, it was more likely to have been arranged from within the regime to forestall his anti-corruption campaign. He was replaced by a more pliant figure in Ali Kafi, but with a tougher new prime minister, Belaid Abdessalam, who at once tackled urban terrorism: he set up special courts and instituted severe punishments. The regime still hoped to persuade the FIS to cooperate, and its two leaders, Abassi Madani and Ali Belhadj (who had been arrested during the disturbances of June 1991), were given 12-year prison terms instead of being sentenced to death.

Unfortunately for Algeria, the country has imbibed a deep culture of violence that stretches back to the original Muslim conquest. It took the French 50 years to conquer Algeria in the 19th century, while in the independence war of 1954–1962, about a million people were killed; both sides massacred whole villages on the other side while the French authorities resorted to torture as a matter of routine. The same pattern reemerged during the war of the 1990s.

The Civil War

Violence escalated steadily through 1993. Already 210 security personnel had been killed during 1992; by October 1993 about 1,000 Islamist sympathizers—FIS or others—had been killed while some 3,800 Islamists had been brought before the new security courts and 240 had been condemned to death. The state of emergency was renewed in February and attacks were launched on prominent figures including Kasdi Merbah, a former prime minister, on 22 August. Intellectuals and soldiers were also targeted by the fundamentalists. The government placed all responsibility for the violence upon the FIS, although the people did not accept this, believing that other extremist Islamist and secular groups were also responsible for the violence.

The government faced growing unpopularity as it failed to control the violence. It called for fresh dialogue, while the political parties—apart from the FLN—remained opposed to it. The regime also became increasingly internationally isolated. On 27 March 1993, Algeria broke diplomatic relations with Iran and then withdrew its ambassador from **Sudan**, accusing both countries of providing support for the Islamist extremists. At the same time the regime attempted to create a common front with the governments of Tunisia and Egypt against Islamic extremism. Relations with Morocco deteriorated, however, after King Hassan criticized the military suspension of the electoral process in Algeria. The conflict developed further during 1994. The State Council called a national meeting of political parties to choose a new president, but nearly all the parties boycotted the call. The HSC then chose Liamine Zeroual as president; he was a former general and had been defense minister.

Zeroual called for a dialogue with the FIS and released a number of FIS prisoners. As a further gesture, in September, Abassi Madani and Ali Belhadj were transferred from Blida prison to house arrest. Madani had written to the president from prison to say the FIS would respect a pluralistic political system that resulted from any future elections. However, the dialogue Zeroual sought failed to materialize since the FIS would not renounce violence. Indeed, violence increased throughout the year as the security forces attempted, unsuccessfully, to destroy the Islamist opposition.

The Islamist opposition now split into two factions: the Groupe Islamiste Armée (GIA)/Armed Islamic Group mainly in and around Algiers; and the Mouvement Islamiste Armée (MIA)/Armed Islamic Movement operating in the east and west of the country. Foreign nationals were now deliberately targeted and more than 60 were killed, which led most countries to withdraw their nationals from Algeria. The government launched a new campaign against the GIA. An Islamist attack upon the secure prison at Tazoult led to 1,000 prisoners escaping, while another attack upon the French embassy resulted in five deaths. The French government then decided to expel FIS supporters from **France**. In November, a former military chief was assassinated in Algiers and an airplane was hijacked. In this case three passengers were killed, but so were four terrorists and in reprisal, in December, four priests were killed. Other killings were less spectacular and did not always make the international headlines, but they continued remorselessly. By the beginning of 1995, estimates suggested that as many as 40,000 people had been killed since January 1992. The split between the GIA and the more moderate FIS grew deeper. In January 1995, the FIS, the FLN, the Socialist Forces Front and the Hamas party met in Rome, where they agreed on the need to end the violence and form a government of national unity to supervise elections. However, the government rejected these proposals, even though they had the backing of France, Italy, Spain, the **United States**, and a majority of the anti-government groups in Algeria. The GIA demanded the punishment of Algeria's leaders. Instead, the government proposed presidential elections for November 1995, and when the time came, President Zeroual was reelected with a comfortable majority. He then attempted further negotiations with the imprisoned FIS leaders.

By this time Algeria was coming under mounting international criticism for its human rights violations, with Amnesty International blaming it for the deaths of 96 prisoners in the Serkadji prison riot at the beginning of the year. There was also growing international concern at the increasing number of extra-judicial killings by the security forces, which were clearly condoned by the government.

The violence continued unabated through January 1996 with car bombings and the now familiar murders of whole communities by throat-cutting by the Islamists. Moderates in the GIA were murdered because they objected to the campaign of throat-cutting and beheading, while in the mountains, away from the media, a ruthless war continued with few witnesses and less information divulged by the government as to what was happening or what form its own retaliatory actions took. Although Algerians acknowledged Zeroual's political skills, they were also aware that he had failed to stop the killings, which by February 1996, were at a weekly rate of between 100 and 150, while every city had its no-go areas. Foreigners were warned to avoid the city center of Algiers because, as a security official put it, "it takes only 20 minutes to arrange a hit." The fundamentalists also attacked newspapers and television and killed many journalists, as they were heavily Francophone and showed some of the worst effects of the violence.

In April 1996, President Zeroual initiated talks with political leaders in the hope of mapping out a new political/constitutional course of action. He proposed reforms that would include banning political parties based on religion or language while requiring parties to draw their support from across the nation and not simply from one region. The president would only be allowed to serve two five-year terms. The parties reacted cautiously; the FIS (which had not been asked to participate in the discussions) rejected the proposals. These, however, were endorsed by a national conference in September and the new constitution was approved in a referendum in November, for which 80 percent of the country's 16.4 million voters cast their ballots producing an 86 percent vote in favor (although opponents claimed the voting had been rigged). Such proposals ensured that a peace with either the FIS or GIA was out of the question. The GIA became increasingly extreme and made headlines first with the kidnapping of seven Trappist monks in March and then with their execution on 21 May. In August the French bishop of Oran, Pierre Claverie, was killed by a car bomb just after meeting the French foreign minister Hervé de Charette. In July the GIA's leader, Djamel Zitouni, was killed though it was far from clear whether by the security forces or by GIA itself because of an internal disagreement. The assassination of the bishop of Oran raised new fears for the French community in Algeria, then estimated at 1,000 strong, many working in the oil industry: at that time a total of 40 French people had been killed since 1993, for the GIA saw France as the principal source of support for the Algerian government. By the end of the year, an estimated 60,000 people had been killed since the violence began in 1992.

By 1996, increasing evidence provided by human rights groups and the international media suggested that government death squads as well as the GIA were responsible for the brutal massacres taking place. Meanwhile, the army had also effectively privatized the war by arming 200,000 civilians as "communal guards" or "self-defense groups" and altogether by 1996 there were 550,000 men under arms in Algeria.

1997: A Crucial Year

By 1997, the repercussions of the war were being felt increasingly in Europe and at the beginning of the year suspected Algerian terrorists were being arrested in France, Italy, and Germany. The civil war was then entering its fifth year and in remote villages entire families had been hacked to death either by the GIA or by the security forces, because their young men were supporters of one or the other side in the struggle. The GIA's savage tactics were increasingly criticized by mainstream Islamists, including the FIS, but to no effect. As a leading human rights lawyer, Ali Yahia, said in Algiers: "In today's Algeria, power is with the army, not the people. There is no counterbalance. The army believes in neither political pluralism nor democracy, but it uses them. It has made the state its private domain, the instrument of its domination, the source of its privileges. There is no military solution because the crisis is primarily a political one, and must be resolved by talks." He also said: "The Algerian people have been taken hostage. The armed groups put pressure on the population through extortion, to win them over. The army and police use the same methods. Whoever captures the people wins the war. Both sides take revenge against the others' families, feeding the civil war."

By this time, while the prime minister claimed that 80,000 people had been killed, the FIS put the figure at 120,000. Figures, however, had become fairly meaningless, and though the president periodically announced a new figure for guerrillas who had been killed, this made no difference to the rate of killing, which continued unabated. April 1997 proved an especially brutal month with village massacres and train bombs. The area worst hit by atrocities—constant throat-slitting massacres in villages—was in the Mitidja Plain to the south of Algiers. What became increasingly clear during the year was that a proportion of these atrocities could be attributed to the security forces rather than the fundamentalists. As Amnesty International reported in May 1997: "More people are dying in Algeria than anywhere else in the Middle East. Time and time again, no one is brought before a court of law. There is just a statement, released to the press, that the killer or killers had been killed." At the same time, there was growing unease in Europe at the backing being provided for the Algerian government, with accusations that the Algerian authorities were able to exercise many pressures upon the French government.

Parliamentary elections were held in June 1997 at which 41.78 percent of the 16.8 million electorate voted. The elections gave the Rallé National Démocratique (RND)/National Democratic Rally 36.3 percent of votes and 156 seats, and its ally, the once all-powerful FLN, 15.3 percent of the votes and 62 seats, providing their coalition with a majority in the National Assembly, although there was little indication that this would alter the course of the war or the government's strategy.

An estimated 5,000 people were killed in Algeria between the June 1997 elections and the end of September, while little reliable information could be obtained from the Algerian authorities about the real state of affairs in the country. Massacres often occurred near army barracks, yet neither the army nor the police intervened until the killers had gone, a fact that reinforced the argument that the army was either directly responsible for massacres or willing to stand aside, assuming that rival factions were at war. The Islamist guerrillas demonstrated astonishing resilience and despite claims that large numbers of them had been killed, showed no signs of slowing down their campaign or becoming less effective; the more honest—or open—members of the government conceded that their roots were deep among the people, their information and infiltration networks extensive, and that there was no obvious end to the violence in sight. The government, it was also claimed by both its opponents in the country and an increasing number of foreign press and other observers, was using its own violence, which was often disguised as the work of Islamist extremists in order to convince the outside world that the fundamentalists were so terrible that no form of dialogue with them would be possible or make any sense. Apart from announced casualties, by October 1997 there had been an estimated 12,000 who had simply "disappeared." These had been made to disappear, moreover, by a government that claimed to be fighting "international terrorism."

Into the New Century

Horrific massacres of civilians took place at the beginning of 1998, with more than 1,300 men, women, and children slaughtered during Ramadan alone. Increasing international concern led the European Union (EU) to send a delegation to Algiers in late January, but though it was received, it achieved nothing, and the Algerian government rejected any offers of outside assistance or mediation or independent inquiry into the massacres. Further, Algeria repeated its complaint that EU countries were not doing enough to crack down on Islamist extremists in Europe. During the first half of the year, the government mounted a series of offensives against Islamist strongholds and claimed that GIA had sustained heavy losses. At the same time, the ceasefire with the Armée Islamique du Salut (AIS) continued to hold and AIS had persuaded several other smaller groups to declare a truce. A clear division had emerged between the Islamist forces for continued violence (GIA) and those who now sought a political solution (AIS).

The fate of the growing numbers of "disparus" attracted increasing international attention. A high-level UN fact-finding mission led by Mario Soares (the former prime minister of Portugal) visited Algeria from July to August, but though it saw a wide range of people (but not members of the banned FIS), its report was criticized by human rights groups for giving too much credence to the views of the Algerian government.

Presidential elections were held in April 1999 and the former foreign minister **Abdelaziz Bouteflika** was elected president. He quickly made contact with the leading members of the banned FIS. In June the military wing of FIS, AIS, agreed to make its ceasefire of October 1997 permanent and offered to cooperate with the security forces against GIA. Abassi Madani, the FIS leader under house arrest, and the FIS constitutional council endorsed the agreement but other FIS supporters claimed it did not provide a political solution to the conflict. In July, 5,000 Islamist prisoners were released and both houses of parliament adopted a law on civil concord that offered an amnesty to Islamist militants not implicated in massed killings, rapes, or bombings. A referendum of September showed 98.6 percent of voters supported the president's peace initiative with an official turnout of 85 percent. However, families of victims of Islamist attacks and the French language press said it was a "shameful capitulation to Islamist violence." GIA remained divided and some GIA members of breakaway groups surrendered to the authorities or joined the AIS ceasefire. In November, Abdelkader Hadrani, the number three in the FIS hierarchy, was assassinated, which was a setback for national reconciliation, and his death was followed by an upsurge of violence before Ramadan, which began on 9 December.

National reconciliation appeared to come closer in January 2000 when an agreement was reached between the government and AIS. This provided a full amnesty for some 3,000 AIS fighters. In return, AIS agreed to disband permanently. Shortly after the mid-January deadline for the amnesty, the interior minister announced that 80 percent of members of armed groups had surrendered to the authorities. Although for the rest of the year there was relative calm in the capital and major cities, large areas of the countryside remained insecure; an average of 200 civilians, soldiers, and rebels were killed every month through the year and the level of violence escalated in December.

Many parts of the countryside continued in a state of insecurity through 2001 and new massacres of civilians occurred in areas that supposedly had been pacified. In April there were bomb attacks in Algiers after two years of calm. Criticism of President Bouteflika's policy of dialogue continued and was intensified after the events of 11 September in the United States. Following the attack on the World Trade Center and Pentagon, the U.S. government placed both the GIA and the Groupe Salafiste pour la Predication et le Combat (GSPC) on a list of terrorist organizations whose assets were to be frozen. The Algerian government was now able to claim that it felt less isolated because there was greater understanding in the West of its battle against terrorism.

Peace at Last?

There were definite signs in 2002 that the civil war was slowly winding down, partly the result of exhaustion, partly due to the success of government tactics. However, armed Islamist groups still mounted attacks upon civilians and the security forces. By the end of the year, independent estimates suggested that there remained only about 1,000 armed Islamists, as opposed to 25,000 in the mid-1990s. During January 2003, about 40 soldiers and members of self-defense groups were killed when a convoy was attacked in the Aures Mountains. The authorities claimed that a number of al-Qaeda officials were in the country assisting the armed groups. In the April 2004 presidential elections Bouteflika won a second term. He pledged to continue his policy of national reconciliation while insisting that terrorism had to be completely eradicated. During the year the leader of the GSPC, Emir Nabil Sahraoui, and three senior aides were killed, but the GSPC continued its attacks and about 50 people a month were killed.

In January 2005, the Interior Ministry announced that GIA had been virtually wiped out after the security forces had killed or arrested its leading members. In February, Bouteflika appointed former president **Ahmed ben Bella** to head the Commission nationale pour l'Amnestie Générale (CNAG)/National Commission for General Amnesty. In an address to the nation on 6 April, Bouteflika said that security had been "largely restored everywhere across the country." But on the following day, in response, the GIA killed 14 civilians in an ambush. On 15 May, 12 Algerian soldiers were killed in the eastern region of Kenchela by rebels of GSPC and, on 7 June, the GSPC killed six and wounded seven members of the communal guard. On 29 September, a national referendum was held on Bouteflika's latest peace plan, a "charter for peace and national reconciliation." Doubts were cast on the official results when the minister of state for the interior and local authorities claimed that 97.37 percent of the voters had approved the charter. The President described the civil war as a "national tragedy." It had cost the country 150,000 lives and $30 billion. Sporadic outbreaks of fighting continued.

AMIN, IDI AMIN DADA (?1925–2003). Idi Amin was born in the northwest of **Uganda**; he joined the Kenya African Rifles in 1946 and served in Kenya during the Mau Mau rebellion. While in the army, he became a heavyweight boxer and played rugby. He was promoted to full lieutenant just prior to Uganda's independence in 1962. He rose rapidly in the new Ugandan army after independence and was promoted by President Milton Obote to the rank of major general; he became army commander in 1968.

By 1970, Obote no longer trusted Amin whom he was preparing to sideline. In January 1971, at the urging of President **Julius K. Nyerere** of Tanzania, who wanted his support in facing **Great Britain**'s Prime Minister, Edward Heath, over the issue of arms for **South Africa**, Obote went to the **Commonwealth** summit at Singapore but, foolishly, failed to deal with Amin before he left. A soldier tipped off Amin that Obote had ordered his arrest and on 26 January 1971, Amin mounted a coup and seized power while Obote was in Singapore. Although he was initially very popular, Amin's government soon revealed itself to be both tyrannical and cruel. He quarreled with Nyerere who gave Obote asylum; he first wooed and then expelled the Israelis, accepting aid from Colonel **Muammar al-Gaddafi**'s Libya instead; and then he expelled the Asian community to Britain. The pressures which these policies created led to a deterioration in the economy.

The majority of the army still supported Amin when, in 1972, supporters of Obote invaded Uganda from Tanzania. They were turned back. However, from about this time onward, killings inside Uganda escalated: tribal vendettas surfaced and Amin played off one group against another and individuals or groups who appeared to pose a threat to his regime were eliminated, often in brutal massacres. By such ruthless policies he created more and more opponents inside the country and, by the end of the 1970s, these began to liaise with his opponents in Tanzania, who had formed the Uganda National Liberation Front (UNLF). In 1978, Amin invaded the Kagera Salient (the stretch of Tanzania between the lakes), thus providing the pro-Obote exiles in Tanzania as well as President Nyerere with an excuse to move against him. The invaders advanced rapidly upon Kampala in early 1979, and despite the presence of 2,000 Libyan troops in his support, Amin was unable to hold his army together. It disintegrated and fled northward to escape the UNLF forces with their Tanzanian allies. On 10 April 1979, Amin escaped from Uganda by helicopter and was given asylum in Saudi Arabia. He left behind a country in turmoil: an estimated 300,000 Ugandans had been killed during his nine years in power and Uganda soon descended into a civil war which would only be terminated in the late 1980s when **Yoweri Museveni** came to power. Amin died at Jeddah, in Saudi Arabia, on 16 August 2003.

ANGOLA (1975–94). Angola suffered from a prolonged civil war in the years following its independence in 1975. The seeds of this conflict, which would devastate much of the country, were sown during the independence struggle, which had been launched against the Portuguese in 1961. In 1956, various radical groups including the communists, had formed the **Movimento Popular para a Libertação de Angola** (MPLA)/Popular Movement for the Liberation of Angola under the leadership of **Agostinho Neto**. In 1966, the **União Nacional para a Independência Total de Angola** (UNITA)/National Union for the Total Independence of Angola was formed under the leadership of **Jonas Savimbi**. These two movements were to become rivals for power during the struggle against the Portuguese and after independence in 1975.

The Portuguese

In January 1961, the Portuguese army in Angola embarked upon maneuvers to overawe part of the rural population, which was becoming restless; the army said that only a few people had been killed, although the nationalists claimed that 10,000 met their deaths. The MPLA dated the beginning of the struggle against the Portuguese from 4 February 1961, when violence erupted in Luanda, and by April of that year the struggle in Angola had become an issue at the **United Nations**. During the 15 years of warfare that followed, many thousands of Angolans were killed or maimed as the Portuguese fought to hold onto their richest African possession. By 1974, however, they were losing their African wars and following the April Revolution in Lisbon which overthrew the Caetano government and brought General **Antonio de Spinola** to power, the decision was made to withdraw from Africa and to stop fighting wars, which by then, **Portugal** knew it could not win. As the Portuguese prepared to withdraw, the bitter rivalries which existed between the liberation movements, based partly on ethnic and geographic divisions, partly on ideology, and partly on leadership ambitions, came to the fore and threatened to plunge Angola into a post-independence civil war. A third movement, apart from Neto's MPLA and Savimbi's UNITA, was **Holden Roberto**'s **Frente Nacional da Libertação de Angola** (FNLA)/National Front for the Liberation of Angola, but this was soon to collapse and disintegrate.

A sort of unity was achieved in January 1975 after the three movements had met in Nairobi in the hope of presenting a united front to the departing Portuguese. But though a transitional government was formed at the end of January, it soon fell apart and by June 1975, fighting between the three movements had spread to the capital, Luanda. By August there was fighting in most parts of the country. When, on 19 September 1975, Portugal announced that it would withdraw all its troops by 11 November, UNITA and the FNLA announced they would establish a common government in Huambo until they had driven the MPLA from Luanda. On 11 November 1975, the MPLA proclaimed the People's Republic of Angola with Neto as president, while at Ambriz the FNLA and UNITA proclaimed the Popular and Democratic Republic of Angola with Roberto as president.

Even at this stage, as the year drew to its close and the Portuguese departed, the coming civil war was overshadowed by foreign interventions and **Cold War** considerations. The **Union of Soviet Socialist Republics** (USSR) hastened to provide the MPLA with military equipment and airlifted 16,000 Cuban troops into the country to support the MPLA government, which at this time controlled 12 of 15 provinces. **France** supported UNITA, which was assisting the **Frente da Libertação do Enclave de Cabinda** (FLEC)/Liberation Front for the Cabinda Enclave, since Cabinda was sandwiched between the two French-speaking countries of Congo (Brazzaville) and **Zaire**. **South Africa** was preparing to invade Angola from **Namibia** in the south to oppose a Marxist regime. Meanwhile, the Portuguese settlers saw no future for themselves in Angola and left in large numbers, crippling the workings of the economy in the process. The disagreements between the liberation movements were a mixture: opposition to the Marxism of the MPLA by the FNLA and UNITA, and also differences arising out of regional ethnic loyalties. But primarily they were factional—about post-independence power and who was to wield it. The civil war, which got under way, was to be both prolonged and complicated by external support for the different factions. Part of this support was motivated by the regional considerations of Angola's neighbors (Zaire, Zambia, and South Africa through Namibia) and part by Cold War considerations, which would involve the People's Republic of China (briefly), the **United States**, the USSR, and **Cuba**. President **Joseph-Désiré Mobutu** of Zaire began by supporting the FNLA, and when it disintegrated he transferred his support to UNITA. The MPLA relied upon Soviet and Cuban support. UNITA was to receive support from the United States, channeled through Zaire by the Central Intelligence Agency (CIA) and South Africa, whose main aim was to destabilize a potentially powerful socialist or Marxist state to the north of Namibia, which it then controlled. The Ford Foundation lobbied Congress to provide $81 million in aid to Zaire, part of it to be used to fund **mercenaries** to fight against the MPLA, while the departing Portuguese provided $60 million in 1975 for the anti-MPLA factions. As a result of these interventions, what might otherwise have been a more limited civil war for post-independence power became instead inextricably bound up with the Cold War.

Civil War: First Phase (1975–80)

While the newly proclaimed MPLA government was recognized by the Communists, the Huambo (FNLA-UNITA) government received only assistance from the United States, South Africa, Zaire, and Zambia but not recognition. In December 1975, the fragile alliance between the FNLA and UNITA collapsed and after heavy fighting the FNLA was driven from Huambo and then from other strongholds by UNITA. In October 1975, as violence in Angola escalated, South Africa sent troops in support of the FNLA and UNITA. A column of 1,500 to 2,000 South African troops moved up the Angolan coast and, by 26 October, had driven the MPLA from Lubango; by the first week of November it had occupied Lobito and then, on 12 November, it took Novo Redondo, which was 160 kilometers north of Lobito. The USSR responded to this South African advance with a massive arms buildup for the MPLA, sending 27 shiploads of arms and between 30 and 40 cargo planes to Luanda to provide T54 and T34 tanks and 12 MiG-21s. By then Cuban troops had also been flown into Angola. The South African advance into Angola persuaded important African states such as **Nigeria** and Tanzania to recognize the MPLA government. Even so, the special **Organization of African Unity** (OAU) summit of January 1976 was split with 22 states recognizing the MPLA government, 22 arguing for a government of national unity and two—**Ethiopia** and **Uganda**—abstaining. South Africa failed to obtain western (meaning U.S.) support for its intervention and on 4 February 1976 pulled its forces back, although retaining positions 80 kilometers inside Angola to establish a cordon north of the Namibian border. This debacle for South Africa was largely caused by the prevalent mood in the United States, since Washington, in the aftermath of the U.S. withdrawal from Vietnam, was not prepared to become involved in a war in Africa with its own troops on the ground.

The position of the MPLA government was greatly strengthened when, on 2 February, 25 African states had recognized it (a simple majority) and it was able to take its seat in the OAU. By late February, 70 states had recognized the MPLA government. Meanwhile, the government in Luanda had launched its own offensive against the FNLA and by mid-February 1976 had overrun most of the FNLA positions in the north of the country. It also launched a second campaign against UNITA strongholds in the south of the country and these too were overrun. The FNLA and UNITA then turned to guerrilla tactics. President Neto and the MPLA now appeared to have won the post-independence succession struggle although he retained the services of the Cuban troops, who would remain in the country until 1991. In June 1976, the government put on a show trial of captured western mercenaries of whom nine were Britons, three Americans, and one Irish: four were executed and the rest sentenced to long prison terms. In March 1976, the South Africans withdrew completely from Angola following mediation by Andrei Gromyko of the USSR and James Callaghan of **Great Britain**.

UNITA now began to turn itself into an effective guerrilla force and, for example, mounted attacks upon the **Benguela Railway**. Fighting between government forces and UNITA became severe during the last months of 1976. Luso, a focus of fighting, was reduced to a ghost town. Despite retreating from Angola in 1976, South Africa's policy for the next decade would be to support UNITA as part of its general destabilization of independent black states on its borders. By the end of 1976, there were an estimated 18,000 Cuban troops in Angola and Neto had increased the size of the MPLA army to 50,000. During 1977, with the collapse of the FNLA, UNITA became the principal opponent of the Luanda government while, to oblige its new South African ally, it declared war on the **South West Africa People's Organization** (SWAPO), which operated from bases in southern Angola. By 1979, the MPLA army had greatly improved its efficiency with Soviet arms and the support on the ground of the Cuban troops. During the years 1977 to 1980, UNITA was on the defensive, with Zaire temporarily refusing it base facilities and South Africa reducing the level of its support.

Civil War: Second Phase (1980–90)

UNITA began to achieve a comeback in the 1980s; in August 1980 it sabotaged oil storage tanks at Lobito. In 1981, South Africa increased its raids into southern Angola, ostensibly in pursuit of SWAPO, but in fact and more often to do damage to the MPLA position. The United States declared it would not recognize the MPLA government and the Senate then repealed its ban on providing aid to UNITA. From this time on, UNITA was to receive varying amounts of U.S. aid through Zaire. Savimbi was now able to claim that UNITA was receiving aid from Saudi Arabia, Qatar, Morocco, Senegal, and Côte d'Ivoire. Late in 1981, Savimbi visited Washington and in 1982, he achieved a diplomatic breakthrough when he persuaded the United States to tie any agreement with the MPLA to the withdrawal of Cuban troops, a line that suited both Washington and Pretoria. Fidel Castro, however, announced that Cuban troops would remain in Angola until South Africa ceased its attacks and had withdrawn from Namibia. By this time South Africa was occupying 125,000 square kilometers of Angolan territory, while its incursions into Angola had become a regular activity for the South African Defence Force (SADF).

The war intensified during 1983, with South African forces damaging the Lomaum Dam on the Benguela to cause intensive flooding in three provinces. President **Jose Eduardo dos Santos** (who had succeeded Neto on his death in 1979) visited Moscow in 1983 to be assured by the new Soviet leader, Yuri Andropov, that Soviet support for his government would continue. During 1984, Savimbi called for a government of national unity and threatened to attack cities if he was ignored (which he was). In July 1984, UNITA cut an oil pipeline in Cabinda and took European hostages including a Briton, in the hope of forcing London to deal directly with UNITA. About 100,000 people were displaced during the year as a result of the UNITA offensive. By 1985, two wars had become intertwined: that of the MPLA government against UNITA, and that of SWAPO against South Africa, which also assisted Savimbi in his fight against the government. When in January 1986, Savimbi again visited Washington, he was received by the State Department as an important political figure. In May the Angolan government launched a massive campaign against UNITA resulting in thousands of **refugees** flooding into Zambia and devastation in central Angola. In September 1986, the U.S. House of Representatives voted 229 to 189 to provide UNITA with $15 million to help stem Soviet expansion in Africa. In 1987, U.S. Assistant Secretary of State Chester Crocker began his long period of mediation to bring an end to the Angola/Namibia crisis, for by that time South Africa no longer denied that its forces were in Angola to help UNITA. In mid-November 1987, South Africa's General Jannie Geldehuys admitted that South African forces had intervened on the side of UNITA in a developing battle near the southeastern town of **Cuito Cuanavale** while Soviet advisers and Cuban troops were supporting the MPLA forces.

The battle of Cuito Cuanavale (1987–88) was to prove a turning point: it was a large-scale conventional battle fought for control of the strategic town which dominated the southeastern part of the country (rather than guerrilla warfare), and Angolan airpower with Cuban help became a real threat to South African air superiority for the first time. Both sides made big claims about casualties inflicted upon the enemy, but what did become clear was the extent of South Africa's involvement and the fact that it was unable to turn the tide of battle in favor of UNITA. The battle attracted increasing international attention, and Nigeria and other African countries offered to send peacekeeping forces to Angola. On 15 November 1987, President dos Santos claimed that there were 3,000 South African troops and 70 armored vehicles in Angola as well as a further 30,000 South African troops along the Namibian border. By mid-January 1988, the South African force had been increased to 6,000 men, with artillery and armored vehicles taking part in the siege of Cuito Cuanavale. Most of the population of 6,500 had been evacuated and MPLA planes were making daily sorties against the encircling troops. Cuito Cuanavale formed part of a line of towns from Namibe on the coast to Lumbala near Zambia, which controlled the Soviet radar system that monitored South African air activity. It was also the government's most southerly base and essential for mounting air attacks upon UNITA headquarters at Jambe. Heavy casualties were sustained on both sides and the government forces, backed by an estimated 40,000 Cubans by then, were showing new confidence in facing the South Africans. By mid-February 1988, the South African forces had been increased to 7,000. At the same time, the South African air force was suffering losses and no longer enjoyed air superiority; the Soviet air defense system (radar) had altered the balance. By the end of the month, Cuito Cuanavale had become one of the largest set-piece battles in Africa since World War II. Its importance was as much psychological as military since it demonstrated, at last, that South Africa was not invincible and that years of warfare had created some extremely tough soldiers able to stand up to the South African military juggernaut. By March the MPLA armed forces, Forcas Armadas Populares de Libertação de Angola (FAPLA), contained 8,000 South African troops and claimed to have shot down 40 South African planes. By June 1988, it was clear that the South African effort to take Cuito Cuanavale had failed while the presence of Cuban forces along the Namibian border demonstrated South Africa's increasing vulnerability. In addition,

Pretoria was fearful of the political effect at home of some 60 white deaths in the Angolan war. Even so, Savimbi visited Washington in June and met President Ronald Reagan who promised his continued backing for UNITA. The stalemate at Cuito Cuanavale and Pretoria's fear that its forces would be trapped and defeated there undoubtedly helped the Chester Crocker peace process.

The Peace Process (1988–90)

Angola was finally ready to accept **linkage** (the term applied to the U.S. policy of linking independence for Namibia to the withdrawal of Cuban troops from Angola) and proposed a timed withdrawal of its Cuban allies in return for independence for Namibia, a withdrawal of South African forces from Angola, and an end to South African and U.S. support for UNITA. Cuba and the USSR now accepted linkage and George Shultz, the U.S. secretary of state, and Eduard Shevardnadze, the Soviet foreign minister, agreed to work together. A series of peace meetings was held throughout 1988 in different venues including London, Brazzaville, Lisbon, Moscow, Cairo, New York, and then Brazzaville again, where an agreement was finally reached at the end of the year. The terms of the December 1988 Brazzaville Protocols were as follows: Cuba would withdraw its (by then) 50,000 troops over 27 months; South Africa would implement UN Resolution 435 in Namibia during 1989 to lead to independence in 1990; a commission composed of representatives from the United States, the USSR, Cuba, Angola, and South Africa would arbitrate complaints over implementation; and the **African National Congress** (ANC) would withdraw its estimated 10,000 cadres from Angola. The final signing of the agreement took place in New York on 22 December 1988. The Namibian peace process began on 1 April 1989, and Namibia became independent on 21 March 1990; all the Cuban troops had been withdrawn as agreed by July 1991.

However, the deal did not also bring an end to the war between the Angolan government and UNITA, and the United States insisted that its continuing aid to UNITA was a separate issue. In 1989, following the Brazzaville agreement, the MPLA government offered an amnesty to UNITA members, although few took advantage of it. President dos Santos also suggested that the United States should recognize his government, but Washington linked recognition to a settlement between the MPLA and UNITA. The war continued throughout 1989, but though UNITA controlled more territory than the government, this did not include any towns. It was then estimated that UNITA had 40,000 trained guerrillas and 30,000 irregulars. The government, on the other hand, had 160 MiGs, helicopter gunships, and an army of 50,000 as well as 50,000 reservists; it also controlled the Cabinda enclave and therefore the oil industry, which yielded an income of $2 billion a year. Various attempts were made by African governments to bring the two sides together and end the war, but these efforts were hardly helped when the United States increased its **aid** to UNITA in 1990 to $80 million.

Results of the Civil War to 1990

By 1990, after 15 years of civil war, which had been preceded by 15 years of struggle against the Portuguese, Angola had been devastated: towns and infrastructure had been destroyed and revenues were reduced to a trickle while almost no economic development had taken place. In 1986 it was estimated that 600,000 Angolans had been displaced out of a population of 8.5 million, and three years later a further 400,000 had become **refugees** outside Angola. A country which has the capacity to be a substantial food exporter was importing 50 percent of its requirements and needed UN food aid. About 20,000 people had lost limbs, mainly through land mines, which was the highest ratio to population in the world. External interventions had ensured that the civil war was both more prolonged and more devastating than it would otherwise have been, as UNITA could not have survived as a fighting force without the backing of the United States and South Africa. The MPLA government had received massive military assistance (possibly worth $2 billion over two years) from the USSR, with up to 1,000 Soviet advisers and 50,000 Cuban troops in the country at the end of the 1980s. U.S. assistance to UNITA was at the rate of $45 million in 1989 and $80 million in 1990 and South African assistance over the 1980s was reckoned at $160 million. The Cubans may have suffered as many as 10,000 dead over the years 1975–1990, though they did not publish any figures. By September 1989, possibly 300,000 Angolans had been killed in the conflict, while $12 billion worth of destruction had been inflicted on the country.

The Conflict Continues (1992–2002)

A tentative peace was negotiated between the two sides in December 1990 and this was followed by talks in Portugal in February and April 1991, leading to the initialing of an agreement on 1 May. This peace accord was signed on 31 May in Lisbon. The ceremony was attended by the U.S. secretary of state, James Baker, and the Soviet foreign minister, Aleksander Bessmertmykh, and it was agreed that the United States, the USSR, and the **United Nations** should monitor the cease-fire and that elections would be held late in 1992. The UN, thereupon, established the United Nations Angola Verification Mission (UNAVEM) to monitor the cease-fire until after the elections. Registration for the elections took place between May and August 1992; the new Assembly was to have 223 seats and the country would be renamed the Republic of Angola. The elections were held over 29–30 September 1992, with the MPLA winning 128 seats and UNITA 71. Neither dos Santos nor Savimbi received 50 percent of the presidential vote, so a runoff was needed. However, Savimbi claimed that the elections were fraudulent and returned to the bush to resume the war, which he did on 30 October, and by the end of November, his forces controlled two-thirds of the country. When the new Assembly convened, the UNITA members did not take their seats.

In January 1993, government forces launched an offensive to drive UNITA out of the towns it had seized; the UN representative in Angola, Margaret Anstee, said that there was "full-scale civil war" again and that the UN mandate was becoming increasingly irrelevant. The renewed fighting, if anything, was more savage than previously, and though the government had some early successes, UNITA then counterattacked and captured Soyo, the northern oil town, and managed to cut Luanda's water supply. However, UNITA had done itself great damage by returning to the bush and refusing to accept the election results, for Washington finally abandoned its long-standing support for UNITA and said its resumption of the use of force was unacceptable. Portugal, the United States, and Russia each claimed that the 1992 elections had been free and fair and on 12 March 1993, the UN

Security Council passed a resolution placing full responsibility upon UNITA for the renewed fighting. The Council insisted that UNITA return to the peace process by 30 April. On 25 March, the U.S. House of Representatives and the Senate passed a joint resolution condemning UNITA and calling for U.S. recognition of the Angolan (MPLA) government. Yet, despite mounting international pressure and the vital change of U.S. policy, UNITA continued the war. On 2 June 1993, the United Nations extended the UNAVEM II mandate for Angola; by that time an estimated two million Angolans were suffering from hunger, drought, or disease. On 21 June, the United States and Angola established full diplomatic relations. In July 1993, the UN representative Alioune Blondin Beye claimed that more than 1,000 people a day were dying from the direct and indirect results of the war. On 9 August, Britain lifted the arms embargo, which it had enforced against Angola since 1975, on the grounds that the government had a "legitimate right to self-defence," and in September, the United Nations implemented a mandatory oil and arms embargo against UNITA. Finally, on 6 October 1993, in response to these pressures, UNITA said it would accept the election results of 1992, and talks between UNITA and UNAVEM, with Portugal, Russia, and the United States in attendance as observers, began in Lusaka. During this "second" war from October 1992 to October 1993, an estimated 100,000 Angolans had perished. On 9 November 1993, Angola's deputy foreign minister, Joao Bernardo Miranda, claimed that the daily death toll that year had reached 2,000, while in February 1994 the United Nations claimed that three million Angolans were in urgent need of assistance.

Half a Peace

Peace talks were held during December 1993 and January 1994, while the United Nations extended its mandate to March 1994. On 17 February 1994, the two sides signed a document that listed five principles of reconciliation, and UNITA reaffirmed its acceptance of the September 1992 election results. Essentially 1994 became a year of bargaining—about new presidential elections and what ministerial jobs would be offered to UNITA, which claimed the three key ministries of Defense, Finance, and the Interior. The government refused adamantly to cede control of Huambo province to UNITA, which claimed it as the heartland of the Ovimbundu people from whom came its main support. Although a treaty was signed on 20 November 1994, fighting continued in various regions and the existing antagonisms appeared as great as ever. Given this state of affairs, foreign donors were reluctant to provide much needed funds for rehabilitation, and less than half the $227 million requested for this purpose by the United Nations was forthcoming. Hopes of a lasting peace were set back throughout the year as UNITA forces repeatedly resumed fighting. During 1995 this state of "on-off" peace continued, with both sides accusing the other of bad faith. Presidents **Nelson Mandela** of South Africa and **Robert Mugabe** of **Zimbabwe** urged dos Santos not to pursue his military successes against UNITA; at the same time, the guarantee of a role in the country's government persuaded UNITA to be more cooperative.

The country as a whole, meanwhile, faced formidable problems. In 1995, the World Food Programme (WFP) earmarked $65 million of aid for 1.2 million displaced persons, such as, refugees and demobbed soldiers. On 8 February 1995, the UN Security Council resolved to send a peacekeeping force of 3,000 to Angola. One of the worst problems facing the country was the need to find and destroy an estimated 26 million land mines. Savimbi finally agreed to meet dos Santos and was supported in his decision by the eighth ordinary Congress of UNITA, which also endorsed the peace of November 1994. The National Assembly created two vice-presidential posts, one of which would be filled by Savimbi, once he had demobilized his army. It was agreed that UNITA should now simply become a political party. Savimbi accepted these terms, including one of the vice presidencies, and the peacekeeping force was then deployed. However, UNITA remained deeply suspicious of the government's intentions and called upon the international community not to supply the government with any more arms. It also claimed that the new army (supposedly an amalgam of the two fighting forces) was behaving arrogantly in areas which had formerly been controlled by UNITA. During 1997, the formation of a government of national unity was repeatedly delayed and the main stumbling block, as always, appeared to be Savimbi. The UN secretary-general, **Kofi Annan**, called for flexibility on both sides; part of the problem lay in the reluctance of UNITA to demobilize its troops, while the UNITA members who had been elected to the National Assembly did not appear to take their seats. The government of national unity and reconciliation had yet to be inaugurated at the end of March 1997 and most of the delay was attributed to Savimbi who insisted that a joint government program be defined before any inauguration took place. The minister of national defense, General Pedro Sebastiao, complained at the quality of the weapons being surrendered by UNITA under the peace terms and the fact that only 6,000 former UNITA guerrillas had been integrated into the Angolan Armed Forces (although 26,000 had been stipulated in the peace agreement).

The Unity and National Reconciliation Government was finally inaugurated on 11 April 1997; it consisted of members of the MPLA-Partido do Trabalho and UNITA, with portfolios allocated according to the November 1994 agreement in Lusaka. Fernando Jose da Franca van Dunem became prime minister. The inauguration ceremony was attended by a number of African leaders including Presidents Frederick Chiluba of Zambia and Nelson Mandela of South Africa, both of whom had assisted in the peace process. But Savimbi refused to attend, claiming that his safety had not been guaranteed. At a sitting of the National Assembly on 9 April, which now included the 70 UNITA members, legislation was passed which granted Savimbi special status as leader of the largest opposition party. On 16 April, the UN Security Council called for the peace process to be completed without delay, including the incorporation of UNITA's fighters in the Angolan Armed Forces and the normalization of state administration throughout the country. The Security Council once more extended the UNAVEM III mandate to 30 June, but wanted to transform its functions into those of an observer mission as soon as possible. In both May and June 1997, the government moved its forces into largely UNITA-controlled areas, especially Lunda Norte, the diamond producing region, which had produced an income of $600 million a year for UNITA, with the **diamonds** being smuggled out through Zaire. The new president of the **Democratic Republic of Congo** (former Zaire) **Laurent Kabila**, however, was not friendly to UNITA, while the MPLA government seemed bent on a new drive to destroy UNITA as a guerrilla force. During the second half of June, UNAVEM III called upon the government to suspend the fighting as it was endangering the peace process.

In July fighting again increased and, according to the government defense minister, General Pedro Sebastiao, UNITA still had 44,000 troops under its command; many of these had deserted their assembly areas while only 11,764 UNITA troops had been integrated into the Angolan Armed Forces. The Assembly condemned UNITA for returning to violence and concealing arms and troops in contravention of the 1994 Lusaka Accord. On 30 June, the mandate of UNAVEM III came to an end; it was replaced by a UN Observer Mission in Angola (UNOMA). On 28 August, the UN Security Council unanimously adopted a resolution to impose further sanctions on UNITA, unless by 30 September the secretary-general was able to certify that UNITA was moving satisfactorily toward compliance with the Lusaka Accord. On 1 September, a UNITA official confirmed that the party would return to government control all territory still in UNITA hands. On 5 September, on Portuguese Radio, Savimbi said he would demobilize UNITA's remaining forces and comply with the other outstanding terms of the Lusaka Accord. Reports through September indicated that large quantities of arms were being handed over to the government and that numbers of UNITA troops were handing in their weapons, with the result that, on 30 September, the Security Council delayed the imposition of new sanctions until 31 October. When this date was reached and UNITA had clearly failed to meet the conditions of the Lusaka Protocol, the UN imposed sanctions upon it. The result was a savage renewal of the war by Savimbi and his UNITA forces: this came to be called Angola's "fourth war."

On 30 March 1998, the government sent an open letter to the UN claiming that UNITA, with 8,000 well-equipped troops (a figure that was later revised upward of 25,000) was preparing for war. The government blamed UNOMA for its failure to prevent UNITA building up its weapons supply. In June, President dos Santos made a number of trips to gather international support: he concluded an arms deal with Russia, attended the Lusophone summit in Cape Verde to strengthen ties with Portugal and other Lusophone states, and obtained promises of support from members of the Southern African Development Community (SADC), which at a summit in Luanda on 1 October, called for "a swift and rapid campaign to rid the region of UNITA." The violence and successful hit and run attacks mounted by UNITA escalated during the second half of 1998. In December the Angolan army launched an all-out attack on UNITA's principal base of Bailundo, effectively declaring war on UNITA by so doing.

On 17 January 1999, UN Secretary-General Annan told the Security Council that Angola was on the verge of breakdown yet, on 20 February, the Security Council voted unanimously to withdraw the 1,000 strong UNOMA force. UNITA managed to beat off two further attacks upon Bailundo while the UN and other aid agencies were flying in food for the populations of towns, such as, Huambo and Cuito, that were virtually besieged by UNITA and had swollen refugee populations. Renewed heavy fighting by government forces took place in September to capture Bailundo and Andulo; Bailundo finally fell to government forces in mid-October and Andulo in November and on 15 November the MPLA Army Commander claimed that 80 per cent of UNITA's "conventional" capacity had been disrupted and 15,000 tons of weapons had been seized. On 31 December, President dos Santos broadcast: "The somber circumstances and despair resulting from successive wars and persistent economic decline are changing. The Angolan people are on the brink of a new era of hope." This statement proved to be more of a hope than a reality for the war went on throughout 2000 and by the end of the year 3.8 million people had been displaced as refugees. UNITA appeared to make a comeback during 2000. There were many allegations of government violence against civilians, including a scorched earth policy in Cuando Cubango and Luanda Sul provinces. In May, the UN Sanctions Committee produced a 54-page report in which it accused President Gnassingbe Eyadema of Togo and President Blaise Campaore of Burkina Faso of supporting UNITA. It also pinpointed **Rwanda** as an important location for gun-running and **diamond** trading and Libreville in Gabon as a refueling center for planes supplying UNITA and breaking sanctions. The war continued throughout 2001 and both the Angolan government and SADC branded Savimbi a war criminal. Sanctions appeared to be largely ineffective in preventing UNITA obtaining the supplies it needed to carry on the war. From May onward, UNITA was carrying out attacks close to the capital and on civilian targets. In late 2001, there was heavy fighting in the central province of Bie while numbers of refugees were crossing into Zambia and Namibia to escape the fighting.

The Death of Savimbi

The death of Jonas Savimbi on 22 February 2002 effectively brought the war to an end. He had led UNITA forces against the government from 1975 to 1992; then, on losing the election of the latter year, he had returned the country to warfare in his determination to become head of state. His most likely successor, General Antonio Dembo, was also killed. The government then offered an amnesty to the rebel fighters. A cease-fire was signed in Luanda on 4 April and UNITA soldiers were offered assistance in returning to civilian life. Thereafter, some 50,000 UNITA troops with up to 300,000 family members moved into government-run assembly areas. However, many of these assembly areas lacked sanitation, clean water, food, and medicines, and UNITA claimed that numbers died because of these poor conditions and about 30,000 were estimated to have left the camps and returned to their homes. The death of Savimbi was the key to achieving a peace. Few other wars in Africa had been so dependent upon and driven by the ambitions of one individual. The government then faced the immense task of rebuilding the nation. The infrastructure was devastated, the country was covered with millions of anti-personnel mines, agricultural production had all but ceased in large areas, and four million people had been displaced as a result of the fighting.

ANNAN, KOFI (1938–). The seventh secretary-general of the **United Nations** and the first to be elected from the ranks of the UN staff, Kofi Annan was also the first black African to hold this post. His first term began on 1 January 1997 and in June 2001, on the recommendation of the Security Council, he was appointed for a second term by acclamation of the General Assembly. His second term of office ended on 31 December 2006. His period of office coincided with momentous world events and his second term was overshadowed by the terrorist attacks in the **United States** of 11 September 2001, the subsequent declaration by President George W. Bush of the "War on Terror," and then the invasions of Afghanistan and Iraq. Annan's priority as secretary-general was to revitalize the UN by a wide program of reforms.

Kofi Annan was born in Kumasi, Ghana, on 8 April 1938 and was educated at the University of Science and Technology in Kumasi and then at Macalester College in St. Paul, Minnesota. He joined the UN in 1962 and served with the World Health Organization (WHO), the UN Economic Commission for Africa (ECA), the UN Emergency Force (UNEF II) in Ismailia, the Office of the **United Nations High Commissioner for Refugees** (UNHCR), and then at UN headquarters in New York as assistant secretary-general for Human Resources Management and Security Coordinator for the UN System and assistant secretary-general for Program Planning, Budget and Finance, and Controller. Between 1992 and 1997, prior to being appointed secretary-general, he served as assistant secretary-general for Peacekeeping Operations and then as under-secretary-general at a time when UN peacekeeping operations reached an all-time high with 70,000 military and civilian personnel deployed.

In April 2000, he issued a Millennium Report, "We the Peoples: The Role of the United Nations in the 21st Century," which called on member states to adopt an action plan to end poverty and inequality. On 10 December 2001, the secretary-general and the United Nations received the Nobel Peace prize, and the Nobel Committee said Mr. Annan "had been pre-eminent in bringing new life to the Organization."

During his last year as secretary-general, Annan made a number of attempts to engage the UN fully in the developing **Darfur** tragedy, but was unable to mount a full-scale operation to prevent the ongoing killing and abuses of human rights.

ANYA-NYA. Anya-Nya (snake poison) was the name of the southern anti-government guerrilla movement that fought against the Khartoum government in **Sudan**'s first civil war in 1956–1972. Anya-Nya II was formed in 1975 by dissident Dinka and Nuer tribesmen who favored secession from the North, although attacks were only launched on police and military targets in 1983. Anya-Nya II, whose leaders had been active in earlier anti-North campaigns, became the armed wing of the Southern Sudan Liberation Front (SSLF). One of its leaders, Lieutenant Colonel William Chuol, had deserted the army in May 1983, taking with him a battalion from the garrison at Nasir to join Anya-Nya. The movement grew rapidly during 1983 because of dissatisfaction in the army at the system of rotating troops between North and South. When a mutiny broke out at Bor, **John Garang** was sent to quell it, but ended by leading it. Differences between the southern factions, however, led to the creation of the **Sudan People's Liberation Movement** (SPLM), which under Garang became the main secessionist movement in the South with its military wing, the **Sudan People's Liberation Army** (SPLA).

Further splits appeared in Anya-Nya and an increasingly beleaguered President **Gaafar Mohammed Nimeiri** tried to turn the divisions in the South to his advantage. He contacted Anya-Nya II, whose membership embraced a number of southern tribes, and encouraged antagonism to the dominant Dinka who were the mainstay of the SPLA. Following Nimeiri's deposition, his successors pursued the same policy with considerable success. Lieutenant Colonel Chuol, the leader of Anya-Nya II, was killed in a clash with the SPLA in August 1985; he was succeeded by Major Gordon Kong who attacked the SPLA as an agent of the Khartoum government's policy. During 1986, Anya-Nya continued to see the SPLA as its main enemy and constant arguments led to a split, with Anya-Nya dividing into two factions in September 1987. The main burden of the war against the North, thereafter, was sustained by the SPLA led by John Garang.

ARMS TRADE. Few African countries have developed any important arms industries of their own—the exceptions being Egypt and **South Africa**—and, in consequence, they are all dependent upon imports to meet their military requirements. In the period since independence, the military has occupied a high profile in a majority of African countries: either the civilian government has found it necessary to appease the military by ensuring that it is well-equipped and in other ways looked after; or, the military itself forms the government, as a result of coups, and sees its first task as building up the strength of its own—military—supporters. In addition, threats of war with neighbors or actual wars, whether civil or international, have been sufficiently frequent as to ensure the perceived need to build up military strength. As a result, a disproportionate share of scarce resources is devoted to military expenditure.

There is a major social dimension to the arms trade as it affects poor countries. Arms purchases by African countries divert resources that otherwise could be used to relieve poverty and improve health and education. Moreover, any increase in the flow of arms into a poor country reinforces the likelihood of violence, depending upon who obtains control of such weapons. Opponents of an unrestricted arms trade have long argued for an Arms Trade Treaty to control the flow of arms, especially to poor countries so as to safeguard their sustainable development and human rights.

During the 1990s, military expenditure in sub-Saharan Africa rose by 47 percent while life expectancy fell to 46 years. In 1999, South Africa agreed to purchase arms, including frigates, submarines, aircraft and helicopters to the value of $6 billion that could better have been used to combat AIDS or otherwise relieve poverty. In 2001, Tanzania, one of the poorest countries in Africa, spent $40 million on a military Watchman radar system that was both too expensive and inappropriate for its needs, and Eritrea and Burundi both spend more on arms than on health and education combined.

In the event of civil wars, participants have been largely dependent, either upon importing arms from their traditional suppliers, or seeking alternatives. Throughout the years of the **Cold War** there were obvious alternative sources of arms supply: the **United States** and its allies and the **Union of Soviet Socialist Republics** (USSR) and its allies. In addition, there is a thriving international arms business that bypasses official national sales channels and is able to supply almost any requirement provided the money to pay for it is available.

In broad terms there are two motives for supplying arms: to support allies (this was always advanced as a justification during the Cold War); and for money—the arms trade, arguably, is the most lucrative in the world. As long as the Cold War lasted, the supply of arms to almost any regime, no matter how reactionary or dangerous, was justified in terms of providing support for an "ally."

The principal arms suppliers to the continent are, first, **Great Britain** and **France**, in the main to their former colonies and especially to the successor regimes that they wished to maintain in power. Secondly, the United States became an important arms supplier within the context of the Cold War, for example, to the anti-Marxist movements such as the **Frente Nacional da Libertação de Angola** (FNLA) and then the **União Nacional para a Independência Total de Angola** (UNITA) in **Angola**. Thirdly, the USSR, which provided arms to Marxist or pseudo-Marxist regimes such as those in Angola, **Ethiopia**, and **Mozambique** (in the first two cases on a massive scale).

Markets and Ideology

Quite apart from particular war situations (**Nigeria**, Angola, Ethiopia, for example), Africa, despite its poverty, represents a substantial arms market for the principal arms-trading nations; and its many military regimes, in particular, were and are in the market for a wide range of military equipment. During the apartheid years, the West claimed that South Africa was, nonetheless, a bastion of the "free world" and therefore continued to arm it; at the same time South Africa, always fearful of sanctions, built up one of the most advanced arms industries on the continent so that, in time, it only looked outside Africa for the most advanced weaponry. In 1994, when open elections were finally held in South Africa and **Nelson Mandela** became the country's president, the principal arms suppliers lined up to provide weapons for the "new" South Africa. What has become apparent is the ease with which African countries at war, or warring factions on the continent, have been able to obtain the arms they require; these are always available, at a price, and by the 1990s the continent was awash with a range of sophisticated war material.

There is another side to the arms trade that is less easy to quantify. Responding to a question in a television interview in 1979, shortly before his overthrow as president of **Uganda**, Godfrey Binaisa said simply that if he had the money he would experience no difficulty in purchasing all the arms and equipment he then needed to face the opponents to his government. He did not have the money. Given the poverty of Africa, it is instructive that in the late 1990s the average expenditure on the military was far greater than that in the advanced economies. In 1997, members of the North Atlantic Treaty Organization (NATO) spent between 1.5 and 3.6 percent of their GDP on their armed forces; many African countries, on the other hand, spent in excess of 4 percent of their GDP on their military establishments and several, such as Nigeria, more than 5 percent.

The supply of arms, whether in the form of assistance to allies (which still has to be repaid) or simply as part of the lucrative worldwide arms business, has ensured that Africa, despite its general poverty, is oversupplied with arms of most descriptions. Moreover, in the 21st century, despite increased efforts by the **United Nations** and other bodies to curtail the flow of arms into Africa, combatants rarely have difficulty in obtaining the arms they require. Furthermore, and mitigating against all efforts to control the flow of arms, the five permanent members of the Security Council—the U.S., Russia, Britain, France, and China—are responsible for 90 percent of all arms traded worldwide.

A breakdown of the percent of GDP allocated to their military establishments by African countries (figures are for 2004) shows that six countries spent more than 5 percent of GDP—Angola 8.8 percent, Burundi 5.6, Eritrea 17.7, Liberia 7.5, Madagascar 7.2, and Morocco 5; eight countries spent between 3 and 5 percent; 25 countries between 1 and 3 percent; and eight below 1 percent. *See also* DIAMONDS; MERCENARIES; MILITARY ASSISTANCE.

– B –

BARRE, MUHAMMAD SIAD (1909–95). Muhammad Siad Barre became president of **Somalia** in 1969, following a bloodless coup. He ruled as an increasingly autocratic, dictatorial figure until his overthrow in January 1991. Barre, who came from a small Darod clan in the south of Somalia, joined the police under the British in 1941 (after their troops had occupied Italian Somaliland during World War II) and rose to the rank of chief inspector. In 1950, when the mandate of Italian Somaliland was returned to the Italians by the British, Barre was sent to Italy for military training. He became part of the national army in 1960 when the two territories—British Somaliland in the north and Italian Somaliland in the south—were joined to form the independent state of Somalia. By 1966 Barre had become a major general and commander in chief of the Somali army. The assassination of President Abdirashid Ali Shirmake in 1969 led to a dangerous power vacuum, and when it became clear that the assembly would elect a new president supported by Prime Minister Mohammed Ibrahim Egal (a northerner), the army seized power in October and Barre made himself head of a Supreme Revolutionary Council (SRC).

Barre soon adopted a personality cult and imposed his own autocratic rule on the country. He propounded an ideology of scientific socialism and moved toward the **Union of Soviet Socialist Republics** (USSR) in his international stance, thereby making an enemy of the **United States**. He forbade, or tried to forbid, clan loyalties (the core of Somali life) and attempted to persuade clan elders in the rural areas to make his ban stick. He embarked upon a policy of wholesale nationalization which covered medical services, schools, banks, electricity, transport, and the control of exports and imports. In 1975, land was nationalized. A mass literacy campaign was launched in 1972 with Somali as the national language, based on the Roman alphabet. The overthrow of **Haile Selassie** in **Ethiopia** and the emergence of the military Dergue under **Haile Mariam Mengistu** in 1974 changed the political balance of the Horn of Africa.

Barre who, despite providing the USSR with a variety of military facilities, including naval facilities at the northern port of Berbera, had also taken the precaution of joining the Arab League (in 1974) to emphasize Somali traditional values, now turned back to the West. Following the Soviet decision to support the Mengistu government in Ethiopia, Barre turned to the United States and expelled the Soviets from the country. His military adventure against Ethiopia during 1977–1978, in which he attempted to capture the **Ogaden** region, was a failure, but U.S. support ensured that Ethiopia did not try to invade Somalia.

During the 1980s, Barre became increasingly autocratic and isolated, while his poor human rights record steadily alienated international opinion. By 1990, he had not only failed to eliminate the Somali clan system, but had produced a situation in which there was escalating fighting both among clans and between clans and the government, so that the country had been reduced to a state of anarchy and Barre was steadily losing control. A final major military campaign was launched against the breakaway northern provinces in 1990 and, though it appeared a military success, nothing really changed. By midyear, the government was forced to impose a curfew on Mogadishu. Barre was obliged to promise political reforms and elections for 1991 but it was too late. By 1 January 1991, the dissident **United Somali Congress** (USC) controlled large parts of Mogadishu.

President Barre appealed for a cease-fire, but this was rejected by the rebels, and on 27 January, the USC announced that it had taken control of the government. Siad Barre fled the capital under army protection and went into exile in **Nigeria**. By the time he fled Somalia, Barre had presided over the collapse of law and order in his country and left behind a civil war situation, which would escalate enormously over the next four years.

BASHIR, OMAR HASSAN AL- (1944–). Born in **Sudan** and brought up as a devout Muslim, Omar Hassan Ahmed al-Bashir graduated as an army officer in 1966 and then went to Malaysia where he attended staff college. He fought with the Egyptian forces in the 1973 Yom Kippur War against Israel. He then gained further military experience fighting the **Sudan People's Liberation Army** (SPLA) in the South of Sudan.

Bashir led the bloodless coup of 30 June 1989, against the government of **Sadiq al-Mahdi**. On taking power, Bashir created a Revolutionary Command Council for National Salvation. Over 100 army officers who were seen as opponents to his coup were arrested. Bashir claimed that his revolution was a national one, though he never held any meaningful talks with **John Garang**, the southern leader. His total support for Islamic fundamentalism soon became apparent. He abolished the constitution, the national assembly, and all political parties and trade unions, closed down the newspapers, and interned about 30 members of the former government. Although efforts were made to hold talks with the SPLA during the latter half of 1989, these met with little success and collapsed on the issue of Sharia law, which he insisted should be imposed countrywide. In April 1990, he had 28 army officers executed on the grounds that they were planning a coup. A second coup attempt in September 1990 was foiled but several officers then defected to the SPLA.

Through the 1990s, the Bashir government continued the war against the SPLA in the South and, though the fortunes of war constantly changed, there was no indication by late 1998 that the situation could be resolved. Meanwhile, the war debilitated the economic and social life of the whole country and devastated the southern provinces where the fighting was taking place. Seen to be wholly under the influence of the extreme National Islamic Front (NIF) and its leader, Dr. Hassan al-Turabi, Bashir steadily led Sudan into greater isolation; in 1995, Sudan quarreled with Egypt over the attempted assassination of President Hosni Mubarak at the **Organization of African Unity** (OAU) Summit in Addis Ababa by Sudanese "hit men." In May 1995, Bashir had former prime minister Sadiq al-Mahdi arrested but released him in August; Sadiq then fled to **Eritrea** where his presence reinforced opposition to Bashir by exiled Sudanese.

In the 1996 presidential elections, Bashir polled four million of 5.5 million votes; Hassan al-Turabi was then elected unanimously as president of the National Assembly. By 1997, Sudan was generally isolated in the Arab world; it had poor relations with the West, which had cut off virtually all aid, and especially poor relations with the **United States**. There was no sign of any letup in the war with the South.

A power struggle between Bashir and Hasan al-Turabi, leader of the National Islamic Front, developed at the end of the 1990s, leading Bashir to declare a three-month state of emergency on 11 December 1999 when he suspended the National Assembly. He rejected accusations that his actions amounted to a coup and announced that new elections would be held at a date to be decided. The confrontation continued through 2000, with Bashir arguing for a move toward democracy and a secular state and al-Turabi objecting to the latter and accusing Bashir of abandoning the cause of Islam. Having won the presidential elections in December 2000, Bashir renewed the state of emergency for a year as his government struggled against the opposition umbrella group, the National Democratic Alliance.

Meanwhile, there were increasing international pressures to bring the war in the south of the country to an end. Bashir, firmly in control after winning the presidential election and having, apparently, sidelined al-Turabi, his principal opponent, began to make serious moves toward a settlement of the war which at last became a real possibility. However, escalating strife in **Darfur** from 2003 onward presented a new and dangerous problem.

BEIRA CORRIDOR. The port of Beira on the **Mozambique** coast has existed since 1889 when it was founded as the headquarters of the Mozambique Company. It was constructed to act primarily as an outlet for the landlocked territories of the interior, rather than for the use of Mozambique itself. The port became a principal outlet for Southern Rhodesia (**Zimbabwe**), Northern Rhodesia (Zambia), Nyasaland (Malawi), and the Transvaal in **South Africa**. It lies at the mouths of the Pangal and Buzi Rivers and faces the Mozambique Channel. A railway runs due west 250 kilometers from Beira to Mutare, just across the border in Zimbabwe, where it joins the Zimbabwe rail network and links into that of Zambia to the north and that of South Africa to the south. The railway is Zimbabwe's shortest and cheapest route to the sea.

The route of this rail line came to be called the Beira Corridor because it runs parallel to the road, the oil pipeline, and the over-head power cables carried the length of the Corridor by pylons. The Beira Corridor assumed great strategic importance during the 1960s following the Unilateral Declaration of Independence (UDI) of November 1965 by the government of Ian Smith in Rhodesia. At that point, the British government established a naval blockade of Beira to prevent the use of the oil pipeline to supply the illegal Rhodesian government.

During the UDI years, **Zimbabwe African National Union** (ZANU) guerrillas frequently attacked the Corridor, which was a Rhodesia lifeline, until independence in 1980. Then the position was reversed and the Corridor became a vital outlet for the new state of Zimbabwe under the government of **Robert Mugabe**. It was attacked repeatedly by the guerrilla forces of **Resistência Nacional Moçambicana** (RENAMO)/Mozambican National Resistance which were supported clandestinely by South Africa in its efforts to destabilize both Mozambique and Zimbabwe. RENAMO had been created with the help of the Rhodesian Central Intelligence Organization (CIO) under Ken Flower in 1975; the CIO had funded RENAMO but after 1980 this task was undertaken by South Africa. During the early 1980s, the Beira railway was either closed or could only be used when trains had heavy military escorts. Zimbabwe then committed up to 3,500 troops to assist the **Frente da Libertação de Moçambique** (FRELIMO)/Mozambique Liberation Front forces to guard both the railway and the Corridor as a whole. South African strategy was to close the railway and so force Zimbabwe to use transport routes to the south. Any interruption to the Beira Corridor route also affected Zambia adversely since a high proportion of its copper was exported through Beira. From 1985 onward, the concentration of both FRELIMO and Zimbabwean troops along the Corridor turned it into a relatively safe area during the brutal latter stages of the civil war in Mozambique. Many Mozambicans came to live along the Corridor where they created shambas and farmed and were able to conduct some business, although still subject to RENAMO attacks.

Mozambique was able to attract substantial aid during the latter years of the 1980s for the rehabilitation of the port at Beira and the upgrading of the railway and road, so that by 1992, Beira had become one of the world's most up-to-date container ports. When the civil war in Mozambique finally came to an end, this meant an immediate boost to the life of the port and the Corridor, which began once more to fulfill its original function of serving the landlocked territories of the interior.

BEN BELLA, AHMED (1918–). The son of a small businessman of Maghuia in the department of Oran, Ahmed ben Bella was born on 25 December 1918. He was educated in the local French school and then at Tlemcen where he first encountered racial discrimination and also came into contact with the developing Algerian nationalist movement. He served with distinction in the French army, which he joined in 1937, and was awarded the Croix de Guerre in 1940 and the Medaille Militaire in 1944.

On his return to **Algeria** after the war, he resumed his nationalist opposition to the French who confiscated his farm as punishment, though that only made him a more determined nationalist. In the later 1940s, ben Bella joined the nationalist underground movement, then led by Messali Hadj, and became a leading member of the "Young Turks." Following the Algerian elections of 1948, which were seen to have been rigged by the governor, ben Bella, along with other young radical nationalists, decided that there was no possibility of achieving independence by peaceful democratic means. They founded a movement within that of Messali Hadj, the **Organisation Secrète** (OS)/Secret Organization, with the object of taking up arms and turning to violence as the only way to obtain independence from **France**. In 1950, an OS raid upon the Oran Post Office to obtain money was led by ben Bella; he was imprisoned by the French, but escaped after serving two years of his sentence. He went underground and then moved to Egypt where he obtained assistance for his activities from revolutionary supporters of the new Nasser government.

Working with other nationalists ben Bella now came to two decisions: to create a new nationalist party—the **Front de Libération Nationale** (FLN)/National Liberation Front—and to launch an armed insurrection. He became a leading member of the FLN, which began to ship arms to Algeria. There were two attempts upon ben Bella's life during 1956—one in Cairo and one in Tripoli. He was then arrested in Algeria by the French when negotiating peace terms with the French Prime Minister Guy Mollet; he was to remain in a French prison from 1956 to 1962. As a result, he was dissociated from the events of 1956–1962 in Algeria and so kept his radical reputation intact.

Ben Bella was released in 1962 after the peace of Evian-les-Bains. Independence saw immediate splits in the ranks of the FLN between the moderates and radicals. The conservative leaders of the FLN formed a provisional government, **Gouvernement Provisoire de la République Algérienne** (GPRA)/Provisional Government of the Algerian Republic, while the radicals at the FLN party congress meeting in Tripoli elected a socialist-oriented government, the Bureau Politique, which ben Bella joined. At this stage, ben Bella needed the support of the chief of the Armée de Libération Nationale (ALN)/National Liberation Army, Colonel **Houari Boumedienne**, which he obtained. In 1963, ben Bella was elected unopposed as president of the Algerian Republic.

In the immediate aftermath of independence Algeria faced huge problems, partly the result of the war, partly due to the departure of almost all the French *colons* (including the administration, leaving the country desperately short of skilled people at all levels), and partly due to the lawlessness that usually follows a civil war with armed gangs disrupting normal life. Ben Bella set about creating a working state out of nothing and with a clear sense of future priorities set aside 25 percent of the budget for education. He embarked upon a policy of nationalizing the huge farms of the former French settlers as well as introducing other agrarian reforms. But the economy sometimes reacted poorly to socialist measures. His radicalism led ben Bella to become an anti-Zionist ally of the Arab states opposed to Israel, while at the same time he attempted to develop cultural and economic relations with France. His humanity appealed to the people and he enjoyed great popularity, but he tended to govern on a day-to-day basis and he notably failed to obtain the full support of the FLN. On 19 June 1965, ben Bella was deposed in a coup mounted by Boumedienne and was subsequently imprisoned for 15 years and only released on 30 October 1980. Twenty-five years later, in 2005, President **Abdelaziz Bouteflika** appointed ben Bella to head the Commission Nationale pour l'Amnestie Générale (CNAG)/National

Commission for General Amnesty as the long-drawn out war between the government and the Islamist fundamentalists appeared to be drawing to a close.

BENGUELA RAILWAY. The Benguela Railway, built between 1903 and 1929, with its railhead at Lobito on the Atlantic coast of **Angola**, became a vital strategic line for transporting copper to the coast for both **Congo** and Zambia during the troubled 1960s. The railway runs a total of 1,350 kilometers from Lobito to Katanga (Shaba Province) in southern Zaire and then continues on to the Zambian Copperbelt. Given Zambia's landlocked position and total dependence upon transport routes through neighboring countries, and once the Unilateral Declaration of Independence (UDI) had been declared in Rhodesia in November 1965, the railway became vital to Zambia, which had to export bulk copper to sustain its embattled economy.

Up to 1973 and the closure of the Zambia-Rhodesia border by the Smith government, some 15,000 tons of copper a month went out along the Benguela Railway, and by May 1974, the amount had climbed dramatically to 45,000 tons a month. The railway was a vital source of revenue for Angola and provided jobs and security for substantial numbers of workers at Benguela and Nova Lisboa as well as providing a basis for further industrial development. During the latter stages of the nationalist war against the Portuguese in Angola, the liberation movements had refrained from attacking the line, although small, spasmodic raids had forced the Portuguese to guard trains and not move goods by night.

Jonas Savimbi, the leader of the **União Nacional para a Independência Total de Angola** (UNITA)/National Union for the Total Independence of Angola, operated from a base near Luso, the point from which trains had to be guarded; Savimbi was the son of a Benguela railway worker but at this time he informed the railway authorities that the line would be safe.

From August 1975 onward, however, as fighting between the liberation movements intensified, the railway no longer provided an outlet for either **Zaire** or Zambia. Bridges were blown up and, for a time, UNITA came to control long stretches of the railway. This UNITA action was a contributory cause leading President **Kenneth Kaunda** of Zambia to recognize the **Movimento Popular para a**

Libertação de Angola (MPLA)/Popular Movement for the Liberation of Angola government of Angola in 1976 and expel UNITA from his country. In 1975, President Kaunda announced that Zambia proposed to build a new line to connect the Copperbelt through Solwezi in northern Zambia direct to the Benguela Railway in Angola, bypassing Zaire, but nothing came of this plan. Although, from time to time, hopes were raised through the 1980s that the Benguela Railway would be reactivated, this proved impossible as the Angolan civil war intensified.

BIAFRA. *See* NIGERIA, CIVIL WAR (1967–70).

BOUMEDIENNE, HOUARI (MOHAMMED BEN BRAHIM BOUKHAROUBA) (1927–78). One of seven children, Mohammed Ben Brahim Boukharouba was born on 23 August 1927, at the village of Clauzel near Guelma in **Algeria**. He obtained his secondary (Arabic) education at Kettani Medersa in Constantine but, when he failed to obtain deferment from conscription into the French army in order to complete his studies, he fled to Egypt. Shortly after arriving in Cairo, however, he gave up his studies to join other Algerian nationalists, most notably **Ahmed ben Bella**, and changed his name to Houari Boumedienne.

In December 1954, after the **Front de Libération Nationale** (FLN)/National Liberation Front had embarked on full hostilities against the French in Algeria, Boumedienne pushed himself forward in a bid to be accepted as a leader of the coming struggle. He was given military training at Hilwan in Egypt and this was followed by a guerrilla course at Nador, 240 kilometers west of Oran, in Morocco. In 1955, he began leading guerrilla attacks against the French in the Oran area. By 1957, Boumedienne had become the commander of Wilaya V, which was one of the six commands of the FLN. In June 1958, Boumedienne was promoted to commander of the Armée de Liberation Nationale (ALN)/National Libération Army in the west, the area covering the Algeria–Morocco border. In September of that year, he became a member of the Conseil National de la Révolution Algérienne (CNRA)/National Council of the Algerian Revolution when its provisional government was established in Cairo. He was then promoted to colonel and placed in command of the ALN General

Staff, which was stationed at Ghardimaou, five kilometers inside Tunisia, by which time he was in command of a force of 30,000 men.

In 1962, following independence, Boumedienne at once became involved in the power struggle between the old guard led by ben Khedda and the radicals led by ben Bella, who had just been released from prison by the French. On 30 June 1962, the provisional government dismissed Boumedienne from the army; he, however, took refuge with the army in Wilaya VI in the Sahara and proceeded to rally the army behind ben Bella. On 20 September 1962, ben Bella won a 90 percent vote as prime minister; on 28 September, he appointed Boumedienne minister of defense. When ben Bella became president on 15 September 1963, Boumedienne became first deputy premier while also retaining his post as minister of defense and army commander, which put him in an exceptionally strong position. By 1964, ben Bella saw Boumedienne as a serious rival for supreme power; he began to undermine his position and nominated Colonel Tahar Zbiri as chief of the army general staff but, in a secret pact with Zbiri, Boumedienne kept control of the army. Next, ben Bella forced Ahmed Medeghri, the minister of the interior and a strong supporter of Boumedienne, to resign. Then, following a warning that ben Bella intended to oust him from his offices during the Afro–Asian Conference due to be held in Algiers, Boumedienne secured the support of the army and seized power in a coup on 19 June 1965, denouncing ben Bella as a "diabolical dictator."

Thereafter, Boumedienne was to rule Algeria until his death in 1978. With regard to Israel, especially after the 1967 Six-Day War, he was to become a leading "hawk." At first, Boumedienne ruled through a 26-member revolutionary council, but after a coup attempt was mounted against him in 1967, he ruled directly. Spartan and austere, he always relied upon the army as his support base. He was responsible for a policy of socialism, but was never extreme, arguing that what people needed were not speeches but "bread, shoes and schools."

BOUTEFLIKA, ABDELAZIZ (1937–). Abdelaziz Bouteflika was born at Tlemcen in western **Algeria** on 2 March 1937; the son of a merchant who emigrated to Morocco, he obtained his education at Oujda in that country. It was there that he joined the Moroccan section of the Union Générale des Étudiants Mohametains Algériens (UGEMA)/General Union of Algerian Muslim Students. In May 1956, in the course of a student strike, Bouteflika abandoned his studies to join the Armée de Libération Nationale (ALN)/National Liberation Army. He was sent to Wilaya V where he became a close friend of the older **Houari Boumedienne**.

In 1960, Boumedienne sent Bouteflika on a mission to seek support for the **Front de Libération Nationale** (FLN)/National Liberation Front from Mali and Guinea in West Africa. Later that year, he was appointed a staff officer under Boumedienne at Ghardimaou in Tunisia. In January 1962, Bouteflika became spokesman for young military leaders and passed on their grievances to the provisional government. Also in 1962, Bouteflika was sent on a secret visit to the still imprisoned ben Bella at Chateau d'Aulnoy in **France**, in the course of which he paved the way for an alliance between ben Bella and Boumedienne. On 20 September 1962, following independence, Bouteflika was elected to the National Assembly for Tlemcen and joined the government on 29 September as minister for youth and sport. A year later, on the assassination of Mohamed Khemisti, Bouteflika was appointed to his job as foreign minister. Although he performed well in this post, Bouteflika was a known supporter of Boumedienne and, as the gulf between Boumedienne and ben Bella widened, the latter took more and more foreign affairs into his own hands. During 1965, Bouteflika became increasingly disenchanted with ben Bella, and his resistance to him convinced Boumedienne that he could obtain sufficient backing for his coup, which he mounted that June. Subsequently, Bouteflika was made a member of the Revolution Council and was to serve Algeria as foreign minister into the 1970s.

Bouteflika was to make a major political comeback in 1999 when he won the presidential elections of April. He at once embarked upon a course of reconciliation in the hope of ending the bitter war between the government and the Islamist extremists and a referendum of September showed 98.6 percent of voters supporting his peace initiative. However, the civil war continued. Criticism of Bouteflika's policy of dialogue intensified after 11 September 2001 when the **United States** declared a war on terror. In the presidential elections of April 2004, Bouteflika won a second term and pledged to continue his policy of national reconciliation. In April 2005,

Bouteflika claimed that security had been "largely restored every-where across the country."

BURUNDI. It is difficult to focus upon civil war in Burundi because for nearly 40 years, from just before independence in 1962, the country has been in a state of potentially explosive civil war between the members of its Hutu majority and Tutsi minority ethnic groups. The violence, when it comes, almost always takes the form of two-way massacres.

Background

Burundi was first incorporated into German East Africa during the European "Scramble" at the end of the 19th century; in 1916, during World War I, it was taken over by Belgian troops from the neighboring Belgian Congo; in 1923, it became part of the Belgian-administered mandate of Ruanda-Urundi created by the newly formed League of Nations. The subsequent Belgian administration emphasized tribal differences and worked through the ruling minority group, the Tutsis, who represented a mere 15 percent of the population, while the Hutus represented 84 percent. Historically, the Tutsis had moved into the region centuries earlier and imposed their rule on the Hutus, a sedentary farming people. This tradition of overlordship had, in effect, been continued by the colonial powers, which used the Tutsis as their agents of government. Burundi, with neighboring **Rwanda** as well as parts of **Uganda**, Tanzania, and the eastern **Democratic Republic of Congo** (formerly **Zaire**), is a region highly sensitive to Tutsi–Hutu antagonisms. These are of long standing. Just before independence in Rwanda, which that country achieved at the same time as Burundi, there was a successful uprising of the Hutus against the Tutsis.

Burundi became independent in 1962 as a kingdom under a Tutsi ruler, Mwami Mwambutsa IV. Growing Hutu unrest led to an uprising in 1965, and while this was brutally put down, the king was forced to flee the country. On 28 November 1966, Michel Micombero carried out a successful coup to make himself president, and the country a republic. Between 1966 and 1972, the Tutsi-dominated government executed a series of purges against the Hutus, especially those with education or in positions of authority, so as to entrench itself in power.

The Events of 1972

In March 1972, ex-King Ntare, who had reigned for less than a year after Mwabutsa's exile prior to the Micombero coup, returned to Burundi, where his appearance sparked off a Hutu coup attempt. This failed and was followed by massive Tutsi reprisals. On 29 April 1972, there followed another Hutu uprising aimed at overthrowing the Tutsi government, and in the south of the country, Tutsis were indiscriminately slaughtered. However, the government had been expecting trouble and a further Tutsi campaign of systematic massacre of Hutus followed. Hutus in the army were eliminated and approximately a third of educated Hutus were targeted and killed. When this Hutu uprising began, Micombero claimed that Ntare had mercenary support to overthrow the government, and both Tanzania and Zaire sent his government limited military assistance. Tutsi casualties were heaviest in the south of the country and about 25,000 Tutsis were forced to flee into neighboring countries as **refugees**.

On the other hand, the Tutsi massacres of educated Hutus were designed to deprive them of their potential leadership. Estimates of the numbers killed vary between 80,000–100,000 and as many as 250,000 dead, while another 500,000 became homeless and about 40,000 became refugees in neighboring countries. Targets among the Hutus included priests, teachers, university students, and about one-fifth of secondary school children, while a Roman Catholic priest claimed that 15,000 bodies were buried in one grave. There was no foreign intervention to prevent the killings and African countries, generally, adopted the attitude that the massacres were an internal affair for Burundi. The state of emergency was lifted on 21 June 1972, when President Micombero claimed that 25,000 Hutus had been in training to carry out massacres of Tutsis. He also claimed that between 50,000 and 100,000 people, mainly Tutsis, had been killed in the south of the country. Other estimates by missionaries downgraded the number of Tutsi deaths to no more than 2,000, while also suggesting that at least 80,000 Hutus had been killed. The immediate result of this civil war of massacres was the emergence of a Tutsi elite with absolute power over all aspects of government. International expressions of shock were not accompanied by any meaningful actions, and in Switzerland the exiled king, Mwambutsa IV, accused the Micombero government of a policy of Hutu extermination. Hutu refugees continued to cross into Tanzania during 1973 and Burundi government planes then bombed the refugee settlements.

A New Phase

In 1976, a coup toppled Micombero and brought Jean-Baptiste Bagaza, also a Tutsi, to power. He pursued a genuine policy of Hutu–Tutsi reconciliation and land reform, which favored the Hutus, but in the period 1984–1987 his government became more intolerant of human rights and, in particular, had a confrontation with the Roman Catholic Church. Bagaza was deposed in another coup of 1987, to be replaced by Major **Pierre Buyoya**, who did not vary his policy much from that of his predecessor. In August 1988, a fresh outbreak of killings took place in the commune of Marangara in Ngozi province and at Ntegi in Kimundu province, and an estimated 10,000 people, mainly Hutus, were killed in the Bujumbura area. The army was Tutsi-controlled, and all arms were also under its control. About 65,000 Hutu refugees crossed the border into Rwanda. The relatively small scale of this uprising demonstrated how absolute Tutsi control of the country was at that time.

In February 1991, Buyoya issued a Charter of National Unity, which granted equal rights to the three ethnic groups, the Hutu, Tutsi, and Twa (1 percent of the population). In November 1991, members of the Palipehutu group killed 270 people in Bujumbura and elsewhere, while by 3 January 1992, the death toll had doubled and 10,000 people had fled as refugees (although European estimates suggested a death toll of 3,000 and 50,000 refugees). Buyoya held the country's first ever multi-party presidential elections on 1 June 1993; he was defeated by Melchior Ndadaye, the first Hutu to become president. Tutsis demonstrated against Ndadaye's victory and there was a Tutsi army coup attempt at the time of his presidential inauguration, though that failed. However, a successful and bloody coup was mounted by the Tutsis on 21 October 1993, in which President Ndadaye was killed. The army, unconvincingly, insisted that it was loyal to the government of the dead president. Massacres took place in many parts of the country and by the end of October the **United Nations High Commissioner for Refugees** (UNHCR) reported that over 500,000 refugees had fled Burundi—342,000 into Rwanda, 214,000 into Tanzania, and 21,000 into Zaire—while by mid-November it was estimated that 150,000 people had been killed. The **Organization of African Unity** (OAU) announced the creation of a force of 200 to protect ministers, while relief agencies were then trying to cope with 800,000 refugees, of whom approximately 100 a day were dying. By 21 December 1993, about 1.5 million people out of a population of 5.6 million had fled their homes to escape violence and as many as 150 a day were dying.

The Events of 1994

On 13 January 1994, the National Assembly appointed another Hutu, Cyprien Ntaryamina, as president. About 100,000 refugees returned home, but the violence continued and on 11 February an international commission reported that the greater part of the army, which was Tutsi, had been actively or passively involved in the coup attempt. Estimates of deaths during 1993 ranged between 25,000 and 200,000. The country was clearly poised for further violence when, on 6 April 1994, President Ntaryamina and President Juvenal Habyarimana of Rwanda were killed when a rocket hit their plane (they had been having discussions about stopping the violence). Surprisingly, the death of Burundi's president did not lead to a breakdown as happened in Rwanda, although violence remained close to the surface. The speaker of the assembly, Sylvestres Ntibantunganga, became president. The government agreed upon a formula of power sharing between the parties, but this provoked extreme Hutus into claiming they had been betrayed. In any case, 95 percent of the security forces remained Tutsi and for the time being they kept the peace.

Hutu extremists in Burundi now began to make contact with their extremist counterparts in the refugee camps outside the country, which contained many Rwandese Hutus. Burundi remained in a state of low intensity civil war through 1995: unofficial Tutsi militias were supported by the Tutsi army; Hutu guerrilla groups looked for further support to the refugee camps for exiles from Rwanda. During March 1995, two suburbs of Bujumbura were cleared of Hutus so that, in effect, the capital became a Tutsi town. At the end of March, some 300 Europeans were airlifted out of the country following the murder of three Belgians. In April, Tutsis massacred 400 Hutus in the Gasorwe region. Violence escalated through the second half of the year. In July, Amnesty International accused the Burundi Security Forces of collaborating with Tutsi extremists to kill thousands of Hutus over the period since 1993. By the end of the year, **United Nations** reports claimed that three or four soldiers were being killed daily and 200 civilians weekly.

In February 1996, the United Nations warned that civil war was taking place in many parts of Burundi and recommended that the world should take preemptive action rather than wait for fresh genocide to occur. Massacres during April accounted for 735 deaths and probably more. At last, there were signs that neighboring countries wanted to intervene, at least tentatively, to prevent further killings and on 25 June 1996, at a regional summit at Arusha, Tanzania, Burundi reluctantly accepted the principle of international intervention. Then, in July, Prime Minister Antoine Nduwayo reversed his position and opposed any international peacekeeping operation. A massacre of 300 Tutsis by militant Hutus at Bugendera in mid-July sparked off another coup on 25 July when the military seized power and installed former President Buyoya in his old job. He claimed: "We have done this to avoid genocide. We want to restore peace and protect the population." In reaction to this coup, however, Kenya, Rwanda, Tanzania, Uganda, **Ethiopia**, and Zaire imposed sanctions on Burundi and by mid-September, Hutu rebels claimed that 10,000 people had been killed since the coup.

Buyoya adopted a policy of all-out war against the Hutu rebels in an effort to inflict a crushing defeat upon them. Defense expenditure for the year increased by 70 percent over 1996 and many of the Hutu peasants were forced to move into "regroupment camps" to prevent them from having contact with the guerrillas. There was no sign of any abatement of the war in 1998 when in January about 1,000 Hutu rebels belonging to the Conseil National pour la Défense de la Démocratie (CNDD)/National Council for the Defense of Democracy attacked a military camp and village close to the capital, Bujumbura. Fighting in the area around Bujumbura continued through February and in late March and early April 1998 an estimated 20,000 people were displaced from their homes near the capital. On 7 April 1998, the New York–based organization, Human Rights Watch, published a report which accused both the government and the Hutu rebels of responsibility for "a massive campaign of military violence" which had seen thousands of civilians killed, raped, or tortured.

The war between the Tutsi army and the Hutu rebels was estimated to have cost 250,000 lives between 1993 and 1999. In September 1999, there was an escalation of rebel activity and the government responded by moving 300,000 Hutu peasants into "regroupment camps." Conditions in these camps were appalling and the UN Security Council urged the government to abandon the policy, but a military spokesman said nothing could be done until the rebels abandoned their "genocidal activity." The ongoing peace process suffered a setback in October when **Julius Nyerere**, the former president of Tanzania, who had been acting as principal mediator, died. The former president of **South Africa, Nelson Mandela**, replaced Nyerere as mediator. He criticized the regroupment policy and President Buyoya promised to dismantle the centers. In August 2000, a power-sharing agreement was reached at Arusha, Tanzania, between the government, the military, and a number of political parties representing both Hutu and Tutsi. The agreement was signed in the presence of Mandela, U.S. President Bill Clinton, and over a dozen heads of state. However, the agreement had to be balanced against the interests of the Tutsi-led army and three Hutu guerrilla forces as well as several Tutsi parties that were absent. This Arusha agreement stipulated a three-year transition period. The arrangement appeared to break down on 26 February 2001 when a majority of the parties to the agreement refused to accept Buyoya as the interim head of the transitional government. The breakdown of the negotiations led the rebel Forces for National Liberation (FNL) to advance into the capital, Bujumbura, from its outskirts and it took the national army 10 days to drive them out again.

In April 2001, South Africa's deputy president, Jacob Zuma, took over as official mediator from Mandela. He organized a meeting between Buyoya and the head of the Hutu-leaning Forces for the Defense of Democracy (FDD), Jean-Bosco Ndayikengurnkige; this meeting sparked Tutsi fears of a Hutu takeover and an attempted putsch followed and general fighting escalated. In May, Buyoya went to South Africa where he met Zuma, Mandela, and President Thabo Mbeki, who reinforced his determination to stand up to Tutsi extremists. A new peace plan was announced at Arusha on 23 July. This laid down that a three-year transitional government would be led by Buyoya for the first 18 months and then by Domitien Ndayizeye, the secretary-general of the Front Burundien pour la Démocratie (FRODEBU)/ Front for Democracy in Burundi, for the second 18 months. Ndayizeye had been elected president in 1993. On the day this agreement was announced, Tutsi soldiers launched another coup attempt. In addition, the two armed Hutu groups, the FDD and FNL, were unwilling to accept the cease-fire. South Africa then sent 7,000 troops to act as peacekeepers. Several new political parties were established in the first months of 2002. There was an upsurge of fighting in May, which caused thousands to flee their homes in northern Bujumbura. The Hutus saw the Tutsi army as a repressive force, the Tutsis regarded it as their only guarantee of security. Intense efforts at mediation during the second half of the year by South Africa and Uganda persuaded the government and the FDD to agree to a cease-fire on 30 December.

In January 2003, President Buyoya and the FDD leader, Pierre Nkurunziza, visited South Africa and asked for additional peacekeeping forces from South Africa, **Mozambique**, and Ethiopia to supplement the 7,000 South African troops already in Burundi. On 30 April, Buyoya gave up the presidency according to the interim agreement and Domitien Ndayizeye, a Hutu, replaced him. He at once guaranteed the safety of the Tutsis and promised to advance preparations for presidential elections in 2004. A new wave of fighting broke out in July and affected 16 out of 17 provinces. The collapse of the cease-fire prompted Zuma to visit Bujumbura where he supported the government of Ndayizeye. In October, President Thabo Mbeki personally intervened as a mediator and brought the FDD leader Nkurunziza and Ndayizeye together in Pretoria where the two men signed a new political and military agreement. Meanwhile, peacekeeping troops from Mozambique and Ethiopia arrived in Burundi. In November, a formal peace was signed between the government and the FDD in the presence of three African heads of state. It was agreed that the FDD should have four ministerial posts, 15 seats in the legislature, and one third of all new civil service and police posts. In addition, FDD military forces were to be integrated into the army while 40 percent of the officer corps was to be drawn from the FDD and top military posts were to be split equally between Hutus and Tutsis.

Putting the power-sharing agreement into operation was the principal concern through 2004. On 6 January, President Ndayizeye created a joint military command of 20 representatives of the army and 13 of the FDD. A few days later the Hutu FDL, which had not accepted the peace process, launched an attack near the capital. During March, 200 members of the FDD reported for training in the new National Defense Forces of Burundi. In April, the FDL signaled its readiness to suspend the armed struggle and Hutu refugees in Tanzania began to return home. In May, the United Nations announced that it would deploy peacekeepers in Burundi to replace the **African Union** forces. The UN Operation in Burundi (ONUB) was to consist of 200 military observers, 125 staff officers, 120 civilian police, and other civilian personnel. The peace process suffered a setback in July when the main Tutsi party, Union pour le Progrès National (UPRONA)/Union for National Progress, rejected the power-sharing constitution which gave 60 percent of the seats in the national assembly (lower house) to Hutus and 40 percent to Tutsis. Further dissension led to the postponement of the elections that had been set for October until 22 April 2005 while the referendum to approve the constitution was twice delayed and then set for 22 February 2005.

2005: A Final Settlement?

In January 2005, new political parties were registered and a National Truth and Reconciliation Commission was established to investigate crimes by both Hutus and Tutsis and suggest measures of reconciliation. The National Referendum was held on 28 February and 92 percent of the voters approved the new constitution. Under the new constitution, the first president would be elected by both houses of the legislature—the National Assembly and the Senate—and thereafter presidents would be popularly elected. The government was to be open to all ethnic affiliations but to be made up of a maximum of 60 percent Hutus and 40 percent Tutsis. A meeting of regional leaders at Entebbe (Uganda, Kenya, Tanzania, and Zambia) with President Ndayizeye agreed to prolong the interim period to allow time for legislative and presidential elections. Local elections were held nationwide on 3 June. The former rebel (Hutu) Conseil National pour la Défense de la Démocratie-Forces pour la Défense de la Démocratie (CNDD-FDD)/

National Council for the Defense of Democracy-Forces for the Defense of Democracy won 57 percent of the seats, Ndayizeye's FRODEBU 23 percent, and the main Tutsi party UPRONA 6.3 percent. The legislative elections were held on 4 July with CNDD-FDD winning 64 out of 118 seats, FRODEBU 30 seats, and UPRONA 24. Pierre Nkurunziza, the candidate of the CNDD-FDD, won the presidential election with 91 percent of the votes of the joint session of the legislature with a combined total of 162 members. He was the sole candidate and replaced Ndayizeye as President of Burundi. Martin Nduwimana of UPRONA became first vice-president in charge of Political and Administrative Affairs. On 10 October, Agathon Rwasa, the chairman of the Party for the Liberation of the Hutu People-Forces for National Liberation (Palipehutu-FNL) (the only rebel faction that was still offering armed resistance) was suspended and Jean-Bosco Sindayigaya was elected chairman in his place. A spokesman then announced that the new leadership would not take up arms against the "properly elected" government of Pierre Nkurunziza. In December, the UN Security Council extended its peacekeeping mandate to 1 July 2006.

BUTHELEZI, CHIEF GATSHA MANGOSUTHU (1928–). Chief Gatsha Buthelezi, leader of **South Africa**'s Inkatha Freedom Party (IFP) and a Zulu chief, became one of the most controversial figures in South Africa during the 1980s. He was born on 27 August 1928, and is related to the Zulu royal family. He graduated from Fort Hare University in 1951, and in 1953 went to work as an interpreter in the Bantu Department in Durban. In June 1970, Buthelezi was elected leader of the Zulu territorial authority and later became its chief minister. He embarked upon a long power struggle with the king and the traditionalists, always insisting that King Goodwill, who was installed on 3 December 1971, should only have ceremonial functions and no power.

At first, Buthelezi opposed the system of Bantustans, which was introduced during the premiership of Hendrik Verwoerd, but then decided to work within the system and became the first prime minister of the Kwa-zulu Bantustan in April 1972. Despite his apparent acquiescence in the Bantustan system, Buthelezi never accepted that it should lead to separate development or full independence, which he rejected as a political option. However, he was a pragmatist in the apartheid world of South Africa in the 1970s.

In 1976, he founded the Black Unity Front, which aimed to create a federation of the homelands; more important for his and Kwazulu's future, he also founded the Inkatha movement, which rapidly achieved a membership of 200,000 and became his power base. Buthelezi was accused of fostering tribalism, and so in 1978 he tried to refute this accusation by creating a black, Coloured and Indian alliance, though he did not succeed. He also claimed to be ready to work with the **African National Congress** (ANC). At the beginning of the 1980s, however, the ANC condemned Buthelezi for his "half and half" policies; he kept his options open and was ready to cooperate with the government. During 1985, which was a turning point for South Africa, there was mounting violence between members of the Inkatha Movement and ANC supporters, although the party was banned in South Africa. This violence occurred mainly in Kwazulu but also in the mining hostels where the two groups were intermingled. The violence continued for the rest of the 1980s and into the 1990s. Buthelezi drew most of his support from rural Zulus, while many of the urban Zulus supported the ANC. Buthelezi probably never had the support of more than 25–30 percent of the Zulus.

After **Nelson Mandela**'s release in February 1990, Buthelezi used the IFP to cause disturbances on a sufficient scale to ensure that he would be treated as a major factor in any political settlement, and though he met Mandela in an effort to bring an end to the IFP-ANC violence, this continued right up to the elections of April 1994. During the long period of negotiations and constitution making (1990–94) Buthelezi played a complex on-off game of politics, sometimes veering one way and sometimes another, but always maintaining his position as far as possible at center stage. His reputation was badly damaged in July 1991 when the *Daily Mail* revealed that the South African government had secretly funded the Inkatha movement to counter the ANC. Only at the last moment did Buthelezi agree to take part in the 1994 elections, in which the IFP obtained 10.5 percent of the votes and won control of Kwazulu-Natal Province. He became a member of the interim government as minister of home affairs.

BUYOYA, PIERRE (1949–). Pierre Buyoya, a Tutsi, was president of **Burundi** from 1987 to 1993, when he lost the country's first ever multi-party elections; he was brought back to power as president by the army in a coup of July 1996. Born on 24 November 1949, Buyoya went to Belgium in 1967 for further studies and followed this with military training, including tank training, before returning to Burundi in 1975. He became the commander of a tank squadron and then went to **France** for further military training (1976–77). After his return to Burundi from France, Buyoya turned his attention to politics and joined the Union pour le Progrès National (UPRONA)/Union for National Progress which elected him to its central committee in 1979. He went to Germany for a third period of military training in 1980–1982.

Although at first close to President Jean-Baptiste Bagaza, Buyoya became increasingly disenchanted with him and so distanced himself from his old colleague. Then, on 3 September 1987, with the support of most of the army, he mounted a successful coup against Bagaza whom he accused of corruption. On taking power he suspended the 1981 Constitution, dissolved the National Assembly, and suspended all UPRONA organizations. Instead, he established a Comité Militaire du Salut National (CMSN)/Military Committee of National Salvation. He failed to pay sufficient attention to the always delicate and usually deeply suspicious relationship between the Tutsis and Hutus with the result that another series of tribal massacres occurred in August 1988. Although the mainly Tutsi army was principally responsible for what happened, Buyoya blamed Hutu **refugees** from abroad for inflaming the Hutus in Burundi.

In the aftermath of these massacres, Buyoya launched a policy of reconciliation and, in October 1988, he appointed a new cabinet in which he gave equal representation to Tutsis and Hutus. At the same time he established a Committee of National Unity, which was to formulate policies designed to reconcile the two ethnic groups. After it had reported in May 1989, Buyoya instructed the committee to prepare a Charter of National Unity. Buyoya worked to eliminate tribalism and, in December 1990, for the first time, the Hutus gained a majority on the Central Committee of UPRONA as well as providing its secretary-general. As a result, some prominent Hutus returned from exile and in February 1991 Buyoya gave Hutus a majority of posts in his new cabinet. In May 1991, he announced that he favored pluralism and began to prepare the country for multi-partyism. In the first ever multi-party presidential elections of 1 June 1993, which he had brought about, Buyoya was defeated by Melchior Ndadaye, who was the first Hutu to become president of Burundi; he was the leader of the opposition Front Burundien pour la Démocratie (FRODEBU)/ Burundian Democratic Front. This Hutu triumph was short-lived.

On 21 October 1993, the Tutsis mounted a bloody coup and by the end of the month 500,000 refugees had fled the resultant massacres. The death of the presidents of Burundi and **Rwanda** on 6 April 1994 brought both countries close to the abyss, although Burundi did not collapse into genocidal massacres as did Rwanda. Even so, Burundi was to experience a state of varying civil war and massacres for the next two years. On 15 July 1996, after months of developing chaos, the military seized power and installed Buyoya as president. On taking office he said: "We have done this to avoid genocide. We want to restore peace and protect the population." Buyoya remained president through to 2003 when, after 18 months as president under the new power-sharing agreement, he stepped down on 30 April to be replaced by Domitien Ndayizeye.

– C –

CABORA BASSA DAM. The Cabora Bassa Dam is the third major hydro-electric project on the Zambezi River, downstream of the Victoria Falls hydro-electric project and the Kariba Dam. It is one of the largest hydro-electric projects in Africa and the world. The dam is situated on the Zambezi, 128 kilometers northwest of Tete, the capital of Tete Province in the north of **Mozambique**. The dam is 170 meters high and 300 meters at the crest and contains a total volume of 510 million cubic meters of water. The dam has created Lake Cabora Bassa, which stretches back 240 kilometers to the border of Zambia; it is 32 kilometers across at its widest point.

The Cabora Bassa Dam project was conceived by the Portuguese when the prospect of losing the war against the **Frente da Libertação de Moçambique** (FRELIMO)/Mozambique Liberation Front nationalists must already have been anticipated as a future possibility. The Portuguese reason for building the dam, since they did not require the potential power for Mozambique, was twofold: to sell the power to **South Africa**, which suffers from a permanent shortage of hydro-capacity; and, by making Cabora Bassa indispensable to South African development, to ensure that South Africa was drawn into the defense of the dam against the military advance of FRELIMO. For these reasons the dam was as much strategic as it was economic in its conception. A consortium of South African, German, and French companies formed the Zambezi Company (ZAMCO) and construction was begun in 1967. The dam was owned by Portugal on the understanding that when the capital costs had been fully repaid by the end of the century, ownership would pass to the government of Mozambique. Power from the dam was to be distributed through the country by 1,600 kilometers of transmission lines and the eventual capacity was to be 3,600 megawatts. The main supply of electricity was always intended for South Africa; it passes along a 1,422-kilometer dual 530-kilowatt transmission line to that country. Incorporated in the whole project were plans to supply power to Malawi and **Zimbabwe**.

During the years of struggle against the Portuguese (1967–75), the dam was frequently attacked by FRELIMO and required a heavy concentration of military forces to guard it. Following independence in 1975, FRELIMO then found the position reversed and instead of attacking, the dam was obliged to defend it against attacks by the **Resistência Nacional Moçambicana** (RENAMO)/Mozambican National Resistance as well as attempts by RENAMO to cut the transmission lines to South Africa. In 1982, for example, supplies to South Africa were cut off for a period of six months. After the transmission lines had been repaired, a special armed force was created to patrol and safeguard the lines from further RENAMO attacks. Peace in Mozambique, which by the mid1990s looked reasonably stable, meant that the transmission lines could be extended to carry extra power to new markets in South Africa as well as Malawi and Zimbabwe, while also feeding supplies into the national grid. The project has yet to achieve its full potential, which is enormous.

CAMUS, ALBERT (1913–60). Albert Camus was one of the outstanding left-wing writers of his period. Brought up with his brother by his mother in a working-class district of Algiers, he found himself naturally in sympathy with the nationalist (Algerian) cause. During 1934–1935 he became a member of the Algerian Communist Party and just prior to World War II, he wrote a number of articles in which he analyzed the social conditions of the Muslims of the Kabyle district. These articles drew attention, 15 years in advance of the Algerian civil war, to the conditions and injustices which were a primary cause of that conflict. He insisted that **France** should live up to its principles of equality and justice in **Algeria**. Yet, in the end, Camus turned out to be only moderately revolutionary, and by 1958 he spoke of not abandoning Algeria to the new imperialism of the **Front de Libération Nationale** (FLN)/National Liberation Front. He argued that the FLN intended to evict 1.2 million Europeans, although this was a mild stance compared with that taken by the more extreme French military.

CENTRAL AFRICAN REPUBLIC (CAR). In April 1996, President Ange-Felix Pattassé faced an army mutiny over unpaid salaries and though the threatened revolt was temporarily calmed, a more serious mutiny erupted in May. As a result, French troops (there was a French military base in the country) became involved: first, to evacuate French citizens, then to patrol Bangui (the capital) and, in effect, to maintain Pattassé in power. The French then negotiated a settlement between the government and the mutinous troops and justified their intervention on the grounds that they were defending a democratically elected president. However, in return for their services, the French imposed Jean-Paul Ngoupandé, CAR ambassador in Paris, upon Pattassé as prime minister with a brief to make a reluctant Pattassé adopt structural reforms that would be acceptable to **aid** donors. By November, relations between the president and his prime minister had reached breaking point and another, more serious army mutiny was launched. The mutineers belonged to the Yakoma tribe of former President André Kolingba. They seized part of the capital and brought the country to the brink of civil war. French troops were again deployed to protect the presidential palace and other key points in the capital. The Franco–African summit, which met in Ouagadougou, Burkina Faso, sent a mediating mission to CAR consisting of four presidents (Burkina Faso, **Chad**, Mali, and Gabon) while the former head of state of Mali, Amadou Toumani Touré, was made facilitator.

New violence surfaced at the beginning of 1997 when mutineers killed two French soldiers in Bangui. The French reacted by attacking the mutineers' positions and several were killed. **France** then announced that it was sending a further 300 soldiers to join the 2,000 already in CAR, although the previous December, the French had begun to phase out their military involvement in controlling the mutiny as they handed over to African troops from the Inter-African Mission to Monitor the Bangui Accords (MISAB). MISAB's mandate was to gather and disarm the mutineers. MISAB consisted of 500 troops from Senegal, Chad, Gabon, Togo, and Burkina Faso with logistical support from France. It was commanded by General Amadou Toumani Touré of Mali. MISAB suffered two setbacks in May and June, but by July the great majority of the mutineers had returned to barracks and the rebels had been disarmed by the end of September. MISAB was to remain in CAR, with the backing of the **United Nations** Security Council, for a further period to supervise a process of reconciliation. In August, meanwhile, France had announced that it was to close its two bases in Bangui and Bouar in 1998 and withdraw all its troops from the country.

On 15 April 1998, MISAB was replaced by the United Nations Mission to the Central African Republic (MINURCA) which "took over" the troops from the five countries that had formed MISAB with additional troops from **Côte d'Ivoire**. France continued to provide logistics and funds and Canada provided some military personnel to bring the total force to over 1,000 troops. How long MINURCA remained in the country would depend upon political and economic reforms. In the presidential elections of September 1999, Patassé won with 51.6 percent of the vote in the first round. The mandate of MINURCA was extended for a further six months in November. However, the elections had resulted in considerable turbulence and there were doubts as to whether the newly retrained army would hold together. Nonetheless, MINURCA withdrew from CAR at the beginning of 2000, although the disastrous state of the economy boded ill for the future. At the end of May, a coup attempt was mounted by supporters of Kolingba and 10 days of fighting in Bangui were the worst since the army mutinies of 1996. This time the revolt was only put down with the assistance of Libyan troops as well as followers of the **Congo** (DRC) rebel leader Jean-Pierre Bemba who crossed the river to assist Patassé's forces. The fighting left 100 dead and resulted in thousands of **refugees** while also further depressing the economy.

Unrest through 2001 included strikes by unpaid civil servants. In November, a power struggle developed between Patassé and his army commander, General François Bozize, who tried to launch a coup. Libyan troops again came to the assistance of Patassé and Bozize fled to Chad. Patassé, however, found himself increasingly dependent upon Libyan troops to maintain him in power. On 26 October 2002, supporters of Bozize launched an attack in Bangui and this was only repulsed after six days of fighting by the Libyan troops and rebel soldiers from DRC. By the end of the year Bozize's supporters, with assistance from Chad, controlled substantial areas in the northwest of the country. In 2003, a new peacekeeping force of 300 troops, this time from the Communauté Economique et Monétaire de l'Afrique Centrale (CEMAC)/Economic and Monetary Community of Central Africa, replaced the Libyans. However, on 15 March, the CEMAC force did not oppose Bozize's troops who entered Bangui when Patassé was absent at a conference. The rebels fired on Patassé's plane when he attempted to return, so he continued to Cameroon and later found asylum in Togo. Bozize was proclaimed president on 16 March and his spokesman said the "interruption of the democratic process was necessary to put things back to square one." At first the **African Union** (AU) refused to recognize the Bozize coup and he was not permitted to send a delegation to the AU summit in **Mozambique**. By the end of the year, however, he had gained considerable acceptance including a resumption of **aid** (including military assistance) from France. President Bozize spent 2004 consolidating his power and preparing for elections in 2005. A Presidential Constitution was drafted and promulgated and this was approved in a referendum of 5 December by 90.4 percent of the votes.

CHAD. Chad became independent from **France** in 1960, and like the other huge countries lying along the Sahel region—Mauritania, Mali, Niger, and **Sudan**—suffered from the north–south divide. The north was poor, many of its people were nomadic, and they were ethnically Arab, Tuareg or Arabicized, and Muslim. The south was more populous, more westernized as a result of colonialism, and the population was black African, following African traditional religions or Christianity rather than Islam. These were mainly settled agricultural people who were better off in both material and educational terms than the nomads of the north. This divide between north and south made the subsequent civil wars easier to understand, though these were greatly complicated by other considerations: struggles between rival contenders for power, the role of Libya, which laid claim to the Aozou Strip in the north, and interventions by France, sometimes urged on by the **United States**, as well as neighbors such as **Nigeria** and **Zaire**.

Background and Beginnings

In 1962, Chad's first post-independence president, François Tombalbaye, made Chad a one-party state and though this political decision was accepted by the south, it was rejected in the north. French troops, which had remained in the north after independence, were withdrawn in 1964 and replaced by sections of the Chad National Army, whose soldiers were recruited from the south. These troops were soon at odds with the local people. A first revolt against southern domination occurred in 1966 at Oueddai; the rebels secured some limited support from Sudan. This and other brief rebellions at this time were uncoordinated and largely ineffective; they were in reaction to taxes, the behavior (and presence) of central government civil servants, and, more generally, because of longstanding northern suspicions of any southern interference. Slowly, these northern rebels came together to create a central organization—the **Front de Libération Nationale du Tchad** (FROLINAT)/Chad National Liberation Front. It was then recognized by the Libyan government (which had its own reasons for intervening in the affairs of Chad) and provided with offices in Tripoli.

The First Phase: 1966–75

The civil war, which gradually developed, was complicated by external factors. It was predominantly a struggle between the widely different peoples of north and south whose various leaders over the years sought power for themselves. But it also involved France, which intervened several times with military force over a period of 20 years on behalf of the government in the south, while Libya provided the principal external support for FROLINAT, which represented the northern rebels. In the later stages of these wars, during the

1980s, the United States became involved, offering financial support to the south and reinforcing France's interventions, largely in order to contain Libyan expansionism.

Dr. Abba Siddick was the first leader of FROLINAT in 1966, but he was soon to be replaced by **Goukouni Oueddei**, who was prepared to rely upon Libyan support. At first, FROLINAT obtained aid from **Algeria**, but from 1971 onward relied upon Libya. Tombalbaye attempted to appease FROLINAT by taking northerners into his cabinet, but his overtures were rejected. In 1968, as the war increased in intensity, France sent an air force contingent to reinforce the government of Tombalbaye, and the following year dispatched 1,600 troops to Chad. Their numbers were reduced in 1971 and withdrawn in 1972, and though their presence had not made a great deal of difference to the fighting on the ground, this first French intervention set a pattern for the future. Following a coup attempt against him, Tombalbaye accused Libya of complicity in the FROLINAT rebellion and broke off diplomatic relations, but this action merely persuaded Libya to recognize FROLINAT. The fighting became serious in the early 1970s with FROLINAT capturing a number of northern towns, including Bardai and Faya-Largeau.

FROLINAT had no discernible ideology apart from race and religion and its consequent determination to control the government. Like many such movements, FROLINAT was subject to internal tensions and splits. Goukouni Oeddei and his **Forces Armées Populaires** (FAP)/Popular Armed Forces proved too independent for Libya's purposes and so it switched its support to the new **Front d'Action Commune** (FAC)/Front for Common Action, which was led by Ahmat Acyl. A third splinter group emerged: the **Forces Armées du Nord** (FAN)/Armed Forces of the North led by **Hissène Habré**.

In November 1972, the governments of Chad and Libya resumed diplomatic relations and signed a pact of friendship. This was no more than a temporary pause for breath, however, for in 1973 Libya moved its own armed forces into the Aozou Strip of northern Chad, which it proceeded to annex. Libya justified this action in terms of a 1935 Franco–Italian Protocol, which had recognized 111,370 square kilometers (43,000 square miles) of northern Chad as part of Italian Libya. Subsequently, France had not ratified the Protocol, but there existed clear grounds for argument as to which country had rights of possession. The region was all the more important because it contained substantial resources of uranium. In 1975, Tombalbaye was ousted in a coup by General Felix Malloum, but he proved unable either to subdue the northern rebels and bring the civil war to an end or to expel the Libyans from the Aozou Strip.

The Second Phase: 1975–1986

Following the seizure of three French hostages by FROLINAT in 1975, Malloum fell out with Paris and ended France's base facilities in N'Djamena, although they were restored the following year. In January 1978, Malloum met Habré, the leader of the FAN; they agreed upon a ceasefire and a new government, which would include FROLINAT members. This was an attempt by Malloum to keep FROLINAT divided, but it broke down as FROLINAT, in reaction, became reunited and proceeded to inflict a series of defeats on the Chad army, capturing Fada and Faya Largeau in the process and splitting the country so that the whole of the north was held by FROLINAT, the south by the government. A ceasefire between the two sides followed, but in April 1978 FROLINAT broke it and its forces advanced on the capital. France intervened again, this time sending a force of 2,500 Legionnaires and several squadrons of fighter-bombers in support of the government. In June, the French and Chadian forces launched a major offensive against FROLINAT and inflicted heavy losses upon it at Ati. As a result, Malloum's government, which had been close to collapse, recovered.

Libya, meanwhile, had committed between 2,000 and 3,000 troops to the support of FROLINAT, so that by mid-1978, both France and Libya were heavily involved in the Chad war. Although the French forces had halted the southward advance of FROLINAT, they had not defeated them. Consequently, the country was divided between the south held by the government supported by France and the north held by FROLINAT supported by Libya. Habré of the FAN now made an agreement with Malloum: the latter would remain as president while Habré would become prime minister; his army, the FAN, would be demobilized and its members integrated into the national army. At this point France supported Habré. The alliance was short-lived and had broken down by December 1978. The FAN had not been disbanded, and by January 1979 FAN troops were clashing with the regular army and proving to be a superior fighting force. Then Goukouni's FROLINAT forces advanced upon N'Djamena to join with Habré in attacking the government, and in a coup of February 1979, Habré ousted Malloum. This coup was followed by a general war, with the Muslim forces from the north massacring black southerners and vice versa.

The Forces Armées du Tchad (FAT)/Armed Forces of Chad were rallied by Colonel Abdelkader Kamougue, a former foreign minister, and military order was re-established. Nigeria now intervened in an effort to counterbalance Libyan influence. The Nigerian government hosted peace talks at Kano in northern Nigeria during March and April 1979. These involved Habré, Goukouni, Malloum, a pro-Nigerian party which had emerged, and Libya, as well as Cameroon, Niger, and Sudan as further putative peacemakers. A cease-fire was agreed upon and a Gouvernement d'Union Nationale de Transition (GUNT)/National Union Transitional Government was established. Habré and Malloum "resigned" and Goukouni was appointed president of GUNT. The various armies were to be integrated. Nigeria then overstepped its role as a peacemaker by trying to impose its own candidate, Mahamat Abba, upon Chad, leading both Habré and Goukouni to quit the conference. On their return to N'Djamena, Habré and Goukouni agreed to form a government of national unity of their own, but this, too, did not last and Chad reverted to factional squabbles and fighting.

In March 1980, fighting broke out in N'Djamena between Kamougue's FAT and Habré's FAN and continued all year. France decided to withdraw and had taken its troops out of Chad by May. Then, in June, Goukouni signed a treaty of friendship with Libya but without consulting the GUNT to which he belonged. An offensive by Habré's FAN in the north resulted in major retaliation by Libyan forces whose planes attacked Faya-Largeau and N'Djamena, while its troops, in combination with those of Goukouni, overran large areas. Backed by 5,000 Libyan troops Goukouni took the capital, N'Djamena; it was a triumph for Goukouni. He now overreached himself by entering into an agreement with Libya's **Muammar al-Gaddafi** for an eventual union of Chad and Libya, an agreement which provoked a major international reaction. The **Organization of**

African Unity (OAU) embarked upon intensive diplomacy, which was backed by both France and the United States, to prevent Gaddafi from extending his influence into Chad and by mid-1981, under strong French pressure, Libya withdrew its forces from N'Djamena. At a meeting in Nairobi in June 1981, the OAU agreed to establish a peacekeeping force, which both France and the United States promised to help finance. This was mounted in December of that year when 2,000 Nigerian troops, 2,000 Zairean, and 800 Senegalese under the command of a Nigerian, Major General Ejisa, arrived in Chad. This force remained neutral, although Goukouni had hoped to use it to destroy the FAN and Habré; instead, the OAU persuaded the Libyans to withdraw, with the result that Habré, in the north, obtained many of their weapons and was able to renew his struggle against Goukouni. His fortunes were again in the ascendant, and in June 1982, Habré took N'Djamena unopposed: Kamougue fled as his support collapsed and Goukouni also fled to Algeria.

By October 1982, Habré had established a government in N'Djamena; not only was the FAN more efficient now than Goukouni's forces, but the latter had lost support in the south by agreeing to Libya's claims in the north. A new pro-Habré Forces Armées Nationales Tchadiennes (FANT)/National Armed Forces of Chad was formed. By 1983, Habré had gained international recognition; however, Goukouni was making a recovery in the north. Habré refused to deal with Libya, which maintained its claim to the Aozou Strip, while the FAN now became riven by factions. In April, fighting broke out between FAN troops and the Nigerians over counterclaims between Chad and Nigeria to islands in Lake Chad, with the Nigerians allying themselves with anti-Habré groups. French **mercenaries** assisted the FAN which, nonetheless, suffered some 300 casualties (dead).

In June 1983, Gaddafi increased the level of Libyan support for Goukouni, but this led to a new French intervention (in part the result of U.S. pressures) with 2,800 troops. These created an east–west line (the Red Line) across the country to prevent Goukouni's forces from coming further south. At this point, violence erupted in the extreme south of the country and Habré was not immediately in a position to bring this under control; numbers of **refugees** from the violence fled into neighboring countries. In the north, Libyan planes bombed Oum Chalouba before being repulsed with heavy losses by Habré's forces. In September 1983, Habré visited France to take part in the Franco–African summit and criticized France for not being prepared to fight the Libyans. The war continued through 1984 with substantial casualties on both sides. In mid-1984, Habré dissolved FROLINAT and replaced it with the Union Nationale pour l'Indépendence et la Révolution (UNIR)/National Union for Independence and Revolution in an effort to create a more evenly balanced north–south government, but it did not work. Further fighting in the south erupted in August 1984 and was met by brutal government repression so that refugees flooded into **Central African Republic** (CAR). The fighting continued to April 1985. In September 1984, France and Libya agreed to withdraw their troops simultaneously from Chad, and by 10 November, all 3,300 French troops had left the country, although Libya kept its forces in the far north. President François Mitterand admitted he had been fooled by Gaddafi. France then made an offer to send troops back to Chad, but Habré refused since he distrusted French motives. Through 1985, Habré consolidated his power in the south and appeared to have brought the rebellion there under control. By October 1985, however, the Libyans had an estimated 4,000 troops in the north of Chad.

The Third Phase: 1986–1990

In February 1986, the civil war became an international war when the Libyans launched an offensive across the 16th parallel of latitude north, the line France had established dividing the country. Gaddafi had assumed that France would not send troops back to Chad, but he had miscalculated. Initially Habré's forces repulsed the Libyan attack; then he appealed to France for aid and French bombers from bases in CAR bombed the Libyan airstrip at Ouadi Doum, northeast of Faya-Largeau. France then established an air strike force in Chad. The United States (in April 1986 the United States had bombed Libya in an attempt to "take out" Gaddafi) now provided Habré with $10 million in **aid**. At the same time, Goukouni's GUNT was disintegrating and many of its members defected to Habré. By mid-November, U.S. arms for Chad were arriving in Douala, Cameroon, and France had sent 1,000 troops to support its air units, and these were deployed along the 16th parallel of latitude. Then, in December,

Habré launched an offensive against the Libyans in the extreme north at Bardai and in the Tibesti Mountains. French aircraft dropped supplies for his forces. Otherwise, despite Habré's urgent requests for their help, the French appeared unwilling to become further involved fighting the Libyans, although they had 1,200 troops along the 16th parallel and a further 4,000 stationed in CAR. Habré, especially, wanted anti-aircraft and anti-tank guns. The Libyans now had an estimated 6,000–8,000 troops in Chad. Only after Habré had pleaded that 20 years of war had wrecked the Chad economy and that he was not strong enough to face Libya unaided, did France agree to drop supplies for his forces, while the United States promised a further $15 million in aid. The French publicly discouraged Habré from attacking the Libyans, but then in mid-December, Goukouni's forces, which had switched to Habré's side the previous October, inflicted a major defeat on the Libyans.

At Bardai, 400 Libyans were killed and 17 of their tanks destroyed. France now agreed to assist Habré, who went north to attack the Libyans and assist the 3,000 Goukouni troops. This juncture represented a rapprochement between Habré and Goukouni's FAP, although Goukouni himself appeared to be a prisoner in Tripoli. These Libyan reversals at the end of 1986 offered the best opportunity yet of bringing the civil war to an end. At the beginning of 1987, Habré's forces launched a major offensive against the Libyans, who were forced to quit most of the towns they had occupied including Ouadi Doum. The Libyans then met with a major defeat at Fada when 784 soldiers were reported killed and 100 (Soviet) tanks were destroyed. Later 130 Libyan prisoners were displayed to the diplomatic corps in N'Djamena. During January, French planes ferried supplies to the north as Habré prepared for a further advance, while Libya built up its forces to an estimated 15,000 men and France sent a further 1,000 troops to Chad. In March 1987, Habré's forces under the command of Hassan Djamous captured Ouadi Doum, which was Libya's base for its strike aircraft: 3,600 Libyans were killed, 700 were captured, and 2,000 died of thirst in the desert as they fled. The Libyans now gave up Faya-Largeau and retreated further north while Habré, at last, appeared able to extend his authority over the whole country. Another 2,000–3,000 Libyan troops were isolated across the border in the **Darfur** Province of Sudan. Many of the Libyan troops were, in fact, mercenaries who had been pressed into the Islamic Pan-African Legion; these were originally people who had gone to Libya to seek work. The Chad war appeared to be deeply unpopular in Libya.

A Precarious Peace

France and Senegal (chair of the OAU) tried to persuade Habré to take the issue of the Aozou Strip to arbitration (April 1987), but Habré refused, stating his determination to recapture it. In August his forces took Aozou town but then were forced to retreat under heavy Libyan air attacks. However, in September FANT forces captured Maater-es-Surra in southeast Libya, destroying 22 aircraft and 100 tanks and killing 1,700 Libyans. Habré now had troops in southern Libya and controlled the whole of Chad; on 11 September 1987, a cease-fire with Libya was agreed upon. However, Habré did not have control of the Aozou Strip and a stalemate between Libya and Chad continued through 1988, especially as France was not prepared to help Habré take over the Aozou Strip, which had been heavily fortified by the Libyans. A breakthrough came in May 1988, when Gaddafi announced his readiness to recognize the Habré government and provide a "Marshall Plan" to reconstruct war-damaged areas of Chad.

Casualties over more than 20 years of civil war, with its various foreign interventions, are extremely difficult to quantify; at times the fighting had only been between Chad factions, at others the French and Libyans were active on either side, and by the end it was a war between Chad and Libya. During the fight for N'Djamena in 1980, between 3,000 and 4,000 people were killed. From 1965 to the end of the 1970s possibly 20,000 people were killed, while a further 30,000 died during the 1980s. The short conflict between Chad and Nigeria in 1983 over Lake Chad resulted in between 300 and 500 Chadians being killed. Claims and counterclaims for casualties were often conflicting and the casualties for 1987 in the fighting with Libya are at best approximations since Chad undoubtedly inflated the figures for Libyan casualties, while Libya played down its losses, which were in the region of 4,000 dead, 200 tanks and 45 aircraft destroyed. Libyan interventions were certainly very costly, but it could rely upon its oil wealth to meet the bill; Chad, on the other hand, is one of the poorest countries in Africa. It was heavily dependent upon French financial and military aid, and French forces came and went three times during the 20-year war. Chad also received financial and military assistance from the United States ($25 million in 1983; $15 million in 1987). The French estimated the cost of maintaining their troops in Chad at approximately $420,000 a day and these interventions were not popular in France. At various stages of the war **refugees** from Chad crossed into Sudan and CAR and in the 1980s, according to the **United Nations High Commissioner for Refugees** (UNHCR), there were up to 25,000 refugees in Darfur Province of Sudan.

Habré's great year of triumph was 1987: he fought the Libyans to a standstill and invaded their territory before obtaining a ceasefire; Gaddafi agreed to recognize his government and provide aid; and finally Libya agreed to go to arbitration over the Aozou Strip. On 31 August 1989, Chad and Libya agreed to spend a year seeking a solution to their differences, while an OAU Observer Force administered the Aozou Strip and France and Libya undertook to withdraw their forces in stages. However, in December 1990, General **Idriss Déby**, who had been in exile in Darfur, Sudan, overthrew Habré in a coup. He released Libyan prisoners who had been held since 1988 and was believed to have received support for his coup from Gaddafi. Nonetheless, on 5 September 1991, Chad and Libya signed a security agreement of bilateral cooperation and both the internal and external wars appeared to have come to an end. On 3 February 1994, the International Court of Justice ruled by 16 to one to confirm Chad's sovereignty over the Aozou Strip, and on 31 May, the Aozou Strip was formally returned to Chad.

CHILD SOLDIERS. The widespread use of child soldiers in Africa's civil wars became a phenomenon of such conflicts during the 1990s and has continued unabated during the present century. In the three years to the end of 2004, more than 100,000 children were abducted, tortured, and sexually abused before being enrolled to fight in Africa's ongoing civil wars. Boys and girls, some as young as nine or 10, are forced to join militias and are subjected to psychological torture to make them malleable for subsequent indoctrination as soldiers. The **Democratic Republic of Congo** had 30,000 child soldiers in its militias: boys were used as fighters or bodyguards for commanders, girls were gang raped by soldiers for entertainment. In **Uganda** the

Lord's Resistance Army (LRA) has used child soldiers for many of the 20 years it has been fighting against the government. Child soldiers have also been used in the **Sudan People's Liberation Army** (SPLA) in **Rwanda** and **Burundi**. The influx of light ammunition into Africa has been a boost for child recruitment since small guns are perfect for use by children. According to the children's rights director at Human Rights Watch, Tony Tate, "If we send light ammunition to these countries, they will be used by children." In West Africa during the 1990s, child soldiers were deployed in large numbers in the civil wars in **Liberia** and **Sierra Leone**.

Efforts by the international community to prevent the use of child soldiers have, so far, met with limited success. In 2002, the **United Nations** introduced a protocol to end the recruitment of child soldiers and though a majority of nations have signed it, the agreement has been routinely violated in Africa. Countries can now be legally tried for using soldiers under the age of 15 through the International Criminal Court in The Hague, but as yet none has been prosecuted. In April 2006, Human Rights Watch reported that as many as 300,000 child soldiers under the age of 18 and some as young as eight had been used in 33 ongoing or recent armed conflicts in almost every part of the world. A high proportion of these were in Africa. Human Rights Watch pointed out the following: that children are uniquely vulnerable to military recruitment because of their emotional and physical immaturity; that lightweight automatic weapons are simple to operate, readily accessible and can be used by children as easily as adults; that children are most likely to become child soldiers if they are poor, separated from their families, displaced from their homes, living in a combat zone, or have limited access to education. They serve in a number of capacities—as porters, cooks, guards, messengers, spies, as well as in combat. Sometimes they are put in the front lines or sent into minefields ahead of older troops and some have been used for suicide missions. Since few peace treaties recognize the existence of child soldiers, the problem of reintegrating them into civilian life is often ignored. In any case, it is likely to be exceptionally difficult with the result that many end up on the street, become involved in crime, or are drawn back into armed conflict.

The United Nations has paid increasing attention to the problem of child soldiers since the mid-1990s and there have been a number of

Security Council resolutions relating to children affected by armed conflict passed in 1999, 2000, 2001, 2003, 2004, and 2005. Graca Machel (now the wife of **Nelson Mandela**) produced a report in 1996 *Impact of Armed Conflict on Children* with the support of the United Nations Centre for Human Rights and the United Nations Children's Fund (UNICEF), which sets out an agenda for action by member states. According to Amnesty International USA, an estimated 30,000 children (described as "night commuter" children) living in northern Uganda, leave home every evening to sleep in urban areas or into the middle of larger camps for internally displaced persons in an attempt to escape the risk of abduction by the Lord's Resistance Army.

CHISSANO, JOAQUIM ALBERTO (1939–). Joaquim Alberto Chissano became president of **Mozambique** on 3 November 1986, on the death of President **Samora Machel**. He took control of the country when it was in the middle of a terrible civil war with no sign of an end to the fighting. Chissano was born on 22 October 1939, in Gaza Province; he attended Xai Xai Secondary School and then graduated from the Liceu Salazar in Maputo, after which he went to **Portugal** for further studies. He returned to Mozambique in 1962, as growing nationalist ferment was about to spark off the long liberation war against the Portuguese, and became one of the founding members of the **Frente da Libertação de Moçambique** (FRELIMO)/ Mozambique Liberation Front.

In 1963, he was promoted secretary to FRELIMO's first leader, Dr. Eduardo Mondlane. Under Mondlane's successor Machel (Mondlane was assassinated in 1969), Chissano was made responsible for security and defense at the FRELIMO training camp at Kongwa in Tanzania. He then became the chief representative of the exile wing of FRELIMO. In 1974, when Machel was still in exile, he appointed Chissano as prime minister of the transitional government, which was established on 2 September of that year. At independence in 1975, President Machel dispensed with the office of prime minister; instead, he made Chissano foreign minister. In this post, Chissano continued to rise in the FRELIMO party hierarchy and was recognized as Machel's number two. He was not involved in the **Nkomati Accord,** which Machel negotiated with **South Africa** (an agreement that did some damage to Machel's reputation), though he accepted it once it came into operation.

Following the death of Machel in an air crash of 19 October 1986, the FRELIMO Central Committee met on 3 November to elect Chissano head of the party and president. Chissano was essentially a political pragmatist and though ideologically a Marxist he sought to obtain allies in the West. He was also tough and forced Malawi to abandon its support for the **Resistência Nacional Moçambicana** (RENAMO)/Mozambican National Resistance. He obtained essential help from both **Zimbabwe** and Tanzania with troops on the ground to fight RENAMO (their task was specifically to guard the **Beira Corridor** and the Nacala rail link to the Indian Ocean ports). After his decision in 1990 to establish a multi-party system in Mozambique and forsake Marxism, Chissano won western support for his fight against RENAMO. Over the period 1990–1992, with many stops and starts, Chissano came to terms with the leader of RENAMO, Afonso Dhlakama, and worked to achieve a lasting peace. In the elections of 1994, Chissano obtained 53.3 percent of the presidential vote to Dhlakama's 33.7 percent. He then faced the monumental task of rebuilding Mozambique after 30 years of war. In 2004, after serving as president for 18 years, Chissano stepped down and was succeeded in the presidential elections at the end of that year by Amando Guebuza.

CHURCHES. The role played by the churches in African civil wars and confrontations has sometimes been important if not crucial to peacemaking while at other times, as for example, in **Burundi** or **Liberia**, **refugees** from massacres have turned to them in the hope of protection. Mediation by the churches in war situations is an expected role and at different levels various African churches, separately or in collaboration, have attempted to mediate in the continent's many civil conflicts. During the civil war in **Nigeria**, for example, the papacy attempted to mediate a peace (a high proportion of Ibos are Roman Catholic) but it had no more success than either the **Organization of African Unity** (OAU) or the **Commonwealth** in this role. Attempts at mediation by Christian churches in **Sudan** failed completely since the government was Muslim and was attempting to impose Sharia law upon the South, even though its people either followed traditional African religions or Christianity but not Islam. When the Archbishop of Canterbury, Dr. George Carey, insisted upon visiting the South of Sudan in January 1994, he only succeeded in creating a diplomatic row between **Great Britain** and Sudan. In Southern Africa (Rhodesia and **South Africa**), some of the churches came to play an increasingly radical role: in Rhodesia during the guerrilla war against the Smith government's Unilateral Declaration of Independence (UDI) (1965–80); and in South Africa during the struggle against apartheid.

In the case of **Mozambique**, the churches deserve considerable credit for the peace that was eventually achieved in 1992 between the government and the **Resistência Nacional Moçambicana** (RE-NAMO)/Mozambican National Resistance. In 1989, as both sides in this war became increasingly exhausted, church officials mounted strenuous efforts during the first half of the year to negotiate a cease-fire and peace. They persuaded RENAMO to take part in a meeting of June 1989 in Nairobi with church leaders. A second meeting in Nairobi between church representatives and Dhlakama was cancelled after government troops attacked RENAMO's Gorongosa base, but in July 1989, Dhlakama did go to Nairobi to meet Mozambique church leaders, and though this meeting produced nothing concrete, it was seen as the start of the peace process. When, finally, a peace agreement between RENAMO and the Mozambique government was signed in Rome on 4 October 1992, by President **Joaquim Chissano** and Afonso Dhlakama, it represented the culmination of two years of negotiations; the three principal negotiators had been President **Robert Mugabe** of **Zimbabwe**, the British businessman "Tiny" Rowland, and the Roman Catholic Church.

Apart from their many efforts at mediation, the churches either directly or in association with humanitarian organizations, such as Christian Aid, have been responsible for much relief work in war affected areas.

COLD WAR. Cold War considerations determined the manner in which the major powers intervened, whether in Africa or elsewhere, during the years 1950 to 1990. In two areas of long-lasting conflict—**Angola** and **Ethiopia**—support for one or the other side was provided on a major scale by the **United States** and the **Union of**

Soviet Socialist Republics (USSR); such support was a constant and sometimes decisive factor in the fortunes of the combatants. Most of the African liberation movements, such as the **African National Congress** (ANC), the **Frente da Libertação de Moçambique** (FRELIMO)/Mozambique Liberation Front, the **Movimento Popular para a Libertação de Angola** (MPLA)/Popular Movement for the Liberation of Angola, the **South West Africa People's Organization** (SWAPO), the **Zimbabwe African National Union** (ZANU) or the **Zimbabwe African People's Union** (ZAPU), sought **aid** especially from the USSR and Eastern bloc countries since for the greater part of their struggles they found little assistance, and certainly not military assistance, forthcoming from the West. One exception was the **União Nacional para a Independência Total de Angola** (UNITA)/National Union for the Total Independence of Angola: since it was fighting the Marxist MPLA government in Angola, which was supported by the Cubans as well as the Soviets, it was able to obtain substantial support from the United States. **Mozambique** was another major theater of war and FRELIMO relied heavily upon assistance from the Communist bloc.

    Zaire under **Mobutu Sesi Seko**, on the other hand, became a conduit for U.S. aid to UNITA. Throughout these years, **South Africa** played its own Cold War card, offering its strategic position as an inducement to the West to turn a blind eye to the iniquities of apartheid which, broadly, the West did for most of the period. Under **Siad Barre, Somalia** was to expel the Americans and invite in the Russians; then, at the time of the **Ogaden War** with Ethiopia, Barre switched sides and the United States, reluctantly, supported Barre in order to have the use of the naval facilities at the port of Berbera. And through most of these years, Kenya offered military facilities to the United States and **Great Britain**.

    Angola illustrates perfectly how the Cold War policies of the two superpowers could turn first the liberation struggle and then the post-independence civil war into an international flashpoint involving the United States, the USSR, **Cuba**, South Africa, and Zaire, and sometimes Britain and the People's Republic of China. **Portugal**, at the beginning of the 1960s, was one of the two poorest non-communist states in Europe; it saw its African colonies, and most notably Angola, as essential to its economic well-being and so determined to hold onto them at all costs. It was a member of the North Atlantic Treaty Organization (NATO) but in fact, with the connivance of the United States and Britain in particular, used armaments that were designated for NATO purposes only to fight its African wars. **Agostinho Neto**, the Marxist leader of the MPLA, called for and obtained massive Soviet aid in 1975 to ensure that he held onto the succession, as Portuguese power disintegrated and his position was contested by both the **Frente Nacional da Libertação de Angola** (FNLA)/National Front for the Liberation of Angola and UNITA. This help included the arrival of an initial 10,000 Cuban troops, which were deployed in 1976 to halt the advance of the South African column that had invaded Angola and was moving up the coast toward Luanda. The scene was set for a Cold War confrontation that would last through to 1990. U.S. President Gerald Ford wanted to intervene militarily in Angola, but Congress vetoed his move—wisely it would seem—in view of the traumatic backlash then taking place as a result of the ignominious U.S. withdrawal from Vietnam. China also became involved briefly in Angola, providing support to both the MPLA and FNLA, although it was soon to withdraw its interest from the region. Once UNITA, of the movements opposed to the MPLA government, had emerged as the main alternative to be supported over the years by both South Africa and the United States, the MPLA government relied for support upon the USSR and Cuba and this it received through to 1990. It is doubtful whether **Jonas Savimbi** and UNITA would have survived—and certainly not with the degree of success they achieved—without U.S. support, which was provided entirely in terms of Cold War calculations while, equally, the MPLA's debt to the USSR and Cuba was enormous. It was also for Cold War reasons that the United States decided to tie the withdrawal of the Cubans from Angola to any Angolan–Namibian settlement, and the subsequent concept of **linkage** played its part in prolonging the war.

The Cold War, then, came to form an ever present background to this and other wars in Africa and it was not until the Soviet leader, Mikhail Gorbachev, had revealed his desire for detente and made plain that the USSR wanted to bring to an end its worldwide confrontations with the United States that the kind of great power involvement which had prolonged the conflict in Angola could at last be terminated. As Angola and other African countries were to learn soon enough, once the Cold War compulsions had been eliminated, the great powers became far more wary of interventions in Africa, as their reluctance to become involved in West and Central African wars during the 1990s demonstrated.

COMITÉ RÉVOLUTIONNAIRE POUR L'UNITÉ ET L'ACTION (CRUA)/REVOLUTIONARY COMMITTEE FOR UNITY AND ACTION. This body was formed in 1954 by young Algerian militants who decided to take arms against French colonialism. They chose **Ahmed ben Bella**, who had escaped French custody in 1952, as their leader, and he, with Belkacem Krim and seven others in Cairo, agreed to head CRUA. They were former members of the **Organisation Secrète** (OS)/Secret Organization. However, though CRUA's goal was to prepare for armed insurrection its effective life was over before the hostilities against the French were launched. On 1 November 1954, it was renamed the **Front de Libération Nationale** (FLN)/National Liberation Front.

COMMONWEALTH. After 1945, as the European empires were steadily dismantled, the great majority of British colonies opted to become members of the Commonwealth, which they saw as a potentially valuable extension of their influence, since it provided them with an added international dimension. Over two explosive African issues—the Unilateral Declaration of Independence (UDI) in Rhodesia and apartheid in **South Africa**—membership of the Commonwealth enabled its African states in particular to exert pressures upon **Great Britain,** which would not otherwise have been possible, and they did this steadily from 1961 (South Africa leaving the Commonwealth over apartheid) and 1965 (UDI in Rhodesia) until both these issues had been satisfactorily resolved in African terms. African membership of the Commonwealth included, in West Africa, **Nigeria**, Ghana, **Sierra Leone**, and The Gambia; in East Africa, Kenya, **Uganda**, Tanzania; in Central Africa, Malawi, Zambia, **Zimbabwe**; in Southern Africa, Botswana, Lesotho, Swaziland; and in the Indian Ocean, Mauritius and Seychelles. South Africa, which had achieved formal international independence under the Statute of Westminster in 1931, left the Commonwealth in 1961 and would only resume membership in 1994 after **Nelson Mandela** had become its first African president. Of these countries—16 including South Africa—no less than five were to experience some form of civil war after independence; these were Nigeria, Sierra Leone, South Africa, Uganda, and Zimbabwe. The Commonwealth was called upon to play a mediating role wherever this seemed practicable.

As the racial confrontation with white-dominated Southern Africa became more menacing during the 1970s and 1980s, four Commonwealth states—Botswana, Tanzania, Zambia, and Zimbabwe—were to play important roles as Frontline States while Lesotho, Malawi, and Swaziland either acted as conduits for the **African National Congress** (ANC) or as recipients of **refugees** (Malawi in particular in relation to the civil war in **Mozambique** during the 1980s). The Commonwealth, through its London-based Secretariat, made several efforts at mediation during the Nigerian civil war, though without success, as well as in relation to the later civil war in Sierra Leone, but it was in the Mozambique war that the Commonwealth played a major role. Mozambique had never been a British colony and was not a member of the Commonwealth; however, as a consequence of its geographical position in Southern Africa, all its neighbors except South Africa—that is, Malawi, Swaziland, Tanzania, Zambia, and Zimbabwe—were members of the Commonwealth during the 1980s when it was torn by civil war, and it was in their combined interests to assist Mozambique. As a result of their pressures, the Commonwealth provided substantial aid to Mozambique through the 1980s and, as a consequence, Mozambique applied to join the association. Once South Africa had rejoined the Commonwealth in 1994, Mandela was able to add his influential voice to the other African states, and at the Auckland Commonwealth Heads of Government Meeting (CHOGM) of November 1995, Mozambique was admitted to membership. This represented a remarkable achievement on the part of the Southern African group of Commonwealth countries.

At the beginning of the 21st century, Zimbabwe faced calls from Britain and Australia for its suspension from the Commonwealth because of the unruly way in which its government was carrying out land reforms and its treatment of the opposition. A special Commonwealth meeting was held in Abuja, Nigeria, in September 2001 at which Zimbabwe agreed that further land reform would be conducted in an orderly fashion without violence. Nothing, however, changed in

Zimbabwe. In 2002 three Commonwealth leaders—President Thabo Mbeki of South Africa, President **Olusegun Obasanjo**, of Nigeria and Prime Minster John Howard of Australia—were appointed as a committee of three to report on the Zimbabwe elections of 9–11 March. They reported that the election "did not adequately allow for a free expression of will by the electors" and on 19 March, the three decided that Zimbabwe be suspended from the Commonwealth for a year. In December 2003, the biennial Commonwealth Heads of Government Meeting (CHOGM) met in Abuja, Nigeria, and after strained debate among six heads of government specially appointed to deal with the Zimbabwe issue, they reported back to the CHOGM that the suspension should continue. However, on 7 December 2003, President **Robert Mugabe** withdrew his country from the Commonwealth.

COMORO ISLANDS. The French-ruled Comoro Islands in the Indian Ocean obtained their independence from **France** in 1974 after a referendum, although one of the four principal islands, Mayotte, voted to remain a French dependency. Over the succeeding quarter century, there was increasing dissatisfaction in the island of Anjouan where separatists argued they were neglected by the government on Grande Comore. On 14 July 1997, two people were killed and a number seriously wounded in clashes between the security forces and the separatist Mouvement du Peuple Anjouaniste (MPA)/Anjouan People's Movement. Further clashes occurred a week later on 22 July after the MPA leader, Abdallah Ibrahim, had been arrested. Following Ibrahim's release on 28 July, tensions again escalated and at a demonstration by a crowd of 7,000 on 3 August, there were demands for independence for Anjouan from the Comoros and a return to French rule. The demonstrators hoisted the French flag, as other separatists did, on the smaller island of Moheli.

France responded to these demands by insisting that it respected the "territorial integrity of the Federal Islamic Republic of the Comoros." The supporters of the MPA named Ibrahim as president of Anjouan and also named a 12-member "Cabinet." The **Organization of African Unity** (OAU) sent Pierre Yere of **Côte d'Ivoire** as its special envoy to the Comoros and began to mediate between the two sides. France, on 11 August, affirmed its support for the OAU and pressed for a fairer distribution of French budgetary **aid** so that

Anjouan would obtain a greater share of this aid than formerly. On 12 August, after a meeting with the separatist leaders, Yere announced that secession was "totally unacceptable." Reconciliation talks under OAU auspices were scheduled for September.

At the beginning of September, however, the government of President Mohamed Taki Abdoulkarim landed between 200 and 300 troops in Anjouan in an attempt to regain control of the island and claimed on 3 September that "the military pacification mission" had "re-established the security of the state . . . without bloodshed." However, by 5 September, it emerged that about 30 soldiers had been killed fighting in Mutsamudu (the capital of Anjouan), as well as some civilians, and that the government forces had suffered a defeat. On 8 September, a spokesman for Abdallah Ibrahim said "the state of Anjouan" had been established and that Ibrahim had been empowered to rule by decree. On 15 September, the separatists were reported to be threatening to kill about 80 soldiers they had taken prisoner should the Moroni government attempt a second attack; the following day the central government affirmed there would be no further attack.

The failure to take Anjouan had repercussions on Moroni where, on 9 September, President Taki dismissed his government and assumed absolute powers. There were reports of an uprising against Taki. On 13 September, Taki set up a State Transition Commission, to include three representatives from Anjouan and two from Moheli where separatists had also staged a revolt, and only two representatives from his dissolved government. On 28 September, Ibrahim announced that Anjouan would hold a referendum on self-determination, on 26 October, and that this would be prior to a conference on the island's future, which was to be organized by the OAU and the Arab League, set to take place in Addis Ababa (**Ethiopia**) at the end of October or early November. The referendum was carried out on 26 October and the following day it was reported that 99 percent of the Anjouan electorate had voted for independence (the referendum was held against the advice of the OAU Secretary General Salim Ahmed Salim). On 29 October, a spokesman for the secessionist administration announced the establishment of a provisional government; this was seen as a prelude to the creation of a constitution for the island and holding elections under its provisions. Apart from Ibrahim as president, Ibrahim Mohamet Elarif was named minister for finance, the budget, trade, and industry; Ali Moumine was named foreign minister; and Ahmed Charikane became minister of state for the presidency, in charge of public relations. On 1 November 1997, the OAU said it did not recognize the legitimacy of the independent Anjouan government and called upon the separatists to attend the Comoran reconciliation conference, which the OAU planned to hold in Addis Ababa, although no date had then been set. Pierre Yere stated, on 10 November, that the OAU planned to deploy a force of military observers in Anjouan; this was rejected by Anjouan, although on 13 November the separatists agreed to attend the Addis Ababa talks. On 25 November, an eight-member OAU force arrived in Moroni and was expected to be joined by 20 soldiers from Tunisia, Niger, and Senegal.

At a meeting under OAU auspices held in Addis Ababa during December 1997, a declaration was drawn up which advocated regional autonomy for the islands. However, Anjouan did not agree to this declaration. Factional fighting on Anjouan during February 1998 led the OAU to warn of the danger of civil war. On 25 February, Abdallah Ibrahim's Anjouan administration conducted a referendum on the island and, on 4 March, it was reported that 99.54 percent of the voters had approved a new constitution, which abrogated the laws of "the Islamic Federal Republic of Comoros." By mid-1998, it seemed likely that Anjouan would continue as a de facto independent island.

CONGO, DEMOCRATIC REPUBLIC OF: AFRICA'S GREAT WAR. A year after he had assumed power in the newly named Democratic Republic of Congo (DRC) in May 1997, when **Mobutu Sese Seko** fled the country, President **Laurent Kabila** faced a new civil war with many of those who had supported him in 1997 now turning against him. In any case, he faced formidable problems in the aftermath of the Mobutu years. There were a number of armed groups in different parts of the country that had to be brought under control if Kabila was to establish a united DRC. Thus, for example, Hutu militants were operating from bases in North Kivu to launch attacks in **Rwanda**. In addition, a number of ethnic groups in both North and South Kivu provinces were in arms and in effect establishing "no go" areas under their control. Furthermore, soldiers of Mobutu's Forces Armées du Zaire (FAZ)/Armed Forces of Zaire were operating on their own and had bases in both **Congo** (**Brazzaville**) and **Central**

African Republic. Kabila lacked a firm base of his own and in Katanga, where he did have some support, there was a growing secessionist movement. In fact, Kabila's victory in 1997 had depended upon the Banyamulenge (ethnic Tutsi of South Kivu) and the armies of **Uganda** and Rwanda, which had their own motives for assisting him. Once Kabila had assumed power, there was a reaction against these allies in Kinshasa and, in particular, resentment at the Tutsi. Moreover, Kabila did not try to form a broad alliance with Etienne Tshikedi's Union pour la Démocratie et le Progrès Social (UDPS)/ Union for Democracy and Social Progress, instead imprisoning critics who formerly had supported him and filling the key posts in his government with members of his own family or ethnic kinsmen from Katanga. Kabila also resisted **United Nations** efforts to investigate human rights abuses and the massacre of thousands of Hutu refugees by his forces in 1997. As a result, the UN team withdrew from DRC in April 1998. **Aid** donors, who had been asked for $1,500 million for reconstruction, only offered $100 million by mid-year.

By July, Kabila was removing Tutsis, whether Rwandan or from his own Banyamulenge, from top positions in the military and the Banyamulenge began to return to South Kivu. Rwanda, which was Tutsi dominated, saw evidence that Kabila was creating training camps for exiled Hutu extremists. On 2 August, the military in Goma and Bukavu mutinied and two weeks later these rebels announced the formation of the Rassemblement Congolais pour la Démocratie (RCD)/Rally for Congolese Democracy and a new civil war was under way. The Banyamulenge, backed by Uganda and Rwanda, represented the core of the rebellion. An academic, Ernest Wamba dia Wamba, was made president of the RCD. At the beginning of this rebellion, on 4 August, the rebels had executed a daring maneuver when they used civilian planes from Goma airport to move several thousand troops to the military base at Kitoma near the port of Matadi. Former FAZ troops at Kitoma joined the rebels and set out for Kinshasa. They occupied the Inga Dam and hydroelectric work and reached the airport at Kinshasa. Kabila appealed to **Angola** and **Zimbabwe** for help and Angolan troops from the Cabinda enclave attacked the rebels in the rear. The Angolan and Zimbabwean air forces then forced the rebels to retreat into northern Angola. In the weeks that followed **Namibia**, Congo (Brazzaville), Central African Republic, **Sudan**, **Chad**, and

Gabon each promised support for Kabila and sent token forces or financial aid. What came to be called Africa's Great War had begun. By the end of August, the rebels had control of a large part of eastern Congo including Kisangani, the country's third town. During September and October, the rebels continued to advance and more Angolan and Zimbabwean troops were committed to Kabila's aid. Those who came to assist Kabila had their price. Angola obtained oil concessions, Zimbabwe copper and cobalt concessions, Namibia **diamonds**.

1999

At the beginning of 1999, there were outbreaks of intense fighting in eastern Congo. The rebels of the RCD were advancing into Katanga and eastern Kasai while a second rebel group, the Movement for the Liberation of the Congo (MLC), led by Jean-Pierre Bemba, was gaining control of territory in the northeast. However, both groups had to take account of the Bembe resistance fighters, the Mai Mai, who were supported by Hutu guerrillas from **Burundi**. Over 9–16 January, the Mai Mai attacked Bukavu; in retaliation, the RCD massacred 500 civilians in a village near Uvira in southern Kivu. By this time, five months of fighting had cost the intervening countries both money and casualties. Uganda and Rwanda backed the rebels; Angola, Namibia and Zimbabwe supported the Kabila government. On 18 January, representatives of these five states met in Windhoek, Namibia, and agreed on the first steps toward a cease-fire. In March, the **Organization of African Unity** (OAU) appointed Zambia's president, Frederick Chiluba, to coordinate peace moves. In April, the Libyan leader, **Muammar al-Gaddafi**, convened a meeting of leaders in Sirte, at which Kabila met Uganda's president, **Yoweri Museveni**, and the two leaders signed a peace agreement. Uganda undertook to train 1,500 Congolese troops to replace its own in eastern Congo. On the home political front, President Kabila accepted the need for a national dialogue but excluded political opponents from taking part, making clear his determination to hold on to power. On 29 May, Rwanda announced a unilateral cease-fire in the Congo.

A summit of participants in the war was held in Lusaka during June at which **South Africa** in particular used its influence to push for an agreement and, on 11 July, an agreement was reached that included: an immediate cease-fire, the incorporation of rebel troops in the national army, and a national dialogue. The agreement was signed by the Kinshasa government and the five intervening states, but not the RCD, which was split between ex-Mobutists and "renovators." Wamba dia Wamba was removed from office. The fighting did not stop however. On 11 October, the Joint Military Commission (JMC) set up by the OAU to monitor the peace (chaired by Algeria's General Lallai Rachid) met in Kampala. All the warring parties took part as well as representatives of the UN, OAU, European Union, and Zambia. However, Rwanda made it a precondition of its participation that ex-soldiers from the former Rwandan army and the Interahamwe militia should be sent back to Rwanda. The Lusaka Accord stipulated that all foreign troops should be withdrawn from the Congo by February 2000. The UN would send 500 peace monitors. In December, the OAU appointed the former president of Botswana, Sir Quett Ketumile Masire, as facilitator of the peace process. Meanwhile, in October, the deposed RCD leader Wamba dia Wamba had set up a new government at Bunia in the northeast; he announced that he would be both president and minister of defense. He created a new party—RCD-Liberation Movement (LM). In December, the RCD Ihanga, the RCD-LM, and the MLC met in Uganda and agreed to form a coalition. By the end of the year, the cease-fire had broken down and Kabila had concluded an arms deal with the People's Republic of China.

2000

There was no sign of any let-up in the war as the new century opened. Rwanda, especially, continued to support the rebels because the DRC continued to harbor armed Interahamwe militia and former Rwandan troops who had been responsible for the 1994 genocide. Less justifiably, Uganda claimed to protect its frontier from rebel encroachments by occupying eastern areas of the DRC where it said anti-Kabila rebels operated. On the government side, both Angola and Zimbabwe were committing greater numbers of troops in support of Kabila, while Namibia also did so on a smaller scale. Thus, a civil war in the DRC had become a regional conflict involving on a substantial scale five of the country's neighbors—Uganda and Rwanda supporting the rebels, Angola, Namibia, and Zimbabwe supporting Kabila. In

January, Kabila called for the unconditional withdrawal from DRC of foreign forces. In February, he offered an amnesty to any rebels who accepted his authority, although the offer was rejected by both the MLC and RCD. In August (after vain efforts by the UN to establish a peacekeeping force), an emergency summit was held in Lusaka by the Southern Africa Development Community (SADC) to break the deadlock. However, Kabila brought the meeting to an end by refusing to accept Masire as mediator; he was angry that his allies did not call on Uganda and Rwanda to withdraw their forces from the DRC.

In a new turn of events, fighting broke out during May and June between the Ugandan and Rwandan forces in the northeast of the country so that Kisangani was freed of foreign troops and the UN was able to deploy peacekeepers there. Although Kabila did agree at the end of the year to the deployment of UN peacekeepers in government-controlled territory, further peace initiatives faced deadlock. At the beginning of 2001, RCD troops, backed by the Rwandans, seized Pweto on Lake Mweru in the southeast and forced 3,000 Zimbabwean and Congolese troops to flee into Zambia.

2001

The DRC entered 2001 after three years of war with no sign of a resolution. Kabila's government only controlled the western third of the country and its hold was far from certain. The north, the east, and the southeast were under the control of rebels who were largely supported and financed by DRC's eastern neighbors Uganda, Rwanda, and Burundi. At the beginning of the year, Kabila said there could be no cease-fire until there had been a total, unconditional withdrawal of all foreign forces. President Museveni of Uganda, however, refused to accept this and was supported by Rwanda's President Paul Kagame whose forces had entered the DRC in order to neutralize the armed forces that had been responsible for the 1994 genocide in his country. These forces were to be found in Kivu and Katanga provinces. Kabila's priority ought to have been to address the security concerns of his eastern neighbors but instead, in January, he organized a peace conference in Gabon that was only attended by carefully selected participants. However, the conference was ignored by the international community and came to nothing.

On 16 January, a member of the presidential guard assassinated Kabila. He was "succeeded" by his son Joseph who immediately demonstrated greater flexibility than his father. He toured **France**, Belgium, and the **United States** and also met Kagame of Rwanda and the UN Secretary-General **Kofi Annan**. Later, in March, he met the former president of Botswana, Quett Masire. A UN report in April condemned the "looting" of the DRC undertaken by members of the armed forces of Uganda and Rwanda. The report suggested that these two countries supported the rebels not due to their own security concerns but from a desire to exploit the DRC's massive resources that were especially abundant in the east of the country. The report noted that Uganda and Rwanda were stripping the DRC of large quantities of minerals including diamonds, copper, cobalt, gold, and coltan, as well as timber and ivory. It reckoned that a third of the 12,000 elephants in the Garamba national park had been slaughtered for their tusks. However, Angola, Zimbabwe, and Namibia, which were also helping themselves to the DRC's resources, were absolved of any wrongdoing on the grounds that they had been permitted to do so by the Kabila government in return for their support. This UN report provided the Joseph Kabila government with recognition, although it was unelected. Kabila allowed the UN to send personnel to monitor the cease-fire between the rebels and the government-controlled part of the country.

In May, urged by Masire the facilitator, the representatives of the different groups met in Lusaka to revive the peace process. Kabila met Kagame and assured him that he would disown the Interahamwe on DRC soil. During May 12, Security-Council ambassadors produced a report that recognized Kabila and his supporters as the government of the DRC. Their report referred to both the RCD and MLC as rebels. At the same time, they stressed the need for dialogue and called for inclusion in the peace talks of unarmed political groups and most notably Etienne Tshisekedi, the opposition leader who had been in exile, but now returned to the country. In May, restrictions on opposition were lifted and the economy was freed: that is, the franc was floated, commercial courts replaced military tribunals, and state control of diamond trading was relaxed. Subsequently, the DRC was visited by delegations from the World Bank, the International Monetary Fund (IMF), and the European Union and these visits led to a new flow of aid into the country. An inter-Congolese dialogue between armed rebels and unarmed civilians was held in Gaborone, Botswana, and appeared to move the peace process forward. In September, UN Secretary-General Kofi Annan visited Kinshasa, Kisangani (then in rebel hands), and Kigali, the capital of Rwanda. Namibia, a supporter of Kabila, confirmed that it had withdrawn its 1,800 troops from DRC.

Despite these encouraging moves, there was much violence during May and June in the east of the country when Hutu extremists crossed from DRC into Rwanda—possibly under DRC pressure—leading to heavy fighting in both northwestern Rwanda and northern Burundi. In September, DRC government troops and their Mai Mai allies attacked RCD positions in the east of the country where the RCD had revealed its inability to administer the territory it controlled or to stop Hutu incursions into Rwanda. Further complications arose when the Rwanda-supported RCD group in Goma and the Uganda-backed group in Kisangani fell to fighting each other. As long as RCD-Goma could not prevent Hutu raids into Rwanda, Kagame was reluctant to withdraw his forces from DRC.

By the end of the year the peace process was stalling. Government negotiators had walked out of a meeting in Addis Ababa in November while the UN had pointed out that the various armed groups had little reason to lay down their arms since the war had allowed them to be self-financing and sustaining as they raped the country of its resources. A UN panel of experts claimed that the Kabila government and its external allies, especially Zimbabwe, shared responsibility for the looting of DRC's natural resources. Apart from the war—or local wars—Joseph Kabila's hold on power was uncertain. His support came from Angola (still at this stage fighting **União Nacional para a Independência Total de Angola** (UNITA)/National Union for the Total Independence of Angola under **Jonas Savimbi** and Zimbabwe, which appeared to regard DRC's resources as a source of profit. There were 9,000 Ugandan troops in DRC supporting the MLC while Ugandan and Rwandan supported rebel factions frequently fought each other. Rwanda had 10,000 troops in DRC to support the government but these Tutsi forces were mainly concerned to limit the activities of the estimated 30,000 Rwandan Hutu troops who had been the perpetrators of the 1994 massacres. On a smaller scale, Burundi had less than 1,000 troops fighting Burundian Hutu rebels either in DRC or in Tanzania. Angola had 2,000 troops in support of Kabila and their numbers were reduced during the year. Angola's principal concern was to take out or limit the UNITA forces operating from DRC as the long civil war in that country continued. Namibia, which had supported Kabila, withdrew its force of 1,800 troops during September. Zimbabwe had 10,000 troops in DRC and both its military and businesses were obtaining deals that allowed them to exploit DRC's natural resources.

2002

A meeting in Sun City, South Africa, between rebel groups and the DRC government took place at the beginning of the year, but reconciliation proved difficult. In March, the peace process suffered a setback when the Goma-based RCD seized Moliro, causing the government negotiators to quit the Sun City talks. The UN Security Council criticized the RCD and by implication its Rwanda backers, but when RCD forces were withdrawn from Moliro, the talks resumed. A tentative peace agreement was reached in April, but this excluded the RCD. The government wanted to create a power-sharing agreement with the Ugandan-backed MLC of Jean-Pierre Bemba and thereby limit the war to the east of the country and isolate the Rwanda-backed RCD. However, this April agreement was criticized by the facilitator, Quett Masire, and opposed by Rwanda, which then sent troop reinforcements across the border in support of the RCD. In May, the RCD was responsible for a series of brutal massacres in Kisangani resulting in renewed UN criticisms of Rwanda's role. A new dimension to the chaos in the country occurred when heavy fighting erupted in the northeast between tribal factions, forcing the Ugandan forces to withdraw. Rwanda then argued that to remove foreign troops (its own) simply meant that huge areas of DRC would come under the control of feuding tribal militias. By this time, these groups had obtained sophisticated weaponry and were strengthening their control over the natural resources that increasingly appeared to be the real object of the various warring groups. The UN now extended the mandate of its UN Mission in DRC (MONUC) and promised to increase its numbers while the government's position was also strengthened by a substantial inflow of World Bank and IMF aid.

South Africa's president Thabo Mbeki, chairman of the new **African Union** (AU), exerted pressure upon Rwanda to enter into direct negotiations with the DRC government and a peace agreement between presidents Paul Kagame and Joseph Kabila was signed in Pretoria on 30 July. Under its terms, the Kabila government agreed to disarm, arrest, or repatriate the Hutu forces in DRC that had been responsible for the 1994 genocide. In return, Rwanda agreed to withdraw its (then) 22,000 troops. Whether the agreement would be implemented was uncertain since Kabila needed the support of the Interahamwe forces and ex-Rwandan Armed Forces (FAR) to liberate the eastern third of the country. Nonetheless, on 17 September, the Rwandan army began to withdraw from DRC and the last 2,000 Zimbabwe troops also began to leave. In keeping with its promise, the Kabila government now banned the Democratic Liberation Forces of Rwanda which represented the Hutu exiles. And under a further agreement with Uganda of 10 September, the latter began to withdraw its troops from the northeast of the country. As a result of these moves, most foreign troops had been withdrawn from DRC by early October while the veteran opposition leader Etienne Tshisekedi was now allowed to take part in open political activities and he went on a tour of eastern DRC held by the RCD. South Africa, whose mediating role had been significant, augmented its contingent of 200 peacekeepers with a further 1,500 troops.

The UN panel on the illegal exploitation of natural resources and other forms of wealth reported in October. First, it underlined the large-scale pillaging that had been carried out by foreign troops and claimed that such pillaging reinforced the self-perpetuating nature of the war in which both local and foreign troops fought as much to exploit resources as to resolve questions of sovereignty and defense. The report called on the Security Council to impose financial sanctions on 29 named companies as well as prominent individuals on both sides in the conflict. The report claimed that the DRC government and its allies, particularly Zimbabwe, had acquired $5 billion of state assets without making payment to the DRC treasury. Subsequently, the Kabila government sacked three ministers and dismissed a number of high-ranking functionaries.

Renewed fierce fighting occurred in mid-October as pro-government militias moved in behind the withdrawing Ugandans and Rwandans. Uvira was taken by Mai Mai forces, although it was then recaptured by the RCD. A new wave of **refugees** fled the fighting. In November, Kabila and Kagame met in Pretoria to review the peace process and, in December, the government met with various rebel groups in Pretoria to work out a settlement. It was agreed that Joseph Kabila should be president for a transitional two year period assisted by four vice-presidents representing the RCD, the MLC, other unnamed opposition members, and the government.

2003

At the beginning of 2003, despite the ceasefire agreed on the previous December, two thirds of the country remained under rebel control. Foreign donors now pledged $2.5 billion for reconstruction, but security was at best fragile. Massacres of civilians in the Beni region of Ituri province in the northeast augured ill for the peace process; the crimes included rape and torture. In March, when the remaining 1,000 Ugandan troops were scheduled to be withdrawn, tensions rose sharply in Bunia, the capital of Ituri province. Then, as chaotic fighting between different tribal groups erupted, Uganda reoccupied Bunia and several neighboring villages. The Ugandans put local Lundu militias (the Lundu are agriculturalists) in control of the area they were vacating, but this led to heavy fighting with the cattle-herding Hema who were supported by Rwanda. Rwandan-backed RCD troops then moved north to challenge the Ugandans and their Lundu allies. The Ugandans finally withdrew from Bunia on 6 May by which time there were 700 UN peacekeepers in the town. Yet, despite their presence, fierce fighting broke out between the local militias. The Hema moved back into the town and expelled the Lundu with a great deal of slaughter. According to Human Rights Watch, killings in Ituri reached 50,000 at this time and led to 500,000 refugees. And according to the U.S. aid agency International Rescue Committee (IRC) the larger conflict that had been set off in 1998 by the Rwandan invasion of DRC had caused the death of between 3.1 and 4.7 million people. Ninety percent of these deaths were due to lack of medical facilities, food insecurity, and generalized violence.

South Africa's Thabo Mbeki worked hard to broker a new peace deal and in April delegates to the Inter-Congolese National Dialogue met in Sun City and agreed on the formation of a government of national unity that would oversee new elections while a new constitution provided a power-sharing formula. Fighting was still taking place during these negotiations, but on 30 June, President Kabila declared the war over. He opened the government to both his armed enemies and civilian opponents. In July, Kabila was installed as head of the new transitional government and three of the four vice-presidencies went to his opponents as did 40 ministerial posts. There remained a series of major problems to settle. No timetable had been set for the demobilization of the belligerents or their incorporation in the national army and they remained in control of large parts of the country. More ominous for the future was the exclusion of Tshisekedi from a leadership post. As a result his party, the Union pour la Démocratie et le Progrès Social (UDPS)/Union for Democracy and Social Progress, decided to stay outside the transitional government and ally itself with the Rwandan-supported RCD. They then denounced the peace process. The transitional government was criticized for being tribally based.

Meanwhile, in June, **France** had sent 1,200 troops to Bunia. They banned the carrying of guns and brought some semblance of peace to the surrounding areas. They withdrew from the town on 1 September to be replaced by the UN Mission in DRC (MONUC), but the peacekeepers were unable to stop the fighting in the outlying areas of Ituri. Local militias, with support from Ugandan and Rwandan generals, acted on behalf of the different factions in government. A confidential UN report of December accused both Rwanda and Uganda of collaborating with members of the transitional government to arm militias that were fighting to gain control of mineral-rich areas of the country. The report further claimed that Tshisekedi was preparing a rebellion in Kasai Oriental with Rwandan support. Rwanda, meanwhile, was using the profits from mining in eastern DRC to purchase arms for the groups it supported, such as the RCD in Goma. It further claimed that 10,000 UPC fighters were under the direct command of the Rwandan army. At the same time, Ugandan "interests" were being secured by three militia groups, one of which was said to be run directly from President Museveni's office in Kampala.

2004

Although 2004 appeared to begin positively with a visit by Thabo Mbeki and a group of businessmen to discuss reconstruction while, in March, Rwanda established an embassy in Kinshasa, the fragile peace was broken at the end of March when former members of Mobutu's presidential guard attempted to mount a coup, and though this failed, it was a reminder of how delicately poised everything was. In Ituri, further fighting erupted between the Lundu, supported by Uganda and Hema. The 4,700 UN peacekeepers had difficulty in maintaining order. Groups of fighters, some consisting of pre-teen **child soldiers**, had become accustomed to a lawless life and exacting taxes from the local population. However, on May 30, militias in the area agreed to lay down their arms and join the peace process. Another threat to the peace was posed by cross border raids from Rwanda; these were in retaliation for movements on the border by Hutu refugees, remnants of the Hutu army that had fled there in 1994. The Rwandan government expressed alarm that the UN peacekeeping force had failed to disarm such forces. At the end of May, several thousand RCD-Goma troops seized control of Bukavu leading Kabila to declare a state of emergency and a "general mobilization." The rebels quit Bukavu after a few days but others seized Walikale from the Mai Mai supporters of Kabila. Walikale was the center of cassiterite production and the price of the mineral had risen sharply in the early months of the year. The government had little control over Katanga, the center of cobalt production, and ever-rising Chinese demand for cobalt meant that large quantities were being smuggled out of the country.

The government's inability to control these strategic centers or its borders demonstrated its overall vulnerability and the weakness of the new army (Forces Armées de la République Démocratique du Congo (FARDC)/Armed Forces of the Democratic Republic of the Congo. In the east, where much of the economic infrastructure had been destroyed, 10,000 UN troops costing $1 million a day appeared to make little difference to the widespread lawlessness. When President Kabila promised to send 10,000 FARDC troops to the east, Rwanda's president threatened to invade DRC to support his proxies. In response to this threat, both Angola and Tanzania offered to send troops to support Kabila. The UN Security Council at once warned foreign countries to stay out of the conflict. In June, the International Criminal Court (ICC) announced that it was setting up a new permanent war crimes court to investigate "crimes" in the DRC. Two warlords, one Lundu and one Hema, were arrested and charged with massacres, rapes, murders, and the use of child soldiers.

Then a scandal engulfed the UN peacekeeping force when a number of them were accused of rape and sexual abuse of children and by December some 50 cases of abuse involving rape, paedophilia, and prostitution had been raised. The situation in the east of the country steadily worsened during the second half of 2004. UN Secretary General Kofi Annan asked for 13,500 fresh troops and a rapid mobile force equipped with 37 helicopter gunships to be sent to DRC. In October, Kabila visited Kisangani in the east and a month later—a sign of growing confidence on the part of the transitional government—suspended six ministers and 10 senior managers of estate-owned companies accused of corruption. When at the end of November, Kabila again threatened to send 10,000 troops to the eastern border, Kagame again threatened to invade the DRC and claimed the right to disarm Hutu rebels in DRC, which the UN had failed to do. In December, RCD-Goma units mutinied against colleagues in the national army and seized the town of Kanyabayonga in North Kivu. Meanwhile, anticipating the arrival of 10,000 of Kabila's troops, refugees began to move out of the eastern provinces. At the end of this chaotic year, the humanitarian organization International Rescue Committee reported that the instability in DRC was the "deadliest crisis" in the world and estimated that the widespread conflict was responsible for 1,000 deaths a day, 98 percent from malnutrition and disease.

2005

The first months of 2005 proved a damaging time for the reputation of the United Nations forces in DRC. The UN Office of Internal Oversight Services (OIOS) reported on 7 January that MONUC troops had sexually abused women and girls, some as young as 13. An initial 72 allegations were investigated and led to 20 case reports. Later, another 150 allegations led to a further 50 case reports. The report said the problems were "serious and ongoing" and that the investigation had not acted as a deterrent. On 25 February, MONUC troops were ambushed in northeast Ituri while patrolling a refugee camp and nine Bangladeshi soldiers were killed. At that time one third of MONUC peacekeepers, some 4,500 soldiers, were stationed in Ituri. In response to the January report on sex abuses, the UN now enforced a "non-fraternization rule" and imposed nighttime curfews on its military bases. Then, on 1 March, MONUC soldiers (Bangladeshis) launched an attack on Loga, 35 kilometers from Bunia, where nine of their soldiers had been killed in February, and killed at least 50 members of the Front Nationaliste Intégrationiste (FNI)/National Integrationist Front, a Lundu militia group which they held responsible for the ambush. The attack was the most deadly to be carried out by the UN since the launch of MONUC in 1999.

A report by Human Rights Watch on 7 March claimed that tens of thousands of young girls and women had been raped or subjected to other sexual violence during the 1998–2003 civil wars. It also claimed that the militias had carried out mass rapes in Ituri province and that as late as October 2004 at least 10 rapes a day were carried out in Bunia. Médecins sans Frontières (MSF) had treated over 2,500 rape victims at its hospital in Bunia since June 2003. On 30 March, the UN renewed the MONUC mandate until 1 October 2005 and extended its arms embargo on North and South Kivu and Ituri district and to any recipient in DRC territory. On 11 April, the DRC government brought a case before the International Court of Justice (ICJ) at The Hague charging Uganda with massive human rights abuses and destruction and looting in its territory and sought compensation. Although Uganda had withdrawn from DRC in 2003 its proxy militias continued to operate in the east of DRC.

A new constitution of DRC was approved by the Chamber of Representatives on 13 May to be put to a national referendum within six months and elections were scheduled to be held in March 2006. Meanwhile, government troops foiled a secession attempt by Katanga where 100 people were arrested, including Andre Tshombe, the son of Moise Tshombe. In June, Human Rights Watch published a report claiming that foreign-financed gold mining was fuelling serious human rights abuses in DRC. The *Curse of Gold* alleged that AngloGold Ashanti (Anglo–American) had provided "meaningful financial aid and logistical support" to the Front Nationaliste Intégrationiste, the Lundu militia, that had been accused of atrocities in

Ituri. The report argued that AngloGold's links with the FNI helped the company obtain gold reserves around Mongbwalu. AngloGold denied it had supplied support for the FNI, but admitted its employees had "given way" to extortion by the FNI. The report also claimed that such gold from DRC was sent to Uganda and thence shipped to global gold markets in Europe and elsewhere. After discussions with Human Rights Watch, the Swiss gold refining company announced the suspension of gold purchases from Uganda.

In September, a new rebel group, the Mouvement Révolutionnaire du Congo (MRC)/Revolutionary Movement of the Congo began operating in Boga and Tshabi in Ituri district. They caused "terror and grief" in the two towns and hundreds of people fled to Bunia. The new group comprised the remnants of a number of other rebel groups: the Patriotic Resistance Front of Ituri (FRPI), the Party for Unity and Safeguarding the Integrity of Congo (PUSIC), Union of Congolese Patriots (UPC), Front for National Integration (FNI), the People's Army of Congo (FARC), and the Rally for Congolese Democracy—KML (RCD-KML). The leaders of the MRC were two notorious officers—Bwambale Kabolele and Bosco Ntaganda. The MRC had been distributing arms and cash to attract new recruits, and according to the Roman Catholic missionary news service (MISMA), it received significant external support, probably from Uganda and Rwanda. Both these countries appeared to remain determined sources of continuing destabilization for DRC. During the month, more than 1,000 soldiers in North Kivu had deserted to join the ranks of another dissident, Brigadier-General Laurent Nkunda. The deserters were mainly Congolese Tutsis. In October, the UN again extended the MONUC mandate to September 2006 and authorized the deployment of an infantry battalion in Katanga. On 13 November, several thousand government troops launched an operation in Dubie region of Katanga to reestablish the state's authority. Dubie had been infiltrated by Mai Mai fighters under their leader Gideon. By late November, 60,000 people had fled their homes and about 300 Mai Mai fighters had been arrested.

On 18 December, a national referendum on the new constitution gave it overwhelming approval by more than 12 million to 2 million votes in a 62 percent turnout. It received the support of most parties in DRC. The constitution provided for a decentralized government and limited the president to two five-year terms. The age for presidential candidates was reduced from 35 to 30 years so that 34-year-old Joseph Kabila could stand. All ethnic groups living in the Congo in 1960 were eligible for citizenship. On 19 December, the ICJ ruled that Uganda should pay compensation and reparations to DRC for occupying the eastern region from 1998 to 2003. The DRC government said it would seek between $6 billion and $10 billion. In its ruling, the ICJ said of the Ugandan forces in DRC that they had committed acts of killing, torture, and other forms of inhumane treatment of the Congolese civilian population, destroyed villages, trained child soldiers, and incited ethnic conflict.

Future Prospects

According to the British medical journal *The Lancet* of 6 January 2006, DRC was suffering the world's worst humanitarian crisis with 38,000 people dying each month from easily treatable diseases. It estimated that some 3.9 million people had died since 1998 as an indirect result of war, mostly from disease rather than violence. The high death rate had continued since the end of the war in 2002 due to insecurity, the collapse of the health system, and inadequate international aid. Further violence and insecurity arose in North Kivu in late January due to the activities of Brigadier-General Laurent Nkunda whose troops had dislodged government detachments in a number of places including Rutshuru, forcing the army to reorganize. The violence continued through February, leading the government to deploy further battalions in defense of Rutshuru. Thousands of civilians fled into Uganda or to Goma to escape the fighting. The security situation also deteriorated in South Kivu when the Hutu rebel Democratic Forces for the Liberation of Rwanda (FDLR) launched attacks on government and other targets. On 13 February, a donor conference was held in Brussels; it launched a UN Humanitarian Action Plan and requested $682 million, although donors only agreed to fund about $100 million. The low response was put down to donor and international fatigue with DRC problems.

In March, a joint MONUC/Congolese army mission in Orientale province had to be abandoned when the Congolese soldiers threatened MONUC personnel and began looting, their behavior demonstrating the unreliability of the army. Ituri province remained highly volatile, with new militias appearing and an army more used to lawlessness and looting than any readiness to accept military discipline. In April, due to logistical problems, the legislative elections and first round of presidential elections were postponed from June to 30 July. The UN Security Council authorized the temporary deployment of an EU force (Eufor R. D. Congo), which had been proposed by Germany, to support MONUC during the election period. Despite continuing violence in the east of the country, there were signs in mid-2006 that the DRC government was slowly extending its control over the country, though security and an abiding peace acceptable to all the people had yet to be achieved.

What must have been one of the most complicated elections in Africa's history and the first to be held in independent Congo was conducted during July 2006. The two principal contenders for the presidency were Joseph Kabila, who had headed the transitional government ever since the assassination of his father Laurent Kabila, and Jean-Pierre Bemba, one of the vice-presidents in the transitional government and the leader of the Mouvement pour la Libération du Congo (MLC)/Movement for the Liberation of the Congo, who had turned his rebel group into a political party. In the 30 July ballot some 16.9 million votes were cast, a 70 percent turnout: Joseph Kabila won 45 percent of the votes, Jean-Pierre Bemba 20 percent. Since Kabila did not obtain 50 percent of the vote, a runoff election between the two leading contenders was set for 29 October 2006. Meanwhile, when the results became known, fighting erupted in Kinshasa between the followers of the two men and was only brought to an end after three days by the UN peacekeepers. There were 17,000 UN peacekeepers in the country who had supervised the election, as well as an additional 1,000 EU troops who had been sent to bolster the UN during the election period. In the runoff at the end of October, Kabila obtained 58 percent of the vote. His defeated rival Pierre Bemba pledged to enter the opposition peacefully.

CONGO, DEMOCRATIC REPUBLIC OF. *See* ZAIRE.

CONGO, REPUBLIC OF (BRAZZAVILLE). The Republic of Congo, often called Congo-Brazzaville after its capital, lay across the Congo River from Leopoldville (later Kinshasa) in the **Republic of the Congo** (later **Zaire**). It was a former French territory and, although much smaller and with fewer ethnic groups than its neighbor, rivalries among these groups and their respective leaders were strong and tenacious. On several occasions, military men carried out coups to oust the politicians in charge. Despite this instability, during the first few decades following independence in 1960, the political system did not collapse, in part due to continued French influence and involvement.

In 1997, however, the situation deteriorated. This was partly triggered by the coming elections. In 1991, under pressure, then President Denis Sassou-Nguesso agreed to multi-party elections when he abandoned Marxism and in August 1992 these elections were won in a fair contest by Pascal Lissouba. New elections were due to be held in July 1997 and the signs were strong that Sassou-Nguesso, who was contesting the presidency, would make a comeback. By 1997 the political situation had become increasingly tense. Many regular army officers came from Sassou-Nguesso's Mboshi tribe and Lissouba, doubtful of army loyalty, had formed a militia from his own Zoulou tribe; these had been trained and equipped by the Israelis. In addition, the mayor of Brazzaville, Bernard Kolelas, had formed his own militia (the Ninjas) from the Kongo tribe. And Sassou-Nguesso had his own "Cobras," another militia.

In June 1997, civil war broke out between supporters of the incumbent president, Pascal Lissouba, and supporters of the former president, Denis Sassou-Nguesso. The war appeared to be a straightforward power struggle between rival politicians and their respective power groups. It was complicated by the fact that French troops were already stationed in Brazzaville; they had been sent earlier in the year to evacuate expatriates from Zaire (later renamed Democratic Republic of Congo) across the river as the **Mobutu Sese Seko** regime collapsed. On 20 April 1997, following three days of mutiny by the sailors at the Brazzaville base, the government dismissed Commander Fulgor Ongobo, commander of the national navy, and Lieutenant Commander Boignbeya, commander of the Brazzaville base. The sailors demanded their dismissal, accusing them of tribalism. The sailors, who were recruited from the south of the country, refused to be transferred to the north; the two commanders came from Cuvette in the north. On

11 May, at Owando, 600 kilometers north of Brazzaville, an attempt was made to assassinate former president Denis Sassou-Nguesso and though he escaped, 12 people were killed in a fight between his followers and supporters of another former president, Joachim Yhombi-Opango, who had been ousted by Sassou-Nguesso and had become an ally of the incumbent president Lissouba. Sassou-Nguesso was visiting the region, a stronghold of his supporters, on an election tour.

Eruption of Violence

Fighting broke out on 5 June 1997 in Brazzaville between the rival militias of President Lissouba and Sassou-Nguesso, after the army had cordoned off Nguesso's house in an apparent attempt to disarm his independent militia. On 7 June, part of the Forces Armées Congolaises (FAC)/Congolese Armed Forces and part of the navy defected to join the Cobra militia of Sassou-Nguesso; they drove loyal troops out of the eastern suburbs of Brazzaville and captured the radio station and barracks at Mpila. As a result, the loyal section of the army was forced to withdraw to the city center. Reinforcements for the president were airlifted to Brazzaville from Pointe Noire: these consisted of 250 loyal FAC paratroopers and 200 Zoulou militiamen. Government forces then began to bombard the rebel-held northern parts of the capital. Widespread looting followed and the Zoulou militia attacked foreigners; one French Legionnaire was killed and seven wounded as they attempted to move French nationals to safety. This provoked wider French intervention and Paris announced that it would send further troops to reinforce the 450 already in the country. Lissouba, meanwhile, accepted an offer by Brazzaville's Mayor Kolelas to attempt to find a solution to the crisis. President Omar Bongo of neighboring Gabon also offered to mediate. By 9 June, Brazzaville had been cut in half by the rival groups, both of whom were employing heavy weapons including artillery.

France now sent 400 more troops and President Jacques Chirac appealed to the two sides to end the fighting. On 11 June, both Lissouba and Sassou-Nguesso ordered cease-fires, but these broke down the next day. France, meanwhile, had secured military control of the airport and, by 15 June, had evacuated a total of 5,000 foreign nationals, mainly to Gabon. On 17 June, a three-day cease-fire was agreed upon while the French troops withdrew and, after further international **mediation**, Mayor Kolelas announced that the two sides would extend the cease-fire for seven days. But the fighting continued despite the cease-fire and, on 21 June, the **United Nations** secretary-general, **Kofi Annan**, asked the Security Council to approve a force of 1,600 international troops to secure Brazzaville airport.

There were reports of atrocities against civilians as well as widespread looting; estimates suggested that as many as 10,000 casualties had occurred, while French military sources said there had been 2,000 deaths by the end of June. On 29 June, Kolelas announced a new ceasefire and said that a nine-point peace plan had been accepted by the two sides, but this agreement collapsed the following day amidst further heavy fighting. The fighting continued throughout July and, by 23 July, it was reported that more than 4,000 people had been killed since the violence began on 5 June. Cease-fire agreements were violated almost as soon as they had been made. Sassou-Nguesso's Front Démocratique et Patriotique (FDP)/Democratic and Patriotic Front questioned the impartiality of Kolelas as a mediator and, on 8 July, the FDP demanded that any future ceasefire should be signed by Lissouba himself, not his prime minister, Charles David Ganao, and should be the prelude to a comprehensive political settlement. On 13 July, Lissouba did sign a ceasefire, although heavy fighting continued. Peace talks were held in Libreville, Gabon, but in the meantime Lissouba asked the Constitutional Court to postpone the presidential elections that were due to take place on 27 July and extend his mandate beyond its expiry date of 31 August. Sassou-Nguesso opposed any extension of the president's mandate and warned that such a move would lead to further fighting. He asked, instead, for the formation of a national government.

The Libreville talks broke down on 19 July; no agreement had been reached on the timing of the elections. On 22 July, the Constitutional Court postponed the presidential poll; this met a furious response from Sassou-Nguesso's supporters. Fighting between the two sides escalated during August and spread to the north of the country, while mediation efforts made no impact. On 1 August, a joint United Nations/ **Organization of African Unity** (OAU) mediation mission arrived in Libreville and after three days of discussion it was reported that both sides had made concessions. Then, on 5 August, Sassou-Nguesso's delegation rejected a plan for a government of national unity and an extension of Lissouba's term beyond 31 August. The talks were effectively suspended. Heavy fighting in Brazzaville in the first half of August also included shells landing in Kinshasa across the river, and the government of the newly installed **Laurent Kabila** responded in kind. By this time fierce fighting was also taking place in the north in the Likouala region, 725 kilometers from Brazzaville, and on 19 August Sassou-Nguesso's forces captured the town of Ouesso.

Fresh talks began in Libreville on 18 August 1997. President Omar Bongo of Gabon proposed a peace plan, but this was rejected by Sassou-Nguesso on 21 August and then by the government delegation two days later. The pro-government radio accused Bongo of favoring Sassou-Nguesso, his father-in-law; the radio also accused France of interfering (France, despite his Marxism in the past, had always seen Sassou-Nguesso as an ally). Heavy fighting continued in Brazzaville. A total of 39 groups and parties, which supported President Lissouba and the opposition Mouvement pour la Démocratie et le Développement Intégrale (MDDI)/Movement for Democracy and Integral Development, signed a power-sharing agreement while heavy fighting continued in Brazzaville (although Sassou-Nguesso's Forces Démocratiques Unies (FDU)/United Democratic Forces did not sign). The agreement came into force on 31 August (the expiry date of Lissouba's presidency) and provided for a government of national unity and the continuation of existing political institutions for an indefinite transitional period. President Lissouba appointed Bernard Kolelas, who was both mayor of Brazzaville and leader of the opposition MDDI, as prime minister with a brief to form a government of national unity and bring an end to the three-month-old civil war. At that point, with the support of 40 parties, Kolelas was seen as the best hope of ending the war.

By mid-September casualties had risen to an estimated 4,000 (official) to 7,000 dead, while 800,000 people had fled Brazzaville, which by then was in ruins. On a visit to Paris, Lissouba said he refused to negotiate with Sassou-Nguesso, whom he regarded as a "common rebel." Sassou-Nguesso confirmed that his Cobra forces were fighting government supporters in the north of the country; interviewed on Radio France Internationale he said he believed there had to be a transitional government to reorganize the state and "organize credible elections" with the support of the international community, and he rejected Kolelas as an appropriate prime minister for this task. A summit of eight African leaders in Gabon called for a UN peacekeeping force, while another appeal was made to the two sides to stop fighting. President Lissouba, who was visiting Kabila in Kinshasa, was represented by Kolelas. Sassou-Nguesso reacted to this summit by saying it took two to install a ceasefire. The countries involved in the summit, apart from Gabon, were Benin, **Central African Republic**, **Chad**, Equatorial Guinea, Senegal, and Togo, with the OAU in the chair.

The Kolelas government got off to a poor start since fighting in Brazzaville forced ministers, including Kolelas, to stay away from their offices. In a radio broadcast, the secretary general of President Lissouba's Union pour la Démocratie Sociale et pan-Africaine, Christophe Moukoueke, urged members of Sassou-Nguesso's party to take up the five posts allocated to them in the new coalition government. Kolelas outlined to the National Assembly three aims of his government: restoration of peace, post-war reconstruction, and presidential elections. However, Sassou-Nguesso's forces now launched a large-scale offensive in Brazzaville, targeting the west and the city center, the Maya Maya airport, the Central Post Office, the headquarters of the armed forces, and other public buildings. Lissouba's transitional government collapsed and Sassou-Nguesso seized the capital. The Executive Secretariat of the FDP announced that Major General Denis Sassou-Nguesso would be sworn in as president of the Republic on 25 October. This took place in the Parliament building, one of the few left standing; the new president gave no date for elections.

The Aftermath

France denied having intervened in the civil war and claimed it had played no role in Sassou-Nguesso's victory. France's foreign minister, Herbert Vedrine, said that France's only goal during the four-month war had been to support the mediation efforts of Gabon, although a foreign ministry spokesman, Jacques Pummelhardt, reacted to Sassou-Nguesso's victory by saying "it is a good thing" and that it is "essential for war-ravaged Congo to commit itself wholeheartedly to the path of nation." Sassou-Nguesso, even in his Marxist days, had always been regarded in Paris as a reliable ally of France and it was clear that France was determined to support the new government.

Deposed President Lissouba called for a campaign of civil disobedience against the new government. The French oil company ELF, the biggest oil company operating in the Congo, had reportedly supported Sassou-Nguesso throughout the war. In early November, President Sassou-Nguesso announced his new government. He also claimed that Lissouba had been supported by troops from the **União Nacional para a Independência Total de Angola** (UNITA)/ National Union for the Total Independence of Angola as well as **mercenaries**. All foreigners who had been detained during the fighting were set free. The president then announced that a peace and reconciliation forum would be held, although Lissouba and his associates would not be invited. On 17 November 1997, Cobra forces (the Sassou-Nguesso militia) demonstrated in Brazzaville to demand integration into the army; some of them (from the north) had seized houses and property of southerners. They claimed they had been forgotten by their leaders. On 21 November, the minister of the interior, Pierre Oba, banned all militia groups and said that in the future only security forces would be allowed to carry arms. The Zoulous, who had supported President Lissouba, were given an ultimatum to return from the bush and lay down their arms. Over the following months it became clear that Sassou-Nguesso had regained full control of the country.

CONGO, REPUBLIC OF THE (LATER ZAIRE). On 30 June 1960, the Belgian Congo, which had emerged out of the Scramble for Africa as the Congo Free State of King Leopold II, became independent as the Republic of the Congo. The country was ill-prepared for independence; political parties had only been allowed during the second half of the 1950s, and not until after riots in 1958 and 1959 did the Belgians begin to modernize their colonial structures in preparation for the coming change. The June date for independence was fixed at a meeting in Brussels in February 1960. The Belgians had created six provincial governments with competencies equal to those of the central government, an arrangement which naturally encouraged an immediate power struggle between the provinces and the center, once the Belgians had gone. In elections that May, one month before independence, **Patrice Lumumba** and his party, the Mouvement National Congolais (MNC)/National Congolese Movement, won the most seats and on 30 May, Lumumba was made prime minister, while Joseph Kasavubu, a politically more moderate rival, became president. They had to rule a vast and unwieldy country with extremely difficult communications, a range of differing ethnic groups, and virtually no trained personnel.

Collapse into Violence

Within days of independence there were riots and then a mutiny by the Force Publique (armed forces) for better pay and conditions. A breakdown of law and order followed, leading to an exodus of Europeans. The problems the new country faced—a left–right struggle at the center, ambitious provincial leaders, a breakdown of law and order, and desperately few people with any kind of training—ensured that breakdown would lead to civil war. The immense mineral wealth of the Congo was another factor of great political importance since a number of western nations—the former colonial power, Belgium, with large-scale investments, the **United States**, and **Great Britain**—were simply not prepared to see this wealth lost to them or destroyed. They had, in consequence, compelling motives for intervention. Almost at once, a power struggle developed between Prime Minister Lumumba, who was accused of "selling" the country to the Soviets, and **Moise Tshombe**, the leading politician of Katanga (now Shaba) Province where the bulk of the country's minerals were located, who was right-wing in his politics and had close ties with western business interests. The Congo was also to be the first black African country into whose affairs (originally quite legitimately through the **United Nations**) the **Union of Soviet Socialist Republics** (USSR) would intervene: up to that time it had been largely a stranger to African politics. This meant that the Congo crisis became inextricably bound up with the **Cold War**. On 11 July, Tshombe announced that Katanga Province was seceding from the Congo; the following day, Lumumba appealed to the United Nations to help restore order and prevent the secession. Belgian troops, whose presence was deeply resented, had remained in the Congo after 30 June and their attempts to restore order made matters worse.

The United Nations

Under its secretary-general, **Dag Hammarskjöld**, the United Nations responded swiftly and sent a mixed force of Swedish and African troops to the Congo to keep the peace. The attempted secession of Katanga was followed by another would-be secession, this time by Kasai Province. As the UN force discovered, the task of maintaining order was formidable: the Congo, Africa's third largest country, covered 2,345,095 square kilometers and consisted of more than 200 ethnic groups. Government forces managed to get control of Kasai Province quickly enough, but were insufficient to subjugate the rebellious Katanga Province. The Belgians, in fact, assisted Tshombe's secession. Belgium had huge stakes in Katanga's mineral wealth; it recruited **mercenaries** to safeguard Tshombe and the mines, while Tshombe himself was an adroit politician. Meanwhile, a power struggle developed between Lumumba and Kasavubu and in September Kasavubu dismissed Lumumba. The military commander, Lt. Col. **Joseph Désiré Mobutu**, then carried out his first coup and created a College of Commissioners to rule the country. Lumumba fell into the hands of the Commissioners and then was taken to Katanga where he was tortured before being murdered. The United Nations failed to intervene on his behalf and was widely blamed for allowing his murder, a black mark against the organization that remained for a considerable time. On 2 August 1961, Kasavubu appointed a new government with Cyrille Adoula as prime minister, and Antoine Gizenga, a Lumumbist, as his deputy. A new crisis arose in September 1961 when Dag Hammarskjöld, on a flight from Ndola in Northern Rhodesia to Katanga in order to negotiate with Tshombe, was killed in a crash that has never been adequately explained. At the end of 1962, UN forces finally moved against Katanga and brought its secession to an end on 15 January 1963. Tshombe went into exile.

Civil War

Events from independence to January 1963, when Katanga's secession was brought to an end, were as much a United Nations effort to restore order as they were a civil war. But after the restoration of central government control, there followed a general deterioration in law and order. First came the Mulele rebellion in Kwilu Province, one of the country's richest regions. Pierre Mulele had served briefly in Lumumba's government. Early in 1964, his followers killed about 150 officials and his rebel army of not more than 4,000 became a major threat to the country's stability. Meanwhile, in March 1964, about 400 members of the Katanga Gendarmerie crossed into **Angola** where Tshombe's white mercenaries gave them military training. In June 1964, the last UN troops left the Congo and in the wake of their departure a new round of violence erupted. In July, Kasavubu invited Tshombe back from exile to replace Adoula as prime minister; Tshombe then raised a force of mercenaries to put down the Mulele rebellion in Kwilu and the northeast, on the **Uganda** border.

By that time, the eastern rebels had come to control about 500,000 square kilometers of territory. The Congolese Army, on the other hand, had virtually disintegrated. On 5 August, the rebels, who had named themselves the Popular Army of Liberation, captured Stanleyville (later Kisangani), the Congo's third town. They allied themselves with the National Liberation Committee, consisting of left-wing exiles and Lumumbists. However, in pitched fighting between the Congolese Army and the rebels on 19 August, some 300 rebels were killed, including Mulele. The United States now intervened; Tshombe had sought its support early in August, and it now sent a number of air force transport planes and 50 paratroop guards, which it put at the disposal of the U.S. Ambassador. Tshombe appealed for African troops to help him fight the rebels and claimed that the rebellion had been stirred up by the People's Republic of China. This was at least a possibility, as the Chinese, operating from their **Burundi** embassy, saw the chance of increasing their influence in the region. On 7 September the rebels, who still held Stanleyville, announced the formation of a government under a former Lumumbist, Christopher Gbeng. Meanwhile, Tshombe's agents were recruiting South African and Rhodesian mercenaries at $280 a month. Tshombe's agents worked hard to secure **Organization of African Unity** (OAU) backing for his position, but when the heads of state meeting took place in Cairo that October, he was refused permission to participate. In fact, Tshombe was dependent upon Belgian support and between 400 and 500 mercenaries led by the notorious Mike Hoare. Some of these mercenaries were then training the Congolese army to retake

Stanleyville. On 24 November 1964, the United States used its transport planes to fly in 600 Belgian paratroopers to retake Stanleyville, where the rebels were holding 1,200 Europeans hostage. A number of these Europeans lost their lives in this operation while the remainder were either rescued or turned up later. The Congolese army, led by mercenaries, followed the Belgian paratroopers into Stanleyville.

Kasavubu, who saw Tshombe developing into a dangerous rival, now dismissed Tshombe whose Confédération Nationale des Associations Congolaises (CONACO)/Council of National Alliance of the Congo appeared to be winning the elections that were held that month. By the end of the month, the rebellion became increasingly disoriented. Even so, it was still dangerous, with forces consisting of the Simbas, including a number of ex-soldiers, and the Jeunesse, young untrained Mulelists who could be fanatical. The rebellion continued into March 1965, but by then the rejuvenated Congolese National Army, led by mercenaries, was winning the war. This army was a law to itself and carried out widespread terror tactics and slaughter among the civilian population. The mercenaries, who by then were being paid $560 a month, were responsible for a growing catalog of brutalities, which included torturing prisoners before killing them.

The Aftermath

On 24 November 1965, General (as he had since become) Mobutu took power, suspending President Kasavubu and his prime minister, Evariste Kimba, who had replaced Tshombe. Mobutu assumed all executive functions and was set to rule the country until his overthrow in 1997, 32 years later. It is impossible to be precise about the nature of the Congo Crisis, as it was called at the time; there were so many interventions—by the United Nations, the Belgians, the United States, big business interests, mercenaries—that it is difficult to say whether it was really a civil war or something else. How much were the attempted secessions of both Katanga and Kwilu foreign inspired? The crucial question about the crisis, which must remain unanswered is: what would have happened in the Congo had there been no interventions from outside?

Estimates of December 1964 suggested that the rebels had killed about 20,000 Congolese and that 5,000 of these had been killed in

Stanleyville. The Congolese Army is reputed to have killed many thousands, often in reprisals, though no figures have been produced. The mercenaries killed people in the villages through which they passed and often did so out of wanton cruelty. Certain European deaths came to 175, less than the figure of 250 originally estimated for Stanleyville, when the Belgian paratroopers retook the town in 1964; many more Europeans were wounded. Possibly 300 Europeans died altogether from beginning to end of the crisis, and their deaths attracted most international media attention. A total figure of 30,000 deaths has been suggested, though the real casualties may have been much higher. Destruction to property and the general collapse of order did enormous long-term damage to the Congo. The interventions of the West were self-serving, having more to do with the preservation of western interests in the country's mineral wealth than any desire to ensure peace. The mercenaries, whose behavior was barbaric, did the white cause in Africa great harm. Apologists for the mercenaries would argue that they were responding to equal barbarism perpetrated by the Congolese rebels whose brutalities against Congolese government officials were often appalling. The end result of this brutal civil war and collapse of order, which for a time made the name Congo synonymous with breakdown in Africa, was to be 32 years of dictatorship and what later came to be called state kleptocracy under Mobutu.

CÔTE D'IVOIRE. The government of President Henri Konan Bedié was overthrown by a coup mounted on 24 December 1999 and replaced by a military junta led by General Robert Gueï. The coup was initiated by members of the para-commando unit who had not been paid for service in **Central African Republic** under the **United Nations**. On the other hand, the speed with which the coup led to a military takeover of key strategic points—the radio station, the President's Office, and the airport—suggested advanced planning that went beyond a pay dispute. The president had returned to Abidjan from abroad on 23 December, on news of unrest, and met a delegation of the mutineers on the 24th. However, at 11:00 a.m. that day, General Gueï broadcast on commercial radio to announce the removal of the president and the dissolution of the government, the National Assembly, the Constitutional Council, and the Supreme Court;

a nine-member Comité National de Salut Publicque (CNSP)/National Committee of Public Salvation replaced them with General Gueï, the former chief of army staff, as the new head of state. The coup sent shockwaves through the region as Côte d'Ivoire had long been regarded as the most successful and developed member of Francophone West Africa. President Bedié took refuge in the French ambassador's residence, but following hostile demonstrations outside the building by members of the military, he was moved to the French military base at Port Bouet. Bedié made a broadcast calling for resistance to the coup, but none was forthcoming. Instead, the gendarmerie joined the military in support of the coup. The French did not make any move to support Bedié and, on 26 December, he left for Togo and then went into exile in **France**. In the immediate aftermath of the coup, the military put an end to the rioting and looting that erupted. Gueï had the support of three high-ranking officers: General Abdoulaye Coulibaly, General Lansana Palenfo, and Lt.-Col. Mathieu Doué. Political prisoners were released including Henriette Diabate, the parliamentary leader of the Rassemblement Démocratique Republicain (RDR)/Democratic Republican Rally, who had been jailed by Bedié the previous November. The RDR's presidential candidate for the October 2000 elections, Alassane Ouattara, returned from exile. The government had been trying to deny him Ivorian citizenship on the grounds that he was a Burkinabé by birth.

The year 2000 began in a mood of uncertainty, although considerable goodwill existed for Gueï who had been a reluctant coup leader, persuaded to take the lead by others. He promised an early return to civilian rule. There was bitter opposition to Ouattara (a northerner) in southern Côte d'Ivoire and it was soon clear that the coup had sparked a wider crisis between south and north. In August, a postponed referendum on the notion of Ivoirité—citizenship—was held and achieved a substantial majority for Ivoirité. An attempt to assassinate Gueï in September was blamed upon Coulibaly and Palenfo, who were dismissed and took refuge in the Nigerian embassy. In October, the courts again ruled that Ouattara could not stand for election as president with the result that the RDR boycotted the elections so that 62 percent of the registered voters did not vote. There were two main contenders for the presidency: Gueï, standing as an independent, and Laurent Gbagbo, who to that point had supported

Gueï's campaign in support of Ivoirité. Gueï who had initially appeared as a reluctant coup maker, now made a determined effort to install himself in power by sacking the electoral commission and proclaiming himself the winner of the election. This move led to his downfall. Gueï's prime minister, Soulemane Diarra, resigned and thousands of Gbagbo's supporters took to the streets in protest. Hours of street battles followed and then army units defected from Gueï who fled the country by helicopter instead of swearing himself in as president. Diarra reinstated the electoral commission and swore in Gbagbo as president. However, supporters of Ouattara now took to the streets demanding new elections. Their demonstrations were bloodily suppressed by the military, which massacred 50 young members of the RDR. Gbagbo then banned Ouattara from standing in the parliamentary elections set for December. When these elections were held, the RDR again boycotted them with the result that most northern constituencies did not vote. Gbagbo's Front Populaire Ivoirien (FPI)/Ivorian Popular Front won a convincing victory while the former ruling party came second. But the exclusion of the RDR and Ouattara, whose support all came from the north of the country, created a dangerous split along ethnic and religious lines.

2001

While Gbagbo had won the December election and defeated Gueï, despite his army support, the new danger came from the north because Ouattara had been prevented from standing. There was growing anti-northern feeling in the south, representing its Christian and tribal differences with the north, a majority of whose people were Muslim and Burkinabé incomers. In January, an attempted anti-Gbagbo coup heightened tensions since it was seen to have covert support from Burkina Faso. Already the anti-northern feeling had led to a mass exodus of some 200,000 Burkinabé workers from the cocoa and coffee plantations. Gbagbo needed to curb the activities of his most militant supporters, many of whom were violently anti-northern, and follow a path of reconciliation. He was supported in this aim by **African Union** President Alpha Oumar Konaré. France also worked to calm the situation in what had been seen in Paris as its show case post-colonial Francophone ally. The economy now appeared to be on the brink of disintegration. Gbagbo, however, would not make the one move that might have saved the situation and that was to recognize the Ivorian nationality of Ouattara. In June, Gbagbo established a National Reconciliation Forum under the chairmanship of Seydou Diarra, a northerner. This brought together the leaders of the different factions, including former president Henri Konan Bedié, Robert Gueï who had returned to the country as a political party leader, and a reluctant Ouattara who, however, could not afford to be absent even though the courts were in the process of considering whether he was Ivorian or Burkinabé (he had formerly served as prime minister for four years under President Félix Houphouet-Boigny). An uneasy period of suspense was to follow, though few people believed that the crisis was over.

2002

The tensions and unrest that had been building up ever since the coup of December 1999 finally exploded in September 2002, following another coup attempt on the 19th of the month. This, apparently, was no more than a mutiny by dissatisfied soldiers, but it soon became clear that the military wanted to take control of the country. Army mutinies occurred simultaneously in five cities. That, in Abidjan, failed but the mutinies in Bouaké in the center-north of the country and in Korhogo in the far north succeeded. Supposedly, these revolts were about the grievances of 750 recruits who had been warned they were to be dismissed, but that was only a pretext. There was serious fighting in Abidjan which cost 300 lives including those of two leading figures: the interior minister Emile Boga Doudou and the former head of state General Robert Gueï who was killed by an assassination squad; the 750 recruits were reputedly his followers, but as in so many such situations, the stories were confused and conflicting. Soldiers, who had defected from the army in the years 1999–2002 and taken refuge in Burkina Faso, had moved back into Côte d'Ivoire and taken over the mutiny in the north where they quickly established control over a wide sweep of country.

Army loyalists failed in their attempt to recapture Bouaké from the rebels who then advanced on the capital Yamoussoukro, but they were halted by French troops. The French units were in Côte d'Ivoire under an existing defense agreement. At the beginning of the mutinies, the French troops had been deployed to evacuate French nationals who wished to leave the country, and the rebels had permitted them to enter Bouaké for this purpose only. By November, the rebels had created a political movement, the Mouvement Patriotique de la Côte d'Ivoire (MPCI)/Patriotic Movement of Côte d'Ivoire under the leadership of Guillaume Soro. A cease-fire negotiated by the **Economic Community of West African States** (ECOWAS) had been put in place but the country had divided between north and south, with the Gbagbo government holding the south, the rebels the north. In the south, growing xenophobia led to attacks upon foreigners from Burkina Faso and Mali who were accused of supporting the rebels. At the end of November, an ECOWAS peace force, comprised of troops from Senegal, Ghana, Niger, Benin, and Guinea-Bissau, was set up, in theory to replace the French, who to that date had been policing the ceasefire. Gbagbo, meanwhile, was reported to be recruiting support from **Angola** and **mercenaries** from **South Africa**. Ouattara, whose inclusion in the government might have prevented the looming disaster, was allowed to leave the country. He had taken refuge in the French embassy—his house had been torched by government loyalists in September.

By the end of 2002, the main military force in the country to maintain some kind of peace consisted of 1,500 French troops (an increase from the 600 allowed under the existing defense treaty). The situation was further complicated by the appearance of two new movements across the border in Liberia: the Mouvement Populaire Ivoirien du Grand Ouest (MPIGO)/Popular Ivorian Movement of the Great West; and the Mouvement pour la Justice et la Paix (MJP)/Movement for Justice and Peace. Both movements were sympathizers of former General Gueï while English speakers were also reported to be members, implying a direct link with the Liberian President **Charles Taylor**. By the end of the year the future looked both gloomy and dangerous and the expectation was for further conflict and national disintegration. At best, Gbagbo only had partial control of the army and government while rising xenophobia in the south was matched by growing separatism in the north.

2003

Côte d'Ivoire entered the new year split in half between north and south with French troops acting as peacekeepers and becoming increasingly unpopular in the process. A peace deal was worked out at Marcoussis south of Paris at which government, the rebel "new forces" (forces nouvelles) from the north, and other minor rebel groups from the West were represented. The deal would allot places to the rebels in a transitional government and ruling powers were divided between the president and the prime minister. A constitutional amendment was also proposed on the question of citizenship, which was a major cause of the rebellion. However, strong opposition to the Marcoussis agreement was at once apparent in the south and riots in Abidjan led Gbagbo to hesitate as to whether he should ratify the agreement and only on 10 March (after two months hesitation), was Seydou Diarra, the prime minister who had been nominated by consensus, sworn in. The rebels did not attend the swearing in for "security reasons" and in any case the swearing in was only achieved after an intervention by Ghana's President John Kufuor who was the current chair of ECOWAS, which had played an important part in brokering the peace agreement.

Fear of economic collapse prevented disintegration, although the country remained partitioned between north and south. Contacts with Côte d'Ivoire's two northern neighbors, Burkina Faso and Mali, both of which had large numbers of their citizens living and working in the north, led to a partial reopening of the northern border in July when Gbagbo declared that the "war" was over. In September, a leading rebel, Sergeant Ibrahim Coulibaly who had been in exile in Burkina Faso, was arrested in Paris for recruiting mercenaries, while a number of rebel "associates" were arrested in Abidjan amid rumors of another planned coup. Tensions increased in October and the government banned public meetings and demonstrations. ECOWAS pressure persuaded the government to exercise greater control over the militias which supported it. At the end of the year rebel members of the government, who had withdrawn from it in September, returned. France, which had increased the strength of its military force to 4,000 troops, agreed to keep them in the country until elections had been held in 2005.

2004

The stalemate between north and south that had lasted through 2003 seemed likely to continue in the new year. In January, President

Gbagbo visited Paris and had apparently cordial talks with President Jacques Chirac. In the north the rebels—"the New Forces"—appeared to be facing internal difficulties. In April, the **United Nations** finally agreed to France's request to send a force of 6,000 peacekeepers to reinforce the 4,000 French troops already carrying out this task. Prior to the arrival of the UN force, a major setback occurred on 25 March, when in Abidjan a peaceful demonstration of opponents of the Gbagbo regime was ruthlessly and bloodily suppressed by government forces. A subsequent UN inquiry found that 120 people had been killed and many more were injured or reported missing. The consequence of this action was the withdrawal of rebel ministers from the transitional government. Intense diplomatic efforts by Africa, Europe, and the UN to ease the newly mounting tensions followed and an African summit was held in Ghana in July, which was attended by the UN Secretary-General **Kofi Annan** and the African Union president, Alpha Oumar Konaré. The summit obtained new commitments from all the parties in Côte d'Ivoire for disarmament in the north and constitutional reforms to repeal the nationality amendment that entrenched "Ivoirité." This citizenship clause insisted that a citizen had two Ivorian parents. Gbagbo and his supporters only accepted this latter condition with bad grace. Subsequently, since the parliament made no moves to implement the summit resolutions, the rebels held on to their arms.

In October, Gbagbo threatened to retake the north by force and in November launched a bombardment of Bouaké, the rebel stronghold. By accident or design his air force killed nine French soldiers when its two Sukhoi-25 bombers (piloted by East Europeans) attacked Bouaké. France reacted immediately by destroying the Ivorian planes on the ground as well as the presidential helicopter gunship. There followed days of bitter anti-French actions including attacks on French schools, property, and individuals. The French government, thereupon, organized a mass evacuation of a large proportion of its 10,000 citizens then in Côte d'Ivoire, and in the process took control of Abidjan airport and the two main bridges. These French actions led to increasing questions as to just what France's role in the country was. On 9 November, rumors of another anti-Gbagbo coup sparked new attacks upon the French whose troops then killed a number of Ivorians: France claimed the number was 20, Côte d'Ivoire that it was 60. At the end of the year, South Africa's president Thabo Mbeki became involved in **mediation** efforts and, though the parliament did amend the constitution on the issue of Ivoirité, Gbagbo insisted that there had to be a referendum on the subject before the amendment could be accepted.

2005

On 1 February, the UN Security Council passed resolution 1584 requesting the secretary-general to create a group of experts to analyze the security situation in Côte d'Ivoire and report back in 90 days. The UN called on the government and the New Forces to cooperate with the UN Operation in Côte d'Ivoire (UNOCI) and to reveal what armaments each side had within 45 days. On 6 April government, rebels, and opposition leaders met in Pretoria and agreed to end hostilities, begin disarmament, and plan elections. After four days of talks, under the chairmanship of Thabo Mbeki, the agreement produced a statement that the parties "hereby solemnly declare the immediate and final cessation of all hostilities and the end of the war through the national territory." The agreement was signed by President Gbabgo, Prime Minister Seydou Diarra, former president Bedié, the leader of the New Force, Guillaume Kisbafori Soro, and the opposition leader Alasanne Ouattara. Under its terms any dispute as to interpretation should be referred to President Thabo Mbeki. On 13 April, he ruled that all Ivorian leaders, including Ouattara, should be allowed to stand in the forthcoming presidential elections. The Forces Armées Nationales de Côte d'Ivoire (FANCI)/Armed Forces of Côte d'Ivoire and the Forces Armées des Forces Nouvelles (FAFN)/Armed Forces of the New Forces met in Bouaké on 16 April and agreed to begin withdrawing all heavy weapons from the frontlines on 21 April. On 14 May, the two sides signed a disarmament agreement to be implemented over the following months with demobilization to take place between 27 June and 10 August. In early June, armed clashes by rival ethnic groups occurred in the west of the country leading to 100 deaths and threatening the country's delicate peace, even though they were not connected to the recent conflict. Hundreds of people fled the villages round Duebone following these clashes between the Guere and Dioula.

The UN Security Council authorized Secretary-General Kofi Annan to appoint a high representative to help prepare for the October presidential elections. He would work alongside Thabo Mbeki who, arising from the Pretoria agreement, also had a key role in organizing the election. On 24 June, UN Resolution 1609 extended the UNOCI mandate to 24 January 2006. On 5 July, Gbagbo used his presidential powers to override his ruling Front Populaire Ivorien (FPI)/Ivorian Popular Front, which had blocked reforms called for by the Pretoria Agreement of April. He also announced that presidential elections would be held on 30 October. However, on 9 September, UN Secretary-General Kofi Annan announced that the October elections would not take place. This followed a statement by the New Forces that they would no longer accept South African mediation because, they claimed, South Africa was biased toward the government. Gbagbo later announced that he would not step down unless an election was held to end his mandate. On 21 October, the Security Council adopted Resolution 1633 on the end of Gbagbo's mandate and the "impossibility of organizing presidential elections on the scheduled date" and decided that Gbagbo should remain in office from 31 October for a period not to exceed 12 months. The resolution called upon Gbagbo to cede some of his presidential powers to a new prime minister to be appointed by 31 October.

The New Forces rejected the UN resolution and, on 31 October, said that they no longer recognized the legitimacy of the Gbagbo government and proclaimed Guillaume Soro, leader of the New Forces, as the new prime minister. Further, the spokesman for the New Forces, Sidiki Konaté, said that the New Forces had started to mobilize in the north and were preparing to undertake "all forms of action to prevent Laurent Gbagbo from believing a single moment that he is head of state of Côte d'Ivoire." Efforts to find a prime minister continued through November and the current AU chairman, President **Olusegun Obasanjo** of **Nigeria**, visited Côte d'Ivoire and had talks with all parties. A presidential decree of 5 December appointed Charles Konan Banny, governor of the Banque Centrale des Etats de l'Afrique de l'Ouest (BCEAO)/Central Bank of West African States as prime minister. On 28 December, Banny announced the formation of a new government that included members of the New Forces. However, the New Forces threatened to boycott the new cabinet because Banny had failed to gain control of the Finance Ministry from Gbagbo supporters.

2006

Developments in Côte d'Ivoire followed a familiar post–civil war pattern of agreements, walkouts, postponements, concessions, as gradually the two sides came—or tried to come—together. January proved an especially fraught month. The UN backed International Working Group (IWG), which had been set up to assist Prime Minister Banny, met on 15 January in Abidjan when it announced that it would not extend the mandate of the Assembly that had expired the previous April. But the National Assembly was a power base for Gbagbo and his supporters responded angrily with the result that, on 27 January, Gbagbo unilaterally extended the life of the National Assembly. Meanwhile, in mid-January, the "Young Patriots" (jeunes patriotes)—youths who supported Gbagbo—took control of areas of Abidjan and attacked migrant businesses and shops. In the west of the country, about 1,000 protesters occupied the base of the UN Operation in Côte d'Ivoire and 300 Bangladeshi peacekeepers were forced to leave the base. On 17 January, the FPI (Gbagbo's party) announced that it was withdrawing from the peace process. It accused the international community of carrying out a "constitutional coup d'état." Obasanjo, a key mediator, flew to Abidjan on 18 January for talks with Gbagbo who subsequently appealed for calm. Nonetheless, rioting and unrest throughout the south continued for several days. On 24 January, the UN Security Council adopted Resolution 1652 to extend the UNOCI mandate (as well as the presence of French troops) until 15 December.

Having gone to the brink of a new round of civil war, all parties drew back in February and on the 28th of the month held talks in Yamoussoukro at which they announced their renewed support for the peace plan contained in UN Security Council Resolution 1633 of 21 October 2005. A statement, without setting dates, "acknowledged the necessity of updating the timetable and immediately resuming dialogue" between the army and rebel leaders. They agreed to meet frequently. A "no war, no peace" situation characterized 2006 to emphasize the fragility of the agreements that had been reached between the different factions. On 2 June, the UN Security Council adopted Resolution 1682 (2006), authorizing an increase in the strength of the UN Operation in Côte d'Ivoire (UNOCI) of up to 1,500 additional personnel until 15 December 2006. There was still a long way to go before a definitive peace could be assured.

CROCKER PLAN. The agreement to end the war in **Angola** that was signed in December 1988 had been negotiated by U.S. Assistant Secretary of State Chester A. Crocker. The plan encompassed the U.S. determination to tie an Angolan peace and independence for **Namibia** to the policy that had come to be known as **linkage**, which would also involve the withdrawal from the region of **Cuba**'s military forces. The plan involved the simultaneous, phased withdrawal of Cuban troops from Angola and of South African troops from Namibia and the holding of **United Nations**–supervised elections in Namibia. At the time (1988) there were an estimated 50,000 Cuban military personnel in Angola.

Tripartite talks were held in a number of venues during 1988 between representatives of Angola, **South Africa**, and Cuba under the chairmanship of Crocker. The final agreement provided for the phased withdrawal of 50,000 Cuban troops over a period of two-and-a-half years to July 1991; independence for Namibia with the implementation of UN Resolution 435 with a United Nations peacekeeping force which should be established in Namibia by 1 April 1989; the withdrawal of South African troops from Angola as well as approximately 10,000 **African National Congress** (ANC) cadres.

The success of the Crocker Plan was ensured by the rapidly approaching end to the **Cold War** confrontations of the previous 40 years and the subsequent agreement between U.S. President Ronald Reagan and Soviet President Mikhail Gorbachev to pursue a policy of worldwide detente. On 1 April 1989, UN Resolution 435 was implemented in Namibia despite a **South West Africa People's Organization** (SWAPO) incursion into Namibia from Angola that might have delayed the plan. In January 1989, Cuba began the withdrawal of its troops two months ahead of the agreed schedule, and in February South African troops began to leave Angola. Namibia became independent on 21 March 1990, when all South Africa's forces were withdrawn from the country.

CUBA. The Cuban intervention on the side of the **Movimento Popular para a Libertação de Angola** (MPLA)/Popular Movement for the Liberation of Angola government in 1975 made a crucial difference to that government's ability to survive in the face of an invasion from **South Africa** and later to win in the ensuing civil war. But though Cuban military assistance was crucial to MPLA survival, Washington was so set against any Cuban international activities that its presence in **Angola** almost guaranteed subsequent U.S. support for **Jonas Savimbi** and the **União Nacional para a Independência Total de Angola** (UNITA)/National Union for the Total Independence of Angola. Moreover, the presence of Cuban forces in Angola led the **United States** to endorse the South African-UNITA suggestion of **linkage**, a policy that tied any settlement in Angola to the withdrawal of Cuban forces.

The Cuban presence in Angola from 1975 to 1990 certainly heightened the **Cold War** aspect of the civil war, although it would be wrong to suggest that this alone brought the Cold War to Angola. **Agostinho Neto**, the leader of the MPLA at this time, was an avowed Marxist and had already ensured the Cold War nature of the conflict. Thus, when the position of his party as the successor to the departing Portuguese was threatened in 1975, he automatically turned to Moscow for support. The MPLA, in any case, had been receiving Communist assistance in its struggle against the Portuguese. In 1975, with the help of Soviet transport, Cuba sent 10,000 troops to Angola to support the MPLA in its fight with the **Frente Nacional da Libertação de Angola** (FNLA)/National Front for the Liberation of Angola and UNITA. The initial 10,000 Cuban troops were steadily increased over the years to about 25,000 in 1987. During the second half of the 1980s the Cubans played a vital role in defending Angola from South African incursions.

Apart from its military personnel, Cuba supplied several thousand technicians (often at quite low levels) as well as medical teams and engineers since Angola had been almost entirely denuded of even elementary skills when the Portuguese departed in 1975. The civil war in Angola continued through the 1980s and the Cuban troops bolstered MPLA resistance to UNITA, which was supported by South Africa. In 1987, which became a climactic year in the war, Cuban troops were increased from about 25,000 to 50,000 and played a vital part in the battle of **Cuito Cuanavale** (1987–88). In the event, Cuito Cuanavale was successfully defended against strong South African intervention, not least because of the Cuban presence and its air defenses. The settlement that was reached during 1988 (the **Crocker Plan**) included the Cuban agreement to withdraw its forces from Angola over a period of 30 months, and the last Cuban forces were withdrawn from Angola in May 1991, ahead of schedule. Thus concluded what had been by far the most effective Cuban intervention in any country.

CUITO CUANAVALE. The battle of Cuito Cuanavale was fought for the town of that name in southeast **Angola** over the better part of a year during 1987–1988 between the **Movimento Popular para a Libertação de Angola** (MPLA)/Popular Movement for the Liberation of Angola government forces, backed by the Cubans, and the **União Nacional para a Independência Total de Angola** (UNITA)/ National Union for the Total Independence of Angola, backed by **South Africa**. It became, in both military and political terms, a turning point in the long civil war and was one of the most important battles to be fought anywhere in Africa since 1945. Cuito Cuanavale was one of a line of forts which stretched from Namibe on the Atlantic to Lumbala near the Zambian border; between them they controlled the Soviet installed radar system which monitored South African air activity. UNITA recognized Cuito Cuanavale as a vital forward position for the Forcas Armadas Populares de Libertação de Angola (FAPLA)/Popular Armed Forces for the Liberation of Angola in an area that otherwise was largely UNITA-controlled, and they therefore laid siege to the town in mid-1987. The town had special importance since it advanced MPLA forces within striking distance of Jambe, the UNITA headquarters. Although South Africa claimed in December 1987 that its forces in Angola had been withdrawn, it became clear by late January 1988 that substantial South African forces were engaged in the siege of Cuito Cuanavale; they were bombarding the town with long-range G5 howitzers. The MPLA government evacuated the 6,500 inhabitants of the town, and the Angolan air force made daily sorties against the UNITA and South African positions.

The South Africans had intervened in force when it became clear that UNITA on its own was not strong enough to halt the MPLA advance on Jambe. As the Crocker negotiations developed through 1988, Washington hoped that a combined UNITA–South African force would be able to defeat the MPLA at Cuito Cuanavale, a development that would make Luanda more amenable to a deal, but the defeat did not occur. By mid-February, as the battle escalated, the South Africans increased their ground troops to 7,000. There were heavy losses on both sides and South Africa was obliged to admit the politically damaging fact in Pretoria of growing white casualties. When South Africa also admitted the loss of one of its Mirage planes, this highlighted the growing intensity of the air war; South Africa had lost air superiority when the balance had been altered by the installation of a Soviet air defense network. The Cubans and Soviets employed SA-8 missiles, the South Africans and UNITA Stinger missiles.

By the end of February 1988, the battle had become one of the largest conventional military clashes in Africa, and the South African force had then been increased to 8,000. The FAPLA held Cuito Cuanavale with about 10,000 troops; it was equipped with Soviet tanks, APCs, and anti-aircraft missiles, and these, in part, were manned by the 50th Division of the Cuban army. A crucial psychological aspect of this conflict was the realization that South Africa had lost its automatic military superiority, something that had been taken for granted until that time. The FAPLA, backed by the Cubans and with years of fighting experience, had become a formidable force in its own right. In March 1988, Angola claimed to have downed 40 South African planes since September 1987, a claim denied by South Africa, although it had certainly lost more planes than the one loss to which it had admitted. The position was becoming all the more serious for South Africa since by 1988 it faced growing internal upheaval. In mid-March South Africa sent a 500-vehicle convoy to reinforce its 8,000-strong force round Cuito Cuanavale. High casualties were being recorded on both sides.

In April 1988, President **Jose Eduardo dos Santos** and the Cubans accepted **linkage**. The peace talks (the **Crocker Plan**) went ahead, and it was agreed that South Africa's forces would be withdrawn and that **Namibia** would become independent. The stalemate at Cuito Cuanavale and the military performance of the Angolans and their Cuban allies convinced South Africa that it could not win and, in fact, was in danger of suffering a catastrophic setback. This realization also helped promote the peace process. At the end of the battle, the South Africans were no longer employing white troops in the front line for fear that white casualties would lead to unwelcome political repercussions at home.

– D –

DARFUR (SUDAN). A new conflict emerged in **Sudan** during February 2003 in the huge western region of Darfur, which covers approximately one fifth of the geographical area of the country. The conflict was between government forces and their regional militia allies, and the Darfur Liberation Front (DLF) which, however, changed its name in March 2003 to the Sudan Liberation Movement/Army (SLM/A). The rebels charged the government with supporting Arab militias in massacring the Fur and other indigenous peoples of the region and demanded a "united and democratic Sudan" that it believed could only be achieved through armed struggle. The government dismissed the rebel accusations and, in its turn, claimed that it was fighting "banditry" in the region. The Khartoum government called upon the SLM/A to bring its rebellion to an end. The situation in Darfur deteriorated throughout the year and created an increasing number of **refugees**, some within the huge region itself and others who fled across the border into neighboring **Chad**. By the end of 2003, Amnesty International claimed that about 500,000 people had been displaced as a result of the conflict. Analysts believed that the recovery of the depressed Sudan economy was dependent upon the achievement of peace in Darfur and the establishment subsequently of a more equitable distribution of the national wealth.

2004

By the beginning of 2004, the war in Darfur had become a matter of international concern; it was to escalate throughout the year. Ironically, while the 21-year-old North–South civil war at last appeared to be coming to an end (*see* SUDAN), the ethnic war in Darfur was becoming more brutal and intense. Black Muslim communities of Darfur that had long complained of the pro-Arab bias of the Khartoum government had finally launched a resistance movement led by the Sudan Liberation Army and the Justice and Equity Movement (JEM). The government, though often denying anything of the kind, appeared to encourage the Arab militia, the Janjawid, to launch attacks upon settled ethnic groups in Darfur. A ceasefire was agreed in April but it made little difference and the program of what was seen in the outside world as ethnic cleansing continued. By mid-2004, an estimated 1.2 million people had fled the region, 300,000 of them into Chad. These refugees presented the international community with a massive problem of chronic food shortage. International food **aid** was often hijacked by the rival militias and aid agencies faced difficult and dangerous conditions as they attempted to bring relief to the refugees. An estimated 50,000 villagers had been murdered and thousands of women were raped and forced into slavery. Pressures upon the Khartoum government by the international community to control the activities of the Janjawid made little or no impression.

The conflict divided Sudan's Islamist movement between the ruling National Congress Party (NCP) and the JEM in Darfur. It created a rift between the westerners in Darfur and the ruling northerners and threatened to split the country once more just when the two sides in the North–South civil war at last seemed on the verge of agreeing to a genuine settlement. One aspect of the war was the longstanding sense in Darfur that successive national governments had treated the region as peripheral to national concerns and, in consequence, had neglected it and deprived it of its proper share of national revenue. Another problem, not fully appreciated by the international community, was the perennial rivalry between the nomads and the settled agriculturalists. This rivalry had long historic roots and the growth of population meant an ever growing pressure upon the region's limited water resources. Renewed cease-fire agreements, after the first one of April 2004, were regularly broken by both sides. **African Union** (AU) military observers arrived in Darfur in July but their operations were temporarily suspended the following December when an AU helicopter was shot down. There was widespread condemnation of the Khartoum government and Janjawid brutality by foreign nations and international agencies including Human Rights Watch, Amnesty International, the **United Nations**, the **United States**, and the European Union (EU). According to Mukesh Kapila, the UN Humanitarian

Coordinator for Sudan, the situation in Darfur was a human disaster. In July, the U.S. Congress described the killings as genocide and increased pressure for military intervention. Meanwhile, the UN had convened a meeting of 36 donor nations and appealed for $236 million to help the victims of the conflict. Non-governmental organizations (NGOs) trying to distribute relief supplies were harassed by both the Sudan army and the Janjawid. The government regarded the NGOs as meddlers in its affairs. The UN Security Council warned in September that non-compliance with earlier UN resolutions to respect a ceasefire could lead to the application of sanctions against Sudan's oil industry. In December, increased violence led the UN to suspend its humanitarian relief operations.

2005

In March, the UN pledged full support for the African Union Mission in Sudan (AMIS), which had been set up to monitor and assist the peace process in Darfur. On 29 March, the Security Council passed Resolution 1591 (2005) by 12-0, with Algeria, China, and Russia abstaining, to strengthen the arms embargo on Sudan and impose a travel ban on those considered responsible for the killings in Darfur. It would freeze the overseas assets of such people. The UN also released new figures which showed that more than 180,000 people had died of hunger and disease over the preceding 18 months in the Darfur conflict, an average of 10,000 a month. A mini-African summit was held in Tripoli, Libya, over 16–17 May at which it was agreed that the AU peacekeeping mission required assistance from the North Atlantic Treaty Organization (NATO) and the European Union (EU). The meeting rejected any foreign interference in Darfur, which it argued should be dealt with in an African context, but was prepared to ask for logistical support in the form of transport, equipment, and communications, which could most readily be supplied by either NATO or the EU. As a result, on 18 May, NATO ambassadors in Brussels approved a formal AU request for assistance. At the same time, NATO insisted that the AU would be "principally responsible" for the Darfur operation. NATO would not put troops on the ground but would help with planning, as well as logistics. At this time the AU had 2,600 troops in Darfur; it had agreed to increase the number to 8,000. On 26 May, donor countries agreed to $200 million to assist the AU operation. On 6 June, the chief prosecutor of the International Criminal Court (ICC), Luis Moreno Ocampo, announced that he would open an investigation into alleged war crimes in Darfur. The Sudan government objected to the timing of the announcement and claimed that it would make rebels "adopt stubborn stances." An international commission of inquiry, established in October 2004 by UN Secretary-General **Kofi Annan** to determine whether or not acts of genocide had occurred in Darfur, had reported (February 2005) that, while widespread crimes in Darfur did not constitute genocide, there was reason to believe that crimes against humanity and war crimes had been committed, hence the ICC investigation.

On 5 July, the government and two rebel groups—JEM and SLM/A—ended their latest round of talks in Abuja, **Nigeria**, by signing a "declaration of principles" that included provisions for the return of internally displaced people and encouraged "reconciliation between various resident groups" in Darfur. Further talks were scheduled for August. On 18 July, Khalil Ibrahim Mohammed, the chairman of JEM, and Minni Arcua Minnawi, the secretary general of SLM/A, signed a peace treaty in Tripoli whose aim was the cessation of hostilities and the improvement of relations between the two groups. On 21 July, while on a visit to Sudan, U.S. Secretary of State Condoleezza Rice stated that the Sudanese government had a "credibility problem with the international community" over Darfur. During October, rebels in western Darfur kidnapped 38 AU peacekeepers near Tine on the Chad border. They were abducted by a breakaway faction of JEM. At the same time, SLM/A killed four Nigerian AU soldiers and two civilian contractors. These attacks led to fears for the safety of the (by then) 6,000 AU peacekeepers. Later that month, the Janjawid militia attacked a government police station in Geneina close to the Chad border. By this time the conflict had become more confused and chaotic. In December, Human Rights Watch issued a report in which it claimed that since July 2003 Sudanese government forces and the Janjawid militia had committed crimes against humanity and war crimes "on a massive scale" during counter-insurgency operations in Darfur. It alleged that the government "at the highest levels" was responsible for abuses in Darfur. There was an angry response in Khartoum. A UN Security Council Resolution 1651 (2005) of 21 December urged the Sudan government and the Darfur rebels then taking part in peace talks in Abuja "to reach without further delay an agreement that will establish a basis for peace, reconciliation, stability and Justice."

2006

It was inevitable that the war in Darfur would have repercussions across the border in Chad where so many refugees had fled, and in January, tensions between Sudan and Chad rose sharply when Chad accused Sudan of supporting the rebel movement, United Front for Democratic Change, that was trying to oust President **Idriss Déby**. On 13 January, the Khartoum government rejected a suggestion put forward by UN Secretary-General Kofi Annan that U.S. and EU troops be sent to Darfur to assist the AU peacekeeping mission. On 20 January, JEM and SLM/A announced that they had agreed to unite as the Allied Revolutionary Forces of Western Sudan. This followed their unity agreement of July 2005 in Tripoli. Darfur was a major topic on the agenda of the AU meeting in Khartoum over 23–24 January. A number of countries, uneasy at the role of the Sudan government in Darfur, worked to block Sudan's campaign to become the next chair of the AU.

A report of 6 February in the British newspaper, *The Guardian*, suggested that Darfur was slipping back into major violence and that as many as 70,000 people had fled the displacement camps. The AU Mission in Sudan blamed the SLM/A for attacking the government-held towns of Shearia and Golo; this had led the Janjawid to attack the refugee camps in reprisal. On 30 April, the Sudanese government announced that it had accepted an AU peace plan for Darfur. However, this was promptly rejected by JEM and SLM/A. The AU proposal would have disarmed the Janjawid and the rebel groups; declared Darfur a transitional region; promised a referendum on further autonomy in 2010; and offered an annual $200 million subsidy to the region. By May, there were increasing signs that the continuing violence and movement of people in Darfur and across the border into Chad was beginning to destabilize the latter country. A peace agreement signed in Abuja in early May was assisted when the United States and **Great Britain** sent senior envoys to support the AU sponsored deal. The agreement included the following provisions: a cease-fire; disarmament of the Janjawid and the Darfur rebels; the rebel factions to have majorities in the three Darfur state legislatures; the integration of rebel forces into the national army; a protection force for civilians; a reconstruction and development fund; provisions to compensate war victims. By the end of May, there was little sign that the peace agreement would stick, for neither the main faction of the SLM/A nor JEM had signed, while the Janjawid militia were spreading their raids ever farther into Chad. Thus, by mid-2006, despite peace agreements, AU efforts, and international pressures by the UN, the U.S., and Britain, there was much continuing violence and little indication that either the Sudan government or the various Darfur factions were seriously trying to implement a peace.

DÉBY, IDRISS (1956–). The man who ousted **Hissène Habré** as **Chad**'s leader in a coup on 4 December 1990, Idriss Déby reaped the benefits of the peace settlement with Libya, although the conclusion of the war had been Habré's achievement. Born in 1956 in eastern Chad, Déby joined the army in 1970, passed through the N'Djamena officer cadet school in 1975, and then qualified as a pilot in France in 1976. In 1978, he threw in his lot with Habré and created an alliance between his own tribe, the Zaghawa, and Habré's tribe, the Daza. He became chief of staff of the **Forces Armées du Nord** (FAN)/Armed Forces of the North and led the campaign that restored Habré to power in 1982 when he led the FAN forces into N'Djamena on 2 June of that year. He then took control of southern Chad. In mid-1983, Déby repulsed the forces of **Goukouni Oueddei**. However, by that time he was becoming too popular and powerful for Habré, who decided to get him out of the way by sending him on a higher officers education training course in Paris.

When he returned to Chad, Habré made him his military adviser. As Habré entrenched his power during 1988, he spread offices and positions among his own Daza tribe and so became less dependent upon Déby and the Zaghawa; Déby saw his influence declining, but failed to create a government power base of his own. On 1 April 1989, Déby was accused of plotting against Habré; with his loyal troops he fought his way clear of N'Djamena and retreated to **Sudan** and exile across the border in **Darfur** Province. His colleague Hassan

Djamous was captured and killed. Déby soon visited Lagos, where he accused Habré's government of tribalism, extortion, and injustice. He then went to Libya to brief **Muammar Gaddafi** on Habré's plans and troop dispositions. With encouragement from the Libyan leader, Déby then created his Mouvement Patriotique du Salut (MPS)/ Patriotic Salvation Movement and made an alliance with the Front du Salut Nationale.

In March 1990, Déby's forces engaged with Habré's troops inside Chad in a number of fierce battles. Then in November 1990, with Libyan **aid**, Déby crossed the border into Chad with his full force and again engaged Habré's forces; he took only two weeks to reach N'Djamena and Habré, whose forces had collapsed and fled the country. On 4 December 1990, Déby became head of state. He established an Executive Committee, which was dominated by his MPS. He quickly managed to persuade other politicians who had fled to accept him as head of state. Déby then detached himself from dependence upon Libya and became the political beneficiary of the Chad–Libyan agreements, which Habré had recently secured. Déby was still in power in 2006 when he faced an increasingly serious threat internally from an opposition movement, the Front Uni pour le Changement (FUC)/United Front for Change, and externally from the presence of **refugees** from Darfur and support for the president's opponents that was provided by the Janjawid from **Sudan**.

DE GAULLE, CHARLES (1890–1970). The French statesman Charles de Gaulle first pursued a military career which culminated in his leadership of the Free French during World War II. He then headed two successive provisional governments in **France** immediately after the liberation, but resigned in 1946 and from that date until 1958 was in opposition. In May 1958, the insurrection in **Algeria** had become so serious and emotive that it threatened to spark off a civil war in France itself. Many Frenchmen looked to de Gaulle as a bastion against subversion and disorder and hoped that if he came to power he would resolve the Algeria problem. On 13 May, thousands of French *colons* (settlers) in Algeria, who were fighting a bitter rear-guard action to prevent the Algerian nationalists from achieving independence, sacked the offices of the governor general and called for the integration of Algeria with France; they supported a return to political power in France of de Gaulle on the (mistaken) assumption that he would uphold their struggle and keep the **Front de Libéra-tion Nationale** (FLN)/National Liberation Front from winning independence for Algeria. The French army in Algeria tacitly approved of these actions. Many Muslims mixed with Europeans during these demonstrations hoping that a solution was in sight.

After careful calculations and a number of statements, notable principally for their ambivalence, de Gaulle became prime minister. On 4 June he visited Algiers to scenes of enthusiasm, but he was careful to give no hint as to his intentions. In October 1958, de Gaulle instituted widespread reforms on behalf of the indigenous Algerian population who were granted the full rights of French citizens. On 30 October at Constantine, he announced a social-political program to help the Muslim population: this included the provision of adequate schools and medical services, the creation of employment, and opening of entrance to the higher ranks of the public service to Muslims. The *colons* now became restless as de Gaulle gave no indication that he would integrate Algeria with France.

Meanwhile, de Gaulle had been given a mandate to reform the French constitution and on the basis of the new constitution, which he enacted, he was elected president of the Fifth Republic on 21 December 1958. In September 1959, de Gaulle declared that the Algerian people had the right to determine their future; in other words, though he wanted close French–Algerian relations, he was prepared to resolve the crisis by granting independence to Algeria. As it became clear to the French community in Algeria that de Gaulle was going to give the country independence on FLN-Muslim terms rather than integrate it with France, settler opposition turned to extremes.

There was a settler uprising against the French government on 24 January 1960, but this collapsed after nine days for want of military support. A more dangerous uprising took place early in 1961, in this case, supported by four leading French army generals two of whom, **Raoul Salan** and Maurice Challe, had served as commanders in chief in Algeria. De Gaulle was unmoved by the protests, the bulk of the army remained loyal, and after three days the uprising collapsed. De Gaulle proceeded to negotiate with the FLN to resolve the civil war in Algeria, which became independent in June 1962, while the vast majority of the one million *colons* quit Algeria and returned to France.

DE KLERK, FREDERIK WILLEM (1936–). The white compromise politician who played a significant role in bringing apartheid to an end, F. W. de Klerk was the last president of **South Africa** under the system of white minority rule. In the 1980s, he was seen as a hardline Afrikaner opponent of any concessions to the black majority and the obvious candidate to succeed President P. W. Botha and safeguard white interests. He was born in Johannesburg on 18 March 1936, and was brought up on National Party (NP) politics in the Transvaal. He practiced as a lawyer in Vereeniging from 1961 to 1972, was chairman of the local NP divisional council, and became Vereeniging's member of Parliament. After holding the post of president of the Senate (to 1976), de Klerk was given a number of ministerial posts—Posts and Telecommunications, Sport and Recreation, Home Affairs, Social Welfare and Pensions, Mines, Environmental Planning, Energy, and Education. In 1985, he led the hardliners in the Cabinet who opposed granting concessions when Botha was preparing to give his so-called Rubicon speech that August. In 1988, he denounced the head of the South African Rugby Board, Dr. Danie Craven, for meeting with the **African National Congress** (ANC)—which he described as a "terrorist" organization—in Harare. In February 1989, following Botha's stroke, he was elected leader of the NP. De Klerk's relations with Botha plummeted through 1989 and, when he proposed to visit President **Kenneth Kaunda** in Zambia, Botha in a rage resigned.

De Klerk succeeded him as president and was sworn in on 15 August. After a general election, de Klerk was unanimously elected president by Parliament on 14 September 1989. At that point he said he was committed to change but did not explain what he intended. His first important move toward change was to release seven leading members of the ANC, including Walter Sisulu. Then, in a speech he delivered on 2 February 1990, de Klerk unbanned the ANC and 32 other banned political organizations and a week later released **Nelson Mandela** unconditionally. In the succeeding four years he presided over the transitional period, which ended with the elections of April 1994 that saw Mandela come to power as South Africa's first black president. It is unlikely that de Klerk foresaw what would happen. When he unbanned the ANC and the other political parties, he opened a Pandora's box; he certainly had not estimated correctly the strength of support that existed for the ANC and probably thought he could remain in power by playing off the ANC against the Inkatha Freedom Party, the different Homelands, and the Pan-Africanist Congress. De Klerk became second vice-president in Mandela's interim government of May 1994. In May 1996, he took the NP out of the government to lead the opposition, but in August 1997, as the NP appeared on the verge of splitting between its left and right wings, he resigned the leadership of the party.

DEMOCRATIC FRONT FOR THE SALVATION OF SOMALIA (DFSS). The Democratic Front for the Salvation of Somalia was formed during September/October 1981 by three Somali dissident groups then stationed in **Ethiopia**. On 27 October the DFSS claimed it had achieved major victories against the regime of **Siad Barre**. The DFSS said its aim was to bring an end to the Barre regime and establish a democratic system under a new constitution; it also wanted to remove U.S. bases from **Somalia** and pursue a non-aligned policy. In October 1982, the DFSS formed a joint military command with the **Somali National Movement** (SNM).

The first Congress of the DFSS was held in February/March 1983; it reelected Colonel Ahmed Abdullah Yusuf as chairman. That February, however, the Somali government claimed that 500 members of the DFSS had surrendered following a government amnesty, although this was denied by the DFSS. Clashes between the DFSS and government forces occurred on varying scales during the years 1982–1987, often along the Ethiopian border region and with Ethiopian support. The DFSS suffered from a good deal of dissension during the 1980s; the rivalry stemmed from differences between members of the three founding organizations. Again, according to the Somali government, a further 200 members of the DFSS defected in 1984 in protest at Yusuf's leadership. In October 1985, Yusuf and a number of his supporters were detained in Ethiopia after a shooting incident, although the real reason was almost certainly that Yusuf had offended the Ethiopians by demanding a reduction of their involvement in DFSS affairs. In March 1986, the DFSS elected Dr. Hassan Haji Ali Mireh as its leader to replace Yusuf.

Although the DFSS was instrumental in the general growth of dissent in Somalia during the 1980s, after its coup in hijacking a Somali

Airways plane to Addis Ababa in 1985, its activities died off and it became an ineffective force in the growing Somali struggle that would soon erupt into full-scale civil war.

DIAMONDS. At a conference of Group of Eight (G-8) foreign ministers held in Berlin during December 1999, British Foreign Secretary Robin Cook proposed a mechanism to curtail the sale of stolen diamonds from such countries as **Angola** and **Democratic Republic of Congo** (DRC) that provided finances to sustain violent conflicts. At the same time De Beers, the world's largest diamond company, announced that it was to introduce measures to prevent the sale of illegal diamonds. During 2001 the world became familiar with the term "blood diamonds" that were used to finance Africa's wars. A voluntary monitoring mechanism to check for "conflict diamonds" was approved on 30 October 2003 by all the participants in the "Kimberley" process that had been established earlier in the year with **United Nations** backing to curb the illicit diamond trade. A plenary session of the Kimberley process was held in Sun City, **South Africa**, and included representatives of 55 countries, the diamond industry, and non-governmental organizations (NGOs). They agreed on a system of "visits" to countries that volunteered to prove their compliance with the Kimberley rules. The agreement was a compromise, as opposed to the original proposal advanced by South Africa, that regular independent monitoring missions should be sent to all diamond producing countries every three years. The two Congos—DRC and Congo Brazzaville—which were at the center of "conflict diamond" allegations, volunteered to host review commissions before the end of the year.

On 9 July 2004, Tim Martin, the Canadian chairman of the Kimberley process, announced that **Republic of Congo (Brazzaville)** had been expelled from the process. This followed the report of a mission that visited the country in June and claimed that the government was not complying with the requirements of the process. The Congo authorities were "unable to account for a massive discrepancy between the scale of rough diamond exports and the absence of any reported production or imports." The Congo review mission also said that large quantities of diamonds—including conflict diamonds—were finding their way from the Congo into the legitimate market. In late October

2004, members of the Kimberley process met in Gatineau, Canada. They noted that considerable progress had been made during the year. In particular, the process had come to encompass the overwhelming majority of the production and trade in rough diamonds. A production report for 2003 showed $8.5 billion in rough diamonds and the issue of 47,598 certificates for more than $20 billion worth of trade. The meeting also noted that eight participant countries had received review visits and that another seven would do so before the end of the year. Russia then took over the chair from Canada. The next meeting of the Kimberley process took place in Moscow during November 2005 when 36 countries, the European Union (EU), and the World Diamond Council were present. The final communiqué of the meeting noted "with great concern" the ongoing illicit production of diamonds in the northern, rebel-controlled regions of **Côte d'Ivoire**, which posed a challenge to the Kimberley Process Certification Scheme (KPCS). The illegal production in the north of Côte d'Ivoire was estimated at 300,000 carats a year and was highly organized. The meeting agreed to a series of measures to prevent the introduction of conflict diamonds from Côte d'Ivoire into the legitimate trade. It was also agreed to carry out a detailed assessment of the volume of rough diamonds produced and exported from Côte d'Ivoire, and members were asked to take action against any of their nationals or companies involved in illicit diamond trade or production in Côte d'Ivoire.

Despite the work of the Kimberley process, it was clear early in 2006 that diamonds were still funding civil wars in Africa as they had done so often in the past. During the 1990s, warlords and rebel groups in countries such as Angola, DRC, **Liberia**, and **Sierra Leone** received billions of dollars from the sale of illicit diamonds, which were used to purchase arms. The trade is widespread in Africa and the Kimberley process appears to have had little more than a superficial impact upon it. Moreover, according to Global Witness international terrorist groups, including al-Qaida, have infiltrated diamond-trading networks to raise funds and they launder huge amounts of money. In recent years, the countries in Africa most associated with the illicit diamond trade are Angola, Côte d'Ivoire, Sierra Leone, and Liberia. In the case of Angola, through most of its long civil war, **Jonas Savimbi** controlled North and South Luanda, the two richest diamond producing provinces, and diamond production gave him an annual revenue of $500 million, which he spent on arms and to keep his troops in the field. In Côte d'Ivoire, the illegal diamond trade was responsible for the upsurge in violence during 2005, since most of the diamond mines are outside the government's control. The UN placed sanctions on Côte d'Ivoire's diamond trade in December 2005. During the brutal civil war in Sierra Leone through the 1990s, the rebel Revolutionary United Front (RUF) largely funded itself by means of the illegal diamond trade and at the height of the war RUF was selling $200 million of illegal diamonds a year. Liberia's diamond trade was still under UN sanctions in 2006 because of fears that neighboring countries were smuggling illegal diamonds into Liberia to be sold on the legitimate markets. The post-civil war government of **Charles Taylor** was heavily involved in the illicit trade.

DOE, SAMUEL (1951–90). The decade of the 1980s, when President Doe ruled, **Liberia** made the civil war of the early 1990s inevitable. Doe came to power by a bloody coup and ruled brutally, steadily creating enemies for himself in the process. From the Krahn tribe, he was born on 6 May 1951; in 1969, he enlisted as a soldier. He was enrolled in the Ministry of Defense Radio Communications School in Monrovia and completed his training in 1971. In 1979, Doe was given training at a camp run by U.S. Special Forces and was then made a master sergeant. On 12 April 1980, he led 17 soldiers into the executive mansion in Monrovia to kill the incumbent president of Liberia, William R. Tolbert, as well as some 30 officials and guards.

Doe then made himself commander in chief and chairman of the People's Redemption Council. He promised he would return the country to civilian rule. His summary execution in public of 13 of Tolbert's senior ministers or associates set the tone of brutality that would mark his subsequent behavior in power. Doe held elections in 1985, though these were widely regarded as rigged; even so, he only narrowly got himself elected president. He became increasingly unpopular thereafter and relied upon oppression and brutality to maintain his position.

By 1989 two rebel leaders, **Charles Taylor** and **Prince Yormie Johnson**, had gathered numbers of dissident troops around them and began military attacks against the regime, but though their actions came under the heading of civil war, they rapidly degenerated into massacres of **women and children** and unnecessarily brutal violence. Even so, by mid-1990 the rebels controlled the greater part of Monrovia, forcing Doe to barricade himself in the executive mansion with a bodyguard of loyal Krahn soldiers. On 9 September 1990, Doe, accompanied by 60 soldiers, left the executive mansion to visit the headquarters of the **Economic Community of West African States** (ECOWAS) military monitoring group, **ECOWAS Monitoring Group** (ECOMOG), to negotiate his own escape from Liberia but he was captured by Johnson's men, tortured, and then killed on 10 September.

DOS SANTOS, JOSE EDUARDO (1942–). Born on 28 August 1942, Jose Eduardo dos Santos became president of **Angola** on the death from cancer of **Agostinho Neto**. Following the charismatic Neto, dos Santos was at first constrained by the situation in which Angola was then trapped, both by civil war and the activities of its neighbors. Only slowly was he able to assert himself and move the country away from Marxism to a putative deal with the **União Nacional para a Independência Total de Angola** (UNITA)/National Union for the Total Independence of Angola.

Dos Santos had joined the **Movimento Popular para a Libertação de Angola** (MPLA)/Popular Movement for the Liberation of Angola at age 19, in 1961, at the beginning of the armed struggle. In 1963, he became the MPLA representative in the Republic of **Congo** (Brazzaville). He visited the **Union of Soviet Socialist Republics** (USSR) for further studies and married a Russian woman. He graduated in petrochemical engineering and oil at Baku University and then (1969–70) in military telecommunications. Back in Angola, dos Santos again took part in the guerrilla fighting, from 1970 to 1974, and in the latter year he was elected to the Central Committee of the Politbureau, placed fifth. He became foreign minister in the 1975 independence government and was instrumental in persuading Zambia to abandon its pro-UNITA policy in 1976. From 1975 to 1978 he was appointed deputy prime minister. Under the political reorganization of 1978, dos Santos became minister of planning and head of the National Planning Commission. Before his death in Moscow on 10 September 1979, Neto appointed dos Santos his deputy and he was unanimously confirmed as Neto's successor by the Central Committee to become president of Angola on 21 September 1979. He pledged to continue Neto's policies.

Angola then faced huge problems: a shattered economy and a civil war against UNITA, which was assisted by **South Africa**. Dos Santos wanted to improve relations with the West while, at the same time, trying to end U.S. and South African support for UNITA and gradually he did improve Angola's image in the West, though not with the **United States**. Slowly the Angolan government came to realize that a settlement could only be achieved if the concept of **linkage** was accepted. By 1988 dos Santos found that both Washington and Pretoria were prepared to enter into an agreement and in order to secure this he began, from mid-1989, to drop party officials who were seen to be too Marxist in Washington. He was assisted in his changing policy by the thaw in U.S.–Soviet relations that accompanied the end of the **Cold War** and the military situation brought about by the stalemate at **Cuito Cuanavale**, which had halted the South African forces supporting UNITA.

The agreement of 22 December 1988, signed in New York, paved the way for an end to the civil war and the gradual introduction of democracy in Angola. At a meeting in **Zaire** at **Mobuto Sese Seko**'s retreat at Gbadolite, dos Santos "shook hands" with UNITA's **Jonas Savimbi**. On 20 March 1991, as part of the peace process, dos Santos promised multiparty democracy for Angola; an agreement was signed in Lisbon on 31 May 1991, and elections were held throughout Angola in September 1992. Although Savimbi refused to accept the election result and returned to the bush to carry on the civil war for another year, which saw very high casualties, this time around dos Santos had near universal international support, while Savimbi finally lost the backing of the United States. A second precarious peace process got under way at the end of 1994, but real peace was only achieved after the death of Savimbi in 2002. In 2005 dos Santos had been president of Angola for a quarter of a century.

– E –

ECONOMIC COMMUNITY MONITORING GROUP (ECOMOG). ECOMOG is the military monitoring group established by the **Economic Community of West African States** (ECOWAS) in 1990 to mount a peacekeeping mission to bring the civil war in **Liberia** under control. The original states providing troops for ECOMOG, under the command of a Ghanaian, General Arnold Quainoo, were **Nigeria**, Ghana, The Gambia, **Sierra Leone**, and Guinea. Nigeria was always to have the largest force of troops on the ground; later, other countries also provided contingents of troops. The ECOMOG force remained in Liberia until the end of the civil war saw the election as president of **Charles Taylor**, one of the principal contenders for power (*see* LIBERIA). ECOMOG was also to attempt a peacekeeping role in Sierra Leone following the development of a civil war in that country from 1992 onward, so that during the 1990s ECOWAS became involved in peacekeeping in two of its member states.

Like all peacekeeping forces, ECOMOG came in for a range of criticisms—being partisan, using too much force, not using enough force, doing too much or too little. Nonetheless, it undoubtedly helped, first to stabilize the situation in Liberia and then to assist the final peace process. More important, for Africa, ECOMOG established a principle of joint military intervention on a regional basis to curtail civil war. What also became apparent as a result of this exercise was the need for external assistance, at least with finance: African states may have the military capacity to carry out a policing operation, but they require logistical support to transport their forces to the operational area and financial assistance to meet the costs. In October 1995 ECOWAS chiefs of staff met in Monrovia to discuss the role of ECOMOG following an appeal by Ghana's President Jerry Rawlings for West African States to contribute to the peace force. Burkina Faso, **Côte d'Ivoire**, Ghana, Nigeria, and Togo pledged to contribute more troops, while the other ECOWAS member countries committed themselves to provide further assistance for the peace process.

In the case of Sierra Leone ECOMOG forces, mainly Nigerian, were able to oust the military regime that had seized power in May 1997, in February 1998, although only in October of that year could they claim major successes against the rebels. The civil war took an ugly turn at the beginning of 1999 when the Revolutionary United Front (RUF) and the Armed Forces Revolutionary Council (AFRC) launched a massive attack upon Freetown. ECOMOG drove them out after two weeks of fighting when 3,000 civilians were killed. Only at the end of 2000 were the ECOMOG forces in Sierra Leone phased out when a **United Nations** force of 13,000 peacekeepers (the largest such UN force in the world at that time) took over.

In Liberia, following Charles Taylor's election victory of 1997, it became possible at the end of the year for ECOMOG to reduce its force in the country though still retaining some troops there, since it appeared that its peacekeeping mission had been accomplished. During 1998, relations between Taylor and ECOMOG were increasingly strained, not least because Taylor was always antagonistic to the Nigerians, and there were a number of confrontations between government and ECOMOG forces. However, by October 1999 the situation in Liberia appeared sufficiently stable that the remainder of the ECOMOG force was withdrawn after ten years of peacekeeping and monitoring. ECOMOG's involvement in these two countries through the 1990s was often controversial; at the same time, the organization was able to improve its peacekeeping skills so that it had come to be regarded as a principal peacekeeping instrument in Africa.

ECONOMIC COMMUNITY OF WEST AFRICAN STATES (ECOWAS). The Economic Community of West African States was established by treaty in Lagos during May 1975; originally it comprised 15 countries: Benin, Burkina Faso, **Côte d'Ivoire**, The Gambia, Ghana, Guinea, Guinea-Bissau, **Liberia**, Mali, Mauritania, Niger, **Nigeria**, Senegal, **Sierra Leone**, and Togo. Cape Verde became the 16th member in 1977. The object of the treaty was to liberalize trade between members and work to create a full customs union by 1990. ECOWAS proceeded slowly and cautiously, aware of the many differences between its constituent members. Nigeria, with its oil wealth and huge population, was, inevitably, the dominant member. When Liberia collapsed into civil war (1989/90), it was soon apparent that outside powers with interests in the country—principally the **United States** and **Great Britain**—did not wish to intervene except to safeguard and remove their nationals. It was equally clear that neither the **Organization of African Unity** (OAU) nor the **United Nations** then had the capacity to intervene. The deteriorating situation in Liberia offered Nigeria (the regional power) and ECOWAS the opportunity to mount a peacekeeping initiative. An ECOWAS peacekeeping role in Liberia at this time was all the more important—and welcome—because the United Nations, especially after the formal end of the **Cold War**, was then reappraising its own peacekeeping capabilities and returning to an earlier view that, where possible, peacekeeping should be carried out by those powers in the region most affected and concerned with any local war.

The ECOWAS initiative in Liberia was an appropriate response to the local situation. In 1990, therefore, ECOWAS organized its own peacekeeping force, the **Economic Community Monitoring Group** (ECOMOG), which originally consisted of military contingents from Nigeria, Ghana, The Gambia, Sierra Leone and Guinea. This ECOWAS intervention received the backing of the OAU and the United Nations and obtained limited financial assistance from the United States. ECOWAS continued to act as a peace broker during 1995/1996 when the worst of the fighting in Liberia was over and slow moves toward peace were under way. The ECOWAS intervention in Liberia had an importance beyond that civil war, since it represented an African attempt to deal with civil war on a regional basis and, hopefully, set a precedent for the future. ECOWAS was also to intervene in the civil war in Sierra Leone that began in 1992, thus establishing the expectation that it would assume a peacekeeping role in the region.

ERITREA. Full details of the war for independence waged against Ethiopia from 1962 to 1991 are treated in the section on Ethiopia since during those years Eritrea was regarded by the international community as part of the larger state.

Eritrea, as a separate entity from **Ethiopia**, became an Italian colony during the Scramble for Africa (1890). At the Battle of Adowa in 1896, the Italians were defeated by the Ethiopian emperor, Menelik, and though Italy was obliged to recognize the independence of Ethiopia, the emperor in his turn had to accept the fact that Eritrea, which Ethiopia had hoped to incorporate into its expanding empire, had instead become an Italian colony. British troops invaded Italian Eritrea during World War II, and following the peace of 1945, it was placed under **United Nations** administration. In 1952 the United Nations decided that Eritrea should be federated with Ethiopia and this took place on 11 September of that year. The Eritreans soon came to resent Ethiopian domination of the federation and during the 1960s began a rebellion against the government in Addis Ababa, which lasted for 30 years. At first this was somewhat spasmodic, but gradually it developed momentum and became part of the wider civil and revolutionary wars that engulfed Ethiopia from the early 1960s until the beginning of the 1990s.

Eritrea finally achieved its independence on 24 May 1993. After 30 years of warfare, it was the successful seizure of Asmara (the main city of Eritrea) by the **Eritrean People's Liberation Front** (EPLF) in May 1991 that made independence possible. A referendum was conducted on 23–25 April 1993: 1,018,000 voters registered for the referendum and of these 800,000 were in Eritrea, 150,000 in **Sudan**, 40,000 in Ethiopia, and 28,000 in the **United States**. A total of 98.2 percent of those eligible to vote did so and 99.8 percent voted for independence. The referendum was monitored by observers from the United Nations, the **Organization of African Unity** (OAU), and various countries. The provisional government (established in 1991) was then replaced by a transitional government that remained in office for four years: in effect, this government was composed of the EPLF leadership. The Central Committee of the EPLF (with additions) became a National Assembly and the EPLF leader, **Issayas Afewerke**, became president of Eritrea. Eritrean independence was recognized by Ethiopia and other countries; it was the first new African country to achieve independent status since **Namibia** in 1990. At the June 1993 OAU summit, Afewerke criticized the organization for having upheld Ethiopia's right to control Eritrea during the previous 30 years. *See also* ERITREAN LIBERATION FRONT (ELF); ERITREAN LIBERATION FRONT-POPULAR LIBERATION FORCES (ELF-PLF).

ERITREA–ETHIOPIA BORDER WAR, 1998–2000. Although this is a war between two independent states, it has many of the attributes of a civil war: Eritrea had been incorporated into Ethiopia at the beginning of the 1960s and had fought a 30-year war to achieve its independence in 1993, while its people and those of Ethiopia were closely related and had fought as allies in the last stages of the war against the regime of **Mariam Mengistu**. Nonetheless, the border dispute between Eritrea and Ethiopia that flared up in May 1998 became the prelude to a devastating two-year war between the two countries. The apparent good relations that had existed since the fall of Mengistu and the achievement of independence by Eritrea had cloaked underlying differences that were brought to the surface by the border dispute. Ethiopia, despite the change of regime in 1991 and its acceptance of Eritrean independence, may well have harbored resentments, both at its loss of power when it no longer controlled Eritrea and because an independent Eritrea deprived it of direct access to the Red Sea and effectively made it a landlocked country. On the other side, the border conflict brought to the fore long-standing Eritrean resentments of former Ethiopian imperialism at its expense.

On 6 May 1998, several Eritrean soldiers were killed near Badme to the northwest of the Tigray region of Ethiopia. In retaliation for these deaths, Eritrean forces seized an area previously administered by Ethiopia, but claimed by Eritrea. Then, over the following months, a series of clashes took place at a number of disputed border points that resulted in hundreds of casualties on both sides. Early in June Ethiopian aircraft bombed Asmara airport. In retaliation, Eritrean planes bombed the Ethiopian towns of Makelle and Adigrat. Serious border fighting came to an end in mid-June, although artillery exchanges continued throughout the year. More ominous for the future, both sides began to build up their military forces, purchasing arms principally from Eastern European countries and the People's Republic of China and both carried on propaganda campaigns against each other. Between June and December, Ethiopia rounded up Eritreans and expelled them to Eritrea and by the end of the year Eritrea claimed that some 40,000 of its people or Ethiopians of Eritrean origin had been deported. In response, Ethiopia claimed that a similar number of Ethiopians had been expelled from Eritrea. And both sides claimed that their nationals had been ill-treated. There were immediate economic consequences for both countries, apart from those associated with increased military expenditure. Thus, Ethiopia had to divert its export/import trade to Djibouti and cross-border trade between the two countries ceased. Prior to the war and possibly acting as contributory causes were the Ethiopian resentment at the high cost of using Assab, the Eritrean port on the Red Sea, and Eritrean anger, following its launch in 1997 of its new currency, the nafka, at the Ethiopian insistence that all trade transactions should be conducted in dollars.

Although both countries claimed to be committed to peace, efforts at mediation by outsiders made little headway. The **Organization of African Unity** (OAU) advanced 11 peace proposals in November, but Eritrea rejected any that called upon it to withdraw from territory it had occupied after 6 May or the return of Ethiopian administration to Badme. Earlier, U.S./Rwandan attempts at mediation had made no progress. Hardliners appeared to be in the ascendant in both countries and the tough stand taken by Ethiopia's prime minister, **Meles Zenawi**, obviously strengthened his political standing. The economy of Eritrea was seriously affected by the war: the port of Assab had come to a virtual standstill while the trade gap widened as a consequence of increased military spending. Remittances from overseas Eritreans became the government's greatest source of income.

1999

A period of eight months "quiet" along the border was broken in February 1999 when Ethiopia launched an attack to retake Badme. This was successful and Ethiopian troops penetrated 30 kilometers into Eritrea. However, a similar attempt to take Zalembessa was a disaster as was an Eritrean attempt to retake Badme at the end of March. In May and June, Eritrea made two more attempts to retake Badme but both were repulsed. These attacks and counter-attacks led to heavy casualties on both sides, an estimated 30,000 each. There were only minor military engagements across the border for the remainder of the year while Ethiopian air attacks upon Assab and Massawa or the Sawa national service center caused little damage.

Mediation efforts during these months failed to produce a cease-fire, although both combatants agreed on an OAU peace framework that included military observers and a new demarcation of the border under UN supervision. Both sides would have to re-deploy their forces outside the occupied areas, according to the status quo prior to 6 May 1999. While the two countries had accepted the next stage in the peace process in July, they had yet to agree on the "modalities of implementation." However, distrust between the two continued and no agreement had been reached by the end of the year. In fact, the conflict widened during 1999, with both sides encouraging third parties to become involved. Thus, Eritrea supported the armed opposition to the Djibouti government and the Front for the Restoration of Unity and Democracy (FRUD) in its attacks upon the railway line to Ethiopia in August and November, thus further damaging the Ethiopian economy. At the same time, Eritrea provided arms and training for the Oromo Liberation Front (OLF) and sent 1,500 fighters into southern Ethiopia with the assistance of the Somali warlord Hussein Aydid. He visited Asmara in February. By August, however, Ethiopia claimed to have killed or captured 1,100 OLF fighters. In October Aydid changed sides and visited Ethiopia. Subsequently, OLF leaders were deported to Eritrea and its office in Mogadishu was closed. In the meantime, Ethiopia had worked with the **Sudan** government to support Eritrean opposition groups in exile. By December 1999, Ethiopia had deported an estimated 65,000 Eritreans while about 22,000 Ethiopians had been expelled the other way.

In September the World Bank announced a moratorium on projects for both countries because of their rising military expenditure. By the end of 1999, an estimated 300,000 people on each side had been displaced by the fighting. Eritrea's, in any case, small and fragile economy had deteriorated through 1999. There were 250,000 mobilized soldiers, heavy military spending, and little activity at the country's ports, especially Assab, which was normally the principal outlet for Ethiopia.

2000: A Fragile Peace

During the first four months of 2000 there was hardly any fighting on the disputed border. Both sides said they accepted the peace framework that had been negotiated by the OAU, although they still disagreed over how it should be implemented. In May, when U.S./ Rwandan-sponsored talks had broken down, and in defiance of a **United Nations** Security Council arms embargo, Ethiopia launched a major offensive and retook Zalembessa and Bada. In addition, Ethiopian troops pushed deep into Eritrea to seize the towns of Senafe and Barentu. Eritrea, now facing defeat, announced its withdrawal from all the areas it had seized in 1998. Subsequent international pressure finally persuaded the two countries to agree to a ceasefire on 18 June. Six months later on 12 December, a formal peace agreement was signed. Under its terms, a UN **peacekeeping** force called the UN Mission to Ethiopia and Eritrea (UNMEE) with up to 4,200 men was sent to patrol the 25-kilometer security buffer inside Eritrea and was to be deployed until the border had been demarcated. By the end of the year, half the UN force was in place, though disagreements over the security zone remained. Both sides continued to deport the nationals of the other side and both complained at the ill treatment received by their nationals and no agreement had been reached about compensation for those who had been deported. However, the repatriation of prisoners was started before the end of the year and Ethiopia began to demobilize 50,000 troops.

At best it was an uneasy peace, with both countries continuing propaganda campaigns against each other while they maintained their support for dissident groups, with Ethiopia backing the Alliance of Eritrean National Forces (AENF), which was the chief anti-government group in Eritrea, while in September 2000 Eritrea hosted a conference in Asmara of six Oromo opposition groups to the Ethiopian government. Estimates suggested that the war had cost more than 70,000 lives and though no detailed costs were available, each side was reckoned to have spent several hundred million dollars purchasing arms from Russia, China, Bulgaria, Libya, and Israel. According to the International Monetary Fund (IMF), the war had led Ethiopia sharply to reduce the amount of money spent on health and education, as well as capital funding. In Eritrea, the final Ethiopian advance had disrupted planting in the main grain producing area and, as a result, dramatically increased the number of people requiring food **aid**.

In Ethiopia during 2001, Prime Minister Meles Zenawi was accused of agreeing to a peace with Eritrea too easily and failing to capture the port of Assab, perhaps one of the underlying reasons for the war. In Eritrea, defeat led to the appearance of open opposition to the autocratic rule of President **Issayas Afewerki**. Uneasy relations between the two countries were a feature of 2002 and in February of that year there was a visit by a 15-member delegation from the UN Security Council to both countries in an effort to encourage them to accept the peace process. In April 2002 the independent Border Commission, which had been set up by the permanent Court of Arbitration in The Hague following the December 2000 peace agreement, set out its "final and binding decision" on the border which both countries were committed to accept. Each side lost and gained territory although Badme, the starting point of the conflict, was not on the Commission maps. Complaints by both sides to UNMEE were ignored. However, the release of prisoners of war continued and in November 2002, Ethiopia repatriated the final group of them. The border dispute rumbled on, thereafter, and both countries demonstrated dissatisfaction with the border ruling of 2002, although there were no renewed hostilities. Tensions between Ethiopia and Eritrea remained high into 2006, with Eritrea's President Isayas Afewerki accusing foreign powers of favoring Ethiopia, while the Eritrean government increasingly rejected the wider international community.

ERITREAN LIBERATION FRONT (ELF). The Eritrean Liberation Front (ELF) was first established in Cairo in 1958 as an Eritrean nationalist party. Its activities through the 1960s were spasmodic rather than effective, and by 1969 a split occurred between the older, more conservative members and young radicals who wanted the movement to shift to the political left. The radicals were supported by leftwing governments in Iraq, Libya, and Syria as well as the Al-Fatah Movement. In 1970 the radicals took control. At the same time, Marxist–Leninists led by Mohammed Nur broke away to form the **Eritrean People's Liberation Front** (EPLF). At that time, the ELF was operating a more systematic guerrilla war from **Sudan** against the Ethiopian government forces and administration.

At the beginning of the 1970s, the ELF forces numbered about 2,700; they worked to obtain the support of the rural population and where they came to control an area or region, they established alternative administrations to those of the Ethiopian government. The ELF divided **Eritrea** into five provinces, each to be administered by a five-man committee, which controlled security, defense, information, and political propaganda. However, in 1975, just after the fall of the Emperor **Haile Selassie**, a second split occurred in the ELF, so that the movement was not able to take advantage of the fluid situation which existed in **Ethiopia** at that time. On this occasion, the breakaway faction was led by Osman Saleh Sabhe, the founder, and his new movement now became the **Eritrean Liberation Front-Popular Liberation Forces** (ELF-PLF). The collapse of the imperial regime of Haile Selassie in Addis Ababa gave a boost to the Eritrean independence movements and led large numbers of Eritreans to join their ranks, and by 1977 the ELF had an estimated 22,000 guerrillas. This year proved to be the climax of ELF's successes; it defied the forces of the new military Dergue that ruled Ethiopia under **Haile Mariam Mengistu** and captured a number of Eritrean towns.

These successes were not to be repeated. In 1978, after it had defeated the Somalis in the **Ogaden** region, the Ethiopian army (freshly armed with Soviet weapons and equipment) turned its attention upon Eritrea and recaptured the towns recently taken by the ELF, which, by 1979, was reduced to controlling only rural areas. The ELF continued its resistance to the Ethiopian government forces until 1980, but in 1981 it was virtually destroyed by the EPLF. There had been attempts by the ELF to work with the EPLF during 1977 and 1978, followed by an agreement of March 1981 between the movements at a meeting held in Tunis, but the agreement did not work and later in 1981, fierce fighting between the ELF and EPLF broke out in Eritrea. Over the years the ELF had obtained support from **Cuba**, the People's Democratic Republic of Yemen, and the **Union of Soviet Socialist Republics** (USSR) (prior to 1975) and from Iraq, Syria, and Libya in the Arab world. When the USSR switched its support to the Dergue of Mengistu in 1975, Cuba also followed suit but, nonetheless, refused to fight against its former allies. The ELF was able to use bases in Sudan throughout the war. The ELF continued as an organization through to the mid-1980s, but its defeat by the EPLF in 1981 destroyed it as an effective liberation movement.

ERITREAN LIBERATION FRONT-POPULAR LIBERATION FORCES (ELF-PLF). The split in the ranks of the **Eritrean Liberation Front** (ELF), which occurred in 1975, gave rise to the new ELF-PLF. This was led by Osman Saleh Sabhe, the founder of the ELF, who was unhappy with the way the ELF was developing. The ELF-PLF was never very effective. It was the smallest of the factions that broke away from the ELF, and though by 1977 it had an estimated 5,000 members, it only lasted to 1980 when Sabhe entered into an alliance with another faction, the ELF-Revolutionary Council. By 1982 the ELF-PLF had become moribund.

ERITREAN PEOPLE'S LIBERATION FRONT (EPLF). Although the Eritrean People's Liberation Front (EPLF) was not the first Eritrean resistance movement to be formed, it became the most effective, and at the end of the long war, its leader formed the government of the newly independent Eritrean state. The EPLF leadership consisted of the more radical-minded members of the **Eritrean Liberation Front**

(ELF) until 1970, when they broke away from that movement to form the EPLF. During the 1970s it grew steadily in strength, sometimes quarrelling with the ELF and sometimes working in alliance with it. Periodically the members of the two movements fought each other until their climactic confrontation of 1981, from which the EPLF emerged victorious.

The two most important leaders of the EPLF were its original secretary general, Mohammed Nur, and his deputy **Issayas Afewerke**, who subsequently became the leader and then the first president of an independent **Eritrea**. The EPLF managed to dominate the rural areas of Eritrea and operated increasingly effectively in the towns as well, where it used terrorist tactics against government officials. In 1977, the EPLF captured the town of Keren, which it had earlier besieged unsuccessfully; at that time it hoped to make Keren the capital of an independent Eritrea. In 1978, when the Ethiopian government brought all its forces to bear upon Eritrea (following the end of the **Ogaden War**), the EPLF sought an alliance with the ELF, and for a time they fought together. But in the period 1978–1980, frequent agreements between the two movements were broken and it was clear that a long-term alliance was not practicable. Fierce fighting for supremacy broke out in 1981 and continued until the EPLF decisively defeated the ELF, which thereafter ceased to be an effective movement. From this time on the EPLF became the dominant Eritrean movement. In 1982 it could field 8,000 fighters. In 1987, Issayas Afewerke became the EPLF secretary general, in effect its leader. In May 1991, EPLF forces seized Asmera and then formed an interim government that ruled Eritrea until the referendum of April 1993, which was followed by full independence. The EPLF formed the government of the new state.

ETHIOPIA. The wars that ravaged Ethiopia from 1961 to 1991 were part civil and part nationalist or anti-colonial revolt, and they were further complicated by a confrontation with **Somalia** (the **Ogaden War** of 1977–78) so that it is difficult to distinguish them from each other. There were three internal wars over these years: the Eritrean war of secession; the Tigrayan revolt against the central government; and the Oromo revolt or revolts. A further complicating factor came from **Cold War** interventions: the **Union of Soviet Socialist**

Republics (USSR) and its allies supported the regime of **Haile Mariam Mengistu**, which came to power in 1975 on the overthrow of **Haile Selassie**, while **Sudan**, for its own geopolitical reasons, supported both the Eritreans and Tigrayans, though the intensity of this support varied over the years. Ethiopia, unlike most African countries, also had a history of colonial expansion under its last emperors and, apart from the brief Italian invasion and occupation by Mussolini (from 1935 to 1941), had not been colonized as had the rest of Africa. This more or less constant state of 30 years of warfare only came to an end in 1991 when Addis Ababa fell to the Ethiopian People's Revolutionary Democratic Front (EPRDF) led by **Meles Zenawi**, which led to the collapse of the Dergue and the flight of Mengistu.

Background and Beginnings

During the Scramble for Africa, Italy established a colony in Eritrea on the Red Sea coast in 1890. Later, the Italians attempted the conquest of Ethiopia but were defeated at Adowa in 1896 by Emperor Menelik II; this was the only major defeat suffered by the European colonizing powers. Under the terms of the subsequent peace between Italy and Ethiopia, Emperor Menelik II had to recognize the Italian colonization of Eritrea, even though Ethiopia saw Eritrea as potentially part of its expanding empire. Mussolini's invasion and occupation of Abyssinia (Ethiopia) in 1935/1936 only lasted until 1941, when British troops operating from East Africa liberated the country; Haile Selassie, who had been in exile in **Great Britain**, was reinstalled as Emperor of Ethiopia while Britain undertook the temporary administration of Eritrea.

After World War II, the question of Eritrea's future was passed to the newly formed **United Nations**, which eventually decided that it should be federated with Ethiopia. The federation came into being on 11 September 1952. By 1958, it had become plain that the government of Haile Selassie intended to absorb Eritrea completely into Ethiopia. In order to prevent full integration with Ethiopia, the **Eritrean Liberation Front** (ELF) was formed in Cairo (1958) under the leadership of Osman Saleh Sabhe and a 10-man revolutionary council. The ELF claimed that full integration into Ethiopia was in violation of the 1952 agreement, and a military wing, the Eritrean Liberation Army (ELA), was formed. The first shots in what became the Eritrean war of secession were fired in September 1961.

The Eritrean War of Secession

On 14 November 1962, the Eritrean Assembly—which had been "packed" for the purpose—voted for complete union with Ethiopia and the following day, the Emperor Haile Selassie abolished Eritrea's autonomous status. The ELF now moved its headquarters to Baghdad, and for the following decade was the most significant liberation group fighting against the government of Addis Ababa. The Popular Liberation Front (PLF) also emerged in the early 1960s; this was a Marxist group and like the ELF demanded independence for Eritrea. Like many other nationalist groups the ELF was plagued by internal dissensions and splits. In 1969, the younger, more militant elements accused the ELF leadership of being too conservative; they moved to the left and were supported by the radical Arab governments—Iraq, Libya, and Syria as well as Al Fatah. Although, during the 1960s, the ELF had been responsible for several aircraft hijackings, which generated a good deal of publicity for its cause, it was otherwise not very effective on the ground, and only after the young militants had taken control at the beginning of the 1970s, did the war escalate with the ELA operating across the border from bases in Sudan to conduct a series of guerrilla campaigns. The ELF then had about 2,500 guerrillas and these won the support of the rural populations amongst whom they moved and so were able to set up a series of administrative districts as alternatives to those of the government. In 1971, the Ethiopian government placed Eritrea under martial law. A second split in the ranks of the ELF occurred in 1970 when another group of Marxists under Mohammed Nur broke away to form the **Eritrean People's Liberation Front** (EPLF). Despite these breakaways, the ELF prospered during the mid-1970s, as the government of Haile Selassie collapsed and the military Dergue took control, and by 1977 had an estimated 22,000 guerrillas in the field.

Mengistu's Dergue was as determined as had been Haile Selassie to prevent Eritrean secession. In 1974 Sabhe demanded recognition of the ELF as the sole representative of the Eritrean people and called for the right to self-determination and a referendum under UN auspices and, on 23 August 1974, the Eritrean deputies resigned from the parliament in Addis Ababa, accusing the government of ignoring Eritrean affairs. The ELF also claimed, at this time, that the Ethiopian government was massacring civilians in Eritrea. In November 1974, the government sent 5,000 army reinforcements to Eritrea, while the ELF claimed that its $2 million of freshly donated weapons from Libya gave its forces military superiority over the 40,000 Ethiopian troops then stationed in Eritrea. By the end of the year, ELF forces were fighting within six miles of Asmara, the Eritrean capital. In January 1975, Radio Ethiopia called upon Eritrean communities to make contact with the guerrillas to persuade them to end their revolt; the government promised to seek a peaceful solution to the conflict. By early 1975, however, ELF forces (now numbering more than 15,000) controlled most of the Eritrean countryside, but when they engaged the Ethiopian army in a major battle outside the town of Keren, they were forced to retreat; later in the year when the revolution in Addis Ababa was at its height, ELF forces almost succeeded in taking Asmara.

At this time, the ELF and EPLF agreed to form a united front and a single military command. The EPLF, meanwhile, had built up its strength and during 1977 captured most of the Eritrean towns, including Keren, which it saw as a future capital for Eritrea, and by the end of the year the Ethiopian forces were more or less confined to four towns—Barentu, Asmara, Massawa, and Adi Caich. By 1978, the EPLF had about 12,000 guerrillas in the field. During 1978, both the ELF and the EPLF took advantage of Ethiopia's confrontation with Somalia in the Ogaden region and cooperated with each other to inflict a series of substantial defeats upon the Ethiopian armed forces. However, once the Ogaden conflict had been resolved in Ethiopia's favor, Addis Ababa was able to bring its full force to bear upon the Eritrean war and the liberation movements were thrown onto the defensive.

Cold War considerations altered the course of the conflict in 1978: the USSR, which had supported the Eritrean struggle against Haile Selassie, now put its full support behind the Marxist Dergue of Mengistu, and the Cubans, who then had 13,000 troops in Ethiopia fighting the Somalis in the Ogaden, did the same. In June 1978, after their victory over the Somalis, the Ethiopians launched a major offensive against the Eritreans with 100,000 troops to recapture most of the towns lost in 1977. By the end of 1978, the ELF had reverted to guerrilla tactics in the rural areas while the EPLF had retreated to the region round Nacfa in the north of the country. The ELF just about maintained its position through to the 1980s but in 1981, as a result of further factional fights and an all-out struggle between the ELF and the EPLF, the latter emerged as the victor in a brutal battle between the two movements and, thereafter, remained the principal Eritrean liberation movement.

The Triumph of the EPLF: 1981–1993

In 1982, the Ethiopian government announced a program of reconstruction for Eritrea—Operation Red Star—and tried to attract an estimated 500,000 overseas Eritreans to return home, but it did not succeed, and though it offered talks to the EPLF, these were only in the context of a united Ethiopia. Talks were held, but they broke down. Mengistu now personally took control of the war in Eritrea and led an attack upon the EPLF stronghold at Nacfa, but this was a failure leading to an estimated 80,000 Ethiopian casualties. In January 1984, the EPLF seized Barentu and then defeated 10,000 Ethiopian troops at Mersa Teklai on the Sudan border, yet the following year both places fell to Ethiopian counterattacks.

Despite these successes, Ethiopian troops were becoming reluctant to serve in the north of Eritrea, which was abandoned to the EPLF in 1986. Another EPLF offensive in December 1987 resulted in a government defeat at Nacfa. In March 1988, the EPLF captured the Ethiopian army's regional headquarters at Afabet and then claimed to have killed one third of the Ethiopian troops serving in Eritrea. Mengistu admitted that the Eritrean rebels were "threatening the sovereignty" of the country. Two new developments became important in 1988: the EPLF began successful attacks upon government food convoys, and the **Tigre People's Liberation Front** (TPLF), fighting its own war against the Addis Ababa government, worked in alliance with the EPLF. Mengistu now attempted to improve relations with Somalia so as to release troops from the Ethiopia–Somalia border region to fight against both the EPLF and TPLF in the north. By 1989, the government was increasingly on the defensive as both the EPLF and TPLF mounted large offensives against it; moreover, the rapidly developing change in the political climate as the Cold War came to an end threatened to cut off Mengistu's principal source of military assistance, the USSR. In 1990, following the fall of Massawa to the EPLF, Mengistu called upon his forces to fight to "the bitter end"; in March of that year, the Soviet leader, Mikhail Gorbachev, called upon Mengistu to negotiate, a clear signal that **aid** would shortly be reduced or cut off.

By the end of 1990, the EPLF was in control of most of Eritrea, including the port of Massawa, while its troops encircled Asmara and were shelling the airport. Soviet aid for Ethiopia, meanwhile, had come to an end. A coup attempt against Mengistu in 1989, though unsuccessful, signaled growing disquiet with his regime. There was a general lowering of morale, while the army faced increasing problems finding enough recruits. The Mengistu regime collapsed during 1991. The newly formed Ethiopian People's Revolutionary Democratic Front (EPRDF) advanced into Gonder Province and then Gojam in February; in April, it took Shawa region prior to entering Addis Ababa. By this time, the EPLF controlled the whole Red Sea coast and had cut off the government's sea lifeline at Aseb. On 21 May 1991, Mengistu fled Addis Ababa and was given refuge in Harare, **Zimbabwe**. The EPRDF occupied Addis Ababa on 28 May, and on 29 May, government forces in Eritrea surrendered to the EPLF.

An Independent Eritrea

The EPLF set up an autonomous administration in Asmara and its leader, **Issayas Afewerke**, formed a provisional government to run the country until a referendum to decide the future of Eritrea could be held.

The war had attracted a number of outside interventions: the USSR supported Mengistu for Cold War reasons; Sudan supported the ELF and then the EPLF for strategic reasons; a number of Islamic countries supported the ELF for religious reasons. Over the years the ELF obtained support from Syria, Libya, Egypt, **Algeria** and, after 1974, from Iraq and China. Both the USSR and **Cuba** provided some support for the ELF prior to the Mengistu revolution when they switched sides. The Ethiopian government supported the **Sudan People's Liberation Army** (SPLA) fight against the Khartoum government as a way of counterbalancing Khartoum's support for the ELF.

The casualties for this war were very heavy, though at best they can only be roughly estimated. In 1974, after 14 years of warfare, estimates suggested that 30,000 had been killed, while 70,000 had been displaced. In 1982, the EPLF released 3,000 Ethiopian prisoners; on their return to Ethiopia they were imprisoned, executed, or re-enlisted. For propaganda reasons—to boost their own morale—both sides exaggerated enemy casualties and played down their own.

In 1988 about 300,000 **refugees** from the war in southern Sudan were in Ethiopia, while 500,000 Eritrean refugees were in the Kassala-Port Sudan region of Sudan. By mid-1988, 500,000 Eritreans were being fed by Christian relief organizations, while 260,000 were being fed by Ethiopian government agencies. When the war finally came to an end, Eritrea required massive food aid. When Addis Ababa fell to the EPRDF, the EPLF would not join with it to form a government since it wished to make plain that Eritrea was separate from Ethiopia. The subsequent interim government in Addis Ababa recognized Eritrea's right to independence, although it was agreed that a referendum on Eritrea's future should be delayed for two years. During 1992 the EPLF established total control over Eritrea and launched a program of reconstruction. It enjoyed widespread support from the people. The economy was in ruins and though the provisional government had not been accorded international recognition, it behaved as though it were the government of an independent state. On 24 May 1993, Eritrea became formally independent with Issayas Afewerke as its first head of state.

The Tigrayan Revolt

Although long part of the Ethiopian empire, the province of Tigre (Tigray) is sufficiently distinctive that its people consider themselves to be a separate nationality. Moreover, for 150 years prior to the Tigrayan Emperor Yohannis IV, who ruled Ethiopia from 1871 to 1889, Tigre had been virtually autonomous. Following the defeat of the Italians by the British in 1941 and the resumption of his throne by Haile Selassie, the British supported Ras Seyoun as the provincial ruler of Tigre, thereby giving rise to the suspicion that they were employing their well-known "divide and rule" tactics. It was thought that the British hoped to detach Tigre from Ethiopia and join it to

Eritrea, which they then controlled. In order to counter British designs, Haile Selassie insisted that Ras Seyoun should remain in Addis Ababa, but his action was counter-productive and led to a Tigrayan revolt, so that by 1943 Haile Mariam, who had led the revolt, and his supporters controlled most of Tigre. In August 1943, the Ethiopian army, supported by British advisers and airpower, attacked the Tigrayan strongholds and the revolt collapsed. However, this abortive revolt highlighted Tigrayan resentments at Ethiopian domination and fostered the idea of an Eritrean–Tigrayan alliance for the future.

Haile Selassie, who had taken the revolt seriously and feared uprisings elsewhere in his empire, now withdrew his unpopular Shoan officials and allowed the Tigrayans to select their own sub-governors. In 1947, he allowed a greater degree of autonomy to Tigre and permitted Ras Seyoun to return to his province. Relations between the Addis Ababa government and Tigre were reasonable for the remainder of Haile Selassie's long reign but, on his fall in 1974, a new Tigrayan nationalist movement emerged to form the TPLF. The TPLF began life as a moderate, pro-western movement, but later moved sharply to the left; its cadres obtained training in Eritrea from the EPLF, while its young radicals wished to overthrow the existing system. The TPLF then turned on its own moderates and eradicated them in a bloody purge. It was only in the latter part of the 1970s that the TPLF became significant; by 1977 and 1978, its future was threatened by the emergence of the militant Ethiopian People's Revolutionary Party (EPRP), which had begun to use terrorist tactics to destroy the TPLF. After the end of the Ogaden War, when Ethiopian forces returned in strength to fight in Eritrea, the TPLF suffered heavy losses. Yet, despite this setback, the movement launched a guerrilla campaign against the government in 1979, captured a number of government posts, and killed hundreds of Ethiopian troops. By August of that year, 70 percent of Tigre was under TPLF control.

The TPLF threatened the government's strategy in Eritrea, since Tigre lay between Addis Ababa and Eritrea, and an alliance between the TPLF and the EPLF would pose a major challenge to the government. By the early 1980s, government forces were suffering a steady rate of casualties as a result of TPLF activities. In 1981, the TPLF assisted the EPLF in its factional fight against the ELF. In 1984, the TPLF made a tactical political error when, in order to attract international assistance, it moved 200,000 "refugees" across the border into Sudan. Most of them simply wanted to return home and did not see themselves as refugees at all; at the same time the move created bad relations with the EPLF, which had 500,000 genuine refugees of its own in Sudan. The result was a series of clashes between the two movements.

During 1985–1986, Ethiopian forces regained control of large areas of Tigre and followed up this success with a program of food distribution, which won it allies among the Tigrayan people. However, in 1987 and 1988, the TPLF launched a new offensive, following the capture of Afabet by the EPLF; when the government moved troops from Tigre to Eritrea, the TPLF promptly overran government garrisons which had been left behind, and by April 1988 the government only controlled the Tigrayan capital, Makele. The TPLF and EPLF were once more working together successfully. At the end of May 1988, the TPLF captured the garrison town of Maychew to the south of Makele and forced the Ethiopian army to retreat farther south to Wolle Province; the TPLF claimed to have destroyed two Ethiopian battalions during fighting round Amba Alage. By this time, the TPLF had about 20,000 soldiers and these were supplemented by local militias who joined them when their own areas were under threat.

Mengistu now called for a nationwide effort to destroy the TPLF, and in a major offensive of June 1988, drove them from six towns which they had occupied. This proved to be one of the last successful military offensives by the Ethiopian armed forces; by mid-1990, as the Mengistu government began to collapse, the TPLF was operating barely 160 kilometers north of Addis Ababa and claimed to have inflicted a massive 22,000 casualties upon the retreating Ethiopian forces. By the end of the year, the TPLF and EPLF were clearly in command of the military situation, while Mengistu's forces were everywhere on the defensive. Meanwhile, in January 1989, the TPLF had created a coalition of forces opposed to the Ethiopian government—the Ethiopian People's Revolutionary Democratic Front (EPRDF)—which consisted of the TPLF as the lead organization, the Ethiopian People's Democratic Movement (EPDM), which was a northern-based Amhara movement, the Oromo People's Democratic Organization (OPDO), and a number of smaller movements. In the first months of 1991, the EPRDF overcame the remaining government forces opposed to it and following Mengistu's flight, entered

Addis Ababa on 28 May 1991. Meles Zenawi, the Tigrayan leader who had assumed the leadership of the EPRDF, now became interim president of Ethiopia. Order was restored in Addis Ababa and the long years of war appeared to have come to an end. There are no reliable figures for casualties on either side in this long struggle, although figures were periodically produced to cover particular engagements; it was claimed, for example, that 4,000 civilians were killed between March and November 1988 by bombing raids against Tigre and that 40 villages were destroyed. And in mid-1990, following the heaviest fighting of the war between government troops and the EPRDF, the latter claimed to have killed or wounded 22,000 government troops.

The Oromo Insurrections

The series of wars waged against the Ethiopian government during the years 1960 to 1990 are explained, in part, by the nature of the Ethiopian state which, essentially, was an empire made up of diverse peoples who had been brought under the rule of its emperors. These were usually Amharas, occasionally Tigrayans, and differed in ethnic origin, religion, and other cultural characteristics from the greater part of the peoples they ruled.

The Oromo people, who live in the south and east of Ethiopia, are not Amharic and comprise 40 percent of the total population. There were earlier Oromo revolts against domination by the Ambaric center and one had been launched in 1928/1929. When the Italians retreated in 1941, they armed the Oromo in the hope that they would harass the advancing British. The Oromo were implicated in the Tigre revolt of 1943. The Oromo of Bale Province, with the local Somalis, revolted from 1963 to 1970. The revolt started as a defiance of the governor of Wabe district when he attempted to collect taxes and this rising led to others, so that by the end of 1965, resistance to government had spread while Bale district itself had become its center. However, both this and other Oromo uprisings were widely dispersed; they were not coordinated. Rather, they were a typical peasant response to oppression, which had a long history and were not a nationalist uprising comparable to the resistance of the Eritreans.

The Oromo leader, Wako Gutu, described himself as a general of Western Somalia and his movement as the Liberation Front of

Western Somalia; his stance, designed to attract Somali support, was counter-productive and only served to increase the wrath of Addis Ababa. Nonetheless, Gutu spread the rebellion from Bale to Boranne and his forces showed some grasp of guerrilla tactics. The Oromo were too diverse and there were too many divisions among them, however, to allow them to achieve any cohesive unity, and their greatest problem was to maintain a united front with their Somali allies. This first Oromo revolt came to an end in 1970 and at that time, of 1,206,000 inhabitants of Bale Province, one million were Oromo, yet the best land was held by the Amhara and the top jobs were held by Christians rather than Oromo Muslims. The Somalis in the east of the country (the Ogaden region) continued their defiance of the government and later joined with the Somalis from across the border in the war of 1977/1978. Although Gutu accepted a government appointment in 1970 and the insurrection appeared to have come to an end, new discontents surfaced after the fall of Haile Selassie. In 1977, during the Ogaden War, the **Oromo National Liberation Front** (ONLF), later OLF, emerged but it was only to have any importance while Ethiopia was at war with Somalia and collapsed once the Somalis had been defeated. The OLF advocated Oromo self-determination and obtained its support from peasant associations but by 1980, although the OLF maintained an office in Mogadishu, little was happening in the field. In 1986, about 70,000 refugees fled into Somalia to escape enforced resettlement. There was renewed fighting between government forces and OLF supporters in 1988 in Wollega district, but the movement never achieved the cohesiveness or the thrust of the Eritrean or Tigre organizations. Following the collapse of the Dergue in 1991, the EPRDF set up an interim government and, in July 1991, a national conference was called to form a governing council to include representatives of regional and ethnic groups. More than 60 political organizations took part in a search for democratic consensus and in June 1992, multi-party local elections were held; in the west the OLF boycotted these elections and on 23 June 1992, the OLF withdrew from the interim government. However, Oromo discontent did not turn into a further revolt and after the secession of Eritrea in May 1993 the Oromo appeared, if with reluctance, to accept the new government. *See also* ERITREA–ETHIOPIA BORDER WAR (1998–2000).

ETHIOPIAN DEMOCRATIC UNION (EDU). This union was one of the several movements that rose and fell during the long Ethiopian civil war or wars. It was formed in 1975, following the fall of Emperor **Haile Selassie**, and represented the center in Ethiopian politics. Its leader was General Iyassu Mengeshu who was in London in 1975, but returned to **Sudan** to head the EDU. For a time, principally by controlling roads in the north of **Ethiopia** that gave access to **Eritrea**, the EDU assisted the Eritrean revolt. The EDU's principal aim was to oppose the forcible imposition of Marxism upon the Ethiopian people; it favored a federal solution to Ethiopia's problems. The movement suffered a military defeat in 1978 and those of its members who were able to do so, fled to Sudan; others who were captured were executed. Thereafter, the EDU became a negligible factor in the ongoing struggles in Ethiopia.

– F –

FANON, FRANTZ (1925–61). Frantz Fanon, whose writings influenced a generation, moved steadily to the political left during his short life and became increasingly anti-French as a result of the appalling behavior of the French in **Algeria** which he witnessed. Frantz Omar Fanon was born in Martinique and died in Washington, D.C. He became a psychoanalyst and social philosopher; he served with the French army during World War II and then completed his studies at the University of Lyons. In 1952, Fanon's book, *Peau noire, masques blancs* (Black Skin, White Masks) was published; in it he recorded his aversion to racism. Fanon served as the head of the psychiatry department of Blida Joinville Hospital in Algeria from 1953 to 1956. In 1954 he joined the Algerian Liberation Movement and in 1956, he became the editor of the **Front de Libération Nationale** (FLN) newspaper El Moudjahid, which was published in Tunis. In 1960 the FLN's provisional government appointed Fanon ambassador to Ghana. His Algerian experiences had a profound, radicalizing effect on Fanon who had treated (at Blida Joinville) both the victims of torture as well as the torturers. His seminal work, *Les Damnés de la terre* (The Wretched of the Earth) was published in 1961, the year of his death. In this work, Fanon urged those people who had been colonized to purge themselves of their colonial degradation. The logic of this was to rise in violent revolt against their European oppressors. Among his other works was *Pour la révolution africaine* (For the African Revolution).

FORCES ARMÉES DU NORD (FAN)/NORTHERN ARMED FORCES. The Forces Armées du Nord came into being in 1978. The FAN was **Hissène Habré**'s faction of the northern Muslim opposition movement, the **Front de Libération Nationale du Tchad** (FROLINAT), and Habré himself was an ardent Muslim nationalist who, by 1978 had been campaigning in the desert for 10 years. Habré and the FAN took part in the 1979 government of national unity in **Chad**, although this was only to last a short time until, in 1980, the factions fell apart, and in the fierce fighting which then took place in the capital, N'Djamena, Habré and the FAN were defeated by the forces of **Goukouni Oueddei**, who was supported by the Libyans. After this defeat, Habré and the FAN retreated to **Sudan** where he re-equipped and retrained his army. Following the Libyan withdrawal of 1981, the FAN reoccupied the towns it had formerly controlled: these included Iriba, Abeche, Adrea, and Gueneda. In 1982, Habré captured Faya-Largeau and by the middle of that year he had ousted Goukouni from N'Djamena to become president. The FAN was always Habré's military instrument, although it failed him in 1990 when he was ousted in a short military campaign by **Idriss Déby**.

FORCES ARMÉES DU TCHAD (FAT)/ARMED FORCES OF CHAD. The Forces Armées du Tchad emerged at the end of the 1970s from the former armed forces, which by then were disintegrating. It was led by Colonel Abdelkader Kamougue, who had previously led the gendarmerie. Although drawing its support from the south, neither FAT nor Kamougue played any part in the 1979 agreement, which created a temporary new government. FAT opposed the Libyan intervention which had been engineered by **Goukouni Oueddei**, even though Libyan forces never came to the southern region where FAT operated. Kamougue was never a very convincing leader or more than a peripheral figure in the complex maneuvers for power, which were then taking place in **Chad**, and late in 1982 he was forced to flee the country as **Habré**'s forces took control of the south.

FORCES ARMÉES POPULAIRES (FAP)/POPULAR ARMED FORCES. The Forces Armées Populaires was the armed faction of the **Front de Libération Nationale du Tchad** (FROLINAT), which had broken away and joined **Goukouni Oueddei**. FAP was his equivalent of **Habré**'s **Forces Armées du Nord** (FAN). In 1981, when Goukouni was at the height of his influence FAP, briefly, was the dominant FROLINAT faction in the country. Goukouni presided over the Government of Unity in **Chad** from 1979 to 1981 and early in 1980, when Habré's FAN attempted a coup, the FAP was able to triumph over its rival, though largely as a result of Libyan support. However, following his agreement of January 1981 to work for a merger of Chad and Libya, Goukouni met so much opposition that he had to reverse his stand and request the Libyan forces to leave Chad. Once the Libyans had withdrawn, Habré was able to stage a comeback; he reoccupied wide areas of the country and cut off Goukouni from his northern allies and Libya.

FRANCE. France, along with **Great Britain**, was one of the two main European colonial powers in Africa and in the post-colonial era was to become more deeply involved in some of the continent's civil wars than was Britain. France maintained military garrisons in several African countries after independence; in theory these were available to assist Francophone countries on request, according to a series of military treaties between France and Francophone Africa, though in practice they also acted as a very obvious reminder of French interests in the region. One reason for the greater French (than British) readiness to intervene in Africa was the fact that the major part of the French empire had been concentrated in Africa with the result that French investment in its African colonies and **aid** to them in the post-independence era were commensurately more important to France than comparable aid and investment from Britain to Anglophone Africa.

In the period after 1945 France, like Britain, saw its worldwide influence declining and determined, as far as was in its power, to bolster its international standing by maintaining close links with former colonies in Francophone Africa. This policy became all the more important after France's forced withdrawal from French Indo-China following the defeat of the French army at Dien Bien Phu in 1954. Through its African connections, France sought to enhance its diplomatic clout and world influence; Paris was assisted in this because of the often close ties which existed between leading French statesmen, such as **Charles de Gaulle** and leading African politicians, such as Félix Houphouet-Boigny of **Côte d'Ivoire** or Leopold Senghor of Senegal, who had sat as elected representatives in the French Assembly. Although the French policy of assimilation was usually more rhetoric than reality, it sometimes produced a closer understanding between French and African politicians than existed between British politicians and their African counterparts.

France pursued this policy in a number of ways: by maintaining strong commercial ties and providing preferential terms for African exports to France; by providing substantial levels of **aid** (often equivalent to two-and-a-half times the level of aid provided by Britain); by maintaining the Franc Zone to bolster Francophone economies; and by a readiness to intervene militarily to support Francophone regimes facing internal or other threats. France also labored to perpetuate the use of the French language in Africa.

In 1945, the French African empire consisted of the following territories: in North Africa—**Algeria**, Morocco, and Tunisia; in West Africa—Cameroon, Côte d'Ivoire, Dahomey (later Benin), Guinea, Mali, Mauritania, Niger, Senegal, Togo, Upper Volta (later Burkina Faso); in Equatorial Africa—**Central African Republic**, **Chad**, **Congo**, Gabon; in East Africa and the Indian Ocean—**Comoro Islands**, Djibouti, Madagascar.

After 14 Francophone African countries became independent in 1960, France made great efforts to prolong its influence on the continent. The long and brutal civil war in Algeria between the *colons* (settlers) and the **Front de Libération Nationale** (FLN) from 1954 to 1962, which brought French control in the Maghreb to an end, saw massive French military involvement with the deployment of up to 500,000 troops in the colony. France intervened several times in Chad during the long wars between north and south in that country, although in this case, France intervened primarily to check Libyan expansion or for reasons of **Cold War** strategy than for any obvious advantages to be gained from Chad itself.

The stationing of a permanent and substantial French garrison in Djibouti, following its independence in 1977, was a source of income to the tiny state and a means of keeping it independent against Somali expansionist ambitions, as well as creating a base that could support French policy in the Gulf and Indian Ocean, as it did during the Gulf War of 1991. French garrisons in a half dozen African states clearly indicated France's readiness to support those Francophone countries which it saw as allies.

The French presence was reinforced by the Franc Zone, which provided for free movement of currency among the Francophone countries that were members, and guaranteed their CFA franc against the French franc. The Franc Zone acted to steady and support the currencies of the Francophone states as well as to ensure that those economies remained closely linked to France. The Zone was created prior to the independence of Francophone Africa and most of France's colonies initially elected to join it; however, Mali left in 1962 (though it rejoined in 1968), Guinea was expelled in 1958 when it opted for complete independence, while other territories which had joined at first subsequently left the Zone. These latter included Mauritania, the Maghreb countries of Algeria, Morocco, and Tunisia, and Madagascar. The Comoro Islands joined in 1976. The former Spanish colony of Equatorial Guinea applied to join the Franc Zone in 1985 and was admitted. All the currencies of the Franc Zone are freely convertible into French francs at a fixed rate.

French readiness to intervene in post-independence Africa resulted from the huge extent of its colonial empire on the continent. France went to considerable lengths to maintain its post-colonial links with Francophone Africa; these comprised language, administrative and educational systems, the Franc Zone, strong two-way trade and investment. Relatively massive injections of French aid acted as a cement to this relationship. The attempt to create a French Community in Africa in 1958 floundered on the decision of Guinea under Sekou Touré to opt for immediate, full independence.

Later, however, under President Georges Pompidou, France inaugurated the system of annual Franco–African summits, and while these were viewed from Paris as a means of enhancing French influence in Africa, they were regarded by African countries as a means of exerting pressures upon France. French military assistance in Africa has to be viewed against this background. France has concluded Mutual Defense Agreements with Central African Republic, Chad, Congo, Gabon, and Mali. In 1961 Central African Republic,

Chad, Congo, and Gabon formed a "Defense Council of Equatorial Africa." France also concluded defense agreements with countries which were not members of the French Community—Benin, Cameroon, Côte d'Ivoire, Mauritania, Niger, and Togo. Following Algeria's independence in 1962, France was permitted to lease the naval base at Mers-el-Kebir and the air base at Bou-Sfer for 15 years; however, these agreements were terminated in 1968 and 1970. Up to 1964/1965 France maintained about 27,800 troops in Africa; then it reduced these garrisons to about 6,000 troops with contingents in Chad, Côte d'Ivoire, Senegal, and Madagascar, although the number of troops was to increase again.

French forces in Africa were not there for ceremonial or diplomatic reasons, but intervened on request and sometimes without being asked. Such interventions took place in Central African Republic, Chad, the Comoro Islands, and Gabon. Following Djibouti's independence in 1977, France stationed some 3,000 troops of the French Foreign Legion in the country as part of a mutual defense pact, and these were used in the 1991 Gulf War, despite Djibouti's support for Iraq. In August 1997, France announced that it was to reduce its military presence in Africa. At that time, France had seven bases in Africa with a total of 8,100 men; the minister of defense, Alain Richard, said these commitments would be reduced to five bases and 6,000 men. The reasons for this retrenchment were partly financial and partly a decision to adopt a less interventionist approach on the African continent. The five main bases would be in Chad, Côte d'Ivoire, Djibouti, Gabon, and Senegal, while bases in Cameroon and Central African Republic would close, although a small contingent was to remain at the airport of Bangui in Central African Republic to maintain a bridgehead for possible future operations. The minister implied in his statement that future French military operations in Africa would either be to assist French citizens or to help "stabilize" Africa, but that they would not be used (as in the past) to "arbitrate between rival forces." The approximate strength of French troops remaining on the continent (1998) would be: Chad (840), Côte d'Ivoire (500), Djibouti (3,200), Gabon (600), Senegal (1,300).

After its African colonies achieved independence, France worked extremely hard to maintain close ties with them, encouraging economic unions between or with them, and making plain by the extent of its investment and readiness to provide military help that it would act as an external resource, always separate from the superpowers during the years of the **Cold War**, that they could call upon for assistance.

France's retrenchments in relation to Africa at the end of the 20th century, were drastically upset by events in Côte d'Ivoire at the beginning of the 21st century, which saw France committing some 4,000 troops to that country in an effort, along with the **United Nations**, to maintain the peace between the rival factions that split Côte d'Ivoire between north and south.

FRENTE DA LIBERTAÇÃO DE MOÇAMBIQUE (FRELIMO)/ MOZAMBIQUE LIBERATION FRONT. As the nationalist determination to oust the Portuguese from **Mozambique** developed, several liberation movements arose in the early 1960s; these merged in 1962 to form the Frente da Libertação de Moçambique (FRELIMO) under the leadership of Dr. Eduardo Mondlane. By 1969, when Mondlane was assassinated, FRELIMO had become a powerful organization, although its cohesion was now threatened by a potential split between the leadership that came from the south of the country and the fighting forces that were mainly drawn from the north. For a short time following Mondlane's death, FRELIMO was ruled by a troika, but before long **Samora Machel**, one of the three who made up the joint leadership, emerged as the undisputed leader. His military ability, as well as his personal charisma, were to alter the character of the guerrilla war against the Portuguese.

As early as 1964, FRELIMO had extended the war into Tete Province in an attempt to prevent the construction of the **Cabora Bassa Dam** on the Zambezi; by 1974 (the year of the coup in Lisbon which toppled the Marcello Caetano government) FRELIMO forces were fighting throughout the northern third of the country and as far south as Manica and Sofala provinces, as well as across the Pungwe river. According to Portuguese sources, 3,815 FRELIMO guerrillas were killed between May 1970 and May 1973. In 1974, as white settler farms came under increasing threats of attack, **Portugal** was forced to transfer 10,000 troops from **Angola** to Mozambique. Meanwhile, FRELIMO claimed that its greatest victories were being achieved among the liberated people of the country, where new freedoms were being introduced. By this last year of the war against the Portuguese, FRELIMO had long been the only liberation movement and so formed the first independence government of Mozambique in 1975. It became the sole (Marxist) ruling party.

The new government faced daunting problems: not only was Mozambique one of the poorest countries in Africa, but it had suffered from nearly 15 years of warfare and the great majority of its people were rural peasants unaccustomed to urban life, although they had now occupied the towns. FRELIMO lacked the discipline necessary for peace and its members were difficult to control; moreover, after a long, brutal war and memories of past oppression, there were demands for reprisals against former enemies or collaborators with the Portuguese. The readiness of the new government to support the **Zimbabwe African National Union** (ZANU) in Rhodesia and the **African National Congress** (ANC) in **South Africa**, ensured the immediate enmity of the illegal Smith regime in Rhodesia as well as that of P. W. Botha's government in South Africa. The result of this enmity was the creation of the **Resistência Nacional Moçambicana** (RENAMO)/Mozambican National Resistance by Ken Flower, the head of the Rhodesian Central Intelligence Organization (CIO), during 1974–1975, in order to destabilize the new FRELIMO government and leadership.

Discontented members of FRELIMO, including many who did not see any quick rewards resulting from their victory, provided recruits for RENAMO, which soon challenged government authority in many rural areas. By the early 1980s, as the Mozambique economy deteriorated and the war against RENAMO escalated, FRELIMO turned from the **Union of Soviet Socialist Republics** (USSR), East Germany, and other Communist countries, which until then had been its principal backers, and sought instead to mobilize western support for its cause. By 1983, the war against RENAMO was going badly, FRELIMO forces in the field were ill-equipped and malnourished (and not paid), and often did not wish to fight at all. The **Nkomati Accord**, which was concluded with South Africa in 1984 by Machel, appeared to make pragmatic sense, even though it was opposed by the hardline members of FRELIMO. In the event, the South Africans did not keep their side of the agreement. By 1988, the greater part of the FRELIMO army, with the exception of a few of the best units, appeared to have disintegrated and the government came to rely increasingly upon troops from **Zimbabwe** and Tanzania to safeguard its vital cross-country railway routes to Beira and Nacala.

In June 1989, a 12-point position paper on how to end the war with RENAMO was issued by FRELIMO and a peace process was initiated. During 1990, the FRELIMO government under President **Joaquim Chissano**, radically altered the constitution to pave the way for the switch from a one-party Marxist state to a multi-party system, and in November the government announced the abandonment of Marxism–Leninism, the creed which had been a cornerstone of FRELIMO until that time. The years 1990–1994 witnessed negotiations that finally produced a ceasefire, then peace followed by an amalgamation of the armies of FRELIMO and RENAMO under **United Nations** auspices. In the legislative elections of 1994, FRELIMO won 44.3 percent of the vote to RENAMO's 37.7 percent and though FRELIMO formed the new government, it was no longer a sole "ruling party" but one of a multi-party system.

FRENTE DA LIBERTAÇÃO DO ENCLAVE DE CABINDA (FLEC)/LIBERATION FRONT FOR THE CABINDA ENCLAVE. FLEC was formed at the end of the 1950s by Luis Ranque Franque; he was temporarily ousted from this post but regained it in 1963. There was a sense of a Cabindan, as opposed to Angolan, entity, which helped FLEC operate on its own. FLEC rejected the 1975 agreement between **Portugal** and the three main Angolan liberation movements—the **Movimento Popular para a Libertação de Angola** (MPLA), the **Frente Nacional da Libertação de Angola** (FNLA), and the **União Nacional para a Independência Total de Angola** (UNITA). Cabinda had a genuine cause for complaint; it had only been incorporated into **Angola** as late as 1958 on the eve of the long independence struggle. FLEC did not take part in the struggles of 1975 between the different factions as the Portuguese withdrew; the governments of both **Congo** (Brazzaville) and **Zaire** favored FLEC, since an independent Cabinda would prove a far easier neighbor for either of them to manipulate than a Cabinda that was part of a Marxist Angola. From 1975 onward, FLEC itself was to suffer from splits and was to be largely ineffective as a guerrilla movement, although the arrival of the Cubans in Angola (including Cabinda) during 1975–1976 helped to promote the influence of FLEC, since the Cubans were seen as Marxists and were not popular in the enclave. The discovery of oil in 1966 had conferred great strategic importance upon Cabinda to the U.S. oil companies operating there, and to the Portuguese as a source of revenue to fight their war, as well as causing its neighbors, Congo and Zaire, to examine the possibility of a takeover. FLEC's chances of breaking away from Angola were never high since from 1975 onward 50 percent of the MPLA government's war costs were derived from Cabinda oil profits. In 1978, FLEC came under the control of Zita Tiago and achieved a series of guerrilla successes against Cuban and MPLA troops during 1979, mainly by sabotaging oil installations. However, FLEC gradually lost its importance during the 1980s, although surfacing from time to time to carry out nuisance attacks.

FRENTE NACIONAL DA LIBERTAÇÃO DE ANGOLA (FNLA)/NATIONAL FRONT FOR THE LIBERATION OF ANGOLA. The FNLA was formed in 1962 by a combination of **Holden Roberto**'s União das Populaçoes de Angola (UPA) and the smaller Partido Democratico Angolano (PDA). The FNLA from its creation was opposed to the Marxist oriented **Movimento Popular para a Libertação de Angola** (MPLA). The FNLA at once strengthened its position by setting up a government in exile in Kinshasa (**Congo**, later **Zaire**)—Governo Revoluçionario de Angola no Exilo (GRAE). In 1963, GRAE received immediate recognition from a number of African countries and the **Organization of African Unity** (OAU); however, this recognition was to be withdrawn in 1971, for by then GRAE was clearly no longer in any position to claim that it was the sole representative of the Angolan people.

Although the FNLA had little success against the Portuguese as a guerrilla movement during the liberation struggle, it was still able to claim the allegiance of the Bakongo people in the north of **Angola** and was one of the three movements, together with the MPLA and the **União Nacional para a Independência Total de Angola** (UNITA), to take part in the independence talks with the Portuguese. Following the end of hostilities between the Portuguese and the liberation movements in 1974, the FNLA sent troops to the capital,

Luanda, but they at once clashed with the far larger MPLA forces that were already there and had to withdraw. By August 1975, a civil war between the different factions appeared inevitable. At this time the FNLA enjoyed the support of Zaire's **Mobutu Sese Seko** and also of the People's Republic of China, which was then prepared to adopt a contrary stance to any followed by the **Union of Soviet Socialist Republics** (USSR), which supported the MPLA. Already in 1974, the Chinese had sent 100 advisers to Kinshasa as well as medical supplies and arms; the level of Chinese **aid** was increased during 1975. Daniel Chipenda, a substantial figure in the MPLA, defected with 1,000 men during 1975 and joined forces with the FNLA, enabling the movement, though only briefly, to capture a number of northern towns. The MPLA soon asserted its military superiority and the FNLA was unable to maintain its grip on northern Angola, so that an estimated 500,000 people sympathetic to the FNLA fled across the border into Zaire as **refugees**, while the FNLA collapsed as an effective movement. On 28 February 1976, Presidents Mobutu and **Agostinho Neto** signed an agreement not to promote military action against one another; the result was an end to base facilities for the FNLA in Zaire.

From this time onward, the FNLA became less and less important in the ongoing struggle for dominance in Angola and the civil war was largely fought out between the MPLA and UNITA. In 1978, the FNLA lost a number of its senior officials who returned home following an amnesty offer by the MPLA government in Luanda. Nonetheless, as late as 1980, the FNLA claimed to control parts of northern Angola. In 1981 Holden Roberto was replaced as the leader of the FNLA by a twosome of Paulo Tuba and Hendrik Vaal Neto.

FRONT D'ACTION COMMUNE (FAC)/FRONT FOR COMMON ACTION. The FAC was one of the many movements which emerged during the long civil war (or wars) in **Chad**; it formed part of the northern Islamic opposition to southern control of the country. FAC came into being by breaking away from the **Front de Libération Nationale du Tchad** (FROLINAT), at first describing itself as the Vulcan Force; its leader was Ahmat Acyl. The FAC operated in the eastern part of Chad and depended for support upon Libya, which was prepared to back it following the brief alliance formed by **Hissène Habré** and **Goukouni Oueddei** in 1979. At this time, Libya saw the FAC as the best means of achieving its own objectives in Chad. FAC members took part in the government of unity of 1979 and then became involved in the fighting a year later when the alliance government disintegrated. The FAC then made the mistake of supporting the Libyan intervention in Chad of 1981, only to find that it had isolated itself once the Libyans withdrew in November of that year. Once Libyan support was withdrawn, the FAC was never a serious player in the civil war and in 1982, following the death in a helicopter crash of Ahmat Acyl, it ceased to exist.

FRONT DE LIBÉRATION NATIONALE (FLN)/NATIONAL LIBERATION FRONT. The Front de Libération Nationale was formed in 1954, once the Muslim nationalists had determined to use violence to oppose continued French control of **Algeria** and the Armée de Libération Nationale (ALN) was its military wing. **Ahmed ben Bella** became the first leader of the FLN, but was soon imprisoned by the French; he had served in the French army and copied guerrilla tactics of Mao and Tito. The brutal repression practiced by the French simply gave impetus to the nationalist resistance and alienated the population, a high proportion of whom had been passive and were illiterate. French brutality and torture were met with terrorism. The FLN received external support from three main sources: Egypt under Nasser provided funds; Morocco and Tunisia, Algeria's two neighbors, provided cross-border sanctuary for FLN forces after achieving their independence in 1956. Friction between the external leadership based in Cairo and the internal leadership conducting the struggle inside Algeria developed, although there was never any doubt that the view of the radicals over the moderates would prevail. Ramdane Abani led the internal FLN and launched the urban terrorist campaign in the city of Algiers during 1957 and, though this was eventually broken by the French, it was only by means of the extensive use of torture, and such brutality served to alienate the mass of the population.

The FLN created military and civil committees throughout the countryside, with the latter acting as alternatives to the French administration, raising taxes, and recruiting new members for the FLN. Military equipment was purchased from Egypt and Syria. The FLN established a government in exile based in Tunis with **Ferhat Abbas** as prime minister, ben Bella (in prison) as his deputy, and Belkacem Krim as minister of defense. This government was recognized as legitimate by Arab countries, the **Union of Soviet Socialist Republics (USSR)**, and the People's Republic of China. In 1958, when **Charles de Gaulle** came to power in **France**, he showed complete realism about Algeria and offered the FLN self-determination, earning the enmity of the *colons* (settlers) and an important section of the army by doing so. The French, despite increasing the number of troops to 500,000 in Algeria, never defeated the FLN, many of whose leaders had a military background. These nationalists became increasingly left-wing as they realized the extent of the gap between the French perception of Algeria and the needs of their people. **Houari Boumedienne**, who had become the leader of the FLN in ben Bella's absence in prison, moved it politically toward a socialist philosophy. At independence in 1962, the FLN emerged as the sole political party to rule Algeria as a socialist, Islamic, one-party state for the next few decades. *See also* ALGERIA, THE ISLAMIST WAR (1992–2006).

FRONT DE LIBÉRATION NATIONALE DU TCHAD (FROLINAT)/CHAD NATIONAL LIBERATION FRONT. The Front de Libération Nationale du Tchad was formed in Algiers in 1966 by Dr. Abba Siddick, who was largely a figurehead. The leadership was disputed by two far more charismatic figures, **Goukouni Oueddei** and **Hissène Habré**. FROLINAT derived its support from the northern peoples, largely nomadic and Muslim, who resented political control by the black non-Muslim south. In 1974, Habré and Goukouni split to lead separate movements of their own: they did so over the issue of the French ethnologist, Françoise Claustre, whom Habré had taken hostage. Libya's **Muammar Gaddafi** then used his influence to persuade Goukouni, who was the leader of the northern Toubou people, to obtain Claustre's release, although this did not happen until 1977. Goukouni's willingness to work with Gaddafi and the Libyans (at one stage agreeing to Gaddafi's proposal of an eventual union between the two countries) proved a turning point in the fortunes of the two leaders. Goukouni's alliance with Libya was never popular, although he regarded it in pragmatic terms as a way of winning the war. After the split between the two men, it was

Goukouni who continued to control a truncated FROLINAT, while Habré formed his own **Forces Armées du Nord** (FAN). Goukouni in his turn created his own army, **Forces Armées Populaires** (FAP) based upon Faya-Largeau in the north, and was to lead it until his influence evaporated. By 1980, following the collapse of the short-lived alliance in a government of national unity between Habré and Goukouni, which had been formed in 1979, about a dozen different groups attempted to gain control of FROLINAT, but its influence and importance waned as other developments and movements came to dominate the politics and fighting.

– G –

GADDAFI, MUAMMAR AL- (1942–). Born in a Bedouin tent in the desert south of Tripoli, Gaddafi was trained as an officer cadet for the Libyan army and in 1969, aged only 28, led a coup of junior officers to oust King Idriss from power. Gaddafi became chairman of the Revolutionary Command Council which was then established (effectively head of state) and remained the leader of Libya thereafter. Charismatic, radical, and unpredictable, he at once challenged the western political position in the Arab Middle East and it was his determination to take control of Libya's oil, which led the other oil states to follow his lead and turn the Organization of Petroleum Exporting Countries (OPEC) into a formidable economic "power," which confronted the West in 1973 following the Yom Kippur War between Israel and its two neighbors, Egypt and Syria.

Libya's oil wealth, compared with the country's small population, meant that Gaddafi could afford to carry out reforms at home while pursuing a range of foreign policies that normally would be beyond the scope of a small state. These included supporting a number of foreign terrorist organizations, quarrelling with Egypt and other Arab states for their failure to take a stronger line against Israel, and confronting both the **United States** and **Great Britain**. In 1981, the U.S. administration of Ronald Reagan accused Gaddafi of sending a hit squad to assassinate the president, and the subsequent U.S.–Libyan quarrel culminated in the U.S. air strike against Libya in April 1986. The accusation that two Libyans were responsible for placing the bomb on Pan Am Flight 103, which blew up over Lockerbie, Scotland, on 21 December 1988, led the United States and Britain to persuade the **United Nations** Security Council to impose sanctions on Libya.

During the 1970s, when he was at the height of his influence and oil wealth, Gaddafi became involved in a number of African countries, either providing financial support for regimes of which he approved or more clandestine support for liberation or opposition movements. He first supported the Eritrean rebels against the government of **Haile Selassie** in **Ethiopia**, then switched sides to support the revolutionary government of **Haile Mariam Mengistu**. He supported the **Sudan People's Liberation Army** (SPLA) in southern **Sudan**, despite his desire to encourage the spread of Islam. In particular, he became involved in the long series of wars in **Chad** and his forces occupied the Aozou Strip in the north of that country, to which he laid claim. He also supported **Uganda**'s dictator **Idi Amin**.

Gaddafi's meddling in other countries earned him opprobrium from the countries concerned, but also succeeded in enraging the West not least, perhaps, because he was doing what it had long seen as its particular prerogative. However, at the end of the century, Gaddafi signaled his desire to come in from the "cold" and aided by the rising world fuel crisis and his country's capacity to meet some of the western demands for oil, he succeeded in achieving a rapprochement with both the United States and Europe. His pledge in 2003 to abandon weapons of mass destruction, led to a rapid improvement in relations with Washington and in 2004 U.S. oil companies that had been operating in Libya before U.S. sanctions were imposed, were allowed to negotiate a return to Libya. In April 2004, following a March visit to Libya by British Prime Minister Tony Blair, Gaddafi made an official visit to Brussels at the invitation of the European Commission. Gaddafi's rapprochement with the Western powers coincided with his attempts to foster and then lead the **African Union** (AU), which replaced the **Organization of African Unity** (OAU) at the beginning of the 21st century. However, Gaddafi's relations with leading Africans, and especially presidents Thabo Mbeki of **South Africa** and **Olusegun Obasanjo** of **Nigeria** were less than cordial after he had rubbished the idea of a New Partnership for Africa's Development (NEPAD) when he said: "We are not children who need to be taught. They (the colonial powers) made us slaves, they called us inferior but we have regained our African name and culture."

GARANG, JOHN (DE MABION) (1945–2005). A Dinka of southern **Sudan**, John Garang was born in 1945, finished his education by taking a B.A. in the **United States** and then, in 1970, on his return to Sudan he joined the **Anya-Nya** movement. Following the peace of 1972, when President **Gaafar Nimeiri** brought the first phase of the civil war in Sudan to an end, Garang was integrated into the Sudan army. He was promoted and reached the rank of lieutenant colonel in 1979 when he went to the United States for further study. When he returned to Sudan, toward the end of Nimeiri's presidency, Garang discovered that in a bid to hold on to power as his popularity steadily slipped, Nimeiri was trying to appease the Islamic fundamentalists by introducing Sharia law throughout the country. By 1982, there were renewed outbreaks of fighting in the South with rebels mounting attacks upon the army. When an army mutiny took place at Bor in the South, Nimeiri sent Garang to deal with it, but instead he joined the rebels and in August 1983 formed the **Sudan People's Liberation Army** (SPLA).

Garang then spent the rest of the year launching SPLA attacks against government targets in the South and was able to halt drilling for oil by Chevron, which had only recently commenced. In March 1984, by which time he wanted to overthrow Nimeiri and form a socialist government, Garang formed the **Sudan People's Liberation Movement** (SPLM). Nimeiri attempted to appease Garang by offering him the vice-presidency and making him coordinator of development in the South, but Garang refused. On 16 April 1985, the military, under General Suwar al-Dahab, mounted a coup and overthrew Nimeiri; Garang ordered a ceasefire, but when he learned Dahab's plans for the South, he renewed the war. A year later, in April 1986, a civilian government under **Sadiq al-Mahdi** came to power; Sadiq offered Garang a place on his Council of Ministers (cabinet), but Garang refused to take part. Talks between Garang and Sadiq were held in Addis Ababa during July 1986, but they did not reach any agreement.

In the years 1986–1989, Garang made a number of territorial (military) gains in the South but the plight of the people worsened, with many starving as a result of the war. In May 1989, Garang announced a one-month cease-fire so as to allow discussions about freezing the proposed imposition of Sharia law. However, this effort at finding a solution was nullified by the coup, which brought General **Omar al-Bashir** to power. Within a month of Bashir's assumption of power Garang made clear his opposition. The gradual moves toward fundamentalism under Bashir, with Dr. Hasan al-Turabi orchestrating them in the background, ensured that the war between North and South would continue. However, by 1990, war weariness in the South produced factionalism and splits in the SPLM, although Garang with reduced forces nevertheless continued fighting.

The war continued through the 1990s with heavy human distress and many thousands of **refugees** created by the fighting. On 10 April 1996, a peace treaty was signed by the Khartoum government and two of the rebel groups in the South. These, however, did not include Garang's faction of the SPLA, and he continued the struggle. After six years of on-off peace negotiations, the government and the Sudan People's Liberation Army/Movement (SPLA/M) signed a number of protocols in Naivasha, Kenya; in January and May 2004 that included a permanent ceasefire and the mechanism for implementing the peace agreement. This was signed in January 2005 and cemented when, on 9 July, Garang was sworn in as the country's first vice-president. Tragically, Garang died in a helicopter crash on 30 July.

GOUVERNEMENT PROVISOIRE DE LA RÉPUBLIQUE AL-GÉRIENNE (GPRA)/PROVISIONAL GOVERNMENT OF THE ALGERIAN REPUBLIC. On 18 September 1958, the **Front de Libération Nationale** (FLN) established a provisional government in exile in Tunis, the GPRA, with **Ferhat Abbas** as its leader. The GPRA, however, soon split into two factions: those who argued that it should concentrate its efforts employing diplomatic pressures to bring about change which would lead to Algerian independence; and those who wanted to intensify the armed struggle. Members of the GPRA and the French government first met secretly at a location outside Paris in June 1960. In August 1961, at a meeting in Tripoli, Ferhat Abbas was removed from the leadership of the GPRA and replaced by ben Khedda, who was then the GPRA's minister of social affairs. At the same time, Belkacim Krim became minister of the interior and Saad Dahlad became foreign minister.

On 19 March 1962, the GPRA and the French government signed the ceasefire agreement at Evian-les-Bains. On 5 July 1962, ben Khedda and the GPRA arrived in Algiers from their exile to take over the provisional administration of **Algeria**. However, the GPRA had outlived its usefulness. Both ben Khedda and Belkacim Krim, who had been the chief FLN negotiatiors at the Evian peace talks, now favored cooperation with **France**, while **Ahmed ben Bella**, who had been elected vice president of the GPRA while still in prison, wanted a complete break with France; instead, he favored a policy of Maghreb unity, nonalignment, and anti-colonialism. Meanwhile, on 30 June the GPRA had dismissed **Houari Boumedienne**, the commander in chief of the Armée de Libération Nationale (ALN), on suspicion of plotting a coup. On 11 July, both Boumedienne and ben Bella returned to Algeria from Morocco and established themselves at Tlemcen as a rival authority to the GPRA, and on 22 July, ben Bella announced the formation of a seven-man Political Bureau which would undertake "the direction of the country, the reconversion of the FLN and ALN, the construction of the state and the preparation for a meeting of the Conseil national de la Révolution Algérienne (CNRA) at the end of 1962."

Support was now rapidly withdrawn from the GPRA, while ALN troops loyal to ben Bella occupied Bone and Constantine. At the same time, other troops under Boumedienne advanced on Algiers and ben Khedda and his cabinet fled. On 4 August 1962, the Political Bureau of ben Bella assumed control of Algeria.

GOWON, YAKUBU (1934–). In July 1966, General Gowon succeeded General Johnson Aguiyi-Ironsi as military ruler of **Nigeria**, led his country through the civil war to keep it united, and then rebuilt it in the aftermath of the war. Born on 19 October 1934, Yakubu Gowon was to become Africa's youngest head of state during a major crisis in its most populous country and see it through successfully.

He underwent officer training in Ghana, then in England at Eaton Hall, followed by Sandhurst during 1955–1956, before going for further training at Hythe and Warminster. He served on the Nigerian **peacekeeping** mission in the **Congo** (1961–62) and was promoted lieutenant colonel in 1963. Following the military coup of January 1966, General Aguiyi Ironsi became head of state; he appointed Gowon chief of staff of the Nigerian Army. Gowon himself was not involved in the second coup of July 1966, but he was chosen as head of state by the northern officers on the death of Ironsi (Gowon came from the Middle Belt in Nigeria) and assumed office on 1 August 1966.

He was determined to restore military discipline, but in October was faced with the massacre of Ibos in the north. He spent the first months of 1967 trying to persuade **Chukwuemeka Odumegwu Ojukwu**, the military leader of the Eastern Region, not to secede, but he failed to do so and, on 29 May 1967, Ojukwu proclaimed the independent state of Biafra. Gowon countered Ojukwu's proclamation of Biafra by declaring a state of emergency and dividing Nigeria into 12 states, a move that resulted in the abolition of the former ethnically based regions. The civil war began in July and rapidly escalated when the Biafrans advanced into Benin State during August. Gowon issued a "code of conduct" to his troops and insisted that Biafran civilians should be treated properly. When Biafra collapsed in January 1970, Gowon made sure that there was no bloodbath and no retribution. Nonetheless, the war had produced much suffering and an estimated one million deaths, mainly the result of starvation.

Gowon's policy of rehabilitation for the defeated Ibos worked, and within a year of their defeat the starvation and disease which had grown to major proportions by the end of the war had been reversed. His policy of rehabilitation was Gowon's greatest achievement. Gowon promised a return to civilian rule by 1975, but he postponed the date in 1974. One of Gowon's last achievements while in power was to preside over the creation of the **Economic Community of West African States** (ECOWAS) that 20 years later was to undertake a peacekeeping role in **Liberia,** which was then ravaged by civil war. Gowon was ousted from power in a bloodless coup of July 1975 and went to study at Warwick University in Britain.

GREAT BRITAIN (BRITAIN). As one of the two principal European powers in Africa (along with **France**) that was in the process of withdrawing from empire in the years after 1945, Britain inevitably became involved at a number of levels in the wars, whether civil or nationalist, which characterized the politics of the continent at this time. Sometimes Britain was involved in its capacity as a colonial power, sometimes as an **aid** donor, and sometimes as a mediator through the **United Nations** or the **Commonwealth**. **Cold War** considerations also influenced the extent of British commitments on the continent. Unlike France, which maintained garrisons in several countries after independence and intervened actively with these troops on a number of occasions, Britain was more circumspect and tried to keep clear of civil war entanglements where this was possible. The British interest in Africa was directed primarily at its former colonies, which joined the Commonwealth at independence, since the greater part, though by no means all, of Britain's trade, investment, and influence lay with these Commonwealth African countries.

Commonwealth African Countries

In West Africa, Britain's ties lay first with **Nigeria** (the largest black African country which became independent in 1960) where the exploitation of oil after independence made it of major importance, and here Britain became deeply involved during the Nigerian civil war of 1967–1970. Another Commonwealth country in West Africa was Ghana (independent in 1957) whose first leader, Kwame Nkrumah, had greatly accelerated the process of independence in the late 1950s with his call for "independence now." The other two Commonwealth countries on West Africa were **Sierra Leone** and The Gambia.

In East Africa, Britain's most important colony, Kenya, was the theater for the Mau Mau uprising against settler rule in the 1950s and the recipient of considerable British investment; following independence Britain made arrangements for regular "tropical" training in Kenya for units of the British army. **Uganda** was the second British colony in East Africa; relations between the two countries were to slump during the **Amin** years (1971–79) when, among other moves, Idi Amin expelled 30,000 Asians to Britain. Britain's other East African colonies were Tanganyika (independent 1961) and **Zanzibar**, whose violent revolution of African versus Arab in January 1964 was followed by the union of Tanganyika and Zanzibar in April 1964 to form the United Republic of Tanzania. After the defeat of the Khalifa's forces by the British at Omdurman in 1898, Britain and Egypt established a condominium over **Sudan**, although in real terms the country was to be British administered until independence at the beginning of 1956. In the 1920s, the British had considered detaching the southern black, non-Muslim, Christian, and traditional religions provinces of Sudan and joining them to its East African empire; had Britain done this, there would have been no civil war in Sudan during 1956–1972 or again from 1983. Britain had one further colony in Eastern Africa: British Somaliland, which formed the "Horn" of Africa. This was joined with former Italian Somaliland in 1960 to form the newly independent Republic of **Somalia**. During the civil war of the 1980s and 1990s, the former British part of the whole attempted to break away to form a separate independent state.

In Central Africa, the ill-fated Central African Federation (CAF) of 1953 represented a British attempt to create a dominion that would inevitably have been white-dominated. After 10 years of rising, African nationalism and violence the CAF was dissolved at the end of 1963 into its three constituent parts: Malawi, the former Nyasaland, became independent in July 1964; Zambia, the former Northern Rhodesia, in October; while Southern Rhodesia, dominated by a white minority opposed to African majority rule, carried out a Unilateral Declaration of Independence (UDI) in November 1965. Neither Malawi nor Zambia was to be affected by civil wars though both, as Frontline States facing the white minority governments in Rhodesia and **South Africa**, were much troubled by events to their south over many years. While Malawi was the only member of the **Organization of African Unity** (OAU) to exchange diplomats with South Africa, Zambia took a principled stand against both UDI in Rhodesia and apartheid in South Africa.

Britain and Southern Africa

President **Kenneth Kaunda** became the chairman of the Frontline States during the 1980s, and Britain found itself under constant pressure from both Zambia and the other Frontline States to initiate tougher action, first against Rhodesia and then South Africa, though it was generally unwilling to do so.

UDI in Rhodesia was maintained for 15 years (1965–80) and involved Britain in a number of acrimonious disputes with the Commonwealth and the OAU as a result. Following the 1979 Lusaka Commonwealth Conference, Rhodesia returned to legality and then became independent as **Zimbabwe** in 1980. Thus Britain was able to maintain correct, if not especially, cordial relations with Zimbabwe during the 1980s when the Dissidents' War took place. The three British High Commission territories—Bechuanaland, Basutoland, and Swaziland—became independent without major problems (except their relations with South Africa) in 1966 (Botswana and Lesotho) and 1968 (Swaziland).

Britain's long historical relationship with South Africa was complicated by white racial antagonisms between Britons and Afrikaners, quite apart from the black–white racial divide, which became acute during the apartheid years (1948–90). These years saw South Africa become progressively more isolated and also saw Britain fighting a rear-guard action to prevent the international application of sanctions to South Africa. This was especially the case during the years of the Margaret Thatcher government in Britain (1979–90). As South Africa moved closer to civil war from 1985 onward, Britain found itself isolated in the councils of the Commonwealth on the issue of sanctions. Once President **F. W. de Klerk** of South Africa had unbanned the **African National Congress** (ANC) and released **Nelson Mandela**, the country moved to the settlement of 1994 when Mandela became president and the whole political atmosphere in Southern Africa changed for the better.

Aid to Africa

At both official and unofficial levels (government and non-governmental organizations), Britain is a major source of aid for Commonwealth African countries, and this has sometimes taken the form of rehabilitation in the wake of civil wars or other political disturbances. British investments in Africa have been broadly concentrated in a few strategic countries, most notably Nigeria, Kenya, and South Africa, and such investments colored the British reaction to the civil war in Nigeria and apartheid in South Africa.

Oil was discovered in Nigeria in the late 1950s, shortly before independence, and was exploited by both British Petroleum and Shell; as a result, when the civil war broke out in 1967, Britain had huge oil stakes (as well as other investments) to defend in Nigeria, a fact that influenced the British attitude toward the civil war. After sitting cautiously on the fence for the first months of the war, Britain came down firmly on the side of the federal government in Lagos.

In the case of apartheid, Britain had huge investments in South Africa, between 60 and 70 percent of all external investments in the country, and these were exceptionally profitable, so that London had a powerful if selfish motive for doing nothing to disturb the state of affairs there. As a result, British governments tacitly supported the apartheid system and sometimes openly defended the position of the Pretoria government while preventing other states from mounting serious pressures upon the apartheid regime. With an estimated 800,000 British passport holders resident in South Africa during the apartheid years, the British used the "kith and kin" argument as an excuse for taking little or no action against apartheid.

Britain did intervene militarily in East Africa in January 1964 to put down army mutinies in Kenya, Uganda, and Tanganyika just after independence; subsequently, it entered into an agreement with Kenya to carry out annual military exercises in the country and have available other facilities as well. The British attitude toward the **Congo** troubles of 1960–1964 was ambivalent, not least because of its substantial investments in **Tanganyika Concessions** (TANKS) and Union Miniere, so that a breakaway Katanga would not have been unwelcome in London; in any case, as a rule, Britain supported right-wing rather than left-wing groups in most of the revolutionary situations which developed in Africa. Under Prime Minister Edward Heath, Britain was unsympathetic to Uganda's Milton Obote, who attended the Commonwealth conference in Singapore in January 1971 in order to support Presidents Kenneth Kaunda and **Julius Nyerere** in opposing the recently announced British intention to sell arms to South Africa. The British, therefore, welcomed the coup that brought Amin to power in Uganda, believing quite wrongly that they would find him easy to manipulate. Instead, he embarked upon policies that reduced Uganda to civil war.

On the whole the major powers, including Britain, tended to ignore the long civil war in Sudan, although a number of British church groups, non-governmental organizations (NGOs), and relief agencies did become involved in the South. The Archbishop of Canterbury, Dr. George Carey, visited the South in 1994 and created an incident with the Khartoum government by so doing. British **mercenaries** were to appear over these years in **Angola**, the Congo, Rhodesia, and elsewhere on the continent.

Tony Blair, who became prime minister of Britain in 1997, demonstrated particular concern for Africa whose problems he famously described as a "sore on the conscience of the world." In 1999, he authorized the dispatch of British troops to Sierra Leone to bolster the United Nations peacekeeping effort at the end of the country's civil war and sent further reinforcements in 2000. His Chancellor, Gordon Brown, worked hard to persuade the Group of Eight (G8) countries to forgive the debts of Africa's poorest countries. And in 2005, the Blair-sponsored Commission for Africa reported and made a number of recommendations as to how the rich countries, in association with Africa, could do more to solve the continent's problems of poverty.

– H –

HABRÉ, HISSÈNE (1936–). Hissène Habré was one of the leading players throughout the long years of civil war in **Chad**, from the beginning of the 1970s until he was ousted from power in the coup of December 1990, which brought **Idriss Déby** to power. The son of a shepherd, Habré was born at Faya-Largeau and became a clerk in the French army. He received rapid promotion and in 1963 became deputy prefect of Moussouro. He was sent to Paris for higher education and returned to N'Djamena in 1971. On his return from Paris, Habré entered government service.

President François Tombalbaye decided to use Habré as a negotiator and sent him to talks with the then head of the **Front de Libération Nationale du Tchad** (FROLINAT), Abba Siddik, who converted Habré to his cause; but though Habré joined FROLINAT he did not approve of Siddik's caution and the two leaders soon quarreled. Habré, therefore, joined **Goukouni Oueddei** and became a joint leader with him of the Forces Armées du Nord (FAN), then concentrated in the Tibesti Mountains. In 1974 Habré, with fewer than 500 troops, attacked the town of Bardai and attracted international attention by taking a German, Christophe Stalwen, and a Frenchwoman, Francoise Claustre, hostage; he demanded ransom and while Germany paid for Stalwen, **France** refused to pay and Claustre remained a hostage until 1977. Habré quarreled with Goukouni over this affair and so decided to break their relationship and operate on his own.

He made a deal with President Félix Malloum to become prime minister in a government of national unity. This did not last and at the end of 1978, Goukouni's forces captured N'Djamena. A fresh government of national unity—Gouvernement d'Union Nationale de Transition (GUNT)—was formed with Goukouni as prime minister, but Habré was not prepared to play number two to him and in March 1980, heavy fighting between their respective forces erupted in the capital. Nine months of fighting in and around N'Djamena followed before Habré's forces were defeated when Libyan troops intervened on behalf of Goukouni. Habré was forced to retreat into exile at the end of 1980, first to Cameroon and then to **Sudan**. While in Sudan, Habré rebuilt his forces. He ignored the efforts of the **Organization of African Unity** (OAU) to bring about a cease-fire and invaded the north of Chad early in 1982; he had a series of successes and captured a number of towns in May and then, on 7 June 1982, he took the capital, N'Djamena. On 19 June, Habré proclaimed himself interim head of state and established a Council of State. He then turned his army against the forces of Abdelkader Kamougue in the south and by August had forced him into exile.

On 21 October 1982, Habré was sworn in as president of Chad and was able to claim that for the first time in 17 years all Chad was under a single ruler. Goukouni now made a recovery and in 1983, in alliance with the Libyans, reconquered the north of the country, taking Faya-Largeau in June. The strength of the Libyan intervention persuaded the **United States**, France, and **Zaire** to send military assistance to Habré. For some time, Habré faced insurrections in the south, despite his defeat of Kamougue, but gradually he overcame these. In 1987, he was able to mount an offensive in the north and to liberate the whole region except for the Aozou Strip. Following President **Muammar Gaddafi**'s speech to the OAU of 25 May 1988, in which he said he would recognize the Chad government, Habré seized the chance to restore diplomatic relations with Libya (the first time since 1982). Goukouni continued to hold out in the north, but Habré managed to attract most of his supporters to join him, including Achiek Ibn Oumar and his troops. In elections, which he staged on 10 December 1989, Habré obtained a 99 percent vote for himself as president for the next seven years.

Habré underestimated both the determination and military skill of his former ally, Idriss Déby, who invaded Chad from Sudan in November 1990. Habré led his forces against Déby, but they were heavily defeated and he was then deserted by most of his troops and obliged to flee to Cameroon. Later he became an exile in Senegal. However, in September 2005 an investigating judge in Belgium charged Habré with crimes against humanity and torture and issued an international warrant for his arrest. The Belgian move followed four years of judicial investigation that had been carried out at the instigation of 21 Chadians living in Belgium under that country's "universal jurisdiction" law, which was designed to allow prosecutions for crimes against humanity, regardless of where they had been committed. In November, Habré was arrested in Senegal but was released on appeal, then re-arrested and placed under house arrest while the case for his extradition to Belgium was put before the current president of the **African Union**, President **Olusegun Obasanjo** of **Nigeria**.

HABYARIMANA, JUVENAL (1937–94). Born in 1937 and army-educated, Juvenal Habyarimana seized power without bloodshed in a coup on 5 July 1973. He ruled **Rwanda** for the next 20 years and though a Hutu was equally ready to act against insurgents of either the Hutu or the Tutsi ethnic groups; he adopted a policy of reconciliation between the two groups. Immediately following the coup in which he ousted Gregoire Kayibanda, he banned all political activity. In 1975, he created the Mouvement Révolutionnaire National pour le Développement (MRND) and made himself sole leader of a one-party state.

On 20 December 1978, a new constitution confirmed Habyarimana in his position as president of Rwanda. Three years later, the elections of December 1981 returned the country's first elected legislature in the form of a National Development Council under the one-party system. In 1983 Habyarimana, the sole candidate, was re-elected president. In 1985, he reorganized the party and set up a school of ideology. He was again elected president in 1988. Economic and social problems, however, mounted during the latter part of the 1980s; these included soil erosion, an increase in population that put further strains upon the economy, and the collapse of coffee prices (Rwanda's staple export); each problem contributed to Habyarimana's growing unpopularity. Responding to pressures for reform, Habyarimana introduced measures that would lead to multi-partyism on 21 September 1990. However, these plans were thrown into confusion when in October 1990, the **Rwanda Patriotic Front** (RPF) mounted an invasion from **Uganda**. The RPF was Tutsi dominated. The invaders were defeated and forced to retreat, but only after months of heavy fighting and severe casualties. Habyarimana then pressed ahead with his reform program and on 10 June 1991, Rwanda became a multi-party state.

Habyarimana hoped to persuade the exiled Tutsis to return home and take part in multi-party elections. Instead, the RPF invaded for a second time, its leadership intent only on taking political control along ethnic lines. On 6 April 1994, the plane carrying Habyarimana and the president of **Burundi**, Cyprien Ntaryamira (they had been holding talks about the joint problems of their two countries), was shot down by Hutu extremists. Both men were killed, and this action sparked off the disaster of ethnic massacres which erupted and continued in Rwanda for six months to claim an estimated one million lives.

HAMMARSKJÖLD, DAG (HJALMAR AGNE CARL) (1905–61).
Dag Hammarskjöld, who was born on 19 July 1905, was the second secretary-general of the **United Nations** and played an active role in the early phases of the civil war in the former Belgian **Congo** before he was killed on 18 September 1961 in a mysterious air crash near Ndola in Northern Rhodesia (Zambia) while on his way for talks with breakaway Congolese leader **Moise Tshombe**, who was attempting to create a separate state of Katanga out of the huge **Republic of the Congo**.

Hammarskjöld was a Swedish civil servant who served in his country's Ministry of Foreign Affairs from 1947 to 1951; then he was sent to the United Nations as vice-chairman of Sweden's delegation. On 10 April 1953, following an interregnum after the resignation of Trygve Lie of Norway, Hammarskjöld was elected secretary-general of the United Nations. He was to be re-elected in 1957 and spent much of his time dealing with peace problems in the Middle East. No other UN secretary-general gathered to himself as much executive power as did Hammarskjöld.

The Congo crisis, which exploded in July 1960 shortly after the Belgian Congo had become independent, faced the United Nations with its first major problem in black Africa. Hammarskjöld was a very independent secretary-general and acted with speed in response to events in the Congo. He answered the appeal for help by the Congolese prime minister, **Patrice Lumumba**, by sending a **peacekeeping** force in July to control the civil strife which had broken out. Hammarskjöld did not have a free run in the Congo for long because in September 1960 the **Union of Soviet Socialist Republics** (USSR) denounced this intervention, despite the fact that Lumumba (the supposed protege of Moscow) had requested such help. During 1960 the Soviet leader, Nikita Khruschev, advanced the concept of a UN troika: that the world body should be run by three secretaries-general, one to represent the West, one to represent the Communist bloc, and one to represent the Third World or Non-Aligned Movement. While the UN peacekeeping operation was in the Congo Lumumba, who became a hero of the Left, was kidnapped and taken to Katanga where he was first tortured and then killed. The United Nations had failed to guard Lumumba and subsequently, made no attempt to rescue him.

Hammarskjöld managed to invest the office of secretary-general with great authority, which included the right to take emergency action prior to gaining the approval of the Security Council. He also made plain he would not be cowed by the **United States**. A controversial figure, and arguably the most outstanding UN secretary-general, Hammarskjöld made African concerns central to UN operations for the first time.

HANI, CHRIS (1942–93). One of the younger generation of the **African National Congress** (ANC) in exile, Chris Hani was born on 28 June 1942, in Transkei. He joined the ANC Youth League in 1957. He attended Fort Hare University from 1959 to 1961, where he studied Latin and Roman history, and completed his studies at Rhodes University before he began work as an articled clerk in Cape Town, although this only lasted until 1963. Hani worked for the South African Congress of Trade Unions (SACTU), but when the ANC was banned he went underground to work for its armed wing, Umkhonto we Sizwe. He proved himself to be extremely able and popular and was elected to the Committee of Seven in Western Cape. In 1962 he was arrested for possessing banned material and charged under the Suppression of Communism Act and sentenced to 18 months in prison. He appealed and went into hiding while on bail.

The ANC now sent him abroad for military training; he was to fight with the **Zimbabwe African People's Union** (ZAPU) in Rhodesia where he learned much of guerrilla warfare. When the government of Botswana banned Umkhonto we Sizwe, Hani was arrested and sentenced to six years in prison; he was freed after two years and went to Zambia. In 1974, following his election to the ANC National Executive, he returned to **South Africa** to build up the organization in the Cape. He then spent seven years in Lesotho. Hani joined the ANC in Zambia in 1982, by which time its headquarters were sited in Lusaka, and became deputy commander in chief of Umkhonto we Sizwe, a post he held until 1987, when he succeeded **Joe Slovo** as its chief of staff.

Always on the radical wing of the ANC, and regarded as the "darling of the left," he quarreled with the leadership about the use of violence against soft targets. Hani returned to South Africa in 1990, following **Nelson Mandela**'s release, and played a leading role in the relaunch of the South African Communist Party (SACP) on 29 July 1990. At the 48th National Conference of the ANC of July 1991, Chris Hani received the most votes from the delegates despite or because of his communist connections. On 10 April 1993, Hani, who was then the leader of the SACP, was assassinated, his death threatening to disrupt the peace talks which were then in progress between the ANC and the government of **F. W. de Klerk**. His assassins were two whites, Clive Derby-Lewis and Janusz Walus.

– J –

JOHNSON, PRINCE YORMIE (c. 1959–). Emerging to prominence during the civil war in **Liberia**, Prince Yormie Johnson began as a military colleague of **Charles Taylor** before parting company with him to form his own guerrilla group. Johnson was a Gio from Nimba county. He joined the army as a young man to become a lieutenant in 1974. He was sent on a training course to Fort Jackson in South Carolina, but after a car crash, he left the army in 1977. He was involved with General Thomas Quiwonkpa, who mounted an unsuccessful coup attempt against President **Samuel Doe** in 1985; the subsequent brutal killing of Quiwonkpa by Doe and the exposure of his body left its mark on Johnson and in 1987, he joined Taylor's **National Patriotic Front of Liberia** (NPFL) in order to oppose Doe. NPLF guerrillas were given training in Libya. Johnson was part of the guerrilla invasion force of Charles Taylor, which crossed into Liberia on 24 December 1989 from **Côte d'Ivoire**.

The immediate reaction of President Doe to the invasion was to repress the Gio and Mano people who lived in the region where the civil war (invasion) had begun, but this simply had the effect of uniting them behind the rebels. Differences between Taylor and Johnson soon emerged, and Johnson proceeded to build up his own following. He opposed Taylor's dependence upon Libyan support; this stance suited the **United States**, which was always ready to support opponents of **Muammar Gaddafi**, and Washington tended to favor Johnson over Taylor. By mid-1990, when the NPLF guerrillas had reached the outskirts of the Liberian capital, Monrovia, Taylor and Johnson were operating separate guerrilla organizations, with Johnson calling his followers the Independent National Patriotic Front. His soldiers were the first to enter Monrovia. Johnson told reporters at this time: "I don't want power. I want a fair election. I will get Doe, he is not going to get away."

Johnson was in favor of external intervention to end the civil war in Liberia and supported the **Economic Community Monitoring Group** (ECOMOG) set up by the **Economic Community of West African States** (ECOWAS). On 9 September 1990, when Doe left the Executive Mansion to visit ECOMOG headquarters for a consultation about his own withdrawal from the country, he was seized by Johnson's guerrillas, interrogated, and tortured before being killed the next day. Other killings or executions were carried out by Johnson's forces at this time. Johnson then cooperated with ECOMOG and turned his troops against Taylor's NPFL. He took part in the series of peace conferences that were held during 1990 and 1991 and became a member of the interim government under **Amos Sawyer**. Johnson promised to assist **Sierra Leone** after it had been invaded by Taylor's NPLF. In August 1991, following a debate in the legislative assembly about his conduct and allegations of killings done in his name, Johnson resigned from the interim government.

– K –

KABILA, LAURENT-DÉSIRÉ (?1943–2001). The victory of Laurent-Désiré Kabila in **Zaire**'s civil war during 1997, when he toppled the corrupt regime of President **Mobutu Sese Seko**, brought a virtually unknown man to the leadership of Africa's third largest country. Kabila became a nationalist at the end of Belgian rule when he supported **Patrice Lumumba**. A Luba from Katanga (Shaba), Kabila studied political philosophy in **France** before becoming a protege of Lumumba and a Marxist. Kabila was implicated in the Simba massacre of civilians in Stanleyville (Kisangani) in 1964. He formed his own political party, the Parti de la Révolution Populaire (PRP)/Popular Revolution Party, which opposed Mobutu for 30 years, although during the years 1964 to 1996, Kabila fought a totally ineffective campaign from his base in the Fizi Mountains bordering Lake Tanganyika. According to Che Guevara, to whom Kabila played host in 1965, there was little of the revolutionary about Kabila. Guevara said: "He displays none of the required discipline of a dedicated revolutionary and is too addicted to drink and women."

Kabila is credited with the kidnapping of three U.S. students and a Dutch researcher in 1975 and making money from smuggling gold. He retained control of a remote area west of the Mitumba Mountains throughout the Mobutu years, although little else is known of his activities. He had a reputation for animosity toward Roman Catholics and Catholic influence in the country and is reputed to have killed Roman Catholics, whom he regarded as opponents, when he was confined to the Fizi Mountains.

Nonetheless, despite much adverse criticism once he had come to power, Kabila did succeed in forging and leading a broad front against Mobutu (something no other opponent of Mobutu had ever managed) and in October 1996, his PRP joined with three other parties to form the Alliance des Forces Démocratiques pour la Libération du Congo/Zaire (AFDL)/Alliance of Democratic Forces for the Liberation of Congo/Zaire.

When Kabila emerged victorious from the civil war in May 1997, as Mobutu's forces disintegrated, outside observers attributed his victory largely to the support of Tutsi troops from both **Rwanda** and **Uganda** rather than to the achievements of his own followers. Little was known of the country's "savior" except that he was nominally of the Left in politics. U.S. Security Council President Bill Richardson said hopefully of Kabila (the **United States** had long been deeply involved with Mobutu's Zaire): "Kabila shows promise of learning from his mistakes and becoming more tolerant in accepting diverse viewpoints."

After he came to power in May 1997, Kabila banned opposition parades, reputedly allowed his forces to massacre thousands of Hutu refugees, held up the **United Nations** human rights investigations, and then expelled the UN representatives. As president of a shattered country, whose economy had been virtually destroyed, Kabila faced formidable problems: general chaos and a breakdown of law and order, some 240 tribes or ethnic groups, smoldering secessionist ambitions in Katanga, and predatory western companies moving in to profit from the economic mess left by Mobutu. Six months after the fall of Mobutu, there appeared to be breakaway tendencies developing in the east of the country.

In mid-1998, the **Congo** faced another civil war, again beginning in the east; the rebels, mainly ethnic Tutsis, were supported by both Rwanda and Uganda in an attempt to prevent the massacre of Tutsis in Kinshasa and elsewhere in the country. When, in August 1998, it appeared that Kabila might lose power, **Angola**, **Namibia**, and **Zimbabwe** committed themselves to supporting Kabila and sent military contingents to his aid. The outcome of these external interventions was to turn a civil war into what became known as "Africa's Great War." Kabila, who at best only had partial control over events in his huge country, was assassinated by one of his own presidential guards on 16 January 2001. His son, Joseph Kabila, gradually became his "successor." *See also* CONGO, DEMOCRATIC REPUBLIC OF: AFRICA'S GREAT WAR.

KAUNDA, KENNETH DAVID (1924–). Kenneth Kaunda, who was president of Zambia from October 1964 to October 1991, played a significant, if external and secondary, role in relation to the wars in the Southern Africa region. Zambia's long western border was with war-torn **Angola**; in the east Zambia bordered the northern Tete Province of war-torn **Mozambique**; and along the Zambezi it was in confrontation with Rhodesia while also having a border along the

Caprivi Strip of **Namibia**, where a guerrilla war was in progress. For the greater part of Kaunda's presidency, "confrontation" with the white-dominated South was the principal concern of Zambian foreign policy, and Zambia's geographic position made it the Frontline State in relation to Rhodesia under Ian Smith and his illegal regime. The nationalist uprising in Angola, which began in 1961, was followed by a second uprising in Mozambique in 1963 and then the Unilateral Declaration of Independence (UDI) in Rhodesia in 1965, so that by the latter year Zambia faced highly destabilized war situations on three borders.

Kaunda, therefore, had a major interest in assisting any moves toward a settlement. When Angola became independent of **Portugal** in 1975, Kaunda at first supported the **Frente Nacional da Libertação de Angola** (FNLA)/National Front for the Liberation of Angola and the **União Nacional para a Independência Total de Angola** (UNITA)/ National Union for the Total Independence of Angola movements in that country; in 1976, following a **Movimento Popular para a Libertação de Angola** (MPLA)/Popular Movement for the Liberation of Angola government offensive against UNITA, about 1,000 **refugees** crossed the border into western Zambia. Shortly afterward, Zambia came to terms with the new Angolan government of **Agostinho Neto** (March 1976) and subsequently impounded a UNITA plane while also closing its airspace to UNITA and the FNLA and prohibiting them to operate from Zambian soil. By the end of 1976, there were 19,000 Angolan refugees in Zambia, whose government then expelled UNITA officials from Lusaka. By March 1977, Zambian–Angolan relations were sufficiently amicable for Kaunda to make an official visit to Angola. From 1984 onward, Lusaka was to act periodically as a venue for peace talks between the Angolan (MPLA) government and U.S. and South African officials. In 1986, UNITA's leader **Jonas Savimbi**, whose forces then controlled a third of Angola, warned Kaunda not to support the Luanda government. An important consideration for Zambia was the **Benguela Railway**, which was used to transport Zambia's copper to Lobito for trans-shipment to Europe, until the line was cut in the later 1970s during the Angolan civil war.

In 1979, by which time Lusaka acted as headquarters for a number of southern African liberation movements, the **Commonwealth** held its biannual heads of government meeting there (in part as a recognition of Kaunda's role in relation to the struggle in the south of the continent); this was the occasion when a breakthrough in relation to Rhodesia was achieved, so that by April 1980, **Robert Mugabe** and the **Zimbabwe African National Union** (ZANU) had won the first universal franchise elections in that country, and an independent **Zimbabwe** was born.

In 1985, Kaunda succeeded **Julius Nyerere** as chairman of the Frontline States, a role he filled until the end of the decade. As a supporter of the liberation movements operating in the south, as an arbiter and finally as chairman of the Frontline States, Kaunda made a substantial contribution to the eventual settlements that were reached in the region.

– L –

LAGU, JOSEPH LAGU YANGA (1931–). Joseph Lagu was born on 21 November 1931, and following school went for training at the Military College, Omdurman. He came from the far south of **Sudan** and was posted there with the army in the early 1960s, when he first met **Gaafar Nimeiri**. On 4 June 1963, Lagu deserted the army and joined the **Anya-Nya** rebels, and on 19 September he launched the first Anya-Nya attack against a government target. The movement, meanwhile, was able to obtain arms from the disintegrating Simba rebel movement in neighboring **Zaire**. For the next seven years, until the beginning of the 1970s, Lagu's forces launched a series of attacks against government targets, such as convoys, bridges, and roads. His rebel forces probably numbered an average of 2,000 over these years, though Lagu claimed as many as 7,000. On 27 March 1972, a peace agreement was signed between the Nimeiri government and the southern rebels at Khartoum, in the presence of the Ethiopian emperor, **Haile Selassie**, to bring to an end the first phase of the civil war. Lagu was now promoted to the rank of general, and his Anya-Nya forces were integrated into the Sudanese army. In 1978, he stood against Abel Alier in the South to become the president of the Executive Council of the Southern Region. In 1980, Lagu resigned his post and new elections were held, this time resulting in a return to power of Alier. Lagu then campaigned for the South to be divided into three regions, a move designed to prevent domination by the Dinkas. Nimeiri adopted Lagu's approach to the problems of the South and appointed him one of three national vice-presidents; then in May 1983 Nimeiri divided the South into Equatoria, Upper Nile, and Bahr al-Ghazal Provinces. However, this division, which the South welcomed, was accompanied by the introduction of Sharia law, which it bitterly opposed, and this latter move once more led to civil war. This time, however, Lagu was sidelined; he was in any case too close to Nimeiri. Instead, **John Garang** formed the **Sudan People's Liberation Army** (SPLA) and the **Sudan People's Liberation Movement** (SPLM) and the second phase of the North–South civil war began. When Nimeiri was ousted from power on 6 April 1985, Lagu's vice-presidency was terminated and he retired to exile in London.

LIBERIA. After a decade of corruption, oppression, and brutality under President **Samuel Doe**, who had seized power in a bloody coup of April 1980, Liberia was ready to erupt. An uprising, which turned into a full-scale civil war, began simply as an explosion of anger against the government in one particular region. Fighting began in Nimba county, near the border with **Côte d'Ivoire**, over Christmas 1989; after 10 days of violence, about 10,000 people had fled as **refugees** into Côte d'Ivoire to escape the violence. The rebels destroyed villages and killed a number of civilians, while large parts of Nimba county fell into rebel hands. The immediate reaction of the government was to place the capital under curfew. A majority of the rebels were Gio people belonging to the principal tribe in Nimba county; they attacked members of the Krahn tribe, from which the president came.

The Rebels

The rebels called themselves the **National Patriotic Front of Liberia** (NPFL); their leader, **Charles Taylor**, had been one of Doe's ministers in the early 1980s but had fled Liberia in 1984, accused of corruption. He took $900,000 with him to the **United States**. Taylor manifestly did not possess the credentials of a crusader against a corrupt regime; he was after power. By mid-January 1990, Côte d'Ivoire announced that 30,000 **refugees** had crossed into its territory to escape "genocide," while Charles Taylor claimed that his forces then numbered 5,000 men. Diplomats in Monrovia then estimated that no more than 50 troops on either side had been killed; the bulk of the casualties were among the civilian population. A clear tribal or ethnic pattern of fighting had emerged: the Gio supporters of Taylor attacked members of the Krahn tribe while government forces retaliated by attacking the Gio. The government sent two battalions of troops to deal with the rebellion, although these proved inadequate. By the end of January 1990, some 50,000 people were believed to be hiding in the bush throughout Nimba country to escape retaliation from government forces.

In April 1990, President Doe rashly claimed that "there is no inch of this nation not under the control of the government." There followed an immediate upsurge of fighting in Nimba county and by the end of the month the United States advised its 5,000 citizens then in Liberia to leave, while British Airways laid on special flights to airlift out **Commonwealth** citizens. By this time, the rebels were within 112 kilometers of Monrovia and their army was reported to be 3,000 strong. It was also rumored that Taylor had obtained Libyan backing. The Liberian army, which faced the rebels, was then 7,000 strong. By early May, according to Africa Watch, the number of refugees fleeing the tribal fighting, which had become increasingly savage, had risen to 300,000. At this stage most of the casualties were either Gio or Mano people.

In mid-May, when he captured Buchanan, the country's second port, Charles Taylor had an estimated 10,000 troops under his command. A week later he captured Kakata, which lay a mere 64 kilometers from Monrovia, and by the end of May he was in a position to attack Monrovia's international airport of Robertsfield. During June, the government forces began to disintegrate as they turned upon one another according to tribe. Taylor, meanwhile, was not prepared to hold talks with the other rebel groups and saw himself as the sole candidate for power. By this time U.S. and British warships lay off Monrovia, ready to evacuate their citizens, while the United States had 2,100 marines on standby for emergency intervention. By the end of June 1990, an estimated 750,000 of Monrovia's population (half the total) had fled as Taylor's NPFL closed in. At this point, President Doe said he would welcome an international **peacekeeping** force if this could be arranged at the conference on Liberia, then being held in **Sierra Leone**.

Discipline in the government forces was fast disappearing: Doe had placed members of his own tribe, the Krahn, in all the top army posts, but many could neither read nor write; at the same time summary executions were taking place and morale was collapsing. The rebels entered the outskirts of Monrovia at the end of June, by which time only about 1,000 government troops remained in the city. Demonstrators now called on Doe to resign. Some 400 Gio and Mano people took refuge in city churches, fearful of government reprisals. By July, Monrovia had become a ghost city and the people who remained waited for the arrival of the rebels; government troops were routed wherever they attempted to confront the rebels. Doe, meanwhile, had barricaded himself in the Executive Mansion where he was guarded by crack troops. Government forces continued to target members of the Gio and Mano tribes, while the rebels sought to kill members of the Krahn tribe. About 6,000 Gio and Mano living in Monrovia sought refuge from government soldiers in churches or the Japanese embassy. By the end of the first week in July, the rebels were bombarding the port area of Monrovia, while members of the army abandoned their uniforms and fled. Gradually Monrovia fell to Taylor's forces, street by street, although Taylor himself (known as "superglue" for his corrupt practices) did not appeal as an alternative head of state to Doe.

Prince Yormie Johnson

At the end of July, two clear groups had emerged: Charles Taylor, who was then at the head of 15,000 rebels, insisted that Doe would not be permitted to leave the country; **Prince Yormie Johnson**, who had been an ally of Taylor but had split from him the previous February, had a force of 7,000 troops of his own. Johnson had tried to persuade the United States to intervene but had been told that the war was an internal Liberian affair; he now described Taylor as a criminal who had received $80 million from Libya's **Muammar Gaddafi** to start a revolution (an unlikely story as far as such a sum of money was concerned). At the end of July, when an estimated 375,000 Liberians had fled into neighboring countries, government forces massacred 600 men, women, and children in a Lutheran church where they had taken refuge. While the ambassadors of the European Community called for an emergency session of the **United Nations** Security Council, government forces in Monrovia mounted a counterattack.

Intervention by West African States

At this stage a number of West African states, under the leadership of **Nigeria**, made plans to intervene and stop the fighting; these were The Gambia, Chana, Guinea, Nigeria, and Sierra Leone. The **Economic Community of West African States** (ECOWAS) prepared a military intervention force under the command of Ghana's Lt.-Gen. Arnold Qainoo while requesting financial assistance from the United States to help cover the costs. In Monrovia itself, President Doe was beleaguered in the Executive Mansion while the city was divided between the forces of Taylor and Johnson. The **Economic Community Monitoring Group** (ECOMOG) was established in Monrovia in the first part of September and on 9 September President Doe—whose position was becoming increasingly precarious—went to the ECOMOG headquarters with 60 followers to discuss his own evacuation from the city; however, he was intercepted by Johnson's men, tortured, mutilated, and killed. After Doe's death, both Taylor and Johnson laid claim to the presidency as did Brig. Gen. David Nimblay, who had been Doe's minister of defense and reputedly responsible for his death squads. ECOWAS now gave its backing to a former politician, **Amos Sawyer**, who was made head of an interim government. He too advanced claims to the presidency. Fighting between the followers of these four would-be presidential candidates was to continue until November when a cease-fire was arranged. By that time (November 1990), casualties were estimated in tens of thousands, the economy was in ruins, and a great deal of property had been wrecked.

Rivalry for the Presidency

It became clear in early 1991 that the cease-fire between the rival factions would not hold, and while Sawyer with his interim government was just able to maintain control in Monrovia, outside the city the rivals fell to fighting one another. The rival groups that emerged were: the Armed Forces of Liberia (AFL) (the remnants of Doe's army) under General Hezekiah Bower; the National Patriotic Front of Liberia

(NPFL) under Charles Taylor; and the Independent National Patriotic Front under Prince Yormie Johnson. The factions met in Lome, Togo, during February where they agreed to convene a national conference in March, although Taylor, who then controlled over half of Liberia, was reluctant to take part. Lome, however, resolved nothing; 14 factions (though not Taylor's NPFL) met, but failed to reach any agreement.

A new international dimension was then added to the situation as clashes occurred along the border of Sierra Leone between Taylor's forces and Sierra Leone government troops (Taylor's forces had crossed into the neighboring country illegally). In June 1991, Sawyer spoke of an ECOMOG supervised peace and this was followed by a meeting during July in Yamoussoukro, Côte d'Ivoire, when Sawyer and Taylor promised to end the fighting. At that time, it was estimated that 15,000 people had been killed; a peace treaty was negotiated in October.

Yet Liberia began 1992 as deeply troubled as ever with no real peace in sight. An electoral commission was established on 13 January to organize elections for mid-year but, meanwhile, the mid-January deadline for handing in arms passed without anyone having complied. Yet another faction—the United Liberation Movement of Liberia (ULIMO) under Ralegh Seekiwe—now materialized and on 4 March 1992, Seekiwe said he would continue fighting. In April at Geneva, Sawyer and Taylor met with ECOMOG and agreed that it should create a buffer zone along the border with Sierra Leone. However, the following August fierce fighting erupted inside Sierra Leone between Taylor's forces and troops of former President Doe. In November another outbreak of bitter fighting occurred between the NPLF and ECOMOG forces in Monrovia. ECOWAS now ordered tougher action through ECOMOG against Taylor's NPFL, which by this time controlled 95 percent of Liberia; it ordered a trade embargo while the Nigerian air force bombed rebel positions around Monrovia. On 19 November 1992, the UN Security Council called for an arms embargo on Liberia.

ECOMOG Action against the NPFL

In January 1993, ECOMOG launched an offensive against the NPFL and on 8 January, its forces sank two ships and seized three others bringing arms to the NPFL. ECOMOG proceeded to drive the NPFL out of Monrovia's suburbs. The withdrawal of Senegal's contingent from ECOMOG meant that its forces were composed of Nigerians (the majority) and troops from The Gambia, Ghana, Guinea, Mali, and Sierra Leone. ECOMOG made substantial military gains early in 1993: its forces retook Kataka from the NPFL and moved along the coast to the port of Buchanan; they captured Lofa County in the north—a total of three Taylor strongholds. In May 1993, reflecting his losses, Taylor launched a campaign of terror against civilians under his control. On 6 June, 450 people in refugee camps were massacred and though at first Taylor and the NPFL were blamed, it later transpired that the massacres had been carried out by the Armed Forces of Liberia composed of former Doe soldiers. After a series of talks brokered by ECOWAS, the **Organization of African Unity** (OAU), and the United Nations, a peace agreement was signed on 25 July 1993 by the interim government (Sawyer), the NPFL, and ULIMO at Cotonou, Benin.

At this time, it was estimated that as many as 150,000 people had died in the civil war, that one third of the population of 2,250,000 had been displaced with 110,000 facing starvation, that widespread damage had been done to towns and villages, while the economy had been brought to a standstill. On 25 August 1993, it was agreed to establish a Council of State with the interim government continuing in office, and that an Africa-wide peacekeeping force (not only ECOWAS) should be assembled. At the end of August, the 35 members of the transitional legislature had yet to be named. Nigeria announced that it intended to withdraw its troops by March 1994. Delays to the implementation of the peace continued, although on 22 September 1993, the UN Security Council adopted Resolution 866 to establish a UN Observer Mission in Liberia (UNOMIL). In February 1994, the Council of State elected David Kpormakor, a member of the Sawyer interim government, as its chairman. Then, in March, in an apparent breakthrough, Charles Taylor announced that his forces would disarm, even though fighting continued in the southeast of the country. There were then between 25,000 and 60,000 men to be disarmed by the peacekeepers.

1994 proved a difficult year—half peace, half violence. On 16 May, the three groups—the interim government, the NPFL, and ULIMO—formed a new government, although ULIMO complained that fighting between the three factions still continued. On 19 July, Taylor complained that his NPFL forces had been attacked by ECOMOG with heavy loss of life; early in August the NPFL held talks with the OAU and UN delegations and the warring factions then met (3 August) and agreed to cease hostilities so that ECOMOG and the United Nations could deploy their peacekeepers. However, further fighting occurred during the month, this time between the NPFL and the Liberian Peace Council. At the end of the year (21 December), all seven (by then) of the warring factions agreed to a cease-fire to come into effect on 28 December. Peace remained elusive through 1995, and negotiations during January in Accra, Ghana, ended without agreement between the factions on the composition of the Council of State, although the cease-fire held. In February, Charles Taylor put forward a new plan under which an old traditional chief, Chief Tamba Tailor, would become chairman of the council while Taylor would be vice-chairman. This was rejected. Fighting then broke out between the NPFL and the Liberian Peace Council and some 35,000 people were forced to flee their homes and take refuge in Buchanan. The fighting, with another massacre at Yosi, continued through April.

Talks continued through the year—at Accra, Ghana, and Abuja, Nigeria, under ECOWAS auspices, and UNOMIL renewed its mandate. Tanzania, which had contributed 300 troops to the peacekeeping force, withdrew these in frustration when no progress was achieved. In July 1995, Taylor was accused of importing arms and raiding across the Guinea border. The factions all met in Monrovia for the first time since the outbreak of the civil war at the end of 1989 and finally settled on the composition of the Council of State (August). It was to have a neutral chairman and two neutral members. A cabinet of 16 was sworn in, while Charles Taylor became one of the six members of the Council of State. Despite the agreement, further fighting occurred at the end of the year. The peace collapsed in April 1996, when bitter fighting erupted in Monrovia, forcing thousands to flee the city. This fighting followed the storming of the dissident General D. Roosevelt Johnson's home (he was the leader of the ULIMO-J faction) by the forces of the NPFL and those of General Alhaji G. V. Kromah of the United Liberation Movement of Liberia (ULIMO-K). General Roosevelt Johnson's home was soon retaken by his supporters who were Krahn tribesmen, and who then went on the offensive against NPFL and ULIMO-K forces. Prince Yormie Johnson's forces now took several hundred hostages. A new cease-fire was arranged and in August a truce was negotiated. At this stage Burkina Faso, Côte d'Ivoire, The Gambia, Mali, Niger, and Togo agreed to provide peacekeeping troops, and the United States promised $30 million in funding.

In November 1996, the peacekeeping force began the task of disarming the rival factions, and by July 1997, UN officials claimed that 15,519 fighters had been disarmed since the process began. Meanwhile, speaking in Monrovia on 14 February 1997, Nigeria's foreign minister, Chief Tom Ikimi, said (for ECOWAS) that elections for president and the legislature would be held on 30 May; and ECOWAS agreed to create a seven member electoral commission to supervise the elections. It was agreed that the ECOMOG force should be withdrawn from Liberia six months after the elections; it would be replaced by a well trained Liberian army and police force. During February 1997, ECOMOG arrested 60 "armed criminals" of the various factions who had not surrendered their weapons and handed them over to the police. As preparations went ahead for the May elections, the fragile peace was threatened by continuing general instability. On 6 March, assisted by the United States and **Great Britain**, some 1,160 troops from Côte d'Ivoire, Ghana, and Mali arrived in Monrovia to reinforce ECOMOG. Large quantities of arms were recovered from the Executive Mansion (headquarters of the Council of State) by ECOMOG, which arrested 11 ex-NPFL fighters. Alhaji Kromah was arrested after four truckloads of arms were recovered from his residence; arms were also found at the residences of Charles Taylor, George Boley, and General Roosevelt Johnson, all former faction leaders. Following disagreements, a meeting of all the presidential contenders was held in Abuja, Nigeria, on 16 May. The elections were rescheduled for 19 July, with 2 August set for runoffs and 6 August for the inauguration of the newly elected government.

The Elections of 1997

Sixteen parties were registered to take part in the elections. The elections resulted in an overwhelming victory for Charles Taylor and his National Patriotic Party (NPP), which took 49 out of 64 seats in the House of Representatives and 21 out of 26 seats in the Senate. Taylor was declared president on 23 July by the Independent Election Commission; he had won more than 70 percent of the votes cast. Speaking on 24 July, Taylor called for national reconciliation and promised "fair play, equality and justice for all."

However, having won the elections, Taylor showed little inclination to share power with former opponents, instead working to destroy opposition groups and especially the United Liberation Movement of Liberia (ULIMO). At the same time, Taylor's relations with the remaining ECOMOG forces were strained and he maintained his support for the rebel forces in neighboring Sierra Leone where civil war continued. During 1998, neighboring states accused Taylor of supporting the Revolutionary United Front (RUF) in Sierra Leone. Since both Sierra Leone and Guinea had contributed contingents of troops to the ECOMOG force in Liberia, it was clear that Taylor's support for RUF was in the nature of settling old scores. Taylor maintained a tight grip on power through 2000, assisted by his control of the country's **diamond** trade. In June, however, Britain persuaded the EU to block the first tranche of $55 million **aid** for Liberia because of its continued support for the RUF. In May 2001, UN sanctions were imposed on Liberia because of its ongoing interference in Sierra Leone. Sanctions included a ban on diamond exports and travel restrictions on senior government officials.

The Disintegration of the Taylor Regime

Taylor's grip on power began to fall apart during 2002. In January, many thousands of Liberians fled the north of the country to escape fighting between government forces and Liberians United for Reconciliation and Democracy (LURD). The fighting spread and gradually came closer to Monrovia forcing Taylor to declare a state of emergency. In March, LURD said it was ready to hold peace talks, but Taylor relied on a military solution. In May, the UN Security Council voted to renew sanctions on Liberia for another year because of its continuing support for the Sierra Leone rebels and in July the secretary-general, **Kofi Annan**, warned that the conflict in Liberia threatened UN peacekeeping efforts in Sierra Leone. The fighting between government forces and LURD continued in January 2003, by which time LURD was receiving assistance from Guinea. Much of the fighting was centered upon the diamond producing towns of Wesua and Wiegiu. In April the U.S., EU, and UN missions in Liberia claimed that thousands of people had been forced to flee their homes and that 14,000, mainly **women and children**, had crossed the border into Guinea. By this time, Guinean troops were fighting alongside LURD against Taylor.

In May, the UN High Commissioner for Refugees (UNHCR) called upon Taylor to step down, saying he was the embodiment of the region's problems. Then on 4 June, Taylor's position was greatly weakened when the Special Court for Sierra Leone (a UN-backed war crimes tribunal) indicted him for war crimes and accused him of "bearing the greatest responsibility for war crimes" during the 10-year civil war in Sierra Leone, which had finally come to an end in 2002. When Taylor was attending a peace conference in Accra, Ghana, a warrant for his arrest was issued, forcing him to leave early and return to Liberia, after saying he would "strongly consider" a government of national unity that did not include him. In June 2003, the rebels laid siege to Monrovia and LURD gave Taylor until 10 June to leave the country. Pressures mounted on Taylor throughout the remainder of June and through July until, on 4 August, ECOWAS peacekeepers began to arrive in Monrovia to a wild welcome from its citizens. On 11 August, Taylor resigned the presidency and fled to Nigeria (from where he was extradited to the Netherlands to stand trial in The Hague for human rights violations). He was succeeded by his vice-president Moses Blah, who at once signed a peace settlement with the rebels. It was agreed to set up an interim government in October to hold office until elections were held in January 2006. Through 2004 Liberia struggled to return to normalcy. Over 5–6 February, a donor conference at UN headquarters in New York pledged $500 million for Liberian reconstruction.

LINKAGE. In 1981, following the election victory of Ronald Reagan and the Republicans, the **United States** adopted a tougher line toward **Angola**; the Washington administration said it would not recognize the government in Luanda while 20,000 Cuban troops remained in the country. At the same time, the U.S. Senate voted to repeal its earlier ban on **aid** to the **União Nacional para a Independência Total de Angola** (UNITA)/National Union for the Total Independence of Angola, and from then onward a regular flow of aid to UNITA was channeled through **Zaire**. **Jonas Savimbi**, the leader of UNITA, was largely responsible for pushing the idea of linking any internal settlement between the **Movimento Popular para a Libertação de Angola** (MPLA)/Popular Movement for the Liberation of Angola government and UNITA to the withdrawal of the Cubans—what became known as linkage—and such a policy also suited **South Africa**, which sought any excuse to prolong its own presence in South West Africa (**Namibia**). In the case of Washington, apart from its rooted antagonism to **Cuba**, linkage provided an excuse for accepting the status quo in Namibia while delaying any decision about Angola. In the case of Pretoria, linkage meant it could prolong both its hold on Namibia and its maintenance of apartheid, as long as Angola remained destabilized.

In response to this new policy of linkage, Cuba's Fidel Castro said in July 1982 that Cuban forces would not be withdrawn from Angola until South Africa had quit Namibia and ceased its attacks upon Angola. Later in the same year Savimbi visited Washington where he received VIP treatment, since his usefulness to Washington, as well as his personal stature had been enhanced as a consequence of the new policy. Through the 1980s, linkage ensured that each side in the Angola equation tied agreement with the other to the withdrawal of the Cubans on the one hand and independence for Namibia on the other. This greatly complicated the chances of achieving a peace and prolonged the war; yet, in the end, it probably assisted Namibia to achieve its independence from South Africa. Despite the objections to linkage, which were maintained through most of the 1980s by the Angolan government and Cuba, eventually both accepted linkage during the 1988 negotiations when the **Crocker Plan** was put into place.

LORD'S RESISTANCE ARMY. *See* UGANDA AND THE LORD'S RESISTANCE ARMY.

LUMUMBA, PATRICE (1925–61). Patrice Lumumba was born on 2 July 1925 at Onalua in Kasai of the small Batetela tribe which was to assist his national appeal as a politician, since he was not the representative of a powerful regional group, as in the case of **Moise Tshombe**. As a young man, Lumumba became active as an évolué (educated African) when he wrote essays and poems for Congolese journals. He applied for and received full Belgian citizenship and obtained a job as a postal clerk, first in Leopoldville (Kinshasa) and then Stanleyville (Kisangani). In 1955, Lumumba became president of a Congolese trade union of government employees, which was not affiliated with any other group. At the same time, he became active in the Belgian Liberal Party in the **Congo**. In 1956, Lumumba went on a tour to Belgium, but on his return to the Congo was arrested and eventually condemned to one year in prison for embezzling post office funds. In October 1958, Lumumba founded the Mouvement National Congolais (MNC)/ National Congolese Movement, which was the colony's first nation-wide political party. In December 1958, Lumumba attended the first All-African People's Conference in Accra; he returned to the Congo a far more militant nationalist as a result of his new experience. In 1959, the Belgian government announced a program to lead the Congo to independence over five years. The more radical nationalists denounced this program, which they claimed was designed to install puppets before independence was achieved, and they boycotted the elections that were a part of it. The Belgian response to opposition was repression.

On 30 October 1959, clashes in Stanleyville led to 30 deaths, and Lumumba was imprisoned on a charge of incitement to riot. The MNC then changed its tactics of boycott and entered the elections; in Stanleyville it secured 90 percent of the votes. In January 1960, Belgium convened a round table conference in Brussels of all the political parties to discuss coming political changes. The MNC refused to take part in the conference without Lumumba, whom the Belgians then released and flew to Belgium. It was agreed that the Congo should become independent on 30 June 1960. National elections were scheduled for the previous May. Lumumba emerged with the strongest following from these May elections and was called on—reluctantly by the Belgians—to form the first African government, which he did on 23 June. However, although Lumumba became prime minister, he was forced to share power with Joseph Kasavubu.

In the two weeks following independence, the Force Publique (Armed Forces)—which strongly objected to its Belgian commander, who remained in place after independence—sought better pay and conditions, and rebelled. Then Tshombe declared the secession of Katanga Province. Belgium sent troops to protect its nationals, and a majority of these were posted to Katanga, where most of the country's minerals were found. In effect, they supported Tshombe's secession. Lumumba, therefore, appealed to the **United Nations**, which sent peace enforcement troops to the country. Lumumba's hold on power was tenuous, however, and he had few trained people under him in government, while the Congolese army was an uncertain factor at this time. The Belgian troops refused to evacuate Katanga and the UN force was unwilling or unable to overcome the secession by Katanga, with the result that Lumumba turned to the **Union of Soviet Socialist Republics** (USSR) for assistance, requesting planes to transport his forces to Katanga. He also called upon independent African countries for help and asked them to meet in Leopoldville that August to work out ways of providing him with assistance.

The West had now become alarmed that Lumumba was "too independent." President Kasavubu, who was a weak figure, favored regional "autonomy." On 5 September 1960, he dismissed Lumumba who, however, denied his authority to do so. Then, on 14 September in his first coup, Colonel **Joseph-Désiré Mobutu** seized power. He came to a working arrangement with Kasavubu, but not Lumumba. In October the United Nations recognized the new Kasavubu government, a move which split the independent African countries broadly into radicals who supported Lumumba and moderates who supported Kasavubu. Lumumba had been given UN protection in Leopoldville, but when he attempted to travel to Stanleyville, which was his main support base, he was captured by Kasavubu forces (2 December); then, on 17 January 1961, he was handed over to Tshombe's regime in Katanga where he was first tortured and then murdered.

After his death, Lumumba became both a national and an African hero, while the fact that the United Nations had failed either to protect him or to rescue him was a scandal that did the world organization great harm. His death also did major damage to Tshombe's reputation. Lumumba was hardly exceptional in his nationalist views nor in his political capacities, but he came to be regarded as an enemy by powerful western interests which were fearful that the Congo, occupying its strategic position in the center of the continent and rich with its vast mineral wealth, would fall into the Communist camp.

– M –

MACHEL, SAMORA MOISES (1933–86). Samora Machel was born in Goza Province and began his adult career as a male nurse in Lourenco Marques (Maputo). He met Eduardo Mondlane, the founder of the **Frente da Libertação de Moçambique** (FRELIMO)/Mozambique Liberation Front, in 1961 but did not hear of the creation of the liberation movement (1962) until 1963 when he left **Mozambique** and joined it in Tanzania. In August 1963 he was sent to **Algeria** for guerrilla training. On his return to Tanzania, he established the first FRELIMO training camp and had under him 250 fully trained fighters when Mondlane launched the struggle against the Portuguese on 25 September 1964. Machel specialized in hit-and-run tactics, always striking at the Portuguese in different places. In 1966, he became FRELIMO's secretary for defense and in 1968, its commander-in-chief. Following the assassination of Mondlane (by letter bomb) in 1969, Machel became one of the troika or three-man council that was appointed to run FRELIMO; in June 1970, however, he was confirmed as the leader of the movement. Despite receiving the bulk of its arms from the **Union of Soviet Socialist Republics** (USSR) or other Communist sources, Machel denied that FRELIMO was a Communist movement: "FRELIMO is a Mozambique party," he insisted. He led the fight against the Portuguese from 1969 to 1974 to become president-in-waiting during the transitional period (1974–75) before the Portuguese departed.

In 1975, Machel became president of an independent Mozambique and almost at once faced a new threat: the insurgency of the **Resistência Nacional Moçambicana** (RENAMO)/Mozambican National Resistance, which was carefully fostered to destabilize the new state, first by Ian Smith's Rhodesia and then, after Rhodesia had become **Zimbabwe** in 1980, by **South Africa**. The civil war which followed, and lasted until 1992, became one of the most brutal in Africa. Machel was a charismatic leader and liked best to be dealing with problems on the spot; he needed all his charisma by the mid-1980s, when the South African–supported civil war waged by RENAMO had brought the country near the point of collapse. As a result Machel was obliged, in 1984, to enter into the **Nkomati Accord** with South Africa; under its terms, Mozambique and South Africa agreed that they would not assist dissidents of either country against the other. Mozambique kept its side of the bargain; South Africa did not. Machel was criticized both by his supporters in Mozambique and by leaders elsewhere in Africa for agreeing to the Nkomati Accord, but at the time he had little alternative. On 19 October 1986, Machel died when his plane crashed in mysterious circumstances as he returned to Mozambique from a meeting with other "frontline" leaders in Lusaka. A pragmatist and soldier, whose role was crucial in both the liberation struggle and guiding Mozambique in its first years of independence, Machel was succeeded by **Joaquim Chissano**.

MAHDI, SADIQ AL- (1926–). Sadiq al-Mahdi was the grandson of Abdul Rahman al-Mahdi, the founder of the Mahdists, whose name in **Sudan** is synonymous with Islam. Educated in Khartoum and at Oxford, Sadiq became the leader of the Umma Party, and on the death of his father in 1959, also became an imam. A man of complexities, Sadiq has often proved indecisive at crucial points in his career. He became prime minister the first time in 1966 when he presided over a coalition government. He tackled the problem of southern dissidence by devolution, creating regional governments, but his efforts were thwarted and he was defeated in 1967 when his uncle, Muhammad Mahjub, became prime minister in his stead. In 1970, following **Gaafar Nimeiri**'s assumption of power, he was accused of treason and went into exile (3 April). Back in Sudan in 1972, he was arrested, only to be released in 1974, when he again went into exile. After reconciliation talks with Nimeiri, Sadiq entered his government in 1977 and joined the ruling Sudan Socialist Union (SSU), but soon found himself in disagreement with Nimeiri's policies and once more went into exile, this time in England.

He was allowed back into the country in 1983, but again fell out with Nimeiri over the question of Sharia law. Sadiq was imprisoned by Nimeiri from September 1983 to December 1984. He contested the post-Nimeiri elections of April 1986 when the Umma Party won the most seats (99) but not an absolute majority, and he became prime minister on 6 May 1986, when he formed a broad-based government. He called upon the rebelling southerners to negotiate. However, the **Sudan People's Liberation Army** (SPLA) under **John Garang** stepped up the war and was only prepared to negotiate if Sadiq first abolished Sharia law. Sadiq wished to apply Sharia law only to the Muslim population of Sudan, but he was hampered in his aim because the Umma Party did not have a clear majority. He therefore called another election for 27 April 1988, when his coalition obtained 196 seats in the 222-seat Assembly; he again tried to negotiate with Garang, but his coalition was weakened in December 1988 when the Democratic Unionist Party (DUP) withdrew to make a tentative peace agreement with Garang and his **Sudan People's Liberation Movement** (SPLM).

Following the DUP defection, Sadiq declared a state of emergency as anti-government demonstrations occurred; at this point, Sadiq turned to the fundamentalists led by Dr. Hassan al-Turabi. This move simply complicated the situation: Turabi and his supporters wanted to impose strict Sharia law; the army opposed this; Sadiq favored a broad-based government and renewed negotiations with the SPLM.

The army seized power under General **Omar Hassan al-Bashir** on 30 June 1989. Sadiq went into hiding, but was found and imprisoned. He was later released, but the new regime saw him as a political threat and again arrested him and kept him in prison until 1996. He then went into exile in **Eritrea**. Sadiq's name was always more important than Sadiq himself, while his background—whatever his own more liberal beliefs might suggest—made it impossible for him to oppose Islamic control in the form of Sharia law with any conviction.

MANDELA, NELSON ROLIHAHLA (1918–). Nelson Mandela, the son of a Thembu chief, was born at Qunu near Umtata, in **South Africa**. In 1938 he went to Fort Hare University to read law. He turned to politics in 1944 when he joined the **African National Congress** (ANC) and formed its Youth League. With his friend, **Oliver Tambo**, he established the first black African law firm in Johannesburg in 1952. He was shortly to lead a nationwide defiance campaign. Mandela became the leader of the Transvaal ANC and in 1953 was banned from public meetings for a period of two years. He was charged with treason in December 1956, but acquitted in March 1961. He organized a massive stay-at-home campaign in opposition to South Africa becoming a republic in 1961 and was arrested under the terms of a state of emergency. He later went into hiding and became known as the "black pimpernel" as he organized ANC opposition from underground.

In 1963, with eight other ANC leaders, Mandela was charged with plotting violent revolution, and at the conclusion of his trial on 20 April 1964, gave a memorable four-and-a-half-hour speech in defense of his actions, which achieved international renown. He was sentenced to life imprisonment on Robben Island. In prison, Mandela became an icon for liberation movements all over the world, as well as for South Africa's opponents of apartheid. In 1982, he was transferred from Robben Island to Pollsmoor Prison near Cape Town, and several times during the 1980s, the government of P. W. Botha made approaches to him promising his release if he would renounce violence. He refused. Following the discovery that he had developed tuberculosis, Mandela was transferred to a house in the Victor Verster Prison, Paarl.

Signalling a fundamental change of policy, President **F. W. de Klerk** announced the unbanning of the ANC and 32 other political parties in a speech he delivered at the beginning of February 1990; Mandela was released unconditionally a week later on 11 February 1990. He was pragmatic in his negotiations with the government and established a personal rapport with de Klerk, but in December 1990 at the ANC consultative conference—the first to be held in South Africa in 30 years—he accused de Klerk of pursuing a double agenda by a policy of destabilizing and attempting to undermine the ANC and its allies. In the fraught four-year period (1990–94), Mandela established his absolute authority over the ANC and, indeed, over most of South Africa. He also traveled the world and obtained huge support for his dream of a new South Africa. Only gradually did de Klerk and the National Party come to see that there was no alternative to the ANC. In the elections of 26–29 April 1994—the first all-race elections in the country's history—the ANC obtained 62.7 percent of the vote.

On 10 May 1994, Nelson Mandela was inaugurated as president of South Africa and head of the government of national unity. Gradually, in the remaining years of the decade, Mandela withdrew from active involvement in the day-to-day running of the state so as to make it easier for his designated successor, Thabo Mbeki, to work himself into authority. Unlike all too many African leaders, Mandela did not cling to power but worked toward his own retirement. On 16 June 1999, Thabo Mbeki was inaugurated as the second democratically elected President of South Africa and Mandela stood down. He became, what for many he already was, an elder statesman and, for example, replaced **Julius Nyerere**, who died in October of that year, as mediator in **Burundi**. He could afford to be outspoken in a way that many African leaders could not and in September 2000, publicly criticized President **Robert Mugabe** of **Zimbabwe** for his "use of violence and the corroding of the rule of law." During the new century, however, Mandela cut down on public engagements.

MEDIATION. Africa's wars have attracted many efforts at mediation by neighboring powers, countries from outside the continent with special interests in Africa, or international organizations. Such efforts have usually been conducted by mediators friendly to one or the other side in the conflict and, more rarely, by genuinely impartial mediators. The three international bodies that have consistently attempted to mediate disputes are the **Organization of African Unity** (OAU), the **United Nations**, and the **Commonwealth**. There have also been African regional efforts at mediation, most notably by the **Economic Community of West African States** (ECOWAS) through the **Economic Community Monitoring Group** (ECOMOG), in both **Liberia** and **Sierra Leone** during the 1990s. **France**'s efforts at mediation in **Chad** and those of the **United States** in **Angola** were important, though in both cases these powers were seen to be partial to one side in the conflict.

In any civil war, the crucial prerequisite for mediation has to be the desire of both sides in the dispute to bring it to an end. If the combatants do not seek peace (which too often has been the case), then, no matter how well disposed the mediators might be, their chances of success are minimal.

Mediation to bring an end to the Angolan civil war (1975–92) was spearheaded by the United States during the long negotiations of 1988 (the **Crocker Plan**); and at that time the approaching end of the **Cold War** meant a degree of U.S.–Soviet collaboration, which would not have been possible at any earlier time. Even so, the negotiations were a long drawn-out affair. In the Liberian civil war of 1990–1994 ECOWAS, led by **Nigeria**, worked hard at mediation, and the ECOMOG **peacekeeping** force played a substantial part in helping bring about a peaceful solution. In this particular case, the efforts of ECOWAS were endorsed and encouraged by the United Nations and the OAU. Indeed, during the 1990s, it became a growing feature of both OAU and United Nations policy to encourage regional peacekeeping efforts.

The Nigerian civil war of 1967–1970 attracted mediation efforts by the Commonwealth, the Vatican, and the OAU, but none succeeded. The OAU, for example, insisted upon a solution within the context of maintaining a single Nigerian state, a condition that was unacceptable as a starting point for a breakaway Biafra. The 1967 OAU summit at Kinshasa appointed a Consultative Peace Committee under the chairmanship of Emperor **Haile Selassie** of **Ethiopia** to mediate the Nigerian dispute, but it made little headway. The OAU continued its mediation efforts through to December 1969, by which time the federal government had all but won the war. At the same time, the secretary-general of the Commonwealth, Arnold Smith, attempted to mediate between the two sides in the Nigerian dispute, but again without success, not least because Biafra saw Britain as biased in favor of the Federal Government. At the beginning of the 21st century, the OAU was replaced by the **African Union** (AU) and one of its first, and hardest, tasks was to attempt to mediate and peace keep in the **Darfur** conflict in **Sudan**.

Mediation in any potential or actual dispute is designed to persuade the two sides to a conflict to resolve their differences peacefully. Such efforts should not be mistaken for either peacekeeping or peace enforcement, which may come later or be undertaken at the same time. In fact, however, such efforts are often in progress simultaneously and become confused with one another in practice.

MENGISTU, HAILE MARIAM (1940–). Haile Mariam Mengistu was born in 1940 and joined the army to become a regular soldier. He came to prominence in 1974 during the coup and subsequent revolution, which overthrew Emperor **Haile Selassie** of **Ethiopia** to end his long-lasting reign. Mengistu was a member of the Armed Forces Coordinating Committee, which soon became the real center of power in the aftermath of the 1974 coup. Other officers, more senior than Mengistu, vied with one another for control of the Committee. On 12 September 1974, the Military Advisory Committee turned itself into the Provisional Military Administrative Council (PMAC), or Dergue, and Mengistu was elected vice-chairman.

Mengistu quickly made his mark on the Dergue as a brilliant speaker and hard worker, coining the revolutionary slogan "Ethiopia first." His dedication and ruthlessness ensured that he would soon emerge on top. There were to be two chairmen of the Dergue, General Aman Mikael Andom and General Teferi Bante, both of whom would be eliminated by Mengistu before he finally became chairman of the Dergue in February 1977; and by 11 November 1977, when Mengistu had Atnafu Abate executed (as a would-be challenger to his authority), only 60 of the original 120 members of the Dergue were left. Under Mengistu's leadership, the Dergue turned Ethiopia into a

Marxist state: land was seized and distributed to state cooperatives, industry was nationalized, and peasant associations carried out land reform programs. Mengistu worked to "civilianize" the government by the creation of a Commission for the Organization of a Party of the Workers of Ethiopia (COPWE), and in 1983, he announced plans for a new People's Democratic Socialist Republic.

In 1986, a draft constitution was published and endorsed in a referendum of February 1987. On 14 June of that year, elections for a national parliament were held and Mengistu and all the members of the ruling politburo of COPWE were duly returned. On 11 September 1987, the national parliament (Shengo) unanimously elected Mengistu president (he was also chief executive, commander in chief of the Armed Forces, and chairman of the Council of Ministers). Throughout these years, Mengistu was faced with the steadily escalating war in **Eritrea** and in 1977–1978, the **Ogaden War**. He obtained massive Soviet military **aid** as well as the assistance of Cuban forces in the war against **Somalia**, but when that war came to an end, his government found that the war in Eritrea had become even fiercer and more intractable.

In 1988–1989, the **Eritrean People's Liberation Front** (EPLF) and the **Tigre People's Liberation Front** (TPLF) launched a combined offensive; by that time it was becoming clear that the war-weary Ethiopian army was not going to win the war. Constant high losses were an important factor sparking off the massive military coup attempt of May 1989, when Mengistu was out of the country. Troops loyal to Mengistu rallied to his cause, however, and Mengistu returned to resume control. Most of the military high command was eliminated. Although he was totally ruthless and a great survivor, Mengistu lacked flexibility and proved incapable of negotiating with the Eritreans or Tigrayans; he continued to prosecute the war long after it was clear he could not win, while his army became steadily more demoralized. On 5 June 1989, the Shengo announced that it was willing to participate in peace talks with the Eritreans, but it precluded any consideration of Eritrean independence, and no progress had been achieved by mid-1990. By May 1991, the rebel forces were closing in on Addis Ababa and Mengistu saw that he was defeated. After sending his family out to **Zimbabwe**, Mengistu himself fled to exile in that country on 21 May 1991, and his regime collapsed.

MERCENARIES. Mercenaries have earned a dubious name for themselves throughout history; their object, as a rule, has been to obtain maximum pay for minimum risks, with the result that those hiring them rarely get value for money. Mercenaries, usually white and recruited from the former colonial powers, became familiar and generally despised figures in Africa during the post-independence period. They were attracted by the wars, whether civil or liberation, that occurred in much of Africa during this time and, as a rule, were to be found on the side of reaction: supporting **Moise Tshombe** in his attempt to take Katanga out of the **Republic of the Congo** (1960–63); in Rhodesia fighting on the side of the illegal Smith regime against the liberation movements; in **Angola**; on both sides in the civil war in **Nigeria**; and in other theaters as well.

The Congo

In the chaos of the Republic of the Congo (1960–66) mercenaries were labeled "les affreux." In Katanga under Tshombe, they were first used to stiffen the local gendarmerie; later they were organized in battalions on their own, numbering one to six commandos, as a fighting force to maintain Tshombe's secession. There were originally 400 European mercenaries in Katanga during the secession; this number rose to 1,500 during the Simba revolt, which affected much of the Congo. These mercenaries came from a range of backgrounds: British colonials, ex-Indian Army, combat experienced French soldiers from **Algeria**, World War II RAF pilots from Rhodesia and **South Africa**, and Belgian paratroopers. The troubles that began in the Congo immediately after independence in July 1960 provided the first opportunity for mercenaries to be employed as fighting units since World War II. These white soldiers fighting in black wars, both then and later, became conspicuous military/propaganda targets in an increasingly race conscious world.

Nigeria

The Nigerian civil war (1967–70) witnessed the use of white mercenaries on both sides, and stories of mercenary involvement and behavior were a feature of that war. Three kinds of mercenary were used: pilots on the federal side; pilots and soldiers on the Biafran side; and relief pilots employed by the humanitarian relief organizations assisting Biafra. Memories of savage mercenary actions in the Congo were still fresh in African minds when the Nigerian civil war began and at first, there was reluctance to use them. Despite a great deal of publicity, the mercenaries played a relatively minor role in the Nigerian civil war, except for air force pilots. French mercenaries led a Biafran force in a failed attempt of December 1967 to recapture Calabar. In Nigeria and elsewhere in Africa, the mercenaries were well aware of the low esteem attached to them and were careful not to put themselves at risk of capture. The Nigerian Federal Code (for the military conduct of the war) said of mercenaries: "They will not be spared: they are the worst enemies." Although both sides in Nigeria were reluctant to use mercenaries, both did so in the end for what they saw as practical reasons, especially because of the shortage of Nigerian pilots. In this war, British mercenaries fought for the federal side against French mercenaries on the Biafran side to perpetuate existing Anglo–French rivalries in Africa; it was the first time since the Spanish civil war of 1936–1939 that contract mercenaries had faced each other on opposite sides.

Mike Hoare, who had become notorious as a mercenary in the Congo, offered his services to each side in Nigeria in turn, but neither wished to employ him. The capacity of Biafra to resist against huge odds was prolonged because Ulli Airport was kept open to the last moment in the war; had it been destroyed, Biafra would have collapsed, but the mercenaries on either side had engaged in a "pact" not to destroy the Ulli runway, since to do so would have put the pilots on both sides—those bringing in supplies to Biafra and those supposedly trying to stop them for the federal government—out of a job. At least some mercenaries in Biafra were involved in training ground forces and helping to lead them, and some of these became partisan for Biafra, though that is unusual. The French government supported the use of its mercenaries in Biafra, since it saw potential political advantage to itself if the largest Anglophone country on the continent should be splintered. Apart from the pilots, however, Biafra got small value for money from the mercenaries it employed.

Why Mercenaries Were Employed

As a rule, the mercenaries offered their services in terms of special skills—such as weapons instructors or pilots—that were in short supply among the African forces at war. The need for mercenaries in most African civil war situations has arisen from the lack of certain military skills among the combatants and the belief that mercenaries are equipped to supply these skills. What emerges repeatedly in the history of the mercenary in Africa—whether in Nigeria, Angola, or elsewhere—is the fact that mercenaries charged huge fees (to be paid in advance) for generally poor and sometimes nonexistent services. As a rule, they were simply not worth the money. The mercenaries always sought maximum financial returns and minimum risks and in Nigeria, for example, helped destroy the notion that white soldiers were of superior caliber to black ones. This was simply not true. Zambia's President **Kenneth Kaunda** notably described mercenaries as "human vermin," a view that had wide credence in Africa, so that their use by any African combatant group presented adverse political and propaganda risks. An assumption on the part of many mercenaries was that they were superior soldiers and would stiffen whichever side they were on; many, in fact, turned out to be psychopaths and racists whose first consideration, always, was money. In general, mercenary interventions in African wars were brutal, self-serving, and sometimes downright stupid and did more to give whites on the continent a bad name than they achieved in assisting those they had supposedly come to support. The desperate, that is the losing, side in a war, would be more likely to turn to mercenaries as a last resort, as happened in Angola during 1975–1976.

Angola

The mercenaries, who became involved in Angola during the chaos that developed as the Portuguese withdrew in 1975, appeared to have learned nothing from either the Congo or Nigeria. As the **Frente Nacional da Libertação de Angola** (FNLA)/National Front for the Liberation of Angola was being repulsed by the **Movimento Popular para a Libertação de Angola** (MPLA)/Popular Movement for the Liberation of Angola and its Cuban allies, the American CIA decided to pay for mercenaries and proceeded to recruit 20 French and 300

Portuguese soldiers for an operation in support of the anti-Marxist FNLA. The CIA recruited French "hoods" for Angola and the French insisted that the CIA should use the services of the notorious Bob Denard. He had already worked for **Joseph Désiré Mobutu** in the Republic of the Congo. It was thought that French mercenaries in Angola would be more acceptable or less offensive than Portuguese mercenaries. Despite this, the Portuguese, having lost their colonial war, allowed and encouraged a mercenary program of their own in Angola, in opposition to the newly installed MPLA government. In fact, the use of mercenaries in Angola in 1975 proved a fiasco. By January 1976, for example, over 100 British mercenaries were fighting for the FNLA in northern Angola. They were joined by a small group of Americans.

One of the most notorious of these British mercenaries, a soldier by the name of Cullen, was captured by the MPLA and executed in Luanda. In February 1976, 13 mercenaries including Cullen were captured by MPLA forces in northern Angola: four were executed, one was sentenced to 30 years in prison, and the others got lesser though long terms of imprisonment.

Later Mercenary Interventions

In 1989, white mercenaries under the Frenchman Bob Denard seized power in the **Comoros Islands** following the murder of President Ahmad Abdallah. At the time, South Africa was paying mercenaries to act as a presidential guard in the Comoros. As the Mobutu regime in **Zaire** collapsed during the latter part of 1996 and 1997, senior French officers were recruiting a "white mercenary legion" to fight alongside Zaire's government forces. In January 1997, it was reported that 12 or more French officers with a force of between 200 and 400 mercenaries—Angolans, Belgians, French, South Africans and Britons, Serbs and Croats—had arrived in Zaire. As **Laurent Kabila**'s forces advanced on Kisangani there was a mass exodus of the population, including the Forces Armées du Zaire (FAZ)/Armed Forces of Zaire troops of Mobutu and many of the mercenaries who had been recruited by the Zaire government. These latter then quit the country.

In summary, mercenaries in Africa, by their brutal behavior and racism, have done great damage to the white cause on the continent; they have proved less than able soldiers; they have often quit when their own lives were in danger rather than do the job for which they had been paid; and with one or two exceptions, the combatants would have been better off without using them.

MILITARY ASSISTANCE. Military assistance and the **arms trade** cannot easily be separated, for the former usually (though not always) depends upon the latter. In Africa's many civil wars, assistance to belligerents has come from two main sources: neighboring countries have often become involved on one or other side, providing cross-border bases, routes for the supply of arms, and sometimes becoming engaged with their own forces; external assistance (from outside the continent) has been provided by the major powers—the **United States**, the former **Union of Soviet Socialist Republics** (USSR), **Great Britain** and **France**, or by lesser powers such as **Cuba**.

In the Algerian civil war (1954–62) France, in the end, committed 500,000 troops to support the *colons*, and though this involvement was part of a French rear-guard action to maintain its colonial control of **Algeria**, it was also supporting one side in a civil war since the *colons*, approximately one million in strength, saw themselves as citizens of Algeria in which they were determined to remain.

Similarly, the Portuguese committed the greater part of their armed forces to the wars in **Angola**, **Mozambique**, and Guinea-Bissau over the years 1960–1975, by which time the three territories had become independent. Most of Portugal's modern military equipment had been supplied by the United States on the understanding that it was used for North Atlantic Treaty Organization (NATO) purposes only, but **Cold War** considerations, especially in relation to Southern Africa, persuaded the West to turn a blind eye to Portugal ignoring its agreements.

Once the Portuguese had quit Angola, a civil war erupted and was to last, with precarious intermissions, until 2002. It was fought between the **Movimento Popular para a Libertação de Angola** (MPLA)/Popular Movement for the Liberation of Angola government and its rival for power, the **União Nacional para a Independência Total de Angola** (UNITA)/National Union for the Total Independence of Angola. From 1975 to 1990, Cuba provided consistent military support for the government with up to 50,000 troops on the ground as well as air cover, and was given back-up by the

USSR, which transported Cuban troops across the Atlantic as well as providing arms. On the other side, the U.S. working mainly through the Central Intelligence Agency (CIA) based in Zaire, supported UNITA as did **South Africa**, whose military interventions on behalf of UNITA played a significant role in the war.

The civil war in **Chad**—1966–1990—witnessed interventions by Libya which aimed to annex the mineral-rich Aozou Strip in the north of the country, and so allied itself with factions rebelling against the government; by France, which intervened with troops on three separate occasions in support of the government; and by the U.S. which provided the government with loans, mainly to thwart Libyan intentions.

In the brief but bloody civil war in the **Republic of Congo** in 1997, France, which in any case had troops stationed in the country, clearly supported Denis Sassou-Nguesso, who succeeded in overthrowing the government of Pascal Lissouba, though whether the diplomatic stance of a great power can be treated as military assistance is open to question.

The long war in **Ethiopia** (1962–93), which led to the independence of **Eritrea**, witnessed Cuban involvement with both troops on the ground and air support, as well as a massive supply of arms by the USSR to the government of **Haile Mariam Mengistu**.

France maintained a number of military garrisons in Africa in the post-independence era—in **Central African Republic**, Chad, **Côte d'Ivoire**, Djibouti, Gabon, Senegal, and Madagascar—and used these to intervene on a number of occasions on behalf of embattled governments. In 1978, for example, France airlifted troops to **Zaire** to oppose a force of several thousand enemies of **Mobutu Sese Seko** who had crossed into Shaba province from Angola and occupied Kolwezi.

The Nigerian civil war (1967–70) attracted major international interest. Britain insisted it would continue to supply arms to the Federal Military Government (FMG) of **Nigeria,** but only those it had supplied on a traditional basis rather than new arms such as aircraft, with the result that the USSR stepped in and provided the FMG with fighter planes (MiGs) and bombers (Ilyushins).

Rhodesia, under the illegal Ian Smith regime, which had made a Unilateral Declaration of Independence from Britain, and South Africa, under its apartheid government, created and then armed the opposition to the Marxist government in Mozambique, and the **Resistência Nacional Moçambicana** (RENAMO)/Mozambique National Resistance carried on a civil war against the **Frente da Libertação de Moçambique** (FRELIMO)/Mozambique Liberation Front government from 1975 to 1992.

During the developing crisis in **Rwanda** (1990–94) that culminated in the holocaust of 800,000 Tutsis and moderate Hutus, Belgium, France, and Zaire each sent troops to support the Hutu government. When in 1978 exiled Ugandans invaded **Uganda** from Tanzania in order to overthrow **Idi Amin**, they were supported by 10,000 Tanzanian troops.

Finally, in the civil war in Zaire that brought an end to **Mobutu Sese Seko**'s long reign and developed into what came to be called **Africa's Great War**, five of the newly renamed **Democratic Republic of Congo**'s neighbors became involved and committed troops in support of one or the other side in the conflict: Rwanda and Uganda on the side of the rebels, Angola, Namibia, and **Zimbabwe** in support of the **Laurent Kabila** government.

Almost all Africa's civil wars attracted support of one kind or another. The military assistance considered here is separate from that provided through the **United Nations** for **peacekeeping** operations. *See also* DIAMONDS; MERCENARIES.

MOBUTU, JOSEPH-DÉSIRÉ (LATER SESE SEKO) (1930–97). Joseph-Désiré Mobutu emerged from the chaos that overwhelmed the **Republic of the Congo** in the early 1960s to become president in 1965. He ruled the country as an increasingly autocratic and dictatorial leader and was ruthless in dealing with any challenges to his authority. He came to treat the state as his personal fief, and by the 1990s, the term state kleptocracy—theft of public assets by the ruling elite—had become synonymous with his rule. He was forced from power in 1997 by a coalition of opponents led by **Laurent Kabila**, who then had the support of **Uganda** and Tutsi-controlled **Rwanda**. He was already suffering from cancer and died of it shortly after relinquishing control of **Zaire**.

In 1950, Mobutu was expelled from school in Mbandaka and conscripted into the Force Publique (armed forces) in which he served for six years and was trained as an accounts clerk in Luluabourg. He left the Force Publique in 1956 and took up a career in journalism in Leopoldville (Kinshasa). In 1958, he went to Brussels where he worked for Infor-congo. He became a member of **Patrice Lumumba**'s Mouvement National Congolais (MNC) and organized its office in Brussels. In 1960, he returned to the Congo as Lumumba's senior private secretary.

At independence, Lumumba appointed Mobutu chief of staff and second in command of the army. As the country disintegrated, Mobutu built his own power base in the army. On 13 September 1960, Mobutu staged a military coup and suspended both President Joseph Kasavubu and Prime Minister Patrice Lumumba to replace them with a College of Commissioners. He allowed Kasavubu back to power while retaining real control through the army. He mounted a second coup on 23 November 1965, and this time he retained power and became president. Thereafter, he pursued a policy of centralizing government and ensuring that he had effective control of all decision-making bodies.

In 1971, Mobutu embarked upon a policy of "authenticity," substituting African for European names, renaming the country Zaire, dropping his own old names (Joseph-Désiré) to become Mobutu Sese Seko, and launching his own party—the Mouvement Populaire de la Révolution (MPR)—which became the sole authorized party. But, though he maintained central political control over his huge country, Mobutu was at best inept at economic management. Zaire became heavily indebted, state expenditure exceeded income by large margins, while bribery and endless corruption became the norm. Through the 1970s and into the first half of the 1980s, the International Monetary Fund (IMF) attempted to bring order to the country's economy by imposing financial discipline, but its measures were unacceptable to Mobutu, who broke with the Fund in 1986.

Mobutu's anti-Communism, as well as the geographic position of his vast country in the center of Africa, made him a natural choice as an ally on the continent for the **United States**. He always supported the opponents of the **Movimento Popular para a Libertação de Angola** (MPLA)/Popular Movement for the Liberation of Angola in **Angola** and allowed Zaire to be used as a conduit for Central Intelligence Agency (CIA) **aid** to both **Holden Roberto**'s **Frente Nacional da Libertação de Angola** (FNLA)/National Front for the Liberation of Angola and **Jonas Savimbi**'s **União Nacional para** a **Independência Total de Angola** (UNITA)/Union for the Total Independence of Angola through the 1970s and 1980s.

By 1990, faced with rising demands for democratic change throughout Africa, Mobutu found himself subjected to growing pressure to permit real democratic opposition to his rule to emerge. The economy of his potentially rich country was in chaos and near to collapse, and in April 1991, he set up a commission to draft a new constitution and allowed political parties freedom to operate. The result came in the form of a mounting crescendo of demands for Mobutu to resign.

The changed world climate of the 1990s, which followed the end of the **Cold War**, the end of U.S. support for Savimbi in Angola, and the endless human rights and "kleptocracy" scandals that made Zaire a byword for corruption, meant that by the mid-1990s, even Mobutu's longterm supporters—the United States and **France**— were beginning to distance themselves from him. The rebellion that broke out at the end of 1996 and saw a sudden and rapid collapse of Mobutu's power in 1997, when Kabila and his Alliance des Forces Démocratiques pour la Libération du Congo/Zaire (AFDL) secured Kinshasa, finally brought his long rule to an end. Kabila proclaimed the establishment of the Democratic Republic of Congo on 17 May 1997. On 7 September 1997, Mobutu died in Morocco.

MOHAMMED, ALI MAHDI (1940–). Ali Mahdi Mohammed, a pragmatic moderate and a businessman, became president of **Somalia** in 1991 after the flight of **Siad Barre**, the country's former president of 21 years. Mohammed first became a schoolteacher and then went to Egypt and Italy during 1963–1966 for training in community health. Back in Somalia he was appointed director of malaria research. He became involved in politics only to be arrested and imprisoned by Siad Barre. After his release from prison, Mohammed turned to business and ran a hotel in Mogadishu. In 1990, he was one of 114 private citizens who signed a letter condemning the policies of the Barre regime; he fled the country when Barre sought to arrest those who had signed the manifesto.

He then raised money to finance the **United Somali Congress** (USC), which had an office in Rome. Mohammed joined the political wing of the USC and returned to Somalia late in 1990, by which time the USC forces had established a foothold in Mogadishu. Mohammed was not a guerrilla fighter; his role was to find the money to finance the USC. His leading position in the USC was contested by General **Muhammad Farah Aideed**, who became its chairman while Mohammed had little personal following outside Mogadishu. Nonetheless, he was put forward as a compromise candidate on behalf of the USC to succeed Barre as the country's president, and following the endorsement of six guerrilla groups (but not of General Aideed) he became interim president of Somalia on 27 January 1991, and his candidacy was approved by 130 elders. However, there was anger at his elevation amongst other freedom fighter groups outside Mogadishu who had not been consulted. Mohammed was sworn in as president of Somalia on 18 August 1991, for a two-year period. His presidency was at once contested by Aideed and the country was plunged into the chaos of renewed civil war. Six years later, when the more charismatic Aideed, who was leader of the Somali National Alliance (SNA) coalition, died of wounds, Mohammed remained as leader of the Somali Salvation Alliance. At the time of Aideed's death, Mogadishu was divided between the two groups and each leader termed himself "president" of Somalia, although this did not include the self-declared republic of Somaliland in the north. The presidency was disputed over the following years as Somalia descended into near civil war again.

MOUVEMENT POUR LA LIBÉRATION DU TCHAD (MPLT)/ MOVEMENT FOR THE LIBERATION OF CHAD. The Chad Liberation Movement came into being in 1978, at a time when **Nigeria**, as a mediator in the **Chad** civil war, was enjoying maximum influence in Chad where the war then threatened to tear the country apart. The MPLT had close ties with Nigerian interests and operated from islands in Lake Chad; its principal influence and support were to be found in western Kanem Province. At one level, the MPLT represented Nigeria's determination to limit Libyan expansionism in Chad, which Lagos saw as a threat to its own interests. The MPLT leaders—in short succession between 1978 and 1981—were Abubakar Abderaman, Idris Adoum Mustapha, and Lool Mahamat Choua. It was never a serious player in the core politics of the civil war.

MOVIMENTO POPULAR PARA A LIBERTAÇÃO DE ANGOLA (MPLA)/POPULAR MOVEMENT FOR THE LIBERATION

OF ANGOLA. The Popular Movement for the Liberation of Angola, always known as the MPLA, was formed from several nationalist groups, including the Communists, in 1956 and, despite factions and divisions and a long bloody struggle against the Portuguese, emerged as the ruling party in **Angola** in 1975. A year later it appeared to have defeated its two main rivals for power—the **Frente Nacional da Libertação de Angola** (FNLA)/National Front for the Liberation of Angola and the **União Nacional para a Independência Total de Angola** (UNITA)/National Union for the Total Independence of Angola. The first president of the MPLA, Mario de Andrade, was succeeded in the leadership in 1962 by **Agostinho Neto**, who was to dominate the movement until his death from cancer in Moscow nearly 20 years later. Despite his Marxism, Neto was always a nationalist first and he was sometimes criticized for not being sufficiently pro-Soviet by hardliners in the MPLA. Indeed, there was an attempt under Nito Alves to oust him from the leadership for this reason in 1975, although this proved unsuccessful. Another MPLA leader, Daniel Chipenda of the Ovimbundu from Lobito, who had represented the MPLA in Dar es Salaam during the 1960s, also attempted unsuccessfully to wrest the leadership from Neto. He was reported to be responsible for two assassination attempts on Neto in 1972 and 1973, and was expelled from the party in 1974 when he joined the FNLA.

Although the MPLA agreed with the other two liberation movements (FNLA and UNITA) to take part in a transitional government following the cease-fire with **Portugal** in October 1974, by March/April 1975 fighting had broken out between the MPLA and the FNLA. Then in August 1975 clashes occurred between the MPLA and UNITA, and the MPLA was obliged to rely upon Cuban troops to maintain its hold on power. Following independence on 11 November 1975, when the MPLA received immediate recognition from Communist countries as the new government of Angola, the scene was set for the long civil war that was to follow, with UNITA as the main enemy. This would continue through to 1994. During the period 1975–1990, the MPLA would rely upon massive Soviet assistance with arms and equipment and up to 1,000 Soviet military advisers as well as a Cuban military presence, which at its greatest extent at the end of the 1980s amounted to some 50,000 troops.

In the wake of negotiations, which took place throughout 1988, and the subsequent slow moves toward power-sharing with UNITA, elections were held in September 1992. The MPLA, meanwhile, had moved away from its overt Marxism and in August 1992, the People's Assembly accepted a new democratic constitution that would permit the new assembly—then about to be elected—to be based upon multiparty democracy; it also agreed to drop the word People's from the name of the country, which would become simply, the Republic of Angola.

MOZAMBIQUE. Mozambique was ravaged by war for nearly 30 years before it slowly returned to peace at the beginning of the 1990s. First came the war of liberation against the Portuguese (1964–75), only to be ended after the change of government in **Portugal** that came with the overthrow of the Marcello Caetano dictatorship in April 1974. Following this event, Portugal signaled its readiness to grant independence to its African territories and Mozambique became independent on 25 June 1975. The great majority of the 250,000 Portuguese settlers, who had held most of the administrative and skilled jobs, left the country at independence to present the **Frente da Libertação de Moçambique** (FRELIMO)/Mozambique Liberation Front government with formidable problems of reconstruction. Mozambique, by almost any standards, was one of the poorest countries in Africa and the world at this time.

Background

As the fighting against the Portuguese in both Mozambique and **Angola** had escalated during the early 1970s, both white-controlled Rhodesia and **South Africa** had provided Portugal with support in its efforts to hold on to power; however, when the Portuguese finally withdrew in the mid-1970s, Mozambique's neighbors embarked upon policies of destabilization in order to undermine the new governments which came to power, since both Salisbury and Pretoria saw these as Marxist opponents of white racialism. By 1975, the **Zimbabwe African National Union** (ZANU) was having an increasingly successful impact upon the Smith regime in Rhodesia and it received immediate backing from the new Mozambique government. The head of Rhodesian security, Ken Flower, who ran the Central Intelligence Organization (CIO), conceived the idea of fomenting civil war in Mozambique by creating and then supporting a rival movement to FRELIMO. Flower originally advanced his idea during talks with his Portuguese and South African security counterparts during 1971 and 1972. At first his suggestion was not adopted, but in March 1974, Flower visited the director general of Security in Lourenco Marques (Maputo), Major Silva Pais, who agreed with his approach. Flower wanted to launch an African group of Flechas (arrows) who would be responsible for "unconventional, clandestine operations." In April 1974, prior to the Lisbon coup which toppled Dr. Marcello Caetano, the Rhodesian CIO began to recruit Mozambicans to form an organization to operate inside Mozambique, in theory without external support, although in practice it would depend first upon Rhodesia and then, after 1980, upon South Africa for assistance. The members of this group became known as the **Resistência Nacional Moçambicana** (RENAMO)/ Mozambican National Resistance, which was usually referred to simply as RENAMO. Flower and the CIO had little difficulty in recruiting dissident Mozambicans during 1974/1975 and such a movement made sense to an increasingly beleaguered Rhodesia.

The Civil War: 1975–1984

The huge exodus of the Portuguese was a contributory cause of the developing chaos: of 250,000 Portuguese at independence in 1975, only 15,000 remained by 1978. As colonialists, the Portuguese had reserved all the skilled posts for themselves and when they went, the greater part of the country's skilled capacity went as well. Moreover, the departing Portuguese carried out wilful acts of destruction of machines and equipment as they left. Once the new FRELIMO government had made plain its political stand—its determination to apply **United Nations** sanctions against Rhodesia and its declaration of support for the **African National Congress** (ANC)—it made itself a natural target for Rhodesian and South African hostility. From 1975 onward, both the Rhodesian and South African military were to make periodic cross-border raids into Mozambique, and for them RENAMO was to prove an invaluable ally, or at least an important nuisance factor.

In the period 1975–1980, as RENAMO gradually built up its capacity to harass the new government, Mozambique found itself beset by four basic problems: the loss of Portuguese skills; the deteriorating state of the economy; the presence in Mozambique of both ZANU and ANC guerrillas, which attracted punitive cross-border raids from Rhodesia and South Africa; and growing dissatisfaction among FRELIMO members who had expected quicker "rewards" once the country became independent. It is not possible to pinpoint exactly when RENAMO resistance to the new government became sufficiently important to warrant the description of either dissidence or civil war. The immediate problems concerned Rhodesia rather than South Africa: there were about 10,000 ZANU guerrillas in the country and growing border violence as Rhodesian security forces and ZANU guerrillas raided back and forth in the two territories. Such conditions provided a perfect cover for RENAMO to launch its activities.

There was to be a state of border war between Mozambique and Rhodesia from 1975 until 1980 when Rhodesia became independent as **Zimbabwe**. In March 1976, obeying UN sanctions, Mozambique closed its border with Rhodesia. In August of that year, after RENAMO spies had provided the information, the Rhodesian Selous Scouts raided across the border to attack the ZANU base camp at Nyadzonia (Pungwe) where they killed about 1,000 members of ZANU, many of them women and children. During 1977, frequent ZANU incursions across the border into Rhodesia led to retaliatory cross-border raids against the ZANU bases in Mozambique. It was, in any case, easier for the Rhodesians to attack these camps than to find the ZANU guerrillas in the Rhodesian bush. President **Samora Machel** claimed that between March 1976 and April 1977 there occurred 143 Rhodesian acts of aggression across the 1,140 kilometer border between the two countries, in which a total of 1,432 civilians, of whom 875 were Rhodesian refugees, were murdered. At the same time, however, there was little evidence of any internal opposition to FRELIMO or of RENAMO guerrillas operating against the government.

The acknowledged opposition to FRELIMO at this time—the United Democratic Front of Mozambique—had failed to obtain arms from Europe for a struggle against the government. On the other hand, RENAMO claimed that its guerrillas were then fighting under the command of six former FRELIMO commanders. By 1978, it had become apparent that the poverty-stricken Mozambique economy was heavily dependent upon three aspects of its connection with South Africa: the transit trade through Maputo; remittances from laborers in South Africa, especially in the mines; and payments for power from the **Cabora Bassa Dam**. Two of these links with South Africa made Mozambique especially vulnerable: both the Cabora Bassa power lines and the transit routes (road and rail) to Maputo and Beira were open to attacks by RENAMO.

By 1979, ZANU was clearly winning the war in Rhodesia and huge new pressures (following the **Commonwealth** heads of government meeting which was held in Lusaka that August) spelled the coming end to the Smith regime in Salisbury. However, in Mozambique the activities of RENAMO had by then become a serious threat to the government; as a result, it was in Mozambique's interest that the struggle in Rhodesia should be terminated. Thus, in December 1979, when the ZANU leader, **Robert Mugabe**, was prepared to abandon the Lancaster House Conference in London and return to the bush, President Machel exerted pressure upon him to come to terms with the British foreign secretary, Lord Carrington.

Once Mugabe had become president of Zimbabwe in April 1980, Flower told him of his CIO role with regard to RENAMO, but Mugabe still kept him in office. In Mozambique the stage was set for an escalation of the civil war, for though independence for Zimbabwe meant the reopening of the joint border and the immediate easing of existing tensions, RENAMO guerrillas were then established in Manica, Sofala, and Tete Provinces. The result was that the government had to deploy substantial forces against the insurgents. Even so, whether RENAMO could really become effective seemed doubtful at that stage: Rhodesia had ceased to be its paymaster and South Africa had to formulate a clear policy in relation to Mozambique. However, Pretoria soon decided upon a policy of maximum economic disruption of its neighbor; it urged RENAMO to attack lines of communication (roads and railways), which served the landlocked countries to its north—Malawi, Zambia, and Zimbabwe and, in particular, to concentrate upon the **Beira Corridor**. In April 1981, RENAMO attacked the Cabora Bassa hydro-electric power station and cut the power lines. At that time, Cabora Bassa supplied 10 percent of South Africa's power; the attack demonstrated that South Africa did not control RENAMO. In June 1981, fierce fighting in the north of Mozambique between government forces and RENAMO guerrillas caused hundreds of refugees to flee into Zimbabwe; they complained of ill-treatment from both sides.

The government now constructed fortified villages (similar to the former *aldeamentos* of the Portuguese) so as to protect and control the rural populations. In July, Machel met with Mugabe to discuss joint security measures. By the end of 1981, RENAMO activities in Manica and Sofala Provinces were sufficiently damaging to lead the government to recall FRELIMO commanders who had been released from service: they were ordered to establish "people's militias" and arm them. During the liberation struggle, FRELIMO's main support had come from the **Union of Soviet Socialist Republics** (USSR), East Germany, and other Communist states; now, however, it felt the need to mobilize support from the West if it was to contain the South African destabilization activities.

During 1982, RENAMO widened the scope of its operations and obtained military equipment from South Africa, while concentrating its attacks upon road and rail links used by the landlocked countries of the interior. In May 1982, the government began a major operation to make the Beira Corridor safe from RENAMO attacks; this included arming civilians living along the Corridor. RENAMO then employed a fresh tactic, that of abducting foreigners who were working in Mozambique in an effort to frighten them into leaving the country. Its efforts paid off when 40 Swedish workers fled to Zimbabwe after two of their number had been killed. Other persons abducted included six Bulgarian workers, while a Portuguese was killed. Fresh strains were added to an already deeply damaged economy when RENAMO attacked the Beira Corridor. In October 1982, Machel was forced to seek assistance from two of his neighbors, Tanzania and Zimbabwe: he asked President **Julius Nyerere** to increase the number of Tanzanian troops in the north of Mozambique—there were 2,000 there already—and asked President Mugabe for assistance in fighting RENAMO. By 1983, RENAMO guerrillas had become active in every province except Cabo Delgado in the north where the Tanzanian troops were stationed. By this time several thousand Zimbabwean troops had been deployed along the Beira Corridor, although the railway line was still being sabotaged.

The Mozambique government mounted a major anti-RENAMO campaign in Zambezia, Mozambique's richest province, and a second campaign in Inhambane Province in the south.

A growing problem for the government was the poor condition of its army: by this time it was ill-equipped, badly malnourished, often unpaid, and its soldiers felt neglected. Such troops, suffering from low morale, did not want to take the field against RENAMO. Twice during 1983 (May and October), units of the South African Defence Force (SADF) raided Maputo, ostensibly to attack ANC bases, but in fact to exert further pressures upon an already harassed government. Also during 1983, Machel visited a number of western countries seeking aid, although the immediate consequence was that the USSR cut off its assistance to Mozambique. South African policy was to put pressure upon the "Frontline" States (which included Mozambique) so that they would not provide the ANC with bases, and Pretoria's support for RENAMO now appeared to be paying dividends.

Under these pressures, Machel was obliged to forge a deal with South Africa. On 16 March 1984, President Machel met South Africa's President P. W. Botha at Nkomati on their joint border; they negotiated the **Nkomati Accord**, by whose terms they would each prevent the activities of opposition groups in the other's territory. Mozambique was obliged to withdraw its support for the ANC and South Africa for RENAMO. The ANC and Nyerere both condemned the Accord, but at the time, Machel had little choice, even though his own leadership was opposed to the agreement. In fact, no decline in RENAMO activity followed. In June 1984, South Africa's foreign minister, "Pik" Botha, went to Maputo to insist that South Africa was keeping its side of the agreement. It did not do so. The government now made members of the ANC in Mozambique live in controlled camps (or leave the country) and reduced the ANC mission in Maputo to 10. Furthermore, about 800 ANC departed from Mozambique to other Frontline States. When Machel visited China and North Korea in July, both countries endorsed the Nkomati Accord, which gave Machel moral support but not much else. During the second half of 1984, RENAMO increased the severity of its attacks, with continuing backing from South Africa, and by August was active in all 10 of Mozambique's provinces.

The Second Phase: 1984–1990

Meetings between representatives of the Mozambique government, RENAMO, and South Africa, during August and September 1984, had proved abortive, and in November 1984, RENAMO mounted a new offensive throughout Mozambique. A strong government counter-offensive destroyed 100 RENAMO bases and resulted in the deaths of about 1,000 guerrillas. During 1985, despite protests by the Maputo government, South Africa made no efforts to restrain RENAMO; nor did it withdraw its support, and by this stage Portugal was also providing aid for RENAMO. The guerrilla tactics now changed: they raided villages and forcibly conscripted villagers to act as porters or soldiers. Some towns also came under siege. In April 1985, RENAMO severed rail links between South Africa and Mozambique. When the country celebrated its tenth independence anniversary in June 1985, President Machel was obliged to tell the people that Mozambique had to remain on a war footing because of RENAMO. At a meeting with Presidents Nyerere and Mugabe in July 1985, the latter promised to commit more troops to fight RENAMO. In August 1985, a joint campaign by FRELIMO and Zimbabwean troops captured the RENAMO headquarters at Casa Banana in Sofala Province. Documents seized in the raid showed that South Africa had provided continuous support to RENAMO ever since the Nkomati Accord, and this led a for-once deeply embarrassed South African government to reply that it had only "technically" broken the Nkomati Accord. The spokesman then blamed Portugal and claimed that the government was unable to control the many Portuguese then in South Africa who "worked to Lisbon's orders."

Slowly, meanwhile, the West was becoming more sympathetic to Mozambique and both the **United States** and **Britain** offered relief aid following the 1985 drought. In addition, Britain offered military training for FRELIMO troops—but in Zimbabwe. A further 5,000 Zimbabwean troops were committed to Mozambique in addition to the 2,000 already there. The year 1986 turned into the worst year of the civil war. In February, RENAMO recaptured Casa Banana and this had to be retaken by Zimbabwean troops in April. The government found that it was spending 42 percent of its revenue fighting RENAMO or preparing to deal with South African incursions. RENAMO concentrated upon cutting railway links, thus reducing government revenues from the transit trade. Then, in a further calculated blow to the government, South Africa announced that it would no longer recruit Mozambicans for its mines or renew the contracts of those already in the Republic. This represented a financial loss in the region of $90 million a year. When President Machel asked President Hastings Banda of Malawi to hand over RENAMO rebels then in his country, Banda instead expelled several hundred into Mozambique where they ravaged the border area. RENAMO then declared war on Zimbabwe.

On 19 October 1986, following a meeting with Presidents **Kenneth Kaunda** and Mugabe in Lusaka, Machel was killed when his plane crashed on its return journey. The crash was never properly explained: South Africa was blamed and a South African mission in Maputo was sacked. South Africa claimed that documents found in the wreckage (the plane crashed just inside the South African border) showed that Zambia and Mozambique were plotting to overthrow Hastings Banda of Malawi. **Joaquim Chissano**, Machel's foreign minister, succeeded him as president and Maputo increased its pressures upon Malawi to end its support for RENAMO, threatening to cut its transit routes through Mozambique. As a result, Malawi reversed its policy and committed 300 troops to help guard the Nacala Railway, which linked Blantyre to the Indian Ocean port of Nacala. The line was then being upgraded and rehabilitated.

The war continued as fiercely into 1987, and President Mugabe agreed to provide further military assistance until the war had been won. By this time an estimated four million Mozambicans were facing starvation or destitution as a result of the civil war and one million people had been forced to leave their homes in Zambezia Province, which was one of the worst affected areas. However, the presence of Tanzanian and Zimbabwean troops, as well as the reversal of Malawi's policy of helping RENAMO, gave the government a new lease of energy to fight the war. A South African raid upon Maputo in May—supposedly against an ANC base—finally spelled the end of the Nkomati Accord. By this time, the Mozambique–Zimbabwe border region had become a semi-war zone.

There were 40,000 Mozambican **refugees** in camps in Zimbabwe and a further 40,000 were thought to be roaming the country in search of work. Zimbabwe rounded these people up and sent them back to Mozambique. A RENAMO incursion into Zambia produced Zambian retaliation and a military pursuit into Mozambique to destroy two RENAMO bases. In July 1987, RENAMO attacked the southern town of Homoine to massacre 424 people, although Chissano claimed that the South Africans were responsible. Further RENAMO attacks in the south included the ambush of a convoy north of Maputo in which 270 people were killed. RENAMO tactics aimed to isolate Maputo. These RENAMO forces operating along the coast were being supplied by sea from South Africa. They attacked the only road linking Maputo with Gaza and Inhambane Provinces. The Mozambican military escorts for convoys proved ineffective and the troops' morale was low. Such attacks close to the capital also had a demoralizing effect upon both the government and the international community living in Maputo. However, internal divisions in RENAMO weakened its onslaught. A leading member, Paulo Oliveira, advocated peace while Afonso Dhlakama, the leader, insisted on continuing the war. In December 1987, following the announcement by Chissano of a law of pardon, some 200 members of RENAMO surrendered in January 1988 and Oliveira defected to the government. The Zimbabwean troops provided essential stiffening for the demoralized Mozambican army; with their help two RENAMO bases were captured in December 1987 and a further three in March 1988.

Meanwhile, under Chissano, Mozambique was moving steadily toward the West: **Great Britain** agreed to a $25 million **aid** package as well as an increase in the military training for FRELIMO, which it was carrying out in Zimbabwe; and in June 1987, Mozambique negotiated a financial package with the International Monetary Fund (IMF). In October 1987, Mozambique was allowed to send an observer mission to the Vancouver Commonwealth Heads of Government Meeting (CHOGM) and a special Commonwealth fund was created to assist Mozambique. In addition, a massive $600 million project to rehabilitate the port of Beira was launched, to be financed (in the main) by funds from the European Community. Mozambique had now come to see the West rather than the Communist bloc as its essential economic resource and savior.

RENAMO activity reached a peak during 1988 with repeated attacks upon communications and villages, with sabotage aimed at the vital Chicualacuala rail line linking Zimbabwe to Maputo. By this time RENAMO had an estimated 20,000 men in the field. Sometimes a force of as many as 600 guerrillas would attack a particular target, though generally RENAMO used small bands of men, often armed only with machetes, who robbed and killed. Half the FRELIMO army appeared to have collapsed or disintegrated and only the better units were able to withstand RENAMO, while government control did not run in large parts of the country. Instead, the government appeared increasingly dependent upon troops from Zimbabwe (10,000) and Tanzania (3,000) to fight RENAMO.

The position was made worse because of the large numbers of refugees created by the war. Sometimes whole villages were massacred. Many RENAMO guerrillas were, in fact, no more than armed bandits, the product of a lawless time. Afonso Dhlakama controlled about half the RENAMO forces. He had worked closely with South African intelligence since 1980 and had undergone training at the South African Special Forces base at Voortrekkerhoogte. South Africa, even after the Nkomati Accord, had made airdrops of supplies to RENAMO. Its other backers were the Portuguese (principally those who had fled in 1975 to settle in South Africa) and right-wing groups in the United States. Part of Pretoria's motive for assisting RENAMO was economic: South Africa wanted to force the landlocked countries to its north—Malawi, Zambia, and Zimbabwe—to continue trading through South Africa and a destabilized Mozambique helped ensure that this happened.

Western aid to Mozambique increased through 1988 while Chissano's government attempted to reactivate the Joint Security Commission with South Africa (it had been set up under the terms of the Nkomati Accord). In Lisbon, Eco Fernandes, who wanted RENAMO to maintain its links with South Africa, was shot. At a time when right-wing U.S. senators were arguing for U.S. aid to RENAMO, U.S. Deputy Assistant Secretary of State Roy Stacey publicly described RENAMO as "waging a systematic and brutal war of terror against innocent Mozambican civilians through forced labor, starvation, physical abuse, and wanton killing." The war produced many contradictions: in May 1988, for example, South Africa offered the Maputo government 82 million rand in military assistance to protect the Cabora Bassa Dam against RENAMO; Mozambique refused the offer of South African troops, but accepted training for 1,500 FRELIMO troops to guard the power pylons. In mid-year the government launched a new offensive against RENAMO.

Peace Negotiations

A possible breakthrough occurred in August when Chissano endorsed a plan advanced by church leaders to meet representatives of
RENAMO in an effort to end the war. In 1989, the U.S. State Department claimed that RENAMO had killed 100,000 people since 1984.
Meanwhile, Malawi had become host to nearly one million refugees
(one in 12 of its population) and early in 1989 refugees from the war
were arriving at the rate of 20,000 a month. And, despite repeated
denials by Pretoria, South Africa continued to support RENAMO. In
April 1989, RENAMO made a conciliatory gesture when it agreed to a
ceasefire to allow food supplies to reach starving people. In June 1989,
President Chissano advanced a 12-point peace plan, provided that
RENAMO would renounce violence and agree to constitutional rule:
by that time, some 3,000 members of RENAMO had accepted the December 1987 government amnesty. Also that June, church leaders met
representatives of RENAMO at one of its strongholds, Gorongosa, and
Dhlakama endorsed the peace move. RENAMO then demonstrated
its readiness to compromise by sacking Artur Janeiro de Fonseca, its
pro–South African external relations minister, and replacing him with
Raul Domingos, formerly chief of staff. Talks scheduled to take place
in Nairobi, Kenya, were called off when the government launched an
attack upon Gorongosa. However, Dhlakama did go to Nairobi for
talks with church leaders at the end of July, and though no agreement
was reached these talks were generally seen to herald the beginning of
a peace process. There was a setback in October 1989, but at the end
of the year, Presidents Daniel arap Moi of Kenya and Robert Mugabe
of Zimbabwe met in Nairobi to urge both RENAMO and the Mozambique government to drop all talk of preconditions. Early in 1990, with
the country facing growing industrial unrest and an army that often
went unpaid for months, President Chissano announced major constitutional changes which had the effect of moving Mozambique into line
with the western democracies. An immediate result of this move was
a U.S. announcement at the end of January that it no longer regarded
Mozambique as a Communist country, while the general effect of these
reforms was to make Mozambique more acceptable to the West.

The end of the **Cold War** played a part in the peace process,
for once Mikhail Gorbachev had come to power in the USSR, he

signaled the withdrawal or ending of Soviet aid and advised the two sides in the war to negotiate a peace. Fighting was to continue through 1990, but in July, the two sides met in Rome for talks arranged jointly by the churches and President Mugabe of Zimbabwe. In November 1990, the government announced the abandonment of Marxism–Leninism and said it would thereafter run the economy according to market forces.

In December 1990, after Zimbabwe's forces had been confined to the Beira and Limpopo Corridors, a ceasefire was negotiated; however, in February, despite the emergence of new political parties as part of the peace process, RENAMO launched new attacks to cut the roads to Malawi in the north. Peace talks were resumed on 6 May 1991, with RENAMO attempting to alter the agenda while its guerrillas continued to launch attacks against the Cabora Bassa power lines and railway links. The talks again broke down, but the following 4 October, a cease-fire was signed by Chissano and Dhlakama. By this time both sides were exhausted: these talks had been brokered by the Roman Catholic Church, President Mugabe, and the British businessman "Tiny" Rowland.

Costs and Casualties

The statistics of this brutal war were horrifying: by 1988 RENAMO campaigns had forced a minimum of 870,000 people to flee the country, had displaced a further one million inside the country, and reduced another 2.5 million to the point of starvation, while approximately 100,000 civilians had been killed and many more wounded or permanently maimed. By the end of the 1980s, famine threatened up to 4.5 million people throughout the country. There are variations on these figures but they each tell the same story. For example, in 1988 the World Food Programme (WFP) reported that there were 420,000 refugees in Malawi, 350,000 in South Africa, 22,500 in Swaziland, 30,000 in Zambia, 64,500 in Zimbabwe, and 15,000 in Tanzania to make a total of 902,000. Other estimates gave a total of 650,000 refugees in Malawi. The government requested (mid-1988) $380 million in emergency assistance to help feed six million people threatened with famine.

By the beginning of 1992, Mozambique was rated (by the World Bank) as having the lowest standard of living in the world.

The Aftermath

In December 1992, the United Nations agreed to send a **peacekeeping** force of 7,500 to Mozambique; its task would be principally to safeguard the transport corridors. However, delays in implementation almost led to disaster and RENAMO withdrew from the peace process. This resumed again and on 14 April 1993 the Zimbabwe troops guarding the Beira and Limpopo Corridors were withdrawn. By the following May 4,721 UN soldiers from five countries, the United Nations Operation in Mozambique (UNOMOZ), had arrived and these were accompanied by additional unarmed units. On 14 June 1993, the repatriation of 1.3 million refugees began under **United Nations High Commissioner for Refugees** (UNHCR) auspices while international donors promised $520 million for humanitarian programs. On 14 August, the Joint Commission for the Formation of the Mozambique Defense Armed Forces (CCFADM) agreed upon a program to create a Mozambique Defense Armed Forces (FADM); 50 officers from either side in the civil war and 540 soldiers were selected for a 16-week training course. On 20 October 1993, the UN secretary-general, Boutros Boutros-Ghali, visited Maputo for talks with Chissano and Dhlakama. A fresh timetable for demobilization was set—this was to be carried out between January and May 1994, with a new army coming into being in September 1994. UN Security Council Resolution 898 of February 1994 authorized the creation of a UN police component to supervise the coming elections.

By March 1994, troops were moving into demobilization centers by which time 6,000 UNOMOZ troops were stationed in the country at a cost to western donors of $1 million a day. By mid-July 1994, 3.2 million voters had registered in areas over which the government had control. RENAMO called for a government of national unity after the elections. During the run-up to the elections, Dhlakama charged FRELIMO with fraud and said RENAMO would not take part in the elections, although on 28 October he reversed this stand and urged his followers to vote. The election results gave Chissano 53.3 percent of the presidential vote and Dhlakama 33.7 percent while, for the legislature, FRELIMO obtained 44.3 percent of the votes and RENAMO 37.7 percent. Dhlakama agreed that RENAMO would accept these results and cooperate with the government. Various offers of aid for reconstruction were now made by western governments.

At first, relations between the ruling FRELIMO government and RENAMO were delicate; Chissano said Dhlakama could not be an official leader of the opposition because he was not a member of the legislature but would, nonetheless, be provided with a salary and other official benefits since he had come second in the presidential election. In March 1995, the Paris Club pledged $780 million in loans and grants to Mozambique; the government also hoped to obtain relief on $350 million of debts. The government launched a program to eradicate poverty. The European Union arranged another package of aid in 1995 worth $65 million to rehabilitate Cabora Bassa and the Beira Corridor. By May 1995, most of the refugees had returned home, and in November 1995, Mozambique was admitted as a full member to the Commonwealth. In 1996 Mozambique embarked upon the long haul of economic and social recovery. It enjoyed much international goodwill at this time and in particular, growing links with the new South Africa, which was ready to provide assistance for its recovery.

MUGABE, ROBERT GABRIEL (1924–). Born at Kutama Mission in Mashonaland on 21 February 1924, Robert Mugabe became a secondary school teacher in 1941 and later went to Fort Hare University in **South Africa** where he earned a B.A. in English (1951). After further teaching in Rhodesia, Mugabe went to Zambia and then Ghana where he met his wife-to-be, Sally, arriving in the country just before it achieved independence. Events in both Zambia and Ghana heightened Mugabe's interest in politics; he returned to Rhodesia in 1960 and began his political career.

He opposed the 1960 constitutional proposals through the National Democratic Party (NDP) and after this, having been banned in December 1961, he became deputy secretary-general of the **Zimbabwe African People's Union** (ZAPU). In 1962, ZAPU was banned and Mugabe himself was restricted. Later he was arrested but jumped bail and fled to Dar es Salaam in Tanzania. In 1963, ZAPU split into two factions and Mugabe joined that, led by the Rev. Ndabaningi Sithole.

Mugabe returned to Salisbury (Harare) in 1964, by which time he had become secretary-general of the **Zimbabwe African National Union** (ZANU); he was again arrested and this time would spend 10 years in detention.

While in detention Mugabe studied; he was also elected to lead ZANU, when the party deposed Sithole after internal dissensions threatened to split it. In the course of the so-called detente exercise of 1974, Ian Smith released the nationalist leaders although, after Herbert Chitepo had been assassinated, Mugabe went to **Mozambique** to take control of the guerrilla war against the Smith government: this had begun in earnest during 1973. The **Commonwealth** Heads of Government Meeting (CHOGM) held in Lusaka during August 1979 led to the London negotiations at Lancaster House of September–December 1979, which produced a formula for **Zimbabwe**'s independence. In the elections of March 1980, Mugabe's ZANU won 57 out of the 80 open seats (20 were reserved on a restricted roll for Europeans) to become the prime minister of Zimbabwe when it became independent on 18 April 1980.

Mugabe included **Joshua Nkomo**, his chief political rival, in his broad-based government of 1980, but the two men fell out in 1982 following the discovery of an arms cache on Nkomo's farm. Nkomo was sacked and his top political lieutenants were arrested. Nkomo then fled into exile in London. The next five years, 1982–1987, witnessed the so-called war of the dissidents: in real terms this was a war between the majority Mashona people (Mugabe's supporters) and the minority Ndebele people (Nkomo's supporters). The Ndebele had moved into western Zimbabwe in the mid- to late nineteenth century when they fought and defeated the Mashona. Mugabe showed complete ruthlessness in his determination to crush the rebellion, and the Fifth Brigade, trained by North Koreans, which was the spearhead of the government forces, earned an especially unpleasant reputation for brutality.

Mugabe's political base was strengthened in 1985, during the middle of the Dissidents' War, when he increased his seats in an election from 57 to 63 and reduced Nkomo's following in the legislature from 20 to 15. Nkomo had returned from exile in August 1983 and gradually, in a series of talks, an agreement was reached on political unity. These talks almost broke down in 1987 and there was a brief eruption of new violence in Ndebeleland, but the talks were resumed at the end of the year and a binding agreement was achieved in April 1988. A change to the constitution of October 1987 had abolished the separate white seats and created an executive president. On 31 December 1987, Mugabe became Zimbabwe's first executive president. At the ZANU congress of December 1989, the formal merger of ZANU and ZAPU took place; in effect this meant the disappearance of ZAPU. This event could be taken to represent the final ending of the civil war.

In August 1998, Mugabe decided to send Zimbabwean troops to the **Democratic Republic of Congo** to assist **Laurent Kabila** who faced a rebellion that threatened to bring his 15-month-old rule to an end.

Serious opposition to Mugabe emerged in May 1999 with the formation of the Movement for Democratic Change (MDC) under Gibson Sibanda and Morgan Tsvangirai. Zimbabwe's intervention in the Congo war with 10,000 troops was deeply unpopular. A referendum of 12 February 2000 to ratify amendments to the constitution, essentially designed to give greater power to the president, was decisively rejected with a 55 percent vote against the proposed amendments. Although publicly accepting defeat, Mugabe then launched a government campaign of retribution and harassment against those who had opposed the change, and especially the MDC. The 4,500 remaining white farmers were targeted and their farms invaded by landless squatters, a campaign that led to a confrontation with **Great Britain**. The confiscation of white-owned farms accelerated through 2001 as the "war veterans" led the occupations and seizures. Apart from the white farmers who lost their farms, many thousands of African farm workers lost their jobs and by the end of the year, an estimated half million Zimbabweans had crossed the Limpopo River into South Africa in the hope of avoiding starvation and finding jobs.

During the first half of 2002, in the run up to presidential elections, there was much government harassment and intimidation of the opposition, including treason charges leveled at the MDC leader, Morgan Tsvangirai, who was challenging Mugabe for the presidency. Manipulation of ballot boxes ensured a Mugabe victory but the international community reacted severely, both the European Union and the **United States** imposing sanctions on Zimbabwe. On 19 May, the Commonwealth suspended Zimbabwe's membership. On 8 September, the remaining 2,900 white farmers were ordered off their land without compensation.

As a result of his policies, Mugabe had turned Zimbabwe into a pariah state while its economy was virtually in free fall. At the end of 2003, Mugabe announced Zimbabwe's immediate withdrawal from the Commonwealth, which had continued to be highly critical of his actions and had voted to suspend Zimbabwe's membership for a further year. Isolated, widely condemned for its undemocratic practices and intimidation of all opposition, nonetheless Mugabe continued to rule Zimbabwe into 2006.

MUSEVENI, YOWERI KAGUTU (1944–). Yoweri Museveni was born in southwest **Uganda**; he studied political science, economics, and law at the University of Dar es Salaam. In 1970 he became an officer of the General Service Unit (GSU), then being created by Akenna Adoko to counterbalance the influence and power of the military. Following **Idi Amin**'s coup of January 1971, Museveni went into exile where he emerged as a prominent opponent of Amin, creating the Front for the National Salvation of Uganda (FRONSA) in 1972; FRONSA established camps inside Uganda. By 1979, FRONSA consisted of a force of about 9,000 men, and Museveni and FRONSA took part in the campaign of 1978/1979 that led to Amin's collapse and flight.

In the brief interim government of Professor Yusuf Lule in mid-1979, Museveni was minister of defense and acted as head of state in Lule's absence. Godfrey Binaisa, Lule's successor as head of state, feared Museveni's ambition and demoted him to the post of minister for regional cooperation. In 1980, when Paul Muwanga replaced the Binaisa government with a Military Commission, he promoted Museveni as vice chairman. Elections were held in December 1980, after the return to Uganda of Milton Obote, and Museveni formed the Uganda Patriotic Movement to fight them. In the event, he and his party were beaten amid much fraud and vote rigging. Museveni then returned to the bush (1981) to build up his own guerrilla movement—the National Resistance Movement (NRM)—whose military arm, the National Resistance Army (NRA), became a formidable force. Following the overthrow of Obote by General Tito Okello in 1985, Museveni hoped to share power but instead was only offered a minor role in the new government. Even so, he signed a peace pact with Okello on 17 December 1985, in Nairobi. However, there were too many differences between the two men and Museveni was too ambitious for the pact to work for long.

Meanwhile, the Ugandan army had got out of control. Therefore, in mid-January 1986, Museveni took to the field and after bitter fighting he and the NRA captured Kampala on 26 January 1986, and on 29 January Museveni was sworn in as president of Uganda. He proclaimed a policy of national reconciliation, but by then Uganda had been deeply troubled for a long time and at least three resistance movements continued to oppose Museveni and his NRA. Over the period 1986 to 1989 Museveni gradually established his authority over the whole country, sometimes offering amnesties, at others pursuing a scorched earth policy. Museveni permitted limited elections to take place in 1989 but postponed full national elections until 1995. Most opposition had been crushed or sidelined by 1990 and during this year Museveni purged his army of Rwandan troops; these then joined the **Rwanda Patriotic Front** (RPF), which was to advance into **Rwanda** during the next three years to overthrow the Rwandan government in 1994. When elections were finally held in 1996, Museveni's grip on power was confirmed.

Although his position as undisputed ruler of Uganda appeared secure after the 1996 elections, he faced significant rebel groups in the north and west of the country. The **Lord's Resistance Army** (LRA) based in Sudan made any proper control or development of the north impossible. The West Nile Bank Front (WNBF) succeeded in making the West Nile region a more or less no-go area. There was also the Allied Democratic Forces (ADF) operating in the Ruwenzori Mountains. Nonetheless, despite these internal threats, Museveni committed troops to the eastern region of **Democratic Republic of Congo** (DRC) in 1998, to fight alongside the Rwandan army against the forces of President **Laurent Kabila** in support of the Congo Tutsis who were in revolt. Museveni justified his intervention in DRC as a way of protecting Uganda's western border, though his troops, working with the Tutsi rebels, in fact sought to oust Kabila.

In June 2000, over 90 percent of the voters cast their votes in favor of retaining the no-party "Movement" advocated by Museveni that effectively created a one party state under him. In March 2001, Museveni won a landslide victory in the presidential election, gaining 69.3 percent of the votes in what was a rough election. His main opponent, Kizza Besigye, only won 28 percent of the votes cast. Museveni maintained his involvement in DRC through the year, but faced increasingly uneasy relations with Rwanda when fighting between units of the Ugandan and Rwandan armies in the DRC brought the two countries close to war. In February 2002, however, Museveni met with President Paul Kagame of Rwanda and the two leaders restored peace between their two countries. In September 2002, Museveni and President Joseph Kabila signed a peace agreement that provided for the withdrawal of Ugandan forces from the north of DRC. The staged withdrawal of Ugandan forces was carried out through 2003.

Museveni executed a political turnabout in 2003 when he advocated a return to multi-party competition at the urging of the **United States** and the European Union. By May, the Ugandan army had withdrawn from DRC, although three militia groups operating in the Ituri region "looked" after Ugandan interests and, according to a **United Nations** report, one of them was run directly from Museveni's office. During 2004 it became obvious that Museveni was determined to engineer a third presidential term for himself, which would mean altering the constitution. Besigye, the chairman of the opposition Forum for Democratic Change (FDC), who had spent four years in exile in the United States, returned to Uganda in October 2005 and on 14 November was arrested on charges of treason, concealment of treason, and rape. He had held a number of political rallies on his return, which attracted large crowds and his supporters believed his arrest was designed to prevent him challenging Museveni. On 14 December, the FDC nominated Besigye as its candidate in the coming presidential election and, on 2 January 2006, the High Court ordered the release of Besigye, clearing the way for him to challenge Museveni in the elections scheduled for 23 February. Despite considerable violence and many irregularities, Museveni obtained a clear victory in the election, winning 59 percent of the votes against 37 percent going to Besigye.

– N –

NAMIBIA. German South West Africa became a mandate of the League of Nations in 1920 and was administered as such by the **Union of South Africa** until 1946, when the newly formed **United Nations** invited its members to place their mandated territories under its system of Trusteeship. South Africa declined to do so, and by its refusal sparked off a confrontation with the United Nations that was to last until 1990. The **South West Africa People's Organization** (SWAPO) was formed in 1960; its object was to campaign for independence from South African control. In 1966, the General Assembly of the United Nations passed Resolution 2145, which revoked the mandate (of the former League) and changed the name of the territory to Namibia. SWAPO, operating from Zambia and Angola, had sent its first guerrillas into the country the previous year and these now clashed with the South African Defence Force (SADF) to spark off a 25-year armed struggle.

The 1970s witnessed a long-drawn-out confrontation between the United Nations and South Africa, with the world body attempting to prise control of Namibia from Pretoria and South Africa, manipulating minority groups to provide the appearance of an "independent" state associated with South Africa. South African–inspired proposals for an independent South West Africa/Namibia were advanced in 1976, but rejected by the United Nations. In 1977, South Africa accepted the so-called western Contact Group of five (the **United States**, **Great Britain**, **France**, West Germany, and Canada) as mediators and intense negotiations took place over the period 1978–1981 between the Contact Group and South Africa. These led to no result, however, especially as SWAPO saw the Contact Group as biased in favor of South Africa.

In 1981 the United States embarked upon its policy of **linkage** whereby it determined that any resolution of Namibian demands for independence should be tied to the withdrawal of Cuban troops from **Angola**. As a result, the Namibian question became entangled in the Angolan war throughout the 1980s and the SADF was to launch a number of cross-border attacks upon government targets in Angola (ostensibly SWAPO bases) as well as SWAPO bases during the course of the decade. By 1986, South Africa had 35,000 troops in Namibia (75 percent of them recruited from Namibians), although SWAPO put the figure much higher. By this time South Africa was conducting a "hearts and minds" campaign in Ovamboland (where many violations of human rights and atrocities by the South African forces and police were committed) aimed at SWAPO sympathizers in an effort to create divisions between them and other smaller ethnic groups. In 1987 the

People's Liberation Army of Namibia (PLAN) launched attacks upon white farming areas (it had previously done so in 1983), while South Africa now admitted that it had substantial forces inside Angola. These became involved in the battle of **Cuito Cuanavale**, which developed into a major set-piece battle involving the **Movimento Popular para a Libertação de Angola** (MPLA)/Popular Movement for the Liberation of Angola government of Angola and its Cuban allies, on the one side, and the **União Nacional para a Independência Total de Angola** (UNITA)/National Union for the Total Independence of Angola and the South Africans, on the other. The South Africans found they no longer enjoyed military superiority and, as a result, entered into a series of talks that went on through 1988, culminating in an agreement of December 1988. Under its terms, South Africa was to withdraw its forces from Angola by August 1989, the Cubans were to phase the withdrawal of their (estimated) 50,000 troops from Angola by mid-1991, and the United Nations Resolution 435 (of 1978) was to be implemented, whereby internationally monitored elections would be held throughout Namibia. The terms of the agreement were carried out by the different signatory states and Namibia became independent on 21 March 1990.

For a quarter of a century, Namibia had been in a state of high tension; most of the guerrilla fighting was confined to Ovamboland in the north or across the border in Angola, and though there was never any likelihood of SWAPO defeating the SADF, its activities, nonetheless, were on a sufficient scale so as to engage a large part of South Africa's armed forces over many years.

NATIONAL PATRIOTIC FRONT OF LIBERIA (NPFL). The National Patriotic Front of Liberia (NPFL) was formed by **Charles Taylor** while in exile in **Côte d'Ivoire**. In 1984 Taylor had fled to the **United States** from **Liberia**, accused of embezzling government funds. He was arrested in the United States and about to be extradited to Liberia when he escaped and returned to Africa where he sought and obtained assistance from Burkina Faso and Libya. He established a base in Côte d'Ivoire where he created the NPFL.

On 24 December 1989, Taylor led 200 members of his NPFL across the border from Côte d'Ivoire into Liberia and launched his revolt. The regular army of President **Samuel Doe** was unable to contain the rebel group, which made a rapid advance through Nimba County where, in any case, the presidential forces were widely unpopular. Within a few months Taylor's force had grown to some 2,000 troops. In February 1990 Taylor's associate, **Prince Yormie Johnson**, broke away from the NPFL and took his own supporters, a substantial number, with him. Johnson now formed his Independent National Patriotic Front of Liberia (INPFL).

During 1990, as the civil war escalated in intensity and the **Economic Community of West African States** (ECOWAS) attempted to mediate a cease-fire, the NPFL either refused to take part in negotiations or rejected the different settlements that were reached. As the most effective of the guerrilla movements, which by mid-1990 controlled the greater part of Liberia, the NPFL was in a position to make any peace impossible without its agreement, even if it was not strong enough to dictate a peace by itself. In March 1991, a frustrated Taylor allowed the NPFL to join forces with dissident groups from **Sierra Leone** under Foday Sankoh in an invasion of Sierra Leone. This action, however, had the effect of ranging the **Organization of African Unity** (OAU) against Taylor and the NPFL. Over the period 1991–1996 (half war, half negotiations), the NPFL became Taylor's political base as well as his fighting force, and in 1997 he finally emerged the victor of the civil war when he won nationwide elections to become the country's president.

NETO, ANTONIO AGOSTINHO (1922–79). Agostinho Neto was president of the **Movimento Popular para a Libertação de Angola** (MPLA)/Popular Movement for the Liberation of Angola from 1962 to his death in 1979, and for the last four years of that time was also president of **Angola**. He was the most important and effective of the nationalists ranged against the Portuguese during the liberation struggle. He was a Mbundu and a "prison graduate," an intellectual, and a guerrilla leader as well as a "poet of protest." An assimilado and scholar, he was a great persuader, though no orator.

He was born on 17 September 1922, the son of a Methodist pastor at Bengo near Catete, 96 kilometers southeast of Luanda. Between 1944 and 1947 he worked in the public health department. Through the Methodist Bishop Ralph Dodge he obtained a scholarship first to Lisbon and then to the University of Coimbra to study medicine, but was sent down for his political agitation and poems (1955–57). He resumed his studies at the University of Porto, from which he graduated in 1958; he returned to Angola as a doctor in 1959.

On 8 June 1960, Neto was arrested in front of his patients in his surgery, and when the villagers went to Catete to protest at his arrest, they were fired upon by the Portuguese police: 30 were killed and a further 200 injured. Neto was held for three months and then sent to Cape Verde before being taken to **Portugal** in October 1961 to be held at Aljube Prison in Lisbon. He escaped from prison in July 1962 and went to Morocco. In August 1962, Neto attended reconciliation talks in Kinshasa between the MPLA and the **Frente Nacional da Libertação de Angola** (FNLA)/National Front for the Liberation of Angola, but they broke down. Over 1–3 December 1962, the MPLA held its national conference in Kinshasa when it elected a 10-man executive and made Neto its president. In 1964, Neto visited the **Union of Soviet Socialist Republics** (USSR) and received promises of financial support for the MPLA. In 1966, he became the recipient of the Joliot–Curie Award by the World Council of Peace. In 1969, as Angola's delegate, he attended the Afro–Asian Solidarity Conference in Khartoum and in 1970 he went to Rome where he was granted an audience by the Pope. He visited the People's Republic of China in 1971 and attended the **Organization of African Unity** (OAU) Conference at Rabat in 1972. On 13 December 1972, he was reconciled with **Holden Roberto** and the FNLA in Kinshasa.

Following the withdrawal of the Portuguese in 1975, Neto became president of Angola on 11 November of that year, although it was not until 1976 that a majority of the OAU recognized his government as the legitimate government of Angola. Neto faced a difficult four years as president from 1975 to 1979. His new administration refused to consider sharing power with the FNLA or the **União Nacional para a Independência Total de Angola** (UNITA)/National Union for the Total Independence of Angola and successfully destroyed the power of the FNLA during 1976. UNITA, however, took to the bush to become a far more formidable force and waged civil war against the government throughout the 1980s after Neto's death. In December 1977, the Neto leadership launched the MPLA government on a Marxist–Leninist course and changed the name of the ruling party to the MPLA-PT (Partido do Trabalho). In December 1978, Neto's position was further enhanced when the posts of prime minister and three deputy prime ministers were abolished and the party structure was reorganized. However, Neto was suffering from cancer and in 1979 went to Moscow for treatment where he died in September.

NIGERIA, CIVIL WAR (1967–70). The state of Nigeria was an artificial British imperial creation whose major ethnic groups—the Hausa-Fulani of the north, the Yoruba of the west, and the Ibo of the east—were each larger in population than most individual African states. **Great Britain** fostered strong regional governments and, moreover, encouraged a sense of regional rivalry, maintaining the balance between the three great regions from the center. There was no historical basis for the unity of these three regions and their different ethnic groups except British imperial convenience. At independence, therefore, the new Nigeria inherited three powerful regions whose interests tended to draw them away from central authority and, once the British had departed, there was intense rivalry as to who should control the center. (However, about two million Ibos from the Eastern Region were dispersed in other parts of Nigeria, many holding jobs in the more conservative Islamic north where they were often resented.) This situation led to increasingly divisive strains once the British had departed and efforts to balance the claims and counterclaims of the three regions failed to satisfy the aspirations of any of them, so that the political structure inherited from the British rapidly broke down over the period 1960–1966.

The 1966 Coup: Military Rule

On 15 January 1966, part of the army, which had been coordinated by Major Chukwuma Nzeogwu from Kaduna, attempted to overthrow the federal system. In the north the premier, Alhaji Sir Ahmadu Bello, the Sardauna of Sokoto, was murdered. The army proclaimed its aims over Kaduna radio—"a free country, devoid of corruption, nepotism, tribalism and regionalism." In the west another leading politician, Chief Akintola, was killed. In Lagos the federal prime minister, Alhaji Sir Abubakar Tafawa Balewa, and the federal finance minister, Chief Festus Okotie-Eboh, were killed. In addition, nine senior army officers were killed. This first coup, which eliminated these major political figures was, nonetheless, aborted when troops loyal to the government under Major-General J. T. Aguiyi-Ironsi, General Officer Commanding the Nigerian Army, restored federal control. The acting president, Dr. Nwafor Orizu (President Azikiwe was then out of the country), announced that the Council of Ministers had decided to hand over power to the military and General Ironsi assumed authority as head of a Federal Military Government (FMG), as well as becoming supreme commander of the Armed Forces. The coup had solved nothing and the regional differences, which threatened Nigerian unity, remained in place. It had, however, brought to an end the first republic and removed a number of leading political figures who were seen to be synonymous with a discredited system. General Ironsi abolished the federal form of government and the regions, unified the top five grades of the civil service, and introduced provincial administrators. He then turned the FMG into a National Military Government (NMG).

The Second Coup

On 29 May 1966, violent anti-Ibo demonstrations took place in the north of Nigeria, many Ibos were attacked and killed and their property destroyed. Two months later, on 29 July, General Ironsi, who was on a tour of reconciliation, and Lt. Col. Fajuyi (the military governor of Western Province) were kidnapped and killed in Ibadan. The death of Ironsi sparked off the second military coup attempt, in which some 200 eastern (Ibo) officers were killed. The north then talked of secession. Following a three-day interregnum Lt. Col. **Yakubu Gowon**, chief of staff, became military head of state on 1 August. At this point, the country was on the verge of disintegration. Gowon granted amnesty to a number of prominent figures who had been detained by the army since the previous January; these included Chief Awolowo, Dr. Michael Okpara (a former Eastern Region premier), and others. On 31 August, Gowon restored the regions which Ironsi had abolished, and conferences of reconciliation were held.

But Lt. Col. **Chukwuemeka Odumegwu Ojukwu**, the regional commander of the Eastern Region (homeland of the Ibos), would not be reconciled. New anti-Ibo demonstrations took place in the north and between 10,000 and 30,000 Ibos were killed during September, resulting in an exodus of Ibos from the north (where there were one million), the west (400,000), and Lagos (100,000) back to the Eastern

Region. The federal government and Ojukwu, who had emerged as the spokesman of the Ibos, failed to find any common ground, and once the Ibos had returned to the Eastern Region from the other parts of Nigeria, demands for secession became much more insistent.

In January 1967, a conference was held under the chairmanship of Ghana's General Joseph Ankrah at Aburi in Ghana in an attempt to prevent a breakdown, but after the event, neither side could agree on what had been decided. On 26 May 1967, in an effort to break the deadlock, Gowon replaced the old regions by dividing Nigeria into 12 states, although the immediate result was to precipitate the civil war with the Eastern Region. The government in Lagos, with the support of most of Africa, was determined to preserve a single Nigeria. Ojukwu called an emergency meeting of the Eastern Nigeria Consultative Assembly to consider the new division of Nigeria. On 27 May, Gowon broadcast to confirm the division into 12 states—six in the north, three in the east, one in the west, one in the midwest, and Lagos. He also proclaimed a state of emergency. The Eastern Nigeria Consultative Assembly rejected the 12 states arrangement and empowered Ojukwu to declare an independent state and, on 30 May 1967, Ojukwu announced the creation of an independent state of Biafra, which covered the Eastern Region; the majority of its people were Ibos. Gowon at once dismissed Ojukwu from the army and as governor of the Eastern Region. The federal government then announced that it would take "clinical police action" to end the secession and the first military move was made on 6 July.

The Civil War

In July 1966, the strength of the Federal army had been a mere 9,000 men but rapid reorganization and recruitment during the succeeding year as the crisis developed (with Ibo troops withdrawing to the Eastern Region) had raised its strength to 40,000 by July 1967. At the beginning of the war the federal government assumed that Biafra would collapse in a matter of weeks. In fact a new Biafran army was created round the nucleus of 2,000 officers and men who had withdrawn from the federal army, and by July 1967 this army was approximately 25,000 strong. When eight battalions of the federal army advanced on Biafra from the north in July, they met stiff resistance from well-prepared Biafran troops. Then, on 9 August 1967, in a provocative challenge to the federal government, the Biafran army mounted an offensive in the west and crossed the Niger to occupy Benin City and the ports of Sapele and Ughelli.

Nigeria's size and economic potential (the country's oil wealth was then becoming apparent) ensured a high level of international interest in the war as well as a readiness on the part of outside powers to intervene. Britain, the former colonial power, had substantial investments in Nigeria which it was determined to defend and the two giant oil companies, British Petroleum and Shell, were heavily involved in the exploitation of the country's oil. At the beginning of the war, Britain tried to sit on the fence but then came down firmly on the side of the federal government and was to be its principal source of light arms throughout the war. **France**, in pursuit of its own geopolitical interests in the region and the hope of increasing its influence generally in western Africa, supported breakaway Biafra which it aided with arms and other assistance through its proxies **Côte d'Ivoire** and Gabon. The **Union of Soviet Socialist Republics** (USSR), which was ideologically opposed to the breakup of a federation, supported the Lagos government; Moscow saw providing assistance to Nigeria as a way of obtaining influence in a region in which, up to that time, it had had little impact, and during the course of the war it supplied about 30 percent of the arms imported by the federal side including MiG fighters and Ilyushin bombers. The **United States** signaled its intention of remaining outside the conflict, although the U.S. secretary of state, Dean Rusk, infuriated the Nigerians by saying at a press conference that "we regard Nigeria as part of Britain's sphere of influence." Both **Portugal** and **South Africa**, which were facing growing problems justifying white minority rule to an increasingly hostile world, supported breakaway Biafra on the general grounds of prolonging a war (and chaos) in the largest independent black African state, so as to bolster their claims on behalf of white minority rule in the south of the continent.

The westward offensive across the Niger mounted by Biafra on 9 August 1967 threatened the whole structure of Nigeria and signaled the beginning of a full-scale civil war. By 17 August, the Biafran forces had crossed the Ofusu River to reach Ore in the Western Region, from where they could threaten both Lagos and Ibadan. On 29 September the Biafran administrator of the newly overrun midwest,

Major Albert Okonkwo, proclaimed an "independent and sovereign Republic of Benin." In response to this threat, General Gowon announced: "From now on we shall wage total war." Federal superiority in both numbers and arms soon began to tilt the balance back in favor of the federal government and on 22 September, the federal counteroffensive led to the rapid reoccupation of the midwest. Then, on 4 October 1967, federal forces occupied Enugu, the Biafran capital, and by the end of the year had captured Calabar, Biafra's second port.

Early in 1968, in quick succession, the federal forces captured Onitsha (a port and commercial center) and then three major towns—Aba, Owerri, and Umuahia. In May 1968 Port Harcourt, Biafra's principal (and last) port, fell to the federal forces. At this juncture in the war (May 1968), when all the major Biafran towns and ports had been lost and it was hemmed in on three sides (north, west, and south), the possibility of Biafran independence had been lost and the sensible course would have been for Ojukwu to make terms with Lagos. Civil wars do not work in such a fashion, however, and the war continued for another year and a half and produced enormous unnecessary suffering.

The federal strategy was to employ siege tactics, which led to starvation of the Ibos because from this point onward, Biafra could only obtain supplies by air. One year after declaring its independence Biafra had been reduced to a tenth of its original size, and for the rest of the war the civilian population was to suffer from growing starvation. Even so, the Biafran forces mounted a successful counterattack in 1969 to retake Owerri for a short time; their forces also re-crossed the Niger, but they did not have sufficient resources to sustain these successes and slow military strangulation by the federal forces took place. Peace efforts were made during December 1969 as the federal forces harried the Biafran government, which was obliged to move from one place to another.

International Support for Biafra

International assistance for Biafra came from a number of sources and for a variety of reasons. These included humanitarian agencies, a handful of African countries (including Rhodesia, which had then embarked upon its Unilateral Declaration of Independence [UDI] under Ian Smith), and Haiti. There was considerable international sympathy for Biafra as a "small loser" and criticisms of the federal government included the charge that it could have made greater efforts to achieve a peace sooner.

Four African countries recognized Biafra: Tanzania (13 April 1968), Gabon (5 May 1968), **Côte d'Ivoire** (14 May 1968), and Zambia (20 May 1968). Haiti recognized Biafra on 23 March 1969, though its reasons for doing so were not obvious. France supplied weapons for Biafra, channeling them through Côte d'Ivoire and Gabon; Portugal supplied arms through Guinea-Bissau. The International Committee of the Red Cross (ICRC), Joint Church Aid, and Caritas provided relief supplies. Biafra obtained a number of old DC-class airplanes from Rhodesia; on the other hand, the federal government, which had no planes, approached the West which, however, refused to supply any on the grounds that to do so would escalate the war. Lagos, therefore, was obliged to turn to the USSR for airplanes, which it then obtained. As early as 6 September 1968, most of the oil-producing areas of Biafra had been taken by federal forces, so that Biafra did not even have oil as a bargaining counter. Even when it was clear that Biafra must lose the war, the Ibos continued to show remarkable faith in Ojukwu. Biafra projected an upbeat propaganda image, both to reassure its own people, and to obtain foreign support. Another aspect of international involvement in the war was the presence of **mercenaries** on both sides; they contributed an especially unwelcome complication. On the federal side they were used as pilots, on the Biafran side as ground troops and trainers as well as pilots.

The basic strategy of the federal army, which in any case enjoyed huge superiority of numbers and arms, was to blockade the shrinking enclave of Biafra and bring about its surrender by starvation. In the end, Biafra was confined to a small enclave of territory that was served by a single airstrip to which supplies were brought in by mercenaries. During December 1969 and early January 1970, the federal army deployed 120,000 troops for its final assault and Owerri (the last town) and Ulli (the solitary airstrip) fell to the federal army over 9–10 January 1970, and the war was over.

The Aftermath

By the end of the war, the federal army had been increased in size to 200,000 troops. Biafra, despite its handicaps, had demonstrated astonishing resilience, even in its darkest days. Biafra's propaganda machine had also fostered the idea that surrender meant genocide, a line that served the dual purpose of persuading its people to fight to the end (or near end) and engendering a good deal of international sympathy for its cause. On 10 January 1970, Ojukwu handed over power to Major General Philip Effiong, his chief of staff, and fled (11 January) to Côte d'Ivoire, where he was given political asylum.

In the course of the war, a number of attempts at **mediation** had been made by the **Organization of African Unity** (OAU), the Vatican, and the **Commonwealth**, though they had little impact. In the case of the OAU, its insistence that any peace had to be in the context of "one Nigeria," ensured that its efforts were rejected by Biafra. The interests of Africa as a whole, whose leaders were wary of any moves that might signal the breakup of states as they had been at independence, ensured that the OAU took this line. **Arms** for the combatants came from a variety of sources: the main suppliers for the federal side were Britain and the USSR, and for Biafra, France and Portugal. The United States, the Netherlands, Czechoslovakia, Italy, and Belgium refused to supply arms to either side.

The war was prolonged unnecessarily by two factors: the Ibo belief, cultivated by its own propaganda, that they were fighting for survival and faced genocide; and because international charities, aided by mercenary airlifts of supplies, provided relief when otherwise Biafra would have been forced to surrender. The war became a cause for various charities whose propaganda "to feed the starving Biafrans," however well-intentioned, in fact prolonged the war and the suffering.

Estimated casualties were 100,000 military (on both sides) and between 500,000 and two million civilians, mainly the result of starvation, while 4.6 million Biafrans became **refugees**. In the end, 900 days of war had not destroyed Africa's largest black state, while Biafra's bid for secession and independence had failed. In the post-war years, Gowon's greatest achievement was to preside successfully over the reintegration of the defeated Ibos into the mainstream of Nigerian life.

Nigeria's recovery after the war was greatly assisted by the OPEC revolution of 1973; the huge increase in the price of oil enabled Nigeria to launch its giant Third Development Plan in 1975. Through the 1970s, and assisted by its new oil wealth, Nigeria was to enjoy a period of major influence in Africa as a whole. On the other hand, the success of the military in the war had given it a taste for permanent rule in peacetime and, regrettably, by 1998 Nigeria had only enjoyed 10 years of civilian rule since independence, as opposed to 28 years of military rule. However, it returned to civilian rule at the end of the century.

NIGERIA: THE DELTA WAR (1995–). The Niger Delta is Africa's largest floodplain. It consists of dense rainforest, sand ridges, mangrove forests, and swamps and is criss-crossed by tidal channels, streams, rivers, and creaks. It is rich in resources consisting of timber, coal, palm oil and, above all, natural gas and oil (an estimated 35 billion barrels of oil). It is densely populated and as one of the largest wetlands in the world, it is almost impossible to patrol with any success. Crime and violence in the Delta region are financed by between 30,000 and 100,000 barrels of oil that are stolen every day. The money from this illegally tapped oil is used to purchase **arms** for the militias or to enrich Nigerian and foreign business people who are only too ready to profit from the chaos in the region, and to finance political ambitions. Despite the huge energy reserves of the Delta, some 70 percent of the 27 million people who live there exist in a state of extreme poverty.

One fifth of U.S. oil imports come from the Delta (2006) and **Great Britain** expects to obtain 10 percent of its gas requirements from the region in the near future. However, such exports are coming under increasing threats of disruption from the local people who have come to see these exports as the theft of their natural resources. The demand for social justice dates spectacularly from the execution of the Ogoni campaigner Ken Saro-Wiwa by the government of President Sani-Abacha in 1995, which was met with universal condemnation. Saro-Wiwa had launched a campaign for social and ecological justice in the Delta in the 1980s. The complications of this war are considerable and include tribalism, gang warfare for control of oil resources, government neglect of the region, corruption, and the activities of the international oil companies. Three ethnic groups compete for control of the region and fight each other: these are the Itshekiri, the Urhobo, and the Ijaw. Warri, a major town in the center of the Delta, is awash with money and attracts people like a frontier town. Described as the "heart and lungs" of Nigeria, Delta oil has provided the Nigerian government with $300 billion income since oil was discovered in 1956. At independence in 1960, each of Nigeria's three regions was allowed 50 percent of the revenues from minerals found within it, while the balance went to the federal government. Too often, however, the regions have received much less. Agitation for a greater share of its oil wealth has had a long history and in 1966, for example, an Ijaw army officer, Isaac Boro, declared a Federal Republic of Niger Delta, though this only lasted for 12 days.

As the violence has escalated in the early years of the present century, more and more people have moved into the safety of Warri. Foreigners employ armed guards and there has grown up an informal network of armed youths who claim to be fighting for the emancipa-tion of the Niger Delta. The size of these youth groups and the scope of their activities are hard to gauge. Official estimates suggest that Nigeria loses 100,000 barrels of oil a day through "bunkering"—the term covering the illegal siphoning off of oil—and it is believed that the activity depends upon the complicity of oil company employees and highly placed government officials as well as soldiers and the militias. According to Human Rights Watch, oil bunkering fuels gang-related violence in the Delta that, for example, killed 1,000 people in 2004.

Asari Dokubo, leader of the Niger Delta People's Volunteer Force (NDPVF), came to prominence when he threatened to blow up all oil facilities in the Delta, a threat that sent the oil price above $50 a barrel. He was arrested in September 2005 and charged with treason at a time when he claimed to have 10,000 followers ready to reclaim control of the Delta's resources on behalf of its people. He later did a deal with the government—an arms swap for cash—which led a faction of the NDPVF breaking away to form the Movement for the Emancipation of the Niger Delta (MEND). However, MEND subse-quently campaigned for the release of Dokubo so it seemed probable that the two factions were working together. A task force created by President **Olusegun Obasanjo** to cut off the supply of oil, arms, and money to the militias—Joint (Military) Task Force (JTF)—created resentment rather than solving anything and itself became involved in oil bunkering.

During 2006 MEND militants began to seize hostages. In January, they stormed a Shell oil vessel and took four foreigners hostage. They issued three demands: that the government release Asari Dokubo; that the impeached governor of Bayelsa State, Diepreye Alemieyeseigha, who was on trial for money-laundering, should be released; and that $1.5 billion approved by the Senate as compensation to communities affected by oil spills should be paid by Shell. Four days later MEND attacked two houseboats and killed 15 JTF soldiers. Two weeks later it released the hostages it had taken on humanitarian grounds. However, apparently in retaliation, three communities were attacked by a JTF helicopter gunship. By April 2006, MEND had waged a four-month campaign of sabotage and kidnap against the oil producers, forcing the companies to cut production by 550,000 barrels a day.

Poverty and neglect are the root causes of this growing violence. Shell, the largest operator, has been forced to evacuate staff and scale back its operations and, though the federal government has often promised to help the Delta region, little has been done. In April 2006, the government announced plans to construct a $1.8 billion highway through the region and create 20,000 new jobs in the military, police, and state oil companies. However, the sense of neglect continues and since the ruling People's Democratic Party (PDP) controls all the seats in state and local government so that there is no effective political opposition, this allows the militias to speak on behalf of the aggrieved majority of people in the Delta region. Even if no full scale war develops, the escalating violence could force the oil companies to close down more of their land-based operations and concentrate only on their offshore activities at a time when acute demands for oil are everywhere increasing.

NIMEIRI, GAAFAR MOHAMMED (1930–). Born on I January 1930, Gaafar Mohammed Nimeiri went from school to military college to become a second lieutenant in 1952. He was an enthusiastic supporter of Egypt's President Nasser and this was to get him into trouble in the course of his army career. He was involved in the overthrow of General Ibrahim Abboud in 1964; then he was posted to Darfur. He went for training at the American Army Command School, Fort Leavenworth, Kansas. When he returned to the **Sudan**, Nimeiri was again implicated in a coup attempt. He served a period at Torit in the South of the country and was then promoted commanding officer of the military school in Khartoum.

On 25 May 1969, Nimeiri carried out a successful coup to overthrow the government of President Ismail al-Azhari. He set up a Revolutionary Command Council. To begin with, Nimeiri worked with the Communists and turned his attention to destroying the power of the Ansar sect; he sent his best troops against 20,000 of their members on Aba Island in the Nile when 1,000 were killed. However, the Communists then turned against him and attempted a coup in July 1971; this was aborted when Colonel **Muammar Gaddafi** of Libya forced the plane carrying their leaders to land at Benghazi and then handed the coup makers over to Nimeiri. Once he had dealt successfully with the Ansar sect and the Communists—the two centers of opposition to his rule—Nimeiri held a plebiscite on 30 September 1971 to become Sudan's first elected president with a 98.6 percent vote.

He then created the Sudan Socialist Union (SSU). At this time Nimeiri was at the height of his influence and popularity. He therefore turned his attention to the war in the South, which had been dragging on since independence. He entered into secret negotiations with the Southern Sudan Liberation Movement and a peace agreement was hammered out by 27 February 1972. It was Nimeiri's greatest political achievement. The peace of 1972 lasted for 10 years, and though the relationship between North and South was never easy, at least it remained without violence for a decade.

Nimeiri tackled a range of economic and development problems through the 1970s, but he met with growing opposition that included another attempted coup in 1976, though in the following year he was again elected to the presidency by a national plebiscite. His economic troubles multiplied so that he entered the 1980s very much on the political defensive. By 1982 there was political in-fighting in the South, the economy was in the doldrums, and political opposition to Nimeiri's rule was growing.

Nimeiri, therefore, turned to the Islamic fundamentalists for support and in 1983 became a "born again" fundamentalist. He introduced Sharia law with its ban on alcohol and punishments by mutilation, but this produced immediate opposition in the South whose population was not Muslim, and led to a renewal of the civil war (violent incidents had occurred from 1982 onward). Nimeiri's program of Islamicization met with stiff opposition and was the principal cause of the renewal of war in the South. Opposition to Nimeiri grew rapidly through 1984 and on 6 April 1985, while he was visiting the **United States**, Nimeiri was deposed in a coup led by Lt. Gen. Suwar al-Dahab.

NKOMATI ACCORD. The Nkomati Accord between **Mozambique** and **South Africa** was signed on 16 March 1984. It was an agreement whereby the two countries would "not allow their respective territory, territorial waters or air space to be used as a base by another state's government, foreign military forces, organizations or individuals which plan to commit acts of violence, terrorism or aggression" against another country. What this meant in practice was that Mozambique would no longer permit the **African National Congress** (ANC) to use Mozambique, either for passage into South Africa or as a base from which to launch guerrilla actions.

As a result of this Accord—by October 1984—800 members of the ANC had either left Mozambique or been expelled. ANC members were given a choice of leaving the country or living in **refugee** camps. As a consequence, ANC activity in South Africa declined significantly for a time, which was the justification for the agreement from Pretoria's point of view. South Africa, in its turn, agreed to end its support for the **Resistência Nacional Moçambicana** (RENAMO)/Mozambican National Resistance.

Mozambique's adherence to this Accord was seen as a sign of desperation at a time when its economy was plummeting and there was no indication that the civil war would come to an end. South African support for RENAMO had included money, weapons, and assistance with information and communications (radio). This was part of Pretoria's "destabilization policy" directed at its neighbors and especially the "Frontline" States, among which Mozambique was numbered.

In the years following the Accord, despite repeated denials, South Africa continued to support RENAMO and constantly broke its Nkomati pledges. As early as December 1984, Mozambique's President **Samora Machel** accused South Africa of breaking the agreement. Further meetings between representatives of the two countries made no difference, and South Africa continued its support for RENAMO. President **Julius Nyerere** of Tanzania condemned the Accord, but in June 1985 at Harare, **Zimbabwe**, he agreed (with President **Robert Mugabe**) to assist Machel in his fight against RENAMO. Zimbabwe then committed troops to Mozambique and Tanzania did so some-what later. At the time, the Nkomati Accord was seen as a victory for white South Africa. It came at the high point of Pretoria's campaign of destabilization against its neighbors, which was pursued throughout the 1980s.

NKOMO, JOSHUA MQABUKO NYONGOLO (1917–99). Joshua Nkomo was born on 19 June 1917 and completed his education in **South Africa** during the years 1941–1945. He stood for the 1953 elections but was not elected; in 1954 he became president of his local (Rhodesian) **African National Congress** (ANC). While overseas on behalf of the ANC in 1959, the Rhodesian premier, Sir Edgar Whitehead, banned the ANC (September 1959). Nkomo then established a London office at Golders Green. In October 1960, when he was still in London, Nkomo was elected in his absence for the National Democratic Party (NDP), which was the successor in Rhodesia to the banned ANC.

A compromiser by nature, Nkomo was prepared to accept the 1961 Rhodesian constitution, which only allotted 15 of 65 seats in the Assembly to Africans, but his party would not accept the deal. On 9 December 1961, the NDP was banned; it was at once replaced by the **Zimbabwe African People's Union** (ZAPU) and once more Nkomo was elected its leader. He was then detained for three months by the government. A division now opened up within the ranks of ZAPU, which split, and a breakaway movement, the **Zimbabwe African National Union** (ZANU), was formed under the leadership of Ndabaningi Sithole and **Robert Mugabe**. On 16 April 1964, Nkomo was banished to Gonakudzingwa in a remote part of Rhodesia, where he was to remain in detention until the "detente" exercise of 1974.

In 1976, he formed the Patriotic Front with Mugabe as joint leader. Following the Lusaka **Commonwealth** meeting of 1979 and the sub-sequent Lancaster House talks in London, in which Nkomo participated, Rhodesia became independent as Zimbabwe on 18 April 1980. In pre-independence elections, however, Mugabe's ZANU had won 57 of the 80 open (African seats), while Nkomo's ZAPU had only taken 20. Nkomo was made minister of home affairs in Mugabe's first cabinet, but he had little power. Mugabe and Nkomo were far apart, both ideologically and temperamentally, and their respective supporters were always clashing.

In January 1981, Mugabe demoted Nkomo to minister without portfolio. Relations between ZANU and ZAPU supporters deteriorated, and then (17 February 1982) caches of arms were discovered on Nkomo's farms and Mugabe claimed that Nkomo was supporting terrorist groups operating in Ndebeleland (the heartland of Nkomo supporters). The government invested Ndebeleland with armed forces and arrested many of Nkomo's leading supporters. On 8 March 1983, Nkomo fled to Botswana and then to London, where he remained until August of that year when he returned to Zimbabwe.

On his return, Nkomo began to discuss national unity with Mugabe. What this would eventually lead to was the submergence of ZAPU in the ruling party, ZANU, as the country under Mugabe moved toward becoming a one-party state. The "Dissidents' War" was to last from 1982 to 1987 and the progress of talks between the government, which had all the power, and ZAPU was to be a slow, on-off affair. However, once ZANU had won the first post-independence elections in 1985—they were bitterly contested—and Mugabe had increased his electoral advantage, reducing ZAPU's seats to 15, the options open to Nkomo and ZAPU had become still more limited. In the end, the unity talks, which took place through 1987, led to an agreement of April 1988 whereby the two parties were merged into a single ZANU. This represented a total victory for Mugabe. Nkomo was made a senior minister without portfolio in the President's Office. On 9 April 1990, Mugabe promoted Nkomo to become one of two vice presidents. He died on 1 July 1999.

NYERERE, JULIUS KAMBARAGE (1922–99). Julius Nyerere, who led Tanganyika to independence and became the country's first president, played a significant role as the chairman of the "Frontline States" in opposing white minority rule in the south of the continent and supporting the various liberation movements belonging to **South Africa** (the **African National Congress**—ANC), Rhodesia (the **Zimbabwe African National Union**—ZANU, and the **Zimbabwe African People's Union**—ZAPU), and **Mozambique** (the **Frente da Libertação de Moçambique** (FRELIMO)/Mozambique Liberation Front). These and other liberation movements were allowed to have offices in Dar es Salaam. Nyerere was a firm friend of **Samora Machel** of Mozambique and provided support for him both as the leader of FRELIMO when he was fighting against the Portuguese prior to independence, and as president of Mozambique when he was fighting the civil war against the **Resistência Nacional Moçambicana** (RENAMO)/Mozambican National Resistance. As the war against RENAMO escalated during the 1980s, Nyerere assisted first Machel and then his successor **Joaquim Chissano** by providing military assistance—up to 3,000 troops—to help guard vital installations, especially the northern railway from Malawi to Nacala, against sabotage. Nyerere opposed the **Nkomati Accord**, which Machel was obliged to enter into with South Africa in 1984, although he recognized that Machel had few options open to him. In 1985, Nyerere stood down from the presidency of Tanzania and was succeeded by Ali Hassan Mwinyi. He had played a notable role as chairman of the "Frontline States" during the preceding years.

– O –

OBASANJO, OLUSEGUN (1937–). Olusegun Obasanjo was a distinguished soldier who made his mark in the Nigerian civil war and later succeeded Murtala Muhammed as Nigeria's head of state (1976–79) before returning the country to civilian rule. He was born of a Yoruba family on 5 May 1937 and joined the army in 1958. He became a lieutenant in 1960 and served on the **United Nations** Congo force. He was then promoted commander of the engineering unit of the Nigerian army. After attending military training courses in England and India he was promoted lieutenant-colonel in 1967, became commander of the Ibadan Garrison (1967–69), and was promoted to full colonel.

During the **Nigerian civil war** he first commanded the Third Infantry Division and then the Third Marine Commando Division, with which he operated on the southeastern front of Biafra. In January 1970, Obasanjo accepted the Biafran surrender. After the war he continued his full-time military career and, on 29 July 1975, he was made chief of staff, Supreme Headquarters, a post he held until 13 February 1976. Then, following the assassination of Murtala Muhammed, Obasanjo took over as head of state. He kept to the announced program to return the country to civilian rule in 1979 when he stood down. In the 1990s he was imprisoned by the country's military ruler, General Sani Abacha, but, following Abacha's death, was released from prison and ran for the office of president in the elections of February 1999, which he won.

OGADEN WAR. The Ogaden War of 1977–1978 between **Ethiopia** and **Somalia** had an important bearing upon the war of secession or civil war being fought in **Eritrea** against control by Addis Ababa, which was then already more than 15 years old. The Ogaden War focused the attention of the superpowers upon the region and brought the **Cold War** to both combatants, since large consignments of military equipment were airlifted to Ethiopia from the **Union of Soviet Socialist Republics** (USSR), which had decided to support the government of **Haile Mariam Mengistu**. The substantial gains made during 1978 by the two Eritrean liberation movements—the **Eritrean Liberation Front** (ELF) and the **Eritrean People's Liberation Front** (EPLF)—were due, at least in part, to the Ogaden War and the fact that the greater share of the Ethiopian military effort had to be concentrated on the Somali frontier.

Although the Ogaden War was not a civil war—it was a war between two states—it nonetheless contained elements of a civil war since the Somalis, a nomadic people, had traditionally moved back and forth across the whole of the Ogaden region for centuries, relying upon its waterholes for their herds, and a significant Somali minority lived in the Ogaden region of Ethiopia. Long-standing antagonisms in the region predated the Ogaden War. When the former colonial territories of Italian Somaliland and British Somaliland were united in 1960 to create an independent Somalia, the new state adopted a flag which included a five-pointed star in its center; three of these points were intended to signify Somalia irredenta—what was then French Somaliland (subsequently Djibouti), the Northeast Frontier Province of Kenya, and the Ogaden.

An Anglo–Ethiopian treaty of 1897 (the year after the Italian defeat at the battle of Adowa) established the border between Ethiopia and British Somaliland; this cut across traditional Somali grazing lands in the Haud, although it was agreed that Somalis could move their cattle into this Ethiopian territory to graze during the wet season. It was this agreement that formed the basis of later Somali claims. By 1908, Ethiopian Emperor Menelik had settled his borders with **France** for French Somaliland, with **Great Britain** for British Somaliland, and with Italy for Italian Somaliland, and each of these agreements recognized that the Ogaden region was part of Ethiopia. However, when Somalia emerged as an independent state in 1960, it did not renounce its claims to the Ogaden, and when the **Organization of African Unity** (OAU) was formed in 1963, Somalia refused to adopt one of its first resolutions: that all members should accept their inherited colonial boundaries.

Clashes occurred along the Ethiopia–Somali border throughout the 1960s and into the 1970s, with Somalia insisting that the Ogaden was part of Greater Somalia. In the mid-1970s, a Somali liberation movement, the **Western Somali Liberation Front** (WSLF), was formed and this movement greatly increased pressures upon Ethiopia during 1975 and 1976, when Addis Ababa was fully occupied trying to absorb the changes brought about by the Mengistu revolution. By early 1977, increasing numbers of WSLF groups were moving into the Ogaden, where they obtained control of substantial areas on the ground, and the Somali armed forces provided these groups with military backup. During June to November 1977, Somalia effectively took control of most of the Ogaden, forcing Mengistu to order general mobilization in August.

Only by 1980 had Ethiopia regained full control of the Ogaden, by which time both the USSR and **Cuba** had become deeply involved in supporting the Ethiopian regime with military supplies (the USSR) and troops and air force on the ground (Cuba), although the main Ogaden War had come to an end by March 1978. One result of this war was the heavy militarization of Ethiopia. In addition, about one million Somalis had become **refugees** in their own country, and tens of thousands of troops and civilians on both sides had been killed or wounded, although no accurate figures were ever available.

OJUKWU, CHUKWUEMEKA ODUMEGWU (1933–). Chukwuemeka Ojukwu was the leader of Biafra throughout the **Nigerian civil war** when the Eastern Region (the heartland of the Ibo people) attempted to secede from the Federation of Nigeria to become a separate state. It was certainly largely due to his capacities and leadership that Biafra was able to last as long as it did. Ojukwu was born on 4 November 1933 into a wealthy family; he completed his education at Oxford before returning to Nigeria, where he joined the army in 1957.

During the first military coup of 1966, Ojukwu was the leader of the loyalist troops in the north of the country. As a result, he was promoted by General J. T. Aguiyi-Ironsi as military governor of the Eastern Region. In October 1966, following the massacre of Ibos in the north, Ojukwu persuaded General **Yakubu Gowon** to withdraw any northern soldiers from the Eastern Region and he then began training and arming his own men. In January 1967, in a final effort to avert a breakaway by the East, Gowon and Ojukwu met at Aburi in Ghana; subsequently, however, each side interpreted whatever had been agreed in a different way and accused the other side of bad faith. Other Ibo leaders appeared to be more ardent for secession than Ojukwu, but as their acknowledged leader he went with the majority and on 29 May 1967, formally declared the secession of the Eastern Region and proclaimed the independent state of Biafra.

Once the war had started, Ojukwu emerged as a ruthless and autocratic ruler, while on the international stage playing for time and sympathy for the plight of beleaguered Biafra. When, at the beginning of 1970, it was clear that Biafra was about to collapse, Ojukwu called an emergency meeting of his cabinet on 8 January and informed it that he would leave Biafra so as to give it a better chance to make peace with the federal government. Ojukwu left Biafra by plane on 11 January 1970 and went into exile in **Côte d'Ivoire** as the guest of President Houphouet Boigny. After 13 years in exile, he was given an official pardon by President Shehu Shagari and allowed to return to Nigeria.

ORGANISATION DE L'ARMÉE SECRÈTE (OAS)/SECRET ARMY ORGANIZATION. The Secret Army Organization was formed by French settlers (*colons*) in **Algeria** who were opposed to General **Charles de Gaulle**'s policy of offering self-determination to the **Front de Libération Nationale** (FLN). The OAS was supported by sections of the French army including four generals—Maurice Challe, Edmond Jouhaud, **Raoul Salan**, and Andre Zeller. In April 1961, these generals made an attempt to seize power in Algeria but failed. Already by that time the OAS had turned to the terrorist use of bombs and shootings in both **France** and Algeria and continued to do so through 1961. Following the agreement of March 1962 at Evian-les-Bains, which set a date for a referendum in Algeria, the OAS attempted to set up a National Council of French Resistance under the leadership of General Raoul Salan, but on 20 April 1962 he was captured by the authorities and the OAS then collapsed amid mutual recriminations.

At its height, the OAS and Salan (its moving spirit) were believed to have the support of as many as 40,000 French troops; however, the French navy and air force remained loyal to the government of de Gaulle. Altogether some 200 army officers were arrested: Salan and Jouhaud were given death sentences in absentia, Challe and Zeller sentences of 15 years.

ORGANISATION SECRÈTE (OS)/SECRET ORGANIZATION. The Organisation Secrète was a paramilitary organization led by **Ahmed ben Bella**, which came into being in **Algeria** prior to the formation of the **Front de Libération Nationale** (FLN). It had split away from the Mouvement pour le Triomphe des Libertés Démocratiques (MTLD)/Movement for the Triumph of Democratic Liberties in 1947 and was to attain a membership of 500. Its most important act of revolutionary violence occurred in 1949 when its members robbed the Oran Post Office. The French police then arrested ben Bella and destroyed the OS during 1950.

ORGANIZATION OF AFRICAN UNITY (OAU). The Organization of African Unity (OAU) was founded in 1963 by an original 30 (later 32) newly independent African states. Its objects were to promote continental unity, defend African sovereignty, eradicate colonialism, promote international cooperation, and improve the life of Africa's people. It modeled itself broadly on the **United Nations**. Of seven stated fundamental principles, the first four were as follows: recognition of the sovereign equality of member countries; non-interference in the internal affairs of countries; respect for the sovereign equality and territorial integrity of each country and its inalienable right to independent existence; and peaceful settlement of disputes. One result of these conditions was to make any efforts at African **peacekeeping** difficult to mount.

The First Summit

The first OAU Heads of State and Government Summit was held in Cairo in 1964, where the most important issues discussed concerned inter-African borders; **South Africa** and apartheid; and decolonization. The OAU suffers from similar defects to the United Nations: collective action can only sometimes be agreed upon; the "integrity" of states means it cannot easily interfere in civil war situations (although this condition appeared to be changing during the 1990s); and its more powerful members can—and do—threaten to pull out or not cooperate if they believe their interests are at risk as a result of OAU resolutions, as happened with Morocco over the Western Sahara dispute in 1984. Even so, the OAU has always attempted to mediate in the continent's many disputes, although its effectiveness has varied enormously. The limitations of the OAU became apparent when it attempted to mediate disputes.

Algeria

In relation to the civil war in **Algeria** during the 1990s between the military-backed government and the Front Islamique du Salut (FIS), the OAU made no effort to intervene.

Angola

When the Portuguese withdrew from **Angola** in November 1975, leaving the country split between rival liberation movements, the OAU called a special summit (12–14 January 1976) to consider Angola. Its members then split, with 22 countries recognizing the **Movimento Popular para a Libertação de Angola** (MPLA)/Popular Movement for the Liberation of Angola, while 22 were in favor of a government of national unity. Two countries—**Ethiopia**, which was hosting the summit, and **Uganda**, whose President **Idi Amin** was in the chair— abstained from voting. However, by February, 25 countries—a clear majority—had recognized the MPLA as the government of Angola and its leader, **Agostinho Neto**, was then able to take his seat at the OAU. Subsequently, the OAU had little influence upon the Angolan conflict.

Burundi

Although it tried to intervene, the OAU at best played a minor role in the brutal, recurring struggle between Hutus and Tutsis in **Burundi** that periodically exploded, as in 1972, 1988, and 1993–1994. In 1993, for example, following the bloody coup of 21 October, which led to the death of President Melchior Ndadaye and was followed by renewed Hutu–Tutsi violence that forced up to half a million people to flee the country and become **refugees**, a regional summit composed of **Rwanda**, Tanzania, and **Zaire** called for the creation of an African stabilization force. The OAU then announced that it would assemble a force of 200 military and civilian personnel to protect government ministers for a six month period, but dropped the idea in the face of objections from members of the Burundi opposition.

Republic of the Congo

When the OAU was formed in 1963, the **Congo** crisis (1960–65 in the former Belgian Congo) had already created havoc in that country for the better part of three years, and the United Nations was involved as a mediator and peacekeeper. Nonetheless, the OAU did become involved in the crisis during 1964 (the first full year of its existence): in September 1964, at the meeting of its foreign ministers in Addis Ababa, a majority supported the claims of **Moise Tshombe** and it appeared that his position (as the leader of secessionist Katanga) might be bolstered by the credibility that would follow OAU recognition. However, the foreign ministers' approval was overturned the following month when Tshombe was refused admission to the heads of state meeting which was held in Cairo. In the meantime, an OAU Congo Committee had been established. In November 1964, at U.S. insistence, Kenya's Prime Minister Jomo Kenyatta called a meeting of the OAU Congo Committee in Nairobi to discuss the crisis at a time when the Congo rebels were holding 1,200 Europeans hostage in Stanleyville. American planes were then used to bring in Belgian paratroopers to rescue the Europeans—including **mercenaries**— and Kenyatta objected that he had been used as a smokescreen while the **United States** and Belgium mounted their rescue operation.

Liberia

In the civil war that devastated **Liberia** (1990–94), the **Economic Community of West African States** (ECOWAS) and its military arm, the **Economic Community Monitoring Group** (ECOMOG), acted as peacekeepers, while the OAU and the United Nations gave their official support and blessing to this regional intervention.

Mozambique

In the long civil war in **Mozambique** (1975–92), the OAU played no role at all. The non-intervention of the OAU, as in this case, may have been dictated by a number of considerations: these include reference to its charter that lays down non-interference in the internal affairs of a member state, although in the case of Mozambique, such an inhibition ought to have been ignored given the extent of South African assistance for the **Resistência Nacional Moçambicana** (RENAMO)/Mozambican National Resistance, lack of resources, or simple disunity of purpose.

Nigeria

The OAU attempted mediation in the early stages of the **Nigerian civil war** (1967–70), but its insistence that a solution had to be "within the context of one Nigeria" meant that its efforts were regarded with distrust by Biafra. In September 1967, the OAU held a summit at Kinshasa (Congo) where an OAU Consultative Peace Committee was established with **Haile Selassie** in the chair, but it made little impact. Africa generally feared that any successful secession by Biafra would encourage secessionist movements in other parts of the continent where states had been created by the merger of often disparate ethnic groups during the colonial era. The OAU made approaches to the Biafran leadership and in July 1968, **Chukwuemeka Odumegwu Ojukwu** visited Niamey (Niger) to address the OAU Commission, but no progress was made. There was a further OAU meeting to discuss Nigeria at Addis Ababa in August 1968, which only Ojukwu attended, while no Nigerians attended a further meeting of April 1969 in Monrovia. A final meeting of the OAU Consultative Peace Committee was held on

1 December 1969, but by then the war was all but over. These meetings held through the years of the Nigerian civil war demonstrated, if anything, the inability of the OAU to influence the course of events.

Rwanda

During the developing crisis that ended in the horrific massacres of 1994 in Rwanda, the OAU never did more than hold a watching brief and had little impact upon events.

Somalia

Similarly, the OAU played little part in restraining the civil war that devastated **Somalia** during the early 1990s. Nor did it achieve much with regard to the countless clashes between Somalia and its neighbors, Ethiopia and Kenya.

South Africa

On the other hand, the stand taken by the OAU in relation to apartheid in South Africa was one of its first initiatives dating from its foundation in 1963, when it passed a resolution that no OAU member should engage in either diplomatic or trade links with South Africa, as long as apartheid was maintained in that country. This was both a statement of African principle and a form of pressure that helped to unite the continent over the primary issue of race. Over the years, the OAU gave official recognition to various southern African liberation movements as the sole representatives of their countries, and in the case of South Africa, gave its support to the **African National Congress** (ANC) during a long struggle, that toward the end, brought South Africa close to civil war.

Neither in the case of **Sudan**'s civil war nor in the years of chaos in **Uganda,** did the OAU play any appreciable role or manage any effective mediation.

Summary

While it is easy to criticize the apparent inability or unwillingness of the OAU to mediate in civil war situations, it must be understood that the organization suffers from the same limitations that inhibit interventions by the United Nations. Moreover, the OAU cannot call upon the resources of the major powers as can the United Nations. However, in the changing climate of the 1990s, a new approach to peacekeeping began to emerge, which emphasized the importance of regional peacekeeping (as for example by ECOMOG in Liberia) to be carried out with the backing of the OAU, in its turn supported by the United Nations. At the end of the century, the OAU agreed to transform itself into the **African Union** (AU).

OROMO NATIONAL LIBERATION FRONT (ONLF). The Oromo people of southern and eastern **Ethiopia** have periodically been in conflict with the government of Addis Ababa, not as a nationalist movement seeking independence, but more moderately in pursuit of better treatment for remote areas, which generally suffered from neglect by the center. The Oromo Liberation Front (OLF) became the Oromo National Liberation Front (ONLF) in 1977 during the Ethiopia–**Somalia** war of that year (the **Ogaden War**). At first the ONLF collaborated with the Somali-Abo National Liberation Front (SALF) from which it obtained assistance, as it also did from the **Western Somali Liberation Front** (WSLF). ONLF mainly appealed to discontented Oromo of Bale, Sidamo, and Haraghe Provinces but, though it presented the central government with periodic insurrections and a limited amount of violence, it was never to be more than an irritant to Addis Ababa.

In January 1980, the ONLF established an office in Mogadishu which facilitated collaboration with the WSLF, and in April 1981, the ONLF claimed that between 2,000 and 3,000 people had been killed or wounded by government-mounted air raids on Oromo tribal areas during the previous March. Although fairly quiescent over the first half of the 1980s, the ONLF took on a new lease on life when it resisted the central government policy of resettlement in Oromo areas—villageization. In the main, however, its military activity was on a small scale. In 1990, it achieved some limited successes against government forces on the **Sudan** border.

OUEDDEI, GOUKOUNI (1944–). Goukouni Oueddei was a central figure in the recurring civil wars and power struggles that troubled

Chad from the mid-1960s until his presidency from 1979 to 1982. Thereafter, his importance declined. Goukouni was born in 1944 of the Toubou tribe and in his early twenties became a guerrilla leader of northern people fighting to prevent domination by the south. The civil war began in the late 1960s as a northern rebellion against the southern-dominated government of François Tombalbaye; Goukouni's four brothers were killed in the early fighting. In 1972, he formed the second army of the **Front de Libération Nationale du Tchad** (FROLINAT)/Chad National Liberation Front and served as second in command to **Hissène Habré**; however, he broke with Habré over the kidnapping of the French archaeologist Françoise Claustre, whom Habré held while demanding ransom money from **France**.

In 1977, Goukouni became leader of the Northern Armed Forces Command Council and then, in March 1978, chairman of the Revolutionary Committee of FROLINAT. Goukouni was now at the height of his influence and would remain the most important figure in Chad until the end of his presidency in 1982. However, he relied upon support from Libya's leader **Muammar Gaddafi** and this dependence was to be a mixed source of strength and weakness. In July 1977, Goukouni's forces captured the northern town of Bardai; he then went on to defeat the government forces in a series of pitched battles, which allowed him to occupy a large area in the north of the country. In April 1979, with **Nigeria** acting as mediator, Habré and Goukouni were persuaded to combine in forming a provisional government in which, at first, Goukouni was a minister of state. Then, at a meeting in Lagos of 14 August 1979, it was agreed that Goukouni would act as president of a Gouvernement d'Union Nationale de Transition (GUNT). However, Habré and Goukouni were unable to work together and in March 1980, fighting erupted between their respective followers in N'Djamena; then in December, after Goukouni had called in Libyan assistance, Habré was forced to flee.

Goukouni, however, had miscalculated by relying upon Libyan support because, though he had hoped to strengthen his own position when he signed an agreement with Libya (that would lead to eventual union between the two coutries) on 6 January 1981, he in fact undermined his own position since the agreement paved the way for permanent Libyan intervention in Chad, which was to lead to growing friction within Chad itself as well as inviting interventions by both

France and the **United States**. Goukouni had grossly underestimated the unpopularity of a Libyan tie-up, which was opposed by almost all interests in the country (in the end the Libyans were to withdraw from Chad under **Organization of African Unity** [OAU] supervision, but that came long after Goukouni had lost power).

In 1982, Habré, who had fled to exile in **Sudan**, launched an offensive in the north of the country from bases in Sudan, and without Libyan support Goukouni's forces collapsed. On 7 June 1982, Habré was able to take N'Djamena unopposed. It was now Goukouni's turn to flee and he went first to Cameroon and then to **Algeria**; he had suffered a major defeat and was deserted by most of his supporters. At the time of this defeat, his troops complained of lack of arms and of their leader's incompetence; he had failed to establish any administration and many of his former ministers changed sides to join Habré. Despite this setback, Goukouni regrouped with Libyan support and in 1983 began to reconquer the north, capturing Faya-Largeau in June 1983 and Abèche in July.

At this juncture Habré appealed to France, which then sent additional troops to Chad, while the United States, which was always opposed to Gaddafi, responded by providing financial **aid**. The French established a line across the 15th degree of latitude north, later advanced to the 16th degree, in order to contain Goukouni's forces and those of his Libyan ally. Goukouni never regained his former ascendancy, and though in 1985 he formed a new Supreme Revolutionary Council of GUNT with himself as president, this soon collapsed. He refused to participate in reconciliation talks with Habré, organized by the OAU in March 1986. He then fell out with Gaddafi and by October 1986 was reported to be under house arrest in Tripoli. Deserted by his former supporters, Goukouni left Libya and went to live in Algeria. Chad and Libya finally settled their differences. After Habré had been ousted from power by **Idriss Déby** at the end of 1990, Goukouni returned to N'Djamena.

– P –

PEACEKEEPING. During the 1990s, as the "control" parameters of the **Cold War** disappeared, many more conflicts arose that required peacekeeping or peace enforcement, and as a result, there followed an upsurge in **United Nations** (UN) peacekeeping activities. Moreover, there was a dramatic change in the nature of the conflicts, representing a decline in conflicts between states and a rise in civil wars within states, some of quite exceptional brutality. Peacekeeping operations are never easy, and each operation needs to ensure that the peacekeeping force is fully equipped to carry out its task—financially, militarily, and politically—but this has by no means always been the case. UN reports have examined the failings that resulted in and lessons to be learned from the atrocities committed against the Bosnian Muslim population in 1995 in the UN-designated "safe area" of Srebenica and in the 1994 genocide in Rwanda. A UN report in 2000 also comprehensively reviewed UN peace and security activities.

The Department of Peacekeeping Operations (DPKO) is the UN operations arm for peacekeeping. It is responsible for the conduct, management, direction, planning, and preparation of all peacekeeping operations. It has to secure, through negotiations with governments, the personnel and equipment required for each operation; provide logistic and administrative support for operations and political and humanitarian missions; control these operations overall; and keep the UN Security Council informed. It must also make contingency plans for future emergencies. In addition, the department coordinates UN activities related to landmines and develops and supports de-mining programs in all peacekeeping and emergency situations.

Between 1948 and 2000 the UN carried out, or attempted to carry out, a total of 54 peacekeeping operations of which 19 concerned Africa. These were in **Angola, Somalia, Democratic Republic of Congo, Mozambique, Sierra Leone, Liberia, Namibia, Ethiopia** and **Eritrea, Central African Republic**, and Western Sahara (in some cases more than one operation in a country). Of these peacekeeping operations, 36 were carried out during the 1990s and into 2000. A majority of the conflicts were civil wars. From 2004 onward the UN became involved in the **Darfur** conflict, both in humanitarian relief operations and working with the **African Union** (AU) to broker a peaceful solution. Over the period 2004–2005, UN Secretary-General **Kofi Annan** maintained a watching brief over a number of countries that had endured recent conflicts. He appointed a new special envoy to Ethiopia and Eritrea when it appeared likely that the war between them (1998–2000) was in danger of renewal.

The UN extended its peacekeeping mission in Sierra Leone and decided that the UN Mission to Sierra Leone (UNAMSIL) should remain in the country from 1 January 2005. As in Sierra Leone, so in Liberia the UN maintained a watching brief in the hope of preventing a return to violence, as the country struggled to return to normality after years of civil war. As the uneasy north–south divide continued in **Côte d'Ivoire,** the UN maintained a 6,000 peacekeeping force alongside an equivalent number of French troops. The UN peacekeeping force in Democratic Republic of Congo made little impact despite its considerable size. At the same time the UN faced its own problems when a grave scandal erupted concerning its forces in DRC, a number of whom were charged with paedophilia, rape, and prostitution. In May 2004, the UN announced that it would deploy a peacekeeping force in **Burundi** to replace the **African Union** (AU) force deployed there in 2003. Over this period the gravest peacekeeping problems concerned Darfur and Democratic Republic of Congo. UN operations are often hampered when rich donor nations are laggard in making promised payments for peacekeeping, the **United States** and Japan (two of the richest) being particular offenders in this respect.

It is UN policy, wherever practicable, to encourage regional powers to undertake peacekeeping operations. In Africa through the 1990s, the **ECOWAS Monitoring Group** (ECOMOG) undertook a number of peacekeeping operations in West Africa, notably in Liberia and Sierra Leone while the AU, which replaced the **Organization of African Unity** (OAU) at the beginning of the 21st century, has undertaken peacekeeping operations, and most especially in troubled **Darfur** where it deployed 7,000 troops during 2006.

PORTUGAL. Throughout the years of the **Cold War,** Portugal was rated with Greece as one of the two poorest countries of Western Europe and it saw economic salvation in its vast southern African colonies of **Angola** and **Mozambique**. This economic salvation was to come in two ways: first, from the wealth of its African colonies which, in the main, meant the oil, diamonds, and coffee of Angola; and second, by the settlement in those territories of peasants from Portugal. Although the Portuguese had first landed in Angola in 1483 and only a few years later in Mozambique, the vast majority of all the Portuguese settlers in those colonies at the beginning of the 1960s had only arrived there in the years since World War II.

Most of the settlers in Angola and Mozambique had been poor farmers back in Portugal, not perhaps much better educated than the Africans over whom they now came to rule, and since their own betterment in Africa was precarious, they resented and resisted any attempts by the Africans to catch up, for example with better education, since this would threaten their own positions. The Portuguese created two fictions about their colonies: that the Africans in their colonies could be assimilated and that the much vaunted policy of assimilation somehow excused their imperialism, even though by 1975 only one-half of 1 percent of the Africans had been accorded "*assimilado*" status; and second, that the overseas territories were an integral part of Portugal. This latter concept persuaded the Portuguese to fight bitter rear-guard wars, to hold on to their territories long after **Great Britain** and **France** had faced the inevitable and granted independence to their African colonies.

Thus, Portugal embarked upon a damaging and immensely costly attempt to hold on to its African possessions and from the early 1960s, as nationalism swept through the continent, Portugal went against the tide and fought its wars in Angola and Mozambique (as well as Guinea-Bissau in West Africa). By the late 1960s, the Portuguese were deploying three armies—in Angola, Mozambique, and Guinea-Bissau—each of which was by then largely on the defensive while the costs became so great that by the beginning of the 1970s, they represented 50 percent of Portugal's total gross domestic product (GDP). These strains upon the economic, social, and political life of Portugal led to the April Revolution of 1974, which ended the long rule of Antonio de Salazar and Marcello Caetano.

General **Antonio de Spinola**, who had fought in all three of the African territories, was a realist rather than a revolutionary who argued quite simply that Portugal could not win its African wars and therefore should withdraw, which it did. These were not civil wars, but rather nationalist wars of liberation against an imperial power. The result of the long years of struggle, however, was to lay the foundations of chaos and disunity that produced the civil wars which followed in the post-independence years. Further, the abrupt withdrawal in 1975 of nearly 500,000 Portuguese from Angola and 250,000 Portuguese from Mozambique deprived the two territories of a high proportion of all available skills for running the administrations and economies.

The nature of the nationalist struggles at the height of the Cold War more or less ensured that Marxist-oriented liberation movements would emerge, as they did; the **Movimento Popular para a Libertação de Angola** (MPLA)/Popular Movement for the Liberation of Angola in Angola and the **Frente da Libertação de Moçambique** (FRELIMO)/Mozambique Liberation Front in Mozambique. These movements attracted military and other assistance from the Communist countries and this, in turn, ensured that opposing though weaker liberation movements, such as the **Frente Nacional da Libertação de Angola** (FNLA)/National Front for the Liberation of Angola in Angola, would receive support from western sources, especially the **United States**, with the result that the post-independence civil wars that erupted in both countries were unnecessarily prolonged. A further complication arose from the fact that many of the Portuguese settlers who quit these territories in 1975 did not return to Portugal but settled in **South Africa**. From there they were prepared to intervene in both Angola and Mozambique, providing support for the **União Nacional para a Independência Total de Angola** (UNITA)/ National Union for the Total Independence of Angola in Angola and the **Resistência Nacional Moçambicana** (RENAMO)/Mozambican National Resistance in Mozambique.

– R –

REFUGEES. According to the **United Nations** (UN), *refugees* is defined as those who have fled their countries because of a well-founded fear of persecution, or for reasons of their race, religion, nationality, political opinion, or membership in a particular social group, and who cannot or do not want to return. The legal status of refugees has been defined in two international treaties: the 1951 Convention Relating to the Status of Refugees, and its 1967 Protocol—which between them spell out rights and obligations with respect to refugees. As of December 2006, 147 countries were parties to one or both treaties.

The Office of the **United Nations High Commissioner for Refugees** (UNHCR) is the most important international body with regard to refugees. Its principal function is to protect refugees and ensure respect for their basic human rights, including their ability to seek asylum. Required assistance for refugees includes helping them during major emergencies; providing regular programs in education, health, and shelter; offering assistance in promoting self-sufficiency and integration; allowing voluntary repatriation; and offering resettlement in third countries. There are also many people living in refugee-like situations: those displaced in their own countries, former refugees who need help when they return home, stateless people, and people outside their own countries not given the full status of refugees. Then there are asylum seekers (found mainly in industrial countries) who have left their countries of origin to apply for recognition as refugees and whose applications are still pending. Most refugees want to return home as soon as circumstances permit, and at any given time, a proportion of all refugees will be in the process of returning home—because the wars or other conditions that turned them into refugees have come to an end.

Internally displaced persons (IDPs) are refugees within the borders of their own countries, usually as the result of civil war, persecution, disasters, or human rights violations. Civil wars are the principal cause of such IDPs, and there were many of those in Africa during the 1990s, for example in **Angola**, **Democratic Republic of Congo** (DRC), and **Burundi**. At the end of the 20th century there were 20 million to 25 million IDPs—more than the total number of refugees worldwide. Each government has primary responsibility for its own IDPs, but governments are often unable or unwilling to do anything about them. While refugees are safeguarded by well-defined international codes, IDPs are often in a worse position. Trapped in a civil war situation, IDPs may find that they are cut off from any form of relief. They may be designated "enemies of the state." And no international conventions cover them. Their needs, however, are the same as those of refugees. They are most likely to obtain assistance from the UNHCR, the International Committee of the Red Cross (ICRC), the UN High Commissioner for Human Rights, or from non-governmental organizations (NGOs). Even so, many are not helped at all because of the very nature of the situations in which they find themselves.

The vast majority of refugees or IDPs are to be found in Third World countries and Africa has been especially affected. Two African regions, the Horn and Southern Africa, have been particularly subject to refugee movements since the 1960s, though other refugee crises have included the Congo in the early 1960s and **Nigeria** during its civil war (1967–70). The 1980s were deeply troubled years in Africa and some 15 African countries were hosts to substantial numbers of refugees and in some cases very high numbers indeed: **Somalia** (700,000), **Sudan** (690,000). The reasons for these refugees varied from region to region. Thus, in Southern Africa there were two broad categories during the period 1960–2000: those fleeing the civil wars in Angola and **Mozambique**, and those fleeing oppression in **South Africa** and **Namibia**.

In 1986, **relief agencies** operating in Angola reported that the number of people displaced by the war were far more numerous than the 600,000 claimed by the Angolan government, and, as is often the case, relief agencies working on the ground are in a better position to provide relatively more accurate figures of suffering and other indications of the scale of a disaster than agencies such as the United Nations or the government of the warring country itself. During the latter half of 1994 in Burundi, following the death of the country's president and the subsequent massacres, relief agencies found themselves trying to cope with an estimated 800,000 refugees, of whom about 100 a day were dying of disease or starvation.

In 1988, the worst year of the civil war in Mozambique, there were over 900,000 refugees from that country in the neighboring states of Malawi, South Africa, Swaziland, Tanzania, Zambia, and **Zimbabwe**, all of whom were in receipt of relief from bodies such as the World Food Programme (WFP). From 1994 into the 21st century, refugees from Rwanda and Burundi were to be found in all the neighboring countries.

Countries worst affected by refugee movements are often those not involved in civil wars themselves; they are the neighbors of warring countries, many of whose citizens cross the borders in search of temporary safety. Two such countries during the 1990s and into the 21st century were Guinea in West Africa and Tanzania in East Africa. In both cases, they received huge influxes of refugees and the way in which they have coped with them illustrates the size and complexity of the refugee problem.

Guinea has been deeply affected by the wars in **Liberia** and **Sierra Leone**. Between 1990–1991, when both countries descended into civil war, and by 2000 Guinea was host to over 500,000 refugees: at the beginning of the latter year there were 350,000 refugees from Sierra Leone and a further 100,000 from Liberia and the situation worsened through 2000 as the war was resumed in Liberia. One result of this huge influx of refugees was the growth of violence against them inside Guinea, since many of them came to be regarded as invaders rather than victims in need of humanitarian assistance. Nonetheless, a large measure of humanitarian assistance was provided by the government of Guinea, the **Economic Community of West African States** (ECOWAS), UN agencies, donor nations, and non-governmental organizations (NGOs). On the downside, however, the areas inhabited by large numbers of refugees became militarized, with armed groups from the refugee camps and the spread of a range of small arms. The United Nations Children's Fund (UNICEF) had a special role in demilitarizing and retraining young refugees. With the end of the civil wars in both Liberia and Sierra Leone, the number of refugees fell sharply and in August 2004 the UNHCR reported a total of 78,318 refugees in Guinea for which it had responsibility.

Tanzania, on the opposite side of Africa, had become host to the largest number of refugees on the continent. At the beginning of 2004 there were 476,000 UNHCR-assisted refugees in the country while, according to Tanzanian government officials, there were also 170,000 Burundians in permanent settlements and an additional estimated 300,000 Burundians illegally settled in Tanzanian villages. Despite being one of the poorest countries in the world, Tanzania has always been a generous host to refugees.

In January 2005, there were 19.2 million refugees of concern to the UNHCR worldwide and these included 4.9 million in Africa. A breakdown by areas shows that in East Africa there were 1,515,142 refugees to be found, principally in Burundi, **Ethiopia**, Kenya, **Rwanda**, **Uganda**, Tanzania (a massive 602,088), and Zambia. In Middle Africa there were 639,372 refugees, principally in **Chad** (from **Darfur**) and DRC (from Rwanda and Burundi). The total of refugees in Northern Africa was smaller at 415,356 and much lower still in Southern Africa, at 45,999. Of the 406,732 refugees in Western Africa, the three most affected countries were **Côte d'Ivoire**, Guinea, and Sierra Leone. (*See* UNHCR for further country statistics.)

RELIEF AGENCIES. Relief agencies may be divided into two broad categories: international agencies that belong to the **United Nations**, such as the **United Nations High Commissioner for Refugees** (UN-HCR) and the World Food Programme (WFP); and national agencies, generally referred to as non-governmental organizations (NGOs), which originated in a particular country but may subsequently have developed a number of affiliates in other countries. Some of the best known of these are Christian Aid, CARE, Médecins sans Frontières, and OXFAM. Such agencies have always played an important role both during and in the aftermath of civil wars.

Many of these NGOs, which are voluntary organizations, represent large constituencies of ordinary people who have become deeply upset by the suffering taking place in other parts of the world and which can so easily be seen on television. These people want to make a contribution to allay such suffering and by working through NGOs, they feel that they are having a direct impact, which gives them a sense of personal involvement.

The work of relief agencies comes under three broad categories: to take relief (food, medicine, clothing) to the victims of civil war violence; to alert the world community to deteriorating conditions; and to act as a lobby calling for international action to bring an end to the fighting. Moreover, such agencies often work in extremely difficult conditions, providing food or other aid in war situations where their personnel may come under fire or face other hardships, including kidnap. Sometimes they insist upon operating in war zones against the wishes of the government of the country, as various agencies in southern **Sudan** did during the 1990s.

The determination of relief agencies to operate in war zones when national governments or international organizations have found their presence an embarrassment has on occasion altered the course of a conflict. Sometimes—in the civil wars in **Nigeria** or **Somalia**, or the situation in Sudan's **Darfur** province, for example—relief agencies have insisted upon intervention against the wishes of the responsible government; and sometimes their intervention has forced the international community to take actions when it would have preferred to remain inactive.

The publicity-generating capabilities of relief agencies are considerable; indeed, these may be seen as their most potent weapon. They can insist upon taking relief supplies to **refugees** in a war situation, and when they do so such action confers upon the agency influence that it may wield in a variety of ways. Moreover, once an agency has become involved in a dangerous situation it can call for protection for its representatives so that they are able to continue with their humanitarian activities. Agencies are frequently responsible for revealing distressing details of suffering that alert public opinion in their "home" country to what is happening, and this in turn may lead to political demands for greater action by the government. Agencies frequently also embarrass governments in countries where they operate by revealing humanitarian scandals.

On the other hand, some agencies cause problems rather than achieving anything positive. They may lack professionalism and exacerbate already complex issues by their presence rather than bringing any effective relief to those in need. But whether they are well- or ill-regarded, relief agencies have become an important factor in civil (and other) war situations and their voice, in a media-oriented age, cannot be ignored. Sometimes such agencies are used as an excuse by governments, which may argue that they should do nothing to interfere with the delivery of humanitarian supplies, when what is needed in reality is a peacekeeping effort that will bring the fighting to an end.

For example, relief agencies played an important role in the **Nigerian civil war** despite objections by the Federal Military Government in Lagos; aid which they supplied to the starving in Biafra prolonged the war in two ways: by providing food and other necessities, which allowed the Biafrans to continue fighting longer than would otherwise have been possible; and by encouraging the hope that more aid would continue to come in the future. An important element in the international attempts at intervention in post–President Barre's Somalia during the first half of the 1990s was the presence in the country of relief agencies demanding protection while they delivered supplies to displaced refugees. Western Christian (and other) relief agencies came and went in the South of Sudan during its long-lasting war with the North.

Relief workers can become partisan in a civil war situation, though, as a rule, the better agencies attempt to be impartial. Yet, however they may be regarded and whatever they manage to achieve, the presence of relief agencies has become an automatic aspect of any war. No matter how they may be regarded by governments (and sometimes they are heartily disliked), these agencies have become a permanent aspect of any war or disaster situation and, as such, have to be taken into account.

RESISTÊNCIA NACIONAL MOÇAMBICANA (RENAMO)/ MOZAMBICAN NATIONAL RESISTANCE. The Mozambique National Resistance, generally known as RENAMO, fought against the **Frente da Libertação de Moçambique** (FRELIMO)/ Mozambique Liberation Front government, which came to power in Mozambique in 1975, through to the peace of 1992. Then, in 1994, RENAMO took part in nationwide elections.

RENAMO was set up in 1975/1976 by Ken Flower, the head of the Central Intelligence Organization (CIO) in Salisbury, Rhodesia, under the illegal Ian Smith government, as a means of destabilizing the new FRELIMO government that supported the **Zimbabwe African National Union** (ZANU), which then maintained a number of base camps in Mozambique. The original members of RENAMO were recruited from Mozambicans who had fled from the war into Rhodesia.

First operative on the Rhodesian border (Flower's CIO hoped that RENAMO would supply it with advance information about ZANU movements), by 1979 RENAMO was disrupting the new government with attacks in Manica and Sofala Provinces. When Rhodesia became **Zimbabwe** in 1980, the new government of **Robert Mugabe** at once withdrew support from RENAMO, but by then Flower had already persuaded the South African government to take responsibility for supporting RENAMO, which it was willing to do since it saw the movement as a means of destabilizing its Marxist neighbor. During 1983 RENAMO was able to carry out offensives in Nampula and Zambezia Provinces and had developed into a major threat to the stability of independent Mozambique. In August 1983, for example,

RENAMO took 24 Swedish aid workers hostage and then forced them to withdraw from the country. On 28 September 1983, the army claimed to have destroyed a RENAMO provincial base at Tome in Luhambane Province. After the signing of the **Nkomati Accord** (which the Mozambique government had assumed would deprive RENAMO of further assistance from **South Africa**), RENAMO claimed that it possessed sufficient war materiel to continue fighting for two years and that it was by then active in all 10 provinces of the country.

RENAMO then demanded an end to the one-party state and the creation of a government of national reconciliation, but after tripartite talks had been launched between the Mozambique government, South Africa, and RENAMO, the latter withdrew (2 November) claiming it was not prepared to accept the presence of South African troops on Mozambique soil. By the end of 1984 RENAMO was deploying 21,000 guerrillas; its main targets were convoys, civilians, and foreign aid workers and it was able to disrupt trade between Mozambique and Malawi and Zambia. The power lines to Beira and Maputo were cut during December 1984 and January 1985, and by this time RENAMO had become a major threat to the stability of Mozambique and was interrupting and damaging most aspects of development.

By July 1985, Zimbabwe had committed some 10,000 troops to Mozambique to assist the government in its fight against RENAMO. On 28 August 1985, a combined Mozambique–Zimbabwe force captured the RENAMO headquarters in Sofala Province, including documents which revealed that South Africa was still supporting RENAMO, despite the promise not to do so enshrined in the Nkomati Accord. RENAMO attacks upon government and civilian targets were to continue unabated during 1986, and in July of that year Mozambique accused Malawi of harboring RENAMO rebels. One of the side affects of RENAMO offensives was a growing influx of **refugees** into South Africa, which then decided to erect an electric fence along a section of its border with Mozambique. In October of that year, thousands of RENAMO forces were expelled from Malawi to return to Mozambique.

The death of President **Samora Machel** in an air crash (19 October 1986) brought **Joaquim Chissano** to power as president of Mozambique; and following a meeting between Chissano and President Mugabe of Zimbabwe (15 January 1987), a joint statement declared that they would increase military operations until RENAMO had been eliminated. On 7 February 1987, a RENAMO spokesman in Lisbon said it was ready for talks with the government, provided that all foreign troops were withdrawn from Mozambique. Meanwhile, beginning in January 1986, British military personnel undertook a series of training programs for FRELIMO troops at a base in Zimbabwe. During 1988 and 1989 RENAMO activities continued unabated; they prevented any development from taking place, certainly in the rural areas, as more and more government resources had to be diverted to the war against them.

By 1990, UNICEF estimated that 600,000 people had been killed in the course of the war, that about 494,000 children had died of malnutrition, and that 45 percent of primary education facilities had been destroyed, as well as many health centers. As RENAMO activity continued during 1990, the government came to realize that it had to negotiate and would not be able to win a purely military victory.

Talks were held through 1990 and government reforms during the year, foreshadowing the abandonment of Marxism and moves toward a market economy and multi-partyism, gave point to the talks. On 3 November 1990, President Chissano said "there is no longer any pretext for anyone to continue the violence," but RENAMO rejected the 1990 constitution because, it argued, the National Assembly was invalid. Negotiations continued through 1991 and 1992, and toward the end of that year, RENAMO finally agreed to take part in national elections. These were held in November 1994, with RENAMO competing in multi-party elections. Though it came second to FRELIMO in the results, it agreed to abide by these. RENAMO had begun as the creature of Smith's Rhodesia to destabilize Mozambique and it had no discernible philosophy but by the end of a bitter war it demanded—and got—multi-partyism. The most obvious lesson of the RENAMO war was that power should be shared.

ROBERTO, HOLDEN ALVARO (1923–). Holden Roberto was the son of a Baptist missionary worker. He was born on 12 January 1923 at Sao Salvador in northern **Angola** and educated in Kinshasa, where he later worked as a clerk. He became involved in nationalist politics in the mid-1950s. In December 1958 he attended the All African Peoples' Conference in Ghana, representing the newly formed União das Populaçoes de Angola (UPA)/Union of the Angolan

People, under the pseudonym of Jose Gilmore. In 1959, Roberto accompanied the Guinea delegation to the **United Nations** in New York in order to argue Angola's nationalist case against **Portugal**. On his return to Africa, he visited Tunis for the second All-African Peoples' Conference and while there, won for UPA the support of Tunisia's President Habib Bourguiba.

In 1960, the new government of **Republic of Congo** (Kinshasa—the former Belgian Congo) gave permission for Roberto to make a weekly broadcast over Radio Kinshasa. In September 1960 Roberto launched the party magazine—Voice of the Angolan Nation—and in December became president of the UPA. In March 1961, fighting in Angola signaled the beginning of the nationalist struggle against Portugal. Roberto then set forth four priorities: land reform, education, economic development, and political nonalignment. On 27 March 1962, Roberto negotiated the merger of the UPA and a second movement, Partido Democratico de Angola, to form the **Frente Nacional da Libertação de Angola** (FNLA)/National Front for the Liberation of Angola with himself as president. The FNLA then formed the Governo Revoluçionario de Angola no Exilo (GRAE)/Revolutionary Government of Angola in Exile.

Both Roberto and the FNLA suffered a major blow in July 1964, when the dynamic **Jonas Savimbi** resigned as vice-president (accusing Roberto of tribalism) and later (1966) formed the **União Nacional para a Independência Total de Angola** (UNITA)/National Union for the Total Independence of Angola. Further internal quarrels wracked the FNLA during 1965 and 1966 to weaken Roberto's hold on the movement. Nonetheless, he obtained the backing of President **Joseph-Désiré Mobutu** of Congo (Kinshasa) and under pressure from him entered into an agreement with the **Movimento Popular para a Libertação de Angola** (MPLA)/Popular Movement for the Liberation of Angola of **Agostinho Neto** in December 1972. According to this agreement, both the FNLA and the MPLA retained their identities, but were to be united under a Supreme Council for Liberation; Roberto became the Council's president while Neto headed the United Military Command. Roberto and Neto met in February 1973 to implement the agreement, but it never really worked, and when the Portuguese withdrew from Angola in 1975 and the country became independent, the two movements, as well as Savimbi's UNITA, rapidly fell out with each other in the power struggle that soon developed into a civil war. By the end of the 1970s, neither Roberto nor the FNLA had any important part to play in the ongoing struggle that resolved itself into a duel between the MPLA, which had become the government, and UNITA.

RUACANA DAM. Angola is heavily dependent upon hydro-electric power, and its swift rivers, falling off the high central plateau, afford many opportunities for the creation of dams. The Cunene River has great hydro potential, although the last stretch of the river forms the boundary with **Namibia** to the south for several hundred kilometers until it reaches the Atlantic. Prior to 1975, **Portugal** and **South Africa** had coordinated plans to create major dams on the river. The object of the joint venture was to provide Namibia, which is deficient in both power and water, with cheap electricity and a permanent water supply for the north of the country. The Ruacana Falls occur where the Cunene River becomes the joint border between Angola and Namibia. A major power station was to be constructed at this point. Inevitably, given the civil war in Angola and the liberation struggle that had been mounted in northern Namibia by the **South West Africa People's Organization** (SWAPO), the dam became a military target in the war, as well as providing South Africa with an excuse for intervention into Angola from Namibia. The first stage of the dam became operational in 1977 and despite Angolan suspicions of South Africa, the Luanda government went ahead with the joint operation. The potential annual output of the Ruacana power development was put at 1,000m kWh. Ruacana provided a classic example of how strategic economic cooperation may continue between enemies, even when a "state of war" or near war exists, and periodically during the period 1975–1990, military incidents were focused upon the dam. In 1991, President **Jose dos Santos** of Angola and President Sam Nujoma of newly independent Namibia met together and agreed upon feasibility studies for further joint developments along the Cunene River.

RWANDA. Only in Rwanda and neighboring **Burundi** does a potential state of permanent or semi-permanent civil war exist between the two ethnic groups—the Hutu and the Tutsi—who make up the vast majority of the population and whose suspicions and hatreds appear to be irreconcilable. It is not easy to apportion blame: for example, how much is the period of colonialism under the Germans and then the Belgians, who became the mandatory power after World War I, responsible for the divisions being perpetuated because they used the classic imperial technique of divide and rule? The minority Tutsi have usually been in the ascendancy when they have ruthlessly dominated the majority Hutu who, in turn, have periodically risen against the Tutsi whenever the opportunity offered. Antagonisms between these two peoples go back centuries, beginning with the arrival in the region of the warrior Tutsi, who conquered the sedentary Hutu and then kept them as a subservient peasant underclass. The Tutsi represent only 15 percent of the total population.

The Colonial Period

Rwanda and Burundi came under German control during the Scramble for Africa; in 1899 Germany united the two territories to make the single colony of Ruanda-Urundi and worked through the dominant Tutsi. In 1916, Belgian troops occupied the colony from the neighboring Belgian Congo and in 1923, the colony became a Belgian mandate from the newly formed League of Nations. In 1945, it became a Trusteeship Territory under the **United Nations**, still under Belgian control. Like their German predecessors, the Belgians also ruled indirectly through the dominant Tutsi minority, thereby entrenching Tutsi belief in their superiority and right to control the Hutu. The Tutsi were to remain in a dominant political position through to the end of the 1950s. On 25 July 1959, King Mutara III died and was succeeded by his son, who was sworn in on 9 October as King Kigeri V. This event provoked a Hutu uprising.

During the first week of November, following the coronation, the Hutu revolted and killed hundreds of Tutsi, forcing many more to flee as **refugees** to Tanzania, **Uganda**, and the Belgian **Congo**. This revolt, described at the time as the "peasants' revolt," marked the determination of the Hutu, as they saw independence approaching, to cast off Tutsi control. The Belgians restored law and order and then proceeded with democratic reforms which, on a tribal basis, were bound to favor permanent political control by the vastly greater number of Hutu (approximately 84 percent of the population). During June and July 1960, the Parti du Mouvement de l'Émancipation du Peuple Hutu (PARMEHUTU)/Party of the Movement for the

Emancipation of the Hutu People under the leadership of Gregoire Kayibanda, won a massive majority in the municipal elections. In January 1961, Rwanda, under the leadership of Kayibanda (although still under Belgian authority), was declared a republic and the king went into exile. A referendum of September 1961 gave overwhelming support for a republic (under Kayibanda and PARMEHUTU) and endorsed the abolition of the monarchy. Belgium recognized (a fait accompli) Rwanda as a republic on 2 October 1961, and then on 1 July 1962, Rwanda became independent under Hutu control, a state of affairs which reversed centuries of Tutsi dominance. Kayibanda became the independent country's first president. Immediately, with full power in their hands, the Hutu deprived leading Tutsis of political and administrative jobs and replaced them with Hutus.

Tutsi Revolt: 1963

On 29 November 1963, a group of Tutsis who were refugees from the events of 1959, assembled across the border in Burundi and then crossed into Rwanda; they were determined to regain control for the Tutsis. They had seized a number of places, some quite close to the capital, Kigali, before government forces beat them back. In December, larger Tutsi raiding parties crossed the borders and bigger clashes took place. These were again repulsed, but this time reprisals against the Tutsis followed and an estimated 20,000 were massacred by the Hutus, while others were forced into exile as refugees. The events of 1963 greatly reduced Tutsi influence in Rwanda, while the brutal massacres were a form of revenge and exorcism by the Hutus, who had for so long been subordinated to the Tutsis. There was a further bout of anti-Tutsi violence in 1973, and a military coup replaced Kayibanda with Colonel **Juvenal Habyarimana** who pursued a more conciliatory policy toward the Tutsis. But a more conciliatory policy was not a solution to differences and hatreds, which periodically appear to be satisfied only after the shedding of blood.

The 1990s

The Tutsis in exile bided their time and planned another attempt at regaining power. In 1990, between 5,000 and 10,000 Tutsis formed the **Rwanda Patriotic Front** (RPF) in Uganda and on 30 September/

1 October 1990, they crossed into Rwanda under the leadership of Major-General Fred Rwigyema, although he was killed in the early fighting. Uganda then sealed its border to prevent further Tutsis moving into Rwanda which, meanwhile, had appealed for help to Belgium, which sent 600 paratroopers (5 October); in addition, **France** sent 300 troops and **Zaire** 500 (later increased to 1,000). By the end of October, Tutsis were being rounded up in Kigali. President **Yoweri Museveni** of Uganda claimed that the rebels had agreed to a ceasefire and President Habyarimana offered peace talks. Uganda had close ties with the Tutsis and there were an estimated 70,000 Tutsi refugees in Uganda at this time. The Rwanda government argued that there was now no available land for these Tutsis to have if they returned.

Over the period December 1990 and January 1991, further Tutsi cross border raids were mounted from Uganda, resulting in about 350 rebel deaths. In mid-January the government, which had previously taken the line that the Tutsi raids were spontaneous, now claimed these had been planned with Ugandan support. On 23 January 1991, between 400 and 600 rebels crossed into Rwanda to occupy the town of Ruhengeri, although they were driven out two days later. A settlement appeared to have been reached in February 1991 when President Ali Hassan Mwinyi of Tanzania presided at a meeting of Presidents Habyarimana and Museveni in **Zanzibar**. A border ceasefire between the two countries was negotiated. Even so, sporadic fighting was to continue through 1991, although this was small-scale. No real solution had emerged, however, and both sides waited for the next development.

In June 1992, representatives of the RPF and the government met in Paris to work out an accord that would bring the civil war to an end, and one was signed in August. Following this, in October, the government agreed to set up a transitional cabinet, which would include all political parties and the RPF, and this agreement was signed at Arusha, Tanzania, on 9 January 1993. Then it was repudiated by the ruling Mouvement Républicain National pour la Démocratie et le Développement (MRNDD)/National Republican Movement for Democracy and Development and by the end of the month, ethnic killing had broken out again. This rapidly escalated during February with hundreds of deaths; at the same time, an estimated one million people fled to escape the killing and became **refugees**.

The RPF then launched a new offensive from Uganda and recaptured Ruhengeri; it was condemned for its action by Belgium, France, and the **United States**. More French troops were sent to Rwanda to support the Hutu government, and a second ceasefire between the government and the RPF was negotiated on 21 February 1993. Both sides in the conflict had been guilty of atrocities. France, thereupon, withdrew its troops to Central African Republic. Talks were held during March in Dar es Salaam, but these proved inconclusive. On 8 May 1993, the government announced a nine-month program to demobilize 13,000 troops and 6,000 gendarmes. A buffer zone between government and RPF forces was established, to be monitored by a neutral Military Observer Group (MOG), which had been created the previous May 1992. On 30 May 1993, the government agreed to assist the return of 650,000 refugees, but on 25 June negotiations were broken off as each side accused the other of preparing a new military offensive. As early as October 1990, the United Nations had created a UN Assistance Mission in Rwanda (UNAMIR), which had a force of 2,500 troops, to help maintain the peace, although its presence does not appear to have inhibited the recurring violence. In March 1994, immediately after negotiating yet another truce, the RPF ambushed and killed 250 government troops. In Kigali, the government reacted by claiming that 500,000 people had fled from this new violence in the north.

The Death of Two Presidents—6 April 1994

On 6 April 1994, the plane carrying President Juvenal Habyarimana of Rwanda and President Cyprien Ntaryamira of Burundi was shot down over Kigali and both presidents were killed as they returned from a meeting with other regional presidents in Tanzania, where they had been seeking a solution to the escalating Hutu–Tutsi violence. This assassination, later attributed to hardline Hutus who were opposed to any accomodation with the Tutsis, sparked off a wave of mass killings in Kigali where the presidential guard went on a rampage. Those killed included the prime minister and three Belgian (UN) soldiers. Within two days the fighting in Kigali had become general and the RPF was engaged in direct fighting with government forces. In Kigali, fighting was more or less indiscriminate and targets included ministers, nuns, and priests, as well as **peacekeeping** troops—Belgians, Bangladeshis, Ghanaians. The killings that took place in the week after the death of the president appeared mainly to be the work of the presidential guard in revenge for his murder. The Belgian and French troops stood ready to evacuate their own nationals; the Red Cross reported that casualties had reached the 1,000 mark.

At this point the leader of the RPF, Paul Kagame, said his forces would restore law and order in Kigali where anarchy reigned and, while the Belgian commander of the UN peacekeeping forces attempted to arrange a new cease-fire, the rebel forces moved into the outskirts of Kigali. French troops took control of Kigali Airport and supervised the evacuation of some 3,000 foreigners. A further 800 Belgian paratroopers arrived. During this first stage of the catastrophe in Kigali, most of those slaughtered were Tutsis.

On 12 April, however, the RPF army, which had grown to about 20,000, fought its way into Kigali, throwing the government into a panic. The government forces began to disintegrate and it was not clear how many of the 30,000 troops remained loyal to the government. One week after the death of the two presidents, about 10,000 people had been killed in Kigali alone. On 13 April, the RPF Radio Muhabura announced that the northern region of Mutara had been liberated. As the chaos grew worse, the UNAMIR force began to leave the country, some in panic; their excuse was that the government had not given them control of the airport. According to Human Rights Watch in New York, between 6 and 19 April about 100,000 people altogether had been killed and it appeared that a campaign of killing had been planned by Hutu extremists weeks before the death of President Habyarimana. Human Rights Watch claimed that "army officers trained, armed and organized some 1,700 young men into a militia affiliated with the president's political party."

By early May up to 200,000 people were believed to have been killed in three weeks of slaughter, while 500,000 refugees had crossed into Tanzania. The withdrawal of the UN troops (on 21 April 1994, the Security Council voted to reduce UNAMIR from 2,500 to 270) and its failure to send in proper peacekeeping forces while it was increasing its presence in Bosnia raised awkward race questions about its policy. On 17 May, however, by which time large numbers had been killed, the Security Council reversed its policy and increased the size of UNAMIR to 5,000, although neither the United States nor the European Union sent troops. The name "Interahamwe" (those who attack together) now emerged as one of the extremist militias drawn from the ranks of the MRNDD. Another group, the "Impuzamugambi" (those with a single purpose), came from the MRNDD's extremist ally, the Coalition pour la Défense de la République (CDR)/ Coalition for the Defense of the Republic. Training for these groups had been under way before the events of 6 April, and a private radio station owned by members of the president's inner circle had begun a campaign against the Tutsi and Hutu opponents of the president. After 6 April, the radio campaign became more virulent.

There were, in effect, two parallel wars taking place: the RPF fight against the government; and the Hutu extremists' actions against both Tutsis and Hutu moderates. By June, an estimated 500,000 people had been killed. On 19 July the RPF, which by then had taken Kigali and most other towns, announced that it had won the civil war and would form a government according to the 1993 Arusha Agreement, although it would exclude members of the discredited MRNDD.

The Aftermath

The French force, which had come to Rwanda in June, withdrew in September, while **aid** agencies concentrated their efforts upon helping the refugees in neighboring Tanzania and Zaire where Hutu militants were infiltrating the refugees to dissuade them from returning home. On 8 November 1994, the UN Security Council established an International Criminal Tribunal for Rwanda to prosecute those responsible for genocide. By the end of 1994, the new RPF government was pushing a policy of reconciliation. Throughout 1995 it faced enormous difficulties: about a quarter of the population remained outside the country as refugees; militant Hutu guerrillas infiltrated the country to destabilize the new regime; the prisons and detention centers were full of people suspected of involvement in the genocide of 1994; and the Interahamwe militants were known to be active in the cross-border refugee camps. Relations with the United Nations (UNAMIR) were poor since the world body was seen to be more concerned with possible violations of human rights by the RPF than with bringing to justice those responsible for genocide. These and similar problems continued into 1996, and though the RPF army was highly efficient, it still only represented the minority ethnic group of the population, the Tutsis, and there were few signs of any new working relationship emerging between Tutsi and Hutu.

By August 1997, most of the two million refugees had returned home and it was reported that large numbers, especially those from the northwestern provinces of Ruhengeri and Gisenyi, had taken up arms and joined the Interahamwe, which had been able to recruit, train, and arm sympathizers while they were in the refugee camps in eastern Zaire (**Democratic Republic of Congo**). Increasing numbers of incidents by the extremists in the northwestern region were reported during 1997, and a visitor to the region in August described it "as like a volcano." Attacks and violent incidents continued into 1998. Despite the victory of the RPF in 1994, no long-term solution to the Hutu–Tutsi confrontation had emerged; the Tutsi RPF had replaced the Hutu government and faced a country in which seething discontent and preparation for further violence characterized the feelings of a large segment of the Hutu majority.

In the years 1998–2006, three problems dominated political life: sporadic uprisings inside the country, especially in the northwest; Rwanda's involvement in the war in Democratic Republic of Congo; and the ongoing trials of the many thousands accused of complicity in the genocide of 1994. The northwest of Rwanda experienced a state of civil war through 1998, during which time President **Laurent Kabila** of DRC was offering training for Hutu members of the Interahamwe then living in DRC. The events of 1994 continued to cast their shadow over Rwanda through to the end of the century and beyond. The involvement of the Rwandan army in the DRC's civil war was primarily in order to end the threat posed by Hutu extremists who wished to liberate Rwanda from Tutsi domination. Meanwhile, tens of thousands of genocide suspects still awaited trial. In 2000 Rwanda faced the threat posed by between 10,000 and 15,000 Hutu-dominated Rwandan army forces, as well as Interahamwe rebels across the border in DRC, and their presence was advanced as the principal reason for Rwandan intervention in DRC. However, clashes between Ugandan and Rwandan forces in DRC during March 2001 led Uganda to describe Rwanda as "a hostile nation"; this elicited the Rwandan response that Uganda was harboring "anti-Rwandan elements." During

May and June, Hutu rebels of the Army for the Liberation of Rwanda began to cross into Rwanda in increasing numbers from DRC. By early August, the Rwandan army claimed to have killed 1,800 of these insurgents and captured 1,000. The ongoing peace process in DRC led to an upsurge of border fighting as Hutu rebels crossed into Rwanda rather than surrender their arms in DRC.

A meeting in February 2002, between Presidents Paul Kagame and Yoweri Museveni, restored peace between their two countries after the confrontation of their forces in DRC the previous year. Meanwhile, much publicity focused upon the trials of genocide suspects. There was major criticism of the International Criminal Tribunal for Rwanda (ICTR) at Arusha since, after seven years, it had tried only nine cases, while the Rwandan courts had tried 6,000 suspects between December 1996 and June 2001. In June, community courts were established throughout Rwanda to speed up the trials of 115,000 "genocide" prisoners.

Hutu rebels in DRC remained a problem and in 2003 estimates suggested that up to 40,000 Hutu militants responsible for the 1994 genocide found shelter in DRC and periodically launched raids across the border. Although Rwandan troops had left DRC in October 2002, their "interests" in DRC (including the illegal extraction of resources) continued to be represented by local allies, and especially the Goma group of the Rassemblement Congolais pour la Démocratie (RCD-Goma)/Rally for Congolese Democracy-Goma. In December 2005, Hutu rebel fighters of the Forces Démocratiques pour la Libération de Rwanda (FDLR)/Democratic Forces for the Liberation of Rwanda returned to Rwanda. The previous March their leader Ignance Murwamashyaka had announced an end to all offensive operations against Rwanda.

The genocide of 1994 still dominated the politics of Rwanda in 2005 as trials of *genocidaires* were in progress at the UN-created International Criminal Tribunal for Rwanda (ICTR), as well as the traditional courts inside the country.

RWANDA PATRIOTIC FRONT (RPF). The Rwanda Patriotic Front was a Tutsi rebel movement formed by Tutsi exiles in **Uganda**. These rebels, calling themselves the RPF, originally invaded **Rwanda** from Uganda over 30 September/1 October 1990, with between 5,000 and 10,000 soldiers under the leadership of Major General Fred Rwigyema, a friend of Uganda's President **Yoweri Museveni**, who had earlier served in the Uganda National Resistance Army (NRA); he was killed in the subsequent fighting. This first RPF attempt to overthrow the Hutu-dominated government of President **Juvenal Habyarimana** did not succeed, yet the RPF was to return and take Kigali in April 1994 and then form the government. At the time of this first RPF invasion of Rwanda, there were an estimated one million Tutsi **refugees** worldwide; they presented a problem which had been ignored for years by the government of Rwanda. The RPF demanded the return home of all refugees and the overthrow of the Habyarimana government which, in its turn, claimed that the RPF stood for the reinstatement of former Tutsi dominance. The defeat of the RPF in 1990 was assisted by Belgian, French, and Zairean troops who were flown into Rwanda at the time. This, however, was not the end of the story.

In 1991, the RPF began to mount cross-border raids and on 23 January 1991, the RPF occupied the town of Ruhengeri for two days before retreating back into Uganda. In June 1992 representatives of the RPF and the Rwandan government met in Paris and by August had agreed to end the civil war; in October 1992 the government created a transitional cabinet which included members of the RPF, but this soon broke down. In January 1993 new outbreaks of ethnic killings occurred and the RPF again came across the border to seize the northern town of Ruhengeri. At this time the RPF was condemned by Belgium, **France**, and the **United States**. Another ceasefire was negotiated on 21 February 1993. Then in May 1993, the Rwanda government agreed to assist the return of 650,000 refugees, which was one of the principal RPF demands. However, these peace negotiations were broken off in June with each side accusing the other of preparing for war.

Another truce was agreed upon in March 1994, but was followed immediately by an RPF ambush of government troops in which 250 of them were killed. The RPF was now steadily advancing upon Kigali, the capital of Rwanda, and two days after the deaths of Presidents Juvenal Habyarimana of Rwanda and Cyprien Ntaryamina of **Burundi** on 6 April 1994, when their plane was shot down by Hutu extremists, the RPF fought its way into the outskirts of Kigali. A week after the death of the two presidents Paul Kagame, the RPF leader, said that his forces would restore law and order in Kigali, and on 12 April 1994, an RPF army of 20,000 fought its way into the center of Kigali. The government collapsed in panic. The RPF later formed a new government which was faced with appalling problems of reconstruction in the aftermath of six months of slaughter (April to September 1994) in which an estimated one million people had died.

– S –

SALAN, RAOUL (ALBIN-LOUIS) (1899–1984). Born on 10 June 1899, Salan was a distinguished French soldier who became the leader of the four senior officers (generals) who led the revolt in **Algeria** in 1961–1962 against the plans of General **Charles de Gaulle** to grant the colony independence. The other three generals were Maurice Challe (1905–77), Andre Zeller (1898–1979) and Edmond Jouhaud (1905–). The four men worked in their **Organisation de l'Armée Secrète** (OAS)\Secret Army Organization to wage a campaign of terror against the Gaullist government both in Algeria and in **France**. They were eventually captured and imprisoned.

Salan was one of France's most decorated soldiers: he gained the Croix de Guerre during World War I; between 1941 and 1943 he served in French West Africa; he went to French Indochina in 1945 and became the commander in chief there in 1952. Salan was posted to Algeria in 1956 by which time the nationalist rebellion had turned into a major war. Ironically, Salan was one of the leading right-wing figures who, in 1958, called for de Gaulle to be returned to power. De Gaulle recognized that France had to grant independence to Algeria and as it became clear that this is what he would do, so Salan, who had imagined de Gaulle would integrate Algeria into France, believed he had been betrayed by the man he had helped bring to power.

He then established the OAS with the help of the other three generals. A coup attempt by the OAS in Algeria on 22 April 1961 failed and Salan was then sentenced to death in absentia. He went into hiding. A year later (20 April 1962) Salan was captured and tried for treason the following May. The high military tribunal which tried him found extenuating circumstances and Salan was condemned to life imprisonment. (General Jouhaud, who had already been sentenced to death, then had his sentence commuted to life imprisonment by de Gaulle.) Under the terms of an amnesty of 1968 Salan, Challe, and Jouhaud were freed. In 1982, President François Mitterand restored Salan's full rank and pension.

SAVIMBI, JONAS MALKEIRO (1934–2002). Jonas Savimbi, the son of a stationmaster on the **Benguela Railway**, was born on 3 August 1934, and educated at the Dondi Mission School, Chilesso, and then at the Silva Ponto Secondary School at Sa da Bandeira. In 1958, with the assistance of a scholarship, he left to study medicine at Lisbon University but went to Switzerland in 1960. In 1961 he became involved in the liberation struggle for **Angola** when he joined **Holden Roberto**'s União das Populaçoes de Angola (UPA) and was made secretary-general. He played a leading part in the creation of the **Frente Nacional da Libertação de Angola** (FNLA)/National Front for the Liberation of Angola during 1962.

Savimbi soon fell out with Roberto, whom he accused of flagrant tribalism. He broke with the FNLA to form his own party, the **União Nacional para a Independência Total de Angola** (UNITA)/National Union for the Total Independence of Angola, in 1966. In the years to 1975, UNITA and Savimbi played a relatively unimportant part in the struggle against the Portuguese, although by that year he was one of the three leaders to sign the Alvor Agreement with the other two liberation movements; later they also negotiated a common front when they met in Kenya. The brief unity achieved by the three groups—UNITA, FNLA, and the **Movimento Popular para a Libertação de Angola** (MPLA)/Popular Movement for the Liberation of Angola—collapsed during 1975 and by mid-year, Savimbi was seeking assistance from **South Africa** and took to the bush preparatory to launching his own war against the MPLA. From 1975 onward, Savimbi based himself in the bush in southeast Angola. He drew his support from the Ovimbundu, the largest ethnic group in Angola, and enjoyed especially strong support in the region round Jambe, his "capital."

Through the 1980s, Savimbi defied all government efforts to dislodge him. He obtained covert **United States** support, which was channeled to him by the Central Intelligence Agency (CIA) through **Zaire**; he also obtained support from South Africa, which wanted to prolong violence in Angola and so keep the country destabilized. Savimbi frequently traveled abroad in search of support for his cause and his efforts in Washington proved particularly rewarding. There he was accorded VIP treatment by the Ronald Reagan administration, as he represented UNITA as a movement struggling against Communism.

The battle of **Cuito Cuanavale** was the turning point in the long civil war in Angola; it led to a decline in Savimbi's military position and influence, while the agreement of December 1988 confirmed the position of the MPLA as the legitimate government of Angola and saw the withdrawal of the South Africans, which was followed by independence for **Namibia** in 1990. After the 1988 agreement the United States continued to support Savimbi, and his forces continued to fight against the government. Savimbi agreed to take part in elections to be supervised by the **United Nations** in September 1992, but when UNITA lost and Savimbi himself failed to win the presidency, he returned to the bush to set off the most destructive year of warfare (October 1992 to October 1993) in the whole civil war. On 20 November 1994, Savimbi signed a peace treaty to bring this second phase of the civil war to an end. Only in 1995 did Savimbi agree to meet President **Jose dos Santos**, and the National Assembly then created two vice-presidencies, one of which was offered to Savimbi. Even so he continued to hold out, sometimes escalating the bush war, and in early 1999 gave no sign of abandoning his bush army or accepting the changes which had taken place in Angola since the 1992 elections. The war continued into 2001, by which time both the government and the Southern African Development Community (SADC) had branded Savimbi a war criminal. Only Savimbi's death, while fighting government forces in Moxico on 22 February 2002, finally signaled the collapse of UNITA and the real possibility of establishing a genuine peace in Angola.

SAWYER, AMOS (1945–). Amos Sawyer, who was a typical middle of-the-road Liberian politician, found himself thrust into prominence during the Liberian civil war when he became a stopgap president heading an interim government. He was born in Greenville on 15 June 1945. After high school, Sawyer went on a student exchange program to the **United States**. He returned home to attend the University of Liberia and graduated with honors in political science.

He again went to the United States where he obtained a Ph.D. at Northwestern University before returning to lecture at the University of Liberia.

In the 1970s he became the chairman of the Provisional National Committee of the Movement for Justice in Africa (MOJA). When Sawyer, a firm pro-democracy figure, ran in 1979 as a candidate for mayor of Monrovia, the government of William Tolbert was so frightened that it postponed the election. Following the coup of April 1980 in which **Samuel Doe** seized power, Sawyer was appointed chairman of a commission to draft a new constitution; this was adopted by referendum in July 1984. Sawyer, however, was not a compatible figure for a tyrant of Doe's stamp. In August 1984 Sawyer launched the Liberian People's Party; a week later he was arrested with others on charges of masterminding a communist plot and his new party was banned. Demonstrations by students at the university demanding his release met with government repression and five students were shot dead. Even so, on 7 October 1984, Sawyer and 10 other detainees were released. Sawyer declared his intention of running against Doe in the presidential elections but he was then banned from politics by Doe and forbidden to hold press conferences. In 1986 Sawyer went to the United States to study for a fellowship; in January 1988 he became a founding member of the Association for Constitutional Democracy in Liberia (ACDL) and was appointed its executive director.

When **Charles Taylor** launched his revolt during Christmas 1989, Sawyer and the ACDL accepted that such a revolt had been inevitable, though they did not support Taylor. In August 1990, at the conference of the **Economic Community of West African States** (ECOWAS) in Banjul, The Gambia, Sawyer was chosen to head an interim government in **Liberia**. He remained in **Sierra Leone** for two months, however, because of the fighting then taking place in Monrovia. On 21 November 1990, Sawyer was flown into Monrovia in a Nigerian helicopter to find that the **Economic Community Monitoring Group** (ECOMOG) only had control of Monrovia while fighting was taking place in much of the rest of the country, which was mainly controlled by Taylor. On 4 January 1991, Sawyer formed a cabinet; he claimed he did not wish to remain in power for more than a year. At the all-Liberia conference held in Monrovia on 15 March 1991, he demanded that elections should be held the following October. At the **Organization of African Unity** (OAU) summit of June 1991, held at Abuja, **Nigeria**, the organization accepted Sawyer as the legitimate leader of Liberia while denying this position to Taylor.

Sawyer presided over a deeply divided Liberia through 1992 when the worst fighting of the civil war occurred as Taylor's troops besieged Monrovia. He also remained as interim president through 1993, although he was taking part in meetings with Taylor's **National Patriotic Front of Liberia** (NPFL) and Kromah's United Liberation Movement of Liberia (ULIMO) in a series of talks to bring an end to the civil war. In February 1994 the new five-man Council of State elected David Kpormakor as chairman and a transition period began on 7 March. At that point Amos Sawyer stood down as Liberia's interim president.

SELASSIE, HAILE (TAFARI MAKONNEN) (1892–1975). Tafari Makonnen was born of the royal line (the same house as the emperor) on 23 July 1892. Small in stature and clever, Tafari was promoted early in his life by Emperor Menelik and in 1910 was made governor of Harar. On the death of Menelik in 1913, his grandson Lij Yasu succeeded him, though he was only to reign for three years before being ousted in a coup. Menelik's daughter, Princess Zauditu, became queen, although Tafari was now named heir to the throne and during her reign of 16 years was to remain her close adviser.

Tafari was a modernizer, aiming to bring **Ethiopia** into the 20th century. Zauditu died on 2 November 1930, and Tafari was crowned Emperor Haile Selassie I. He continued the reforms which he had initiated under Zauditu until the Italian invasion of his country launched by Mussolini in 1935. In June 1936 Haile Selassie appeared before the League of Nations (Ethiopia had joined at his instigation in 1923) and appealed to the conscience of the world against Italian aggression. He then went into exile in **Great Britain**.

In January 1941, Haile Selassie returned to Ethiopia with British troops and on 5 May (exactly five years after the Italian conquest) entered Addis Ababa. The British, however, did not wish to give him a free hand in his reconquered territory. By persistent diplomacy in stages—an Anglo–Ethiopian agreement of 1942 and a second one of 1944—Haile Selassie managed to regain full control over Ethiopia by 1945. He then began a new series of reforms, especially in the fields of education and communications. He played an important role in the politics of emerging Africa and it was a tribute to his role that when the **Organization of African Unity** (OAU) was established in 1963, its headquarters were sited in Addis Ababa.

In 1952 the former Italian colony of **Eritrea** was federated with Ethiopia, and at first the arrangement worked smoothly but when, in 1962, Ethiopia forced through the full integration of Eritrea (by packing the Assembly) the Eritreans objected and their objections quickly turned into open rebellion. This decision proved to be a turning point in the career of Haile Selassie, and the war of secession waged by Eritrea from 1962 onward became the principal problem facing the emperor during his last decade.

Through the late 1960s and the early 1970s, Haile Selassie played an important role in African affairs, especially as a **mediator**, as he proved by helping end the long civil war in **Sudan** in 1972. But at home he was becoming increasingly reactionary and losing popular support in the process. By 1973 the Eritrean war had become a major drain on the economy and there was no sign of any breakthrough; then the country was devastated by the drought and famine of that year. Haile Selassie, unfortunately, could not or would not bring himself to acknowledge just how severe conditions had become and so did not take the actions necessary to meet the emergency; his mismanagement or lack of leadership provided the army with the excuse to take power.

It was not a sharp, total coup but one perpetrated in stages (the "creeping revolution"): first the army demanded better conditions, and the people imagined that it would also redress their grievances; Haile Selassie was retained as a nominal head of state until 12 September 1974, when he was deposed. A year later, on 27 August 1975, he died (he may have been murdered).

SETIF. The town of Setif, situated in the Tell Atlas range, is the center of Setif Province of northern **Algeria**. It was the scene of an uprising against French rule in 1945 that acted as a prelude to the Algerian war of 1954–1962. On 8 May 1945, riots broke out in Setif when the police challenged Algerians (Muslims) who were carrying nationalist flags during the celebrations of the Allied victory over the Germans in Europe. Their action was a protest at continuing colonial rule. In the disturbances which followed the first demonstration, about 100 European settlers were killed; then, in retaliation, between 6,000 and 8,000 Muslims were massacred. Official French statements claimed that 88 Frenchmen and 1,500 Algerians had been killed as a result of the anti-riot operations carried out by the police and military. On the other hand, the nationalists claimed that 45,000 Algerian people were killed. Independent observers placed the death toll at 10,000 to 15,000, which was far higher than the official French figures, but much lower than the nationalist ones. The accuracy of the figures was less important than the fact of a massive and brutal reprisal, which "gave notice" that the French settlers and the colonial authorities would oppose ruthlessly any moves toward independence. **Ferhat Abbas**, then the outstanding nationalist figure, was arrested and his organization, Les Amis du Manifeste et de la Liberté (AML)/Friends of the Manifesto and of Liberty, was proscribed. Further disturbances took place in October 1945 and May 1946. A pattern of violence had been established which would erupt again in 1954 to dominate Algeria for the succeeding eight years.

SIERRA LEONE. During 1991 Sierra Leone became involved in border fighting with the forces of **Charles Taylor**, the Liberian warlord, and his **National Patriotic Front of Liberia** (NPFL). The government sent 2,150 men to its southern border to combat the Liberians and then requested assistance from the **United Nations** and **Nigeria**. By May 1991 as many as 5,000 civilians as well as Liberian **refugees** were reported to have been killed in the border fighting; it appeared that Taylor was trying to gain control of the diamond-producing region of southern Sierra Leone. This fighting, at first, was in the nature of a spillover from the civil war in **Liberia** and had not taken on a separate Sierra Leone dimension.

On 30 April 1992, a military coup was mounted in Freetown. President Joseph Momoh was overthrown and fled to Guinea, and Captain Valentine Strasser became head of state after first acting as chairman of a National Provisional Ruling Council (NPRC). The new government's first priority was to end the border war with **Liberia**. Sierra Leone contributed troops to the **Economic Community of West African States'** (ECOWAS) peacekeeping force, the **Economic Community Monitoring Group** (ECOMOG) in Liberia.

The Revolutionary United Front

Meanwhile a dissident Sierra Leone group—the Revolutionary United Front (RUF)—based across the border in Liberia, periodically mounted attacks upon government and other targets in Sierra Leone. At the end of 1993 the government claimed a string of military successes against the RUF in the eastern districts which border on Liberia, and that December the Supreme Council of State (SCS) felt able to predict an early end to the insurgency and offer a cease-fire and amnesty. By that time two years of warfare with the RUF had devastated the eastern province, which contains the **diamonds** that are a major source of Sierra Leone's export earnings, and had created an estimated 800,000 refugees.

The successes of 1993 were dashed in 1994. On 11 January 1994, government forces captured a rebel-held center near Pujehun in southern Sierra Leone. Later in the month, however, the rebels killed 100 civilians and razed several villages. Sierra Leone obtained military assistance from Ghana and renewed its offer of a ceasefire and amnesty. But on 30 June 1994, a RUF attack on the village of Telu resulted in 58 civilian deaths and those of two soldiers. In August the government launched a series of attacks upon RUF positions near the diamond-mining center at Kenema. The RUF forces, meanwhile, extended their operations to new areas and took a number of hostages. The war led to rifts in the security forces between junior and senior officers and between the SCS and Captain Strasser and the soldiers at the front; 14 senior officers were dismissed and disaffected soldiers turned to banditry in the war zones. In November 1994, 12 soldiers were executed for murder and armed robbery. The government, which by this time had lost the initiative, again offered negotiations to end the rebellion.

Developing Chaos

The fighting during the first half of 1994 had made it impossible to carry out the voter registration needed for a referendum on the draft constitution (for May), in preparation for a return to civilian rule and district council elections due that November. Dialogue with the RUF proved difficult since it was impossible to determine either its leadership or its aims. In the meantime the economy had collapsed; a revival depended upon an end to the fighting. Further widespread fighting occurred through much of the country early in 1995 and the RUF appeared able to strike at will; its forces overran the bauxite and rutile mines and seized hostages. The closure of the mines deprived the government of 70 percent of its export earnings and many thousands of people fled to Guinea to become refugees. In February, however, government forces retook the Sierra Rutile Mine from the rebels (it is the most important single export earner as well as largest employer in the country).

The government claimed that the RUF was acting as a pawn for Charles Taylor's NPFL in Liberia; there was great uncertainty as to why the outbreak against the government had occurred at all and just what the RUF represented. A favored theory was that the RUF had been created or sponsored by the NPFL in order to undermine the Sierra Leone government since it had supported ECOWAS intervention in Liberia.

Most Lebanese businessmen now fled the country. In mid-1995 Captain Strasser again sought a settlement with the RUF but instead it continued its raids, and in mid-December 1995 it attacked a village only 65 kilometers from Freetown. By this time the government had expanded the army to 13,000 and the war was taking up 75 percent of budget revenues yet, despite this huge effort, the government was unable to contain the RUF, let alone defeat it. The government had also obtained assistance from South African **mercenaries** (through Executive Outcomes) and Russian helicopter crews. The war appeared to abate at the end of 1995, first because the war in Liberia had finally ended and second because of general revulsion at the rebel atrocities. Although a government-RUF meeting was held in Abidjan on 2 December 1995, the RUF refused to take part in the elections planned for February 1996 without first obtaining an end to government hostilities and the withdrawal from Sierra Leone of foreign troops.

The Return to Civilian Rule

On 16 January 1996, a bloodless coup was mounted to topple Strasser and replace him with Brigadier General Julius Maada Bio. Elections for a return to civilian rule were still held in February and the Sierra Leone People's Party (SLPP) won 36 percent of the vote in a turnout of slightly under 50 percent. After a second round of voting, Ahmed

Tejan Kabbah of the SLPP was installed as president in March. Despite fighting throughout the election period, 750,000 voters of the 1.6 million who had registered, cast their votes. Negotiations with the RUF, whose leader had eventually emerged as Foday Sankoh, were brokered by **Côte d'Ivoire** and took place through the year; a peace agreement was finally signed on 30 November 1996. The agreement covered an immediate ceasefire, the disarming of the RUF, and its reconstitution as a political party.

It soon became clear, however, that the promised peace was unlikely to work. The rebels were unwilling to disarm and Sankoh declared that there was "no trust and confidence" between the two sides. In March 1997 the minister of defense, Hinga Norman, accused the RUF of violating the 1996 peace accord. It was reported that thousands of displaced persons were discouraged from returning home from resettlement camps because of the upsurge of violence. Then, on 12 March, it was reported from Lagos that Sankoh had been arrested there and was being kept under guard. On 15 March, Philip Sylvester Palmer, a senior RUF official, announced from Abidjan that the RUF had ousted Sankoh from the leadership. President Ahmed Tejan Kabbah welcomed Sankoh's overthrow and expressed his readiness to work with a new RUF leadership. At the end of March members of the RUF, loyal to Sankoh, took a number of hostages from the anti-Sankoh RUF leadership in an attempt to obtain Sankoh's release from Lagos and his reinstatement as RUF leader.

The Coup of 1997

On 25 May 1997, a little-known army major, Johnny Paul Koroma, was released by rebels from Freetown's central prison to head a coup, and President Kabbah was forced to flee to Guinea. There was looting in Freetown by soldiers, the houses of ministers were searched, and five ministers arrested. On 28 May, Koroma announced the abolition of the constitution and a ban on political parties. The coup was condemned by the international community and Nigeria said it was prepared to lead a regional military intervention to crush the coup and restore the ousted president. The country was plunged into chaos once more. More than 900 American and other Western citizens were airlifted to safety from Freetown by U.S. Marines and the American

Embassy advised all its nationals to leave the country and later closed down. A further 400 British and **Commonwealth** citizens were evacuated on the last commercial flight out before the rebels sealed the ports and airports. The British High Commission remained, though it maintained a low profile.

Following the coup the Commonwealth secretary general, Chief Emeka Anyaoku, gave his blessing to a Nigerian-led military intervention to crush the coup and Nigeria, Ghana, and Guinea sent extra troops and armored personnel carriers to Sierra Leone. Despite these pressures the coup leader, Major Koroma, gave no signs of surrendering and was reported to have linked up with soldiers of Sankoh's rebels of the RUF who, supposedly, had abandoned their rebellion. Koroma himself did not appear to command any widespread support. Nonetheless, the coup leader named a 20-member council including Sankoh as vice-chairman and also including three members of Sankoh's Revolutionary United Front. On 2 June the Nigerians secured control of the international airport and their warships shelled the western end of Freetown, directing their fire at the military headquarters which were being used by the rebel coup leaders. Nigeria, in effect, used the ECOWAS force it had been leading in Liberia to oppose the coup in Sierra Leone.

Chaos and lawlessness persisted through June, despite Nigerian efforts to restore the ousted government. Banks and government offices remained closed, workers protested, and many people feared to leave their homes. By mid-June about 300,000 people had fled the country. Koroma promised a return to civilian rule in 18 months but he ignored proposals advanced by Ghana, Nigeria, and **Great Britain** to restore peace. Although more Nigerian and other ECOWAS troops airlifted into Freetown brought the total to 4,600, at first they seemed unable to gain control or arrest Koroma and the other coup makers.

On 17 June, promising peace and a return to democracy, Koroma was sworn in as president of Sierra Leone. Koroma's Armed Forces Ruling Council (AFRC) accepted the deployment of ECOMOG and UN **peacekeeping** troops in Freetown (it had no alternative), but the instability in Freetown continued and violence escalated in the east of the country between the forces of Koroma and those loyal to the ousted President Kabbah. The Koroma government was to hold out for the rest of the year; it was banned from attending the

Commonwealth Heads of Government Meeting (CHOGM) held in Edinburgh, Scotland, in October 1997, while Kabbah was invited to attend by Britain's Prime Minister Tony Blair. In February 1998 the ECOWAS forces under Nigerian leadership made a new and determined attempt to oust the rebel government. They bombed Freetown, forcing thousands to flee the city. There was widespread chaos and the World Food Programme (WFP) reported that more than 200,000 people were in urgent need of food **aid**. By the middle of February, as Nigerian troops closed in on the center of Freetown, the capital was reported to be in a state of anarchy with many people killed indiscriminately and little discipline amongst the junta troops. By 21 February the Nigerian force had fought its way into the center of the city and Koroma and his junta fled.

There was great relief and rejoicing. Koroma's regime was totally cynical in its stated objects; it simply said that it felt (like the earlier junta under Captain Strasser) that it was entitled to enrich itself at the expense of the country. This is what it had done—or tried to do—during its nine-month tenure of power. As the country began to recover from the fighting, it became clear that prior to this coup, the Sierra Leone army and the rebel RUF had in fact colluded with each other during the earlier fighting in which 20,000 people, nearly all civilians, had been killed since 1991, while a high proportion of the entire population had been displaced. The soldiers on both sides had simply been intent on pillage for their own enrichment. The Nigerians found they were regarded as liberators and, after they had freed the capital, promised to mop up and rid the country of the remnants of the junta supporters.

A False Dawn

On 10 March 1998, President Ahmed Tejan Kabbah returned to Freetown after nine months in exile to be met with a hero's welcome. A number of West African heads of state, including Nigeria's military dictator General Sani Abacha, flew to Freetown to welcome him and the city enjoyed a day of celebrations instead of chaos and bloodshed, which had been its previous lot. The restored president told the huge crowd in the National Stadium that "the people of Sierra Leone have suffered too long" and that he would do everything in his power to reconstruct the country. The task he faced was enormous: after seven years of civil war the economy was in ruins, few crops had been planted, thousands of people were displaced. Sierra Leone had the world's lowest average life expectancy at 42 years. The country would be obliged to rely upon foreign **aid** until the economy could generate income again.

Unfortunately, that was not the end of the story for, during 1998, although Koroma himself was in hiding, the RUF reorganized its forces to carry on the war so that by the end of the year the commander of the RUF forces, Sam Bockarie, announced (28 December) that a major attack upon Freetown was about to be launched. There was savage fighting in the outskirts of Freetown during early January 1999 between the RUF and the Nigerian-led ECOMOG forces; the rebels claimed to control large parts of Freetown and Sam Bockarie insisted that his forces would not cease fighting until Foday Sankoh, who had been detained under sentence of death since October 1998, was freed. On 7 January, President Kabbah agreed to free Sankoh, provided the rebels accepted the 1996 peace agreement, but the rebels rejected these terms. On 9 January, the ECOMOG forces, joined by Nigerian reinforcements, launched a counterattack and drove the rebels from the center of Freetown. Peace talks, with Foday Sankoh in attendance, were then held in Conakry, the capital of Guinea, while a ceasefire was in place. ECOMOG forces seized control of Freetown port on 19 January to enable food aid to arrive. Estimates at the end of January 1999 suggested that 3,000 people had been killed during the month's fighting in the capital. The political future looked bleak. Fighting continued over the first months of the year and the RUF forces remained within 20 miles of Freetown, while they appeared to control about 60 percent of the country.

Pressure was mounted upon President Kabbah to restart peace negotiations and a ceasefire was agreed at Lome, Togo, in May. The agreement laid down that a ceasefire should go into force on 24 May; that fresh talks should start on 25 May; that both sides should retain their existing territorial positions; that humanitarian **relief agencies** should be given access to rebel-held areas; that prisoners should be released; and that the United Nations should deploy peacekeeping monitors. On 7 July this agreement was finalized; Foday Sankoh was released and given a vice-presidency in the interim government while there was to be an amnesty for war crimes and rebel participation in the government. International condemnation of the blanket amnesty for war crimes followed. There were continuing violent clashes in the north of the country. Six thousand UN peacekeepers now arrived in the country—the UN Mission to Sierra Leone (UNAMSIL). However, by the beginning of 2000 it was obvious that the civil war had not come to an end and, if anything, it looked set to become even worse. In February, the deterioration in relations between the two sides persuaded the UN Security Council to increase the number of peacekeepers to 11,000 (by the end of the year to 13,000), which made it the largest peacekeeping force in the world at that time. It had replaced the ECOMOG force that had been withdrawn. The peace agreement of July 1999 collapsed in May 2000 when the RUF abducted 500 UNAMSIL peacekeepers, an action which led to full-scale fighting between the RUF and the Sierra Leone Army.

On 8 May, in Freetown, 10,000 demonstrators marched to the house of Foday Sankoh, the RUF leader who was still, nominally, part of the interim government, to demand the release of the UN hostages. Sankoh's bodyguards fired on the crowd, killing 19, and Sankoh escaped. As this was happening, Britain deployed 1,000 troops in Sierra Leone and there followed a series of defeats for the RUF. The UN hostages were released, Sankoh was captured, and President Kabbah said his immunity would be lifted and he would be put on trial. In August the RUF recommitted itself to the peace process. This, however, was thrown into jeopardy when the West Side Boys (WSB) militia kidnapped 11 British soldiers near Freetown. These were later released but British soldiers stormed the WSB headquarters to kill 25 and capture others. In November Britain sent a further 500 troops to Sierra Leone, as there were growing doubts as to whether the RUF intended to keep the peace. Presidential and legislative elections due for February and March 2001 were postponed due to the deteriorating security situation.

In March, the UN Security Council extended the UNAMSIL mandate and authorized an increase in its numbers to 17,500. The situation appeared to improve on 18 May when the RUF and the pro-government militia, the Kamajor, agreed to end hostilities. Their agreement followed a successful Kamajor campaign that had pushed the RUF forces back into their last stronghold of the **diamond** fields. At the end of May the RUF and Kamajor disarmed some 2,500 of their fighters and the RUF freed 600 **child soldiers** for demobilization. The RUF insisted that the transitional government should be inaugurated by the end of September, but the government refused to be rushed. In September the UN again renewed the UNAMSIL mandate and announced that 16,000 RUF and pro-government militia forces had been disarmed. Britain, meanwhile, was scaling down the number of troops it had deployed in Sierra Leone and by the end of September there were only 450 in the country. By the year's end UNAMSIL had 17,500 peacekeepers in Sierra Leone and claimed that 30,000 fighters had given up their arms since the May agreement.

Peace at Last?

In January 2002, President Kabbah officially declared that the civil war was over while UNAMSIL claimed that altogether 45,000 fighters had been disarmed. The government decided to set up a war crimes court. Government troops with British military advisers were deployed on the Liberia and Guinea borders ahead of the May presidential elections. In February Britain's Prime Minister, Tony Blair, visited Sierra Leone. Under a UN voluntary repatriation scheme, 300 refugees returned home from Liberia although 70,000 remained there. In March, Kabbah lifted the four year state of emergency and Foday Sankoh and 41 other RUF members were charged with murder. Kabbah was reelected for a further five year term in May, his party (the Sierra Leone People's Party—SLPP) taking 83 of 112 seats while his chief rival, Ernest Koroma of the All People's Congress won 27 seats.

After 10 years of civil war, 50,000 deaths, savage brutalities, and the training and use of child soldiers, the war was finally over. It had involved Sierra Leone's two neighbors, Liberia and Guinea, and drawn in the United Nations, ECOMOG, and Britain. In July 2002, a Truth and Reconciliation Commission was inaugurated and in December, judges to sit on the Sierra Leone Special Court for war crimes were sworn in. The last British troops left the country in July, while the UN Security Council agreed to maintain UNAMSIL, at least until mid-2003. The last UN troops left the country at the end of 2005.

SLOVO, JOE (1926–95). One of the outstanding white opponents of apartheid in **South Africa**, who was both a leader of the South

African Communist Party (SACP) and the **African National Congress** (ANC), Joe Slovo was born in Lithuania in 1926 and moved to South Africa as a child. He became a lawyer and specialized in political cases; he married Ruth First, another lifelong opponent of apartheid. In 1950, the SACP was outlawed and Slovo was made a banned person: his freedom was restricted and he was not allowed to give interviews. He then joined the ANC. In 1955 he helped to draft the ANC's Freedom Charter. He was charged with treason in 1956, although the charges were dropped in 1958.

Slovo became a founding member of Umkhonto we Sizwe (the armed wing of the ANC) and following the Sharpeville Massacre of 21 March 1960, which many saw as the starting point of more organized violent opposition to apartheid, he was detained for four months. In 1963, he went into exile. He became chief of staff of Umkhonto we Sizwe and the most influential South African white in exile. He was based in Maputo, **Mozambique**, during the later 1970s and into the 1980s; and in 1982 his wife, Ruth First, was killed by parcel letter bomb. After the conclusion of the 1984 **Nkomati Accord** between Mozambique and South Africa, Slovo moved to Lusaka, Zambia, where the ANC headquarters were sited. In June 1985, he became the first white member of the ANC executive. In August 1987, Slovo resigned as chief of staff of Umkhonto we Sizwe, although he stayed on the ANC executive as well as remaining leader of the SACP. He worked to achieve closer ANC–SACP links.

Following the unbanning of the ANC and other banned political organizations by President **F. W. de Klerk** in February 1990, Slovo returned to South Africa from exile on 27 April 1990, and said he returned in a spirit of conciliation. In July 1990, he relaunched the new-style South African Communist Party of which he became secretary-general. He played a major part in the negotiations between the ANC and the government over the period 1991–1993 and then, following the elections of April 1994, he was appointed minister of housing in the government of national unity and won wide respect for his work in that ministry. He died of cancer in Johannesburg on 6 January 1995, and was mourned by a large dedicated following.

SOMALI NATIONAL MOVEMENT (SNM). The Somali National Movement was founded in 1981 by Somali exiles then living in London. They were Issaqs from northern **Somalia** (the former British Somaliland) who were opposed to the government of **Siad Barre** and what they saw as the neglect of the north by the politically dominant south. The SNM was also opposed to Barre's "socialism" and wanted to restore a mixed economy. The SNM supported moderate Islamic nationalism.

The first guerrilla actions by the SNM were launched in 1982; in 1983 members of the SNM attacked the prison at Madera to the south of Berbera to release 700 prisoners, a few of whom were political detainees. At a meeting with the **Democratic Front for the Salvation of Somalia** (DFSS) in Addis Ababa during 1982, the two movements had agreed to work together in opposition to the government but this "alliance" never amounted to anything and before long, the SNM and DFSS were pursuing their separate agendas. At the 1983 SNM Congress, the central committee adopted as its chairman Ahmed Muhammad Silyango for 1984. However, at this time (1983–86), SNM guerrilla activities were never more than an irritant to the government. In 1987, however, the SNM claimed more substantial victories against the government, killing several hundred of its troops in northern and central Somalia. During May 1987, the SNM captured seven senior members of the Somalia National Security Service (SNSS) who gave information about the extent to which the ranks of the SNM had been infiltrated. That month the SNM also captured Hargeisa Prison and released prisoners. The SNM was able to increase the level of its activities again in 1988.

However, dissension now arose in the ranks of the SNM between the Islamic fundamentalists who opposed the Marxists in the leadership and the policy of dependence upon Ethiopian support and the rest. An agreement between Somalia and **Ethiopia** of 11 April 1988 led to the closure of SNM bases on Ethiopian territory, although this had a contrary effect to that hoped for by the government in Mogadishu for it strengthened the SNM, which was then forced to fight harder to establish its bases in the north of the country. Major fighting took place during 1988 in Hargeisa, which forced the **United Nations** to airlift foreigners to safety while about 1,000 people were killed in the fighting. From June 1988 a full-scale civil war was waged in the north by the SNM and government forces, and between June and August, according to the **United Nations High Commissioner for**

Refugees (UNHCR), some 225,000 people became **refugees** as a result of the fighting.

In the period 1989–1992, as the rest of Somalia was torn by civil war, the SNM was able to declare an independent Republic of Somaliland, and though this did not receive international recognition, it nonetheless proceeded to act as though it was fully independent under its President Mohammed Ibrahim Egal.

SOMALIA. Modern Somalia was created in 1960 by the unification of British Somaliland and the former Italian Somaliland, which had been made a Trusteeship Territory of the **United Nations** in 1945. Somali claims upon the territory of neighboring African states (**Ethiopia**, Kenya, and Djibouti) meant an uneasy relationship with all three. Following its defeat by Ethiopia (aided by the Cubans and massive Soviet military supplies) in the **Ogaden War** of 1977–1978, the government faced mounting problems including a deteriorating economy and growing strains between the north (former British Somaliland) and the south (former Italian Somaliland). Two nationalist separatist groups opposed to the government of President **Siad Barre** emerged after the Ogaden War; these were the **Somali National Movement** (SNM) in the north and the **Democratic Front for the Salvation of Somalia** (DFSS). During the early 1980s, however, neither the SNM nor the DFSS made much impact, even though by 1978 Barre had become increasingly politically isolated and on the defensive, which led him to adopt ever more dictatorial policies.

The DFSS, which had been formed in 1981, brought into a single movement three dissident groups from the Mudagh region of Somalia. The DFSS enjoyed some early successes but was soon to suffer (as did many such movements) from growing internal dissension. The SNM, which was also launched in 1981 (in London), became the more formidable of the two movements. Its appeal was to the people of the north who favored secession. In 1982, the SNM established its headquarters across the Somali border in Ethiopia from where it organized unrest in the northern towns and periodically launched cross-border raids against government targets. The SNM gathered its recruits from the Issas of the north and obtained financial support from dissident businessmen who objected to Barre's economic (socialist) policies. On several occasions the SNM and the DFSS attempted to overcome their differences and combine but without success. During the early 1980s, most actions by the SNM or DFSS were not of great significance and were more of an irritant to the government than a threat. In 1983, the SNM attacked the prison in Madera to release several hundred prisoners some of whom were political. Such actions focused attention upon general grievances rather than anything else and led Barre to announce an amnesty for dissidents and provide increased development funds for the north. In October 1985 the SNM claimed it had killed 160 government soldiers in Hargeisa; a year later, in December 1986, it claimed to have killed 120 government troops in Burao District. The DFSS did not achieve any comparable successes, although its forces occupied a strip of land along the Ethiopian border during 1985. The movement was riven by factions, however, and in 1986 the Ethiopian government reduced its support for the DFSS.

Civil War in the North

The situation began to change during 1987: anti-government demonstrations in Hargeisa were met with mass arrests and a curfew while the SNM, from bases in Ethiopia, launched a series of guerrilla attacks upon government targets and then isolated Hargeisa and cut the road to Djibouti. Early in 1987, in Burao region, the SNM engaged government forces in a major clash on the border with Ethiopia (with Ethiopian assistance). The government claimed to have killed 300 Ethiopians and destroyed four tanks while admitting to 30 casualties (dead) of its own. In May 1987, the SNM again claimed to have captured Hargeisa as well as Burao and Berbera, although foreign observers dismissed these claims, which were denied by the government. The tense situation was made worse by the drought which affected much of Somalia that year, leading the government to proclaim a state of emergency. Barre, faced with a border dispute with Ethiopia and an intransigent SNM in the north, found his own position becoming weaker. By 1988 the SNM rebellion had turned into a full-scale civil war.

Barre managed to obtain an agreement with Ethiopia in April 1988 whereby Ethiopia withdrew its support for the SNM, yet in May the SNM was able to launch a full-scale offensive during which it captured Burao and several smaller towns. Then the SNM attacked Hargeisa and laid siege to the port of Berbera. The government no longer denied SNM claims, but bombed and shelled the towns that had fallen into the hands of the SNM. Estimates of June 1988 suggested that some 10,000 people had been killed in the fighting while 100,000 had fled into Ethiopia as **refugees**. Western governments then evacuated their personnel from northern Somalia. Using terror tactics in Hargeisa, government troops shot rebel sympathizers and left their bodies in the streets as an example to the civilian population, while about 1,000 people were treated in Hargeisa Hospital for wounds. Although on 5 June, President Barre insisted that life had resumed as normal in the north after what he described as SNM suicide attacks, this complacency was not supported by subsequent developments. It was clear that the SNM had made important advances in the north, where it enjoyed considerable sympathy because of its demands for greater autonomy.

During July, government forces launched a major military operation to regain control of the northern towns and both sides claimed they controlled the same towns. Much of Hargeisa was destroyed in the fighting, up to 120,000 refugees were reported to have arrived in Ethiopia, while Amnesty International confirmed that Somali government troops had massacred large numbers of the civilian population of Hargeisa. The fighting of mid-1988 turned a number of towns into rubble, while an estimated 50,000 people lost their lives. Hargeisa, formerly with a population of 500,000, was reduced to a ghost town with 14,000 buildings destroyed and a further 12,000 heavily damaged. Burao was also wrecked. The SNM, which had suffered heavy casualties in the fighting, now reverted to guerrilla tactics. In October 1988, the government claimed to control most of the main roads in the north. The fighting had cost the government about 40 percent of its annual revenues.

In January 1989, the government in Mogadishu changed its tactics and sought to win foreign support for a program that would end the war; it offered economic and political reforms and amnesties as well. The government also attempted to rebut charges of human rights abuses, but refused to hold talks with the SNM. The signs, however, were of growing disenchantment with Siad Barre among his own supporters with influential Somalis leaving the country (including

Barre's wife who went to Kenya); a U.S. State Department report, *Why Somalis Flee*, accused the Somali army of extreme brutality and of murdering 5,000 members of the Issaq clan who supported the SNM. By this time, between 30,000 and 50,000 members of the SNM were located in Djibouti from where they crossed the border at night to carry out guerrilla activities against government forces. Although "neutral" in the war, Djibouti sympathized with the SNM. By the end of 1989 the SNM was clearly in the ascendant in the north, while President Barre had been deserted by his most important ally to this time, the **United States**, which had taken the place of the **Union of Soviet Socialist Republics** (USSR) in 1976. While the country waited for Barre's inevitable fall from power, the SNM had yet to work out a policy for its future. Most economic activity in the north had come to a standstill while the government had concluded a secret deal for military assistance from **South Africa**. In January 1990 the American human rights group Africa Watch claimed that government forces had killed between 50,000 and 60,000 civilians as well as driving 500,000 into exile over the preceding 19 months; the majority of these had been Issas. President Barre just managed to hold on to power through the year, although most of Somalia was under the control of different rebel groups: the SNM held most of the north; the **United Somali Congress** (USC) controlled much of the center; while the Somali Patriotic Movement was active in the south; and armed gangs were busy terrorizing the capital, Mogadishu.

The Fall of President Barre

In May 1990, the Mogadishu Manifesto, signed by 114 politicians and intellectuals, called upon Barre to resign his office. On 6 July 1990, the presidential guard fired into the crowd in the football stadium in Mogadishu, when it jeered a speech by Barre, to kill 60 people. By this time it was clear that the government was disintegrating and that Barre himself was losing control. During December 1990, the USC took control of various districts in the capital and 500 people were killed in two days of fierce fighting, and President Barre was reported to be in a bunker under siege by the rebels. Finally, in January 1991, he fled the country leaving behind him chaos, with half a dozen factions vying for control and an escalating civil war. The

USC proclaimed an interim government under its leader **Ali Mahdi Mohammed** as president. On 18 May 1991, the SNM proclaimed an independent Somaliland Republic in the north (in effect former British Somaliland) with the SNM chairman, Abd ar-Rahman Ahmad Ali Tur, as president. In an effort at **mediation**, President Hassan Gouled Aptidon of Djibouti called a conference in July 1991 of the various Somali groups, but the meeting was boycotted by both the SNM and the chairman of the USC, General **Muhammad Farah Aideed**.

Civil War in Mogadishu: The U.S. Role

In September 1991, a power struggle for control of Somalia erupted in Mogadishu between the followers of the USC-appointed President Mohammed and those of General Aideed. The situation deteriorated through 1992 as famine and starvation affected a growing number of the population, and armed bands acting independently controlled their own areas and held people and food relief supplies for ransom. The **United Nations** intervened in mid-1992 in the hope of restoring order, and its failure to do so persuaded U.S. President George H. W. Bush to authorize the use of 28,000 U.S. marines (under UN auspices) to protect relief columns in Somalia from the depredations of rival clan groups. This U.S.-led United Nations Task Force (UNTAF) arrived in Somalia in December 1992, and in January 1993, began to search for weapons in Mogadishu and other population centers; on 7 January the U.S. commander, General Robert Johnson, announced that his troops had opened up supply routes to the famine-affected areas and that a "new phase" in Somalia was about to begin. However, the Americans quickly came up against resistance in Mogadishu, including sniper fire against their troops, and it was clear the various parties vying for power did not intend to accept U.S. mediation. General Aideed, who was soon to be demonized by the U.S. authorities in Somalia, had meanwhile formed the Somali National Alliance (SNA) with a military wing, the Somali Liberation Army (SLA).

Early in January, the marines destroyed an SLA arms cache and killed 30 Somalis in the process. Then, on 13 January 1993, the U.S. forces suffered their first casualty when a marine was shot dead and what had begun as a policing action began to appear more aggressive. By the end of January 1993 there were some 24,000 U.S. Marines and a further 13,600 troops from other countries in Somalia, serving under the UN umbrella. Tensions now arose between the United States and the United Nations over the role of the U.S. forces: while Washington wanted to withdraw its troops from Somalia by April 1993, the United Nations argued they had to remain longer to be of any use in controlling the situation. At the end of February, Aideed and his SLA went on the offensive in Mogadishu following the rumor that the United States favored one of Aideed's rivals. The SLA barricaded streets and fought running battles with the U.S. marines and attempted to storm both the U.S. and French Embassies. During the last week of February, about 100 people were killed in Mogadishu street fighting between members of the SNA and supporters of General Mohammed Siyad Hersi Morgan, a son-in-law of former President Barre.

During March the United States continued to pull out its troops and UN Secretary-General Boutros Boutros-Ghali named 1 May 1993 as the date for the **peacekeeping** operation to be handed over to the United Nations, when it would become the UN Operation in Somalia II (UNOSOM-II). The United States indicated it would leave 5,000 troops as its contribution to UNOSOM-II, which would have a total force of 20,000 as well as a civilian staff of 2,500. In reaction to further fighting in Kismayu that March the U.S. commander sent in his quick reaction force of 500 marines to restore order and bolster the U.S.–Belgian garrison; and the operation resulted in the deaths of about 100 Somalis.

A national reconciliation conference was held in Addis Ababa on 15 March 1993, at which Ali Mahdi Mohammed, who had proclaimed himself president of Somalia and claimed he enjoyed the allegiance of 11 other factions, hoped to form a transitional government until elections could be held. General Aideed, instead, argued for the creation of an effective regional authority first. However, by the end of March the conference had agreed to establish a Transitional National Council as a temporary Supreme Authority. In May 1993 the U.S.-led UNTAF handed over authority to the United Nations, and UNOSOM-II came into effect under the command of a Turkish general. UNOSOM was to be composed of 20,000 troops drawn from 35 countries; it would have authority to act anywhere in Somalia and use whatever means were necessary to disarm the warring factions, maintain peace, and safeguard **relief** workers. UNOSOM-II was to have at best an uneasy history and its operations in Somalia reflected little credit upon the United Nations, while troops from several of the countries taking part were later accused of brutality and atrocities.

While these developments were taking place, the north proceeded as though it were an independent country and, on 5 May 1993, Mohammed Ibrahim Egal was elected president of the self-proclaimed northern state of Somaliland (former British Somaliland). On 5 June a battle was fought in Mogadishu between Pakistani (UN) troops and the SNA in which Pakistani casualties came to 23 dead and 50 wounded. There were similar Somali casualties. Pakistan called for punitive action to be mounted against Aideed. The United States sent reinforcements from the Gulf, the Security Council condemned the unprovoked attack upon UNOSOM forces, and UNOSOM proceeded to launch a series of attacks against the SNA and Aideed. While such action may have satisfied the countries whose troops had been targets, it could hardly be described as peacekeeping. Following air attacks by U.S. aircraft on SNA targets, Aideed accused the U.S. government of attacking civilians. On 13 June, Pakistani troops fired on demonstrators in Mogadishu, killing 20 and wounding 50; there appeared to be little constraint on the part of the UNOSOM forces and not much evidence of control from above. The United Nations then made the mistake of ordering the arrest of Aideed, and UNOSOM-II mounted a massive manhunt for him throughout Mogadishu; 31 UN soldiers were killed in the course of the month as the unsuccessful manhunt proceeded. The death of three Italian (UN) soldiers led to demands by the opposition in Rome for the withdrawal of the Italian contingent, while Italy blamed U.S. belligerency for the deaths. Italy demanded a greater say in the control of UNOSOM-II and on 12 August, withdrew its forces from Mogadishu. There was growing criticism of the United States for its "macho" attitude and especially of Admiral Jonathan T. Howe, who was the U.S. Special Representative in Somalia.

Another operation to capture Aideed was mounted on 12 July with no greater success; it resulted in 54 deaths and 174 wounded. In August the elite U.S. Rangers raided a house in which they thought to find Aideed, but took UN and French aid workers prisoner instead. By August 1993 the U.S. forces in Somalia were acting as though their operation was a vendetta against Aideed rather than as part of a larger UNOSOM operation. A further 200 Somalis were killed on 9 September when a U.S. helicopter fired on a crowd in Mogadishu; there were seven UN casualties (Nigerians). On 22 September 1993, the UN Security Council adopted Resolution 865 that would bring the UNOSOM-II operation to a close in March 1995. Another battle of October 1993 in Mogadishu resulted in the deaths of 300 Somalis and 18 U.S. marines, while a U.S. helicopter pilot and Nigerian soldier were taken hostage. The United Nations changed its policy following a visit to Mogadishu on 9 October by UN Assistant Secretary General for Peacekeeping Operations **Kofi Annan** (later to be secretary-general); he claimed that UN casualties were too high and therefore argued that "some sort of judicial process" should investigate Aideed's responsibility for UN deaths. This represented a major about-face: it was an admission that the demonizing of Aideed and the long effort to find and arrest him had been a failure, especially for the United States, which had pushed the policy. On 27 October, UN Secretary-General Boutros Boutros-Ghali announced that the United Nations would reconsider Resolution 837, which had authorized the arrest of Aideed.

U.S. President Bill Clinton called for the creation of a new Somali government and announced that all U.S. troops would be withdrawn from Somalia by 31 March 1994, whether or not a settlement had been reached. Germany, Belgium, France, and Sweden in turn announced their intention to withdraw their troops from Somalia early in 1994, although Pakistan expressed its readiness to commit a further 5,000 troops to UNOSOM-II. On 16 November 1993, the United Nations formally abandoned the search for Aideed and instead set up a Commission of Inquiry into responsibility for attacks upon UN forces. Then on 18 November, it renewed the UNOSOM-II mandate until 31 May 1994. Talks, which included Aideed, were held in Addis Ababa but they broke down in mid-December. The end of 1993, which had been a disastrous year for the reputations of both the United Nations and the United States in Somalia, saw the withdrawal of a large proportion of the U.S., German, Italian, and French forces, then under UNOSOM command.

The Withdrawal of the United Nations Force

On 4 February 1994, the United Nations emphasized that its mandate was peacekeeping and reconciliation as opposed to enforcement. Further fierce fighting took place in Kismayu during February between the followers of Aideed and supporters of Mohammed. Violence continued during the first half of 1994 as UN troops were withdrawn. In the south the principal contenders for power remained General Muhammad Farah Aideed and his SNA and Ali Mahdi Mohammed and his "Group of Twelve." The breakaway Republic of Somaliland in the north was relatively peaceful during most of 1994, though violence occurred there toward the end of the year. The main problem throughout the country was to contain and disarm the various military—or militarized—groups; much of Somalia had been controlled by armed gangs ever since the end of Barre's rule. By 25 March 1994, after the withdrawal of the U.S. and European contingents, UNOSOM-II was reduced from 29,000 to 19,000 troops drawn mainly from Africa and Pakistan. Aideed and Mohammed met in Nairobi, Kenya, during March 1994 and agreed to form a government of national reconciliation, but this did not last and in May further fighting erupted in Mogadishu when Aideed's forces seized the airport. Other fighting occurred in Kismayu between Aideed's ally Ahmad Omar Jess and the militia of Mohammed Morgan. There was also dissension in the ranks of the SNA. The United Nations, meanwhile, following its low-profile policy, was still unable to bring the situation under control, although the loss of life was less than under its more aggressive policy: 15 of its "non-intervening" soldiers were killed in four incidents as were several journalists.

In the north a split developed between Egal, who wanted the Republic of Somaliland to break away from Somalia, and Abd ar-Rahman Ahmed Ali Tur, who did not, and this led to fighting in Hargeisa during October. On 19 December 1994, fighting again broke out in Mogadishu between the forces of Aideed and Mohammed resulting in casualties of 20 dead and 125 wounded. When the UNOSOM mandate was renewed in October to last until 31 March 1995, there was no indication that the clan fighting was any nearer to an end. During March 1995, the last UNOSOM-II forces were evacuated from Somalia by an international fleet and 1,800 U.S. marines. The exercise had been a disaster for the United Nations.

After the United Nations

Although the withdrawal of the UNOSOM forces was not followed by a return to civil war, the country remained divided: apart from the breakaway "Republic of Somaliland" in the north, other areas had also become "independent" on a local basis. There was no effective central government and no country had recognized the breakaway republic of the north. In addition to the north, other divisions were as follows: Mogadishu, the port, and the immediate hinterland were split between the factions of Aideed and Ali Mahdi Mohammed (who was still the nominal president), with each trying to unite people behind the SNA and the Somali Salvation Alliance (SSA) respectively; northeastern Somalia and the port of Boosaaso were controlled by the Somali Salvation Democratic Front (SSDF); in the far south (the valley of the Jubba) the forces of General Morgan held Kismayo, while those of Colonel Ahmad Omar Jess held the interior; between the Jubba and Shebeli Rivers yet another faction, comprised of the Rahanwayu clans, had created its own supreme council.

Aideed's power appeared to wane during 1995 and he faced a split in the ranks of the SNA when one of his allies, the businessman Osman Hassan Ali Ato, defected to join Ali Mahdi Mohammed. In June 1995, when the USC voted to replace Aideed as chairman with Ali Ato, Aideed's supporters elected Aideed "president" of all Somalia, though it was an empty gesture. Between September and December 1995, Aideed was engaged in fighting in the south as he attempted to reassert control over the Rahanwayu clans. In the north, Ali Tur (who opposed the secession of the Republic of Somaliland) allied himself with Aideed and the SNA to fight against the self-proclaimed President Mohammed Ibrahim Egal. During the early part of 1996 Aideed achieved a number of military successes against the Rahanwayu Resistance Army (RRA), capturing Xuddur in January and Diinsoor and Doolow in March. At the same time, however, the SNA was weakened by the split between Aideed and his former ally Osman Hassan Ali Ato; their forces clashed near Marka during March as they fought to control the rich banana region. Fighting between SNA groups broke out in Mogadishu in April and Ato created an enclave of his own in the battered capital where sporadic fighting continued to the end of the year. In the south, the RRA recaptured Xuddur in May. On 1 August 1996, Aideed died of wounds received during a battle in Mogadishu on 24 July; his death threw the future of the SNA into doubt, although his son, Hussein Aideed, immediately became the movement's leader.

The Next Phase

At the end of 1996 Somalia remained divided between faction leaders: from time to time fighting erupted in Mogadishu and elsewhere; the country was physically ruined with tens of thousands of people maimed by the endless violence; and the outside world had ceased to bother about the country's plight. Yet if the world had turned away from the problems of Somalia, the disastrous UN intervention had left its mark upon the world community. Instead of Somalia providing the first example of a peacekeeping operation under the "new world order" proclaimed by President Bush in the immediate euphoria following the end of the **Cold War**, it had led to the humiliation of both the United Nations and the United States and put in jeopardy any further effective UN peacekeeping operations. The peacekeepers became increasingly unsure as to whether their task was to enforce peace, no matter at what cost, or try to keep peace between warring factions. There was little cooperation between the various peacekeeping forces and the most obvious lesson for the United Nations was how little its members either respected it or were prepared to ensure its success. Nonetheless, a third Somali National Salvation Council (NSC) met in Addis Ababa, Ethiopia, during January 1998 in the continuing search for a peace settlement for the country. This proved elusive.

The period 1998 to 2000 was generally disturbed, but in May 2000 a Somali reconciliation and government conference met at Asta in Djibouti and by August a 245-member Transitional National Assembly based upon a complex clan system had been chosen and on 27 August, Abdiqasim Salad Hasan (a former minister under Barre) was sworn in as president. Despite endorsement of this settlement by the Inter-Governmental Authority for Development (IGAD), the Arab League, the United Nations, and the European Union, the chances of the arrangement lasting looked precarious. Faction leaders and "warlords" had not taken part; nor had the Republic of Somaliland (former British Somaliland) in the north, nor the separate "Puntland" administration. The assembly members and government were supposed to move into Mogadishu by the end of the year but failed to take control of the city. In the meantime Ethiopia, which was opposed to any overtly Islamist government in Somalia, continued to support factions that rejected the new government. The situation did not improve during 2001. The Transitional National Government (TNG) manifestly failed to establish its authority over the whole country; nor was any progress made in reconciling the faction leaders and warlords who had refused to take part in the Arta conference of the previous year. In March, at a meeting in Ethiopia, 12 of the faction leaders established the Somali Reconciliation and Restoration Council (SRRC). In October Kenya's President Daniel arap Moi hosted two reconciliation conferences in Nairobi (the second in December), but the SRRC leaders boycotted them because the TNG claimed to be the sole legitimate authority in Somalia.

In any case, major new complications followed the events of 11 September in the United States. The U.S. government identified Somalia as a "failed" state and possible haven for Osama bin Laden and there was much concern that the U.S. was planning an attack. The U.S. placed the Somali-based Islamist group, Al-Itihaad al-Islamia (AIAI) on its list of terrorist organizations and the SRRC claimed that AIAI had close links with both the TNG and al-Qaida. Little progress toward genuine reconciliation was achieved during 2002, although IGAD set up a Technical Committee of Djibouti, Ethiopia, and Kenya in Khartoum to organize a Somali Peace and Reconciliation Conference. This, however, achieved nothing. Moreover, the TNG failed to establish its authority outside Mogadishu and serious fighting occurred inside the city in May. During 2003, outbreaks of violence by the warlords and their factions undermined the peace process that in any case appeared to have little real support inside Somalia. The IGAD peace conference proposed federal arrangements to include the Republic of Somaliland and a transitional government for a four-year period, after which the TNG would initiate a dialogue of "national unity." On 5 July the IGAD conference announced that it had reached agreement, but President Abdiqassim Hasan rejected the agreement on the grounds that it would divide the country, recognize the Republic of Somaliland, and was adopting an anti-Islamic line. The president then dismissed his prime minister and speaker of the Transitional National Assembly for signing the agreement on behalf of the TNG. Two faction leaders denounced the agreement and criticized Ethiopian influence over the peace process. During the last months of 2003, the influence of the TNG declined sharply. Its three-year mandate had expired in August and it only controlled about a quarter of Mogadishu.

The peace process had stalled in September 2003 and after much political maneuvering, a new president was sworn in on 14 October 2004: Colonel Abdullahi Yusuf, a former leader of the Somali Salvation Democratic Front, assumed his office in Nairobi. His proposed prime minister and cabinet were both rejected by the TNG in Mogadishu, and Abdullahi then requested peacekeepers from the **African Union** (AU). The government hoped to return to Mogadishu in January 2005. Meanwhile, there was further fighting between factions in the south of the country.

President Ahmed Abdullahi Yusuf and his prime minister, Ali Mohammed Gedi, returned to Somalia from Kenya on 24 February 2005 for the first time since their government had been formed in October 2004. Thousands turned out in the streets of Mogadishu to welcome them. They wanted to determine whether security considerations would allow the government to move to Mogadishu. In March, a chaotic session of the Somali government meeting in a Nairobi hotel ended in violence between members. The transitional legislature voted to block peacekeepers from Djibouti, Ethiopia, and Kenya and agreed to request peacekeepers from **Uganda** and **Sudan**. The prime minister, Gedi, would not accept this since it barred countries that had played a major part in bringing the new government into being. Arguments continued through May as to where the government should be sited: in Mogadishu or the southern town of Baidoa. An AU demobilization plan led 14 faction leaders to withdraw their militias to camps outside Mogadishu with the eventual object of unifying them under one command.

During May 100 members of the legislature, led by the speaker, Sharif Hasan Shaykh Adan, moved to Mogadishu and began removing illegal roadblocks. However, both the president and the prime minister insisted the government could not return to Mogadishu until the city was fully pacified. At the end of May fierce fighting erupted in Baidoa, a preferred seat for the government at that time. In mid-June, Prime Minister Gedi and his supporters in the transitional legislature and cabinet moved from Kenya to establish a government base in Jowhar, 90 kilometers north of Mogadishu. The Mogadishu warlords opposed the move since they wanted the government in the capital under their influence. On 6 November, when Gedi visited Mogadishu from the Jowhar base, there was an attempt to assassinate him; on 14 November heavy fighting broke out in the capital. To the end of the year, Mogadishu remained under the control of warlords and Islamists opposed to the Yusuf government, and intimidation, abduction, and assassination appeared to be the norm in the capital where al-Qaida operatives, Jihadi extremists, Ethiopian security services, and Western-backed counter-terrorism agents all operated.

The rift between President Yusuf and Speaker Adan was patched up on 5 January 2006 when they met in Aden, Southern Yemen. Their quarrel was about the siting of the government, then in Jowhar. In principle, they agreed the government should first move to Baidoa from Jowhar and then to Mogadishu. Finally, the transitional legislature (200 of its 275 members), which had been selected in August 2004 in Kenya, met for the first time in Somalia on 26 February in Baidoa. President Yusuf told the legislature: "Somalis are fed up with hostilities, displacement and endless violence. The people want peace, freedom and to live under the rule of law."

Instead, over 22–25 March, heavy fighting took place in Mogadishu resulting in some 93 deaths. The fighting was between the Islamic Courts' militia and a newly created coalition of warlords and businessmen—the Alliance for the Restoration of Peace and Counter-Terrorism (ARPCT). The Islamic Courts' militia was led by Sheikh Sharif Ahmed Siyar, who was accused of having links with al-Qaida. His militia numbered 1,500 well-armed members who appeared to be better disciplined than the other militias. Their numbers were sometimes augmented by fighters who agreed with the Islamic Courts' faith-based agenda and were opposed to the warlords. The ARPCT included warlords and controlled the greater part of Mogadishu including the airstrips around the city. According to the Islamic Courts, the Alliance was funded by the U.S. Horn of Africa counter-terrorism force, the Djibouti-based Combined Joint Task Force-Horn of Africa (CJTF-HOA). There was fierce fighting in Mogadishu throughout May between the Islamic Courts' militia and the ARPCT. President Yusuf complained, on a visit to Sweden, that the U.S. was funding the ARPCT and that it would do better to give the money to his government. About 170 people were killed during the month, though neither side gained any territory.

By early July 2006, however, the Islamists had come out on top when the last warlord fighting in Mogadishu surrendered after two days of battles in which 140 people were killed. Abdi Awale Qaybdiid was the last of an alliance of warlords backed by the United States. The Islamists now controlled most of Mogadishu and a moderate Islamic leader, Sheikh Sharif Ahmed, said: "From today onward, we promise the world that this city is safe. We need to overcome tribalism and the Somali enemies. There are so many enemies and in order to defend ourselves against them we need to unite." The prime minister, Gedi, called for international peacekeepers to help the government restore stability, but the Islamic Courts said Somalia did not need any foreign troops. Moderates within the Islamic Courts claimed they only wanted to bring law and order to Somalia after 15 years of chaos, but in June the Union of Islamic Courts named as its chairman Sheikh Hassan Dahir Aweys who, the U.S. claimed, had links with al-Qaida.

Tensions were heightened dramatically on 20 July when Ethiopian troops crossed the border into Somalia to support the Yusuf government in Baidoa and threatened to crush the Union of Islamic Courts. The Islamists then threatened to take Baidoa, prompting Ethiopia's information minister, Berhan Hailu, to say that his country would use "all means at our disposal to crush the Islamist group" if it tried to attack Baidoa. (Ethiopia clearly feared the establishment of an extremist Islamic state in Somalia.) By this time, however, it was clear that the Baidoa-based government had little power and less authority while the Islamists in Mogadishu had created a semblance of law and order in the capital and had taken down the security checkpoints which the warlords had used to exact money with the immediate result of lowering the price of food.

The Ethiopian intervention brought a new dimension to the Somali troubles and seemed more likely to unite Somalis behind the Islamists than prevent them from forming a government. The leader of the Islamist militias, Sheikh Hassan Dahir Aweys, called for a holy war against Ethiopia and said that Ethiopia was bolstering the puppet regime of President Yusuf, whom he described as a "servant of Ethiopia." About 5,000 Ethiopian troops had crossed into Somalia, though neither the U.S. nor any member of the UN Security Council condemned the intervention. Observers linked the Ethiopian invasion with the U.S.-led war on terror and claimed that Washington supported the Ethiopian move. Osama bin Laden, in a tape recording, had backed the Union of Islamic Courts, whose leader Sheikh Aweys was on the American most wanted list of terrorists. The British Foreign Office at the end of July gave its unequivocal backing to the Yusuf government and said that leading members of the Islamist movement should be *persona non grata* in any future coalition. Hours later, 19 members of the Yusuf government resigned at the same time that the Islamists took over the presidential palace in Mogadishu. The resigning ministers accused the government of taking orders from Ethiopia. By early August 2006, effective power in Somalia appeared to lie with the Islamic Courts, the Yusuf government in Baidoa was on the verge of collapse, the Ethiopians had intervened, almost certainly with American backing, while most indications suggested the beginning of a new conflict in which the Islamists would emerge the victors.

By November 2006, the peace talks between the transitional government and the UIC had broken down while observers were predicting an all-out war, especially as Ethiopia had moved between 6,000 and 8,000 troops to the border and seemed determined to prevent an Islamist government coming to power in Somalia. According to the TNG foreign minister, Ismael Mohamoud Hurreh, a war would erupt if the Islamic Courts were "not checked definitively." The previous October, Ethiopia's prime minister, Meles Zenawi, had admitted that a few hundred Ethiopian soldiers were in Somalia as "military advisers" while Hurreh claimed that Ethiopia would come to the assistance of the TNG in Baidoa, should the UIC move against it. Meanwhile, **Eritrea** which was still in dispute with Ethiopia over their border, was reputed to have sent 2,000 troops to Somalia to support the UIC. By December 2006, tension in the Horn of Africa was rising and the possibility of an armed conflagration appeared imminent.

SOUSTELLE, JAQUES-ÉMILE (1912–90). Jaques-Émile Soustelle was an anthropologist and politician who played a significant part in bringing **Charles de Gaulle** back to power in **France** in 1958. He was born on 3 February 1912, and took part in anthropological work during the 1930s to earn a doctorate from the Sorbonne in 1937. He was a strong leftist and became secretary-general of the Comité de Vigilance des Intellectuels Antifascistes. In 1940 he joined the Free French under the leadership of de Gaulle. In 1942 Soustelle became the Free French Commissioner for Information; from 1943 to 1944 he directed intelligence operations in **Algeria**. He was a member of the Constituent Assembly from 1945 to 1946 and in de Gaulle's post-war government, he held the post of minister of information. Between 1947 and 1952, Soustelle was secretary-general of de Gaulle's Rassemblement du Peuple Francais (RPF)/Rally of the French People and from 1951, he led the party in the National Assembly.

In 1955, Prime Minister Pierre Mendes-France appointed Soustelle governor general of Algeria after the rebellion there had started. The settlers (*colons*) began by viewing him with intense suspicion, but later they came to regard him as their chief and best spokesman as he advocated the economic and political integration of Algeria in France. In 1956, he was recalled to France by the government of Guy Mollet. Back in the National Assembly between 1956 and 1958, Soustelle led the Gaullists and became known as the "destroyer of ministries" as he attacked successive policies to deal with the Algerian crisis—he was credited with bringing down three governments. In May 1958, Soustelle returned to Algeria to become the leader of the rebel settler Comité de Salut Public (CSP)/Committee of Public Safety. Working with the Algerian rebels, parts of the army opposed to Algerian independence and other disgruntled elements in France, Soustelle assisted in the downfall of Pierre Pflimlin's government in May 1958. De Gaulle then came to power and, once more, appointed Soustelle minister of information; then, in January 1959, de Gaulle made Soustelle minister for Sahara and atomic affairs.

Soustelle did not accept de Gaulle's Algerian policy, once he saw that it was leading to independence, and he left the government in 1960. In 1961 he went into exile and in 1962, a warrant was issued for his arrest; he was accused of plotting against the state. He only returned to France in 1968, following a general amnesty, to resume his academic career. He was again elected to the National Assembly for the years 1973–1978.

SOUTH AFRICA. The imposition of the apartheid laws across the board in South Africa, following the National Party election victory of

1948, consolidated the position of white racial dominance, which had existed for generations. South Africa had been colonized twice: first by the Dutch at the Cape in the 17th century; then by the British, who took the Cape from the Dutch during the Napoleonic wars and retained it at the peace of 1814. During the nineteenth century the Boers, a name given to the descendants of the Dutch settlers, moved away from the Cape to escape British control and established the Boer republics of the Orange Free State and Transvaal, while the British moved along the eastern seaboard to establish a new colony of Natal. In both cases the Boers and British fought against, and then colonized, the black peoples of the regions they occupied. A final confrontation between the British and the Boers occurred in the latter years of the nineteenth century, culminating in the Anglo–Boer War of 1899–1902.

In 1910 the Union of South Africa, comprising the four territories—Cape Province, Natal, the Orange Free State, and Transvaal—became a Dominion of the British Empire; but political power in the Union had been transferred to the white minority and over the succeeding years, the black majority was to find itself both discriminated against and deprived of a political voice in the affairs of South Africa. At the same time there existed sharp divisions and antagonisms between the two white racial groups, the British and the Boers, who from this time onward came to be called Afrikaners. The fact that English and Afrikaans were made the two official languages of the Union of South Africa served to emphasize the difference between the two dominant white groups.

It became an increasing certainty over the years that a clash between the white minority and the black majority was bound to arise and was likely to be violent. Between 1948, when the National Party under Daniel Malan came to power and the word apartheid (the Afrikaans word for apartness, which from this time on would signify the separation of the races) entered international usage, and 1960, the year of the Sharpeville Massacre, the white minority under the leadership, first of Malan, then of Johannes Strijdom and Hendrik Verwoerd, entrenched white power at the expense of the other racial groups.

The Apartheid Struggle: 1960–1990

The Sharpeville Massacre of March 1960 marked the beginning of the final long struggle by black South Africans to achieve political emancipation. From 1960 onward, not only was South Africa increasingly a police state but the military had as its first task, not defending the country from external aggression, but controlling the internal enemies of the white state: that is, the black majority. The apartheid system was designed to entrench white minority power at the expense of the black majority and it did so in two ways: first, by separating every aspect of activity as between blacks and whites to make plain that to belong to the white racial group conferred privileges that were denied to the black majority; and second, by differentiating job opportunities and remuneration so that blacks neither were, nor could aspire to be, equal to the whites.

This white-dominated system was opposed by the **African National Congress** (ANC), which had been formed in 1912 and was Africa's oldest political party, with as its core philosophy the belief in multiracial solutions. During the 1940s and 1950s, the ANC attempted by peaceful political means to persuade the ruling white minority to begin the process of sharing power, but to no avail. During this period young radical Africans, notably **Nelson Mandela** and **Oliver Tambo**, moved into the leadership of the ANC and by the end of the 1950s, had become convinced that it should turn to armed opposition to the ruling National Party. It was the Pan-Africanist Congress (PAC), however, rather than the ANC which called for a peaceful protest in 1960 that was to take the form of Africans assembling before police stations and burning their passes. At Sharpeville, the police panicked and fired on the crowd and the Sharpeville Massacre of 21 March 1960 became a defining point in the long struggle. Shortly afterward both the ANC and the PAC were banned, and Mandela then decided to go underground to lead resistance to the government.

In 1962, the General Assembly of the **United Nations** called on its members to break diplomatic relations with South Africa; it was the beginning of a new phase in a long battle against the apartheid system. In 1963–1964, Mandela and other ANC leaders were arrested and tried in what became known as the Rivonia treason trial, leading to life imprisonment for Mandela and other ANC leaders. There had been an outflow of investment funds from South Africa following the Sharpeville Massacre, but by 1964 the economy was recovering, while the government believed it had achieved effective control over its black majority.

Despite this, between 1960 and 1976 South Africa became an increasingly embattled state: Harold Macmillan's "Wind of Change" speech, which had preceded the Sharpeville Massacre by only six weeks; the banning of the ANC, PAC, and other African political organizations; the imprisonment or exile of black leaders; and the progressive installation of more apartheid laws ensured growing world condemnation and gradually turned the Republic into an international "pariah" state. As South Africa's isolation increased and the world became more critical, so the groundwork was laid for what an increasing number of observers predicted would be a bloodbath when the black majority finally revolted.

The Soweto Uprising of 1976

The Soweto Uprising of 1976 was the most violent in South Africa's history. It was sparked off by schoolchildren (the later "comrades") who objected to the proposed introduction of Afrikaans as a language of instruction in the schools (English was then the medium). Riots broke out on 16 June 1976, causing many deaths and much destruction of property as well as leading to the arrest of many rioters. Soweto (the "southwestern township") of four million became a battleground between the rioters, most of whom were youngsters, and the police. Although the attempted introduction of Afrikaans into the schools was the spark which ignited the riots, the townships had long been simmering with unrest and waiting for an occasion to explode. The riots spread and affected townships in the Rand, Pretoria, Natal, and the Cape; Indian and Coloured youths as well as blacks took part in them. They represented a spontaneous explosion of anger against a deeply unjust system. The authorities only regained control after three weeks of rioting, although further flare-ups continued for some months. One consequence of the riots was the exodus of large numbers of youths to countries to the north where they joined the ranks of the ANC.

From this time onward, the white authorities became far more edgy in the constant expectation of further troubles with the result that the government became even more repressive and ready to impose new restrictions upon the black population. Even so, the Soweto Uprising proved a partial victory for the black townships;

the idea of using Afrikaans as a medium of instruction in black schools was dropped and electricity was extended to the townships. By the end of 1976, the official death toll resulting from the riots was given as 360, although the unofficial figure was 500. In addition, 1,381 people, the majority under 18 years, were convicted of offenses and 528 were given corporal punishment. Nineteen trials were held under the Terrorism Act, and 697 people were detained for security reasons.

Developing Resistance

In the years from Soweto (1976) until the elections of 1994, South Africa became an increasingly violent place with civil disturbances becoming more insistent. A new wave of violence affected the country in 1984: this was both spontaneous and organized against the government and was set off by the proposed constitutional reforms, which gave Asians and Coloureds (but not the Africans) assemblies of their own. By the end of the year the newly formed Confederation of South African Trade Unions (COSATU) had become a spokesman for reform; it demanded the release of Nelson Mandela, the abolition of the pass laws, and an end to foreign investment. Growing black resistance to the government during 1985 (the 25th anniversary of the Sharpeville Massacre) took the form of rent strikes, boycotts, and demonstrations; troops as well as the police were deployed in the townships. There was also much black-on-black violence with necklacing (the practice of putting an old tire filled with kerosene around the neck of a victim and setting it on fire) of informers or collaborators and many townships became ungovernable. On 21 July 1985, a state of emergency was declared in 36 magisterial districts (black townships). The state of emergency was lifted in March 1986, then reimposed on 12 June. Under its terms, an estimated 23,000 people were detained. The violence continued, and in the townships there emerged street-level mini-local governments.

A number of new black organizations emerged, and by 1986 the United Democratic Front (UDF) claimed 600 affiliates and more than two million members; it was a front for the banned ANC. Under these pressures the government committed itself to abolishing the apartheid system. The anti-government pressures mounted during 1987 when

650,000 households took part in rent boycotts; over 5–6 May 1987, a national general strike brought three million workers and students out. There was a second strike on 16 June. These strikes represented the largest ever industrial action in the country's history. The government maintained a state of emergency throughout 1988: the UDF and other organizations were banned, further restrictions were imposed on the press, and young whites began to refuse to do their national service for conscientious reasons. Casualties (dead) over the period 1984 to 1988 were at the rate of 3.2 a day during the emergency, while between September 1984 and December 1985, an official estimate put the dead at 1,000, though unofficial estimates suggested higher figures. Another estimate gave a total of 1,776 killed including 56 members of the security forces in the two years to September 1986.

The Final Phase to the Elections of 1994

Parallel with the anti-government violence was the escalating confrontation, which began in the mid-1980s, between the followers of Chief **Mangosuthu Buthelezi** and his Inkatha Freedom Party (IFP) and the UDF. In essence, Chief Buthelezi had launched a challenge to the UDF for a special place for himself and the Zulu Nation in the changing political scene: the UDF, which had been formed in 1983, stood for the exiled and banned ANC, and a fight against the government; the IFP stood for tribal (Zulu) power, and when it became clear that the Inkatha Movement was losing some of its Zulu support to the UDF, Buthelezi entered into an unholy alliance with the government. Inkatha members would attack UDF supporters while the police refused to intervene to stop the fighting or came very tardily onto the scene of action. The white government was only too pleased to see blacks fighting blacks, especially if it appeared that this would weaken the ANC and its supporters. During 1987 about 498 people died in Inkatha–UDF clashes, and in the first nine months of 1988 another 511 people were killed in such clashes. By March 1990, after the release of Mandela, an estimated 3,000 Africans had been killed in these Inkatha–UDF clashes. By this time there was also clear evidence that Inkatha had worked closely with the police in order to keep in check the UDF (ANC) and boost Buthelezi's chances of personal political advancement.

In the four years from March 1990 to the first all-person elections of April 1994, there was much, often daily, violence which might have developed into full-scale civil war, the majority of it being part of the ANC–Inkatha confrontation. In May 1990 the ANC (by then unbanned) agreed formally to assist the government in curbing violence, and in August of that year it also agreed to bring to an end the armed struggle which it had launched in 1961. Between February and 30 June 1990, there were more than 1,000 ANC–Inkatha deaths; and between July 1990 and August 1991 a further 2,000 deaths. Demonstrations during 1991 by the right-wing Afrikaner Resistance Movement (AWB) also gave rise to fears of white–black violence. Though the estimates for the period 1990 to 1992 vary, it was a time of very considerable violence with one estimate of July 1992 putting the deaths over the period since 2 February 1990 (the date of President **F. W. de Klerk**'s speech unbanning the ANC) as high as 7,000.

During 1993, a breakthrough was achieved in the negotiations between the government and the ANC, after de Klerk had conceded that the ANC represented the majority of the Africans. Even so, it was still a dangerously volatile year and major violence might have followed the assassination of **Chris Hani**, the general secretary of the South African Communist Party, though this did not happen. By 18 November 1993, an interim constitution had been negotiated and the various parties began to prepare for elections to be held in April 1994. Tension remained high, especially since Buthelezi threatened to boycott the elections. Right up to April 1994, it was far from clear which groups would take part in the elections; and by mid-April 1994, an estimated 10,000 people had died in the violence of the preceding four years. Finally, however, at the end of April 1994, South Africa went to the polls and the ANC won a clear majority under the leadership of Nelson Mandela, who became the country's first black president. *See also* GREAT BRITAIN.

SOUTH WEST AFRICA PEOPLE'S ORGANIZATION (SWAPO).
The South West Africa People's Organization was created in 1960 to fight the illegal occupation of South West Africa (**Namibia**) by **South Africa**; in 1966, from the Caprivi Strip in the north of the country, it launched an armed struggle against the South Africans who were in control of Namibia. The story of SWAPO's fight for

independence is not that of a civil war, but SWAPO also became involved in the affairs of **Angola** during the years after 1975 when that country achieved independence. From 1975 onward, Angola afforded SWAPO invaluable assistance by providing it with bases from which it could operate across the border into Namibia. At the same time, this provided South Africa with an excuse to raid across the border into Angola, which it did on frequent occasions between 1975 and 1990. Dimo Hamaambo became the effective military commander of SWAPO by the early 1970s and established his headquarters at Cassinga in Angola. The South Africans first raided Cassinga in a cross-border attack in 1978. South African raids across the border from Namibia into Angola were usually justified in terms of "taking out" SWAPO bases, although they were principally designed to provide assistance to the **União Nacional para a Independência Total de Angola** (UNITA)/National Union for the Total Independence of Angola in its fight against the **Movimento Popular para a Libertação de Angola** (MPLA)/Popular Movement for the Liberation of Angola government in Luanda.

Under Hamaambo, SWAPO created a People's Liberation Army of Namibia (PLAN) which was dispersed along the Namibian border in three sectors. Hamaambo had 3,000 guerrillas under his command, although no more than 400 were active in Namibia at any one time. New recruits crossed the border into Angola without great difficulty, though some returned home disillusioned; most training for SWAPO guerrillas was carried out inside Angola by Cubans and (after 1978) by East Germans. Periodically, SWAPO guerrillas in Angola would join with government (MPLA) forces to attack UNITA; and right up to the settlement of 1990, SWAPO guerrillas in Angola played an important support role for the government in its war against UNITA. Thus, in November 1987 South African forces engaged SWAPO in Angola and lost 10 black and two white soldiers killed, although the opposition in South Africa claimed the attack had really been against Cuban and government forces. The South African Defence Force (SADF) later claimed that 150 SWAPO guerrillas had been killed in this raid.

Namibian independence was finally achieved at the end of the 1980s. In 1988, under the **Crocker Plan**, Angola, **Cuba**, and **South Africa** negotiated a peace plan under which **United Nations** peacekeeping troops would move into Namibia during 1989 and the South

Africans would then withdraw. This plan was almost wrecked in April 1989 when SWAPO forces in Angola crossed the border into Namibia and in two weeks lost some 300 killed by SADF forces. This move by SWAPO nearly proved a catastrophe and might have brought an end to the peace process. It did, however, demonstrate how bases in Angola had always been an important factor in the SWAPO war against the South Africans. Namibia became independent on 21 March 1990.

SPINOLA, ANTONIO DE (1910–96). On 25 April 1974, a group of Portuguese army officers carried out a coup in Lisbon to bring an end to the longest-lasting authoritarian regime in modern European history, one which began with a military coup in 1926. President Americo Tomas and Premier Marcello Caetano were deposed and flown to Madeira; later they were allowed to go into exile in Brazil. The Movimento das Forças Armadas (MFA)/Movement of the Armed Forces seized power in an almost bloodless coup and proclaimed an end to 48 years of dictatorship. By that time **Portugal** had become weary of the ever-growing burden of 13 years of colonial warfare in Africa, and there was little resistance to the coup-makers. Caetano handed over power to General Antonio de Spinola. General Spinola had been the most successful Portuguese general in Africa and had fought with distinction in all three of the colonial wars there—in Guinea-Bissau, **Mozambique**, and **Angola**. Although he was no radical, Spinola had encapsulated the growing discontents of the army in his book, *Portugal and the Future*, which was published in February 1974; in it he challenged the government's military solutions for Africa, ridiculed its so-called civilizing mission, and advocated a settlement. He met with a sympathetic response from the lower ranks of army officers, who were discontented with their conditions.

The coup of April 1974 was wildly popular and few mourned the passing of the regime. The Movement of the Armed Forces handed over the government to a Junta of National Salvation, and General Spinola became acting president. Spinola's importance—he was only to act as president until September 1974—was to ensure the end of Portuguese colonialism in Africa. As a result, he also paved the way for the subsequent power struggles that followed in both Angola and Mozambique. The new government quickly reached agreements with the Partido Africano da Independência da Guine e Cabo Verde (PAIGC)/African Party for the Independence of Guine and Cape Verde in Guinea-Bissau and the **Frente da Libertação de Moçambique** (FRELIMO)/Mozambique Liberation Front in Mozambique, so that by the end of July 1974, Spinola could announce the "immediate recognition" of the right to independence of the peoples of the three African territories. The secretary-general of the **United Nations**, Kurt Waldheim, then visited Portugal and gave the full backing of the world body to the new Portuguese policy toward its African colonies. Portugal reaffirmed its readiness to grant independence to Guinea Bissau, Cape Verde, Mozambique, Angola, and Sao Tome and Principe. Moreover, Portuguese troops were given orders to fight alongside the nationalist guerrillas, should the white settlers attempt to seize power.

In September 1974, a confrontation developed in Portugal between moderates and left-wing army officers; Spinola's provisional government therefore banned the extreme right-wing organization, the Portuguese Nationalist Party (PNP), as signs increased of a potential right-wing countercoup. The Left then forced Spinola to ban a planned demonstration of the so-called silent majority. Spinola thereupon resigned, to be replaced by General Francisco Costa Gomes, the chief of staff of the Armed Forces, as president. Spinola had played a crucial role in persuading Portugal to abandon its military efforts to hold on to its African colonies, presiding over the vital six-month period in which Portugal accepted the end of its African empire.

SUDAN. Since independence in 1956, Sudan has suffered from civil war between the dominant Arabicized and Muslim peoples of the North and the black non-Muslim peoples of the South, though this war is divided between the first period, from 1955–1972, and a new phase, which began in 1983/1984 and continued into the 21st century. The underlying causes of this war are threefold: historical, with the North viewing the South as a source of slaves; religious, with the North being overwhelmingly Muslim, and the South Christian or other African religions; and racial, a division between the Arab or Arabicized peoples of the North and the black Nilotic peoples of the South.

Under the British administration from 1898 to 1956, the peoples of the North and South were kept largely separated; indeed, during the 1920s, **Great Britain** considered detaching southern Sudan from the whole and integrating it into an East African Federation based upon Kenya. The civil war, which broke out after independence in 1956, was occasioned by southern fears of northern dominance. Prior to 1956, as independence approached, there was growing resentment in the South at the prospect of control from Khartoum and following the coup of 1958 by General Ibrahim Abboud, his government introduced new measures whose object was to spread Islam and the Arab language—these were opposed in the South. The government then increased southern fears by giving civil service and other posts in the South to northerners while education in the South, which had been conducted in English by Christian missionaries, was henceforth to be conducted in Arabic and geared toward Islam. A strike in southern schools in 1962 saw many students flee into neighboring countries.

The Formation of Anya-Nya

Some 500 former soldiers of Equatoria Province (the most southerly province of Sudan) formed the **Anya-Nya** movement, whose original objective was guerrilla opposition to northern domination. Its first leader, Emidio Tafeng, invented the name Anya-Nya, which means snake poison. During 1962–1964, foreign Christian missions were expelled from the South, and in September 1962, the Anya-Nya led a rebellion in eastern Nile Province. The Anya-Nya now established training camps in **Uganda** and **Zaire**, and by the end of 1964, Anya-Nya members numbered 2,000. By this time also the greater part of the Sudan army had been moved to the South of the country to deal with the rebellion. Between 1965 and 1969, a series of coalition governments ruled Sudan: amnesties were offered to the rebels, and several North–South conferences were held, but these did not come up with a solution and the war, which at this stage was a low intensity affair, continued. The main victims of the war were the peasant farmers, many of whom became refugees. By 1968, the Anya-Nya had approximately 10,000 members and called themselves the Anya-Nya Armed Forces (ANAF) but, though they had established a revolutionary government, they did not appear to have any thought-out policies for the future. By 1969, the Khartoum government was taking the rebellion sufficiently seriously to use the air force to attack rebel hideouts in the bush while destroying villages in rebel areas to create large numbers of **refugees**.

Nimeiri Comes to Power

On 25 May 1969, Colonel **Gaafar Mohammed Nimeiri** and a group of young army officers mounted a coup and seized power. In the South, the war became more intense and in October 1970 there was heavy fighting, with Anya-Nya forces attacking convoys and destroying bridges; the government retaliated by launching a major offensive. Following the coup attempt against his government of 19–21 July 1971, Nimeiri took far greater powers and made the Sudan Socialist Union (SSU) the country's sole political party. In the South, Major General **Joseph Lagu** replaced Tafeng as leader of Anya-Nya. Lagu then entered into secret peace talks with Nimeiri. Meanwhile 20,000 soldiers of the Sudan army (two-thirds) were committed to the war in the South: Egyptian pilots were flying MiG 21s for the government, while Israel was accused of aiding the Anya-Nya. It was Nimeiri's achievement to bring this first civil war, which had lasted on and off for 17 years, to a close.

By 1972 the Anya-Nya had come to represent the black South, which was deeply suspicious and resentful of the Arab/Muslim North. On 27 March 1972, the Addis Ababa Agreement was reached between the government of Nimeiri and Joseph Lagu and the Anya-Nya. Under its terms the three southern provinces—Bahr al-Ghazal, Equatoria, and Nile—were to be given regional autonomy with a legislative assembly, an executive, and a president who would be national vice-president. Southerners were to be given jobs, especially in the police and army. At the time of the ceasefire, about 12,000 Anya-Nya came out of the bush; half of them were to join the army, and Lagu became the commanding officer in the South. The peace worked for a time. Nimeiri agreed that Sudan should not become an Islamic republic and the South gave up its aim of secession. Nimeiri then called an international conference in Khartoum to help rehabilitate the South and resettle an estimated 250,000 refugees.

During this first civil war (1955–72), an estimated 500,000 people died, mainly as a result of starvation and disease. During the year following the Addis Ababa Agreement, 1,190,000 displaced persons emerged from the bush or exile to return to their homes in the South.

Their resettlement was assisted by the **United Nations** and its agencies and various non-governmental organizations (NGOs) with approximately $20 million in aid. During 1973, 6,000 Anya-Nya were admitted into the army and a further 9,000 returned to their villages, while Nimeiri was given a hero's welcome in the South.

The Second Civil War

By 1983, 10 years after his triumphant visit to the South as the peacemaker, Nimeiri was deeply unpopular, his power visibly on the wane. In order to bolster his position, he began to make concessions to the Islamic fundamentalists who did not wish to maintain the 1972 agreement with the South. Instead, the fundamentalists demanded that Sudan should become an Islamic state and that Sharia law should be extended to the South. In September 1983, after the South had been divided into three separate regions, each with its own governor and assembly and Sharia law had been introduced, the civil war resumed. This time the rebels renamed themselves, the **Sudan People's Liberation Movement** (SPLM) and their armed forces the **Sudan People's Liberation Army** (SPLA).

The SPLA embarked upon guerrilla warfare, threatening both towns and communications, and its disruptive tactics prevented the distribution of food and led to famine, as well as creating new waves of refugees who fled across the borders into neighboring countries. Opposition to Nimeiri mounted through 1984, while the application of Sharia law in the South created great resentment. Egypt protested at the severity of the Sharia punishments. In September 1984, under international pressure and after several abortive coup attempts, Nimeiri lifted the state of emergency, rescinded the division of the South into three regions, and removed the application of Sharia law as far as the South was concerned. However, his moves came too late to stop the developing war and by March 1985, the SPLA had won control of large areas in the South.

On 6 April 1985, the minister of defense, General Abdel Rahman Suwar al-Dahab, ousted Nimeiri from power in a successful coup. The new government then offered the South three seats on the Interim Council for a 12-month period before a return to self-rule. The new government did not rescind Sharia law, however, with the result that the war continued while the state of famine in the South grew worse. In the elections of April 1986, the Umma Party of **Sadiq al-Mahdi** won 99 of 264 seats and he became prime minister of a coalition government. Voting for the 37 southern seats was suspended because of the continuing military activities of the rebels. **John Garang**, the new leader of the SPLA, had already met Sadiq in Addis Ababa on 31 July 1985, but their meeting produced no solution.

The root of the conflict was the determination of the Muslim North to impose Sharia law upon the non-Muslim South. Ever since the rise of the Mahdi in Sudan during the 1880s, the North had been deeply affected by fundamentalist Islamic influences and though Sadiq al-Mahdi was willing to compromise, he was also a direct descendant of the Mahdi and so found himself torn between his wish to solve the political problem and his desire to preside over an Islamic state.

By 1986, the war had taken on a more international dimension, with **Ethiopia** supporting the SPLA in the South while Sudan was supporting the secessionist Eritreans in the North. Sudan, by this time, was deeply in debt to the tune of $18 billion and subject to international pressures to end the war. Yet the war increased in intensity during 1987 and in April of that year, in one of its worst incidents, 1,000 Dinka people were massacred near el-Dhaein in Darfur Province. Sadiq now included members of the National Islamic Front (NIF) in his government, and this served to frighten the South further as to the North's intentions.

Through 1988 a principal factor operating in the South was starvation, and international **relief agencies** were often unable to reach those most in need. Sadiq was re-elected in April and his government then proposed that punishments under Sharia law should be made more severe. By late 1988, an estimated one million displaced people from the South had moved into camps immediately south of Khartoum, while the SPLA attacked food relief convoys. The year was characterized by endless political maneuvering, but no breakthrough was achieved; the NIF adopted the slogan "No peace without Islam." By the end of the year some 250,000 people had died of starvation, since neither the government nor the SPLA would permit food to be taken to those in need. At the beginning of 1989 the SPLA, numbering possibly as many as 40,000, mainly Dinka, controlled the greater part of the South, while government forces were restricted to three major towns and a number of small garrisons.

An increasingly chaotic political situation in Khartoum was brought to an end in June 1989 when the military carried out a successful coup and the "National Movement for Correcting the Situation" under Brigadier **Omar Hassan al-Bashir** suspended the constitution, and dissolved Parliament and all political parties. Bashir became minister of defense and chief of staff. By this time the war was costing a virtually bankrupt government in Khartoum about $1 million a day. As head of the Ansar sect, Sadiq had been unable to abolish Sharia law. Bashir held talks with Garang but it soon became clear that he too was a prisoner of the fundamentalists and would do nothing about Sharia law, which remained at the heart of the South's grievances. The United Nations estimated that by the end of 1989, 500,000 people had died since the resumption of the civil war in 1983. Clashes between Muslim tribesmen and non-Muslim Shilluk resulted in a massacre of 600 early in 1990. By that time Juba, the capital of the South, had an estimated population of 300,000 of whom 200,000 were refugees. During 1991 and 1992 the war continued while periodic proposals for cease-fires or talks were advanced, though none brought any concrete results.

Outside Sudan, the tragedy of this war in southern Sudan was largely ignored by the international community and no serious attempts to halt it were mounted. By 1992, seven million Sudanese suffered from food shortages and three million were either refugees or displaced within the country, while there were constant revelations by Amnesty International, Africa Watch, and other organizations of violations of human rights. During 1993, talks were held in Abuja, **Nigeria**, and Nairobi, Kenya, but they proved abortive. In May 1993, the United Nations pinpointed 1.5 million people in the South who required food aid, of whom 600,000 were by then wholly dependent upon UN supplies. In October 1993, the military Revolutionary Command Council (RCC) dissolved itself and Sudan reverted to civilian rule with Bashir now assuming the presidency. The year also witnessed fierce faction fighting among the rebels themselves, and this produced a new exodus of refugees into Uganda.

In February 1994, the Khartoum government launched a massive military operation against the SPLA. At the same time, the United Nations made an urgent appeal for humanitarian aid to meet the needs of another 100,000 displaced people. Peace talks were held in Nairobi in March and May 1994, but again produced no results, while the plight of the refugees and homeless steadily deteriorated. The war continued at a lower level of intensity during 1995 and made very few international headlines, though in July the London-based Africa Rights group accused the government of undertaking a campaign of genocide against the Nuba people in Kordofan Province. Sudan accused Uganda of assisting the SPLA in the South, while Uganda made a counter-accusation that Khartoum was assisting Christian fundamentalist rebels in northern Uganda and suggested that Israel was involved as well. Renewed fighting in January 1997 resulted in a new wave of refugees crossing into the western districts of Ethiopia; the **United Nations High Commissioner for Refugees** (UNHCR) reported 4,000 refugees at Asosa on the border, with another 15,000 waiting to cross the border "in a desperate state of famine." On 13 January, President Bashir called for a Jihad against the enemies of Islam, following reports that the SPLA (estimated then at 30,000 in strength) had captured Kurmuk and Qaissan, 600 kilometers southeast of Khartoum, and was threatening the Damazin Power Station which supplies the capital. These rebel gains coincided with the new threat posed by the alliance between the SPLA and the Northern Democratic Alliance (NDA) based in **Eritrea**. This had become effective in December 1996 when Sadiq al-Mahdi arrived as an exile in Eritrea. The government accused Ethiopia of attacking Kurmuk and Qaissan, although this was denied in Addis Ababa; nonetheless, Khartoum called for an emergency meeting of the UN Security Council to discuss the question.

The war brought a crisis to Khartoum at the beginning of 1997. On 14 January, Khartoum University was closed so that students could "join the army and fight Ethiopian aggression." On 17 January the town of Mabam in southern Blue Nile Province fell to the rebels, and on 21 January Garang claimed that SPLA troops had killed 300 government soldiers at Abu Shameina, south of the Damazin Dam, and a further 150 at al-Keili. The government denied these claims. President Bashir alleged that rebels were massing along the Ugandan border and called upon Uganda to prevent them from launching attacks from Uganda; on 26 January government troops attacked a rebel base near the Uganda border. Then, on 27 January, Uganda's President **Yoweri Museveni** asked the **Organization of African Unity** (OAU) to declare the Sudanese civil war a colonial conflict, so as to permit other African countries to provide material support to the rebels. During February, the government arrested dozens of suspected saboteurs and four opposition leaders for alleged complicity in the SPLA January offensive. On 19 February, **Nelson Mandela**, who had already met John Garang in December 1996, announced that he was to hold talks with President Bashir in an effort to mediate the war. At the same time, Shaikh Zaid Bin Sultan al-Nahajan of the United Arab Emirates offered to mediate between Sudan and the Eritrean-based National Democratic Alliance (NDA).

In renewed fighting during March, the SPLA claimed to have taken two government-held towns on the Uganda border—Kaya and Gumali—and heavy fighting took place between government troops and rebels supported by Ugandans. In mid-March the SPLA claimed to have captured Yei, including taking 1,000 government troops prisoner as well as capturing 15 tanks and four artillery pieces. On the Eritrean border, the government was more successful and recaptured the strategic town of Chali from the NDA, although two days later the NDA claimed to have taken it back again. There were heavy casualties on both sides. On 25 March, the SPLA claimed it had gained control of the whole southern border and had expelled government forces from the White Nile and Equatoria states. During April 1997, both the NDA in the northeast and the SPLA in the South, claimed victories against the government. Claims and counterclaims by both sides presented a confusing picture, though overall it seemed plain that the government was very much on the defensive.

The government lodged a protest with the United Nations that both Eritrea and Uganda had sent troops to fight in Sudan. On 22 April, Uganda admitted that its forces had entered southern Sudan. In the northeast the NDA was forced to retreat from Aqiq, which it had taken earlier in the month. After announcing a victory over Ugandan forces in the South, with more than 300 soldiers killed and several tanks destroyed, the government signed a peace agreement (21 April) with six southern factions which had broken from the SPLA. There would be a referendum on self-determination for the South after four years, the suspension of legislation imposing Sharia law on the South, and an amnesty for members of the six groups. These were: South Sudan Independence Movement (SSIM); Bahr al-Ghazal group of the SPLA; Bor group; Equatoria Defense Force;

Independence Movement; United Sudanese African Parties. John Garang described the agreement as "a sham."

New Peace Negotiations

On 10 May 1997, Presidents Bashir and Museveni met in Nairobi under the chairmanship of Kenya's President Daniel arap Moi in an attempt at reconciliation and "to start a new chapter of cooperation." Moi proposed that a summit of the Inter-governmental Authority on Development (IGAD), which covers Djibouti, Eritrea, Kenya, Ethiopia, **Somalia**, Sudan, and Uganda, should act as a forum. Meanwhile, fighting continued throughout May with the government acknowledging the loss of Rumbek. At the end of May the Khartoum daily *Alwan* reported a buildup of unidentified troops near the Eritrean–Ethiopian border. Tensions with Eritrea increased in June and the Khartoum government ordered a "maximum state of mobilization" (7 June). A plot to blow up the National Assembly was attributed to a Sudanese national—Adil Mahjub—who was reputedly backed by Eritrea and Egypt, although both countries denied any involvement. On 15 June the SPLA announced the capture of Yirol, northwest of Juba, and was reported to have killed many of the 1,000-strong garrison: this cut off government access to Juba. On 23 June the Eritrean government accused Sudan of plotting to assassinate President **Issayas Afewerke**. On 9 July 1997, the government accepted a framework for peace negotiations at the annual IGAD summit. President Bashir, however, said that the framework was not binding; Garang said he would not negotiate unless the framework was binding on both sides. The IGAD Declaration included the separation of religion and the state, the principle of self-determination for the largely non-Muslim South of Sudan, and the recognition of the country as multiethnic. Until this point the Khartoum government had argued that such a declaration threatened the country's sovereignty. In the meantime, the SPLA was making further military advances and had opened a new front in Upper Nile State.

The quarrel between Sudan and Eritrea grew worse during July 1997, with each side accusing the other of violations of borders, assassination attempts, and assorted misdemeanors. President Bashir met with President Mandela in Pretoria on 12 August, when they both called for a ceasefire in Sudan. On 19 August Mandela announced he would host direct talks between Bashir and Garang on 26 August, but in the event, Garang did not turn up. Meanwhile, on 7 August, President Bashir had sworn in the leader of the South Sudan Independence Movement (SSIM) as chairman of the newly established Southern States' Coordination Council. His choice of the SSIM among the six southern breakaway groups was most calculated to anger the SPLA. Despite these various maneuvers, peace talks between government and SPLA representatives opened in Nairobi, Kenya, on 28 October, under the aegis of IGAD and as a result of earlier **mediation** attempts by **South Africa**'s President Mandela. The talks were chaired by Kenyan Foreign Affairs Minister Kalonzo Musyoka. The Sudanese government delegation was led by External Relations Minister Ali Uthman Muhammad Taha, though it was not clear whether John Garang would take part. Fighting, meanwhile, continued through the month with the SPLA claiming a number of victories. The peace talks were adjourned on 11 November without having achieved any progress. They resumed in April 1998. Garang blamed the government, which had rejected the SPLM claim for full statehood.

On 10 December 1997, U.S. Secretary of State Madeleine Albright held a meeting in Kampala, Uganda, with members of the NDA and John Garang of the SPLA after the United States had imposed economic sanctions on Sudan in November for its alleged support of terrorist activities and bad human rights record. The government of Sudan, meanwhile, had held gubernatorial elections in 10 southern states under the agreement with the six breakaway factions; the southern states were to be administered by former rebel Riek Machar over a four-year period with the assistance of 10 elected governors. Claims by the government that large numbers of the SPLA had surrendered during January 1998 were countered by SPLA claims of further victories. There were no signs through 1998 and into 1999 that the war would end or that any proposed peace meetings would be likely to resolve the fundamental differences which divide North and South.

The Long Road to Peace

During 1999 both Egypt and Libya tried to bring about a reconciliation between the Sudan government of al-Bashir and SPLA leader John Garang, but without success. Speaking in Geneva at the UN

Human Rights Commission in March, Garang stated that the SPLA mission was to end the civil war and achieve a peace by the creation of two separate but confederal states. A major problem that divided North and South was the new Islamic constitution that had passed into law that January. Military setbacks in the South led the president to dismiss the minister of defense, the army commander, and his senior staff. The new defense minister was General Abd al-Rahman Sior al-Khatim. The war continued unabated through 2000 and a number of towns and military garrisons changed hands, while both sides sustained substantial casualties. The Inter-Governmental Authority for Development held meetings in February, May, and December, trying to reconcile the Sudan government and the SPLA but without success: the government wanted to maintain Sharia law, the SPLA insisted on the separation of church and state. As in 2000, IGAD worked through 2001, advocating self-determination for the South but with no more success. In August the government established a ministerial committee to pursue an end to the fighting and review the Libyan–Egyptian peace initiative that insisted upon Sudanese unity. The fighting, however, continued. In February UNICEF lifted 2,800 demobilized southern **child soldiers** from the frontline. Government operations against the SPLA in the Nuba mountains during May led to the deaths and displacement of civilians, while fighting in Bahr al-Ghazal led to the displacement of 30,000 people. The Khartoum government was infuriated when the U.S. allocated $10 million to the SPLA. Oil and its ultimate control was a key issue in any settlement proposals.

2002: A New Peace Momentum

Intense diplomatic activity throughout 2002 brought Sudan appreciably closer to a peace agreement between North and South. In January Britain and Norway held talks with President al-Bashir and SPLA leader John Garang. Later, the U.S. presidential envoy to Sudan, John Danforth, persuaded the two sides to agree on a six-month ceasefire in the Nuba mountains. The agreement was signed in Switzerland and endorsed by the **African Union** (AU). IGAD, Libya, and Egypt maintained pressure upon Khartoum and the SPLA. The U.S. envisaged two parallel systems for Sudan—one for the predominantly Muslim North and another for the non-Muslim South. Despite these talks and negotiations, the fighting continued, and in June the SPLA captured Kapota in Equatoria, some 50 kilometers from the Kenyan border. This represented a major battlefield triumph for the SPLA. Also in June, as a response to American, British, Norwegian, and European Union (EU) pressures, negotiations between the government and SPLM under IGAD auspices were opened in Machakos, Kenya. The talks led to the signing on 20 July of a memorandum that offered the South self-determination and freedom from Sharia law. Following a ceasefire, the accord offered the South the option of seceding after a six-year transitional period. In July President al-Bashir went to Uganda where he met Garang for the first time. Egypt, however, was unhappy with the accord since it was opposed to the possible breakup of Sudan.

However, the peace process was suspended following the capture of Torit by the SPLA on 30 August. Torit had formerly served as SPLA headquarters until 1992 when it fell to government forces. Its repossession by SPLA forces threatened Juba, the capital of the South, which was a government stronghold. The SPLA had used tanks and heavy artillery in the capture of Torit, demonstrating that it was militarily more powerful than just a guerrilla army. Government forces recaptured Torit in early October. Increasing its pressures for peace, in October U.S. President George W. Bush signed the Sudan Peace Act, which provided for economic sanctions against Sudan and U.S. financial assistance to the SPLA, if a peace agreement had not been signed by March 2003. A temporary ceasefire was then agreed; it was to last as long as the talks in Machakos continued. Little progress was made to the end of the year, but in January 2003, negotiations were renewed in Kenya. Discussions focused upon power sharing, whether Sharia law should be imposed in Khartoum, and the question of wealth sharing or how to divide oil revenues. The negotiations were assisted by the International Monetary Fund, the World Bank, and the EU. These slow moves toward full agreement were given a boost when the U.S. refrained from applying sanctions to Sudan, as it had threatened, and when the UN Human Rights Commission did not censure the government for its record. Even so, by July the peace process appeared to be stalling again but was given a new incentive to continue when the U.S. Congress passed the Sudan Peace Act and allocated $180 million for humanitarian and development programs.

In September, the two sides signed a security framework agreement under which the government would scale back its forces in the South from 100,000 to 12,000 and the SPLA would withdraw its forces from the North. This troop redeployment was to be completed within 30 months of a full peace agreement.

Although the **Darfur** crisis overshadowed the peace process throughout 2004, a number of protocols were agreed at Naivasha in January and May. These covered wealth sharing (oil revenues were to be shared equally between North and South); a referendum was to be held on the status of Abyei, the Nuba Mountains and southern Blue Nile province, which were in the North but occupied by SPLA forces; security; and Sharia law in Khartoum, which would not apply to Christians or other non-Muslims. A two-thirds majority would be required to change the constitution of southern Sudan. A number of issues remained to be resolved and meetings in Kenya continued to the end of the year. The final peace accord was signed on 9 January 2005 in Nairobi, when the SPLM/SPLA leader John Garang and the first vice-president, Ali Osman Muhammad Taha, signed a peace agreement that brought to an end the 21-year civil war, Africa's longest, which had caused two million deaths and displaced four million people. It was the climax to 30 months of intense negotiations. The agreement was signed in the presence of President al-Bashir, 11 other African heads of state, and the U.S. Secretary of State Colin Powell. The signing marked the beginning of a six-month "pre-interim" period during which a new constitution would be prepared to form a transitional government in Khartoum and a separate administration in the South. A six-year transitional period would begin in July and national elections would be held before the third year. At the end of the six-year period, the South could vote on whether or not to secede. The peace agreement was favorably endorsed in concrete terms by the international community on 12 April, when donors meeting in Oslo pledged $4.5 billion in **aid**.

Aftermath

The peace suffered a potentially disastrous setback when, on 30 July, John Garang, who had been sworn in as first vice-president on 9 July, was killed in a helicopter crash. The news of his death sparked serious rioting in Khartoum and other cities. In his inaugural speech on 9 July, as first vice-president, Garang had said that peace in Sudan had become "a reality" and called for consensus. Garang's deputy, Salva Kiir Mayerdit, assumed the leadership of the SPLM and on 11 August was sworn in as Garang's successor. A new government of national unity was formed on 20 September. On 21 October Mayerdit announced the formation of the first cabinet of the autonomous region of South Sudan.

SUDAN PEOPLE'S LIBERATION MOVEMENT (SPLM)/SUDAN PEOPLE'S LIBERATION ARMY (SPLA). The Sudan People's Liberation Movement with its military wing (the two terms SPLM and SPLA are often used interchangeably) emerged from a split in **Anya-Nya II** in November 1983. Colonel **John Garang**, who became the leader of the SPLM, had defected from the Sudanese army after being sent by President **Gaafar Nimeiri** to quell an incipient army revolt at Bor; instead he led the rebels to join the Anya-Nya. When he first created the SPLM, Garang was not so much a secessionist as a reformer who demanded a better deal for the South. He demanded an end to Sharia law, an end to French **aid** in **Sudan** (**France** was responsible for the Jonglei Canal development, which was opposed in the South since it split the territory in two), and an end to the proposed oil pipeline project by Chevron, which was seen in the South as a means of depriving it of its oil for the benefit of the North. Attempts at reconciliation between North and South over the period 1983–1985 failed, and the SPLM emerged as the main opponent of the Khartoum government.

Garang now came to view the SPLM as a national liberation movement opposed to a corrupt and oppressive government though not, as yet, as a secessionist movement. The two main grievances advanced by the SPLM were the imposition of Sharia law on the non-Muslim South and the exploitation of the South's resources for the benefit of the North. In the mid-1980s, SPLA activity was mainly confined to the center of Bahr al-Ghazal and eastern Upper Nile near the Ethiopian border. The SPLA did not control the whole of the South, and much of Equatoria Province (the southernmost part of the country) remained outside the rebellion since its people, traditionally, were hostile to the Dinka people to the north of them and the Dinka were

Garang's principal supporters. When Nimeiri was overthrown in April 1985, the SPLM refused to take part in the new administration. The administration proceeded to provide logistical support to the fractured Anya-Nya II in order to widen the gap between it and the SPLA. Libya, which had been backing the SPLA, now withdrew its support, but **Ethiopia** continued to provide the SPLA with assistance. In October 1985, Garang said the ideology of the SPLA was "Sudanism and Nationalism" and he insisted that he wanted national unity based upon cultural diversity.

Negotiations between the SPLM and the National Alliance for Salvation (the government) were attempted during 1986, and the Koka Dam Declaration of March 1986 set forth the conditions under which the SPLM would be prepared to take part in a national conference. The SPLM refused to recognize the validity of the 1986 elections; instead, it intensified its military campaign in the South, now aiming to control Equatoria Province and cut off its capital, Juba. Garang and **Sadiq al-Mahdi** held talks in Ethiopia during July 1986 and agreed to maintain contact, but they came to no agreement to end the war. The SPLA increased the tempo of the fighting through 1988, and though government forces held Juba, Torit, and Bor with garrisons, Garang claimed they were confined to these towns and could not move more than 5 kilometers from them. During the course of 1988, the population of Juba was swelled by the influx of 200,000 refugees. The longer the war lasted the more intractable both sides became. The SPLA continued the war through the 1990s and by 1997–1998 appeared to have control over wide areas of the South, although the situation was fluid and towns or regions changed hands with frequency. The SPLA remained a formidable force through to 2005 and the peace that brought an end to the long civil war.

– T –

TAMBO, OLIVER REGINALD (1917–93). Oliver Tambo was born on 27 October 1917, in Pondoland, **South Africa**, and was educated at Fort Hare University from 1938 to 1941 when he obtained a B.Sc. He taught at St. Peter's Sunday School from 1943 to 1947 but in the latter year he turned to law and became an articled clerk in a solicitor's firm. In 1952, with his friend **Nelson Mandela**, he established the first African legal partnership in Johannesburg. Tambo was a founding member of the **African National Congress** (ANC) Youth League in 1944; he became its national secretary and then national vice president before being elected to the ANC executive in 1949. In 1952 Tambo was banned from attending public meetings for two years under the terms of the Suppression of Communism Act. He was secretary-general of the ANC from 1955 to 1958 when he became deputy president general. In 1956, by which time he had become a marked man as far as the authorities were concerned, he was arrested and charged with treason, but the case was dropped. On 28 March 1960, a week after the Sharpeville Massacre and just before Parliament declared a state of emergency, by agreement with the ANC executive, Tambo left South Africa in order to lead the anti-apartheid struggle from abroad. He was not to return to South Africa for 30 years.

In 1965, Tambo set up ANC headquarters in Morogoro, Tanzania. He spent half his time on the move throughout the world propagating the ANC anti-apartheid cause. On the death of Chief Albert Luthuli (21 July 1967), Tambo became the acting president of the ANC and for the next 20 years he publicized the ANC, addressed anti-apartheid meetings, raised funds, and kept the international ANC alive. From 1987 onward, working from the ANC headquarters in Lusaka, Zambia, Tambo held talks with white liberals and businessmen from South Africa. Tambo always insisted that the ANC, though revolutionary, should be seen to have clean hands.

On 9 August 1989, Tambo suffered his third stroke, and went for prolonged treatment to a clinic in Stockholm. He finally returned to South Africa on 13 December 1990 to open the first ANC conference in the country in 30 years. At the 48th National Conference in Durban in July 1991, Tambo was made honorary national chairman of the ANC while Nelson Mandela assumed the presidency. He died of a final stroke on 24 April 1993.

TANGANYIKA CONCESSIONS (TANKS). In the convoluted story of the **Congo** crisis (1960–65), the influence of big business was never far from the action. The mining companies—Tanganyika Concessions (TANKS) and its Belgian-associated company Union

Minière du Haut-Congo—were deeply involved in the Congo, mainly in Katanga Province, and played an influential role behind the scenes in support of the right-wing forces at work in the country.

Tanganyika Concessions had been formed by Sir Robert Williams in 1899 to develop a terminus on the southern extremity of Lake Tanganyika for Rhodes's Cape to Cairo railway and to provide a steamer service on the lake. TANKS was granted a 2,000-square-mile mineral concession by the British South Africa Company in Northern Rhodesia (now Zambia), and it was Williams's agent, George Grey, who discovered the copper deposits first at Kansanshi, in what became the Zambian Copperbelt, and then in Katanga. Williams then obtained a concession from King Leopold of the Belgians to explore mineral deposits in Katanga. In 1906 Union Minière du Haut-Congo was formed by TANKS and its Belgian associates. Williams also obtained a concession from the Portuguese government for the construction of a railway through **Angola** to Katanga—what eventually became the **Benguela Railway**. In the 1930s TANKS set up companies in Kenya and **Uganda**. In 1950 TANKS moved its domicile from London to Salisbury (Harare) and in 1964 from Salisbury to Nassau, Bahamas.

Williams was the first person to realize the significance of the Katanga copper deposits and was a cofounder of the exploiting company, Union Minière du Haut-Congo. He also found that Katanga was a center of conflicting economic, financial, and political interests, which it remained from the end of the Scramble for Africa through to the history of modern **Zaire**. Up to and after the Congo crisis of 1960–1965, TANKS held a 17.6 percent share in Union Minière du Haut-Congo. Just how much influence these companies exerted during the Congo crisis will probably never be known; it was certainly extensive and antagonistic to African nationalist aspirations.

TAYLOR, CHARLES (1948–). Over Christmas 1989, Charles Taylor launched a revolt against **Samuel Doe**, president of **Liberia**, with an original force of 200 men; by mid-1990, he had gained control of the better part of the country and had effectively brought an end to Doe's rule. Of mixed parentage—his father was an American—Charles Taylor was born in 1948. In the 1970s he went to the **United States** where he attended Bentley College in Waltham, Massachusetts. In 1980 Taylor returned to Liberia as part of a delegation representing the 30,000 U.S.-based Liberians. Shortly after his return (Taylor had been invited by President William R. Tolbert of Liberia to lead the delegation back to Liberia in order to witness moves toward democracy), he said publicly that he had been misled as to the true state of the country. At this time he appeared to support the main opposition party, the Movement for Justice in Africa (MOJA). A few weeks later Samuel Doe seized power in a coup and he made Taylor managing director of the General Services Agency, which was the government procurement agency.

In 1984, Taylor left Liberia for the United States; he was then accused of defrauding the General Services Agency of $900,000. In the United States, Taylor was arrested and was to be extradited to Liberia when he broke from prison, left the United States, and returned to Africa. Taylor obtained backing from Burkina Faso and Libya for his coming confrontation with Doe and established his base in **Côte d'Ivoire** with the support of President Felix Houphouet-Boigny. He then established the **National Patriotic Front of Liberia** (NPFL).

On 24 December 1989, Taylor crossed the border from Côte d'Ivoire into Liberia and launched his revolt with 200 men. He proved to be an apt general and charismatic leader and within months his guerrilla force had increased to 2,000. By June 1990, despite the defection of **Prince Yormie Johnson**, Taylor had reached Monrovia and was fighting his way through the suburbs; he then controlled most of the country. On 27 July 1990, Taylor announced that Doe's government had been dissolved and that he was replacing it with a National Patriotic Assembly of Reconstruction with himself as president. At this stage the **Economic Community of West African States** (ECOWAS) intervened in Liberia and created its own military force, the **Economic Community Monitoring Group** (ECOMOG), to do so; in August ECOMOG occupied Monrovia. Taylor was opposed to the ECOWAS intervention but was unable to prevent it. Over the four-year period (1990–1994) that followed, Taylor was to be a reluctant signatory to various ceasefire agreements and an on-off negotiator with ECOWAS and the other factions that had emerged. Doe himself had been killed on 10 September 1990. Taylor refused to attend the All-Liberia Conference in Monrovia on 15 March 1991, and later that month his NPFL invaded **Sierra Leone** in support of dissident forces there. This led the **Organization of African Unity (OAU)** to oppose Taylor's ambitions.

Taylor, whose opposition had done more than anything else to bring down the Doe regime, was reluctant to give up his arms and disband his forces in order to take part in a peace process from which he might not emerge as national leader. Various attempts were made during 1992 to persuade Taylor to join the peace process, but these he constantly resisted; instead, he was in conflict both with the ECOMOG forces and also those loyal to former President Doe, and fierce fighting took place. Taylor continued to oppose the peace process during 1993 and would not approve the distribution of ministerial jobs in an interim government. Although in July 1994, Taylor claimed that his NPFL had been attacked by ECOMOG, nonetheless in August he agreed with the other warring factions to cease hostilities and cooperate with ECOMOG. Even so, further fighting continued spasmodically into 1995 with the NPFL opposed to the Liberia Peace Council; in July 1995, the NPFL was accused of importing **arms** and carrying out raids into Guinea. At the end of this year, however, Taylor became one of six members of the Council of State. In 1996 Taylor continued to be at odds with the peace and reconciliation process (only, it would seem, because he was maneuvering to make sure he took the presidency) and his maneuvers paid off. When elections were finally held in Liberia during July 1997, Taylor won the presidential polls with 70 percent of the votes cast. The elections, which saw 65 percent of the population vote for Taylor, were declared free and fair by international observers and the elevation of Taylor to the presidency finally brought the long civil war and its dangerous aftermath to an end. As Liberians said of Taylor's victory: "He who spoil it, let him fix it."

Once in power, Taylor did not honor the peace agreement but packed the administration with his supporters. His continued involvement in the war in Sierra Leone in which he supported the rebel Revolutionary United Front (RUF) led to international condemnation. By October 1999, however, the domestic political situation appeared sufficiently stable to allow the remaining ECOMOG forces to be withdrawn from Liberia. Taylor maintained a tight grip on power through 2000 while continuing to support the rebels in Sierra Leone and did so through 2001 as well. At the end of that year, Bishop Michael Francis accused Taylor's government of injustices and failing to uphold basic human rights. By 2002, growing opposition to Taylor threatened to plunge Liberia into a second civil war as the rebel Liberians United for Reconciliation and Democracy (LURD) began attacking government forces in the north of the country. Nonetheless, Taylor was still sufficiently in command of the situation that in September he was able to lift the state of emergency that he had imposed. But by April 2003, the LURD rebels had gained control of the greater part of Liberia and Taylor was further and fatally weakened in June when the UN-backed Special Court for Sierra Leone indicted Taylor for war crimes and accused him of "bearing the greatest responsibility for war crimes, crimes against humanity, and serious violations of international humanitarian law" during the 10-year civil war in Sierra Leone, during which he had backed the rebels. Taylor was attending peace talks in Accra, Ghana, when an arrest warrant for him was given to the police. He told delegates to the talks that he would "strongly consider" a government of national unity in which he was not a member. Then he left so as to escape arrest. In Monrovia his regime was on the point of collapse and on 11 August, Taylor formally resigned the presidency and fled to **Nigeria**.

On 31 May 2004, the Special Court for Sierra Leone ruled that Taylor should stand trial for war crimes and that his immunity as a former head of state did not apply because the court was international. In March 2006, the Liberian government requested Nigeria to extradite Taylor to Liberia to stand trial for war crimes. On 25 March President **Olusegun Obasanjo** announced that Nigeria would allow Taylor's extradition. On 28 March it was reported that Taylor had disappeared from his exile house in Calabar, but he was captured by the Nigerian police the next day near the Cameroon border. He was at once delivered to Monrovia and thence to Freetown in Sierra Leone. The Special Court in Sierra Leone asked the International Criminal Court (ICC) in The Hague to allow the trial to be held there for security reasons and this was agreed by the UN Security Council in June. Taylor first appeared before the ICC in The Hague in July 2006.

TIGRE PEOPLE'S LIBERATION FRONT (TPLF). The province of Tigre in **Ethiopia** had a long tradition of asserting its "independence" against the central government in Addis Ababa, often by means of guerrilla warfare. Following the downfall of **Haile Selassie** and his government, the Tigre People's Liberation Front was set up in 1975 with assistance from the **Eritrean Liberation Front** (ELF), which was already waging a war of secession against Addis Ababa. Since the province of Tigre lies between **Eritrea** and Addis Ababa and controls the line of communication between them, an alliance between the ELF and TPLF posed a major threat to the Ethiopian government. At first the TPLF was allied to the conservative Ethiopian Democratic Union (EDU), which also opposed the Marxist government of **Haile Mariam Mengistu** but, before long, the TPLF switched its support to the more radical **Eritrean People's Liberation Front** (EPLF), which emerged as the leading force in Eritrea after destroying the power of its rival, the ELF. The TPLF, meanwhile, was taken over by the young radicals and the EDU was eliminated in Tigre Province. The TPLF mounted its first major campaign against the government in 1979 and, following a four-month offensive in central and western Tigre, the Ethiopian government claimed, prematurely, to have eliminated the TPLF.

During 1980, the TPLF captured a number of towns and claimed to have gained control of the major part of Tigre Province. Its representatives in Khartoum claimed that 80,000 people had been displaced and that churches, schools, and mosques had been destroyed in government retaliation raids for TPLF successes. During 1981 and 1982, the TPLF again claimed to have mounted a number of successful actions against government forces and that it controlled 90 percent of the province. TPLF successes were due to a number of causes: the failure of the government to extend its re-education program to Tigre Province, demoralization among government troops, and the fact that the TPLF was working closely with the EPLF. In February 1983 the government launched a major offensive against the TPLF with some 50,000 troops; it dislodged its bases and cut its links with the EPLF to the north. Despite this, the TPLF claimed it had killed 4,000 government troops over a two-month period. The government launched a second major offensive against the TPLF in September 1983 but again failed to destroy it. Early in 1984, the TPLF claimed it had inflicted a further 5,000 casualties on the Ethiopian forces and taken another 1,000 prisoners. In April 1984, the TPLF entered into a cooperative agreement with the **Western Somali Liberation Front**

(WSLF). The year saw massive relief operations to counter famine in Ethiopia; during these, the TPLF captured Konem, the largest famine relief center in the country, to disrupt the distribution of supplies. Then, between October and December 1984, about 80,000 Tigre **refugees** crossed into **Sudan**.

In 1985, the government launched another major offensive against the TPLF and made considerable advances, in part because the TPLF did not receive backing from the EPLF, which claimed it had artificially created the refugees who had fled into Sudan, thus detracting from the help which the international community was providing for Eritrean refugees who were genuine. The war continued through the 1980s with the balance turning against the Ethiopian government, and in 1988 the TPLF was able to mount a major offensive to capture a number of towns on the vital (for the government) road to Asmera. On 27 February 1989, the Ethiopian garrison at Mekele, the Tigrayan capital, fell to the EPLF after the TPLF had blocked the Axum-Gondar road. In Khartoum on 1 March 1989, the TPLF claimed it had liberated all of Tigre from the forces of Mengistu's government.

By this time, the TPLF and the EPLF were again cooperating closely with each other. On 14 June 1989, the TPLF offered talks with the government, provided the EPLF was also invited to take part; the TPLF insisted that it did not intend to secede from Ethiopia (like the EPLF), but wanted political reforms to be carried out for the whole country. By this time Mengistu was entirely on the defensive and was forced to extend conscription in a last effort to raise fresh troops. It was clear the government was losing the war. Heavy fighting continued at the end of the year and into 1990. As the war reached a climax and victory came closer **Meles Zenawi**, the leader of the TPLF, decided to widen both his base and his appeal; therefore, in February 1989, he established the Ethiopian People's Revolutionary Democratic Front (EPRDF), which was to incorporate other organizations opposed to the government as well as the TPLF. As a result, the EPRDF claimed to represent the main anti-government forces apart from the EPLF and it put Zenawi in a position to take over as head of state, once Mengistu had been toppled. In January 1991 the EPRDF held its first congress, with Zenawi as its chairman; he jettisoned his earlier Marxist ideology and adopted instead a pragmatic approach to post-war reconstruction which would appeal to the international community. It was as leader of the EPRDF rather than the TPLF that Zenawi and his forces entered Addis Ababa in May 1991. The **United States** supported the EPRDF at this time so that it could restore order. Zenawi would shortly become president of Ethiopia.

TSHOMBE, MOISE (1919–69). Moise Tshombe, who was born on 10 November 1919, at Musumba in the Belgian Congo, became a key player in the disastrous civil war of 1960–1965. Tshombe came from a wealthy family and inherited a considerable business, but on its failure he turned to politics and served in the Katanga Provincial Council from 1951 to 1953. In 1959 Tshombe became president of the Confédération des Associations Katangaises (CONAKAT)/ Confederation of Katangese Associations; this party was supported by Tshombe's own tribe, the Lunda, who were also present in northern **Angola**, and by the Belgian mining group, Union Minière du Haut-Congo, which, together with **Tanganyika Concessions** (TANKS), controlled the copper mines.

With the approach of independence in 1960, Tshombe proposed that an independent Congo should consist of semi-autonomous provinces working together in a loose confederation, a solution that would have favored the mining companies. These and other confederal suggestions were rejected in favor of a centralized state as proposed by **Patrice Lumumba**. In the first national elections of May 1960, CONAKAT won only eight of 137 seats in the Congolese parliament. In Katanga Province, however, CONAKAT was the main party and won the provincial elections. Tshombe became the president of Katanga; then, two weeks after the independence of the **Republic of the Congo**, following the mutiny of the Force Publique on 11 July 1960, Tshombe declared Katanga an independent state.

After the murder of Lumumba, in which Tshombe was probably implicated, he negotiated briefly with President Joseph Kasavubu of the Congo to end the secession of Katanga, but the talks broke down. Tshombe was able to maintain his secession for three years and was supported in doing so by both Belgium and various financial and mining interests. Finally, in January 1963, **United Nations** forces invaded Katanga and defeated Tshombe's troops to reunite Katanga with the rest of the Congo. Tshombe fled to Spain.

In July 1964, President Kasavubu recalled him to act as prime minister and put down the Mulelist Revolt in eastern Congo. Tshombe was then dismissed in October 1965 (supposedly for using the services of white **mercenaries**) and he returned to Spain. In exile, Tshombe was generally reviled in Africa as a stooge of western interests and feared as a possible interventionist in the future. In June 1967, Tshombe was kidnapped while on a flight over the Mediterranean and taken to **Algeria** where he was imprisoned. Algeria would not hand him over to **Joseph-Désiré Mobutu**, who had meanwhile emerged as president of Congo, and he died of a heart attack on 30 June 1969, still in detention. Although he was accused of being a pawn of western commercial interests and was seen as a stooge of the West in Africa, in fact Tshombe was an able politician in his own right as well as being highly ambitious; had it not been for the United Nations' intervention, he might have made Katanga's secession more permanent. Had he done so, he would have deprived Congo (later **Zaire**) of its principal mineral wealth while enabling Katanga to be a relatively rich, viable state on its own.

– U –

UGANDA AND CIVIL WARS (1966–90). The state of civil war (or wars) in Uganda over the years 1966–1990 is hard to categorize. The first phase consisted of the destruction of the Kabaka of Buganda's power by Milton Obote. The second consisted of the brutalities and massacres carried out by **Idi Amin** in order to keep himself in power. The third phase was the war that led to his overthrow. The fourth phase was the civil war that resulted in the ouster of Obote for the second time (following his return to rule Uganda after the overthrow of Amin) and the assumption of power by **Yoweri Museveni**.

When Uganda became independent in 1962, a power struggle at once developed between the central, modernizing government of Prime Minister Milton Obote and the representatives of the conservative kingdoms, whose most important figure was the Kabaka of Buganda, Freddie Mutesa II. This confrontation between the Kabaka and the central government came to a head in 1966 when, in February of that year, Obote suspended the constitution and assumed full constitutional powers. In April 1966, Obote made himself president under a new constitution; the Lukiko (the Buganda Parliament) denounced the new constitution and then in May announced Buganda's secession from Uganda. Obote's response was to declare a state of emergency and send the army to arrest the Kabaka and his followers. After some stiff fighting, Obote emerged the victor, the Kabaka fled to England, and the old Ugandan system of loosely united kingdoms was brought to an end. Instead, Uganda had become a centralized republic.

The Years of Idi Amin

On 25 January 1971, Major General Idi Amin (who had commanded the army against the Kabaka in 1966) seized power in a coup he mounted while Obote was in Singapore attending the **Commonwealth** conference. Obote went into exile in Tanzania, whose President **Julius Nyerere** was a close friend and generally sympathetic to Obote's radical views. In July 1971, and again in September 1972, pro-Obote supporters crossed into Uganda from Tanzania in the hope of ousting Amin. They were repulsed on both occasions. As a result of these incursions and Nyerere's known support for Obote, a state of tension between Uganda and Tanzania developed and characterized the relations between the two countries through to the end of the 1970s and Amin's overthrow. In 1978 exiled Ugandans, supported by 10,000 Tanzanian troops, invaded Uganda and this time succeeded in bringing about Amin's downfall in April 1979. The period of Amin's rule (1971–79) was marked by the disappearance and murder of many prominent Ugandans who were seen as a threat to Amin. In addition, estimates suggest that 250,000 Ugandans were killed under Amin while many others fled the country. The fall of Amin led to a period of rapid changes of government: President Yusuf Lule was followed by President Godfrey Binaisa, who in turn was ousted in favor of a military commission headed by Brigadier David Oyite-Ojok.

Obote Returns

Obote returned to Uganda in May 1980 to lead his Uganda People's Congress (UPC) and in December 1980 he won the elections, taking 68 of 126 seats, although these results were widely regarded as having been rigged. Although 1981 and 1982 could not be described as years of civil war, there was much violence aimed at the government and many complaints of unruly behavior and indiscipline on the part of Obote's army. Violence against the government increased dramatically in 1983, and in the area north of Kampala, an estimated 100,000 **refugees** from escalating violence in the north found themselves targets for an army that was clearly out of control. By 1984, guerrillas opposed to the government were attacking targets ever closer to Kampala; and though the army launched a series of campaigns against these guerrillas, it was civilians in central Uganda who appeared to be the main targets (and victims) of army retaliatory activities. By early 1985, much of Uganda was in chaos; and while anti-government rebels were more and more in evidence and increasingly successful in attacking government targets, there was also a steady rise in the rate of government reprisals. The opponents now emerged as the National Resistance Army (NRA) of Yoweri Museveni; in 1985 the NRA went on the offensive in the west of the country. Although opposition to Obote did not come only from the NRA, this, nonetheless, was the most cohesive and disciplined organization to challenge his power. On 22 July 1985, the army mounted a coup and ousted Obote from power. He fled to Zambia.

Another Interregnum

Brigadier Tito Okello had seized control of Kampala in the army coup; he then excluded Museveni and the NRA from a share in the government, instead making Paul Muwanga (who had been Obote's vice president) prime minister. This appointment convinced Museveni and the NRA that the new government would continue Obote policies and that there would be no essential changes. When the government proceeded to enlist former Amin soldiers in the army, the NRA was confirmed in its opposition. Okello, who realized he had underestimated the NRA, then dismissed Muwanga and met representatives of the NRA in Nairobi, under the chairmanship of President Daniel arap Moi of Kenya, in an effort to resolve their differences. A peace was negotiated between Okello and the NRA on 17 December 1985; Okello, however, did not keep his side of the agreement, which included a withdrawal of all his forces from Kampala and a seat for the NRA on the new Military

Council. In mid-January 1986, Museveni and the NRA renewed the civil war and after suffering heavy casualties in the fighting for Kampala, Okello withdrew to the east, sacking Kampala first.

The Triumph of Museveni and the NRA

On 29 January 1986, Museveni was sworn in as president of Uganda. Okello and his forces had retreated eastward from Kampala, but they then turned north and did great damage in the villages through which they passed, although failing to gain any support. Okello's army then disintegrated, the soldiers threw away their weapons and either merged into the countryside or fled to **Zaire**. The NRA, which was the military wing of the National Resistance Movement (NRM), showed a restraint that was unique in the 16 years of on-off civil war and massacres to which Uganda had been subject, and this restraint added greatly to the appeal exercised by the victorious NRM of Museveni. In March 1986, Museveni declared that the civil war was over—he certainly appeared to be in firm control of events—but he spoke too soon. Attacks by dissidents were mounted on a range of targets through 1986 and 1987. In mid-1987, the Federal Democratic Movement brought its alliance with Museveni to an end and joined with the Ugandan People's Democratic Movement in the hope of overthrowing Museveni. At the end of 1986, meanwhile, 6,000 followers of Alice Lakwena, a priestess of a religious sect in the north, prepared to overthrow Museveni. Lakwena and her ill-armed followers added yet another dimension of violence to a country which had known little else for years; they were defeated in November 1987 by the NRA, although not before 1,490 of them had been killed. Violence continued through 1988, although the NRA was clearly in the ascendant. In midyear the Ugandan People's Democratic Army came to terms with the Museveni government and it did seem possible by the end of 1988 for the government to claim that 20 years of civil war had at last come to an end.

The Aftermath

An estimated 300,000 Ugandans were killed under Amin between 1971 and 1979, especially among the Acholi and Lango tribes. Others fled the country. In 1985 Paul Ssemogerere, the leader of the

Democratic Party, claimed in **Great Britain** that 500,000 people had died between 1980, when Obote returned to power, until his overthrow in 1985. In 1986, Museveni claimed that altogether 800,000 Ugandans had been killed under Amin, Obote, and Okello. Killing and lawlessness continued during the first years of Museveni's rule. As many as 100,000 Ugandans were driven out of the country as refugees at various times over these years. At the beginning of the 1990s, Uganda's greatest need was simply a period of peace so that reconstruction and economic development could take place.

UGANDA AND THE LORD'S RESISTANCE ARMY (LRA). In 1987 an offshoot of Alice Lakwena's Holy Spirit Movement had become a separate though similar rebel force in Uganda. This was the Lord's Resistance Army under the leadership of Joseph Kony. In the years that followed it appears to have been treated as a nuisance or ignored rather than taken seriously by President **Yoweri Museveni**'s government. This attitude changed in the mid-1990s. In 1996 the LRA launched a number of attacks in northern Uganda to cause many deaths. It did not have any clear political objectives. During 1997 the Ugandan army, which was in a state of discontent and widely involved in smuggling and other corrupt activities, proved an ineffective instrument against the LRA, which operated from bases in southern **Sudan**. LRA tactics were to ravage a district and then withdraw to Sudan. The government now adopted a policy of moving civilians from these war-torn districts into protected villages, although these proved unpopular and did not work well. The north of the country appeared to be becoming a no-go area. During 1998 rebel activities in the north and north-western parts of Uganda increased and apart from the LRA, two other rebel groups began to make an impact. The first of these was the West Nile Bank Front (WNBF), which made the West Nile area a virtual no-go zone. The second rebel group was the Allied Democratic Forces (ADF) in the Ruwenzori Mountains. LRA activities in the north made any meaningful development impossible.

By 1999 the LRA, which was supported by the Sudanese government, was making frequent raids into northern Uganda—especially Gulu district—with the result that it had more or less ruined the local economy and created growing disaffection among the Acholi people who lived there. In May, President Museveni offered Kony an amnesty, but it seemed unlikely that this would be accepted as long as the LRA was allowed to operate from Sudan. Both the WNBF and the ADF achieved a higher profile during the year. The WNBF was based in **Zaire** and obtained its arms in that country. The ADF, operating in the west of the country, comprised a fundamentalist Islamic sect, the Tabliqs, and remnants of the rebel National Army for the Liberation of Uganda. The ADF launched a number of attacks in Bundibugyo district, which was isolated by the Ruwenzori Mountains. ADF activities during the year led to 90 deaths and left some 70,000 people homeless. In November 6,000 troops of the People's Defense Force, who had been specially trained in mountain warfare, launched an offensive against the ADF. The next two years saw less action, though there was no sign that the LRA was ready to give up its war against the government.

In 2002, Uganda agreed not to support the **Sudan People's Liberation Army** (SPLA) in return for Sudan allowing a force of 10,000 Ugandan troops to cross into southern Sudan to root out the LRA. However, "Operation Iron Fist" as it was termed, proved a failure and to drive the point home, the LRA attacked a UN **refugee** camp in northern Uganda to massacre 50 civilians. Throughout 2003 the LRA carried out hit and run attacks on villages and trading centers in parts of northern Uganda. Many civilians were killed and many children abducted, while attempts at negotiating an end to the war proved abortive. Furthermore, government forces became increasingly demoralized as they seemed quite unable to put down the insurgency. LRA activity forced the government to increase its defense expenditure, despite Uganda's withdrawal from **Democratic Republic of Congo**.

By 2004, according to the United Nations Children's Fund (UNICEF), 1.6 million people had been displaced by LRA activities while its fighters included many **child soldiers**—Acholi children who had been abducted, with the boys being forced to be soldiers and the girls sex slaves. Despite the years of its existence, the LRA had still not come up with any meaningful political agenda or creed and its troops readily indulged in rape, murder, robbery, and the abduction of children. Following the massacre of 200 refugees in a camp at Lira, in the Langi region, the government changed its tactics. Instead of arming local militias to defend protected villages, it decided to deploy the army once more. Then in November 2004 a temporary truce was agreed, to be followed by talks in December. The **United Nations** representative Jan Egeland described the LRA war as "the biggest neglected humanitarian crisis in the world." The December talks broke down and on 1 January 2005 the LRA ambushed government soldiers to injure four, while President Museveni ordered the army to resume full operations against the LRA, thus ending the ceasefire that had begun the previous November.

On 22 January a senior LRA commander, Brig.-Gen. Michael Acellam-Odong, was captured with two wives and three children of Kony, the LRA leader. In mid-February another leading LRA commander, Brigadier Sam Kolo, surrendered to the government. He had led the delegation to the December 2004 peace talks and now told a news conference that he was surrendering "for the sake of peace in northern Uganda." The army commander Lt.-Gen. Aronda Nyakairama told the same news conference that Kolo's surrender was the direct result of the army strategy of "fighting and talking." On 11 July an army spokesman, Lt.-Col. Shaban Bantariza, announced that Maj.-Gen. Owar Lakati, chief of staff of the LRA, had been killed in mid-June as well as Kony's eldest son. He said that the deaths had occurred in a battle on 14 June in Palabek village, 460 kilometers north of Kampala. He added that the LRA command structure was "finished" and that the rebels were operating as individuals.

On 13 October, the International Criminal Court (ICC) issued arrest warrants for five LRA leaders. The five were Joseph Kony, his deputy Vincent Otti and three commanders—Okot Odhiambo, Dominic Ongwen, and Raska Lukwiya. Kony faced 33 counts including 12 for crimes against humanity for rape and sexual enslavement, and 21 counts for war crimes including attacks on civilians, murder, and forced enlistment in the army of children. In March 2006, the Civil Society Organizations for Peace in Northern Uganda published a report that claimed the rate of deaths in northern Uganda was three times higher than in Iraq and that the 20-year insurgency had cost $1.7 billion. The report was released ahead of the arrival in Uganda of the UN humanitarian chief Jan Egeland who was to hold meetings with non-governmental organizations (NGOs), ministers, and Uganda-based UN officials. Nearly two million people had been driven from their homes during the insurgency and forced to live in government-constructed camps for protection. The report estimated that 25,000 children had been abducted by the LRA during the long war.

Unexpectedly, in a video tape sent to news agencies on 24 May 2006, Joseph Kony insisted that he was not a terrorist and wanted "peace." The tape was made in Sudan at a meeting earlier in May between Kony and other LRA leaders and Riek Machar, a Sudanese vice-president. Machar had delivered Kony's request for peace talks on 13 May to President Museveni who gave Kony until the end of July to end all hostilities. The ICC reacted angrily to the idea of an amnesty for Kony and insisted that he should be arrested and tried for war crimes. As talks approached toward the end of July, and despite Jan Egeland's description of the LRA's activities as "terrorism of the worst kind," a Kenyan spokesman said: "President Yoweri Museveni has declared that the Uganda government will grant total amnesty to the leader of the Lord's Resistance Army, Joseph Kony, despite the International Criminal Court indictment, if he responds positively." The LRA deputy leader Vincent Otti ordered all LRA field commanders to cease all forms of hostilities against the Ugandan army at the beginning of August. By mid-August it seemed possible that a peace was at last in sight. After the usual "hiccups" and delays, the peace talks, which had begun in Juba during July, were re-started. According to a diplomat involved in the process, "Kony does not want a military position or a seat in government. He just wants to go home. He's been living in the bush for 20 years." The humanitarian situation in northern Uganda was appalling and, depending upon whether a peace could be achieved, nearly two million people living in refugee camps have to return to their homes and most of the people living in such camps are dependent upon food **aid** from the World Food Programme.

UNIÃO NACIONAL PARA A INDEPENDÊNCIA TOTAL DE ANGOLA (UNITA)/NATIONAL UNION FOR THE TOTAL INDEPENDENCE OF ANGOLA. The National Union for the Total Independence of Angola was formed after its founder, **Jonas Savimbi**, broke away from the earlier liberation movement, the **Frente Nacional da Libertação de Angola** (FNLA)/National Front for the Liberation of Angola, founded by **Holden Roberto**. Savimbi left the FNLA in 1964 and set up UNITA in 1966. He had studied medicine in Lisbon, then law and politics in Switzerland, and undergone guerrilla training in the People's Republic of China during 1965. Then he returned to Africa and established himself in Zambia. President **Kenneth Kaunda** of Zambia supported Savimbi from the time he established UNITA in 1966 until 1976, the year following **Angola**'s independence, when he was obliged to choose sides in the civil war that had broken out in Angola.

During the fight against the Portuguese, Savimbi had directed UNITA from inside Angola and this enabled him to create a popular base of support among the Ovimbundu people. The **Benguela Railway** passed through UNITA-controlled territory and this allowed UNITA to attack it and force it to close through most of the 1970s. When independence was achieved in 1975, UNITA established itself at Huambo (former Nova Lisboa). In August 1975, UNITA formally declared war on the **Movimento Popular para a Libertação de Angola** (MPLA)/Popular Movement for the Liberation of Angola, once it became clear that the MPLA leadership did not intend to share power with the other liberation movements.

However, Savimbi's decision to fight the MPLA meant that he had to seek assistance from outside and this forced him to turn to the least acceptable source of help in African eyes—**South Africa**. Once **Agostinho Neto** and the MPLA had assumed de facto power as the rulers of Angola on 11 November 1975, UNITA and the FNLA proclaimed their own joint Democratic People's Republic of Angola with their capital at Huambo. Their separate government was not accorded any recognition. By February 1976, UNITA had been driven from all its town strongholds including Huambo by MPLA forces and then was forced to fall back upon guerrilla tactics, operating from the bush. During the remainder of the 1970s, UNITA achieved only a few minor successes, but it survived as an organization and gradually built up its forces with support from South Africa, channeled through **Namibia**. By the beginning of the 1980s, UNITA was able to carry out acts of sabotage in Luanda and claimed to control 12,000 guerrillas, almost certainly an exaggeration.

Then UNITA managed to obtain backing from the **United States** and Savimbi embarked upon a campaign of successful diplomacy in selling the concept of his "democratic" cause. After Ronald Reagan became president, the United States embarked upon its policy of

linkage, insisting that any settlement of the war in Angola or independence for Namibia had to be linked to the withdrawal of Cuban troops from Angola. In 1981, the U.S. Senate voted to end the ban on **aid** to Savimbi and later that year, when Savimbi visited Washington, he achieved a major breakthrough when linkage was formally put in place. UNITA maintained its war against the Angolan government forces throughout the 1980s with both South African and U.S. support, thus ensuring that the struggle in Angola became very much a part of worldwide **Cold War** confrontations. It was not until the crucial battle of **Cuito Cuanavale** over 1987–1988 that the situation changed in favor of the Luanda government. Negotiations were conducted through 1988 between the two sides in Angola plus the United States, the **Union of Soviet Socialist Republics** (USSR), **Cuba**, and South Africa; during the course of the year Savimbi visited Washington (June), and President Reagan personally reiterated U.S. backing for his cause. The war continued through 1989 and 1990 and the United States increased its aid to UNITA from $45 million in 1989 to $80 million in 1990. However, a tentative MPLA–UNITA peace was concluded in December 1990 and a date for countrywide elections was later agreed.

The elections were held in September 1992: the MPLA won 128 seats and UNITA 71, but neither **Jose dos Santos** nor Savimbi obtained the required 50 percent presidential vote. However, in October 1992 Savimbi and UNITA renewed the war and over the ensuing year it reached its most savage dimensions, causing an estimated 100,000 deaths. By renewing the war, UNITA lost the support of its most important ally, the United States, and at the end of 1993 and into 1994 was obliged to return to the negotiating table with the government in Luanda. A slow and tortuous peace process dragged on into 1998, but UNITA escalated the war again in 1999. The death of Savimbi in 2002 brought an end to the war. UNITA then became the main opposition party to the ruling MPLA government.

UNION OF SOVIET SOCIALIST REPUBLICS (USSR). Apart from the Suez crisis of 1956, the USSR had no involvement on the African continent until the post-colonial age, which really began with the exchange of ambassadors in West Africa–Ghana in 1957, and Guinea, which had quarreled with **Charles de Gaulle's France** and was seen to be Marxist, in 1958. In broad terms, Soviet involvements in Africa paralleled those of the **United States** and were in support of Marxist regimes or liberation movements. The USSR was at first a supporter of the intervention in the **Congo** by the **United Nations** in 1960, although it soon broke ranks with the western powers to support **Patrice Lumumba** while the West supported Joseph Kasavubu or **Moise Tshombe**. The USSR and, more generally, the Communist bloc countries were quick to support liberation movements in southern Africa, especially the **African National Congress** (ANC), which in any case was supported in its turn by the South African Communist Party (SACP), as well as the **South West Africa People's Organization** (SWAPO), the **Frente da Libertação de Moçambique** (FRELIMO)/Mozambique Liberation Front, the **Movimento Popular para a Libertação de Angola** (MPLA)/Popular Movement for the Liberation of Angola, and the **Zimbabwe African National Union** (ZANU).

Soviet **aid** was rarely extensive and most of it, apart from a certain amount of "gesture" aid, was concentrated upon left-wing regimes or movements that were either clearly pro-Moscow and anti-West or, in the case of liberation movements, those whose increased effectiveness as a result of Soviet aid would embarrass the West. Support for liberation movements included funding, military and political training, and scholarships to the USSR. In southern Africa, in particular, support for liberation movements could be represented as anti-racist, as opposed to the West, which could generally be seen as supporting the white minority regimes or at least doing nothing to upset their hold on power. In terms of Africa's wars, the USSR was to be a major player in three theaters: **Angola**, **Ethiopia**, and **Mozambique**.

Angola

Given **Portugal**'s membership of the North Atlantic Treaty Organization (NATO), it was inevitable that one or more of the liberation movements in Angola should turn to the USSR for support, and in the case of the MPLA, it had received Soviet backing long before Portugal's withdrawal in 1975. Then, once the Portuguese had withdrawn and a power struggle for the succession ensued, the three liberation movements sought assistance from outside; Soviet and other Communist support for the MPLA was matched by U.S. and other western support for the **Frente Nacional da Libertação de Angola** (FNLA)/ National Front for the Liberation of Angola and later the **União Nacional para a Independência Total de Angola** (UNITA)/National Union for the Total Independence of Angola, ensuring that a **Cold War** dimension was brought to Angola.

During 1975 the USSR sent massive **arms** supplies to the MPLA while **Cuba** sent troops. Thereafter, from 1975 to 1990 and the Angola settlement, the USSR and Cuba were to be the principal external sources of aid for the MPLA which had formed the new post-independence government. In mid-1976, Andrei Gromyko of the USSR and James Callaghan of **Great Britain** between them acted as mediators to guarantee that the South African–financed Calueque Dam should be left out of war calculations and then to persuade **South Africa** to withdraw its troops trom Angola. During the course of the decisive battle of **Cuito Cuanavale** (1987–88) in southern Angola, General Jannie Geldenhuys of the South African Defence Force (SADF) argued that South Africa had only intervened after Soviet and Cuban troops had gone to the assistance of the MPLA government forces. In 1987, despite claims by **Jonas Savimbi** that UNITA forces had killed a number of Soviet troops, this was denied by Moscow, though not their presence in Angola. South African propaganda constantly exaggerated the extent of Soviet support for liberation movements in southern Africa.

What did alter the balance during the battle of Cuito Cuanavale was the installation of a Soviet air defense network which deployed SA-8 missiles and ground-based radar to detect South African incursions. Moreover, at Cuito Cuanavale some 10,000 MPLA troops were equipped with Soviet tanks, APCs, and anti-aircraft missiles. Soviet SA-8 missiles and radar destroyed the air superiority, which South Africa had enjoyed up to that time. However, over this period (1988–89), in the new climate of perestroika, the USSR was prepared to negotiate with the United States to find a resolution to the long Angolan war. In June 1988, talks were held in Moscow between U.S. Assistant Secretary of State **Chester Crocker** and Soviet Deputy Foreign Minister Anatoly Adamishin, and they set 29 September (the 10th anniversary of Resolution 435 on **Namibia**) as the target date for an Angolan solution. A series of meetings that year, which involved both the United States and the USSR, finally produced an agreement in Brazzaville (December 1988). By 1989, with momentous changes under way in the USSR itself and a peace agreed upon in Angola, the USSR was content to phase out its involvement in Angola.

Ethiopia

Soviet involvement in Ethiopia was crucial to the long struggle in that country, first in its war with **Somalia** (1977–78), although that was not a civil war; and then in relation to the long secessionist war fought by **Eritrea** against domination from Addis Ababa which, strictly speaking, was not a civil war either. The USSR had become a substantial aid donor to Somalia after **Siad Barre** came to power in 1969 and sought an alternative source of support for his socialism to the West which, in any case, would not support his expansionist plans. The Somali relationship with the USSR was never particularly easy and in 1974, as a form of reassurance, Barre joined the Arab League. Then, following the revolution in Ethiopia, which brought a Marxist regime to power under **Haile Mariam Mengistu**, Moscow decided to throw its weight behind the new regime which controlled a potentially far more valuable African ally than Somalia.

The importance of Soviet support became clear during 1977, when the Ethiopian government was on the defensive: in the north the war against the Eritrean secessionists was going badly; in the east Somalia had invaded the Ogaden Province with initial devastating effect; and in the center the Dergue had yet to make the new revolution stick. Mengistu was desperate for military assistance and this he received on a massive scale. Though no precise figures were ever disclosed, western estimates suggested that Soviet military assistance between May and December 1977 came to between $850 million and $1 billion. This aid (which would have to be paid for either from Ethiopia's rich coffee crop or by Libyan financial assistance) included a formidable list of military equipment: 60 MiG 21s, 12 MiG 23s, 300 T54/55 medium tanks, 30 T-34 light tanks, 300 armored cars, 40 BTR-152 armored personnel carriers, six 57mm towed anti-aircraft guns, and a number of 155mm and 185mm guns. Such massive aid helped turn the fortunes of the **Ogaden War**.

Mozambique

The USSR provided substantial aid to FRELIMO in its long libera-tion struggle against Portugal (1963–75); subsequently it became a firm backer of the independence government formed by FRELIMO following the departure of the Portuguese; but though the USSR provided substantial economic support after 1975, as well as military advisers (several hundred), it never became committed or as deeply involved in Mozambique as it did in Angola. Moreover, growing support for Mozambique from the **Commonwealth** and the Euro-pean Union during the 1980s (for example, European financial and technical assistance for the rehabilitation of the port of Beira) meant that FRELIMO attitudes toward both the USSR and Marxism began to change and became more ambivalent than those of the MPLA government in Angola. Thus, when at the end of January 1990 the U.S. State Department formally declared that it no longer regarded Mozambique as a Communist state, this could be taken as the point when Soviet interest in backing the government came to an end. In any case, by then the breakup of the Soviet system was imminent.

Other Soviet Involvement

During the **Nigerian civil war**, Soviet support to the Federal Military Government (FMG), principally with military equipment including MiG fighters and Ilyushin bombers, was designed to enable Moscow to obtain a footing and influence in a region of Africa where, to that date, it had had little impact. The USSR supplied about 30 percent of the Nigerian FMG's arms requirements; it was early in the war, when Biafra obtained a number of old DC aircraft from Rhodesia, that the FMG turned to Moscow for the supply of war planes. Even so, throughout the war Soviet military supplies to Nigeria averaged no more in value than $6 million a month, while those from Britain amounted to $20 million a month. There is little evidence, however, that this supply of arms to Nigeria during the civil war made any ma-terial difference to Soviet trade or influence once the war had ended.

The USSR was a firm supporter of the African National Congress (ANC) in South Africa through the long years of the anti-apartheid struggle, and here its influence was assisted by the close alliance that was established between the ANC and the South African Communist Party (SACP). It is arguable that Soviet support for the liberation movements in southern Africa was counterproductive, since it made it easier for Pretoria to defend its system on the grounds that it was fighting against the advance of Communism. The West, which over many years showed itself deeply reluctant, for both racist and profit reasons, to put adequate pressures upon South Africa, welcomed South African claims that it was fighting against the spread of Communism, since this made it easier for western governments to continue their support for the South African regime. This situation allowed Soviet propaganda to cast the West in a racist light.

UNITED NATIONS. The United Nations has responded in a variety of ways to the wars fought in Africa over the post-independence decades. Sometimes it attempted the role of peacemaker, but more usually acted as a peacekeeper after a ceasefire had been reached. The United Nations has been involved especially in **Angola**, **Burundi**, **Congo (Zaire)**, **Liberia**, **Mozambique**, **Rwanda**, **Sierra Leone**, **Somalia**, and **South Africa** as far as civil wars are concerned, with varying degrees of success or failure.

Congo

On 12 July 1960, in the newly independent **Republic of Congo**, the day after **Moise Tshombe** had announced the secession of Katanga Province, **Patrice Lumumba**, the prime minister, appealed to the United Nations to help restore order and keep the Congo united as a single country. Lumumba hoped that a UN presence would make the Belgians withdraw and would prevent the Congo from becoming a pawn in **Cold War** confrontations. UN Secretary-General **Dag Hammarskjöld** responded swiftly to Lumumba's request and UN troops—Swedish and African—soon arrived in the new state. However, a power struggle then developed between President Joseph Kasavubu and Prime Minister Patrice Lumumba, which the latter lost. Hammarskjöld probably underestimated the determination of western interests to control the Congo because of its strategic position and mineral wealth, the latter largely controlled by Belgian and British business interests. The Congo represented the first UN intervention in sub-Saharan Africa, where it encountered some of the pitfalls which awaited it when faced by powerful western political and economic interests determined to continue controlling a newly "independent" African state. The failure of the United Nations force to rescue Lumumba, who was captured and taken to Katanga where he was murdered, was long seen by black Africa as something worse than a simple failure. The UN mission remained in the Congo for four years, and given the Cold War conditions prevailing at the time and the bitter confrontation between the **United States** and the **Union of Soviet Socialist Republics** (USSR), its role became increasingly difficult and controversial. Hammarskjöld himself was killed in September 1961 in the crash of a flight to Katanga from Northern Rhodesia for talks with Tshombe. Only at the end of 1962 did the United Nations act to end Katanga's secession. The UN force was finally withdrawn from the Congo on 30 June 1964; its withdrawal was followed by another wave of violence. The UN Congo intervention undoubtedly prevented a far worse breakdown occurring in that country and established a number of precedents for the future, though it was far from being fully successful or universally acclaimed.

Angola

Three UN missions—the UN Angola Verification Mission (UNAVEM I, II, and III)—worked in that country between 1988 and 1996. Following the December 1988 negotiations in New York, when South Africa, **Cuba**, and Angola signed agreements that would end the civil war and bring **Namibia** to independence, the UN Security Council established the UN Angola Verification Mission to monitor the redeployment of the Cuban troops away from the Namibian border and then their withdrawal from Angola over an 18-month period. UNAVEM I had 70 soldiers and 20 civilians and did not meet any problems with this assignment—the Cubans went as they had agreed to do. In March 1992, the Security Council mandated its mission to observe and monitor the elections which were to be held that September. It increased the numbers of UNAVEM to 450 unarmed observers and then a further 100, while an additional 400 observers were sent to Angola during the actual month of the elections.

These numbers proved woefully insufficient to cover such a huge country in which elections had never been held before. Fighting followed the 1992 elections when **Jonas Savimbi** and the **União Nacional para a Independência Total de Angola** (UNITA)/National Union for the Total Independence of Angola returned to the bush to renew the war. The UNAVEM mandate was due to expire on 31 January 1993, but both sides to the dispute asked for a renewal. The new UN secretary general, Boutros Boutros-Ghali, asked that the UN mission be reduced to 60, that these be withdrawn to Luanda, and that they should then be withdrawn entirely on 30 April 1993, unless peace had been achieved by that date. However, the UNAVEM mandate was again renewed on 2 June 1993, and in July the new UN representative in Angola, Alioune Blondin Beye, claimed that over 1,000 people a day were dying from the direct or indirect consequences of what was then seen as the world's worst war. The United Nations again extended the UNAVEM mandate and called upon UNITA to end the fighting; on 26 September 1993, the UN implemented a mandatory oil and **arms** embargo against UNITA. On 6 October 1993, UNITA announced that it would accept the election results of 1992, and at the end of October talks were resumed in Lusaka between UNITA, UNAVEM, and the three observer countries—**Portugal**, Russia (which had taken over the role of the former USSR), and the United States. The United Nations again extended its mandate until 16 March 1994. However, although throughout the crisis the United Nations kept extending the mandate of UNAVEM, the Security Council was not prepared to send troops on the scale required either to escort convoys of supplies or to break sieges of the towns.

On 21 November 1994, the Security Council welcomed the signing of the Lusaka Protocol by the Angolan government and UNITA, and at the end of the year, UNAVEM II was restored in strength to 476. In February 1995, Security Council Resolution 976 established UNAVEM III, "to help the country's factions to restore peace and achieve national reconciliation."

Further breakdowns and constant suspicion between the government and UNITA continued through 1995; had there been massive UN peacekeeping forces present, the story might have been different. It was the tiny size of the UNAVEM force in Angola which led to disaster, including the second phase of civil war (1992–93), which caused an estimated 100,000 deaths. The lesson of Angola would seem clear: once it is obvious that the parties involved are determined to ignore the UN presence, then either the United Nations should withdraw or else increase the size and effectiveness of its presence until this cannot be ignored. Neither option was adopted in Angola.

Burundi

In 1995 the United Nations sent a mission to Burundi to assess the situation in the aftermath of developments during 1994. At this stage Burundi could be described as being in a state of low-intensity civil war, with Tutsi militias and Hutu guerrillas operating unofficially and causing periodic explosions of violence. The **United Nations High Commissioner for Refugees** (UNHCR) was encouraged by the Security Council to look at the situation in the refugee camps in Tanzania and Burundi itself. At most, during 1995, the United Nations played a peripheral role in a situation of developing and more or less continuous violence in which 800,000 people (15 percent of the population) had become **refugees**. The UNHCR was responsible for delivering emergency relief to these refugees. Intervention to prevent a disaster was clearly required, yet, according to Sir Anthony Parsons, a former British ambassador to the United Nations, following the death of President Melchior Ndadaye, the Security Council "confined itself to verbal condemnation of the coup, a tribute to the dead president and murdered ministers and a call to the secretary-general to monitor developments, bring the murderers to justice and to assist the parties in returning the country to constitutional legality."

Indeed, there was every sign that the major powers which made up the permanent membership of the Security Council were determined to keep clear of any Burundi entanglement. The UN Special Rapporteur for Human Rights in Burundi condemned torture, arbitrary detention, and massacres and said the situation in Burundi revealed "an increasing genocidal trend." Intervention plans had already been devised by UN Secretary General Boutros Boutros-Ghali in February 1996, but the auguries were not good and a proposal to station a rapid reaction force in Zaire was vetoed by the United States. Boutros-Ghali then put up a second plan for intervention troops to be on standby in their own countries while the situation in Burundi was monitored, these troops being ready for quick deployment if required. It was estimated that should such a force meet resistance in Burundi following an intervention, it would need to be 25,000 strong. The United States, **France**, and **Great Britain** and the former mandatory power, Belgium, each refused to earmark troops for such a purpose. In any case, the government of Burundi was opposed to any outside intervention, including any by the United Nations. In New York the Security Council warned against a military coup and the then under-secretary-general for peacekeeping, Kofi Annan, said that with the necessary political support, a force could be deployed in a week. The U.S. ambassador to the United Nations, Madeleine Albright, first said that under no circumstances would Washington tolerate a government in Burundi installed by force, but then added that the United States would not offer any fighting forces to the United Nations for intervention. The coup that ousted Ndadaye duly took place on 25 July 1996, and **Pierre Buyoya** became president. The United Nations ordered all non-essential UN personnel to leave the country.

Rwanda

In 1993, as a result of the fighting between Rwandan government forces and the **Rwanda Patriotic Front** (RPF) operating out of **Uganda**, both Rwanda and Uganda requested the Security Council to station observers along their joint border. A UN observer to Mission Uganda-Rwanda (UNOMUR) was therefore deployed on the Ugandan side of the border in September 1993. The United Nations was then requested to provide a **peacekeeping** force to guarantee public security and this led to the creation of the UN Assistance Mission in Rwanda (UNAMIR) in October 1993, which replaced UNOMUR. Its task was to help create a transitional government. UNAMIR was provided with a force of 2,500 troops as well as civilian police. By the end of 1993, an initial success, some 600,000 Rwandan refugees had returned home. Following the deaths of the two presidents of Burundi and Rwanda on 6 April 1994, the presidential guard in Kigali went on the rampage; 800 Belgian paratroopers arrived to evacuate foreigners (about 3,000) and by 12 April, the RPF was fighting its way into the capital. Within two weeks of 6 April the UN peacekeepers began to quit the country, some clearly in panic. The UN forces left because, they claimed, the government refused to give them control of the airport. On 19 April 1994, the UN special envoy, Jacques-Roger Booh-Booh, stated that if the warring parties did not reach an agreement on a cease-fire "it must be very clear we shall not stay here." Booh-Booh also said, in answer to the question as to whether the United Nations was about to abandon Rwanda, "We came to assist Rwanda, but we cannot impose any solution on the Rwandan people, who have to help us to help them."

As the slaughter continued, the UN Security Council adjusted UNAMIR's mandate three times—21 April, 17 May, and 8 June—to make it an effective instrument for protecting civilians. On 25 May 1994, UN Secretary-General Boutros-Ghali condemned the Rwandan killings as genocide and described the world's unwillingness to do anything as "a scandal." But states which had burnt their fingers in Somalia or were involved in Bosnia were reluctant to take on a Rwandan commitment. After the United States had refused to approve the dispatch of 5,500 troops to Rwanda, the Security Council accepted a French offer of 2,500 troops for one month to provide temporary security and humanitarian **aid** for the refugees, then estimated at 100,000 and more. The French, acting on their own rather than as a formal UN force, were regarded with suspicion by the new Tutsi-dominated Rwandan government because of France's former role in training the Hutu army. They withdrew in August.

The UNAMIR force then replaced the French, as various African countries pledged contingents. On 8 November, the Security Council agreed to the setting up of an international tribunal to try persons accused of genocide and other crimes committed in Rwanda in the period since 6 April 1994. On 21 November, the UN secretary-general asked the Security Council to send 12,000 troops to stem the violence then occurring on a daily basis in the refugee camps in Zaire and Burundi, and to protect relief workers. During 1995 the UNHCR faced the huge problem of persuading one million refugees in camps in Zaire and Tanzania to return home. By then Hutu extremists had seized control of food distribution. Although Boutros-Ghali called on the Security Council to back an international force or support efforts of local countries, he got no response. As exiled Hutus worked to destabilize the new Rwandan government, the UN Security Council (August 1995) lifted its 1994 arms embargo on Rwanda and then established a commission of inquiry to collect information about the supply of arms to former Rwandan government forces. In December 1995, the Security Council adjusted UNAMIR's mandate and reduced its contingent from 5,600 to 1,800 troops. Meanwhile, in March 1995, the Security Council had passed Resolution 978 (recalling its earlier Resolution 955 of November 1994) which had set up the International Criminal Tribunal for Rwanda (ICTR). It called on all states to arrest and detain anyone suspected of genocide. The abysmal record of the United Nations in Rwanda demonstrated that the international community simply did not wish to become involved.

Somalia

The gradual collapse of central government in Somalia under **Siad Barre** occurred during the last years of the 1980s, until he was forced to flee the country in January 1991. When finally Barre went, Somalia was in chaos and the country was controlled by a number of warring factions and clans, while international **relief agencies** were trying to deliver food and other humanitarian supplies to the thousands of people who had been turned into refugees by the fighting. On 31 January 1991, the UN Security Council imposed an arms embargo on Somalia, called for a cease-fire, and requested the secretary-general to contact all parties to bring about a peace settlement. An initial cease-fire was secured, and 40 UN observers arrived in Mogadishu to supervise it. The fighting soon recurred and the number of refugees fleeing the country increased.

In April 1992 the Security Council created a UN Operation in Somalia (UNOSOM) to help end hostilities and promote reconciliation between the warring factions. It also had as its task, safeguarding the delivery of humanitarian aid. By May 1992, however, only a small proportion of relief was actually reaching those in need and about 3,000 refugees a day were crossing into Kenya. The secretary-general therefore increased the strength of UNOSOM, specifically to enable more escorts to be available for the humanitarian supply convoys. In September 1992 the first troops (500) arrived in Somalia to support UNOSOM. A further four units of 750 troops each were authorized, as well as 700 logistics personnel. Their task was to guard supplies at the ports. This brought total UNOSOM strength to 4,200. Prior to becoming secretary-general of the United Nations, Boutros Boutros-

Ghali had compared the readiness of the West to intervene in Yugoslavia with its reluctance to do anything in Somalia in unflattering terms. From May to October 1992 the secretary-general's representative in Somalia, the Algerian Muhammad Sahnoun, tried to persuade the Somali warlords and regional countries to permit outside troops to protect humanitarian food supplies from looters. But in October Sahnoun resigned, accusing both the United Nations and the relief agencies of bureaucracy and lethargy while they allowed Somalia to descend into a "hell" where 300,000 (mainly women and children) had died in 18 months. Then, on 25 November 1992, after one of its relief ships had been attacked, the United Nations suspended its formal program of relief shipments. On 30 November the secretary-general asked the Security Council to authorize a military operation to safeguard relief workers, and this was agreed on 30 December.

Meanwhile, the outgoing U.S. president, George H. W. Bush, had authorized the use of 28,000 U.S. troops in Somalia (under UN auspices) to safeguard relief columns. These troops became part of the UN Task Force (UNTAF) and began to land in Somalia on 9 December 1992. The relationship between the U.S. troops and the United Nations was uneasy from the beginning; in particular, the aggressive tactics of the U.S. troops were seen to be a barrier to effective peacekeeping. By the end of January 1993, there were 24,000 U.S. troops (nominally under UN control) and 13,600 from other countries in Somalia, and by early February tensions had arisen between the United States and the United Nations as to the manner in which control of the U.S.-led intervention should be handed over to the United Nations. Washington wanted to withdraw its forces after two months. On 4 May 1993, a Security Council resolution gave operational command in Somalia to UNOSOM II, which was empowered to disarm warlords in order to safeguard the delivery of supplies to their targets. By mid-1993, the UN force was meeting bitter opposition from the Somali National Alliance (SNA) of **Muhammad Farah Aideed**, and U.S. aircraft were attacking SNA targets. By August the Americans had come to see the arrest of Aideed as their priority aim. The U.S. determination to target Aideed as the principal source of problems for the UN operation brought things to a climax in late 1993.

On 22 September the Security Council passed Resolution 865 to end the UNOSOM II mandate by March 1995. On 19 October 1993, the U.S. Rangers were withdrawn from Somalia. On 7 November Aideed warned he would end the ceasefire agreed on 9 October should U.S. troops (which had been withdrawn from them) return to the streets of Mogadishu. On 16 November the United Nations accepted an Aideed suggestion to appoint a special commission to examine the charges against him; this was a face-saving device to allow the United Nations to abandon its June resolution to arrest Aideed. U.S. President Bill Clinton then announced that U.S. troops would be withdrawn from Somalia by 31 March 1994—a year earlier than the UN authorization of 22 September 1993. The U.S. intervention in Somalia led to exceedingly poor U.S.–UN relations, and once Clinton had announced the withdrawal date for U.S. troops, their ground forces showed great reluctance to be further involved in Somalia, even while there, and in 1994 the United States refused absolutely to become involved in Rwanda.

Once the U.S. forces had departed, the UN Operation in Somalia was rapidly reduced in size and scope of operations. In January 1994, Boutros-Ghali reported that the international community was suffering "unmistakable signs of fatigue" over Somalia. In February 1994, the Security Council renewed the UNOSOM mandate, but it then had fewer than 19,000 troops following the departure of the U.S. force. On 1 June 1994, a commission of inquiry investigating Somali attacks on UN personnel said member nations were not prepared "to accept substantial casualties for causes unrelated to their national interest." This finding had major implications for future UN operations. During the remainder of 1994 efforts to stop the fighting between warring factions failed, and UNOSOM forces were mainly confined to fortified compounds in Mogadishu (which effectively nullified the reason for their presence in Somalia). On 4 November 1994, the Security Council decided to recall UNOSOM II by 31 March 1995, whatever the situation in Somalia; on 2 March 1995, all UN troops were withdrawn from the country. The UN operation in Somalia had been a failure.

Mozambique

By 1990, after 15 years of civil war, both sides in Mozambique—the government forces and the dissident forces of the **Resistência**

Nacional Moçambicana (RENAMO)/Mozambican National Resistance—were sufficiently wearied of the endless fighting that they were prepared, during 1990–1992, to make major efforts to find a peaceful solution to their conflict. A ceasefire agreement was reached on 4 October 1991, and the need for its supervision and assistance in implementing a peace became a matter of urgency. On 16 December 1992, the UN Security Council decided to send a peacekeeping force (UNOMOZ) to Mozambique; it would consist of 7,500 troops, police, and civilians to oversee the disarming of the two sides and to monitor elections. The UN force would also protect the vital railway links (the **Beira** and Maputo Corridors) to countries of the interior. During the early months of 1993 it was touch and go, whether fighting would be renewed until the first 100 UN troops arrived on 15 February. In April, RENAMO withdrew from the ceasefire and **Zimbabwe** withdrew all the troops which had been in Mozambique supporting the government. However, the situation became less precarious in May when 4,721 UN troops and support units arrived in the country; in June the UNHCR began to repatriate 1.3 million refugees, and international donors pledged $520 million for humanitarian aid.

Following a visit to Maputo by Secretary-General Boutros-Ghali, who held talks with President **Joaquim Chissano** and the RENAMO leader Afonso Dhlakama, an electoral commission was established on 20 October 1993 to supervise the elections of October 1994, and the UNOMOZ mandate was extended to cover the elections. By March 1994 troops were arriving at 40 demobilization centers and 6,000 UNOMOZ troops were deployed around the country. The peace process was clearly working. UNOMOZ was costing its western donors $1 million a day. The UN operation in Mozambique was a success story and this was due to two key factors: it had adequate forces on the ground (unlike the operation in Angola); and it was directed by an exceptionally able special representative, the Italian Aldo Ajello. The process of demobilizing the armed forces of the two sides was well advanced before the elections took place; 80,000 **Frente da Libertação de Moçambique** (FRELIMO)/Mozambique Liberation Front and 20,000 RENAMO troops had passed through the demobilization centers. In the event, Chissano won the elections with 53 percent of the vote, while Dhlakama took 33 percent of the vote.

South Africa

The United Nations, arguably, was more consistent in its steadfast opposition to apartheid in South Africa than over many other issues; apartheid was condemned every year after 1949 in the General Assembly, and much tougher sanctions against South Africa would have been applied except that, in the climate of the Cold War, Britain and the United States shielded and where necessary, used their vetoes to protect the apartheid state. As a result, apart from condemnations, there was little the United Nations was able to do except keep the issue of apartheid before the international public. In 1962 the General Assembly called on members to break diplomatic relations with South Africa, boycott its goods, and refuse to sell it arms. Also that year, the United Nations established its Special Committee against Apartheid. In 1965, when the Ian Smith government in Rhodesia made its Unilateral Declaration of Independence (UDI) from Britain, the ensuing crisis diverted attention for a while from South Africa. In 1966 the UN General Assembly proclaimed 21 March (the anniversary of the Sharpeville Massacre) as the International Day for the Elimination of Racism. Throughout the 1970s, as far as it was able and often in a difficult Cold War climate, the United Nations maintained pressures against apartheid and upon South Africa. In 1982 the General Assembly proclaimed an International Year of Mobilization of Sanctions against South Africa. In 1989, as things fell apart in South Africa, the General Assembly adopted a Declaration which listed the steps that the South African government should take to create a climate for negotiations. After President **F. W. de Klerk** came to power (in September 1989) and began to dismantle the apartheid system—unbanning the **African National Congress** (ANC), releasing **Nelson Mandela**, and paving the way for talks between all races and political groups, UN Secretary-General Javier Perez de Cuellar sent a mission to South Africa to report on progress according to the 1989 UN Declaration.

On 13 December 1991, the General Assembly called for all nations to begin restoring sporting, cultural, and academic ties with South Africa. In 1992, Nelson Mandela addressed the United Nations and called upon it to lift sanctions against South Africa. Secretary General Boutros-Ghali appointed the former U.S. secretary of state,

Cyrus Vance, as his special representative in South Africa, and the United Nations deployed its services to assist the transition from white to majority rule. Under UN Resolution 772 (of 1992), 30 observers were sent to South Africa to help implement the National Peace Accord. Thus, at last, the United Nations had established a presence in South Africa with its UN Observer Mission in South Africa (UNOMSA). By 1993 there were 100 UNOMSA observers in South Africa and the United Nations was able to play an important part in monitoring the April 1994 elections.

Liberia

The civil war in Liberia, which erupted at the end of 1989, rapidly escalated during January 1990 so that an estimated 50,000 people were thought to have been driven into hiding in the bush of Nimba country. The war, which was launched by **Charles Taylor**, a former minister of President **Samuel Doe**, was begun in order to bring Doe's 10-year rule, which the U.S. human rights group Africa Watch described as a reign of terror, to an end. In July 1990, a split occurred in the rebel ranks and a second group under **Prince Yormie Johnson** broke away. In August 1990, the European Community ambassadors in Liberia called for an emergency session of the UN Security Council.

An initiative to end the civil war was now mounted by the **Economic Community of West African States** (ECOWAS), and an **Economic Community Monitoring Group** (ECOMOG) led by Nigeria intervened in Liberia with substantial forces. On 19 November 1990, the UN Security Council called for a "general and complete" arms embargo on Liberia. In relation to this civil war the United Nations maintained a low profile and encouraged the regional powers, working through ECOMOG, to take the initiative. Under the terms of UN Security Council Resolution 788 of 1992, which called upon the factions in Liberia to respect the peace process, Secretary-General Boutros Boutros-Ghali sent a special representative, Trevor Gordon-Somers, to assess the situation. On 12 March 1993, the secretary-general submitted a special report to the Security Council, and on 26 March the Security Council adopted Resolution 813, which reaffirmed its support for the Yamoussoukro IV Accords (in **Côte d'Ivoire**) that had been reached by the contending parties as representing the best chances for peace. In August 1993 the Security Council dispatched 30 military observers to Liberia to monitor the ceasefire negotiated at a summit in Benin the previous 25 July, which had been held under the auspices of ECOWAS, the **Organization of African Unity (OAU)**, and the United Nations. Under Resolution 866 of September 22 1993, the United Nations established a UN Observer Mission in Liberia (UNOMIL). This was the second UN mission (the first was the UN–OAS mission in the Dominican Republic, 1965–66) to be undertaken in collaboration with another organization—ECOMOG. It was almost certainly a precedent for the coming years in Africa. The United Nations played a secondary role to ECOMOG in Liberia; nor was it keen to become more deeply involved, given its many other commitments at the time. The importance of the Liberian intervention was the readiness of the United Nations to accept a subsidiary role to a regional organization. The Security Council established a voluntary trust fund to assist ECOMOG.

Conclusions

The civil wars in Africa during the 1990s—and especially those in Angola, Burundi, Liberia, and Somalia, most of which continued or were revived in the 21st century—taught the United Nations some bitter lessons; primarily, that the international community was not prepared to become involved in such situations simply because the United Nations asked for a commitment. The reluctance of the United States to support many UN activities must also be seen as a crippling drawback for the world body: the United States has both the financial means and the military capacity to move troops anywhere in the world quickly and in the numbers required to make an impact. A major UN peacekeeping operation is not possible—or is most unlikely to succeed—unless at least one major western military power (which in reality means the United States, Britain, or France) is prepared to become involved on a substantial scale, since they alone have the capacity for rapid military deployment. The wars in Africa during the 1990s have raised other questions for the United Nations: Should it intervene against the wishes of both sides in a civil war in order to impose a peace (for example in Burundi or Somalia)? Does it have the right to insist upon the delivery of humanitarian aid to those in need, regardless of any existing war situation?

During the 1990s, Africa learned that its troubles rate low on the international scale, since other regions of the world are seen to be of greater national and strategic interest to the powers with the capacity to intervene. In the case of Somalia (a lesson for both the United Nations and the United States), it was made clear by a bungled operation that peacekeepers must try both to be and be seen to be impartial. Another important lesson that will be ignored at peril is the fact that the presence of the international media has now become an automatic adjunct to any UN operation; the result is to keep such an operation in the limelight while also, unfortunately, ensuring that nations taking part in any UN exercise are likely to play to the international gallery in terms of their own contributions and that any mishaps will immediately be picked up by the media. The United Nations must expect to be cast in the role of scapegoat for failures while the big powers will take the credit for successes. Finally, the willingness of the major powers to be part of UN interventions will be related to their estimate of their own interests.

In the first years of the 21st century, apart from ongoing commitments, the United Nations was principally concerned with the civil war in **Darfur**, what had come to be called Africa's Great War in **Democratic Republic of Congo**, and the new flashpoint in West Africa of **Côte d'Ivoire.**

UNITED NATIONS HIGH COMMISSIONER FOR REFUGEES (UNHCR). The office of the United Nations High Commissioner for Refugees was created in 1950, both to protect **refugees** and to find and promote solutions to their problems. Throughout the 1980s and into the 1990s, the number of conflicts which affected Africa, meant that a high proportion of all UNHCR resources were devoted to African refugee problems; in the mid-1990s approximately half the world's refugees were to be found on the African continent. The UNHCR has worked to alleviate the suffering of refugees from the conflicts in **Angola, Ethiopia, Liberia, Mozambique, Somalia, Darfur** and Southern Africa generally, and in many cases the UNHCR has had to deal with refugees who have fled civil wars in their own countries—for example, the large numbers which moved into Malawi during the 1980s to avoid the civil war in Mozambique. The numbers involved run into the millions: in 1991, for example, the total of refugees worldwide was 17 million, of whom nearly half were then in Africa. As the civil wars developed in Liberia and then **Sierra Leone** during the first half of the 1990s, so the UNHCR was alerted to move in and alleviate refugee conditions as far as it had the resources to do so. The UNHCR becomes involved in all substantial refugee problems and has played a significant role in Africa over the years since 1960.

African countries most affected by refugee problems at the beginning of 2005 are listed below. The figures in the table that follows include refugees from another country, returned refugees, and internally displaced persons. Only those countries with 100,000 or more refugees are listed here.

Country	Population of Concern to UNHCR
Burundi	150,696
Ethiopia	116,027
Kenya	249,310
Uganda	252,382
Tanzania	602,256
Angola	105,145
Chad	260,064
Democratic Republic of Congo	213,520
Algeria	169,055
Sudan	845,867
South Africa	142,907
Côte d'Ivoire	119,832
Guinea	145,571
Liberia	603,700
Regional totals	
Eastern Africa	1,683,067
Middle Africa	763,279
Northern Africa	1,128,900
Southern Africa	164,718
Western Africa	1,119,171
Total	4,859,135

(*Source:* UNHCR)

UNITED SOMALI CONGRESS (USC). The United Somali Congress (USC) emerged as an umbrella organization at the end of the

1980s for those groups opposed to the collapsing **Siad Barre** government of **Somalia**. It was formed by exiles meeting in London and Rome; and in 1990 the USC and the **Somali National Movement** (SNM) and Somali Patriotic Movement joined forces to overthrow Barre. At first the USC gained control of central Somalia, but during the second half of 1990 it became involved in fighting against government forces all over the country and finally moved into the capital, Mogadishu. In December 1990, after two days of fierce fighting, the USC occupied parts of Mogadishu. Then in January 1991, President Barre fled the country. The USC then proclaimed an interim government under **Ali Mahdi Mohammed**; however, the USC was subsequently rent by divisions when **Muhammad Farah Aideed** became its chairman and used it as a power base to oppose Mohammed taking power as the country's president.

UNITED STATES. During most of the post–World War II period, Africa as a continent (apart from the Arab Mediterranean) did not feature high in terms of U.S. international priorities. For much of the **Cold War**, when huge political changes were taking place in Africa, Washington "left" the continent to **Great Britain** and **France** as the major ex-colonial powers that between them exercised the principal external influence in the region. American detachment from African problems was made clear in 1967 when, at the beginning of the **Nigerian civil war**, the U.S. secretary of state, Dean Rusk, made a notorious gaffe at a press conference at which he said: "We regard Nigeria as part of Britain's sphere of influence"—a remark that did not go down well in Lagos. In general, the United States saw Africa as lying at the lower end of the scale of its international interests and was largely content, as a result, to leave interventions in the continent to the European powers. There were to be several important exceptions to this general rule during the years 1960–1990; these were **Angola**, **Ethiopia**, **Liberia**, **South Africa**, and **Zaire**. U.S. involvement in Africa increased wherever and whenever the Cold War came to affect any part of the continent.

Angola

The United States was especially concerned with the post-independence civil war that ravaged Angola from 1975 to 1994;

this, in turn, followed 15 years of nationalist struggle against the Portuguese, which only ended with **Portugal**'s withdrawal in 1975. Throughout the years of its involvement in Angola, the United States used Zaire as a base for the Central Intelligence Agency (CIA) from which to provide military supplies for the **União Nacional para a Independência Total de Angola** (UNITA)/National Union for the Total Independence of Angola. Once the **Movimento Popular para a Libertação de Angola** (MPLA)/Popular Movement for the Liberation of Angola, which was seen as Marxist and pro-Moscow, had come to power in November 1975 as the government of Angola, the United States persuaded Gulf Oil (which operated the Cabinda oil fields) to suspend royalties to the government in Luanda. This step represented the beginning of U.S. involvement in the coming Angolan civil war. However, in 1975 the United States was in no mood to become deeply embroiled in an Angolan war situation since it was still reeling from its ignominious withdrawal from Vietnam. Thus, when South Africa intervened militarily in Angola in October 1975, U.S. Secretary of State Henry Kissinger refused to endorse its action and the South Africans were obliged to withdraw. Yet, despite Kissinger's insistence that South Africa was on its own and would not obtain U.S. support or backing for its intervention, in fact the United States soon became responsible for providing covert support to UNITA through the CIA, operating from Zaire. Furthermore, the increasing involvement of **Cuba** in Angola on the side of the government acted as a spur to U.S. activity, for Washington was determined to counter what it saw as Cuban "subversion."

During the 1980s, the United States, with the ready connivance of both Pretoria and UNITA, tied the issue of the withdrawal of Cuban troops from Angola to that of a war settlement and independence for **Namibia**, a policy which became known as **linkage**. The visit to Washington by UNITA's leader **Jonas Savimbi** in January 1986, when he was well received by the State Department, emphasized U.S. commitment to one side in the Angolan civil war. In September 1986 the U.S. House of Representatives voted 229 to 189 to provide $15 million in **aid** to UNITA to help stem the tide of Soviet expansion in Southern Africa. In 1987 the U.S. assistant secretary of state for African affairs, Chester Crocker, began the long series of negotiations to end the Angolan war, always insisting that Cuban troops should leave Angola as a quid pro quo for Namibian independence; his proposals became known as the **Crocker Plan**. Through 1987 to December 1988, talks involving the United States, the **Union of Soviet Socialist Republics** (USSR), South Africa, Angola, and Cuba were held in various venues until agreement was finally reached at Brazzaville in December 1988 (and then ratified in New York); under the terms of the agreement Cuba agreed to withdraw its troops from Angola over 27 months and South Africa agreed to implement UN Resolution 435 concerning Namibia, which finally became independent in March 1990. At the same time, the **African National Congress** (ANC) withdrew its cadres from Angola. However, the agreement did not cover U.S. relations with UNITA, and President **Jose dos Santos** complained that there could be no peace in Angola until the United States ceased its support for UNITA.

Despite this, the United States continued to provide aid to UNITA ($45 million in 1989, $80 million in 1990) until it resumed the war against the government in October 1992, after losing the elections. U.S. support for UNITA at this stage undoubtedly helped prolong the civil war. It was only in January 1993 that the United States finally said that UNITA's resort to force after losing the September 1992 elections was unacceptable. Then, on 25 March 1993, the Senate and the House of Representatives passed a joint resolution condemning UNITA.

Liberia

The historical ties between the United States and Liberia ensured U.S. intervention, if only negatively to remove U.S. citizens, once that country was plunged into civil war at the beginning of the 1990s. In April 1990 the United States advised its 5,000 citizens, then in Liberia, to leave. Later in the year, President **Samuel Doe** claimed that he had authorized U.S. marines to come ashore to assist in his defense. At that time there were 2,100 marines in the U.S. flotilla that was lying offshore. Shortly before he was killed, the United States offered to take Doe out of the country so as to prevent further bloodshed, though nothing came of the offer. In the end it was the **Economic Community Monitoring Group** (ECOMOG), the military intervention force of the **Economic Community of West**

African States (ECOWAS), which intervened in the civil war while the United States provided a measure of financial support.

Elsewhere in Africa

In contrast to its interventions in Angola, the United States played only a small role in **Mozambique** during the last phases of that country's civil war. Once the **Frente da Libertação de Moçambique** (FRELIMO)/Mozambique Liberation front government had formally abandoned Marxism in 1989, the United States became more inclined to assist the peace process (it had first condemned the dissident group **Resistência Nacional Moçambicana** [RENAMO]/Mozambican National Resistance in 1988) and in January 1990 publicly accepted that Mozambique was no longer a Marxist state.

The U.S. decision to intervene in **Somalia** at the end of 1992 appeared to be motivated at least as much by internal politics as by an appreciation of what needed to be done in Somalia. The U.S.-led multinational UN Task Force (UNTAF), including 28,000 marines, arrived in Somalia in December 1992; its object was to secure supply routes to famine-afflicted areas. However, the U.S. forces soon met opposition and before long had made the capture of **Muhammad Farah Aideed** their primary objective, an objective which was not achieved but whose pursuit made U.S. forces unacceptable as impartial peacekeepers. In the end the U.S. intervention increased rather than diminished the rate of casualties and led the United States to withdraw its forces a year ahead of the UN requirement. The U.S. intervention in Somalia turned into a public relations disaster for the United States and soured relations between Washington and the United Nations. One result, almost certainly, was the subsequent refusal of the United States to become involved in any kind of **peacekeeping** in **Rwanda** during the genocidal massacres of 1994.

One of the first occasions, when the United States became involved in black Africa, was in the Congo crisis of 1960–1964, when it found itself in direct conflict with the USSR. The United States committed itself to support **Moise Tshombe** when in 1964 he became (briefly) prime minister of the **Republic of the Congo**; with Belgium, the United States was responsible for the military mission to rescue whites, including **mercenaries**, trapped in Stanleyville (Kisangani).

Subsequently, once **Joseph-Désiré Mobutu** had seized power in the Congo (later Zaire), the United States was to support him and use his country as a CIA base in Africa (especially in relation to Angola) right through the period of his dubious rule in that country.

The 21st Century

In the aftermath of the 11 September 2001 terrorist attacks in the United States, American concerns were especially directed toward developments in the Middle East—Israel/Palestine, Iraq, Afghanistan, and Iran. U.S. interest in Africa was focused upon oil and the fight against terrorism and in a number of conflicts, especially those in West Africa, it maintained a low profile. However, the U.S. played a leading role in brokering the peace between North and South in **Sudan** and there were growing signs during 2006 that it was again becoming involved in Somalia when it became increasingly likely that Somalia would come under an extremist Islamic government. *See also* ARMS TRADE; MILITARY ASSISTANCE.

– V –

VAN DUNEM, PEDRO DE CASTRO "LOY" (c. 1942–). Trained in Moscow, Pedro Van Dunem became **Angola**'s foreign minister on 23 January 1989, at a crucial point in the country's history when peace negotiations to end the long civil war were in progress. He had been appointed third deputy prime minister to President **Agostinho Neto** in 1976, but lost this job in December 1978 when the party, the **Movimento Popular para a Libertação de Angola** (MPLA)/ Popular Movement for the Liberation of Angola, was reorganized and a number of posts were abolished. He was given another job under Neto in 1979, but only after **Jose dos Santos** became president in September 1979, following Neto's death, did he rise to prominence in government.

Dos Santos first appointed Van Dunem as minister of oil and natural resources, which gave him important international contacts through the oil companies working in the Cabinda enclave, including Gulf Oil. Van Dunem had not been close to Neto and supporters of

the former president opposed Van Dunem's promotion to the Politbureau in 1983. In July 1987 he was given the additional portfolio
of minister of state for production, which placed him in charge of
the ministries of oil, agriculture, industry, transport, public works,
and fisheries. Then, on 23 January 1989, he succeeded his name-
sake, Afonso Van Dunem, as minister of foreign affairs just at the
time when it seemed possible that negotiations might bring an end
to the country's long-lasting and devastating civil war. He was to be
criticized by fellow Politbureau members as he tried to deal with the
complexities of the problem of integrating **Jonas Savimbi** and the
União Nacional para a Independência Total de Angola (UNITA)/
National Union for the Total Independence of Angola. On 1 March,
1990, Van Dunem met **South Africa**'s foreign minister "Pik" Botha
to pave the way for normalization of Angolan–South African relations. He continued to negotiate with UNITA for the eventual peace
(which UNITA later broke) and elections of 1992.

– W –

WESTERN SOMALI LIBERATION FRONT (WSLF). The Western
Somali Liberation Front (WSLF) came into being in 1975 during the
aftermath of the fall of Emperor **Haile Selassie,** when ethnic Somalis
in the **Ogaden** region of **Ethiopia** hoped to take advantage of the prevailing confusion in their neighbor to detach the region from Ethiopia.
Both the 1960 Somali Constitution and that of 1969 (the Revolutionary
Charter) included the aim of unifying all Somali territory; Mogadishu
saw the Ogaden as part of **Somalia** and not part of Ethiopia. Although
the activities of the WSLF were not directly a part of the civil war in
Ethiopia, they played a significant role in bolstering the Somali cause
and, therefore, diverting troops from the war against the **Eritrean
People's Liberation Front** (EPLF) and the **Tigre People's Libera-
tion Front** (TPLF). The WSLF also worked with the **Oromo National
Liberation Front** (ONLF) against the government of Addis Ababa.

On 4 September 1977, the WSLF claimed all territory east of a line
running from Moyak on the border with Kenya through Awash to El
Adde on the border with Djibouti. In 1977 the WSLF launched a full-
scale war against the Ethiopian authorities with the aim of detaching

the Ogaden from Ethiopia and, initially, the Ethiopians were quickly driven from the region. The WSLF was supported by regular Somali forces. However, following the withdrawal of the Somali forces from the Ogaden in March 1978, in the face of a massive Ethiopian and Cuban counteroffensive, the WSLF once more resorted to guerrilla tactics in the region. In May 1978 the WSLF and the smaller Somali Abo Liberation Front (SALF) agreed with the **Eritrean Liberation Movement-Popular Liberation Forces** (ELF-PLF) to work together against Soviet, Cuban, and other interventionists in the region. Heavy fighting occurred in the Ogaden through 1979 and 1980, and the WSLF claimed to control 90 percent of the area. But in the second half of 1980, the WSLF suffered heavy losses and Ethiopia recovered almost all the Ogaden territory it had lost. Greatly weakened, the WSLF continued guerrilla activities through the first half of the 1980s, though without making any major new impression upon the situation in the Ogaden, which remained under Ethiopian control.

WOMEN AND CHILDREN. Women worldwide have traditionally been treated as both subordinate and inferior to men, and only in recent times have these perceptions changed, mainly though not exclusively in Western societies, although feminist organizations are still fighting major battles to achieve full equality for women on all fronts. Traditions of male dominance are ingrained in many societies, and this is particularly the case in Muslim societies where the subordinate role of women is justified according to Islamic teaching.

Women play a crucial role in economic and social development: they manage (in many parts of the world) between 50 and 80 percent of food production, processing, and marketing, and run 70 percent of small business enterprises. This is the case in much of Africa with the result that when a country is wracked by civil war and women are unable to carry on their normal work, this has a devastating impact upon that country's normal production and wealth creation.

A significant majority of all **refugees** and displaced persons resulting from war are women and children and a majority of civilians caught up in wars or the crossfire of wars are women who have come to show great resilience and resourcefulness in coping with war's disasters: the destruction of their homes and possessions, and the break-up and deaths of their families. Women face great dangers and much suffering in wars, although their plight could be considerably improved if existing humanitarian laws were fully respected which, unfortunately, is all too rarely the case. In 2006 the International Committee of the Red Cross (ICRC) produced a significant study, *Women Facing War*, which is especially timely given the number of wars in Africa—and worldwide—at the present time. Countless children, those least able to defend themselves, suffer the traumas of war alongside women and many women, in appalling conditions, have been driven to survive for the sake of their children.

Women may also be fighters and as such, they should be treated with the same respect as men when found wounded or captured although, at the same time, they are equally subject to rules that prohibit illegal acts or crimes against humanity. International humanitarian law grants general protection to all war victims; it also provides for specific protection for women in war. Too often its rules are ignored. If properly observed, the suffering of women in war would be greatly reduced. An ICRC Guidance Document translates the findings of *Women Facing War* into practical advice for individuals and other organizations concerned with humanitarian programs and covers how to cope with the needs of women, such as physical safety, access to health care, food and shelter in situations of armed conflict. Coping with physical and sexual violence may be the first priority; later women have to come to terms with missing relatives, widowhood, or life in refugee camps.

Over 11–12 May 2006, a Second International Policy Conference on the African Child: Violence Against Girls in Africa was held in Addis Ababa. In **Democratic Republic of Congo** during Africa's so-called Great War, there were many sexual crimes committed against women and girls by combatants from all sides, including **United Nations** peacekeepers. Similar crimes were committed against women and girls in the civil wars in **Liberia** and **Sierra Leone** through the 1990s and in both countries the activities of **child soldiers** became notorious. Abducting children, both boys and girls, and using them either as soldiers—boys, or as sex slaves—girls, has become endemic in Africa's wars and was especially pronounced during the long course of the war in **Uganda** waged by the Lord's Resistance Army.

The United Nations has devoted much attention to the problems of women through its Commission on the Status of Women, the United Nations Fund for Women (UNIFEM), and other of its specialized agencies. A significant advance in the status of women in Africa took place in January 2006, with the inauguration of the continent's first woman president, Ellen Johnson Sirleaf, as president of Liberia.

– Z –

ZAIRE (DEMOCRATIC REPUBLIC OF THE CONGO). By 1996 Zaire had been ruled by **Mobutu Sese Seko** since 1965, and he and his regime had become notorious for corruption and self-aggrandizement at the expense of the state and people of Zaire. Mobutu appeared to treat Zaire as though it were his personal fief rather than a country for which he had any responsibilities as a ruler. The country's enormous mineral wealth had been frittered away and from being one of the world's principal copper producers, it had deteriorated to such an extent by 1996 that output had been reduced by neglect and corruption, as well as the breakdown of normal commercial–industrial activities, to a mere 34,000 metric tons. Only the production of **diamonds** (17.3 million carats in 1996) provided the government with an important source of revenue and a large part of this was siphoned off by smuggling or other illegitimate operations. The gross national product by the beginning of the 1990s stood at $8.1 billion while per capita income was one of the lowest in Africa at $220. Mobutu had proved himself a master at political manipulation—promising reforms, then reneging on his promises, playing off one group against another, and ruling through a clique whose positions depended entirely upon presidential patronage. The country was ripe for revolution; the question was who would provide it.

Prelude to Civil War

In April 1996, the government announced that the country's first multiparty presidential and legislative elections would be held in May 1997. These elections would be preceded by a constitutional referendum in December 1996. Mobutu once more had salvaged a deteriorating personal position. In 1993 he had been under growing international pressure to institute political reforms. Then, following the 1994 crisis in **Rwanda**, when an estimated one million people had been massacred and a further million or more had crossed into Zaire as **refugees**, the international community had relaxed its pressures upon Mobutu since his cooperation was required in dealing with the enormous refugee crisis. In August it was reported that Mobutu had prostate cancer and had undergone surgery in Lausanne.

The Banyamulenge Rebellion

President Mobutu was still absent from Zaire, recovering from his operation, when a major rebellion of the ethnic Tutsis (Banyamulenge) in eastern Zaire broke out. The Great Lakes region in any case was in turmoil as a result of the troubles in Rwanda and **Burundi**, and the rebellion had been sparked off by the huge numbers of Hutu refugees who had moved into Zaire as a result of the Tutsi triumph in the civil war in that country. The Banyamulenge had been in eastern Zaire for more than 200 years and had established themselves in the Mulenge Hills and then in Uvira. They had become disenchanted with Mobutu's government in 1981 as a result of his policy of divide and rule, under which he had deprived them of their Zairean citizenship. The first fighting had occurred during September 1996, when Zaire accused the Rwandan government of arming the rebels; this was denied, although the **Rwanda Patriotic Front** (RPF) government was predominantly Tutsi and sympathized with the Banyamulenge cause. The extremist Hutu Interahamwe militia, who operated among the refugees, had attacked the Banyamulenge and been supported in doing so by the Forces Armées du Zaire (FAZ)/Zairean Armed Forces. Earlier in 1996 the Hutu militia had cleared thousands of the Banyamulenge from the region of Masisi in North Kivu so as to use the area as a base for cross-border raids into Rwanda, which had come under the control of their rivals, the Tutsis, as a result of the events of 1994. In September 1996 the Hutus had turned upon the Banyamulenge of South Kivu region, but found the 400,000-strong population well armed and ready to repel them. On 8 October 1996, the situation was inflamed when the deputy governor of South Kivu, Lwasi Ngabo, said the Banyamulenge had six days to leave the country or be "exterminated and expelled." This sparked off another exodus of refugees from the region, but about 4,000 young Banyamulenge men began to attack FAZ units, which proved ill-disciplined and put up little effective resistance.

They also attacked refugee camps where the Interahamwe were based, and these attacks in turn sparked off a new movement of the one million refugees inside Zaire. As a result of these attacks, the **United Nations High Commissioner for Refugees** (UNHCR) reported on 21 October that following four days of fighting, the 12 refugee camps in the Uvira area were empty and that 250,000 refugees were on the move, many hiding in the surrounding hills.

The Zaire government, which was unable to control the situation, accused Burundi and Rwanda of setting off the conflict; it claimed that both countries had helped to train and arm the Banyamulenge. The Rwandan government, however, had become deeply frustrated by the presence in the Zaire refugee camps of the Interahamwe militia (which it blamed for the initial genocidal massacres of 1994) and the fact that it believed the government of Zaire was willing to protect the Interahamwe. The situation was ripe for a civil war in Zaire and an international war between Zaire and Rwanda. On 29 October, the Zaire government declared a state of emergency in Kivu region and imposed military rule in order to "eliminate all subversive networks." Despite this, by the end of the month the FAZ soldiers were reported to be fleeing the region and the rebels appeared about to seize control of a large area of western Zaire. In two weeks of fighting the rebels had captured the town of Bukavu and were advancing upon Goma, the capital of North Kivu, while they had already captured its airport which provided access to the region for FAZ troops and relief workers.

The quick success of the rebels and their high degree of coordination suggested to outside observers that they were receiving support from the Rwandan government. This was reinforced by the admission on 30 October by Rwanda that it had deployed troops in eastern Zaire, although solely as a response to the shelling of Cyangugu in Rwanda by Zairean troops the previous day. Rwanda's vice president and minister of defense, Paul Kagame, warned: "If Zaire brings the war to us, we shall fight Zaire." He also repeated his country's support for the Banyamulenge and said Rwanda would not allow Zaire to force them into Rwanda as refugees. He insisted that his country was not helping the Banyamulenge rebels, but also said that "people who want to exterminate others must be resisted." Thus, at the beginning of November 1996, Zaire and Rwanda were close to open hostilities, the FAZ was in disarray, and the Banyamulenge rebels appeared to have emerged with sudden cohesion as a potentially formidable force to challenge the government. The threat of a huge refugee crisis, as well as a war between Zaire and Rwanda, led the international community to plan for a possible military intervention. However, by the end of November the refugee crisis appeared to have been brought under control, although the rebellion against the Mobutu government was gaining momentum.

The Emergence of Kabila

Early in November, **Laurent Kabila** emerged as the leader of the rebels and claimed to be the coordinator of the Alliance des Forces Démocratiques pour la Libération du Congo-Zaire (AFDL)/Alliance of Democratic Forces for the Liberation of Congo-Zaire. Kabila had been an opponent of Mobutu since the 1960s: he now claimed that the AFDL represented five dissident groups—the Banyamulenge, the People's Revolutionary Party (a Marxist group founded by Kabila), Luba rebels from southern Kasai, Shaba rebels, and Kissasse's rebels (a group led by Andre Ngandu Kissasse, who was now acting as the military commander of all the rebels). Following the capture of Goma on 2 November, in which the rebels were assisted by the Rwandan army, the AFDL had gained control of North and South Kivu Provinces. In Kinshasa, the capital of Zaire, there was an angry backlash against this setback; crowds demanded war against Rwanda and Burundi, and Tutsi homes and businesses were attacked. There were fears of a coup by the FAZ against a demoralized government, especially as Mobutu himself was still out of the country. On 15 November, an advance UN-sponsored military team arrived in eastern Zaire to assess the situation and decide whether full-scale military intervention by the international community was the best way to deal with the huge refugee problem. Suddenly, however, the refugees began to stream back into Rwanda; this followed an attack upon the Interahamwe in Mugunga by a joint AFDL–Rwandan army force. As a result, most of the countries which had offered to make troops available for a UN intervention now withdrew their offers, and the idea was abandoned. At the same time, the AFDL began to consolidate its control of Kivu region and on 22 November announced that new political and administrative authorities in South Kivu had been sworn in; on 25 November a similar announcement was made in relation to

North Kivu. Kabila also announced that the aim of the AFDL was to liberate the entire country and said, "Ours is a national movement, not a local one."

On 17 December, Mobutu returned to Zaire and took charge of the situation, which, he said, "is threatening the territorial integrity and the very survival of Zaire as a sovereign and independent state." By that time the AFDL had created an effective buffer zone between the rest of Zaire and Burundi, Rwanda, and **Uganda**. The AFDL now controlled security in the region and was cooperating with the **relief agencies** dealing with the refugees. Reports suggested that the AFDL was in receipt of assistance from Zaire's eastern neighbors. Mobutu appointed a new chief of general staff, General Mahele Lyoko Bokungu, and called upon all political leaders to unite to resolve the crisis. He called for a government of national unity. On 24 December Mobutu appointed a new cabinet, keeping Leon Kengo wa Dondo as prime minister; however, he did not include in his new government anyone from the radical opposition Union pour la Démocratie et le Progrès Social (UDPS)/Union for Democracy and Social Progress of Étienne Tshisekedi. Government troops launched a counteroffensive against the rebels at the end of December.

Initial reports in January 1997 suggested that the rebellion had lost its momentum and that fighting had broken out among the rebels. The government claimed the rebels were backed by Uganda and Rwanda. Even so, the AFDL entered the year in control of a band of country 600 kilometers long bordering Uganda, Rwanda, and Burundi, which it called the "Democratic Congo." At this time the proclaimed goal of the AFDL was the town of Kisangani, which lay 600 kilometers west of Goma. There was clearly some dissension in AFDL ranks and this appeared to center upon the Mai Mai warriors, locals hostile to the Tutsis. On 21 January, the death was reported of the AFDL military leader, Andre Ngandu Kissasse, when tackling dissident Mai-Mai forces. Meanwhile, Mobutu's government was recruiting foreign **mercenaries**; senior former French officers were said to be creating a "white legion" of mercenaries to fight with the Zairean government forces (FAZ). There were reports of heavy fighting involving the mercenaries at the end of January. On 28 January, Kabila claimed his forces had blocked a mercenary-FAZ advance and wiped it out. On 30 January, the government accused Uganda of invading Zaire with 2,000 troops.

Rapid Rebel Advances

Rebel advances during February led Mobutu to fly from the south of France (where he had gone in January for further medical treatment) to Morocco in the hope of persuading King Hassan to send troops to assist him. On 4 February 1997, government officials claimed that troops from **Chad**, Morocco, and Togo would be flown in to support the government. In the east of the country, meanwhile, the AFDL was making steady advances and the FAZ appeared everywhere in retreat. By 8 February a rebel column was advancing on Kisangani, which was guarded by FAZ troops and a detachment of Serbian mercenaries. The whole situation was complicated by the continuing presence in eastern Zaire of large numbers of Hutu refugees from Rwanda; many of them had fled into the forest to escape the possibility of revenge massacres by Tutsis. Government jets from Kisangani, flown by mercenaries, bombed towns held by the rebels, including Bukavu, in mid-February but this did not stop the rebel advance. On 22 February, the rebels took the town of Kalima on the way to Kisangani; three days later FAZ troops supposedly defending Kindu, which lay to the west of Kalima, began looting the town before they retreated. By 28 February, Kindu had fallen and the rebels were within 100 kilometers of Kisangani.

At this point, President **Nelson Mandela** of **South Africa** attempted a peace initiative; he announced that Kabila would visit South Africa to take part in talks with Mobutu. The AFDL continued its rapid advance along the Zaire River during March, while FAZ troops were reported to be fleeing in disarray. On 8 March, the exiled former Hutu commander of the Rwandan army, General Augustin Bizimungu, fled from Kisangani with his deputy, abandoning their Hutu troops who had been fighting with the FAZ to stem the AFDL advance. On 10 March, the Paris daily *Liberation* claimed that the advancing AFDL forces were massacring any Hutus they found. By 11 March, with AFDL forces closing in on Kisangani from three sides, a mass exodus of civilians began. Kisangani fell to the rebels over 15–16 March 1997, the rebels meeting little resistance as FAZ troops changed sides. The rebels now controlled the greater part of the country's diamond-producing region, and two key towns—Mbuji-Mayi, the diamond town, and Lubumbashi, capital of the copper- and cobalt-producing province of Shaba—were both within the grasp of the AFDL. By this time the AFDL controlled about a quarter of the country. On 16 March Kabila met the UN envoy Muhammad Sahnoun, but rejected a UN cease-fire plan and insisted upon a face-to-face meeting with Mobutu. Members of the Mobutu family were reported to be quitting the country for Brazzaville in the neighboring **Republic of Congo**.

Mobutu returned to Zaire and accepted the resignation of Prime Minister Kengo wa Dondo. Despite South African and other pressures to meet with Mobutu and negotiate a cease-fire, Kabila and the AFDL were clearly bent on pursuing the war until complete victory had been gained. On 25 March, as a sign of desperation in Kinshasa, Mobutu's party, the Mouvement Populaire de la Révolution (MPR)/Popular Movement of the Revolution, announced its readiness to share power with the AFDL. On 2 April, Mobutu confirmed his longtime opponent, Étienne Tshisekedi, as prime minister, in what looked like another desperate expedient to defer the inevitable collapse of his regime. In announcing his cabinet, however, Tshisekedi left six places vacant for AFDL members, but the rebels at once announced that they had no intention of taking part in the government. By 8 April, as the rebels advanced steadily on the capital, Kinshasa, parts of the city were in a state of anarchy with soldiers using teargas to disperse crowds demonstrating in favor of Tshisekedi and thus against Mobutu himself. The **United States**, **Great Britain**, **France**, and Belgium now moved troops into Brazzaville, across the Zaire River, in readiness to evacuate their nationals from Kinshasa. On 9 April government forces again used teargas against supporters of Tshisekedi and prevented him from entering the parliament building; he was arrested, and later Mobutu announced he had dismissed him. Mobutu then appointed General Likulia Bolongo, the former minister of defense, as head of what in effect was a military government. Meanwhile, the advance of the AFDL had become unstoppable.

The Last Phase: Collapse of Mobutu Regime

Lubumbashi, capital of the mineral-rich province of Shaba, fell to rebel forces on 9 April 1997. Many FAZ troops in Lubumbashi defected to the AFDL. In Washington, a U.S. government spokesman called upon Mobutu to step down. On 10 April, in Goma, Kabila held a press conference at which he gave Mobutu three days to step down or his forces would move on Kinshasa. On 12 April, Mobutu said he was prepared to meet Kabila but said the latter should ask him "politely." On 13 April, the AFDL made plain it would resume its advance on Kinshasa; in the capital, panic followed a report that AFDL forces were already infiltrating the city. On 14–15 April, Kinshasa was brought to a standstill by a strike of Tshisekedi supporters demanding that Mobutu should stand down. On 16 April, Kabila flew to South Africa for talks with President Mandela and it was announced that a meeting between him and Mobutu had been arranged, but subsequent complications made it seem doubtful. By 22 April, the rebels were closing in on Kinshasa from two sides and France, Mobutu's last external supporter, called for a government of transition to be formed. During 23–24 April, the towns of Ilebo, Tshikapa, and Dowete fell to the rebels, which allowed them to cut many of Kinshasa's supply routes. Rebel forces then entered Bas-Zaire Province to the west of Kinshasa. An announcement from Cape Town, on 29 April, said that Kabila and Mobutu would meet on a South African warship on 2 May in international waters.

A row developed between Kabila and the UNHCR about the Hutu refugees in eastern Zaire; mounting evidence suggested that AFDL forces had committed atrocities against the refugees. Kabila gave the UN 60 days from 27 April to repatriate all Hutu refugees from eastern Zaire. The meeting between Kabila and Mobutu on a South African warship, the Outeniqua, finally took place on 4 May and though Mobutu agreed to step down, the way in which this would be done was not agreed. Following the meeting, Kabila told journalists he had given Mobutu eight days to go; he said his forces were then only 80 kilometers from Kinshasa. He made it plain he would not agree to a ceasefire and that his forces would continue to advance on all fronts. The collapse of the talks signaled an exodus from Kinshasa, and the United States advised its citizens to leave Zaire at once. A battle in Kenge, 200 kilometers from Kinshasa, on 8 May resulted in hundreds of deaths. The same day, Mobutu flew to Libreville, Gabon, for a summit of five countries—**Central African Republic**, Chad, Congo, Equatorial Guinea, and Gabon—which endorsed Mobutu's plan for his withdrawal and called on the military to prepare the country for elections. The plan was rejected by the AFDL. Mobutu returned to

Kinshasa on 10 May, and on 14 May the city was reduced to inactivity by a one-day strike called by Tshisekedi in protest at Mobutu's refusal to surrender power. Further talks scheduled for 14 May on the Outeniqua did not take place when Kabila refused to attend.

Finally, on 16 May, the minister of information, Kinkicy Mulumba, announced that Mobutu "had decided to leave the capital" and had "ceased all intervention in the affairs of state." Mobutu first flew to Gbadolite in northern Zaire; then, on 19 May, he flew to Togo and later went on to Morocco. The Swiss government announced that it had frozen all assets belonging to Mobutu or his family which were then held in Switzerland. It transpired that the senior military officers had told Mobutu they could not guarantee the defense of Kinshasa. The chief of staff, General Mahele Lyoko Bokungu, had made contact with the rebels and said he saw no reason to put a city of five million at risk for one man (Mobutu). On 16–17 May, Mobutu's presidential guard, including his son Captain Mobutu Kongolo, went on the rampage in Kinshasa killing those they regarded as traitors, including General Bokungu. Some 177 people were killed.

The New Democratic Republic of Congo

AFDL troops entered Kinshasa on 17 May, and Kabila announced the establishment of the Democratic Republic of Congo of which he would be president. (Mobutu had changed the name to Zaire in 1971 as part of his Africanization policy.) In a broadcast to the nation, Kabila said he would do everything possible to "guarantee peace, national unity, and the security of the people and their property." He announced the dissolution of all government institutions and the creation of a constituent assembly to draft a new constitution. He also said that several senior officers of FAZ had been in contact with him to confirm their loyalty and obedience to the new authority. The population of Kinshasa welcomed the AFDL troops into the city and Tshisekedi's Union pour la Démocratie et le Progrès Social (UDPS)/ Union for Democracy and Social Progress welcomed the new regime on 19 May. **Angola**, Rwanda, Uganda, and Congo (Brazzaville) recognized the new government, while western countries indicated support but as yet no recognition. On 18 May, the UN representative, Muhammad Sahnoun, said he had received a clear pledge from

Kabila that the AFDL would show maximum cooperation with the relief agencies looking after Rwandan refugees.

Kabila arrived in Kinshasa on 20 May and set up a transitional government. It became clear that there was no place in it for Tshisekedi and his UDPS. On 26 May the new government, for security reasons, ordered the suspension of all political parties within Kinshasa; this included a ban on demonstrations—some had taken place in protest at Tshisekedi's exclusion from government. On 29 May, Kabila took the oath of office with full executive presidential powers. In June, Kabila announced his government priorities: elections would be held after two years but first, during an interim stage, its object was to restore order and then to change the country's external policy and image while the economy was to be run on socialist lines. Priorities for the country were the construction of roads, the establishment of mechanization centers to modernize agriculture, and the electrification of the entire country. Tshisekedi was briefly arrested on 26 June after addressing a rally of his supporters; following demonstrations he was released the next day. On 7 September 1997, Mobutu died in Morocco. *See also* CONGO, DEMOCRATIC REPUBLIC OF: AFRICA'S GREAT WAR.

ZANZIBAR. A small though violent revolution, rather than civil war, occurred in Zanzibar in mid-January 1964 when the African majority, many of whom were the descendants of slaves, revolted against the dominant Arab minority. Zanzibar had been the center or "depot" for the Arab slave trade in East Africa over several centuries and only ceased to play this role when the slave trade across the Indian Ocean to the Gulf was brought to an end in the second half of the nineteenth century, largely as a result of British intervention in the region. In 1890, **Great Britain** established a protectorate over Zanzibar and was to rule the island for the ensuing 74 years, using the Arab minority as the ruling elite under British direction.

Zanzibar became independent at the end of 1963; and of a population of 300,000 some 50,000 were Arab. At independence on 10 December, the Arabs had control of all the political levers of power and the African majority was deeply dissatisfied, more so as it had witnessed in the preceding few years the rapid achievement of independence in one African state after another on the mainland. On

12 January 1964, the self-styled "Field Marshal" John Okello, who came from **Uganda,** led a number of ex-policemen in a revolt which toppled the government of Sultan Seyyid Jamshid ibn Abdullah who went into exile. There were only 700 insurgents but in a short time they had got control of the island. A new government was named under the leadership of Abeid Karume as president. Initially, its members were drawn from both the Afro-Shirazi party, which was African, and the Umma (Arab) party. This new government was at once recognized by the Communist powers—the **Union of Soviet Socialist Republics** (USSR), the People's Republic of China, the German Democratic Republic (GDR)—and the **Cold War** had come to East Africa. After Karume had formed his government, the position of Okello remained unclear; on 14 January Okello pronounced the death sentence on a number of former ministers and for several days he was to claim equal authority with the government.

In order to secure its position, the government requested police assistance from Tanganyika, which sent 200 policemen to its aid. About 500 Arabs had been killed in the immediate resistance to the Okello revolution; three weeks later about 2,500 people were in prison or detention centers and of these, 400 were political prisoners. A different estimate suggests that up to 5,000 Arabs had been killed, while a further 5,000 had gone into exile. Okello, who was seen as an embarrassment in Zanzibar as well as in Uganda and Kenya, left the island in February. The government of Karume became closed and secretive and for years was to be regarded by the West (it was the height of the Cold War) as a potential jumping-off ground for Communist subversion on the mainland.

On 23 April 1964, President **Julius Nyerere** of Tanganyika proposed a union of Tanganyika and Zanzibar; this took place on 27 April when Karume became first vice-president of the United Republic of Tanganyika and Zanzibar. In October 1964, the country changed its name to the United Republic of Tanzania. The Zanzibar revolution was an African inspired revolt against an Arab domination associated with the slave trade that went back centuries; however, because of Zanzibar's strategic position off the East African coast and the speed with which Communist countries recognized the new government, the West reacted by assuming that the turn of events had been Communist-inspired and was part of a Cold War challenge to its interests in Africa.

Nyerere himself was unhappy at the prospect of an independent Marxist-oriented Zanzibar off the coast of Tanganyika, hence his offer of union, which was accepted.

ZENAWI, "MELES" LEGASSE (1955–). Born on 9 May 1955, in Adua, Legasse Zenawi adopted the name Meles as a nom de guerre when he was leading the **Tigre People's Liberation Front** (TPLF). He abandoned his university studies in 1974 to set up the Marxist–Leninist League of Tigre, the northern province of **Ethiopia** that played such a crucial role in the long war in that country, which only ended with the downfall of **Haile Mariam Mengistu** in 1991. Zenawi was opposed to Mengistu from the time he assumed power following the fall of **Haile Selassie**, and with a small group of supporters he launched the TPLF. Over the succeeding decade, the TPLF came to control the greater part of Tigre Province, despite massive military campaigns against it by the large, well-equipped Ethiopian army. Zenawi was opposed to the rival Tigre Liberation Front (TLF) which, he claimed, had murdered its political opponents, and in the end, the TPLF eliminated the TLF. Since the **Union of Soviet Socialist Republics** (USSR) and **Cuba** supported Mengistu, Zenawi and the TPLF required an alternative Marxist model and so they cited the Albanian example, although it is possible to detect an element of African humor in this choice. In January 1989 the TPLF entered into an alliance with the Ethiopian People's Democratic Movement (EPDM) and together they formed the Ethiopian People's Revolutionary Democratic Front (EPRDF) which Zenawi led (he was appointed chairman of the Supreme Council of the EPRDF). By March 1990 the EPRDF forces were only 160 kilometers from Addis Ababa, where they consolidated their position before the final push on the capital.

In January 1991, at the first EPRDF Congress, Zenawi demonstrated his pragmatism by abandoning much of his Marxist ideology and advocating parliamentary democracy and a measure of market forces for the economy. Following the flight of Mengistu, the EPRDF forces entered Addis Ababa on 28 May 1991 and established an interim government. Zenawi agreed to the right to self-determination for **Eritrea**. Zenawi showed great restraint once he had control of Addis Ababa and made plain he was ready to share power with the other ethnic communities. After a series of talks in July 1991, a new government drawn from members of all the allied movements was formed; and on 22 July 1991, Zenawi was elected head of state by the ruling transitional council, and then, from 1995, prime minister.

ZIMBABWE. Latent antagonisms exist between the two principal ethnic groups in Zimbabwe: the Mashona who account for approximately 71 percent of the population, and the Ndebele who represent about 16 percent. The Ndebele under Mzilikazi moved into what is now Zimbabwe from **South Africa** in 1837. From 1870 the Ndebele were led by Lobengula, and under him they expanded eastward to absorb some of the less warlike Mashona until they reached their maximum spread in the 1880s. Then the Europeans moved into the region and both groups were to become part of the white-dominated colony of Southern Rhodesia.

During the course of the long nationalist struggle against white rule that lasted from 1950 to 1980 the Mashona broadly, though not exclusively, became members of the **Zimbabwe African National Union** (ZANU), while the Ndebele adhered in the main to the **Zimbabwe African People's Union** (ZAPU). In the final years before independence (1976–80) ZANU and ZAPU, under pressure from the Frontline States, reluctantly came together to form the Patriotic Front against the illegal white regime of Ian Smith. When pre-independence elections were held (under the terms of the 1979 Lancaster House agreement) in March 1980, there was considerable inter-party violence between members of ZANU and ZAPU. The election gave **Robert Mugabe**'s ZANU 57 seats (of the 80 African seats) while **Joshua Nkomo**'s ZAPU only won 20 seats. This defeat came as a great shock to Nkomo and ZAPU, particularly because Nkomo had been seen as one of the father figures of African nationalism. Everyone, however, had underestimated the strength of tribal affiliations in the elections. The independence government of Mugabe felt its position was precarious: there were civil wars in **Angola** and **Mozambique**; South Africa had embarked upon its policy of destabilizing its neighbors; and Mugabe was distrustful of the whites with their 20 entrenched seats—most of them had been firm supporters of the Smith minority government. In these circumstances Mugabe saw any form of dissidence as a threat, and when it came from the opposition

Ndebele whose leader, Nkomo, had a wider African reputation than himself, he reacted to it ruthlessly.

Immediately following independence, ZANU and ZAPU maintained an uneasy alliance with Nkomo and other of his supporters in the government; however, underlying tensions soon came to the surface. There were problems integrating the two armies and outbreaks of violence gave Mugabe the excuse to extend the state of emergency through 1980. In September 1980, Mugabe ordered the police and the army to take action against dissidents.

The Dissidents' War

Fighting between ZANU and ZAPU supporters, which erupted in Bulawayo during November 1980, left 50 dead. Further clashes took place in February 1981 in both Bulawayo and Gwero; many of the dissidents were ex-guerrillas who had never come out of the bush. Nkomo tried to persuade his followers who were dissidents to lay down their arms. He was at first unsuccessful, although some of them did so later, though only after another 200 people had been killed. Suspicions and tension between the ruling ZANU and ZAPU increased throughout 1981 until the government decided to disarm the remaining guerrillas. Nkomo's supporters believed this would weaken his bargaining position in relation to Mugabe. In theory, disarmament had been completed by May 1981. The government had then reduced the size of the army by 50 percent, for it was costing the new government 20 percent of its budget. Early in 1982, Nkomo denounced Mugabe's moves toward socialism and turned down the suggestion that ZANU and ZAPU should merge into a single party. On 17 February 1982, Mugabe dismissed Nkomo and three other ZAPU ministers. Subsequently, the government claimed that there was a connection between the Rhodesian Front of Ian Smith and ZAPU in an apparent coup attempt, when four whites were found guilty of a plot to overthrow the government. In April, the government claimed it had discovered ZAPU camps where men were being trained to act against the government. Nkomo publicly condemned the dissidents but he was nonetheless put under investigation. The violence increased through May and June 1982: dissidents attacked the prime minister's house and also that of Enos Nkala, a prominent member of ZANU who was also an Ndebele (and therefore seen as a traitor by some members of ZAPU). In Bulawayo, government forces arrested hundreds of people in a search for dissidents. A meeting was held between Mugabe and Nkomo during August but solved nothing. The tension was made worse by the army's Five Brigade, which was recruited from members of ZANU and trained by North Koreans; it was stationed in Matabeleland where it became notorious for its brutalities against actual or suspected dissidents. The steady increase of violence through 1982 culminated on 24 December in a series of incidents in which cars, buses and a train were attacked: three people were killed and 21 were injured.

In March 1983, after an arms cache had been discovered on his farmland, Nkomo fled, first to Botswana and then to London. The war continued through 1983. In August of that year Nkomo returned to Zimbabwe and resumed his seat in Parliament where he met with a hostile reception from the majority of ZANU members. In February 1984 the government imposed a dusk-to-dawn curfew over an area of 6,500 square kilometers of southern Matabeleland, and large numbers of troops were moved into the area to seek out the dissidents. At this point the **churches** accused the government of allowing its troops to perpetrate atrocities and refusing to let food reach areas affected by drought if these were also areas where the dissidents were active.

Climax of the War

Dissident activity spread beyond the core area during the second half of 1984. In November 1984, Senator Moven Ndhlovu of ZANU was assassinated at Beitbridge; his death was followed by riots, and Mugabe dismissed the last two members of ZAPU who were still in his cabinet. He then said ZAPU should be declared an enemy of the people. ZAPU officials were detained, and at the end of November a leading ZAPU supporter of Nkomo was assassinated. The elections of 1985 were carried out in an atmosphere of extreme bitterness between ZANU and ZAPU, with organized violence directed at ZAPU candidates. In Bulawayo ZANU and ZAPU supporters fought pitched battles. ZANU won the election, increasing its number of seats from 57 to 63, while ZAPU's seats were reduced to 15. Enos Nkala remained prominent in ZANU. He was minister of home affairs and especially tough on the dissidents, threatening to destroy ZAPU; as a result he was denounced as a turncoat by ZAPU, a denunciation which served only to emphasize the tribal nature of the Dissidents' War.

During the second half of 1985, following the elections, the government brought great pressure to bear upon ZAPU members: senior officials were arrested, ZAPU was evicted from its headquarters in Harare, and Nkomo had his passport confiscated. The end object of these government maneuvers was to force ZAPU to merge with ZANU and become part of a one-party state. As a result, Nkomo was forced to enter into talks with Mugabe, and these so-called unity talks were to be held on and off through 1986 and 1987. In fact, Mugabe held all the cards—numbers, the army, legitimacy, and patronage—and it became clear that either ZAPU came to terms with the ruling ZANU or fought on in a war it could not win. By March 1986 Nkomo had effectively surrendered to Mugabe's strategy and that month, with Enos Nkala, he appealed for peace in Matabele and then criticized those of his supporters who were endangering the unity talks. In July 1986, 100 people were arrested in Beitbridge under the terms of the state of emergency; then in October Nkala announced the release of all ZAPU detainees. The government was playing a "cat and mouse" game with ZAPU. Even so, the war continued through 1987. An agreement was nearly achieved in August 1987; when this failed the government initiated another crackdown on ZAPU.

The Settlement

The breakthrough came suddenly at the end of 1987 when a unity agreement was announced on 22 December; in essence, unity meant the elimination of ZAPU as a political party. Mugabe now became executive president of Zimbabwe and increased the size of his cabinet to 27, so as to include former ZAPU ministers. An amnesty for guerrillas was announced, provided they surrendered their weapons by 3 May 1988. The war had been one of winners and losers, the Mashona having won the 1980 elections, the Ndebele having lost them, yet refusing to accept the fact. Estimates of deaths according to official sources were 3,000, though they were almost certainly much higher.

The Dissidents' War in Zimbabwe followed a pattern that recurred elsewhere in Africa: there is a fight for independence; the dominant group forms the government; the lesser group feels excluded and therefore threatened; it revolts; it loses; it joins the winners. The war had come at a bad time for Zimbabwe, which was desperate to develop its economy and solve its many social/poverty problems after the Smith years, while also being vulnerable to the destabilization tactics which South Africa directed against the Frontline States through the 1980s. In the years of unity which followed, the disparate figures of Mugabe (austere, intellectual, dry) and Nkomo (the father figure of nationalism) in fact became complementary to one another in what by then had become a de facto one-party state. The report of an investigation by the Catholic Commission for Justice and Peace appeared in the press in Zimbabwe during May 1997 (a copy of the report had been sent to President Mugabe). It confirmed that atrocities had been committed by government troops in Matabeleland between 1983 and 1987, and that the North Korean-trained Five Brigade (Gukurahundi) had massacred 20,000 people in the region.

ZIMBABWE AFRICAN NATIONAL UNION (ZANU). The Zimbabwe African National Union (ZANU) came into being in 1963 when the Rev. Ndabaningi Sithole split away from the **Zimbabwe African People's Union** (ZAPU) to form the new organization. ZANU was a radical nationalist movement, which early adopted a policy of guerrilla warfare against the white regime, especially after Ian Smith came to power in 1964. ZANU was outlawed in August 1964; only after 1972 did it become increasingly militarily successful, by which time it was operating in the eastern part of Rhodesia from bases in **Mozambique**. Following the death by assassination of Herbert Chitepo in Zambia, President **Kenneth Kaunda** closed ZANU offices in Lusaka; and **Robert Mugabe**, the leader of ZANU who had been released from detention by the Smith government during the 1974 detente exercise, moved his headquarters to Maputo in Mozambique. ZANU became increasingly effective during the 1970s, and by 1979 on the eve of the **Commonwealth** Heads of Government Meeting in Lusaka, which led to the Lancaster House talks in London at the end of the year, ZANU had 10,000 guerrillas operating inside Rhodesia.

The **Organization of African Unity** (OAU) and other international pressures persuaded ZANU and ZAPU to form the Patriotic Front in 1976 so that the two movements pursued a joint strategy against the Smith regime, but little trust existed between the two organizations. When universal elections were finally held in Rhodesia in March 1980, ZANU under Mugabe won an absolute majority of the 80 African seats—57 to ZAPU's 20; this was also an absolute majority when the 80 African and 20 white seats were combined. As in so many African countries, tribal and ethnic differences or simple rivalry for power led to post-independence confrontations and violence, including civil war, and this happened in newly independent **Zimbabwe**. ZANU was mainly composed of Shona people, and though it experienced internal factions and splits, it enjoyed an absolute majority since the Mashona comprised over 70 percent of the population. Mugabe, by predilection, wanted to make Zimbabwe a one-party state. ZAPU under **Joshua Nkomo** was bitterly disappointed at the election results—Nkomo had long seen himself as the leader of an independent Zimbabwe.

It was clear to Mugabe that if he wanted to make Zimbabwe a one-party state, he had first to destroy the power of ZAPU. ZANU became the ruling party in April 1980, although several ZAPU leaders, including Nkomo, were given appointments in the independence government. When the former guerrilla armies of ZANU and ZAPU were combined into a new national army in 1980, there were 20,000 members of the Zimbabwe African National Liberation Army (ZANLA), the ZANU army, and these were antagonistic to the members of the Zimbabwe People's Revolutionary Army (ZIPRA), ZAPU's army. By 1982 hostility between ZANU and ZAPU had developed into open violence, and for the next five years Zimbabwe was to suffer from what became known as the Dissidents' War. When it became clear at the time of the 1985 election that the Ndebele and Nkomo could not win either the election or the war, Nkomo began to negotiate with Mugabe.

The negotiations, in real terms, were one-sided since Mugabe held all the trump cards; in effect he demanded the disbanding of ZAPU. An agreement was reached at the end of 1987, and ZAPU ceased to exist as a political party early in 1988 when Nkomo and other ZAPU leaders rejoined the government and Zimbabwe became a de facto one-party state. The disappearance of ZAPU as a political party represented the triumph of ZANU and the Shona people over their old enemies the Ndebele and their party, ZAPU.

ZIMBABWE AFRICAN PEOPLE'S UNION (ZAPU). The Zimbabwe African People's Union was the successor to the Rhodesian **African National Congress** (ANC). It was founded by **Joshua Nkomo** in 1961 and was banned by the white minority government in 1964 and forced thereafter to operate from headquarters in Dar es Salaam, Tanzania, or later from Lusaka, Zambia. James Chikerema led ZAPU during the years 1964–1969 when Nkomo was detained; and though at first ZAPU turned to the People's Republic of China for **aid**, in 1965 it decided to accept aid from the **Union of Soviet Socialist Republics** (USSR) instead. ZAPU was never to be sufficiently militant under Nkomo's leadership to satisfy the more radical of his followers, with the result that the party split in 1963 when the breakaway faction led by Rev. Ndabaningi Sithole formed the **Zimbabwe African National Union** (ZANU).

ZAPU launched its first guerrilla raids into Rhodesia from Zambia in 1967, though these had only a limited impact. Factional fights between Shona and Ndebele members of ZAPU split the organization from 1969 to 1970 when Chikerema, who was a Shona, left ZAPU to form another movement, the Front for the Liberation of Zimbabwe (FROLIZI). When at the end of 1972, ZANU launched major guerrilla attacks upon the Smith regime in the northeast of Rhodesia (they would continue through to 1979), Nkomo held back from any full commitment of his forces while he negotiated with the Smith government in an attempt to achieve a deal that would bypass ZANU, but he failed. Only in 1976 did ZAPU guerrillas infiltrating Rhodesia from Botswana become a major factor in the war. ZAPU recruits from this time on were from the Ndebele and loyal to Nkomo. By 1978 there were 1,250 effective ZAPU guerrillas and by 1980 possibly 3,000. From 1976 onward, ZAPU's guerrillas (the Zimbabwe People's Revolutionary Army—ZIPRA) received highly sophisticated training from Cuban instructors in **Angola** and Zambia, or from training in the USSR. Nkomo never committed all his forces to the fight against Smith in Rhodesia; he held back up to 5,000 members of ZAPU in Zambia (1976–80) ready for use in what he saw as a coming post-independence struggle with ZANU. Following independence in 1980, these 5,000 ZAPU loyalists returned to **Zimbabwe**: some were integrated in the new national army; others took to the bush and became dissidents in the later Dissidents' War.

Bibliography

CONTENTS

Introduction	434
General	435
Algeria	438
Angola	439
Burundi and Rwanda	442
Central African Republic	447
Chad	448
Congo, Democratic Republic of the, and Zaire	450
Congo, Republic of	455
Côte d'Ivoire	455
Darfur (Sudan)	455
Eritrea	456
Ethiopia	459
Liberia	461
Mozambique	464
Namibia	466
Nigeria	467
Sierra Leone	468
Somalia	470
South Africa and Southern Africa	475
Sudan	482
Uganda	485
Zimbabwe (Rhodesia)	486

INTRODUCTION

Although there is a wide range of published material about contemporary Africa, the literature is uneven and particularly in relation to ongoing civil wars or other disturbances. These may rate a good deal of attention in the press, but the student must wait for more considered appraisals in book form. Thus, between 1998 and 2003, what has come to be called Africa's Great War, which has been fought in the Democratic Republic of Congo with a number of its neighbors taking part and has resulted in an estimated 3.5 to 5 million deaths, has attracted far less attention than Iraq where casualties do not remotely approach the lower estimate for the Congo. Much research in this field must rely upon accounts appearing in the press, a huge if varied quantity of reports on the internet, and more considered articles appearing in weekly or monthly magazines: some, like *Time Magazine* or *The Economist* are not specifically concerned with African affairs, but deal with particular aspects of Africa from time to time. The student, therefore, must search the media as well as seeking appropriate publications.

The serious student will need to examine the background to a civil war, as well as reports on the war itself, since it is in the country's history that the underlying causes of any war are to be found. Below are listed a few books that are of particular value in this respect. First, two "global" examinations of Africa over the last half-century that examine many of the causes of present conflicts are (my own) *Africa: A Modern History* and Martin Meredith's *The State of Africa*. Mark Duffield's *Global Governance and the New Wars* examines problems behind wars and the causes of conflicts. Joanna Macrae's *Aiding Recovery* relates the use of aid to the aftermath of wars. Two other books, *Africa Works: Disorder as Political Instrument* by Patrick Chabal and Jean-Pascal Daloz and *The Criminalization of the State in Africa* by Jean-Francois Bayart, and others provide important insights into the way African states operate. If we look at a few of the wars in Africa, the following books offer oversights that will fill in many of the gaps that media reports fail to cover. For the Islamist War in Algeria, Hugh Roberts, *The Battlefield Algeria 1988–2003;* for Angola and Mozambique, Patrick Chabal and others, *A History of Postcolonial Lusophone Africa*, and Tony Hodges, *Angola from Afro-Stalinism to Petro-Diamond Capitalism*; for the

Congo (DRC), Georges Nzongola-Ntalaja, *The Congo: From Leopold to Kabila*; for an unusual personal insight into modern Nigeria, Karl Maier, *The House Has Fallen: Nigeria in Crisis*; for Rwanda there is an African Union report, *Rwanda: The Preventable Genocide*, and Scott Peterson, *Me Against My Brother*; finally, two books about Sudan, Douglas H. Johnson, *The Root Causes of Sudan's Civil Wars,* and Julie Flint and Alex de Waal, *Darfur: A Short History of a Long War.*

Of particular interest is the *Historical Dictionary of Multinational Peacekeeping* in the War Series and *The Historical Dictionary of SubSaharan African Organizations* in the International Organizations Series.

General information on all the African countries concerned can be found in the Scarecrow Press series Historical Dictionaries of Africa, as well as Historical Dictionaries of International Organizations; Historical Dictionaries of Religions, Philosophies, and Movements; and Historical Dictionaries of War, Revolution, and Civil Unrest. The books in these series, like the present volume, include a chronology, introduction, dictionary, and bibliography. They are periodically updated and any new editions can be found at www.scarecrowpress.com. Apart from the media and Internet, a number of yearbooks provide coverage of African affairs:

Africa South of the Sahara (yearbook) Europa Publications
The Middle East and North Africa (yearbook) Europa Publications
Britannica (yearbook)
The Annual Register (yearbook) Keesings Worldwide
Keesings Contemporary Record (monthly)

There is a range of African magazines, mostly published on a monthly basis, such as *Africa Confidential, Jeune Afrique, New African.*

GENERAL

Adepoju, Aseranti. "The Dimension of the Refugee Problem in Africa." *African Affairs* 81 (1982): 21–35.
Africa Review, The World of Information. Saffron Walden, UK. Annually from 1976 to 2004.

Anthony, Constance G. "Africa's Refugee Crisis: State Building in Historical Perspective." *International Migration Review* 25: 3 (1991): 574–91.

Arnold, Guy. *Africa: A Modern History.* London: Atlantic Books, 2005.

———. *Historical Dictionary of Aid and Development Organizations.* Lanham, Md.: Scarecrow Press, 1996.

———. *Historical Dictionary of the Non-Aligned Movement and the Third World.* Lanham, Md.: Scarecrow Press, 2006.

———. *The Maverick State: Gaddafi and the New World Order.* London: Cassell, 1996.

———. *Political and Economic Encyclopaedia of Africa.* Harlow, UK: Longman Current Affairs, 1993.

———. *Wars in the Third World since 1945.* London: Cassell, 1995.

———. *World Government by Stealth: The Future of the United Nations.* Basingstoke, UK: Macmillan, 1997.

Bayart, Jean-Francois, Stephen Ellis, and Beatrice Hibou. *The Criminalization of the State in Africa.* Oxford: The International African Institute in association with James Currey, 1999.

Baynham, Simon. *Military Power and Politics in Black Africa.* London: Croom Helm, 1986.

Black, Jeremy. *Why Wars Happen.* London: Reaktion Books, 1998.

Bruce, Neil. *Portugal: The Last Empire.* North Pomfret, Vt.: David and Charles, 1975.

Burchett, Wilfred, and Derek Roebuck. *The Whores of War: Mercenaries Today.* Harmondsworth, UK: Penguin Books, 1977.

Chabal, Patrick, and Jean-Pascal Daloz. *Africa Works: Disorder as Political Instrument.* Oxford: The International Africa Institute in association with James Currey, 1999.

Chaliand, Gerard. *Armed Struggle in Africa with the Guerrillas in Portuguese Guinea.* New York: Monthly Review Press, 1967.

Clayton, A. *The Wars of French Decolonization.* Harlow, UK: Macmillan, 1994.

Davis, Brian L. *Qaddafi, Terrorism, and the Origins of the U.S. Attack on Libya.* New York: Praeger, 1990.

Duffield, Mark. *Global Governance and the New Wars.* London: Zed Books, 2001.

Elliott-Bateman, Michael, ed. *The Fourth Dimension of War.* Manchester: Manchester University Press, 1970.

Europa. *Africa South of the Sahara.* London: Europa Publications. Annually since 1971.

First, Ruth. *The Barrel of a Gun: Political Power in Africa and the Coup d'Etat.* London: Allen Lane, The Penguin Press, 1970.

Fomerand, Jacques. *Historical Dictionary of the United Nations*. Lanham, Md.: Scarecrow Press, 2006.

Gorman, Robert F. *Historical Dictionary of Refugees and Disaster Relief*. Lanham, Md.: Scarecrow Press, 2000.

Griffith, Ieuan L. L. *An Atlas of African Affairs*. London: Methuen, 1984.

Janowitz, M. *Military Institutions and Coercion in Developing Nations*. Chicago, 1977.

———. *The Military in the Political Development of New Nations*. Chicago: University of Chicago Press, 1964.

Lee, J. M. *African Armies and Civil Order*. London: Chatto and Windus, 1968.

Legum, C., and John Drysdale, eds. *Africa Contemporary Record Annual Survey*: Documents. London: Rex Collings and African Publishing. Annually 1968/69–1989/90.

Lemarchand, Rene. *The Green and the Black: Qadhafi's Policies in Africa*. Bloomington, Ind.: Indiana University Press, 1988.

Lewis, William H. *Peacekeeping: The Way Ahead?* Washington, D.C.: National Defense University, 1993.

Lofchie, Michael F. *Zanzibar: Background to Revolution*. Princeton, N.J.: Princeton University Press, 1965.

MacRae, Joanna. *Aiding Recovery*. London: Zed Books, 2001.

Majdalany, Fred. *State of Emergency*. London: Longman, 1962.

Martin, Michel L. *From Algiers to N'Djamena: France's Adaptation to Low-Intensity Wars 1830–1987*. London: Brassey's (UK), 1989.

Mays, Terry M. *Historical Dictionary of Multinational Peacekeeping*. Lanham, Md.: Scarecrow Press, 2003.

Mays, Terry M., and Marle W. Delauncey. *Historical Dictionary of International Organizations in Sub-Saharan Africa*. Lanham, Md.: Scarecrow Press, 2002.

Meredith, Martin. *The State of Africa*. London: Free Press, 2005.

Parker, Richard B. *North Africa: Regional Tensions and Strategic Concerns*. New York: Praeger, 1987.

Pomeroy, William J., ed. *Guerrilla Warfare and Marxism*. London: Lawrence & Wishart, 1969.

Rosberg, Carl G., and John Nottingham. *The Myth of Mau Mau*. New York: Praeger, 1966.

Segal, Ronald. *The Race War*. London: Cape, 1966.

Simons, Geoff. *Libya: The Struggle for Survival*. Basingstoke, UK: Macmillan Press, 1993.

Smith, Joseph, and Simon Davis. *Historical Dictionary of the Cold War*. Lanham, Md.: Scarecrow Press, 2000.

Thayer, George. *The War Business: The International Trade in Armaments.* London: Weidenfeld and Nicolson, and Paladin, 1969 and 1970.

U.S. General Accounting Office. *UN Peacekeeping: Lessons Learned in Managing Recent Missions.* Washington, D.C.: U.S. Government Printing Office, 1993.

Woronoff, Jon. *Organizing African Unity.* Metuchen, N.J.: Scarecrow Press, 1970.

Zimmerman, Tim. *Coercive Diplomacy and Libya.* Boulder, Colo.: Westview Press, 1994.

ALGERIA

Ageron, Charles-Robert. *Modern Algeria: A History from 1830 to the Present.* London: Hurst, 1991.

Bennoune, Mahfoud. *The Making of Contemporary Algeria, 1830–1987.* Cambridge: Cambridge University Press, 1988.

Caute, David. "Fanon in Algeria." In *Fanon.* London: Fontana Modern Masters, 1970.

Gordon, David C. *The Passing of French Algeria.* London: Oxford University Press, 1966.

International Institute for Strategic Studies. *The Maghreb: The Rise of Radical Islam*, 109–16. London: International Institute for Strategic Studies, 1992.

Leveau, Remy. *Algeria: Adversaries in Search of Uncertain Compromises.* Chaillot Papers. Paris: Western European Union Institute for Security Studies, September 1992.

Middle East Watch. *Human Rights Abuses in Algeria: No One Is Spared.* New York: Middle East Watch, 1994.

Naylor, Philip C. *Historical Dictionary of Algeria.* Lanham, Md.: Scarecrow Press, 2006.

O'Ballance, Edgar. *The Algerian Insurrection, 1954–62.* London: Faber and Faber, 1967.

O'Brien, Connor Cruise. *Camus.* London: Fontana Modern Masters, 1970.

Pickles, Dorothy. *Algeria and France: From Colonialism to Cooperation.* New York: Praeger, 1963.

Quandt, William B. *Revolution and Political Leadership: Algeria, 1954–1968.* Cambridge, Mass.: Massachusetts Institute of Technology, 1969.

Royal United Services Institute. *Confronting Militant Islam: Egypt and Algeria*, 278–90. London: Royal United Services Institute, 1994.

Spencer, Claire. *The Maghreb in the 1990s: Political and Economic Developments in Algeria, Morocco and Tunisia.* Adelphi Paper 274. London: International Institute for Strategic Studies, 1993.

Werth, Alexander. *De Gaulle*. Harmondsworth, UK: A Pelican Original Penguin, 1965.

ANGOLA

Africa Watch. *Arms Trade and Violation of the Laws of War Since the 1992 Elections*. New York: Africa Watch, 1994.

———. *Angola: Civilians Devastated by 15-Year War*. New York: Africa Watch, 1991.

———. *Angola: Violations of the Laws of War by Both Sides*. London: Africa Watch, 1989.

———. *Between War and Peace: Arms Trade and Human Abuses Since the Lusaka Protocol*. New York: Africa Watch, 1993.

———. *Land Mines in Angola*. New York: Africa Watch, 1993.

Aguilar, Renato. *Angola 2000: Coming out of the Woods?* Report for the Swedish Agency for International Development Cooperation, Department of Economics, University of Gothenburg, Sweden, 2001.

Alberts, D. J. "Armed Struggle in Angola." In *Insurgency in the Modern World*, edited by B. O'Neill et al., 235–68. Boulder, Colo.: Westview Press, 1980.

Alexiev, Alexander. *U.S. Policy in Angola: A Case of Nonconstructive Engagement*. Santa Monica, Calif.: The Rand Corporation, 1986.

Amstee, Margaret J. "Angola: The Forgotten Tragedy: A Test Case for U.N. Peacekeeping." *International Relations* 9: 6 (December 1993): 495–511.

———. *Orphans of the Cold War: The Inside Story of the Collapse of the Angolan Peace Process, 1992–93*. Basingstoke, UK: Macmillan, 1996.

Barnett, Don, and Roy Harvey, eds. *The Revolution in Angola: MPLA Life Histories and Documents*. New York: Bobbs Merrill, 1972.

———. *With the Guerrillas in Angola*. Seattle, Wash.: Liberation Support Movement, 1970.

Bender, Gerald J. "Angola: History, Insurgency and Social Change." *Africa Today* 19: 1 (Winter 1972): 30–36.

———. *Angola under the Portuguese*. London: Heinemann, 1978.

———. "The Continuing Crisis in Angola." *Current History* 82: 482 (March 1983): 124–25, 128, 138.

———. "The Limits of Counter-Insurgency: An African Case." *Comparative Politics* 4: 3 (1972): 331–60.

Birmingham, David. *Trade and Conflict in Angola*. Oxford: Clarendon Press, 1966.

———. "The Twenty-Seventh of May: An Historical Note on the Abortive 1977 Coup in Angola." *African Affairs* 77: 309 (October 1978).

Brennan, T. O. *Uprooted Angolans: From Crisis to Catastrophe*. Washington, D.C.: U.S. Committee for Refugees, 1987.

Breytenbach, Cloete. *Savimbi's Angola*. Cape Town: Howard Timmins, 1980.

Bridgland, Fred. *Jonas Savimbi: A Key to Africa*. New York: Paragon House, 1987.

————. *The War for Africa: Twelve Months that Transformed a Continent*. Gibraltar: Ashanti Publishing, 1990.

Bruce, Neil. *Portugal: The Last Empire*. Newton Abbot, UK: David and Charles, 1975.

————. *Portugal's African Wars*. London: Conflict Studies, 1973.

Cann, John P. *Counterinsurgency in Africa: The Portuguese Way of War, 1961–1974*. Westport, Conn.: Greenwood Publishing, 1997.

Chabal, Patrick, et al. *A History of Postcolonial Lusophone Africa*. London: Hurst, 2002.

Chilcote, R. H., ed. *Protest and Resistance in Angola and Brazil: Comparative Studies*. Berkeley: University of California Press, 1972.

Crocker, Chester A. "Peacemaking in Southern Africa: The Namibia-Angola Settlement of 1988." In *The Diplomatic Round 1989–1990*, 9–34. Boulder, Colo.: Westview, 1991.

Davidson, Basil. *In the Eye of the Storm: Angola's People*. Harmondsworth, UK: Penguin, 1972.

————. *Walking 300 Miles Through the Bush of Eastern Angola*. Pasadena, Calif.: Munger Africana Notes, 1971.

Dietrich, Christian. "Have African-Based Diamond Monopolies been Effective?" *Central Africa Minerals and Arms Research Bulletin* 2, 18 June 2001.

Dreyer, Ronald. *Namibia and Angola: The Search for Independence and Regional Security, 1966–1988*. Geneva: Programme for Strategic and International Security Studies, 1988.

Felgas, Helio. *Guerre em Angola*. Lisbon: Livraria Classica Editoria, 1961.

Global Witness. *A Rough Trade, The Role of Companies and Governments in the Angolan Conflict*. London: Global Witness, 1998.

————. *A Crude Awakening: The Role of the Oil and Banking Industries in Angola's Civil War and the Plunder of State Assets*. London: Global Witness, 1999.

————. *All the President's Men*. London: Global Witness, 2002.

Guimaraes, Fernando Andersen. *The Origins of the Angolan Civil War: Foreign Intervention and Domestic Political Conflict*. London: Macmillan, 1998.

Hallett, Robin. "The South African Intervention in Angola." *African Affairs* 77: 308 (July 1978): 347–86.

Hare, P. *Angola's Last Best Chance for Peace: An Insider's Account of the Peace Process*. United States Institute for Peace, Washington, D.C., 1998.

Heitman, Helmoed-Romer. *War in Angola: The Final South African Phase.* Gibraltar: Ashanti Publishing, 1990.

Hodges, Anthony. *Angola from Afro-Stalinism to Petro-Diamond Capitalism.* Oxford: James Currey, 2001.

———. *Angola: Anatomy of an Oil State.* Oxford: James Currey, 2001.

Hodges, Anthony, and Walter Viegas. *Country Strategy Study.* Norwegian People's Aid, Luanda, 1998.

Humbaraci, A., and N. Muchnik. *Portugal's African Wars.* Basingstoke, UK: Macmillan, 1974.

James, W. Martin. *Historical Dictionary of Angola.* Lanham, Md.: Scarecrow Press, 2004.

———. *A Political History of the Civil War in Angola, 1974–1990.* New Brunswick, N.J.: Transaction Publishers, 1992.

Kitchen, Helen. *Angola, Mozambique, and the West.* Washington Paper 130. Washington D.C.: Center for Strategic and International Studies, 1987.

Klinghoffer, Arthur Jay. "The Angolan War: A Study in Regional Security." *The Jerusalem Journal of International Relations* 8: 2/3 (1986): 142–59.

———. *The Angolan War: A Study of Soviet Policy in the Third World.* Boulder, Colo.: Westview, 1980.

Krott, Rob. "Battle for Cabinda." *New African* (March 1998): 12–15.

McFaul, Michael. "Rethinking the 'Reagan Doctrine' on Angola." *International Security* 14: 3 (Winter 1989/1990): 99–135.

Memorias da Guerra Colonial. Lisbon: Andromeda, 1984.

Minter, William. *Apartheid's Contras: An Inquiry into the Roots of War in Angola and Mozambique.* London: Zed Books, 1994.

Monje, Scott Christopher. "Alliance Politics in Escalating Conflict: The Soviet Union and Cuba in Angola, 1974–1991." Ph.D. Diss., Columbia University, 1995.

Okuma, T. *Angola in Ferment.* Boston: Beacon Press, 1962.

O'Neill, Kathryn, and Barry Munslow. "Angola: Ending the Cold War in Southern Africa." In *Conflict in Africa,* edited by Oliver Furley, 183–98.

Papp, Daniel S. "The Angolan Civil War and Namibia: The Role of External Intervention." *Making War and Making Peace: Foreign Intervention in Africa,* 161–96. Washington, D.C.: United States Institute of Peace, 1993.

Pazzanita, Anthony G. "The Conflict Resolution Process in Angola." *Journal of Modern African Studies* 29: 1 (March 1991): 83–114.

Rivers, Bernard. "Angola: Massacres and Oppression." *Africa Today* 21: 1 (Winter 1974): 41–45.

Somerville, Keith. "Angola—Groping Towards Peace or Slipping Back Towards War?" *Terrorism and Political Violence* 8: 4 (Winter 1996): 11–39.

Steenkamp, Willem. *Borderstike: South Africa into Angola*. Durban: Butterworth, 1983.

Stevens, Christopher. "The Soviet Union and Angola." *African Affairs* 75: 299 (April 1976): 137–51.

Stockwell, John. *In Search of Enemies: A CIA Story*. London: Andre Deutsch, 1978.

UN. *Angola: The Post-War Challenges*. UN Common Country Assessment 2002, United Nations System in Angola, Luanda, 2002.

UNICEF. *State of the World's Children 2001*. United Nations Children's Fund, New York, 2001.

UNITA Central Committee. *Angola: Seventh Year*. Leyden: International University Exchange Fund, 1968.

United States Committee on Foreign Affairs. Subcommittee on Africa, House of Representatives. *Legislation to Require That Any United States Government Support for Military or Paramilitary Operations in Angola Be Openly Acknowledged and Publicly Debated*. Washington, D.C.: U.S. Government Printing Office, 1986.

Valentim, Jorege Aliceres. *Qui Libère l'Angola?* Brussels: Michele Coppens, 1969.

Venter, A. J. "Why Portugal Lost Its African Wars." In *Challenge: Southern Africa within the African Revolutionary Context*, edited by A. J. Venter, 224–72. Gibraltar: Ashanti Publishing, 1989.

Wheeler, Douglas L. "African Elements in Portugal's Armies in Africa." *Armed Forces and Society* 2: 2 (1976): 235–50.

Wheeler, Douglas L., and Rene Pelissier. *Angola*. London: Pall Mall Press, 1971.

Windrich, Elaine. *The Cold War Guerrilla: Jonas Savimbi, the U.S. Media, and the Angolan War*. Westport, Conn.: Greenwood Press, 1992.

———. "Media Coverage of the Angolan War." *Africa Today* 39: 1/2 (1992): 89–99.

Wolfers, Michael, and Jane Bergerl. *Angola in the Front Line*. London: Zed Books, 1983.

BURUNDI AND RWANDA

Abdulai, Napoleon, ed. *Genocide in Rwanda: Background and Current Situation*. London: Africa Research and Information Center, 1994.

Adelman, Howard, and Astri Suhreke, eds. *The Path of a Genocide: The Rwandan Crisis from Uganda to Zaire*. New Brunswick, N.J.: Transaction Publishers, 1999.

Africa Watch. *Arming Rwanda: The Arms Trade and Human Rights Abuses in the Rwandan War*. New York: Africa Watch, 1994.

————. *Beyond the Rhetoric: Continuing Human Rights Abuses in Rwanda.* New York: Africa Watch, 1993.

————. *The Crisis Continues.* New York: Africa Watch, 1995.

————. *Genocide in Rwanda: The Planning and Execution of Mass Murder.* New York: Africa Watch, 1996.

————. *Rearming with Impunity: International Support for the Perpetrators of the Rwandan Genocide.* New York: Africa Watch, 1995.

————. *Stoking the Fires: Military Assistance, Arms Trafficking, and the Civil War in Burundi.* New York: Africa Watch, 1997.

African Rights. *Rwanda: "A Waste of Hope": The United Nations Human Rights Field Operation.* London: African Rights, 1995.

————. *Rwanda: Not So Innocent—When Women Become Killers.* London: African Rights, 1995.

————. *Rwanda: Death, Despair and Defiance.* London: African Rights, 1995.

————. *Rwanda: Who Is Killing, Who Is Dying, What Is to Be Done?* London: African Rights, 1994.

African Rights and Human Rights Watch/Africa. *Genocide in Rwanda, April–May 1994.* New York: African Rights and Human Rights Watch/Africa, 1994.

African Union. *Rwanda: The Preventable Genocide.* Addis Ababa: Organization of African Unity, 2000.

Amnesty International. *Burundi: Appeals for an Inquiry into Army and Gendarmerie Killings and Other Recent Human Rights Violations.* New York: Amnesty International, 1992.

————. *Burundi: Killings of Children by Government Troops.* New York: Amnesty International, 1988.

————. *Burundi: Sectarian Security Forces Violate Human Rights with Impunity.* New York: Amnesty International, 1992.

————. *Rwanda: Mass Murder by Government Supporters and Troops in April and May 1994.* London: Amnesty International, 1994.

————. *Rwanda: Persecution of Tutsi Minority and Repression of Government Critics, 1990–1992.* New York: Amnesty International, 1994.

————. *Reports of Killings and Abductions by the Rwandese Patriotic Army, April–August 1994.* New York: Amnesty International, 1994.

————. *Rwanda: Arming the Perpetrators of the Genocide.* London: Amnesty International, June 1995.

Anderggen, Anton. *France's Relationship with Sub-Saharan Africa.* Westport, Conn.: Praeger, 1994.

Argent, Tom, Jeff Drumatra, and Katie Hope. *A Selected Chronology of the Rwanda Crisis, April 5, 1994–September 30, 1994.* Washington, D.C.: U.S. Committee for Refugees, 1994.

Aupens, Bernard. "L'Engrenage de la Violence au Burundi." *Revue Française d'Etudes Politiques Africaines* 8: 91 (1973): 48–69.

Ba, Mehdi. *Rwanda: Un Génocide Français*. Paris: L'Esprit Frappeur, 1997.

Bangoura, D. "Violence Politique et Insécurité au Rwanda." *Defénse Nationale* 51: 8 (1995): 137–45.

Barnett, Michael. *Eyewitness to a Genocide: The United Nations and Rwanda*. Ithaca, N.Y.: Cornell University Press, 2002.

Bayart, J. F., and G. Massiah. "La France au Rwanda." *Temps Modernes* 50: 583 (1995): 217–27.

Bodnarchuk, Kari. *Rwanda: A Country Torn Apart*. Minneapolis: Lerner Publications, 2000.

Bowman, Michael, Gary Freeman, and Kay Miller. "U.S. Policy: No Samaritan: The U.S. and Burundi, State Department Reply." *Africa Report* 18:4 (1973): 32–39.

Cairns, Edmund. *A Safer Future: Reducing the Human Cost of War*. Oxfam, 1997. [Contains materials on international tribunals.]

Carr, Rosamund Halsey. *Land of a Thousand Hills: My Life in Rwanda*. Harmondsworth, UK: Viking Penguin, 1999. (With Ann Howard Halsey.)

Chretien, Jean-Pierre. *L'Afrique des Grands Lacs: Deux Mille Ans d'Histoire*. Paris: Aubier, 2000.

Clarence, W. "The Human Rights Field Operation in Rwanda: Protective Practice Evolves on the Ground." *International Peacekeeping* 2: 3 (1995): 291–308.

Connaughton, R. M. "Military Support and Protection for Humanitarian Assistance: Rwanda, April 1994–December 1994." *SCSI Occasional Series*, No. 18. Camberley, UK: Staff College, 1996.

Dagne, Theodore. *Rwandan Crisis: A Chronology August 1994, June 1995*. Washington, D.C.: Library of Congress, 1995.

Dallaire, Romeo A. *Shake Hands with the Devil: The Failure of Humanity in Rwanda*. Toronto: Random House Canada, 2003.

De Saint-Exupery, Patrick. *L'Inavouable: La France au Rwanda*. Paris: les Srenes, 2004.

Des Forges, Alison. *Leave None to Tell the Story: Génocide in Rwanda*. New York: Human Rights Watch and International Federation of Human Rights, 1999.

Destexhe, Alain. *Rwanda, Essai sur le Génocide*. Brussels: Editions Complexe, 1994.

———. "The Third Genocide." *Foreign Policy* 97 (Winter 1994–95): 3–17.

Doyle, Mark. "Battered." *Focus on Africa* 5: 1 (January/March 1994): 4–8.

Drumtra, Jeff. *Life After Death: Suspicion and Reintegration in Post-Genocide Rwanda*. Washington D.C.: U.S. Committee for Refugees, Feb. 1998.

Eggars, Ellen K. *Historical Dictionary of Burundi.* Lanham, Md.: Scarecrow Press, 2006.

Eltringham, Nigel. *Accounting for Horror: Post-Genocide Debates in Rwanda.* London: Pluto Press, 2004.

Essack, Karrim. *Civil War in Rwanda.* Dar es Salaam: Newman Publishers, 1991.

Evans, Glynne. *Responding to the Crisis in the African Great Lakes.* London: International Institute for Strategic Studies, 1998.

Feil, Scott R. A *Rwandan Retrospective: Developing an Intervention Option.* Carlisle Barracks: Army War College, 1997.

Forscher, Romain. "The Burundi Massacres: Tribalism in Black Africa." *International Journal of Politics* 4: 4 (1974/1975): 77–87.

Franche, Dominique. *Rwanda: Généalogie d'un Génocide.* Les Petits livres, 1997.

Goldstone, Richard J. *For Humanity: Reflections of a War Crimes Investigator.* New Haven, Conn.: Yale University Press, 2000.

Goose, Stephen D., and Frank Smyth. "Arming Genocide in Rwanda." *Foreign Affairs* 73: 5 (September/October 1994): 86–96.

Gourevitch, Philip. *We Wish to Inform You That Tomorrow We Will Be Killed with Our Families.* London: Picador, 1999.

Human Rights Watch Arms Project. *Arming Rwanda: The Arms Trade and Human Rights Abuses in the Rwandan War.* New York: Human Rights Watch Arms Project, 1994.

Jones, Bruce D. *Peacemaking in Rwanda: The Dynamics of Failure.* Boulder Colo.: Lynne Rienner, 2001.

Kamukama, Dixon. *Rwanda Conflict: Its Roots and Regional Implications.* Kampala: Fountain Publishers, 1993.

Kay, Reginald. *Burundi Since the Genocide.* London: Minority Rights Group, 1987.

Keane, Fergal. *Season of Blood: A Rwanda Journey.* Harmondsworth, UK: Viking Penguin, 1995.

Klinghoffer, Arthur Jay. *The International Dimension of Genocide in Rwanda.* New York: New York University Press, 1998.

Korner, P., and K. Schlichte. *Invasion in Rwanda.* Hamburg: Universität Hamburg, Institut für Politische Wissenschaft, 1991.

Kuperman, Alan J. *The Limits of Humanitarian Intervention: Genocide in Rwanda.* Washington, D.C.: Brookings Institution Press, 2001.

Laffin, John. "Invasion of Rwanda." In *The World in Conflict 1991*, edited by John Laffin, 185–88. London: Brassey's, 1991.

Lemarchand, Rene. "Burundi: Ethnicity and the Genocidal State." In *State and Violence and Ethnicity*, edited by P. L. van den Berghe, 89–111. Niwot, Colo.: University Press of Colorado, 1990.

———. *Burundi: Ethnocide as Discourse and Practice.* Washington, D.C.: Woodrow Wilson Center Press and Cambridge University Press, 1994.

Linden, Ian. *Church and Revolution in Rwanda.* New York: Holmes and Meier, 1977.

Maigret, Frederic. *Le Tribunal Pénal International pour le Rwanda.* Paris: Pedone, 2002.

Mamdani, Mahmood. *When Victims become Killers: Colonialism, Nativism, and the Genocide in Rwanda.* Princeton, N.J.: Princeton University Press, 2001.

Melvern, Linda R. *Conspiracy to Murder: The Rwanda Genocide and the International Community.* London: Verso, 2004.

———. *A People Betrayed: The Role of the West in Rwanda's Genocide.* London: Zed Books, 2000.

Metz, Steven. *Disaster and Intervention in Sub-Saharan Africa: Learning from Rwanda.* Carlisle Barracks, Pa.: Strategic Studies Institute, U.S. Army War College, 1994.

Mordani, Dario. "Ruanda: Il Ritorno dall'Inferno." *La Rivista Militare* 5 (September/October 1994): 50–57.

Mutabazi, Claude. *La Position Sociale de l'Officier Rwandais.* Kigali: Ecole Supérieure Militaire, 1987.

Ndagijimana, F. *L'Afrique Face à Ses Défis: Le Problème des Refugiés Rwandais.* Geneva: Arunga, 1990.

Newbury, Catherine. *The Cohesion of Oppression: Clientship and Ethnicity in Rwanda, 1860–1960.* New York: Columbia University Press, 1988.

Nyaminani, Andre. *Le Role des Forces Armées Rwandaises dans le Développement National.* Kigali: Ecole Supérieure Militaire, 1987.

Omaar, Rakiya. *Rwanda: Death, Despair and Defiance.* London: African Rights, 1994.

Orth, Rick. "Four Variables in Preventive Diplomacy: Their Application in the Rwanda Case." *The Journal of Conflict Studies* 17: 1 (Spring 1997): 79–100.

Pearn, John. *Reflections of Rwanda.* Brisbane: Amphion Press, 1995.

Peterson, Scott. *Me Against My Brother.* New York: Routledge, 2000.

Power, Samantha. *A Problem from Hell: America and the Age of Genocide.* New York: Harper Perennial, 2003.

Reed, William Cyrus. "Exile, Reform, and the Rise of the Rwanda Patriotic Front." *Journal of Modern African Studies* 34: 3 (September 1996): 479–501.

Ress, David. *The Burundi Ethnic Massacres.* Lewiston, N.Y.: Mellen, 1992.

———. "Rwanda: An Existence Threatened." *Africa Research Bulletin* (Political Series) (21 July 1994).

———. "Rwanda/Burundi: Anatomy of the Crisis." *New African* (June 1994): 11–16.

Ronayne, Peter. *Never Again? The United States and the Prevention and Punishment of Genocide since the Holocaust.* Lanham, Md.: Rowman and Littlefield, 2001.

Segal, Aaron. *Massacre in Rwanda.* London: Fabian Society, 1964.

Shoumatoff, Alex. "Flight from Death." *The New Yorker* (20 June 1994): 44–55.

Sitbon, Michel. *Un Génocide sur la Conscience.* Paris: L'Esprit Frappeur (no. 36), 1998.

Taylor, Christopher C. *Sacrifice as Terror: The Rwandan Genocide of 1994.* Oxford: Berg, 1999.

Twagilamana, Aimable. *Historical Dictionary of Rwanda.* Lanham, Md.: Scarecrow Press, 2007.

United States House Committee on Foreign Affairs. *Recent Violence in Burundi: What Should be the U.S. Response?* Washington, D.C.: U.S. Government Printing Office, 1988.

"U.S. Troops and Assistance to Rwanda." *Foreign Policy Bulletin* 5: 2 (September/October 1994): 2–9.

Uvin, Peter. *Aiding Violence: The Development Enterprise in Rwanda.* West Hartford, Conn.: Kumarian Press, 1998.

Watson, Catherine. "After the Massacre." *Africa Report* 34: 1 (January/February 1989): 51–55.

———. *Exile from Rwanda: Background to an Invasion.* Washington, D.C.: U.S. Committee for Refugees, 1991.

Weinstein, Warren, and Robert Schrire. *Political Conflict and Ethnic Strategies: A Case Study of Burundi.* Syracuse University, N.Y.: Maxwell Schools of Citizenship and Public Affairs, Syracuse University, 1976.

Williame, Jean-Claude. *Les Belges au Rwanda: le Parcours de la Honte.* Numero special. Brussels: Complexe, 1997.

CENTRAL AFRICAN REPUBLIC

Boulvert, Yves. "Centrafrique, l'horrible année." *Le Nouvel Afrique-Asie* (Paris), no. 148 (January 2002): 12–13.

———. "Centrafrique—Pourquoi Bozizé a Joue son va-tout." *Jeune Afrique L'Intelligent* (Paris) 2131 (13–18 November 2001).

Kalck, Pierre, and Xavier Kalck. *Historical Dictionary of the Central African Republic.* Lanham, Md.: Scarecrow Press, 2006.

Kpatinde, Francis. "Monsieur Propre est arrivé." *Jeune Afrique—L'Intelligent* (Paris) 2203 (30 March–5 April 2003): 21–23.

Kromash, Neil. *Swimming Upstream, External Dependence and Political Change.* University of Washington, Independent Research Paper, May 4, 1998.

Laeba, Oscar. "La crise Centrafricaine de l'été 2001." *Politique Africaine* (Paris) 84, Editions Karthala (December 2001): 163–75.
Marchés Tropicaux et Méditerranéens. Special Centrafrique, no. 2940 (15 March 2002): 554–90.
Ngoupande, Jean-Paul. *Chronique de la crise Centrafricaine 1996–1997. Le syndrome Barracuda.* Paris: L'Harmattan, 1999.
Nwago, Jean-Baptiste. *L'économie Centrafricaine.* Paris: L'Harmattan, collection Etudes Africaines, 2002.
Profil Republique Centrafricaine. *Courrier International* (Bruxelles), 177, (October–November 1999).
Sempere, Jean-Francois. "ISTOM—Le Centrafrique, Un pays à la derive." *Marchés Tropicaux et Méditerranéens* (22 June 2001): 1278–81.
Soudan, Francois. "Qui a voulu tuer Patassé?" *Jeune Afrique—L'Intelligent* 2121 (4–10 September 2001).
Vie du President M. Ange-Felix Patassé. Biographie officielle. Bangui: SERAD (Webmaster: Franck Salvador), 2002.

CHAD

Akbakoba, C. N. O. "The OAU Forces in Chad." *Nigerian Journal of International Affairs* 8: 2 (1982).
Amnesty International. *Chad Never Again? Killimgs Continue into the 1990s.* London: Amnesty International, 1993.
Amoo, Sam G., and I. W. Zaerman. *Mediation by Regional Organizations: The Organization of African Unity (OAU) in Chad.* Mediation in International Relations: Multiple Approaches to Conflict Management. Basingstoke, UK: Macmillan Press, 1994.
Beri, H. M. L. "Civil War in Chad." *Strategic Analysis* 10: 1 (April 1986): 40–49.
Bouquet, Christian. *Tchad: Génèse d'un Conflict.* Paris: L'Harmattan, 1982.
Boyd, Herb. "Chad: A Civil War without End?" *Journal of African Studies* 10: 4 (Winter 1983/84): 119–26.
Brandily, M. "Le Tchad Face au Nord 1978–79." *Politique Africaine* 16 (December 1984): 4563.
Buijtenhuijs, Robert. "La Rébellion Tchadienne: Guerre Nord-Nord ou Guerre Nord-Sud." *Politique Africaine* 1: 1 (March 1989): 130–35.
———. *Le FROLINAT et les Guerres Civiles du Tchad (1977–1984): La Révolution Introuvable.* Paris: Karthala, 1987.
———. *Le FROLINAT et les Révoltes Populaires du Tchad 1965–1976.* Paris: Mouton, 1978.
Charlton, Roger, and Roy May. "Warlords and Militarism in Chad." *Review of African Political Economy* 45/46 (1989): 12–25.

Codo, Leon. "Les Etats-Unis, la France et le Conflit Tchadien: Co-Gestion de la Crise ou Rivalité d'Influence." *Géopolitique Africaine* 9 (October 1988): 81–121.

Cox, J. J. G. "Chad: France in Africa." *Army Quarterly and Defence Review* 188: 2 (1988): 161–67.

Decalo, Samuel. *Historical Dictionary of Chad*. Lanham, Md.: Scarecrow Press, 1997.

Dunn, Michael C. "Chad: The OAU Tries Peacekeeping." *The World Today* 5: 2 (February 1982): 182–88.

El-Kikhia, Mansour O. "Chad: The Same Old Story." *Journal of African Studies* 10: 4 (Winter 1983/1984): 127–35.

Froelich, J. F. *Tensions in Chad*. Adelphi Paper no. 93. London: International Institute for Strategic Studies, 1972.

Gatta, Gali Ngothe. *Tchad: Guerre Civile et Désagrégation de l'Etat*. Paris: Présence Africaine, 1985.

Gautron, Jean-Claude. "La Force de Maintien de la Paix au Tchad: Eloge ou Requiem." *Année Africaine* (1981): 167–89.

Hogot, P. "Les Guerres du Tchad, 1964–1983." *Etudes* (October 1983): 303–16.

Ingold, François Joseph Jean. *L'Appel de l'Afrique Primitive: Juin-Aout au Tchad*. Paris: Grund, 1945.

International Institute for Strategic Studies. *Conflicts in Africa*. Adelphi Paper no. 93. London: International Institute for Strategic Studies, 1972.

Joffee, E. G. H. "Libya and Chad." *Review of African Political Economy* 21 (1981): 84–102.

Kelley, Michael P. *A State in Disarray: Condition of Chad's Survival*. Boulder, Colo.: Westview Press, 1986.

Lanne, Bernard. "Les Causes Profondes de la Crise Tchadienne." *L'Afrique et l'Asie Modernes* 140 (1984): 3–14.

———. "Conflits et Violences au Tchad." *Afrique Contemporaine* 180 (October/December 1996): 52–61.

———. *Tchad-Libye: La Querelle des Frontières*. Paris: Karthala, 1982.

Lapie, Pierre Olivier. *Le Tchad Fait la Guerre*. Algiers: Imprimerie Heintz, 1943.

Lefevre, Eric. *Tchad 1983 Operation Manta*. Paris: Lavauzelle, 1984.

Lemarchand, Rene. "Chad: The Misadventures of the North-South Dialectic." *African Studies Review* 29: 3 (September 1986): 27–41.

Magnant, J. P. "Tchad: Crise de l'Etat ou Crise de Gouvernement?" In *Etats de l'Afrique Noire: Formations, Mécanismes et Crise*, edited by J. F. Medard, 173–203. Paris: Karthala, 1992.

Martin, Guy. "Security and Conflict Management in Chad." *Bulletin of Peace Proposals* 21: i (1990): 37–47.

Ndovi, Victor. "Chad: Nation-building, Security and OAU Peacekeeping." In *Africa in World Politics: Changing Perspectives*, edited by Stephen Wright and Janice N. Brownfoot, 140–53. Basingstoke, UK: Macmillan, 1987.

Ngansop, Guy Jeremie. *Tchad: Vingt ans de Crise*. Paris: L'Harmattan, 1986.

Otayek, Rene. "L'Intervention du Nigeria dans le Conflit Tchadien." *Le Mois en Afrique* 18: 209/210 (1983): 51–66.

Robinson, Pearl T. "Playing the Arab Card: Niger and Chad's Ambivalent Relations with Libya." In *African Security Issues: Sovereignty, Stability, and Solidarity*, edited by Bruce E. Arlinghaus, 171–84. Boulder, Colo.: Westview Press, 1984.

Spartacus, Colonel. *Operation Manta: Les Documents Secrets*. Paris: Plon, 1985.

St. John, Robert Bruce. *Historical Dictionary of Libya*. Lanham, Md.: Scarecrow Press, 2006.

Thompson, Virginia, and Richard Adloff. *Conflict in Chad*. Berkeley: Institute of International Studies, University of California, 1969.

Whiteman, Kaye. *Chad*. London: Minority Rights Group, 1988.

Wright, J. *Libya, Chad and the Central Sahara*. London: Hurst, 1989.

Zartman, I. W. *Conflict in Chad*. Boulder, Colo.: Western Press, 1986.

CONGO, DEMOCRATIC REPUBLIC OF THE, AND ZAIRE

Republic of the Congo, 1960–1970

Abi-Saab, Georges. *The United Nations Operation in the Congo, 1960–1964*. London: Oxford University Press, 1978.

Adeniran, Tunde. "The Relationship Between the OAU and the UN: A case Study of the Congo Crisis, 1960–1964." *Nigerian Journal of International Affairs* 14: 1 (1988): 112–23.

Beauregard, J. P. "UN Operations in the Congo 1960–1964." *Canadian Defence Quarterly* 19 (August 1989): 27.

Brookings Institution. *United Nations Peacekeeping in the Congo, 1960–1964*. 4 vols. Washington, D.C.: Brookings Institution, 1966.

Chakravarty, B. *The Congo Operation, 1960–63*. Delhi: Historical Section, Ministry of Defence, Government of India, 1976.

Clark, S. J. G. *The Congo Mercenary: A History and Analysis*. Johannesburg: South African Institute of International Affairs, 1968.

Collins, C. J. L. "The Cold War Comes to Africa: Cordier and the 1960 Congo Crisis." *Journal of International Affairs* 47: 1 (Summer 1993): 243–69.

"The Congolese Coup of 1960." In *Casebook of Insurgency and Revolutionary Warfare: 23 Summary Accounts*, 301–14. Special Operations Research

Office. Washington, D.C.: The American University Special Operations Research Office, 1962.

Dodenhoff, George H. "The Congo: A Case Study of Mercenary Employment." *Naval War College Review* 21: 8 (April 1969): 44–70.

Dorn, A. Walter, and David J. H. Bell. "Intelligence and Peacekeeping: The UN Operation in the Congo, 1960–64." *International Peacekeeping* 2: 1 (1995): 11–33.

Durch, William J. "The UN Operation in the Congo." In *The Evolution of UN Peacekeeping: Case Studies and Comparative Analysis,* edited by William J. Durch, 315–52. New York: St. Martin's Press, 1993.

Epstein, Howard M., ed. *Revolt in the Congo, 1960–1964.* New York: Facts on File, 1965.

Gleijeses, Piero. "Flee! The White Giants Are Coming": The United States, the Mercenaries, and the Congo, 1964–65." *Diplomatic History* 18:2 (1994): 207–37.

Hatch, John. "The Congo: Hostages, Mercenaries and the CIA." *The Nation* (14 December 1964): 452–55.

Hoare, Michael. *Congo Mercenary.* London: Robert Hale, 1971.

Holmes. John. "The United Nations in the Congo." *International Journal* 16:1 (1960/61): 1–16.

James, Alan. *Britain and the Congo Crisis, 1960–63.* Basingstoke, UK: Macmillan, 1996.

Kalb, Madeleine G. *The Congo Cables: The Cold War in Africa—From Eisenhower to Kennedy.* New York: Macmillan, 1982.

Lefever, Ernest W. *Crisis in the Congo: A UN Force in Action.* Washington, D.C.: Brookings Institution, 1965.

———. *Uncertain Mandate: Politics of the UN Congo Operation.* Baltimore, Md.: John Hopkins Press, 1964.

Legum, Colin. *Congo Disaster.* Baltimore, Md.: Penguin Books, 1961.

Martelli, George. *Experiment in World Government: An Account of the United Nations Operation in the Congo, 1960–1964.* London: Johnson, 1966.

Merriam, Alan P. *Congo: Background of Conflict.* Evanston, Ill.: Northwestern University Press, 1961.

Mohan, Jitendra. "Ghana, The Congo, and the United Nations." *Journal of Modern African Studies* 7: 3 (October 1969): 369–406.

Nzongola-Ntalaja, Georges. *The Congo: From Leopold to Kabila.* London: Zed Books, 2002.

Odom, Thomas P. *Dragon Operations: Hostage Rescue in the Congo 1964–1965.* Fort Leavenworth, Kans.: Combat Studies Institute, 1993.

Ramos, Francisco J. "The United Nations and the Congo Crisis." *Military Review* 45:11 (November 1965): 50–57.

Reed, David. *111 Days in Stanleyville.* New York: Harper and Row, 1965.

Schmidl, Erwin A. "The Battle of Bukavu, Congo 1960: Peacekeepers Under Fire." *Small Wars and Insurgencies* 8: 3 (Winter 1997): 25–40.

Simmonds, R. *Legal Problems Arising from the United Nations Military Operations in the Congo.* The Hague: Martinus Nijhof, 1968.

Vandewalle, Frederic J. L. A. *L'Ommengang: Odysée et Réconquête de Stanleyville, 1964.* Brussels: Le Livre Africain, Collection Temoinage Africain, 1970.

Verhaegen, Benoit. *Rébellions au Congo.* Brussels: C.R.I.S.P., 1966.

Zaire, 1970–1997

Amnesty International. *Zaire: Reports of Torture and Killings Committed by the Armed Forces in Shaba Region.* New York: Amnesty International, 1986.

Aronson, David. "The Dead Help No One Living: A Return to Congo." *World Policy Journal* 14: 4 (Winter 1997/98): 81–96.

Bangoura, Dominique. "L'Armée au Zaire dans une Période de Transition Politique." *Defence Nationale* 50 (1994): 123–34.

Bobb, F. Scott. *Historical Dictionary of Zaire.* Lanham, Md.: Scarecrow Press, 1999.

Boyne, Sean. "Rebels Repel Zaire Counter-Offensive." *Jane's Intelligence Review* 9: 4 (April 1997): 278–81.

———. "The White Legion: Mercenaries in Zaire." *Jane's Intelligence Review* 9: 6 (June 1997): 278–81.

Coquery-Vidrovitch, Catherine, et al. *Rébellions—Révolutions au Zaire.* 2 vols. Paris: L'Harmattan, 1987.

Cornevin, R. *Le Zaire.* Paris: Presses Universitaires de France, 1977.

Ekpebu, L. B. *Zaire and the African Revolution.* Ibadan: Ibadan University Press, 1989.

Erulin, Phillipe. *Zaire: Sauver Kolwezi: UN Réportage Photographique.* Paris: Eric Baschet Editions, 1979.

———. "Truth or Credibility: Castro, Carter, and the Invasions of Shaba." *International History Review* 18: 1 (February 1996): 70–103.

Glickson, Roger. "The Zairean Armed Forces." *African Defence* (December 1990): 38–39.

Gras, Yves. "L'Opération Kolwezi." *Mondes et Cultures* 45 (8 November 1986): 691–715.

Grip. *Congo-Zaire: La Colonisation: L'Indépendance, Le Régime Mobutu—et Demain?* Brussels: Groupe de Recherche et de l'Information sur la Paix (GRIP), 1989.

Kelly, S. *America's Tyrant: The CIA (Central Intelligence Agency) and Mobutu of Zaire.* Lanham, Md.: University of America Press, 1993.

Khanduri, Chandra B. "The Profile of a Commanding Officer." *Journal of the United Service Institution of India* 119: 495 (1989): 81–88.

Leslie, Winsome J. *Zaire: Continuity and Political Changes in an Oppressive State*. Boulder, Colo.: Westview Press, 1993.

Meisler, Stanley. "Crisis in Katanga." *MHO: The Quarterly Journal of Military History* 5: 1 (1992): 70–80.

Ngonzola-Ntalaja, Georges, ed. *The Crisis in Zaire: Myths and Realities*. Trenton, N.J.: Africa World Press, 1986.

Odom, Thomas P. *Shaba II: The French and Belgian Intervention in Zaire in 1978*. Fort Leavenworth, Kans.: Combat Studies Institute, 1993.

Ogunbadejo, Oye. "Conflict in Africa: A Case Study of the Shaba Crisis, 1977." *World Affairs* 141:3 (1979): 219–34.

Prunier, Gerard. "The Geopolitical Situation of the Great Lakes Area in Light of the Kivu Crisis." *Refugee Survey Quarterly* 16 (1997): 1–25.

———. "The Great Lakes Crisis." *Current History* 96 (May 1997): 193–99.

Rieff, David. "Real Politik in Congo: Should Zaire's Fate Have Been Subordinate to the Fate of Rwandan refugees?" *The Nation* 265 (July 7, 1997): 16–21.

Rikhye, Indar jit. *Military Adviser to the Secretary General: UN Peacekeeping and the Congo Crisis*. London: Hurst; New York: St. Martin's Press, 1993.

Rosenblum, Peter. "Endgame in Zaire." *Current History* 96 (May 1997): 200–205.

Sauldie, Madan. "France's Military Intervention in Africa." *Africa* 77 (January 1978): 43–49.

Schatzberg, Michael G. "Military Intervention and the Myth of Collective Security: The Case of Zaire." *Journal of Modern African Studies* 27: 2 (June 1989): 315–40.

———. *Mobutu or Chaos? The United States and Zaire, 1960–1990*. Philadelphia, Pa.: University Press of America, 1991.

Schmidt, Rudolf. "Zaire After the 1978 Shaba Crisis." *Aussen Politik* (English ed.) 30: 1 (1979): 88–99.

Sergent, Pierre. *La Légion Saute sur Kolwezi*. Paris: Presses de la Cite, 1978.

United Nations. *Zaire Human Rights Practices, 1995*. March 1996.

United States Congress/House. Subcommittee on Africa. *Zaire: Collapse of an African Giant?* Hearing Held on April 8, 1997. 105th Congress, 1st Session. Washington, D.C.: U.S. Government Printing Office, 1997.

Willame, J. C. "Zaire: Etat de Crise et Perspectives Futures." *Refugee Survey Quarterly* 16 (1997): 26–41.

Yahemtchouk, Romain. *Les Deux Guerres di Sahara: Les Relations entre la Belgique, la France et le Zaire*. Brussels: Institut Royal des Relations Internationales, 1988.

Young, M. C., and T. Turner. *The Rise and Decline of the Zairean State.* Madison: University of Wisconsin Press, 1985.

Democratic Republic of the Congo, 1997–

Abdulai, N. *Zaire: Background to the Civil War.* London: AEIB, 1997.

Boissonade, Euloge. *Kabila clone de Mobutu?* Paris: Ed. Moreux, 1998.

Braeckman, Colette, et al. *Kabila prend le pouvoir: les prémices d'une chute—la campagne victorieuse de l'ADFL-le Congo d'aujourd'hui.* Brussels: GRIP, 1998.

———. *L'enjeu congolais: l'Afrique centrale après Mobutu.* Paris: Fayard, 1999.

De Villers, Gauthier, and Jean-Claude Willame, in collaboration with Jean Omasombo and Erik Kennes. *République Démocratique du Congo: chronique politique d'un entre-deux guerres, Octobre 1996-Juillet 1998.* Brussels: Institut Africain-CEDAF, 1998.

Doom, Ruddy, and Jan Gorus, eds. *Politics of Identity and Economics of Conflict in the Great Lakes Region.* Brussels: VUB University Press, 2000.

Goyvaerts, Didier. *Conflict and Ethnicity in Central Africa.* Tokyo: Institute for the Study of Languages and Cultures of Asia and Africa, Tokyo University of Foreign Studies, 2000.

Hochschild, A. *King Leopold's Ghost.* London: Macmillan, 1999.

International Crisis Group. *Scramble for the Congo: Anatomy of an Ugly War.* Nairobi and Brussels: ICG Africa Report No. 26, 2000.

Janssen, Pierre. *A la cour de Mobutu.* Paris: Ed. Michel Lafon, 1997.

Madsen, Wayne. *Genocide and Covert Operations in Africa, 1993–1999.* Lewiston, N.Y.: Edwin Mellen Press, 1999.

Ngbanda Nzambo-ku-Atumba, Honore. *Ainsi sonne le glas! Les derniers jours du Maréchal Mobutu.* Paris: Ed. Gideppe, 1998.

Nzongola-Ntalaja, Georges. *From Zaire to the Democratic Republic of the Congo.* Uppsala, Nordiske Afrikainstitutet, 1999.

Reyntjens, Filip. *La guerre des grands lacs.* Paris: L'Harmattan, 1999.

Weiss, Herbert F. *War and Peace in the Democratic Republic of the Congo.* Uppsala: Nordiska Africainstitutet, 2000.

Wesley, Michael. *Casualties of the New World Order: The Causes of Failure of UN Missions to Civil Wars.* New York: St. Martin's Press, 1997.

Wilungula, B. Cosma. *Fizi 1967–1986: le maquis de Kabila.* Brussels: Institut Africain-CEDAF, 1997.

Young, Crawford. "Zaire: The Anatomy of a Failed State," in David Birmingham and Phyllis M. Martin (eds.), *History of Central Africa: The Contemporary Years since 1960.* London: Longman, 1998.

CONGO, REPUBLIC OF

Association Rupture-Solidarité. *Congo-Brazzaville: Dérives politiques, catastrophe humanitaire, désires de paix.* Paris: Editions Karthala, 1999.

Ayessa, B., and J. P. Pigasse. *Brazzaville Chronique 1999.* Brazzaville: Editions Adiac, 2000.

Decalo, S., V. Thompson, and R. Adloff. *Historical Dictionary of the People's Republic of the Congo.* 3rd ed. Lanham, Md.: Scarecrow Press, 1996.

MacGaffrey, J., and R. Bazenguissa-Ganga. *Congo-Paris: Transnational Traders on the Margins of the Law.* Oxford: James Currey Publications, 2000.

Ndaki, G. *Crises, mutations et conflits politiques au Congo-Brazzaville.* Paris: L'Harmattan, 1998.

Obenga, B., and J. C. Makimouna-Ngoualak. *Congo-Brazzaville: diagnostic et strategies pour la création de valeur.* Paris: L'Harmattan, 1999.

Obenga, T. *L'Histoire sanglante du Congo-Brazzaville (1959–1997).* Paris: Présence Africaine, 1998.

Pigasse, J.-P. *Congo: Chronique d'une guerre annoncée.* Brazzaville: Editions ADIAC, 1998.

Sassou-Nguesso, D. *Le Manguier, le fleuve et la souris.* France: Jean-Claude Lattes, 1997.

CÔTE D'IVOIRE

Adebajo, Adekeye. *Building Peace in West Africa.* International Peace Academy Occasional Papers Series. Boulder, Colo.: Lynne Rienner Publishers, 2002.

Bedie, H. Konan. *Les chemins de ma vie: Entretiens avec Eric Laurent.* Paris: Plon, 1999.

Bouquet, Christian. *Géopolitique de la Côte d'Ivoire.* Paris: Arman Colin, 2005.

Diarra, S. *Les faux complots d'Houphoüet-Boigny.* Paris: Editions Karthala, 1997.

La Politique Africaine. Vols. 78, 89, 92, and 98.

Mundt, R. *Historical Dictionary of the Côte d'Ivoire (Ivory Coast).* Lanham, Md.: Scarecrow Press, 1996.

Reno, William. *Warlord Politics and African States.* Boulder, Colo.: Lynne Rienner Publishers, 1998.

Soro, Guillaume. *Pourquoi je suis devenu un rébelle. La Côte d'Ivoire au bord du gouffre.* Paris: Hachette, 2005.

DARFUR (SUDAN)

Amnesty International. "Darfur, Sudan: UN Security Council Must Challenge Human Rights Violations." London: 2 September 2004.

Amnesty International. "Sudan: Who Will Answer for the Crimes?" London: 18 January 2005.

Collins, Robert O. "Disaster in Darfur." *African Geopolitics* 15–16 (Summer–Fall): October, 2004.

De Waal, Alex, and A. H. Abdesalam. "Islamism, State Power and Jihad in Sudan," in Alex de Waal (ed.), *Islamism and its Enemies in the Horn of Africa.* London: Hurst, 2004.

Flint, Julie, and Alex de Waal. *Darfur: A Short History of a Long War.* London: Zed Books, 2005.

Human Rights Watch. "Darfur Destroyed." New York: 9 May 2004.

———. "Darfur Documents Confirm Government Policy of Militia Support." New York: 20 July 2004.

———. "Sudan: Janjaweed Camps Still Active." New York: 27 August 2004.

ICID (International Commission of Inquiry on Darfur). "Report to the United Nations Secretary-General, Pursuant to Security Council Resolution 1564 of 18 September 2004." United Nations. Geneva: 25 January 2005.

Power, Samantha. "Dying in Darfur." *The New Yorker.* New York: 30 August 2004.

Ryle, John. "Disaster in Darfur." *New York Review of Books.* New York: 12 August 2004.

ERITREA

Abbay, A. *Identity Jilted? The Divergent Paths of the Eritrean and Tigrayan Nationalist Struggles.* Lawrenceville, N.J.: Red Sea Press, 1998.

"Africa: EPLF Claims Major Victory." *Defense and Foreign Affairs Weekly* (4–10 April 1988): 3–4.

Bell, John Bowyer. "Endemic Insurgency and International Order: The Eritrean Experience." *Orbis* 18: 2 (Summer 1974): 427–50.

Berger, Carol. "Eritrea: The Longest War." *Africa Report* 32: 2 (March/April 1987): 30–32.

Boyce, Frank. "The Internationalizing of an Internal War: Ethiopia, the Arabs, and the Case for Eritrea." *The Journal of International and Comparative Studies* 5: 3 (1972): 51–73.

Campbell, John Franklin. "Rumblings Along the Red Sea: The Eritrean Question." *Foreign Affairs* 48:3 (April 1970): 537–48.

Cheek, James. "Ethiopia: A Successful Insurgency." In *Low Intensity Conflict: On Threats in a New World,* edited by Edwin G. Corr and Stephen Sloan, 125–49. Boulder, Colo.: Westview Press, 1992.

Cliffe, Lionel, and Basil Davidson. *The Long Struggle of Eritrea.* Trenton, N.J.: The Red Sea Press, 1988.

Cliffe, Lionel, Basil Davidson, and Bereket Habte Selassie, eds. *Behind the War in Eritrea*. Nottingham, UK: Spokesman, 1980.

Connell, Dan. *Against All Odds*: *A Chronicle of the Eritrean Revolution*. Trenton, N.J.: The Red Sea Press, 1993.

Diamond, Robert A., and David Fouquet. "American Military Aid to Ethiopia—and Eritrean Insurgency." *Africa Today* 19: 1 (Winter 1972): 37–43.

Doornbos, M., and A. Tesfai, ed. *Post-conflict Eritrea: Prospects for Reconstruction and Development*. Lawrenceville, N.J.: Red Sea Press, 1999.

Ellington, Lloyd. "The Origins and Development of the Eritrean Liberation Movement." In *Proceedings of the Fifth International Conference on Ethiopian Studies*, edited by Robert L. Hess, 613–28. Chicago: University of Illinois at Chicago Circle, 1979.

———. "Eritrea: Divided We Fall." *Arabia* (March 1987): 32–33.

———. "Eritrea: Food Aid Was Military Cover." *African Concord* (5 February 1988): 9–10.

———. "Eritrea: War and Drought." *Horn of Africa* 4: 1 (1981): 20–28.

Eritrean Liberation Front. *The Eritrean Revolution*. Beirut: ELF Foreign Information Center, 1977–78.

———. *The Eritrean Revolution*: *Sixteen Years of Armed Struggle*. Beirut: ELF Foreign Information Center, 1977.

———. *The National Democratic Revolution Versus Ethiopian Expansion*. Beirut: ELF Foreign Information Center, 1979.

———. *Political Programme*. Beirut: ELF Foreign Information Center, 1975.

Eritrean People's Liberation Front. EPLF: *Serving the Masses on the Medical Front*. New York: EPLF, 1976.

———. *National Democratic Programme of the Eritrean People's Liberation Front*. N.p., 1977.

Erlich, Haggai. *The Struggle Over Eritrea, 1962–1978*. Stanford, Calif.: Hoover Institute, 1982.

Firebrace, James, with Stuart Holland. *Never Kneel Down*. Trenton, N.J.: The Red Sea Press, 1985.

Gebre-Medhin, Jordan. "The EPLF and Peasant Power in Eritrea." *Horn of Africa* 5: 4 (1982/1983): 46–50.

———. *Peasants and Nationalism in Eritrea: A Critique of Ethiopian Studies*. Trenton, N.J.: The Red Sea Press, 1989.

Gilkes, Patrick. "The Battle of Af Abet and Eritrean Independence." *Northeast African Studies* 2: 3 (1995): 39–51.

Heiden, Linda. "The Eritrean Struggle." *Monthly Review* 30: 2 (1978): 13–28.

Henze, Paul B. "Eritrea: The Endless War." *The Washington Quarterly* 9: 2 (Spring 1986): 23–36.

Johnson, Michael, and Trish Johnson. "Eritrea: The National Question and the Logic of Protracted Struggle." *African Affairs* 80: 319 (April 1981): 181–95.

Kaplan, Robert D. *Surrender or Starve: The Wars Behind the Famine.* Boulder, Colo.: Westview Press, 1988.

Killion, Tom. *Historical Dictionary of Eritrea.* Lanham, Md.: Scarecrow Press, 1998.

Kinnock, Glenys. *Eritrea: Images of War and Peace.* London: Chatto and Windus, 1988.

Lobban, Richard. *Eritrean Liberation Front: A Close-Up View.* Pasadena, Calif.: Munger Africana Library Notes, 1972.

———. "The Eritrean War: Issues and Implications." *Canadian Journal of African Studies* 10: 2 (1976): 335–46.

Machida, Robert. *Eritrea: The Struggle for Independence.* Trenton, N.J.: The Red Sea Press, 1987.

Negash, T., and K. Tronvoll. *Brothers at War.* Oxford: James Currey, 2000.

Papstein, Robert. *Eritrea: Revolution at Dusk.* Trenton, N.J.: The Red Sea Press, 1991.

Pateman, Roy. *Eritrea: Even the Stones Are Burning.* Trenton, N.J.: The Red Sea Press, 1990.

———. "The Eritrean War." *Armed Forces and Society* 17: 1 (Fall 1990): 81–98.

Peninou, Jean Louis. *Eritrea: The Guerrillas of the Red Sea.* New York: EFLNA, 1975.

Pool, David. *Eritrea: Africa's Longest War.* London: Anti-Slavery Society, 1980.

———. *From Guerrillas to Government.* Oxford: James Currey, 2001.

Research and Information Center on Eritrea. *Revolution in Eritrea: Eyewitness Reports.* Rome: Research and Information Center on Eritrea, 1979.

Semere, Haile. "The Roots of the Ethiopian-Eritrean Conflict." *Issue* 15 (1987): 9–17.

Sherman, Richard. *Eritrea: The Unfinished Revolution.* New York: Praeger, 1980.

Silkin, Trish. "Women in Struggle: Eritrea." *Third World Quarterly* 5: 4 (October 1983): 909–13.

Smock, David R. "Eritrean Refugees in the Sudan." *The Journal of Modern African Studies* 20: 3 (September 1982): 451–65.

Wilson, Amrit. *Women and the Eritrean Revolution: The Challenge Ahead.* Trenton, N.J.: The Red Sea Press, 1991.

With, Peter. *Politics and Liberation: The Eritrean Struggle, 1961–1986.* Aarhus, Denmark: University of Aarhus, 1987.

Young, John. "The Tigray and Eritrean People's Liberation Fronts: A History of Tensions and Pragmatism." *The Journal of Modern African Studies* 34: 1 (1996): 105–20.

ETHIOPIA

Abate, Yohannis. "Civil-Military Relations in Ethiopia." *Armed Forces and Society* 10: 3 (Spring 1984): 380–400.

———. "The Legacy of Imperial Rule: Military Intervention and the Struggle for Leadership in Ethiopia, 1974–78." *Middle Eastern Studies* 19 (January 1983): 28–42.

Baffour, Agyeman-Duah. *The United States and Ethiopia: Military Assistance and the Quest for Security, 1953–1993.* Lanham, Md.: University Press of America, 1994.

———. "The U.S. and Ethiopia: The Politics of Military Assistance." *Armed Forces and Society* 12: 2 (Winter 1986): 287–306.

Baissa, Lemmu. "The Oromo and the Quest for Peace in Ethiopia." *Transafrica Forum* 9: 1 (Spring 1992): 57–68.

Baynham, Simon, and Richard Snailham. "Ethiopia." In *World Armies*, edited by John Keegan, 206–11. New York: Facts on File, 1979.

Clapham, Christopher. "Ethiopia: The Institutionalisation of a Marxist Regime." In *The Political Dilemmas of Military Regimes*, edited by Christopher Clapham and George Philip, 255–76. Totowa, N.J.: Barnes and Noble Books, 1985.

———. *Transformation and Continuity in Revolutionary Ethiopia.* Cambridge: Cambridge University Press, 1988.

Colleta, Nat J., et al. *Case Studies of War-to-Peace Transition: The Demobilization and Reintegration of Ex-Combatants in Ethiopia, Namibia, and Uganda.* Washington, D.C.: World Bank, 1996.

David, Steven. "Realignment in the Horn: The Soviet Advantage." *International Security* 4: 2 (Fall 1979): 69–90.

"Ethiopia." In *World Police and Paramilitary Forces*, edited by John Andrade, 179. New York: Stockton Press, 1985.

"Ethiopia: Conquest and Terror." *Horn of Africa* 4: 1 (1981): 8–19.

"Ethiopia's Hidden War: The Oromo Liberation Struggle." *Horn of Africa* 5: 1 (1982): 62–67.

Giorgis, Dawit Wolde. *Red Tears: War, Famine and Revolution in Ethiopia.* Trenton, N.J.: Red Sea Press, 1989.

Harbeson, John W. *Military Rule and the Quest for a Post-Imperial Ethiopia.* New York: Praeger, 1987.

Henze, Paul B. *Eritrean Options and Ethiopia's Future*. Santa Monica, Calif.: The Rand Corporation, 1989.

―――. *Ethiopia and Eritrea: The Defeat of the Dergue and the Establishment of New Governments*. Washington, D.C.: United States Institute of Peace, 1993.

―――. *Mengistu's Ethiopian Marxist State in Terminal Crisis: How Long Can It Survive? What Will Be Its Legacy?* Washington, D.C.: The Rand Corporation, 1990.

―――. *Rebels and Separatists in Ethiopia: Regional Resistance to a Marxist Regime*. Washington, D.C.: The Rand Corporation, 1985.

―――. *Russians and the Horn: Opportunism and the Long View*. Marina del Rey, Calif.: European American Institute for Security Research, 1983.

International Security Council. *The Horn of Africa: A Strategic Survey*. New York: International Security Council, 1989.

Korn, David A. "Ethiopia on the Verge of Disaster." *Journal of Third World Studies* 7: 1 (Spring 1990): 20–40.

―――. *Ethiopia, the United States, and the Soviet Union*. Carbondale: Southern Illinois University Press, 1986.

Lefebvre, Jeffrey A. *Arms for the Horn: U.S. Security Policy in Ethiopia and Somalia, 1953–1991*. Pittsburgh, Pa.: University of Pittsburgh Press, 1991.

―――. "Donor Dependency and American Arms Transfers to the Horn of Africa: The F-5 Legacy." *Journal of Modern African Studies* 25: 3 (September 1987): 465–88.

Legum, Colin, and Bill Lee. *Conflict in the Horn of Africa*. London: Rex Collings, 1977.

Makinda, Samuel M. *Superpower Diplomacy in the Horn of Africa*. London: Croom Helm, 1987.

Mathias, Hilletework. "Superpowers in the Horn of Africa: The Ethiopian-Somali Border Conflict." Ph.D. diss., Howard University, 1988.

Morelli, Anthony. *The Role of U.S. Military Assistance in Ethiopia*. Montgomery, Ala.: Air University, 1970.

Pankhurst, R. *The Ethiopians*. Oxford: Blackwell, 1999.

Papp, Daniel S. "The Soviet Union and Cuba in Ethiopia." *Current History* 76: 445 (March 1979): 110–14, 129–30.

Payton, Gary D. "The Soviet-Ethiopian Liaison: Airlift and Beyond." *Air University Review* 31: 1 (November/December 1979): 66–73.

Prouty, C., and E. Rosenfeld. *Historical Dictionary of Ethiopia and Eritrea*. 2nd ed. Lanham, Md.: Scarecrow Press, 1994.

Shehim, Kassim. "Ethiopia, Revolution, and the Question of Nationalities: The Case of the Afar." *The Journal of Modern African Studies* 23: 2 (June 1985): 331–48.

Shindo, Eiichi. "Hunger and Weapons: The Entrophy of Militarisation." *Review of African Political Economy* 33 (August 1985): 6–22.

Shinn, David H., and Thomas P. Ofcansky. *Historical Dictionary of Ethiopia.* Lanham, Md.: Scarecrow Press, 2004.

Tareke, Gebru. "Preliminary History of Resistance in Tigrai (Ethiopia)." *Africa* 39: 2 (1984): 201–26.

Tekle, Amare. "Military Rule in Ethiopia (1974–87): The Balance Sheet." *Horn of Africa* 13/14: 3/4 (1990/1991): 38–58.

Tiruneh, Andargagnew. *The Ethiopian Revolution, 1974–1987: A Transformation from an Aristocratic to a Totalitarian Autocracy.* Cambridge: Cambridge University Press, 1993.

Tola, Babile. *To Kill a Generation: The Red Terror in Ethiopia.* Washington, D.C.: Free Ethiopia Press, 1989.

U.S. House Select Committee on Hunger. *Ethiopia and Sudan: Warfare, Politics, and Famine.* Washington, D.C.: U.S. Government Printing Office, 1988.

Viaud, Pierre. "Ethiopia: La Guerre Oubliée des Trois Fronts." *Afrique Contemporaine* 135 (July/September 1985): 46–52.

Woodward, Peter. "Ethiopia and the Sudan: The Inter-State Outcome of Domestic Conflict." *Contemporary Review* 230 (May 1977): 231–34.

——. *War or Peace in North-East Africa?* London: The Center for Security and Conflict Studies, 1989.

Wubnen, Mulatu, and Yohannis Abate. *Ethiopia: Transition and Development in the Horn of Africa.* Boulder, Colo.: Westview Press, 1988.

LIBERIA

Adeleke, Ademola. "The Politics and Diplomacy of Peacekeeping in West Africa: The ECOMOG Operation in Liberia." *Journal of Modern African Studies* 33: 4 (December 1995): 569–93.

Adibe, C. E. "The Liberian Conflict and the ECOWAS-UN Partnership." *Third World Quarterly* 18: 3 (September 1997): 471–88.

Africa Watch. *Easy Prey: Child Soldiers in Liberia.* New York: Africa Watch, 1994.

——. *Liberia: A Human Rights Disaster.* New York: Africa Watch, 1990. Also in *Liberian Studies Journal* 16L 1 (1991): 129–55.

——. *Liberia: Cycle of Abuse. Human Rights Violations Since the Cease-Fire.* New York: Africa Watch, 1991. Also in *Liberian Studies Journal* 17:1 (1992): 128–64.

——. *Liberia: Flight From Terror. Testimony of Abuses in Nimba County.* New York: Africa Watch, 1990. Also in *Liberian Studies Journal* 15: 1 (1990): 142–61.

————. *Liberia: Waging War to Keep the Peace: The ECOMOG Intervention and Human Rights*. New York: Africa Watch, 1993. Also in *Liberian Studies Journal* 18: 2 (1993): 278–318.

Alao, Abiodun. *Peace-Keeping in Sub-Saharan Africa: The Liberian Civil War*. London: Brassey's, 1993.

Anderson, John Lee. "The Devil They Know." *The New Yorker* (27 July 1998): 34–39, 42–43.

Ankomah, B. "Liberia on a Knife edge." *New African* 328 (March 1995): 10–14.

Asibey, Andrew Osei. "Liberia: Political Economy of Underdevelopment and Military 'Revolution Continuity of Change.'" *Canadian Journal of Development Studies* 2: 2 (1981): 386–407.

Barrett, L. "The Siege of Monrovia." *West Africa* (23–29 November 1992): 816–18.

Berkeley, B. "Liberia between Repression and Slaughter." *The Atlantic* 270: 6 (December 1992): 52–64.

Brehun, Leonard. *Liberia: The War of Horror*. Accra: Adwinsa Publications, 1991.

Clapham, Christopher. *Liberia*. Basingstoke, UK: Macmillan, 1994.

Clayton, Anthony. *Factions, Foreigners and Fantasies: The Civil War in Liberia*. Camberley, UK.: Conflict Studies Research Centre, 1995.

Conteh-Morgan, E. "ECOWAS: Peacekeeping or Meddling in Liberia." *Africa Insight* 23: 1 (1993): 36–41.

Curtis, P. K., and B. Branama. *Liberia's Civil War*. Washington, D.C.: Library of Congress, 1995.

Dunn, D. Elwood, Amos J. Begon, and Carl Patrick Burrows. *Historical Dictionary of Liberia*. Lanham, Md.: Scarecrow Press, 2001.

Fleischman, Janet. "Human Rights and the Civil War in Liberia." *Liberian Studies Journal* 19: 2 (1994): 173–82.

Gershoni, Yekitiel. "War without End and an End to a War: The Prolonged Wars in Liberia and Sierra Leone." *Africa Studies Review* 40: 3 (December 1997): 55–76.

Howe, Herb. "Lessons of Liberia: ECOMOG and Regional Peacekeeping." *International Security* 21: 3 (Winter 1996/97): 145–76.

Hubbard, Mark. *The Liberian Civil War*. London: Cass, 1998.

Husband, Mark. "Targeting Taylor." *Africa Report* 38: 4 (July/August 1993): 29–32.

Iweze, C. Y. "Nigeria in Liberia: The Military Operations of ECOMOG." In *Nigeria in International Peacekeeping 1960–1992*, edited by Margaret A. Vogt and E. E. Ekoko, 216–43. Oxford: Malthouse Press, 1993.

Joyce, James F. "Madness in Monrovia: What Led to the Liberian Bloodbath." *Commonweal* 123 (June 1996): 9–11.

Keih, George Klay. "The Obstacles to the Peaceful Resolution of the Liberian Civil Conflict." *Studies in Conflict and Terrorism* 17: 1 (1994): 97–108.

Kufuor, K. O. "Starvation as a Means of Warfare in the Liberian Conflict." *Netherlands International Law Review* 41: 3 (1994): 313–32.

Magyar, Karl P., and Earl Conteh-Morgan, eds. *Peacekeeping in Africa: ECOMOG in Liberia*. Basingstoke, UK: Macmillan, 1998.

Marley, Anthony D. "Too Many Cooks in the Kitchen: International Intervention in Liberia." *Small Wars and Insurgencies* 8: 2 (Autumn 1997): 109–24.

Newsom, David D. (Williams, Abiodun). *Regional Peace Making: ECOWAS and the Liberian Civil War*. Boulder, Colo.: Westview Press, 1992.

Nmoma, Veronica. "The Civil Crisis in Liberia: An American Response." *The Journal of African Policy Studies* 1 (1995): 71–78.

———. "The Civil War and the Refugee Crisis in Liberia." *The Journal of Conflict Studies* 17: 1 (Spring 1997): 101–25.

Nolte, G. "Combined Peacekeeping: ECOMOG and UNOMIL in Liberia." *International Peacekeeping* 1: 2 (1994): 42–45.

Nwokedi, Emeka. *Regional Integration and Regional Security: ECOMOG, Nigeria and the Liberian Crisis*. Bordeaux: Centre d'Etude d'Afrique Noire, 1992.

Ofodile, A. C. "The Legality of ECOWAS Intervention in Liberia." *Columbia Journal of Transnational Law* 32: 2 (1994): 381–418.

Okolo, Julius Emeka. "Liberia: The Military Coup and Its Aftermath." *The World Today* 37:4 (April 1981): 149–57.

O'Neill, William. "Liberia: An Avoidable Tragedy." *Current History* 92 (May 1993): 213–15.

Outram, Quentin. "Cruel Wars and Safe Havens: Humanitarian Aid in Liberia, 1989–1996." *Disasters* 21: 3 (1997): 189–203.

———. "'It's Terminal Either Way': An Analysis of Armed Conflict in Liberia, 1989–1996." *Review of African Political Economy* 24: 73 (September 1997): 355–71.

Reno, Williams. "Foreign Firms and the Financing of Charles Taylor's NPFL." *Liberian Studies Journal* 18: 2 (1993): 175–87.

———. "Reinvention of an African Patrimonial State: Charles Taylor's Liberia." *Third World Quarterly* 16: 1 (1996): 109–20.

Richards, Paul. "Rebellion in Liberia and Sierra Leone: A Crisis of Youth?" In *Conflict in Africa*, edited by Oliver Furley, 134–70. London: Tauris Academic Studies, 1995.

Riley, Stephen P. *Liberia and Sierra Leone: Anarchy or Peace in West Africa?* London: Research Institute for the Study of Conflict and Terrorism, 1996.

———. *War and Famine in Africa*. London: Research Institute for Study of Conflict and Terrorism, 1994.

Ruiz, Hiram A. *Liberia: Destruction and Reconstruction*. Washington, D.C.: U.S. Committee for Refugees, 1992.

———. *Uprooted Liberians: Casualties of a Brutal War*. Washington, D.C.: U.S. Committee for Refugees, 1992.

Sesay, Max Ahmadu. "Civil War and Collective Intervention in Liberia." *Review of African Political Economy* 23: 67 (1996): 35–52.

Tanner, Victor. "Liberia: Railroading Peace." *Review of African Political Economy* 25: 75 (March 1998): 133–47.

Vogt, Margaret A., ed. *The Liberian Crisis and ECOMOG: A Bold Attempt at Regional Peacekeeping*. Lagos: Gabumo Publishing Company, 1992.

———. "Nigeria's Participation in the ECOWAS Monitoring Group ECOMOG." *Nigerian Journal of International Affairs* 17: 1 (1991): 101–22.

Weissman, Fabrice. "Liberia: Dérrière le Chaos, Crises et Interventions Internationales." *Relations Internationales et Strategiques* 23 (Fall 1996): 86–92.

Weller, M., ed. *Regional Peacekeeping and International Enforcement: The Liberian Crisis*. Cambridge: Cambridge University Press, 1994.

Yekutiel, Gersoni. "From ECOWAS to ECOMOG: The Liberian Crisis and the Struggle for Political Hegemony in West Africa." *Liberian Studies Journal* 18: 1 (1993): 21–43.

MOZAMBIQUE

Africa Watch. *Landmines in Mozambique*. New York: Africa Watch, 1994.

Alden, C., and M. Simpson. "Mozambique: A Delicate Peace." *Journal of Modern African Studies* 31: 1 (1993): 109–30.

Andersson, H. *Mozambique: A War against the People*. Basingstoke, UK: Macmillan, 1992.

Azevedo, Marco, Emmanuel Nnadozie, and Tome Mbuia Joao. *Historical Dictionary of Mozambique*. Lanham, Md.: Scarecrow Press, 2003.

Baynham, Simon. *Military Power and Politics in Black Africa*. London: Croom Helm, 1986.

Cahen, Michael. *Mozambique: Analyse Politique de Conjoncture*. Paris: Indigo Publications, 1990.

Campbell, Horace. "War, Reconstruction and Dependence in Mozambique." *Third World Quarterly* 6: 4 (October 1984): 839–67.

Chan, S. *War and Peace in Mozambique*. Basingstoke, UK: Macmillan, 1998.

Chingono, M. "War, Social Change and Development in Mozambique: Catastrophe or Creation of a New Society?" Ph.D. diss., University of Cambridge, 1994.

Cline, S. *Anti-Communist Insurgents in Mozambique: The Fight Goes On*. Washington, D.C.: United States Global Strategy Council, 1989.

Darch, Colin. "Are There Warlords in Mozambique?" *Review of African Political Economy* 45/46 (1989): 34–49.

Fauvet, Paul. "Roots of Counter-Revolution: The Mozambique National Resistance." *Review of African Political Economy* 29 (July 1984): 108–21.

Finnegan, William. *A Complicated War: The Harrowing of Mozambique.* Berkeley: University of California Press, 1992.

————. "A Reporter at Large." *The New Yorker* (22 May 1989): 43–76, and (29 May 1989): 69–96.

Hall, Margaret. "The Mozambique National Resistance Movement (RENAMO): A Study in the Destruction of an African Country." *Africa* 60: 1 (1990): 39–68.

Hanlon, J. *Mozambique: The Revolution Under Fire.* London: Zed Books, 1984.

Harries, Patrick. "Mozambique's Long War." *Social Dynamics* 15: 1 (1989): 122–31.

Hoile, David. *Mozambique: A Nation in Crisis.* London: Claridge Press, 1989.

Howe, Herbert M. "National Security." In *Mozambique: A Country Study*, edited by Harold D. Nelson, 241–84. Washington, D.C.: U.S. Government Printing Office, 1984.

Human Rights Watch. *Conspicuous Destruction—War, Famine and the Reform Process in Mozambique.* New York: Human Rights Watch, 1994.

Hume, C. R. *Ending Mozambique's War: The Role of Mediation and Good Offices.* Washington, D.C.: United States Institute of Peace Press, 1994.

Isaacman, Allen. "Mozambique." *Survival* 30: 1 (January/February 1988): 14–38.

————. "Mozambique and the Regional Conflict in Southern Africa." *Current History* (May 1987): 213–16, 230.

Jaster, Robert S. "The Security Outlook in Mozambique." *Survival* 27: 6 (November/December 1985): 258–64.

Kanji, N. "War and Children in Mozambique: Is International Aid Strengthening or Eroding Community-Based Policies?" *Community Development Journal* 25:2 (April 1990): 102–12.

Kyle, S. "Economic Reform and Armed Conflict in Mozambique." *World Development* 19: 6 (June 1991): 637–49.

Legum, Colin. "The MNR." *CSIS Africa Notes* 16 (15 July 1983).

Meldrum, Andrew. "Mozambique Special Report: The Most Brutal War." *Africa Report* 33: 2 (May/June 1988): 23–28.

Metz, Steven. "The Mozambique National Resistance and South African Foreign Policy." *African Affairs* 85:341 (October 1986): 491–507.

Minter, William. *Apartheid's Contras: An Inquiry into the Roots of War in Angola and Mozambique.* London: Zed Books, 1994.

———. "The Mozambican National Resistance (RENAMO) as Described by Ex-Participants." *Development Dialogue* 1 (1989): 89–132.

Morgan, Glenda. "Violence in Mozambique: Towards an understanding of RENAMO." *The Journal of Modern African Studies* 28: 4 (December 1990): 603–19.

Morrison, J. Steven. "The Battle for Mozambique." *Africa Report* 32:5 (September/October 1987): 44–47.

Nilsson, Anders. "From Pseudo-Terrorists to Pseudo Guerrillas: The MNR in Mozambique." *Review of African Political Economy* 57 (July 1993): 60–71, and 58 (November 1993): 34–42.

Nkiwane, Solomon M. "Humanitarian Considerations in Mozambique and Zimbabwe: Problems of Security." *Issues in Peacekeeping and Peacemaking.* Basingstoke, UK: Macmillan Press, 1990.

Panizzo, Enny. "Les Enfants dans la Guerre, le Cas de Mozambique." *Afrique Contemporaine* 180 (October/December 1996): 142–59.

Synge, Richard. *Mozambique: UN Peacekeeping in Action, 1992–94.* Washington, D.C.: United States Institute of Peace, 1992.

United States Institute of Peace. *Conflict and Conflict Resolution in Mozambique.* Washington, D.C.: United States Institute of Peace, 1992.

U.S. Senate Committee on Foreign elations. *Mozambique and United States Policy.* Washington, D.C.: U.S. Government Printing office, 1987.

Vershuur, Christine, et al. *Mozambique: Dix Ans de Solitude.* Paris: L'Harmattan, 1986.

Vines, Alex. "Disarmament and Mozambique." *The Journal of Modern African Studies* 28: 4 (1990): 191–205.

———. *RENAMO: Terrorism in Mozambique.* London: James Currey, 1990.

Wilson, K. B. "Cults of Violence and Counter-Violence in Mozambique." *Journal of Southern African Studies* 18: 3 (1992): 527–82.

Young, Tom. "The MNR/RENAMO: External and Internal Dynamics." *African Affairs* 89: 357 (October 1990): 491–509.

NAMIBIA

Cocker, Christopher. "Peacekeeping in Southern Africa: The United Nations and Namibia." *The Journal of Commonwealth and Comparative Politics* 19: 2 (July 1981): 174–86.

Cullinan, Sue. "SWAPO and the Future of Namibia." *South Africa International* 15: 3 (January 1985): 141–49.

Dale, Richar. "The Armed Forces as an Instrument of South African Policy in Namibia." *Journal of Modern African Studies* 18: 1 (March 1984): 57–71.

Department of Information and Publicity. SWAPO of Namibia. *To Be Born a Nation: The Liberation Struggle for Namibia.* London: Zed Press, 1981.

Grotpefer, John J. *Historical Dictionary of Namibia*. Lanham, Md.: Scarecrow Press, 1994.

Herbstein, Denis, and John Everson. *The Devils Are among Us: The War for Namibia*. London: Zed Press, 1989.

International Defence and Aid Fund. *Apartheid's Army in Namibia: South Africa's Illegal Military Occupation*. London: International Defence and Aid Fund, 1982.

Jaster, Robert. *South Africa in Namibia: The Botha Strategy*. Lanham, Md.: University Press of America, 1985.

———. *The 1988 Peace Accords and the Future of South-Western Africa*. London: International Institute for Strategic Studies, 1990.

Katjavivi, Peter H. *A History of Resistance in Namibia*. London: James Currey, 1988.

Leys, Colin, and John S. Saul. *Namibia's Liberation Struggle: The Two-Edged Sword*. Athens: Ohio University Press, 1995.

Moleah, Alfred T. *Namibia: The Struggle for Liberation*. Wilmington, Del.: Disa Press, 1983.

Toase, Francis. "The South African Army: The Campaign in South West Africa/Namibia Since 1966." In *Armed Forces and Modern Counter-Insurgency*, edited by F. W. Beckett and John Pimlott, 190–221. New York: St. Martin's Press, 1985.

UN Council for Namibia. *The Military Situation in and Relating to Namibia: A Report of the United Nations Council for Namibia*. New York: United Nations, 1983.

———. *The Military Situation in and Relating to Namibia: Report Dated 3 April 1986 of Standing Committee 11 of the United Nations Council for Namibia*. New York: United Nations, 1987.

NIGERIA

Aguolo, Christian. *Biafra: The Case for Independence*. Santa Barbara: University of California, 1969.

Ajayi, J. F. Ade, and A. E. Ekoko. "Transfer of Power in Nigeria: Its Origins and Consequences." In *Decolonization and African Independence: The Transfer of Power, 1960–1980*. New Haven, Conn.: Yale University Press, 1988.

Armstrong, R. G. *The Issues at Stake, Nigeria 1967*. Ibadan, 1967.

Awolowo, Obafemi (Awo). *The Strategy and Tactics of the People's Republic of Nigeria*. London, 1970.

Azikiwe, Nnamdi. *Peace Proposals for Ending the Nigerian Civil War*. London, 1969.

Baker, Pauline H. "Nigeria: The Sub-Sahara Pivot." *Emerging Powers: Defence and Security in the Third World*. New York: Praeger, 1986.

Buhler, Jean. *Tuez-Les Tous! Guerre de Secession au Biafra*. Paris: Flammarion, 1968.

Collis, Robert. *Nigeria in Conflict*. London: Secker and Warburg, 1970.

Cronje, Suzanne. *Britain's Unfinished Business: Nigeria and the World*. London: Sidgwick and Jackson, 1972.

Ekwe-Ekwe, Herbert. *Conflict and Intervention in Africa: Nigeria, Angola, Zaire*. Basingstoke, UK: Macmillan, 1990.

Forsythe, Frederick. *The Biafra Story*. Harmondsworth, UK: Penguin, 1969.

Hatch, John. *Nigeria: Seeds of Disaster*. London: Secker and Warburg, 1971.

Kirke-Greene, A. H. M. *Crisis and Conflict in Nigeria: A Documentary Source Book, 1966–1970*. 2 vols. London: Oxford University Press, 1971.

Nwanko, Arthur A., and Samuel U. Ifejika. *The Making of a Nation: Biafra*. London: Hurst, 1969.

Okeke, Godfrey C. *The Biafra War: A Human Tragedy*. London, 1969.

Okolo, Julius Emeka. "Nigeria." In *International Political Economy Series*, 125–46. Basingstoke, UK: Macmillan, 1994.

Oyewole, Anthony, and John Lucas, *Historical Dictionary of Nigeria*. Lanham, Md.: Scarecrow Press, 2000.

Samueals, Michael A., ed. *The Nigeria-Biafra Conflict*. Washington, D.C.: Center for Strategic International Studies, Georgetown University, 1969.

Schwartz, Walter. *Nigeria*. London: Pall Mall Press, 1977.

St. Jorre, John de. *The Nigerian Civil War*. London: Hodder and Stoughton, 1972.

Uwechwe, Raph. *Reflections on the Nigerian Civil War*. London: O. I. T. H. International Publishers, 1969; and New York (revised): Africana Publishing Corporation, 1971.

Waugh, Auberon, and Suzanne Cronje. *Biafra: Britain's Share*. London: Michael Joseph, 1969.

SIERRA LEONE

Amnesty International. *The Extrajudicial Execution of Suspected Rebels and Collaborators*. London: International Secretariat of Amnesty International, 1992.

———. *Sierra Leone: Prisoners of War? Children Detained in Barracks and Prison*. London: International Secretariat of Amnesty International, 1993.

Bridge, T. D. "Sierra Leone under Attack: Border Conflict." *The Army Quarterly and Defence Journal* 122: 1 (January 1992): 9–12.

By Our West African Correspondent. "Coup in Sierra Leone." *The Army Quarterly and Defence Journal* 122: 2 (April 1992): 230–33.

Dixon-Fyle, Mac. "Reflections on the Role of the Military in Civilian Politics: The Case of Sierra Leone." *Australian Journal of Politics and History* 35: 2 (1989): 211–19.

Fyle, C. Magbaily. *Historical Dictionary of Sierra Leone*. Lanham, Md.: Scarecrow Press, 2006.

Gershoni, Yekutiel. "War without End and an End to War: The Prolonged Wars in Liberia and Sierra Leone." *African Studies Review* 40: 3 (December 1997): 55–76.

Kandeh, J. D. "What Does 'Militariat' Do When It Rules: Military Regimes: The Gambia, Sierra Leone and Liberia." *Review of African Political Economy* 23: 69 (September 1993): 387–404.

Korama, Abdul K. *Sierra Leone: The Agony of a Nation*. Freetown: Andromeda Publications, 1996.

Musa, S., and J. Lansana Musa. *The Invasion of Sierra Leone: A Chronicle Of Events of a Nation under Siege*. Washington, D.C.: Sierra Leone Institute for Policy Studies, 1993.

Olonisakin, Funmi. "Mercenaries Fill the Vacuum." *The World Today* 54: 6 (June 1998): 146–48.

———. "Sierra Leone and Beyond: Nigeria and Regional Security." *Jane's Intelligence Review* 10: 6 (June 1998): 44–46.

Rahill, J. "The Military in Sierra Leone Politics: An Overview." *Sierra Leone Review* 3: 1 (1994): 71–78.

Reno, W. "Privating War in Sierra Leone." *Current History* 96: 610 (May 1997): 227–30.

Richards, Paul. *Fighting for the Rain Forest: War, Youth and Resources in Sierra Leone*. Oxford: James Currey, 1996.

———. "Rebellion in Liberia and Sierra Leone: A Crisis of Youth?" In *Conflict in Africa*, edited by Oliver Furley, 134–70. London: Tauris Academic Studies, 1995.

Riley, Stephen P. *Liberia and Sierra Leone: Anarchy or Peace in West Africa?* London: Research Institute for the Study of Conflict and Terrorism, 1996.

———. "Sierra Leone: The Militariat Strikes Again." *Review of African Political Economy* 24: 72 (June 1997): 287–92.

Shearer, David. "Exploring the Limits of Consent: Conflict Resolution in Sierra Leone." *Journal of International Studies* 26: 3 (1997): 845–60.

Venter, A. J. "Sierra Leone's Mercenary War: Battle for the Diamond Fields." *International Defense Review* 28: 11 (1995): 65–68.

Zack-Williams, A. B. "Kamajors, 'Sobel' and the Militariat: Civil Society and the Return of the Military in Sierra Leonean Politics." *Review of African Political Economy* 24: 73 (September 1997): 373–80.

Zack-Williams, A. B., and Stephen Riley. "Sierra Leone: The Coup and Its Consequences." *Review of African Political Economy* 56 (March 1993): 91–97.

SOMALIA

Abdi, Mohamed Kuslow. "The Genesis of the Somali Civil War: A New Perspective." *Northeast African Studies* 1: 1 (1994): 31–46.

Abdullahi, M. D. *Fiasco in Somalia: U.S.-UN Intervention.* Pretoria: Africa Institute, 1995.

Adam, H. M. "Somalia: Militarism, Warlordism or Democracy?" *Review of African Political Economy* 54 (1992): 11–26.

Adibe, Clement. *Managing Arms in Peace Processes: Somalia.* New York: United Nations Institute for Disarmament Research, 1995.

Afrah, Mohamoud M. *Mogadishu: A Hell on Earth.* Nairobi: Copos, 1993.

———. *The Somali Tragedy: The Comprehensive Dossier That Recreates the Terror and Destruction in Somalia.* Mombasa: Mohamed Printer, 1994.

Africa Watch. *Somalia: A Government at War with Its Own People.* New York: Africa Watch, 1990.

African Rights. *Land Tenure: The Creation of Famine and Prospects for Peace in Somalia.* London: African Rights, 1993.

———. *The Nightmare Continues: Abuses Against Somali Refugees in Kenya.* London: African Rights, 1993.

———. *Somalia: Human Rights Abuses by the United Nations Forces.* London: African Rights, 1993.

———. *Somalia: Operation Restore Hope: A Preliminary Assessment.* London: African Rights, 1993.

African Rights and Mines Advisory Group. *Violent Deeds Live On: Landmines in Somalia and Somaliland.* London: African Rights and Mines Advisory Group, 1993.

Ahmed, A. I. "Somalia: Roots of Anarchy." *Indian Journal of African Studies* 5: 1 (1992): 14–26.

Allard, C. K. "Lessons Unlearned: Somalia and Joint Doctrine." *Joint Force Quarterly* 9 (1995): 10–59.

Annan, K. "Peacekeeping in Situations of Civil War." *New York University Journal of International Law and Politics* 26: 4 (1994): 623–32.

Ayittey, G. B. N. "The Somali Crisis: Time for an African Solution." *Policy Analysis* 205 (1994): 136.

Bariagaber, Assefaw. "The United Nations and Somalia: An Examination of a Collective Clientelist Relationship." *Journal of Asian and African Studies* 31: 3/4 (December 1996): 162–77.

Baynham, Simon. "Somalia: Operation 'Restore Operation.'" *Africa Insight* 23: 1 (1993): 17–23.

Bercuson, David. *Significant Incident: Canada's Army, the Air Borne, and the Murder in Somalia.* Toronto: McClelland and Stewart, 1996.

Biswas, A. "The Crisis in Somalia: The U.S./UN Intervention." *Africa Quarterly* 34: 2 (1994): 193–210.

Blumenthal, Sidney. "Why are we in Somalia?" *The New Yorker* (25 October 1993): 48–60.

Bolton, John R. "Wrong Turn in Somalia." *Foreign Affairs* 73: 1 (January/February 1994): 56–66.

Bongartz, Maria. *The Civil War in Somalia: Its Genesis and Dynamics.* Uppsala: Scandinavian Institute of African Studies, 1991.

Booker, B. M. "Somalia: The Roots of Today's Conflict." *Strategy and Tactics* 171 (1994): 53–61.

Borchini, C., and M. Borstelmann. "The PSOP in Somalia: The Voice of Hope." *Special Warfare* 7: 4 (1994): 2–10.

Bradbury, Mark. *The Somali Conflict: Prospects for Peace.* London: OXFAM, 1993.

Breen, Robert. *Through Aussie Eyes: Photographs of the Australian Defence Force in Somalia.* Canberra: Department of Defence, 1994.

Bryden, Matt. "Somalia: The Wages of Failure." *Current History* 94: 591 (1995): 145–51.

Bush, Kenneth D. "When Two Anarchies Meet: International Intervention in Somalia." *The Journal of Conflict Studies* 17: 1 (Spring 1997): 55–78.

Calchi Novati, G. "Somalia: Storia di una Crisi." *Africa e Mediterraneo* 2:4 (1993): 7–17.

Chopra, Jaret, Age Eknes, and Toralv Nordbo. *Fighting for Hope in Somalia.* Oslo: Norwegian Institute of International Affairs, 1995.

Clarke, Jeffrey. *Frustration and Failure: International Response to the Somali Crisis.* Washington, D.C.: U.S. Committee for Refugees, 1992.

Clarke, Walter S. *Somalia: Background Information for Operation Restore Hope, 1992–93.* Carlisle Barracks, Pa.: U.S. Army War College, 1992.

Crocker, Chester A. "The Lessons of Somalia: Not Everything Went Wrong." *Foreign Affairs* 74: 3 (1995): 2–8.

DeLong, Kent, and Steven Tuckey. *Mogadishu: Heroism and Tragedy.* Westport, Conn.: Praeger, 1994.

De Waal, Alex. *Somalia: No Mercy in Mogadishu: The Human Cost of the Conflict and the Struggle for Relief.* New York: Physicians for Human Rights/Africa Watch, 1992.

Dichl, R. F. "With the Best of Intentions: Lessons from UNOSOM I and II." *Studies in Conflict and Terrorism* 19: 2 (1994): 153–77.

Doyle, Mark. "A Dangerous Place." *Africa Report* 38: 6 (November/December 1993): 38–45.

Drysdale, John G. *Whatever Happened to Somalia?* London: Haan Associates, 1994.

Dworken, Jonathan T. "Restore Hope: Coordinating Relief Operations." *Joint Force Quarterly* 8 (1995): 14–20.

———. "Rules of Engagement: Lessons From Restore Hope." *Military Review* 74: 9 (September 1994): 26–34.

Fair, Karen V. "The Rules of Engagement in Somalia—A Judge Advocate's Primer." *Small Wars and Insurgencies* 8: 1 (Spring 1997): 107–26.

Farer, T. "The UN in Somalia: Understanding the Point of Departure." *Cambridge Review of International Affairs* 8: 1 (1994): 55–62.

Farrell, T. "Sliding into War: The Somalia Imbroglio and U.S. Army Peace Operations Doctrine." *International Peacekeeping* 2: 2 (1995): 194–214.

Fasano, P. "Somalia: La Lunga Notte, l'Alba Tragica." *Africa e Mediterraneo* 2:4 (1993): 55–64.

Freeman, W., R. Lambert, and J. Mims. "Operation Restore Hope: A USCENTOM Perspective." *Military Review* 73: 9 (September 1993): 61–72.

Ghalib, Jospech E. *The Cost of Dictatorship: The Somali Experience.* New York: Lilian Barber Press, 1995.

Greenfield, Richard. "Barre's Unholy Alliance." *Africa Report* 34: 2 (March/April 1989): 65–68.

———. "Siad's Sad Legacy." *Africa Report* 36: 2 (March/April 1991): 13–18.

Guleid, Abdulkarim Ahmed. *"Somaligate": The Decision to Suppress Democracy in Somalia.* Munich: Davies Consulting, 1992.

Halim, Omar. "A Peacekeeper's Perspective of Peacebuilding in Somalia." *Journal of Democracy* 9: 2 (April 1998): 71–86.

Heinrich, Wolfgang. *Building the Peace: Experiences of Collaborative Peacebuilding in Somalia, 1993–1996.* Uppsala: Life and Peace Institute, 1998.

Hirsch, John L., and Robert B. Oakley. *Somalia and Operation Restore Hope: Reflections on Peacemaking and Peacekeeping.* Washington, D.C.: United States Institute of Peace, 1995.

Howe, Jonathan T. "The United States and the United Nations in Somalia: The Limits of Involvement. " *Washington Quarterly* 18: 3 (1995): 49–62.

Hussein, Ali Dualeh. *From Barre to Aideed: The Story of Somalia and the Agony of a Nation.* Nairobi: Stellagraphics, 1994.

Issa-Salwe, A. M., and C. M. Cissa-Salwe. *The Collapse of the Somali State.* London: Haan, 1994.

Lewis, I. M. *A Modern History of Somalia: Nation and State in the Horn of Africa.* Harlow: Longmans, 1980.

Little, Peter D. *Somalia: Economy Without State.* Oxford, James Currey, 2003.

Lorenz, F. M. "Confronting Thievery in Somalia." *Military Review* 74: 8 (August 1994): 46–55.

———. "Law and Anarchy in Somalia." *Parameters* 23: 4 (Winter 1993/ 94): 27–41.

———. "Weapons Confiscation Policy during the First Phases of Operation 'Restore Hope.'" *Small Wars and Insurgencies* 5: 3 (1994): 409–25.

Makinda, Samuel M. *Seeking Peace from Chaos: Humanitarian Intervention in Somalia.* Boulder, Colo.: Lynne Rienner Publishers, 1993.

Melander, Goran. *Refugees in Somalia.* Uppsala: Scandinavian Institute of African Studies, 1980.

Merchant, D. P. "Peacekeeping in Somalia: An Indian Experience." *Army Quarterly and Defence Journal* 126: 2 (1996): 134–41.

Michaelson, M. "Somalia: The Painful Road to Reconciliation." *Africa Today* 40: 2 (1993): 53–73.

Miller, L. L., and C. Moskos. "Humanitarians or Warriors: Race, Gender and Combat Status in Operation Restore Hope." *Armed Forces and Society* 21: 4 (1995): 615–37.

Mubarak, Jamil Abdalla. *From Bad Policy to Chaos in Somalia: How an Economy Fell Apart.* Westport, Conn.: Praeger, 1996.

Mukhtar, Mohamad Haji. *Historical Dictionary of Somalia.* Lanham, Md.: Scarecrow Press, 2003.

Natsios, Andrew S. "Humanitarian Relief Interventions in Somalia: The Economics of Chaos." *International Peacekeeping* 3: 1 (Spring 1996): 68–91.

Omaar, Rakiya. "The Best Chance for Peace." *Africa Report* 38: 3 (May/ June 1993): 44–48.

———. "Somaliland: One Thorn Bush at a Time." *Current History* 93: 583 (May 1994): 232–36.

Patman, Robert G. "Disarming Somalia: The Contrasting Fortunes of United States and Australian Peacekeepers during United Nations Intervention, 1992–1993." *African Affairs* 96 (October 1997): 509–33.

Prendergast, John. *The Bones of Our Children Are Not Yet Buried: The Looming Specter of Famine and Massive Human Rights Abuse in Somalia.* Washington, D.C.: Center of Concern, 1994.

———. *The Gun Talks Louder Than the Voice: Somalia's Continuing Cycles of Violence.* Washington, D.C.: Center of Concern, 1994.

Ruhela, Satyapal. *Mohammed Farah Aideed and His Vision of Somalia.* New Delhi: Vikas Publishing House, 1994.

Sahnoun, Mohamed. *Somalia: The Missed Opportunities.* Washington, D.C.: United States Institute for Peace Press, 1994.

Samatar, Ahmed I. *The Somali Challenge: From Catastrophe to Renewal?* Boulder, Colo.: Lynne Rienner Publishers, 1994.

Saxena, S. C. "Peacemaking and Peacekeeping Efforts in Somalia." *Africa Quarterly* 35: 3 (1995): 65–73.

Sica, M. *Operazione Somalia: La Dittatura, l'Oppositione, la Guerra Civile.* Venice: Marsilio, 1994.

Simons, Anna. *Networks of Dissolution: Somalia Undone.* Boulder, Colo.: Westview Press, 1996.

Smith, S. Somalia: *La Guerre Perdue de l'Humanitaire.* Paris: Calmann Levy, 1993.

Stevenson, Jonathan. "Hope Restored in Somalia?" *Foreign Policy* 91 (Summer 1993): 138–54.

———. *Losing Mogadishu: Testing U.S. Policy in Somalia.* Annapolis: Naval Institute Press, 1995.

Stratford, Trisha. *Blood Money.* London: Penguin Books, 1997.

Thakur, Ramesh. "From Peacekeeping to Peace Enforcement: The UN Operation in Somalia." *The Journal of Modern African Studies* 32: 3 (September 1994): 387–410.

United States. *Military Operations in Somalia.* Washington, D.C.: U.S. Government Printing Office, 1993.

United States Committee on Armed Services. House of Representatives. *Administration's Plan for Continued U.S. Military Participation in U.N. Operations in Somalia.* Washington, D.C.: U.S. Government Printing Office, 1994.

United States Subcommittee on Africa. House Committee on Foreign Affairs. *Somalia: Prospects for Peace and Stability.* Washington, D.C.: U.S. Government Printing Office, 1995.

"UNOSOM II Mandate Renewed, Humanitarian Aspect Stressed." *UN Chronicle* 31: 3 (September 1994): 21–23.

U.S. General Accounting Office. *Somalia: Observations Regarding the Northern Conflict and Resulting Conditions.* Washington, D.C.: U.S. General Accounting Office, 1989.

U.S. House Committee on Foreign Affairs. *Withdrawal of U.S. Forces from Somalia.* Washington, D.C.: U.S. Government Printing Office, 1994.

U.S. Senate Committee on Armed Services. *Operation Restore Hope, the Military Operation in Somalia.* Washington, D.C.: U.S. Government Printing Office, 1993.

Walker, J. "Every Man a Sultan: Indigenous Responses to the Somali Crisis." *Telos* 103 (1995): 163–72.

Weil, Robert. "Somalia in Perspective: When the Saints Come Marching In." *Review of African Political Economy* 57 (July 1993): 103–9.

Weiss, T. G. "Overcoming the Somalia Syndrome—Operation Rekindle Hope?" *Global Governance* 1: 2 (1995): 171–88.

SOUTH AFRICA AND SOUTHERN AFRICA

General

Arnold, Guy. *The Last Bunker: A Report on White South Africa Today.* London: Quartet, 1976.
———. *South Africa: Crossing the Rubicon.* Basingstoke, UK: Macmillan, 1993.
Bunting, Brian. *The Rise of the South African Reich.* Harmondsworth, UK: Penguin, 1969.
Clough, Michael. *The United States, Cuba, and Southern Africa: From Confrontation to Negotiation.* Boulder, Colo.: Westview Press, 1989.
Cooper, Allan D. *Allies in Apartheid: Western Capitalism in Occupied Namibia.* Basingstoke, UK: Macmillan, 1988.
Davis, Stephen M. *Apartheid's Rebels: Inside South Africa's Hidden War.* New Haven, Conn.: Yale University Press, 1987.
Desmond, Cosmas. *The Discarded People: An Account of African Resettlement in South Africa.* Harmondsworth, UK: Penguin, 1971.
Dreyer, Ronald. *Namibia and Angola: The Search for Independence and Regional Security (1966–1988).* Geneva: Program for Strategic and International Security Studies, 1988.
Hanlon, Joseph. *Beggar Your Neighbours: Apartheid Power in South Africa.* London: Catholic Institute for International Relations and James Currey, 1986.
Hay, Robin. *Civilian Aspects of Peacekeeping.* Ottawa: Canadian Institute for International Peace and Security, 1991.
International Institute for Strategic Studies. *Africa: Southern Africa: No Improvements.* London: International Institute for Strategic Studies, 1988.
Jaster, Robert. *A Regional Security Role for Africa's Front-Line States.* Aldershot: Gower, 1985.
———. *The Defence of White Power: South African Foreign Policy under Pressure.* London: International Institute for Strategic Studies, 1988.
Kan, Owen Ellison. *Disengagement from Southwest Africa: Prospects for Peace in Angola and Namibia.* New Brunswick, N.J.: Transaction Books, 1991.
Kentridge, M. *An Unofficial War: Inside the Conflict in Pietmaritzburg.* Cape Town, 1990.
Legum, Colin. *The Battle Fronts of Southern Africa.* New York: Africana Publishing, 1988.
Parker, Frank J. *South Africa: Lost Opportunities.* Lexington, Mass.: Lexington Books, 1984.

Rotberg, Robert I. *Africa, the Soviet Union, and the West.* Washington, D.C.: Scholarly Resources, 1986.

Secenbers, Christopher, and Nicholas Southey. *Historical Dictionary of South Africa.* Lanham, Md.: Scarecrow Press, 2000.

Somerville, Keith. *Southern Africa and the Soviet Union: From Communist International to Commonwealth of Independent States.* Basingstoke, UK: Macmillan, 1993.

Sparks, Allister. *The Mind of South Africa: The Story of the Rise and Fall of Apartheid.* London: Heinemann, 1990.

Steenkamp, W. *South Africa's Border War, 1966–1989.* Gibraltar: Ashanti Publishing, 1989.

UK Foreign and Commonwealth Office. *Britain in Southern Africa: A Force for Peaceful Change and Development.* London: UKFCO, 1989.

Uttley, Garrick. *Globalism or Regionalism? United States Policy towards Southern Africa.* Adelphi Papers no. 154. London: International Institute for Strategic Studies, 1979.

Civil War

Aitchison, J. "The Civil War in Natal." *South African Review* 5 (1990): 457–73.

Alao, Abiodun. *Brothers at War: Dissident and Rebel Activities in Southern Africa.* London: I. B. Taurus, 1994.

Albright, David E. "South Africa's Changing Threat Perceptions and Strategic Response." *In Depth* I (Spring 1991): 114–215.

Amnesty International. *South Africa: State of Fear.* New York: Amnesty International, 1992.

———. *South Africa. Torture, Ill-Treatment and Executions in African National Congress Camps.* New York: Amnesty International, 1992.

Anglin, Douglas G. "The Life and Death of South Africa's National Peacekeeping Force." *Journal of Modern African Studies* 33: 1 (March 1995): 21–52.

Arthur, Paul. "Some Thoughts on Transition: A Comparative View of the Peace Processes in South Africa and Northern Ireland." *Government and Opposition* 30: 1 (Winter 1995): 48–59.

Barber, James. "BOSS in Britain." *African Affairs* 82 (July 1983): 311–28.

Barber, Simon. "South Africa beyond Apartheid." *Optima* 35: 3 (September 1987): 118–25.

Baynham, Simon. "Defence and Security Issues in a Transitional South Africa." *International Affairs Bulletin* 14: 3 (July/September 1990): 4–14.

Bennet, Mark, and Deborah Quin. "Political Conflict in South Africa: Data Trends 1984–1988." Indicator Project South Africa. Durban: University of Natal, Center for Social and Development Studies, 1991.

Birch, Carole. "Prospects for Security and Stability in the New South Africa." In *Brassey's Defence Yearbook*, 1995, 300–22. Edited by Centre for Defence Studies, King's College London. London and Washington, D.C.: Brassey's, 1995.

Boister, Neil B., and Kevin Ferguson-Brown, eds. *South African Human Rights Yearbook*, 1992. Vol. 3. New York: Oxford University Press, 1994.

BOSS: *The First Five Years*. London: International Defence and Aid Fund, 1977.

Brewer, John D. *Black and Blue: Policing in South Africa*. Oxford: Clarendon Press, 1994.

———. "Some Observations on Policing and Politics: A South African Case Study." *Policing and Society* 4: 2 (1994).

Breytenbach, Willie. "South Africa Within the African Revolutionary Context." In *Challenge: Southern Africa within the African Revolutionary Context*, edited by A. J. Venter, 63–90. Gibraltar: Ashanti Publishing, 1989.

Brogden, Michael. "Reforming Police Powers in South Africa." *Police Studies* 17: 1 (1994): 25–44.

Brogden, Michael, and Clifford D. Shearing. *Policing for a New South Africa*. London: Routledge, 1993.

Bryoska, Michael. "South Africa: Evading the Embargo." In *Arms Production in the Third World*, edited by Michael Bryoska and Thomas Ohlson, 193–214. Philadelphia, Pa.: Taylor and Francis, 1986.

Butts, Kent Hughes, and Steven Metz. *Armies and Democracy in the New Africa: Lessons from Nigeria and South Africa*. Carlisle Barracks, Pa.: U.S. Army War College, 1996.

Camerer, Lala. *Costly Crimes: Commercial Crime and Corruption in South Africa*. Halfway House, South Africa: Institute for Security Studies, 1997.

Cammack, Diana. "South Africa's War of Destabilisation." *South African Review* 5 (1990): 191–208.

Cawthra, Gavin. *Brutal Force: Apartheid War Machine*. London: International Defence and Aid Fund for Southern Africa, 1986.

———. *Policing South Africa: The South African Police and the Transition from Apartheid*. London: Zed Books, 1993.

Crocker, Chester A. *South Africa's Defence Posture: Coping With Vulnerability*. Beverly Hills, Calif.: Sage, 1981.

Davis, Dennis, and Mana Slabbert. *Crime and Power in South Africa*. London: Global Book Resources, Johannesburg: David Philip, 1985.

Dodd, Normal L. "The South African Army in 1986." *Armed Forces* 5 (July 1986): 98–109.

du Pisani, Andre. *Beyond the Barracks: Reflections on the Role of the SADF in the Region*. Johannesburg: South African Institute of International Affairs, 1988.

Etherington, Norman, ed. *Peace, Politics and Violence in the New South Africa*. London: Hans Zell, 1992.

Frankel, Philip H. *Pretoria's Praetorians: Civil-Military Relations in South Africa*. Cambridge: Cambridge University, 1984.

Frankel, Philip H., Noam Hines, and Mark Swilling, eds. *State, Resistance and Change in South Africa*. Kent, UK: Croom Helm, 1988.

Glickman, Harvey, ed. *Toward Peace and Security in Southern Africa*. New York: Gordon and Breach Science Publishers, 1990.

Grundy, Kenneth W. *The Militarization of South African Politics*. Bloomington: Indiana University Press, 1986.

———. *Soldiers without Politics: Blacks in the South African Armed Forces*. Berkeley: University of California Press, 1983.

———. "South Africa's Regional Defense Plans: The Homeland Armies." In *South Africa in Southern Africa: The Intensifying Vortex of Violence*, edited by Thomas M. Callaghy, 133–51. New York: Praeger, 1983.

Gutteridge, William F. "The Military in South African Politics: Champions of National Unity?" *Conflict Studies* 271 (June 1994): 1–29.

———. *South Africa: From Apartheid to National Unity, 1981–1994*. Brookfield, Vt.: Dartmouth Publishing, 1995.

———. "South Africa's Defence and Security Forces: The Next Decade." In *Change in South Africa*, edited by John E. Spence, 50–64. New York: Council on Foreign Relations, for the Royal Institute of International Affairs, 1994.

Hamber, Brandon. *Living with the Legacy of Impunity: Lessons for South Africa About Truth, Justice and Crime in Brazil*. Johannesburg: Centre for the Study of Violence and Reconciliation, 1997.

Hanlon, Joseph. *Apartheid's Second Front: South Africa's War Against Its Neighbours*. New York: Penguin, 1986.

Heitman, Helmoed-Romer. "South Africa's Arsenal." *Military Technology* 18: 11 (December 1994): 10–32.

Hills, Alice. "Towards a Critique of Policing and National Development in Africa." *Journal of Modern African Studies* 34: 2 (1996): 271–91.

Hough, Michael. "Revolt in the Townships." In *Challenge: Southern Africa within the African Revolutionary Context*, edited by A. J. Venter, 389–410. Gibraltar: Ashanti Publishing, 1989.

Howe, Herbert M. "The SADF Revisited." In *South Africa: Twelve Perspectives on the Transition*, edited by Helen Kitchen and J. Coleman Kitchen, 78–92. Westport, Conn.: Praeger, with the Center for Strategic and International Studies, Washington, D.C., 1994.

———. "The South African Defence Force and Political Reform." *Journal of Modern African Studies* 32: 1 (March 1994): 29–51.

Human Rights Watch. *Impunity for Human Rights Abuses in Two Homelands: Reports on KwaZulu and Bophuthatswana*. New York: Human Rights Watch, 1994.

———. *The Killings in South Africa: The Role of the Security Forces and the Response of the State*. New York: Human Rights Watch, 1991.

———. *Prison Conditions in South Africa*. New York: Human Rights Watch, 1994.

Jane's Intelligence Review. *Whither South Africa's Warriors?* Special Report no. 3. Surrey, UK: Jane's Information Group, 1994.

Jaster, Robert S. *South Africa and Its Neighbours: The Dynamics of Regional Conflict*. London: International Institute for Strategic Studies, 1986.

———. "The South African Military Reassesses Its Priorities." In *South Africa: Twelve Perspectives on the Transition*, edited by Helen Kitchen and J. Coleman Kitchen, 66–77. Westport, Conn.: Praeger, with the Center for Strategic and International Studies, 1994.

Jaster, Robert S., Moeletsi Mbeki, Morley Nkosi, and Michael Clough. *Changing Fortunes: War, Diplomacy, and Economics in Southern Africa. South Africa: Time Running Out*. South Africa Update Series. New York: Ford Foundation, Foreign Policy Association, 1992.

Karis, Thomas G. "South African Liberation: The Communist Factor." *Foreign Affairs* 65: 2 (Winter 1986–87): 267–87.

Kauppi, Mark Veblen. "The Republic of South Africa." In *The Defense Policies of Nations: A Comparative Study*, edited by Douglas J. Murray and Paul R. Viotti, 476–519. 2nd ed. Baltimore: Johns Hopkins University Press, 1989.

Keller, Bill. "Island of Fear: Inside a SOWETO Hostel." *The New York Times Magazine* (20 September 1992): 32–37, 48–49.

Kempton, Daniel R. *Lessening Political Violence in South Africa: The CODESA Decision*. Washington, D.C.: Georgetown University, Institute for the Study of Diplomacy, 1994.

Khadiagala, Gilbert M. "The Front Line States, Regional Interstate Relations and Institution Building in Southern Africa." In *Toward Peace and Security in Southern Africa*, edited by Harvey Glickman, 131–61. New York: Gordon and Breach Science Publishers, 1990.

Kitchen, Helen, and J. Coleman Kitchen, eds. *South Africa: Twelve Perspectives on the Transition*. Westport, Conn.: Praeger, with the Center for Strategic and International Studies, 1994.

Kynoch, Gary. "The 'Transformation' of the South Africa Military." *Journal of Modern African Studies* 34: 3 (September 1996): 441–57.

Landgren, Signe. *Embargo Disimplemented: South Africa's Military Industry*. New York: Oxford University Press, 1989.

Leonard, Richard. *South Africa at War: White Power and the Crisis in Southern Africa*. Westport, Conn.: Lawrence Hill, 1983.

Levin, Nadia, Kindiza Ngubeni, and Graeme Simpson. *Meeting the Challenge of Change? Notes on Policing and Transition in South Africa*. Johannesburg: Centre for the Study of Violence and Reconciliation, 1997.

Lodge, T. "People's War or Negotiation? African National Congress Strategies in the 1980s." *South African Review* 5 (1990): 42–55.

McDougall, Gay J. *South Africa's Death Squads*. Washington, D.C.: Lawyers' Committee for Civil Rights under Law. Southern Africa Project, 1990.

Manganyi, N. Chabani, and Andre du Toit, eds. *Political Violence and the Struggle in South Africa*. New York: St. Martin's Press, 1990.

Marais, Etienne. *Police-Community Relations: The Natal Conflict and the Prospects for Peace*. Johannesburg: Centre for the Study of Violence and Reconciliation, 1996.

———. *Policing the Periphery: Police and Society in South Africa's Homelands*. Johannesburg: Centre for the Study of Violence and Reconciliation, 1997.

Mare, Gerhard. *Brothers Born of Warrior Blood*. Johannesburg: Ravan Press, 1992.

Marks, Monique. *Community Policing, Human Rights and the Truth Commission*. Johannesburg: Centre for the Study of Violence and Reconciliation, 1998.

Mathews, Anthony S. "South African Security Law and the Growth of Local and Regional Violence." In *Apartheid Unravels*, edited by R. Hunt Davis Jr., 18–32. Gainesville: University Press of Florida, 1991.

Mathews, M. L., Philip B. Heymann, and Anthony S. Mathews. *Policing the Conflict in South Africa*. Gainesville: University Press of Florida, 1993.

Mills, Greg. "The Security Forces in a New South Africa." *The World Today* 47: 3 (March 1991): 43–47.

Minty, Abdul S. *South Africa's Defence Strategy*. London: Anti-Apartheid Movement, 1969.

Moleah, Alfred T. "South Africa Under Siege: The Ever-Deepening Crisis of Apartheid." *Without Prejudice* 1 (Fall 1987): 58–84.

Moorcroft, Paul L. *African Nemesis: War and Revolution in Southern Africa (1945–2010)*. London: Brassey's, 1990.

Murray, Douglas J., and Paul R. Viotti, eds. *The Defense Policies of Nations: A Comparative Study*. Baltimore, Md.: Johns Hopkins University Press, 1994.

Navias, Martin. "The Future of South Africa's Arms Trade and Defence Industries." *Jane's Intelligence Review* 6: 11 (November 1994): 522–24.

———. "South Africa's Security Challenges." In *Jane's Intelligence Review. Whither South Africa's Warriors?* Special Report no. 3. Edited by Robert Hall and Ian Kemp, 4–6. London: Jane's Information Group, 1994.

Ohlson, Thomas, and Stephen John Stedman, with Robert Davies. *The New Is Not Yet Born: Conflict Resolution in Southern Africa*. Washington, D.C.: Brookings, 1994.

Ottaway, Marina. "Liberation Movements and the Transition to Democracy: The Case of the A.N.C." *Journal of Modern African Studies* 29: 1 (1991): 83–114.

Rakgoadi, Pakiso Sylvester. *The Role of Self-Defence Units (SDUs) in a Changing Political Context*. Johannesburg: Centre for the Study of Violence and Reconciliation, 1997.

Robert, Bernhard. "South Africa's Nuclear Weapons: A Defused Time Bomb?" *Aussenpolitik* 44: 3 (July 1993): 232–42.

Roherty, James M. *State Security in South Africa. Civil-Military Relations Under P. W. Botha*. Armonk, N.Y.: M. E. Sharpe, 1992.

Rotberg, Robert I., ed. *South Africa and Its Neighbours: Regional Security and Self-Interest*. Lexington, Mass.: Heath, 1985.

Seegers, Annette. "Current Trends in South Africa's Security Establishment." *Armed Forces and Society* 18: 2 (Winter 1992): 159–74.

———. "The Military in South Africa: A Comparison and Critique." *South Africa International* 16: 4 (April 1986): 192–200.

———. *The Military in the Making of Modern South Africa*. London: Tauris Academic Studies, 1996.

———. "South Africa's National Security Management System, 1972–90." *Journal of Modern African Studies* 29: 2 (June 1991): 253–73.

Spence, John E. "South Africa's Military Relations with Its Neighbors." In *Military Power and Politics in Black Africa*, edited by Simon Baynham, 291–316. New York: St. Martin's Press, 1986.

Steenkamp, Willem. "Arrnscor Today—Selling Arms to the Enemy." In *Challenge: Southern Africa within the African Revolutionary Context*, edited by A. J. Venter, 470–500. Gibraltar: Ashanti Publishing, 1989.

Switzer, Les. *Power and Resistance in an African Society: The Ciskei Xhosa and the Making of South Africa*. Madison: University of Wisconsin, 1993.

Szeftel, M. "Manoeuvres of War in South Africa." *Review of African Political Economy* 51 (1991): 63–76.

Vale, Peter. "The Search for Southern Africa's Security." *International Affairs* 67: 4 (October 1991): 697–708.

Van Rooyen, Johann. *Hard Right: The New White Power in South Africa*. New York: I. B. Tauris, 1994.

Venter, A. J. *The Chopper Boys: Helicopter Warfare in Africa*. Halfway House, South Africa: Southern Book Publishers, 1994.

Winter, Gordon. *Inside BOSS: South Africa's Secret Police*. Harmondsworth, UK: Penguin Books, 1981.

SUDAN

Abegunrin, Olayiwola. "The Arabs and the Southern Sudan Problem." *International Affairs* 60: 1 (Winter 1983/84): 97–105.

Africa Watch. *Children of Sudan: Slaves, Street Children and Child Soldiers.* New York: Africa Watch, 1995.

———. *Civilian Devastation: Abuses by All Parties in the War in Southern Sudan.* New York: Africa Watch, 1994.

———. *"Denying the Honour of Living": Sudan, a Human Rights Disaster.* New York: Africa Watch, 1990.

———. *Eradicating the Nuba.* New York: Africa Watch, 1992.

———. *Inside Bashir's Prisons.* New York: Africa Watch, 1991.

———. *The Ghosts Remain: One Year After an Amnesty Is Declared, Detention and Torture Continue Unabated.* New York: Africa Watch, 1992.

———. *The Lost Boys: Child Soldiers and Unaccompanied Boys in Southern Sudan.* New York: Africa Watch, 1994.

———. *New Islamic Penal Code Violates Basic Human Rights.* New York: Africa Watch, 1991.

———. *The Secret War against the Nuba.* New York: Africa Watch, 1991.

———. *War in South Sudan: The Civilian Toll.* New York: Africa Watch, 1993.

African Rights. *Facing Genocide: The Nuba of Sudan.* London: African Rights, 1995.

Allen, Tim. "Full Circle? An Overview of Sudan's 'Southern Problem' Since Independence." *Northeast African Studies* 11: 2 (1989): 41–66.

Amnesty International. *The Ravages of War: Political Killings and Humanitarian Disaster.* New York: Amnesty International, 1993.

Arnold, Guy. "Sudan: North-South, an Old Pattern of Mistrust." In *Wars in the Third World Since 1945*, Guy Arnold, 397–406. London: Cassell, 1991.

Badal, Raphael Koba. "Sudan: The Role of Religion in Conflict Situations." *Horn Review* 1: 1 (1991): 27–39.

Berger, Carol. "The War in the South." *Africa Report* 31: 4 (July/August 1986): 64–67.

Beshir, Mohammed Omar. *The Southern Sudan: Background to Conflict.* London: C. Hurst, 1968.

———. *The Southern Sudan: From Conflict to Peace.* London: C. Hurst and Company, 1975.

Carter, Nick. "At War with Its People." *Africa Report* 37: 6 (November/December 1992): 65–67.

———. "Slaughter in the South." *Africa Report* 35: 3 (May/June 1990): 21–24.

Chand, David D. "The Sudan Civil War: Is a Negotiated Settlement Possible?" *Africa Today* 36: 3/4 (Summer/Fall 1989): 55–63.

Clark, Colin S. "The Vanishing Famine." *Africa Report* 32: 1 (January/February 1987): 68–70.

Collins, Robert O. "Civil War in Sudan." *Journal of Third World Studies* 5: 1 (Spring 1988): 66–83.

Daly, Martin W., and Ahmad Alawad Sikainga, eds. *Civil War in the Sudan.* London: British Academic Press, 1993.

Deng, Francis M. "Africa's Dilemmas in the Sudan." *The World Today* 54: 3 (March 1998): 72–74.

De Waal, Alex. *War in Sudan: An Analysis of Conflict.* London: Peace in Sudan Group, 1990.

Eprile, Cecil L. *Sudan: The Long War.* London: Institute for the Study of Conflict, 1972.

———. *War and Peace in the Sudan, 1955–1972.* London: David and Charles, 1974.

Fitzgerald, Mary Anne. "What Prospect for Peace?" *Africa Report* 30: 6 (November/December 1985): 11–14.

Flint, Julie. "The Unwinnable War." *Africa Report* 38: 6 (November/December 1993): 46–49.

Garang, John. "An Historical Perspective." *Horn of Africa* 8: 1 (1985): 21–25.

Glickson, Roger C. "Counterinsurgency in Southern Sudan: The Means to Win?" *The Journal of Conflict Studies* 15: 1 (Spring 1995): 45–59.

Heraclides, Alex. "Janus or Sisyphus? The Southern Problem of Sudan." *Journal of Modern African Studies* 25: 2 (June 1987): 213–32.

Husband, Mark. "While the People Starve." *Africa Report* 38: 3 (May/June 1993): 36–39.

Johnson, Douglas H. *The Southern Sudan.* London: Minority Rights Group, 1988.

———. *The Root Causes of Sudan's Civil Wars.* Oxford: James Currey, 2003.

Kasfir, Nelson. *One Full Revolution: The Politics of Sudanese Military Government, 1969–1985.* New York: Praeger, 1987.

Khalid, Mansour. *The Government They Deserve: The Role of the Elite in Sudan's Political Evolution.* London: Kegan Paul International, 1990.

———, ed. *John Garang Speaks.* London: Kegan Paul International, 1987.

Kok, Peter Nyott. *Governance and Conflict in Sudan, 1985–1995: Analysis, Evaluation and Documentation.* Hamburg: Deutsches Orient-Institut, 1996.

Kyle, Keith. "The Southern Problem in the Sudan." *The World Today* 22: 12 (December 1955): 512–19.

Land, Thomas. "The Scorpion Bites in Sudan's Civil War." *East African Journal* 7: 6 (June 1970): 44–46.

Lesch, Ann Mosely. "Confrontation in the Southern Sudan." *Middle East Journal* 40: 3 (1986): 410–28.

———. "Prolonged Conflict in the Sudan." In *Prolonged War: A Post-Nuclear Challenge*, edited by Karl P. Magyar and Constantine Danopoulos, 99–129. Maxwell AFB, Ala.: Air University Press, 1994.

Lobbon, Richard Andrew, Robert S. Kramer, and Carolyn Fluehr Lobbon. *Historical Dictionary of the Sudan*. Lanham, Md.: Scarecrow Press, 2002.

Lusk, Gill. "Les Crises du Mouvement Armée Sud-Soudanais." *Politique Africaine* 50 (June 1993): 32–44.

Mahmoud, Fatima Babiker. *Calamity in Sudan: Civilian versus Military Rule*. London: Institute for African Alternatives, 1988.

Makinda, Samuel M. "Sudan: Old Wine in New Bottles." *Orbis* 31:2 (1987): 217–28.

Mathews, Daniel Koat, and Rebecca Joshua Okwaci. "Position of the SPLM/SPLA in Peace and Conflict in Sudan." *Horn Review* 1: 1 (1991): 51–55.

Mawsom, Andrew N. M. "War, Famine and Fight in Sudan 2. Murahaleen Raids on Dinka, 1985–1989." *Disasters* 15: 2 (1991): 137–50.

Minority Rights Group. *Sudan: Conflict and Minorities*. London: Minority Rights Group, 1995.

O'Ballance, Edgar. *The Secret War in Sudan, 1955–1972*. London: Faber and Faber, 1977.

Prah, K. K. "African Nationalism and the Origins of War in the Sudan." *Lesotho Law Journal* 2: 2 (1986): 179–96.

Prendergast, John. *Sudanese Rebels at a Crossroads: Opportunities for Building Peace in a Shattered Land*. Washington, D.C.: Center of Concern, 1994.

Prunier, Gerard. *From Peace to War: The Southern Sudan (1972–1984)*. Hull, UK: University of Hull, 1986.

Scott, Philippa. "The Sudan People's Liberation Movement (SPLM) and Liberation Army (SPLA)." *Review of African Political Economy* 33 (August 1985): 69–82.

Shields, Todd. "Starving the South." *Africa Report* 34: 1 (January/February 1989): 63–66.

———. "A Tragedy in the Making." *Africa Report* 36: 2 (March/April 1991): 54–57.

———. "Stated Position of the Rebels." *Horn of Africa* 8 1 (1985): 39–46.

Thomas, Graham F. *Sudan: Struggle for Survival*. London: Darf Publishers, 1994.

———. *Sudan 1950–1985: Death of a Dream*. London: Darf Publishers, 1990.

Wai, Dunstan, ed. *The Southern Sudan: The Problem of National Integration.* London: Oxford University Press, 1973.

Wakoson, Elias NyamLell. "The Sudanese Dilemma: The South-North Conflict." *Northeast African Studies* 9:3 (1987): 43–59.

Wolfers, Michael. "Race and Class in Sudan." *Race and Class* 32: 1 (1981): 65–79.

UGANDA

Crisp, Jeff. "Uganda Refugees in Sudan and Zaire: The Problem of Repatriation." *African Affairs* 85: 339 (1986): 163–80.

Flew, C., and A. Urquhart. *Strengthening Small Arms Controls: An Audit of Small Arms Control Legislation in the Great Lakes Region and the Horn of Africa.* London: Saferworld and SaferAfrica, 2004.

Foster, Byarugaba Emansueto. *Rwandese Refugees in Uganda.* Uppsala: Scandinavian Institute of African Studies, 1989.

Furley, Oliver. *Uganda: A Second-Phase Bid for Legitimacy under International Scrutiny.* Basingstoke, UK: Macmillan, 1992.

———. *Uganda's Retreat from Turmoil?* London: Institute for the Study of Conflict, 1987.

Gersoney, R. *The Anguish of North Uganda: Results of a Field-based Assessment of the Civil Conflicts in Northern Uganda.* Kampala: USAID, 1997.

Gingyera-Pinyewa, A. *Uganda and the Problem of Refugees.* Kampala: University of Makerere Press, 1998.

Gomes, N., and K. Mkutu. *Breaking the Cycle of Violence: Building Local Capacity for Peace and Development in Karamoja, Uganda.* Kampala: Pax Christi, 2004.

Human Rights Watch. *Stolen Children: Abduction and Recruitment in Northern Uganda.* New York: Human Rights Watch, 2003.

International Crisis Group. *Building a Comprehensive Peace Strategy for Northern Uganda.* Africa Briefing 27, Brussels: International Crisis group, 2005.

Kasozi, A. *The Social Origins of Violence in Uganda.* Kampala: Fountain Publishers, 1998.

Lomo, Z., A. Naggaga, and L. Hovil. *The Phenomenon of Forced Migration in Uganda: An Overview of Policy and Practice in an Historical Context.* Working Paper no. 1, Kampala: Refugee Law Project, 2001.

Merkx, J. "Refugee Identities and Relief in an Africa Borderland: A Study of Northern Uganda and Southern Sudan." *Refugee Survey Quarterly* 21 (1 and 2): 113–46, 2002.

Pirouet, M. Louise. *Historical Dictionary of Uganda.* Lanham, Md.: Scarecrow Press, 1995.

ZIMBABWE (RHODESIA)

Acland, J. H. B. "The Rhodesia Operation." *Guards Magazine* (Summer 1980): 46–50.

Alao, Charles. "The Metamorphosis of the 'Unorthodox': The Integration and Early Development of the Zimbabwe National Army." In *Soldiers in Zimbabwe's Liberation War*, edited by Ngwabi Bhebe and Terence Ranger, 104–17. London: James Currey, 1995.

"An Outline History of the Rhodesian Air Force." *Aerospace Historian* 23: 1 (1976): 36–42.

Arbuckle, T. "Rhodesian Bush War Strategies and Tactics: An Assessment." *Journal of the Royal United Services Institute* 124: 4 (1979): 27–32.

Archer, J. M. "The Zimbabwe National Army—A Personal View." *British Army Review* 72 (December 1982): 62–65.

Armstrong, Peter. *Operation Zambezi: The Raid Into Zambia.* Salisbury: Welston Press, 1979.

Baldock, R. "Towards a History of Insurgency in Rhodesia." *Rhodesian History* 5 (1974): 97–102.

Barber, James. *Rhodesia: The Road to Rebellion.* London: Oxford University Press, 1967.

Barclay, G. St. John. "Slotting the Floppies: The Rhodesian Response to Sanctions and Insurgency, 1974–1977." *Australian Journal of Defence Studies* 1: 2 (1977): 110–20.

Barwell, J. "Railways at War." *Heritage of Zimbabwe* 6 (1986): 70–75.

Beckett, Ian F. W. "The Rhodesian Army: Counter-Insurgency, 1972–1979." In *Armed Forces and Modern Counter-Insurgency*, edited by Ian F. W. Beckett and John Pimlott, 163–89. New York: St. Martin's Press, 1985.

Bhebe, Ngwabi, and Terence Ranger, eds. *Soldiers in Zimbabwe's Liberation War.* London: James Currey, 1995.

Black, Colin. *Fighting Forces of Rhodesia: The Background and the Present State of Vigilance.* 2 vols. Salisbury: H.C.P. Anderson, 1974.

Bratton, Michael. "Settler State, Guerrilla War, and Rural Underdevelopment in Rhodesia." *Rural Africana* 4/5 (Spring/Fall 1979): 115–29.

Brown, Neville. "Military Sanctions Against Rhodesia." *Venture* 17: 12 (January 1966): 7–12.

Bruton, James K. "Counter-Insurgency in Rhodesia." *Military Review* 59: 3 (March 1979): 26–39.

Burke, G. K. "Insurgency in Rhodesia: The Implications." *RUSI and Brassey's Defence Yearbook*, 1978–78, 26–40. London: RUSI and Brassey's, 1980.

Catholic Commission for Justice and Peace in Rhodesia. *Civil War in Rhodesia: Abduction, Torture and Death in the Counterinsurgency Campaign.* London: Catholic Institute of International Relations, 1976.

———. *Rhodesia: The Propaganda War.* Salisbury: Catholic Institute of International Relations, 1977.

Chan, Steven. *The Commonwealth Observer Group in Zimbabwe.* Gweru: Mambo Press, 1985.

Charlton, Michael. *The Last Colony in Africa: Diplomacy and the Independence of Rhodesia.* Oxford: Basil Blackwell, 1990.

Chiwewe, W. A. "Zimbabwe's Defence Forces: Nine Years of Transformation and Consolidation, 1980–1989." *Zimbabwe News* 20: 4 (April 1989): 49–53.

Cilliers, J. K. *Counterinsurgency in Rhodesia.* London: Croom Helm, 1985.

Cohen, Barry. "The War in Rhodesia: A Dissenter's View." *African Affairs* 76: 305 (October 1977): 483–94.

Cowderoy, Dudley, and Roy C. Nesbit. *War in the Air: Rhodesian Air Forces, 1935–1980.* Alberton: Galago Publishing, 1987.

Coyle, R. G., and C. J. Millar. "A Methodology for Understanding Military Complexity: The Case of the Rhodesian Counter-Insurgency Campaign." *Small Wars and Insurgencies* 7: 3 (Winter 1996): 360–78.

Czech, Kenneth P. "Rhodesia's Brutal Second Matabele War." *Military History* 12: 7 (March 1996): 50–56.

Dachs, Anthony J. "The Course of African Resistance in Southern Rhodesia." *Rhodesian History* I (1970): 95–101.

Davidson, Basil, Joe Slovo, and Anthony R. Wilkinson. *Southern Africa: The New Politics of Revolution.* London: Pelican, 1976.

Downie, N. "Rhodesia: A Study in Military Incompetence." *Defence* 10: 5 (1979): 342–45.

Ellert, Henrik. *The Rhodesian Front War: Counter-Insurgency and Guerrilla Warfare, 1962–1980.* Gweru: Mambo Press, 1993.

Evans, Michael. *Fighting Against Chimurenga: An Analysis of Counter Insurgency in Rhodesia, 1972–79.* Salisbury: Historical Association of Zimbabwe, 1981.

———. "Gukurahundi: The Development of the Zimbabwe Defence Forces, 1980–1987." *Strategic Review for Southern Africa* 10: 1 (May 1988): 1–37.

Fire Force Exposed: The Rhodesian Security Forces and Their Role in Defending White Supremacy. London: Anti-Apartheid Movement, 1979.

Flower, Ken. *Serving Secretly: An Intelligence Chief on Record: Rhodesia into Zimbabwe, 1964–1981.* London: John Murray, 1987.

Gann, Lewis H., and Thomas H. Henrikson. *The Struggle for Zimbabwe: Battle in the Bush.* New York: Praeger, 1981.

Good, Robert C. *UDI: The International Politics of the Rhodesian Rebellion.* London: Faber and Faber, 1973.

Gregory, Martyn. "The Zimbabwe Election: The Political and Military Implications." *Journal of Southern African Studies* 7: 1 (1980): 17–37.

Gutteridge, William. "Rhodesia: The Use of Military Force." *World Today* 21: 12 (December 1965): 499–503.

Hull, Richard W. "The Continuing Crisis in Rhodesia." *Current History* 78:455 (March 1980): 107–9, 133–34.

———. "Rhodesia in Crisis." *Current History* 76: 445 (March 1979): 105–9, 137–38.

Jaster, Robert. "The Rocky Road to Lancaster House: Lessons From the Rhodesian Conflict." *South Africa International* 18: 2 (1987): 102–29.

Jokonya, T. J. B. "The Effects of the War on the Rural Population of Zimbabwe." *Journal of Southern African Studies* 14: 2 (1988): 304–22.

Kirk, Tony. "Politics and Violence in Rhodesia." *African Affairs* 74: 294 (1975): 3–38.

Kriger, Norma. "The Zimbabwean War of Liberation: Struggles Within the Struggle." *Journal of Southern African Studies* 14: 2 (1988): 304–22.

——— . *Zimbabwe's Guerrilla War: Peasant Voices.* Cambridge: Cambridge University Press, 1992.

Learmount, J. H. "Reflections from Rhodesia." *RUSI: Journal of the Royal United Services Institute for Defence Studies* 125: 4 (December 1980): 47–55.

Liberation Support Movement. *Zimbabwe: The Final Advance. Documents on the Zimbabwe Liberation Movements.* Oakland, Calif.: LSM, 1978.

Lovett, John. *Contact: Rhodesia at War.* Salisbury: Galaxie Press, 1977.

MacKinley, John. "The Commonwealth Monitoring Force in Zimbabwe/Rhodesia, 1979–1980." In *Humanitarian Emergencies and Military Help in Africa,* edited by Thomas G. Weiss, 36–60. New York: St. Martin's Press, 1990.

Malcolm, Ian, and Dave West. "The Air Force of Zimbabwe." *World Airpower Journal* 29 (Summer 1997): 110–19.

Marston, R. "Resettlement as Counter-Revolutionary Technique." *Journal of the Royal United Services Institute* 124: 4 (1979): 46–49.

Martin, David, and Phyllis Johnson. *The Chitepo Assassination.* Harare: Zimbabwe Publishing, 1985.

———. *The Struggle for Zimbabwe: The Chimurenga War.* London: Faber and Faber, 1981.

Maxey, Kees. *The Fight for Zimbabwe: The Armed Conflict in Southern Rhodesia since UDI*. London: Rex Collings, 1975.

McLaughlin, Janice. *On the Frontline: Catholic Missions in Zimbabwe's Liberation War*. Harare: Baobob Books, 1996.

Moorcroft, Paul L. "Rhodesia's War of Independence." *History Today* 40: 9 (September 1990): 11–17.

Moorcroft, Paul L., and Peter McLaughlin. *Chimurenga! The War in Rhodesia, 1965–1980*. Marshalltown: Sygma/Collins, 1982.

Moore-King, Bruce. *White Man Black War*. Harare: Baobob Books, 1988.

Morris-Jones, W. H. *From Rhodesia to Zimbabwe: Behind and Beyond Lancaster House*. Studies in Commonwealth Politics and History, no. 9. Ilford: Frank Cass, 1980.

Palmer, Robin H. "War and Land in Rhodesia." *Transafrican Journal of History* 1: 2 (1971): 43–62.

Pongweni, A. J. C., ed. *Songs That Won the Liberation War*. Harare: College Press, 1982.

Raeburn, Michael. *Black Fire: Accounts of the Guerrilla War in Rhodesia*. London: Julian Friedmann, 1978.

Ranger, Terence O. "Bandits and Guerrillas: The Case of Zimbabwe." In *Banditry, Rebellion and Social Protest in Africa*, edited by Donald Crummey, 373–96. London: James Currey, 1986.

———. *Peasant Consciousness and Guerrilla War in Zimbabwe: A Comparative Study*. Berkeley: University of California Press, 1985.

———. "War, Violence and Healing in Zimbabwe." *Journal of Southern African Studies* 18: 3 (1992): 698–707.

Ransford, Oliver. *Bulawayo: Historic Battleground of Rhodesia*. Cape Town: A. A. Balkema, 1968.

Rao, P. C. "The Rhodesian Crisis and the Use of Force." *African Quarterly* 6 (January/March 1967): 285–96.

Reid-Daly, Ron. "War in Rhodesia: Cross-border Operations." In *Challenge: Southern Africa within the African Revolutionary Context*, edited by A. J. Venter, 146–82. Gibraltar: Ashanti Publishing, 1989.

Reid-Daly, Ron, and Peter Stiff. *Selous Scouts: Top Secret War*. Alberton, South Africa: Galago Press, 1983.

Reynolds, Pamela. "Children of Tribulation: The Need to Heal and the Means to Heal War Trauma [Zimbabwe 1970s]." *Africa* 60: 1 (1990): 1–38.

Rotberg, Robert I. "Winning the War for Zimbabwe." *Orbis* 24: 4 (1982): 1045–53.

Rothchild, Donald. "Rhodesian Rebellion and African Response." *African Quarterly* 5 (1966): 184–96.

Rubert, Steven C., and Rikert Rasmussen. *Historical Dictionary of Zimbabwe*. Lanham, Md.: Scarecrow Press, 2001.

Rupiah, Martin R. "Demobilisation and Integration: 'Operation Merger' and the Zimbabwe National Defence Forces, 1980–1987." In *Demobilisation and Reintegration of Former Combatants in Africa*, edited by Jakkie Cilliers, 27–43. Halfway House, South Africa: Institute for Defence Policy, 1995.

———. "Peacekeeping Operations: The Zimbabwean Experience." In *South Africa and Peacekeeping in Africa*, edited by Jakkie Cilliers and Mark Shaw. Vol. 1. Halfway House, South Africa: Institute for Defence Policy, 1995.

Rustin, Bayard. "The War Against Zimbabwe." *Commentary* 68: 1 (1979): 25–32.

Scott, Leda. *Women and the Armed Struggle for Independence in Zimbabwe (1964–1979)*. Edinburgh: Centre of Africa Studies, University of Edinburgh, 1989.

Serapiao, Luis Benjamin. "Zimbabwe's Military Intervention in Mozambique." *African Studies Association Papers* 29: 91 (October/November 1986): 1–25.

Singh, Harjinder. "Armed Struggle and Zimbabwean Independence." *Africa Quarterly* 20: 3/4 (1981): 88–106.

Stedman, Stephen John. *Peacemaking in Civil War: International Mediation in Zimbabwe, 1974–1980*. Boulder, Colo.: Lynne Rienner Publishers, 1991.

Stiff, Peter. *See You in November*. Alberton, South Africa: Galago, 1985.

Sutcliffe, Robert. "The Use of Force in Rhodesia." *Venture* 19 (April 1967): 5–7.

Vambe, Lawrence. *From Rhodesia to Zimbabwe*. Pittsburgh, Pa.: University of Pittsburgh Press, 1976.

Verrier, Anthony. *The Road to Zimbabwe, 1890–1980*. London: Cape, 1986.

Waldman, Selma. "Armed Struggle in Zimbabwe: A Brief Chronology of Guerrilla Warfare, 1966–74." *Ufahamu* 5: 3 (1975): 4–10.

Weinrich, A. K. H. "Strategic Resettlement in Rhodesia." *Journal of Southern African Studies* 3: 2 (1977): 207–9.

Weiss, Ruth. *Zimbabwe and the New Elite*. London: British Academic Press, 1994.

Wilkinson, A. R. "The Impact of the War." *Journal of Commonwealth and Comparative Politics* 18: 1 (1980): 110–23.

———. *Insurgency in Rhodesia, 1957–1973*. London: Institute for Strategic Studies, 1973.

Woollacott, Robert. *Winged Gunners*. Harare, privately printed, 1994.

ZIPA. *Zimbabwe People's Army*. Oakland, Calif.: Liberation Support Movement, 1976.

About the Author

Guy Arnold is a freelance writer who has long specialized in the subject of north–south relations in Africa. Widely traveled in Africa and Commonwealth countries, he has worked with the Overseas Development Institute in Great Britain and was Director of the Africa Bureau (a nongovernmental lobby group) from 1968 to 1972. He has also acted as a consultant in this field from time to time. He is the author of more than 40 books and his publications on Africa include *Aid in Africa, Kenyatta and the Politics of Kenya, The Maverick State: Gaddafi and the New World Order, Modern Kenya, Modern Nigeria, The Last Bunker: A Report on White South Africa Today, South Africa: Crossing the Rubicon,* and *The New South Africa.* His latest book on Africa is *Africa: A Modern History.* His books on the Third World as a whole include *Aid and the Third World, The Third World Handbook, Wars in the Third World since 1945, The Resources of the Third World, The End of the Third World,* and *World Government by Stealth: The Future of the United Nations.*

In the Scarecrow series of historical dictionaries, Arnold has contributed the *Historical Dictionary of Aid and Development Organizations, Historical Dictionary of the Crimean War,* and, most recently, the *Historical Dictionary of the Non-Aligned Movement and Third World.* He has also published books on the state of Britain, including *Brainwash: The Cover-Up Society* and *Britain's Oil,* and a number of travel books and children's information books. He has lectured on international affairs for many years.